MORE PRAISE FOR

# STILL BRAVE

"Faculty and students at all levels of higher education; community activists; policy-makers; and those just plain curious to read the very best scholarship on race and gender will welcome the publication of this volume. James, Foster, and Guy-Sheftall have put together a political, creative, truly interdisciplinary anthology. They have crafted a narrative of Black Women's Studies over the past twenty-five years that will sustain the field in the twenty-first century. They are to be congratulated."

—Claire G. Moses, editorial director of *Feminist Studies* and professor of Women's Studies, University of Maryland

"Radiant with intellectual energy, this sequel to *But Some of Us Are Brave* will be as indispensable to Women's Studies scholars of every race, age, ethnicity, and theoretical orientation as its precursor was. The writers whose classic and contemporary essays are collected here address an exhilarating range of multidisciplinary and multicultural issues, from religion to sexuality to the history of Black feminist criticism—including a closing riff on the Obama daughters and Pecola Breedlove—with verve, wit, passion, and sophistication."

—Sandra M. Gilbert, Distinguished Professor of English Emerita, University of California, Davis

"First Lady Michelle Obama embodies both the dearest hopes and deepest fears of so many African American women. Her fierce advocacy for her children, the power of her embodied self, her broad appeal to Americans of all races and classes suggest the realization of a Black feminist dream. But the essays in *Still Brave* remind us of the fraught terrain on which First Lady Obama stands. They demonstrate how Black women must remain "nice girls" or risk being swiftly punished by an American public with little familiarity with or respect for the diverse, authentic realities of Black women.

The authors of *Still Brave* allow us to glimpse this stunning diversity of Black women's lives across differences of age, color, class, sexual orientation, and religious belief. They illuminate the social and political context, meanings, and burdens that frame Black women's lives. They open space for politically meaningful anger, push back against rigid norms of respectability, and map the contributions of African American women's unique and varied perspectives.

In short the book is courageous, necessary, and exquisitely edited. It is a true testament to the scholar to whom it is dedicated."

—Melissa Harris-Lacewell, associate professor of Politics and African American Studies, Princeton University

The Combahee River Collective ■ Cheryl Clarke ■ Alice Walker ■ Audre Lorde ■ bell hooks ■ Elsa Barkley Brown ■ Deborah K. King ■ Barbara Ransby ■ Michael Awkward ■ Jacquelyn Grant ■ Barbara Christian ■ Nikol G. Alexander-Floyd ■ Evelyn M. Simien ■ Monica A. Coleman ■ Patricia Hill Collins ■ Paula Giddings ■ Ann duCille ■ Angela Y. Davis ■ Cassandra Shaylor ■ Adrienne Davis ■ Cathy J. Cohen ■ Evelynn M. Hammonds ■ Josephine Beoku-Betts ■ Wairimũ Ngarũiya Njambi ■ Lorraine O'Grady ■ Farah Jasmine Griffin ■ Black Men for the Eradication of Sexism ■ Joy James ■ June Jordan ■ Stanlie M. James ■ Carole Boyce Davies ■ Violet Eudine Barriteau ■ Cheryl A. Wall

# STILL BRAVE

## THE EVOLUTION OF BLACK WOMEN'S STUDIES

Stanlie M. James ▪ Frances Smith Foster
▪ Beverly Guy-Sheftall ▶ Editors

THE FEMINIST PRESS
AT THE CITY UNIVERSITY OF NEW YORK
FEMINISTPRESS.ORG

Published in 2009 by the Feminist Press at the City University of New York
The Graduate Center, 365 Fifth Avenue, Suite 5406
New York, NY 10016

Publication of this book was made possible, in part, by funds from the Ford Foundation.

Second printing, January 2010

**Library of Congress Cataloging in Publication Data**

Still brave / edited by Stanlie M. James, Frances Smith Foster, and Beverly Guy-Sheftall. — 1st ed.
    p. cm.
  ISBN 978-1-55861-611-0
1. African American women. 2. Feminism. 3. Feminist theory. 4. Women, Black  I. James,
Stanlie M. (Stanlie Myrise) II. Foster, Frances Smith. III. Guy-Sheftall, Beverly.
  E185.86.S765 2009
  305.48'896073--dc22
                                                                    2009029454

*For Nellie Y. McKay*

# CONTENTS

## III  BODY AND SOUL

## IV  TO BE YOUNG, GIFTED, AND BLACK

## V FROM THIS MOMENT ON . . .

## EPILOGUE

# Introduction

Merely to use the term "Black women's studies" is an act charged with political significance. At the very least, the combining of these words to name a discipline means taking the stance that Black women exist—and exist positively—a stance that is in direct opposition to most of what passes for culture and thought on the North American continent.
—Gloria T. Hull and Barbara Smith, 1982

## Some of Us Were Brave

The creation in 1969 at San Diego State University of the first Women's Studies program marked the emergence of Women's Studies as a distinct entity within higher education in the United States. Some two decades later Clark and Emory Universities pioneered the Women's Studies Ph.Ds. In the fall of 2002 representatives of doctoral programs in the United States, along with others interested in establishing such programs, met at Emory University for the first national conference on the Ph.D. in Women's Studies.

According to the National Women's Studies Association (NWSA), by 2009, there were more than six hundred departments and programs and over ten thousand courses in Women's Studies in the United States, with the largest number of students in any interdisciplinary field. Women's Studies as a discrete area of study has also expanded internationally with programs, departments, and courses now found in Africa (Uganda, South Africa, Senegal, and Nigeria for example), Europe, Canada, Mexico, Argentina, Costa Rica, the Caribbean, India, Indonesia, China, Korea, and Japan. Doctoral programs continue to emerge in the U.S. and other countries.

During the 1970s Phase I of the evolution of Women's Studies in the academy focused on the establishment of the field as a separate discipline. The 1980s ushered in Phase II, which could be considered the coming-of-age of the Women's Studies movement as programs and eventually departments became acknowledged and even respected units within more colleges and universities. However, Phase II was also marked by critical disagreements. Some agreed with leaders such as Florence Howe who wrote in 1982:

> The major thrust of the second decade will be toward directing the movement outward, toward "mainstreaming." Despite a decade of new scholarship, Women's Studies has so far made little progress toward its "ultimate strategy" of transforming the established male-biased curriculum.[1]

This process of bringing about a gender-balanced curriculum was an attempt to "de-ghettoize" Women's Studies and to incorporate it into the rest of the academic enterprise. The objective was to include feminist scholarship and other new scholarship on women within all of the disciplines by initiating curriculum transformation projects in diverse academic settings throughout the country. Curricular transformation was complicated, however. Gatekeepers (not always male) of the established curriculum created obstacles, but often the more serious challenges were within the Women's Studies movement itself. Some declared that the goal was to balance, mainstream, and integrate Women's Studies into the academic curriculum. Others rejected this as an "add-and-stir" approach and espoused radical paradigm shifts that would "transform" the institution itself.[2] Most Women's Studies advocates argued, however, that it was not "either-or," but rather "both-and." Separate Women's Studies courses, they believed, must exist alongside gender-balanced courses within the disciplines.

Despite the important, even transformative, work of the Women's Studies movement during both phases, many advocates, particularly women of color, were marginalized and increasingly frustrated by unexamined claims about a universal sisterhood in feminist theorizing. Lesbians critiqued institutionalized heterosexism and the relative invisibility of lesbian experience within the emerging scholarship on women and gender. Black women critiqued Women's Studies scholars and curriculum integration projects for their relative lack of attention to questions of racial, ethnic, class, or cultural difference in definitions of womanhood almost from the very inception of the women's movement. Johnnella Butler, who co-directed the first curriculum integration project between Women's Studies and Ethnic Studies, asserted: "Women are separated from each other by race, class, ethnic group, religion, nationality, and culture so that they appear to share more of a common identity with men of their own immediate group than with women outside that group."[3]

One of the hardest-hitting critiques of the insensitivity of Women's Studies to race, class, and ethnicity can be found in the pioneering work of Black feminist theorist bell hooks, who declared:

Our [Black feminist scholars'] collective work . . . made it possible for individuals active in the feminist movement to demand that Women's Studies courses acknowledge that they claimed to be talking and teaching about women, when the actual subjects of study were white women. This was an important breakthrough, which has had and continues to have profound impact on [the] feminist movement and feminist scholarship in the United States. However, the insistence on recognizing differences among women and of ways the intersection of race, sex, and class determine the nature of female subjectivity, has not sufficiently altered hierarchical structures within Women's Studies and feminist scholarship. Most programs continue to focus central attention on white women, as though they represent all women, subordinating discussions of Black women and other nonwhite groups.[4]

Although Black women had been instrumental in helping establish Black Studies, the field remained male centered, while Women's Studies privileged middle-class white women as the norm for what it meant to be female. Because Black Studies and Women's Studies failed to adequately address the unique experiences of women of African descent in the United States and around the world, a few brave women created a new field—Black Women's Studies—to provide a conceptual framework for moving women of color from the margins to the center of Women's Studies; for incorporating gender analyses into Black Studies; and to be a catalyst for initiatives such as bringing "Minority Women's Studies" (as it was called) into core curricula in diverse academic settings.

The most noteworthy developments in the evolving field of Black Women's Studies came from a multi-racial group of women. Some were scholars who had been teaching and conducting research on Black women since the 1960s and who built upon the work of foremothers such as Maria W. Stewart, Edmonia Lewis, Anna Julia Cooper, Frances E.W. Harper, Zora Neale Hurston, Margaret Walker, and Lorraine Hansberry. Others included artists, activists, entrepreneurs, ministers, and organizers committed to improving the lives of Black women and their communities. From the beginning, too, Black Women's Studies was enhanced by a younger group of women (and a few progressive men) who were usually students or junior faculty inspired by particular individuals to embrace the emerging scholarship on race/gender/sexuality. Within a relatively short period, they produced Black feminist and womanist theories, scholarly resources, visual art, films, and interdisciplinary scholarship that eventually impacted "mainstream" Women's Studies.

Nineteen-seventy was a significant year for the emerging concepts of race/gender/class and intersectional approaches to the study of women. Among the significant publications were Alice Walker's *The Third Life of Grange Copeland,* Maya Angelou's *I Know Why the Caged Bird Sings,* and Toni Morrison's *The Bluest Eye. The Black Woman,* a pioneering collection of critical writings by and about Black women edited by Toni Cade, also appeared in 1970. Though Cade's work was rarely acknowledged by white academic feminists for its significance in the development of Women's Studies, *The Black Woman* was foundational to the field of Black Women's Studies, in part through its inclusion of the distinct voices of a variety of Black women (not just academics), and its cogent arguments differentiating their experiences from those of both Black men and white women. Cade's work preceded by two years Gerda Lerner's 1972 documentary history *Black Women in White America,* which is often erroneously cited as having ushered in Black Women's Studies.[5]

Pioneering works neglected by white feminist historians and social scientists but fundamental to the establishment of Black Women's Studies include Rosalyn Terborg-Penn and Sharon Harley's 1978 anthology, *The Afro-American Woman: Struggles and Images.* The groundbreaking works of La Frances Rodgers-Rose (*The Black Woman*) and Filomina Chioma Steady (*The Black Woman Cross Culturally*) were the first edited social science anthologies on Black women. These scholars and others paved the way for bell hooks, Darlene Clark Hine, Paula Giddings, Bonnie Thornton Dill, Elsa Barkley Brown, Rose Brewer, Mary Helen Washington, and Patricia Hill Collins, all of whom are now more visible to the white feminist academic community.

A significant development in the evolution of Black Women's Studies was the emergence of feminist literary criticism.[6] Black women had been excluded from both African Americanist and feminist critical canons, but early on Black feminist literary critics made visible a rich tradition of Black women writers going back to the nineteenth century.[7] These scholars disrupted a largely male narrative that was being used to construct an African American literary tradition. In this regard, the work of Barbara Smith, Mary Helen Washington, Barbara Christian, Deborah McDowell, Nellie Y. McKay, Hortense Spillers, Gloria T. Hull, Hazel Carby, Frances Smith Foster, Beverly Guy-Sheftall, Claudia Tate, Cheryl Wall, Mae Henderson, Carole Boyce Davies, Gloria Wade-Gayles, Valerie Smith, and Miriam DeCosta Willis, among many others, comes to mind—as well as Alice Walker, who is responsible for rescuing Zora Neale Hurston from the shadows. The founding of *SAGE: A Scholarly Journal on Black Women* (hosted by the Women's Research and Resource Center at Spelman College) in 1983 was a major milestone in promoting research on women of African descent around the world. *SAGE* signaled the coming-of-age of Black Women's Studies in many ways and illustrated the importance of studying the intersection of race, gender, and class within Women's Studies.

Gloria Hull, Patricia Bell Scott, and Barbara Smith were among the first to recognize this critical mass of brave Black women activists, artists, scholars, intellectuals, and community leaders who were responsible for the development of Black Women's Studies. In 1982, they published with the Feminist Press the foundational text with the cogent title that says it all: *All the Women Are White, All the Blacks Are Men, But Some of Us Are Brave: Black Women's Studies*. The editors explain the origins of this book, which most of us simply call *Brave*, in no uncertain terms:

> Women's studies courses . . . focused almost exclusively upon the lives of white women. Black studies, which was much too often male-dominated, also ignored Black women. . . . Because of white women's racism and Black men's sexism, there was no room in either area for a serious consideration of the lives of Black women. And even when they have considered Black women, white women usually have not had the capacity to analyze racial politics and Black culture and Black men have remained blind or resistant to the implications of sexual politics in Black women's lives.[8]

### From *Brave* to *Still Brave*

> We wanted it to be a source for as many readers as possible. . . . The necessary link between academics and activism is best summarized in the words from the introduction: 'The bias of Black Women's Studies must consider as primary the knowledge that will save Black women's lives'. . . . In the year 2000, with our lives and the lives of all our communities still in danger, our struggle continues and much work remains to be done.
>
> Barbara Smith (2000)

It is a testament to the inevitability of change that even foundational texts come to need revision, expansion, or supplementation. And the time came when Florence Howe, former long-time editor of the Feminist Press, extended an invitation to Nellie Y. McKay to edit a twentieth anniversary edition of *Brave*. McKay, a professor at the University of Wisconsin-Madison, agreed to do so with three stipulations: that the Feminist Press would confirm that Gloria (Akasha) Hull, Patricia Bell Scott, and Barbara Smith were not interested in updating the volume; that Stanlie M. James, also a professor at Wisconsin and a regular collaborator with McKay, would co-edit the new volume, and that the Press also confirm that Hull, Scott, and Smith were comfortable with McKay and James undertaking the new project.

Once these stipulations were agreed upon, and with the previous editors' blessings, McKay and James began what they called the *Brave* Project, using the collaborative, consultative form of transdisciplinary Black feminist scholarship. They brainstormed together, read and re-read *Brave*, and consulted widely. They took pains to include individuals with different disciplinary, methodological, generational, and political perspectives as they pondered what a new edition of *Brave* should contain.

They then invited a heterogeneous group to participate in the symposium Are All the Women Still White?: Globalizing Women's Studies, held at the University of Wisconsin-Madison, June 8–10, 2000. Invited participants included Michael Awkward, Kimberlé Crenshaw, Carole Boyce Davies, Evelynn M. Hammonds, Darlene Clark Hine, Tara Hunter, Deborah K. King, Jacqueline Jones Royster, Beverly Guy-Sheftall, and Deborah Gray White, as well as professors Linda Green, Freida High Tesfagioris, and Gloria Ladson Billings, librarian Emilie Ngo Nguidjol, and graduate students from the University of Wisconsin. Participants facilitated discussions around questions implied by the symposium's title as well as core issues surrounding the future of Black Women's Studies. They were invited to identify critical research questions for Black Women's Studies in the twenty-first century and to assess similarities and differences from questions addressed in the 1982 edition of *Brave*. The conveners also asked the participants to consider the kinds of materials and courses that would be critical to the ongoing development of Black Women's Studies. McKay and James expected the symposium to provide them with suggestions for updating the original volume and for commissioning a few additional articles. Then, as editors, they would simply write a forward and introduction and that would be it!

The symposium began comfortably enough. McKay's welcome included a short, informal presentation entitled "21st Century Vision: Why We've Come Together." James shared a letter from Barbara Smith who was unable to attend but wanted to express her delight with the proposal to revise *Brave* in a manner that would allow it to continue to make a difference in the new century, especially in the lives of Black women. Smith stated, "I know Akasha, Pat, and I are genuinely grateful to them [McKay and James], and I also feel that new life will be breathed into the book and into the field of Black Women's Studies as a whole because of the unique insights and perspectives that each of you bring to this project."

After the editors' introductions and the previous editors' gracious blessings, Beverly Guy-Sheftall disrupted the agenda when she stated that while

*Brave* was clearly historic, groundbreaking, and critical in the development of Black Women's Studies, she did not find it particularly useful for teaching in the undergraduate classroom given the disciplinary focus of most courses. Which courses, for example, might be appropriate for the adoption of such a text, if one was not teaching a Black Studies or Women's Studies course? Others noted that *Brave* was a kind of hybrid text—that although it did not easily lend itself for classroom use as a textbook, it was one of the few resources available for Black Women's Studies courses. Some said its usefulness was as a reference tool because it included important resources such as bibliographies and syllabi at a time when the field was just beginning to emerge and before the advance of the ubiquitous web. Historians Darlene Clark Hine, Deborah Gray White, and Tara Hunter reminded the group that there were no articles on African American women's history in the original text and that for two decades, they and others had been working diligently to address that silence through the development of a sub-field of Black women's history. They had brought with them a bibliography of the work historians had produced in the years since the publication of *Brave*.

The agenda was scuttled as lively and far-ranging discussions questioned the practicality and relevance of the symposium's original assumptions. Participants asked questions such as: Was the envisioned updated anthology intended as a reference or a classroom textbook? Should new essays be commissioned that would assess the state of Black Women's Studies? Should the emphasis be on Black Women's Studies in the twenty-first century? Should the task of updating *Brave* be mainly to include the most important or groundbreaking articles that had been published since 1982? They debated including updated bibliographies, course syllabi, relevant web sites, videographies/filmographies, listings of Black women's organizations, special issues of journals,[9] conference proceedings, an atlas of Black women in the U.S., and key rulings on legal issues and their impact on the lives of Black women. They explored the implications of creating a Black Women's Studies presence in cyberspace. They generated a list of themes for inclusion in the new text, such as religion/spirituality, health, male/female and female/female relationships, sexuality, and science/technology. They discussed topics such as biraciality, identity, hair, color caste, and color consciousness and their impact on Black women. And they lamented the absence in the original text of a diasporic or global dimension. After three days of intense discussion, a consensus emerged that the *Brave* Project should provide a catalyst for critical discourses that would further the development of Black Women's Studies in the twenty-first century.

Originally, McKay and James hoped to have the new manuscript ready for publication in 2002 in time for the twentieth anniversary of the first edition. After the symposium, they realized that they were entrusted with a much more profound task than they had imagined. Not only would they need to entirely reconceptualize the new *Brave*, but their vision would have to be expansive enough to address the numerous accomplishments that had occurred in the field of Black Women's Studies and the evolution of Black feminisms since 1982. Their colleagues had thoroughly impressed upon them the magnitude of their task. The symposium had underscored the importance of a new *Brave* project and their need to figure out how to get it right. While they were certainly energized by the symposium, they were also in a state of shock!

After countless emails, letters, and conversations with symposium participants and with others who had not attended,[10] they realized that getting it right would require a thorough review of the literature that had appeared since the publication of *Brave*. It meant exploring new disciplinary, interdisciplinary, and transdisciplinary discourses that incorporated a Black feminist perspective and/or analyzed critical issues of concern to Black women. It also meant acknowledging and exploring the diasporic and cross-cultural dimensions of Black women's experiences no matter where they lived in the world.

By 2004 the editors had collected more than two hundred articles that were important enough to merit consideration for inclusion in the new anthology. Many were "nominated" by symposium participants, while others were already highly anthologized and had become canonical texts. Some original essays were submitted by authors who had heard of the project and wished to be included. Many of them were groundbreaking texts from various disciplines that covered a broad range of topics and issues. Others were smart, provocative, informative essays that built upon earlier works. As the editors immersed themselves in this extraordinary body of scholarship it became exceedingly clear that *Still Brave* would be to *Brave* as daughters often are to their mothers. The two volumes would share a common ancestry and keep the family resemblance, but they would be distinctly different and the product of different eras.

*But Some of Us Are Brave* ultimately had drawn together the thinking and scholarship of a relatively small group of intrepid pioneers engaged in creating a new field of study. In the years since its publication, the field of Black Women's Studies has moved beyond mainly literature and history[11] to encompass additional disciplines, particularly sociology, anthropology, political science, economics, religion, the arts, law, and the natural sciences. Since the 1980s, Black Women's Studies has been indelibly stamped by interdisciplinary, cross-disciplinary, and multi-disciplinary research and theorizing from a range of locations—African Diaspora Studies, popular culture, Black queer studies, communications and journalism, rhetoric, theology, feminist science studies, and critical race theory. Definitions have been refined and a broad range of Black feminist and womanist theories have emerged. Perhaps one of the most interesting developments is that the theorists, advocates, and practitioners of Black Women's Studies no longer feel as compelled to present a united front. Their willingness to disagree has fostered lively debates and even tensions that have enriched the field. There have been sustained efforts to establish cross-disciplinary alliances within the academy as well as efforts to develop coalitions outside the academy, all of which create a more heterogeneous and engaged Black Women's Studies community.

Clearly McKay and James had a changeling on their hands and a mandate to recognize and appreciate its heritage and its evolving future. Unfortunately, something else became clear as well. Nellie Y. McKay's courageous struggle with cancer had given her time to finish many things, but the *Brave* Project would not be one of them. In true McKay fashion, before she died in January 2006, she instructed James to inform Beverly Guy-Sheftall and Frances Smith Foster that they would be sharing the co-editing responsibilities with her to develop a second generation anthology.

Nellie Y. McKay and Black Women's Studies: A Symposium was convened at the University of Wisconsin-Madison on April 1, 2006, to celebrate McKay's life.[12] In her remarks at the celebration, James issued a public invitation to Foster and Guy-Sheftall, and the three of them met with Florence Howe to begin planning their collaboration on the project. They agreed to review as many of the articles already collected as possible and to make suggestions for additional articles that should be reviewed as potential contributions to the new volume. Only after such an extensive review process could they begin to think about the shape and content of the new volume. The *Brave* Project was becoming *Still Brave*.

## Anthologies, Joan Little, and Sweet Honey In the Rock

Anthologies are historical narratives. Historical narratives help us define who we think we are, where we believe we come from and where we imagine we can go . . . anthologies—especially those we read as historical or authoritative—carry cultures, order experiences and share visions. Anthologies refute, defend and recommend.

Frances Smith Foster, 2007

The roots of "anthology" are "anthos," which means "flower," and "logia," which is a "collection" or "garland." A flower collection or garland can be unique, often is beautiful, but always is more than the sum of its parts. An anthology is, actually, an artifice and artifact of its editors. When Frances Smith Foster and Beverly Guy-Sheftall joined the project they knew *Still Brave* could not be a sequel to the original anthology. But what would it be? Which flowers in what order would both commemorate and inspire? After numerous discussions, intense debates, but no actual arguments, the three editors agreed that *Still Brave* would be an anthology that provides a retrospective on the state of Black Women's Studies since the publication of *Brave*. We wanted a collection that was compelling and accessible to scholars, intellectuals, students, and anyone with curiosity and questions about Black Women's Studies. We wanted to build a bridge between the past and the future. We wanted the book to be expansive, leading readers toward particular perspectives while simultaneously suggesting, even requiring, counter-anthologies with different arrangements, different selections. And we wanted to do this in a way that provided wisdom beyond the published words which we, like Smith, Hull, and Scott, believe is crucial for transforming lives. A huge challenge was organizational structure. We finally decided to signify via a representative anecdote and references to music.

We start with a story. Once upon a time, before *Brave*, in 1975 to be more precise, Joan Little (pronounced Joanne), a twenty-year-old Black woman, was raped by a prison guard. In and of itself that was not unusual, but this time the plot changed a bit. Joan Little avenged herself by stabbing her assailant with the ice pick he had used to subdue her. She was charged with first degree murder. Histories, oral and scholarly, tell us that, too, was not unusual. However, Joan Little was the first Black woman to be acquitted of the charge of murdering a white man. The lesson is, however, not in the jury's verdict. It is in how it happened. Joan Little's case was won because many people, mostly women, were incensed enough to organize and to publicize her plight, despite the fact that she was not, as some folk said, the best kind of victim around which to build a movement. Little was no Rosa Parks or even an Angela Y. Davis. She was not an educated, middle-class activist whose actions were anticipated if not precipitated by organized groups. Little was the kind of woman whom middle-class folk tried to ignore or uplift without getting close enough to be stained by the encounter. She had been convicted of breaking and entering, receiving stolen property, and larceny, and was serving time in prison.

According to Minnie Bruce Pratt, "The historic campaign that saved Little from execution or life in prison was the first successful U.S. struggle to assert the right of African-American women to self-defense against white rapists."[13] The press gave it a lot of play and many activists wrote about the case. But, if any of us recall it, we do so no doubt because we have heard, or heard about, the ballad composed and performed by Sweet Honey in the Rock. One of the most salient aspects of the lyrics to "Joan Little" is the way they resonate with a conflict experienced by many more "respectable" women (especially those of us who are Black): "My mama always told me . . . leave that no good woman alone . . . you gonna be judged by the company you keep." And it marks a moment when "nice girls" publicly agreed with "not nice girls" that Joan Little was their sister, their mother, themselves.

We tell this story not only because it continues to be significant for us today as we consider and evaluate with whom and for what we stand, but also because it bears witness to the essential role of music, which is sound and sense, song and poetry, in our lives and—quiet as it's kept—in the academy.

This story points to the direction we took in choosing essays for *Still Brave*. We believe that each selection is a classic, a benchmark, a turning point, or a moment of startling clarity in Black Women's Studies. We doubt that any of these articles were written with the intent of bringing its author fame, and given that academic writing is rarely financially lucrative, they were not written to gain fortune. But we believe that, as is the case with Joan Little, the individual action had collective impact. We have arranged these individually published pieces, written from within and across various disciplines, into communities of thought and moment. For the most part we have ordered them chronologically within sections, and named each section, each neighborhood, each family of thought, with a line from a song we believe represents, reaffirms, and reconstructs the pieces into a whole. In so doing, we acknowledge and honor the presence and prescience of music in Black Women's Studies and other cultural contexts as well as in the history of African peoples.

By placing these essays in company with others, we also change them. Readers who begin with the first one and read sequentially interpret each in context with the others. Reading them chronologically allows a sense of evolution, but it should not suggest a deliberate progression or direct call and response. One of the unfortunate truths of the academy is that too often, too many of us work in silos without adequate communication or collaboration with others in different parts of the university, in different colleges and universities, and—especially—with those who are not in the academy. Another tendency that we lament, and one reason why this collection exists, is the pervasive tendency to ignore or minimize what preceded us and to assume that the latest is the greatest! We are not encouraging evaluation on the basis of the most recent interpretations. We are encouraging interpretation that considers the time and circumstances of each essay or proclamation.

The title of each section in this collection refers to a song also relevant to time and circumstance in African America. In this way, we acknowledge that Black Women's Studies did not develop in an intellectual vacuum but was and is affected by our oral traditions and shared situations. For example, the first section, "The Way We Were," refers less to Barbra Streisand's rendition than it does to Gladys Knight and the Pips' version of those lyrics. African Americans undoubtedly knew both versions, but the way Gladys Knight and the Pips sing the rhythms and harmonies as well as the words with which they introduce their recording make it pure Sankofa. In other words, whereas Streisand sings nostalgia, their interpretation of "The Way We Were" envisions our future by reviewing our past. This song is the soundtrack as we begin *Still Brave* with The Combahee River Collective statement that was included in *But Some of Us Are Brave.* At least two of the editors of *Brave*, Barbara Smith and Gloria Hull, participated in the collective, a group that split off from the National Black Feminist Organization partly to provide a more welcoming community for Black lesbians. The collective is generally acknowledged as formulating the term "identity politics." Arranged in chronological order are other formative pieces, many of which are from defining collections of their era. Years and moments not included mark the inevitable incompleteness of recollection.

Sweet Honey in the Rock sings that every woman who has ever loved a woman ought to stand up and call her name and we feel the inclusivity and particularity of their music creates a space for multiple interpretations and singular celebration. "I Call My Name" riffs on the lyrics to Sweet Honey in the Rock's "Every Woman." Continuing the theme of "identity politics," but spotlighting improvisation and adaptation, this section offers a panorama of questions and concerns addressed time and again. It insists upon the political and personal implications of naming and defining one's self for oneself, the importance of language itself, especially as it concerns who and what defines Black Women's Studies. Jacquelyn Grant's 1986 essay, "Womanist Theology," in content and context, leads into a more intense consideration of the power of naming, but also returns us to The Combahee River Collective. Monica A. Coleman's "Must I Be Womanist?," published twenty years later, shows the changing same. Patricia Hill Collins also contributes to these discourses around identity by providing a gendered critique of the controversial Afrocentrism perspective.

The section "Body and Soul" stresses the inseparability of identities—gender, race, class, religion, and sexuality. If a reader is inclined to think that sexuality, violence, health, and other material aspects of life are fairly recent concerns, she need only recall Joan Little or The Combahee River

Collective. "Body and Soul," as composed by Coleman Hawkins and Duke Ellington in the first part of the twentieth century, is a jazz classic. "Body and Soul," as Anita Baker sang it in the latter part of that century, also assumes the inextricability of the physical and emotional self. But Baker's version has a Black woman's sassiness that declares she's wasted enough time trying to live other people's versions of herself. This "Body and Soul," like the essays in the section it heralds, affirms every day becoming better as the Black woman's strength to trust her own definitions, dreams, and expectations grows.

"To Be Young, Gifted and Black" was a favorite song of Nellie Y. McKay, to whom this volume is dedicated. This anthem has been recorded by many artists and used as mantras for many brave Black women. It invites numerous positive interpretations. One of our favorites is the 1978 rendition by Nina Simone, one among the legions of activist/artists whose contributions have not been studied enough. In this section we offer a small sample of the various contributions and conversations begun earlier but carried on today. Here we see the relatively young field of Black Women's Studies challenging traditional disciplines such as history, art history, sociology, and literary studies to acknowledge and seriously address the intersectionality of identity.

Ella Fitzgerald's rendition of "From This Moment On" celebrates the joy of companionship. Its lyrics acknowledge the blues songs of the past, but declare that from now on "whoop dee doo" songs are in order. The struggle continues, but numbers bring strength. Our concluding section comes full circle as a Sankofa honoring of the future that our past makes possible because we have placed in company writings that enlarge and enhance one another. The first selection, "Mission Statement" from Black Men for the Eradication of Sexism, echoes the first section, and represents the growth of Black male feminism.

The editors recognized, unhappily, that this volume could not adequately represent the robust, nuanced and complicated presence of Black Women's Studies and Black feminisms in Africa and the Diaspora. We did, however, include in this section essays that represent the global reach of the field of Black Women's Studies and the usefulness of Black feminist perspectives as an analytical tool for the development of human rights and the analyses of contemporary political events.

We joyfully acknowledge that the field of Black Women's Studies has greatly expanded and continues to transcend U.S. borders, but we also recognize the limitations of space that required us to develop criteria for inclusion in this anthology—a complicated process.[14] *Still Brave* does attempt to capture the evolution of Black Women's Studies since the landmark publication of *All the Women Are White, All the Blacks Are Men, But Some of Us Are Brave*. We know that our choices are not free from biases.

We were guided by the following principles in our editorial process. We would include foundational, influential essays from a range of disciplines by both established and young scholars. Although many scholars included here have produced important bodies of work in Black Women's Studies, we decided to choose only *one* essay from any individual. This was a difficult decision and resulted, for example, in our not including Angela Y. Davis's important essay on Black women and slavery because we wanted to include her pioneering work on prisons; or Evelynn M. Hammonds' powerful essays on Black female sexuality because we wanted to include her groundbreaking work on race, gender, and HIV/AIDS. Another guideline was to include essays that were more or less free of disciplinary jargon and employed more accessible language so that the collection would be appropriate for the general reader, including undergraduates. We were also drawn to articles that employed interdisciplinary approaches, were review essays of feminist discourse surrounding an important topic, or engaged important debates such as the usefulness of "feminism" vs. "womanism." We chose not to include excerpts from longer works or essays that have been heavily anthologized and are more accessible.[15]

Probably the most difficult and controversial decision we made was to focus, as noted above, on Black Women's Studies within and about the United States. At a time when U.S.-centric and nationalist perspectives are being challenged, our decision seems almost unthinkable. However, it was simply impossible to do justice to the pioneering and voluminous scholarship about Black women in Africa and the African Diaspora since the publication of *Brave*. This is why we felt compelled to narrow our focus. We anticipate that a second volume will engage the transnational.

Like its "foremother," then, *Still Brave* is limited. It does not include reference materials such as course syllabi because so many can now be found on the web. Not all of the disciplines or areas of study that have been impacted by Black Women's Studies are represented here, such as philosophy, film studies, and popular culture. We have not included Black feminist scholarship on hip hop culture, for example the exciting work of Tricia Rose and Gwendolyn Pough.[16] Excerpts of lengthy essays have not been included because of our decision to publish only complete works. The collection, while expansive, is not a comprehensive retrospective on the evolution of the field. Like all anthologies, it does not include many essays that belong here. We especially regret having excluded essays that focus on a particular individual or organization, or highly specialized essays from particular disciplines, such as art history or Black feminist science studies.[17]

However imperfect this new Black Women's Studies reader might be, we are indebted to Barbara Smith, Gloria Hull, and Patricia Bell Scott for showing us the way and creating a space for the development of one of the most significant curricular and scholarly interventions in the U.S. academy. We are also convinced that the lives of Black women here and around the globe have been enhanced by these ongoing research and activist projects.

*Still Brave* is not a sequel to *But Some of Us Are Brave*. It is a praise song to those who gave us that gift, that garland of flowers. *Still Brave* recognizes the courage it takes to respond to, yet not imitate, a major political and academic achievement. Having completed this task, we are humbled and yet heartened as we send this out to you—our own bouquet, our own song of ourselves.

Stanlie M. James
Frances Smith Foster
Beverly Guy-Sheftall

## Notes

1. Florence Howe, "Feminist Scholarship, the Extent of the Revolution," *Change* 14 (April 1982): 6.

2. Johnnella E. Butler and John C. Walters, eds. *Transforming the Curriculum: Ethnic Studies and Women's Studies* (Albany: State University of New York Press, 1991), xix.

3. Butler, "Difficult Dialogues," *Women's Review of Books* 6 (February 1989): 16.

4. bell hooks, "Feminism and Black Women's Studies," *SAGE: A Scholarly Journal on Black Women* 6 (Summer 1989): 54.

5. Accounts of stages of development in U.S. women's history, even the new social history, rarely took into account Black women's history, which includes a number of important texts that impacted the evolution of Black Women's Studies. See especially Sharon Harley and Rosalyn Terborg-Penn, eds., *The Afro-American Woman: Struggles and Images* (Port Washington, N.Y.: Kennikat Press, 1978); Paula Giddings, *When and Where I Enter: The Impact of Black Women on Race and Sex in America* (New York: Morrow, 1984); Angela Y. Davis, *Women, Race, and Class* (New York: Vintage, 1981); Deborah Gray White, *Ar'n't I a Woman? Female Slaves in the Plantation South* (New York: Norton, 1985); and the invaluable 16-volume series, *Black Women in U.S. History*, edited by Darlene Clark Hine, et al. (Brooklyn, NY: Carlson, 1990).

6. See Barbara Smith's "Toward a Black Feminist Criticism," *Conditions: Two* (1977), 27, the first theoretical essay on Black feminist criticism. Three years later, Deborah McDowell's "New Directions for Black Feminist Criticism," *Black American Literature Forum* 14 (October 1980): 153, called for a clearer definition of "the black feminist aesthetic," and delineated the major tasks that would confront the Black feminist critic over the next decade. Earlier, the pioneering work of Mary Helen Washington called atten-

tion to the distinctive work of Black women writers. See her "Black Women Image Makers," *Black World* (August 1974), and her two pioneering anthologies, *Black-Eyed Susans: Classic Stories by and about Black Women* (Garden City, NY: Anchor, 1975) and *Midnight Birds: Stories by Contemporary Black Women Writers* (Garden City, NY: Anchor, 1980). *Sturdy Black Bridges: Visions of Black Women in Literature*, edited by Roseann P. Bell, Bettye J. Parker, and Beverly Guy-Sheftall (New York, NY: Doubleday, 1980), was the first anthology of Black women's literature and it had a diasporic dimension as well. Barbara Christian's *Black Women Novelists: The Development of a Tradition, 1892–1976* (Westport, Conn.: Greenwood Press, 1980) was the first full-length study of the novels of Black women. For an excellent overview of Black feminist criticism, see Cheryl Wall, ed., *Changing Our Own Words: Essays on Theory, Criticism, and Writing by Black Women* (New Brunswick, NJ: Rutgers University Press, 1989). The publication of Alice Walker's "In Search of Our Mothers' Gardens: The Creativity of Black Women in the South," in *Ms.* (May 1974), posits a theory of Black female creativity; Walker probably designed the first course on Black women writers which she taught in 1977 at Wellesley College.

7. See Farah Griffin's review essay in this volume, "That the Mothers May Soar and the Daughters May Know Their Names . . ." for a comprehensive assessment of Black feminist criticism.

8. Hull, Scott, and Smith, *All the Women Are White, All the Blacks Are Men, But Some of Us Are Brave* (New York, NY: Feminist Press, 1982), p. xx–xxi. See also Beverly Guy-Sheftall and Patricia Bell Scott, "Black Women's Studies: A View from the Margin," in *Educating the Majority: Women Challenge Tradition in Higher Education*, Pearson, Shavlik, and Touchton, eds. (New York/London: American Council on Education/Collier Macmillan, 1989); a special issue of *SAGE: A Scholarly Journal on Black Women* focusing on Black Women's Studies, vol. 6, no. 1 (Summer 1989); and the three volume *Africana Women's Studies Series* (Atlanta, GA: Africana Women's Center, Atlanta University, 1984), which includes course syllabi and bibliographies.

9. These would include the special issue of *Conditions: Five, the Black Women's Issue*, vol. 2, no. 2, 1979, edited by Lorraine Bethel and Barbara Smith.

10. At one point Elizabeth Higginbotham, an original contributor to *But Some of Us Are Brave*, even came to Madison and spent a day with McKay and James to discuss the Brave Project and offer suggestions on how to proceed and what to consider for inclusion, especially from a social scientist's perspective.

11. When it was published, the sixteen volume series, *Black Women in United States History* (Brooklyn, NY: Carlson Publishing Company, 1990), edited by Darlene Clark Hine, Elsa Barkley Brown, Tiffany R.L. Patterson, and Lillian S. Williams, was the most comprehensive collection of scholarship on Black women's history in the U.S. It included seminal essays, such as Angela Y. Davis's pioneering essay, "Reflections on the Black Woman's Role in the Community of Slaves," *Black Scholar* 3 (December 1971): 4–15, which rewrote the history of slave resistance, as well as journal articles, unpublished dissertations, and conference proceedings.

12. For commentaries on McKay's life and work see "Nellie McKay Tribute" a special issue of *African American Review* vol. 40, no. 1, Spring 2006.

13. "A look back at the Joann Little Case," March 9, 2006: www.workers.org/s006/us/joann-little-0316

14. While *But Some of Us Are Brave* focused on the U.S., the field of Black Women's Studies was always global. Filomina Chioma Steady, ed., *The Black Woman Cross-Culturally* (Cambridge, Mass.: Schenkman, 1981), was particularly significant because

of its diasporic emphasis and its cross-cultural approach to the experiences of women of African descent. See also the groundbreaking *Women in Africa and the African Diaspora*, edited by Rosalyn Terborg-Penn, Sharon Harley, and Andrea Benton Rushing (Washington, DC: Howard University Press, 1987), which provides a theoretical framework for dealing with women of African descent, and includes a pioneering essay by Steady on African feminism. The global reach of Black Women's Studies is also underscored by Andree Nicola McLaughlin's establishing at Medgar Evers College in 1987 the pioneering International Cross-Cultural Black Women's Studies Institute: A Global Network. The network created a series of world conferences that began in the summer of 1987 in London; subsequent gatherings took place in New York, Zimbabwe, Auckland, Aotearoa (New Zealand), Germany, Venezuela, Hawaii, South Africa, Russia, Costa Rica, Trinidad and Tobago, Japan, and Panama. The Institute fosters international cooperation among women from economically developing nations, promotes peace, advocates for human rights, and provides opportunities for women of diverse cultures to exchange information, share experiences, identify resources, and build linkages.

It is also instructive to consider the gendered aspects of the early history of Black Studies, which has been largely invisible to scholars. This "herstory" of the development of the field concerns itself with a little known organization, the International Council of Women of the Darker Races, which emerged as a result of the racial uplift impulses and international educational projects of the Black women's club movement in the U.S. Organized by several prominent club women in 1924, most notably Margaret Murray Washington, founder of the Tuskegee Women's Club in Alabama and the Council's president, its purpose was to study the history of peoples of color throughout the world, particularly in West Africa, India, Haiti, and Cuba, and to disseminate knowledge about them for the purpose of engendering racial pride. Study groups, which were called Committees of Seven, were also formed to infuse public school curricula with material on Blacks and other people of color. Field trips were organized to gain firsthand experience of other cultures. The Council also studied the situation of women and children of color transnationally. Margaret Murray Washington taught a course at Tuskegee on the condition and status of women throughout the world that clearly illustrated Black women's awareness of the importance of gender long before there was a women's studies movement within the mainstream academy.

15. These would include Evelyn Brooks Higginbotham, "African-American Women's History and the Metalanguage of Race," *Signs* 17 (Winter): 251–74; Hortense Spillers' landmark essay, "Mamma's Baby, Papa's Maybe: An American Grammar Book," *Diacritics* 17 (1987): 64–81; Deborah K. King, "Multiple Jeopardy, Multiple Consciousness: The Context of a Black Feminist Ideology," *Signs* 14 (1): 42–72; Kimberlé Crenshaw, "Mapping the Margins: Intersectionality, Identity Politics, and Violence Against Women of Color," *Stanford Law Review* 43 (July 1991): 1–50.

16. See Tricia Rose, *Black Noise: Rap Music and Black Culture in Contemporary America* (Hanover, NH: University Press of New England, 1994) and *The Hip Hop Wars: What We Talk About When We Talk About Hip Hop—And Why It Matters* (New York: Basic-Civitas Books, 2008); Gwendolyn D. Pough, *Check It While I Wreck It: Black Womanhood, Hip Hop Culture, and the Public Sphere* (Northeastern University Press, 2004); Gwendolyn Pough, Elaine Richardson, Aisha Durham, Rachel Raimist, eds., *Home Girls Make Some Noise: Hip Hop Feminist Anthology* (Mira Loma, CA: Parker Publishing, 2007); T. Denean Sharpley-Whiting, *Pimps Up, Ho's Down: Hip Hop's Hold on Young Black Women* (New York: New York University Press, 2008); Joan Morgan, *When Chick-*

*enheads Come Home to Roost: A Hip-Hop Feminist Breaks It Down* (New York: Simon and Schuster, 2000).

17. Under the rubric of Black feminist science studies, there is a growing body of scholarship on science, medicine, and technology and reproductive rights by Black women academics. The work of Evelynn M. Hammonds, Deborah Grayson, Vanessa Gamble, Diann Jordan, Stephanie Athey, and others is particularly useful. See several anthologies that include Black women: *Gender and Scientific Authority*, edited by Barbara Laslett, Sally G. Kohlstedt, Helen Longino, and Evelynn M. Hammonds (Chicago: University of Chicago Press, 1996); *Women, Science and Technology: A Reader in Feminist Science and Technology*, eds., Mary Wyer, Mary Berbercheck, et al (New York: Routledge, 2001); *Science, Medicine and Technology in the 20th Century: What Difference Has Feminism Made?*, eds., Angela Creager, Elizabeth Lunbeck and Londa Schiebinger (Chicago: University of Chicago Press, 2006); *Undivided Rights: Women of Color Organize for Reproductive Justice*, eds. Jael Silliman, Marlene Gerber Fried, Loretta Ross, and Elena R. Gutierrez (Cambridge, MA: South End Press, 2004); and Jennifer Nelson's *Women of Color and the Reproductive Rights Movement* (New York: New York University Press, 2003). Evelynn M. Hammonds' co-authored book (with Rebecca Herzig and Abigail Bass), *The MIT Reader on Race and Gender in Science* (Cambridge: MIT Press, 2009) and her *The Logic of Difference: A History of Race in Science and Medicine in the United States, 1850–1990* (Chapel Hill: University of North Carolina Press, 2009) are foundational texts in Black feminist science studies. Recent work on the Black female body and Black female sexualities are also important. See Evelynn M. Hammonds, "Toward a Genealogy of Black Female Sexuality: The Problematic of Difference," in M. Jacqui Alexander and Chandra Talpade Mohanty, eds., *Feminist Genealogies, Colonial Legacies, Democratic Futures* (New York: Routledge, 1997) and "Black (W)holes and the Geometry of Black Female Sexuality," *differences: A Journal of Feminist Cultural Studies*, vol. 6, nos. 2 & 3, 1994: 127–45; Dorothy Roberts, *Killing the Black Body: Race, Reproduction and the Meaning of Liberty* (New York: Pantheon, 1997); Kimberly Wallace Sanders, ed., *Skin Deep, Spirit Strong: The Black Female Body in American Culture* (Ann Arbor: University of Michigan Press, 2002); Tricia Rose, *Longing to Tell: Black Women Talk About Sexuality and Intimacy* (New York: Picador, 2004).

**Note:** Throughout this anthology we have kept the original capitalization to remain true to the author's preference at the time of writing. We have also maintained the original footnote formats, which vary from essay to essay.

# THE WAY WE WERE

**A Black Feminist Statement**

*The Combahee River Collective*
1978

We are a collective of black feminists who have been meeting together since 1974.[1] During that time we have been involved in the process of defining and clarifying our politics, while at the same time doing political work within our own group and in coalition with other progressive organizations and movements. The most general statement of our politics at the present time would be that we are actively committed to struggling against racial, sexual, heterosexual, and class oppression and see as our particular task the development of integrated analysis and practice based upon the fact that the major systems of oppression are interlocking. The synthesis of these oppressions creates the conditions of our lives. As black women we see black feminism as the logical political movement to combat the manifold and simultaneous oppressions that all women of color face.

We will discuss four major topics in the paper that follows: (1) The genesis of contemporary black feminism; (2) what we believe, i.e., the specific province of our politics; (3) the problems in organizing black feminists, including a brief herstory of our collective; and (4) black feminist issues and practice.

### 1. The Genesis of Contemporary Black Feminism

Before looking at the recent development of black feminism, we would like to affirm that we find our origins in the historical reality of Afro-American women's continuous life-and-death struggle for survival and liberation. Black women's extremely negative relationship to the American political system (a system of white male rule) has always been determined by our membership in two oppressed racial and sexual castes. As Angela Y. Davis points out in "Reflections on the Black Woman's Role in the Community of Slaves," black women have always embodied, if only in their physical manifestation, an adversary stance to white male rule and have actively resisted its inroads upon them and their communities in both dramatic and subtle ways. There have always been black women activists—some known, like Sojourner Truth, Harriet Tubman, Frances E. W. Harper, Ida B. Wells Barnett, and Mary Church Terrell, and thousands upon thousands unknown—who had a shared awareness of how their sexual identity combined with their racial identity to make their whole life situation and the focus of their political struggles unique. Contemporary black feminism is the outgrowth of countless generations of personal sacrifice, militancy, and work by our mothers and sisters.

A black feminist presence has evolved most obviously in connection with the second wave of the American women's movement beginning in the late 1960s. Black, other Third World, and working women have been involved in the feminist movement from its start, but both outside reactionary forces and racism and elitism within the movement itself have served to obscure our participation. In 1973 black feminists, primarily located in New York, felt the necessity of forming a separate black feminist group. This became the National Black Feminist Organization (NBFO).

Black feminist politics also have an obvious connection to movements for black liberation, particularly those of the 1960s and 1970s. Many of us were active in those movements (civil rights, black nationalism, the Black Panthers), and all of our lives were greatly affected and changed by their ideology, their goals, and the tactics used to achieve their goals. It was our experience and disillusionment within these liberation movements, as well as experience on the periphery of the white male left, that led to the need to develop a politics that was antiracist, unlike those of white women, and antisexist, unlike those of black and white men.

There is also undeniably a personal genesis for black feminism, that is, the political realization that comes from the seemingly personal experiences of individual black women's lives. Black feminists and many more black women who do not define themselves as feminists have all experienced sexual oppression as a constant factor in our day-to-day existence.

Black feminists often talk about their feelings of craziness before becoming conscious of the concepts of sexual politics, patriarchal rule, and, most importantly, feminism, the political analysis and practice that we women use to struggle against our oppression. The fact that racial politics and indeed racism are pervasive factors in our lives did not allow us, and still does not allow most black women, to look more deeply into our own experiences and define those things that make our lives what they are and our oppression specific to us. In the process of consciousness-raising, actually life-sharing, we began to recognize the commonality of our experiences and, from that sharing and growing consciousness, to build a politics that will change our lives and inevitably end our oppression.

Our development also must be tied to the contemporary economic and political position of black people. The post-World War II generation of black youth was the first to be able to minimally partake of certain educational and employment options, previously closed completely to black people. Although our economic position is still at the very bottom of the American capitalist economy, a handful of us have been able to gain certain tools as a result of tokenism in education and employment which potentially enable us to more effectively fight our oppression.

A combined antiracist and antisexist position drew us together initially, and as we developed politically we addressed ourselves to heterosexism and economic oppression under capitalism.

## 2. What We Believe

Above all else, our politics initially sprang from the shared belief that black women are inherently valuable, that our liberation is a necessity not as an adjunct to somebody else's but because of our need as human persons for autonomy. This may seem so obvious as to sound simplistic, but it is apparent that no other ostensibly progressive movement has ever considered our specific oppression a priority or worked seriously for the ending of that oppression. The mere names of the pejorative stereotypes attributed to black women (e.g., mammy, matriarch, Sapphire, whore, bulldagger), let alone cataloguing the cruel, often murderous, treatment we receive, indicates how little value has been placed upon our lives during four centuries of bondage in the Western hemisphere. We realize that the only people who care enough about us to work consistently for our liberation is us. Our politics evolve from a healthy love for ourselves, our sisters, and our community, which allows us to continue our struggle and work.

This focusing upon our own oppression is embodied in the concept of identity politics. We believe that the most profound and potentially the most radical politics come directly out of our own identity, as opposed to working to end somebody else's oppression. In the case of black women this is a particularly repugnant, dangerous, threatening, and therefore revolutionary concept because it is obvious from looking at all the political movements that have preceded us that anyone is more worthy of liberation than ourselves. We reject pedestals, queenhood, and walking ten paces behind. To be recognized as human, levelly human, is enough.

We believe that sexual politics under patriarchy is as pervasive in black women's lives as are the politics of class and race. We also often find it difficult to separate race from class from sex oppression because in our lives they are most often experienced simultaneously. We know that there is such a thing as racial-sexual oppression that is neither solely racial nor solely sexual, e.g., the history of rape of black women by white men as a weapon of political repression.

Although we are feminists and lesbians, we feel solidarity with progressive black men and do not advocate the fractionalization that white women who are separatists demand. Our situation as black people necessitates that we have solidarity around the fact of race, which white women of course do not need to have with white men, unless it is their negative solidarity as racial oppressors. We struggle together with black men against racism, while we also struggle with black men about sexism.

We realize that the liberation of all oppressed peoples necessitates the destruction of the political-economic systems of capitalism and imperialism as well as patriarchy. We are socialists because we believe the work must be organized for the collective benefit of those who do the work and create the products and not for the profit of the bosses. Material resources must be equally distributed among those who create these resources. We are not convinced, however, that a socialist revolution that is not also a feminist and antiracist revolution will guarantee our liberation. We have arrived at the necessity for developing an understanding of class relationships that takes into account the specific class position of black women who are generally marginal in the labor force, while at this particular time some of us are temporarily viewed as doubly desirable tokens at white-collar and professional levels. We need to articulate the real class situation of persons who are not merely raceless, sexless workers, but for whom racial and sexual oppression are significant determinants in their working/economic lives. Although we are in essential agreement with Marx's theory as it applied to the very specific economic relationships he analyzed, we know that this analysis must be extended further in order for us to understand our specific economic situation as black women.

A political contribution which we feel we have already made is the expansion of the feminist principle that the personal is political. In our consciousness-raising sessions, for example, we have in many ways gone beyond white women's revelations because we are dealing with the implications of race and class as well as sex. Even our black women's style of talking/testifying in black language about what we have experienced has a resonance that is both cultural and political. We have spent a great deal of energy delving into the cultural and experiential nature of our oppression out of necessity because none of these matters have ever been looked at before. No one before has ever examined the multilayered texture of black women's lives.

As we have already stated, we reject the stance of lesbian separatism because it is not a viable political analysis or strategy for us. It leaves out far too much and far too many people, particularly black men, women, and children. We have a great deal of criticism and loathing for what men have been socialized to be in this society: what they support, how they act, and how they oppress. But we do not have the misguided notion that it is their maleness, per se—i.e., their biological maleness—that makes them what they are. As black women we find any type of biological determinism a particularly dangerous and reactionary basis upon which to build a politic. We must also question whether lesbian separatism is an adequate and progressive political analysis and strategy, even for those who practice it, since it so completely denies any but the sexual sources of women's oppression, negating the facts of class and race.

### 3. Problems in Organizing Black Feminists

During our years together as a black feminist collective we have experienced success and defeat, joy and pain, victory and failure. We have found that it is very difficult to organize around black feminist issues, difficult even to announce in certain contexts that we *are* black feminists. We have tried to think about the reasons for our difficulties, particularly since the white women's movement continues to be strong and to grow in many directions. In this section we will discuss some of the general reasons for the organizing problems we face and also talk specifically about the stages in organizing our own collective.

The major source of difficulty in our political work is that we are not just trying to fight oppression on one front or even two but instead to address a whole range of oppressions. We do not have racial, sexual, heterosexual, or class privilege to rely upon, nor do we have even the minimal access to resources and power that groups who possess any one of these types of privilege have.

The psychological toll of being a black woman and the difficulties these present in reaching political consciousness and doing political work can never be underestimated. There is a very low value placed upon black women's psyches in this society, which is both racist and sexist. As an early group member once said, "We are all damaged people merely by virtue of being black women." We are dispossessed psychologically and on every other level, and yet we feel the necessity to struggle to change our condition and the condition of all black women. In "A Black Feminist's Search for Sisterhood," Michele Wallace arrives at this conclusion:

> We exist as women who are black who are feminists, each stranded for the moment, working independently because there is not yet an environment in this society remotely congenial to our struggle—because,

being on the bottom, we would have to do what no one else has done: we would have to fight the world.[2]

Wallace is not pessimistic but realistic in her assessment of black feminists' position, particularly in her allusion to the nearly classic isolation most of us face. We might use our position at the bottom, however, to make a clear leap into revolutionary action. If black women were free, it would mean that everyone else would have to be free since our freedom would necessitate the destruction of all the systems of oppression.

Feminism is, nevertheless, very threatening to the majority of black people because it calls into question some of the most basic assumptions about our existence, i.e., that gender should be a determinant of power relationships. Here is the way male and female roles were defined in a black nationalist pamphlet from the early 1970s.

> We understand that it is and has been traditional that the man is the head of the house. He is the leader of the house/nation because his knowledge of the world is broader, his awareness is greater, his understanding is fuller and his application of this information is wiser. . . . After all, it is only reasonable that the man be the head of the house because he is able to defend and protect the development of his home. . . . Women cannot do the same things as men—they are made by nature to function differently. Equality of men and women is something that cannot happen even in the abstract world. Men are not equal to other men, i.e., ability, experience, or even understanding. The value of men and women can be seen as in the value of gold and silver—they are not equal but both have great value. We must realize that men and women are a complement to each other because there is no house/family without a man and his wife. Both are essential to the development of any life.[3]

The material conditions of most black women would hardly lead them to upset both economic and sexual arrangements that seem to represent some stability in their lives. Many black women have a good understanding of both sexism and racism, but because of the everyday constrictions of their lives cannot risk struggling against them both.

The reaction of black men to feminism has been notoriously negative. They are, of course, even more threatened than black women by the possibility that black feminists might organize around our own needs. They realize that they might not only lose valuable and hard-working allies in their struggles but that they might also be forced to change their habitually sexist ways of interacting with and oppressing black women. Accusations that black feminism divides the black struggle are powerful deterrents to the growth of an autonomous black women's movement.

Still, hundreds of women have been active at different times during the three-year existence of our group. And every black woman who came, came out of a strongly felt need for some level of possibility that did not previously exist in her life.

When we first started meeting early in 1974 after the NBFO's first eastern regional conference, we did not have a strategy for organizing, or even a focus. We just wanted to see what we had. After a period of months of not meeting, we began to meet again late in the year and started doing an intense variety of consciousness-raising. The overwhelming feeling that we had is that after years and years we had finally found each other. Although we were not doing political work as a group, individuals continued their involvement in lesbian politics, sterilization abuse and abortion rights work, Third World Women's International Women's Day activities, and support activity for the trials of Dr. Kenneth Edelin, Joan Little, and Inez Garcia. During our first summer, when membership had dropped off considerably, those of us remaining devoted serious discussion to the possibility of opening a refuge for battered women in a black community. (There was no refuge in Boston at that time.) We also decided around that time to become an independent collective since we had serious disagreements with NBFO's bourgeois-feminist stance and their lack of a clear political focus.

We also were contacted at that time by socialist feminists, with whom we had worked on abortion rights activities, who wanted to encourage us to attend the National Socialist Feminist Conference in Yellow Springs. One of our members did attend and despite the narrowness of the ideology that was promoted at that particular conference, we became more aware of the need for us to understand our own economic situation and to make our own economic analysis.

In the fall, when some members returned, we experienced several months of comparative inactivity and internal disagreements which were first conceptualized as a lesbian-straight split but which were also the result of class and political differences. During the summer those of us who were still meeting had determined the need to do political work and to move beyond consciousness-raising and serving exclusively as an emotional support group. At the beginning of 1976, when some of the women who had not wanted to do political work and who also had voiced disagreements stopped attending of their own accord, we again looked for a focus. We decided at that time, with the addition of new members, to become a study group. We had always shared our reading with each other, and some of us had written papers on black feminism for group discussion a few months before this decision was made. We began functioning as a study group and also began discussing the possibility of starting a black feminist publication.

We had a retreat in the late spring, which provided a time for both political discussion and working out interpersonal issues. Currently we are planning to gather together a collection of black feminist writing. We feel that it is absolutely essential to demonstrate the reality of our politics to other black women and believe that we can do this through writing and distributing our work. The fact that individual black feminists are living in isolation all over the country, that our own numbers are small, and that we have some skills in writing, printing, and publishing makes us want to carry out these kinds of projects as a means of organizing black feminists as we continue to do political work in coalition with other groups.

### 4. Black Feminist Issues and Practice

During our time together we have identified and worked on many issues of particular relevance to black women. The inclusiveness of our politics makes us concerned with any situation that impinges upon the lives of women, Third World, and working people. We are of course particularly committed to working on those struggles in which race, sex, and class are simultaneous factors in oppression. We might, for example, become involved in workplace organizing at a factory that employs Third World women or picket a hospital that is cutting back on already inadequate health care to a Third World community, or set up a rape crisis center in a black neighborhood. Organizing around welfare or daycare concerns might also be a focus. The work to be done and the countless issues that this work represents merely reflect the pervasiveness of our oppression.

Issues and projects that collective members have actually worked on are sterilization abuse, abortion rights, battered women, rape, and health care. We have also done many workshops and educationals on black feminism on college campuses, at women's conferences, and most recently for high school women.

One issue that is of major concern to us and that we have begun to publicly address is racism in the white women's movement. As black feminists we are made constantly and painfully aware of how little effort white women have made to understand and combat their racism, which requires among other things that they have a more than superficial comprehension of race, color, and black history and culture. Eliminating racism in the white women's movement is by definition work for white women to do, but we will continue to speak to and demand accountability on this issue.

In the practice of our politics we do not believe that the end always justifies the means. Many reactionary and destructive acts have been done in the name of achieving "correct" political goals. As feminists we do not want to mess over people in the name of politics. We believe in collective process and a nonhierarchical distribution of power within our own group and in our vision of a revolutionary society. We are committed to a continual examination of our politics as they develop through criticism and self-criticism as an essential aspect of our practice. As black feminists and lesbians we know that we have a very definite revolutionary task to perform and we are ready for the lifetime of work and struggle before us.

## Notes

1. This statement is dated April 1977.
2. Michele Wallace, "A Black Feminist's Search for Sisterhood," *The Village Voice*, 28 July, 1975: 6–7.
3. Mumininas of Committee for Unified Newark. *Mwanamke Mwananchi (The Nationalist Woman)*, Newark, N.J., c. 1971: 4–5.

## Lesbianism
### An Act of Resistance

*Cheryl Clarke*

1981

For a woman to be a lesbian in a male-supremacist, capitalist, misogynist, racist, homophobic, imperialist culture, such as that of North America, is an act of resistance. (A resistance that should be championed throughout the world by all the forces struggling for liberation from the same slave master.) No matter how a woman lives out her lesbianism—in the closet, in the state legislature, in the bedroom—she has rebelled against becoming the slave master's concubine, viz. the male-dependent female, the female heterosexual. This rebellion is dangerous business in patriarchy. Men at all levels of privilege, of all classes and colors, have the potential to act out legalistically, moralistically, and violently when they cannot colonize women, when they cannot circumscribe our sexual, productive, reproductive, creative prerogatives, and energies. And the lesbian—that woman who, as Judy Grahn says, "has taken a woman lover"[1]—has succeeded in resisting the slave master's imperialism in that one sphere of her life. The lesbian has decolonized her body. She has rejected a life of servitude implicit in Western, heterosexual relationships, and has accepted the potential of mutuality in a lesbian relationship—*roles* notwithstanding.

Historically, this culture has come to identify lesbians as women, who over time, engage in a range and variety of sexual-emotional relationships with women. I, for one, identify a woman as a lesbian who says she is. Lesbianism is a recognition, an awakening, a reawakening of our passion for each (woman) other (woman) and for same (woman). This passion will ultimately reverse the heterosexual imperialism of male culture. Women, through the ages, have fought and died rather than deny that passion. In her essay "The Meaning of Our Love for Women Is What We Have Constantly to Expand," Adrienne Rich states:

> . . . Before any kind of feminist movement existed, or could exist, lesbians existed: women who loved women, who refused to comply with behavior demanded of women, who refused to define themselves in

relation to men. Those women, our foresisters, millions whose names we do not know, were tortured and burned as witches, slandered in religious and later in "scientific" tracts, portrayed in art and literature as bizarre, amoral, destructive, decadent women. For a long time, the lesbian has been a personification of feminine evil.

. . . Lesbians have been forced to live between two cultures, both male-dominated, each of which has denied and endangered our existence . . . . Heterosexual, patriarchal culture has driven lesbians into secrecy and guilt, often to self-hatred and suicide.[2]

The evolving synthesis of lesbianism and feminism—two women-centered and -powered ideologies—is breaking that silence and secrecy. The following analysis is offered as one small cut against that stone of silence and secrecy. It is not intended to be original or all-inclusive. I dedicate this work to all the women hidden from history whose suffering and triumph have made it possible for me to call my name out loud.

The woman who embraces lesbianism as an ideological, political, and philosophical means of liberation of all women from heterosexual tyranny must also identify with the worldwide struggle of all women to end male-supremacist tyranny at all levels. As far as I am concerned, any woman who calls herself a feminist must commit herself to the liberation of *all* women from *coerced* heterosexuality as it manifests itself in the family, the state, and on Madison Avenue. The lesbian-feminist struggles for the liberation of all people from patriarchal domination through heterosexism and for the transformation of all socio-political structures, systems, and relationships that have been degraded and corrupted under centuries of male domination.

However, there is no one kind of lesbian, no one kind of lesbian behavior, and no one kind of lesbian relationship. Also there is no one kind of response to the pressures that lesbians labor under to survive as lesbians. Not all women who are involved in sexual-emotional relationships with women call themselves lesbians or identify with any particular lesbian community. Many women are only lesbians to a particular community and *pass* as heterosexuals as they traffic among enemies. (This is analogous to being black and passing for white with only one's immediate family knowing one's true origins.) Yet, those who hide in the closet of heterosexual presumption are sooner or later discovered. The "nigger-in-the-woodpile" story retells itself. Many women are politically active as lesbians, but may fear holding hands with their lovers as they traverse heterosexual turf. (This response to heterosexual predominance can be likened to the reaction of the black student who integrates a predominately white dormitory and who fears leaving the door of her room open when she plays gospel music.) There is the woman who engages in sexual-emotional relationships with women and labels herself *bisexual*. (This is comparable to the Afro-American whose skin-color indicates her mixed ancestry yet who calls herself "mulatto" rather than black.) Bisexual is a safer label than lesbian, for it posits the possibility of a relationship with a man, regardless of how infrequent or non-existent the female bisexual's relationships with men might be. And then there is the lesbian who is a lesbian anywhere and everywhere and who is in direct and constant confrontation with heterosexual presumption, privilege, and oppression. (Her struggle can be compared to that of the Civil Rights activist of the 1960s who was out there on the streets for freedom while so many of us viewed the action on the television.)

Wherever we, as lesbians, fall along this very generalized political continuum, we must know that the institution of heterosexuality is a die-hard custom through which male-supremacist institutions insure their own perpetuity and control over us. Women are kept, maintained, and contained through terror, violence, and spray of semen. It is profitable for our colonizers to confine our bodies and alienate us from our own life processes as it was profitable for the European to enslave the African and destroy all memory of a prior freedom and self-determination—Alex Haley notwithstanding. And just as the foundation of Western capitalism depended upon the North Atlantic slave trade, the system of patriarchal domination is buttressed by the subjugation of women through heterosexuality. So, patriarchs must extol the boy-girl dyad as "natural" to keep us straight and compliant, in the same way the European had to extol Caucasian superiority to justify the African slave trade. Against that historic backdrop, *the woman who chooses to be a lesbian lives dangerously*.

As a member of the largest and second most oppressed group of people of color, as a woman whose slave and ex-slave foresisters suffered some of the most brutal racist, male-supremacist imperialism in Western history, the black lesbian has had to survive also the psychic mutilation of heterosexual superiority. The black lesbian is coerced into the experience of institutional racism—like every other nigger in America—and must suffer as well the homophobic sexism of the black political community, some of whom seem to have forgotten so soon the pain of rejection, denial, and repression sanctioned by racist America. While most political black lesbians do not give a damn if white America is negrophobic, it becomes deeply problematic when the contemporary black political community (another male-dominated and male-identified institution) rejects us because of our commitment to women and women's liberation. Many black male members of that community seem still not to understand the historic connection between the oppression of African peoples in North America and the universal oppression of women. As the women's rights activist and abolitionist,

Elizabeth Cady Stanton, pointed out during the 1850s, racism and sexism have been produced by the same animal, viz. "the white Saxon man."

Gender oppression (i.e., the male exploitation and control of women's productive and reproductive energies on the specious basis of a biological difference) originated from the first division of labor, viz. that between women and men, and resulted in the accumulation of private property, patriarchal usurpation of "mother right" or matrilineage, and the duplicitous, male-supremacist institution of heterosexual monogamy (for women only). Sexual politics, therefore, mirror the exploitative, class-bound relationship between the white slave master and the African slave—and the impact of both relationships (between black and white and woman and man) has been residual beyond emancipation and suffrage. The ruling class white man had a centuries-old model for his day-to-day treatment of the African slave. Before he learned to justify the African's continued enslavement and the ex-slave's continued disfranchisement with arguments of the African's divinely ordained mental and moral inferiority to himself (a smokescreen for his capitalist greed) the white man learned, within the structure of heterosexual monogamy and under the system of patriarchy, to relate to black people—slave or free—as a man *relates* to a woman, viz. as property, as a sexual commodity, as a servant, as a source of free or cheap labor, and as an innately inferior being.

Although counterrevolutionary, Western heterosexuality, which advances male supremacy, continues to be upheld by many black people, especially black men, as the most desired state of affairs between men and women. This observation is borne out on the pages of our most scholarly black publications to our most commercial black publications, which view the issue of black male and female relationships through the lens of heterosexual bias. But this is to be expected, as historically heterosexuality was one of our only means of power over our condition as slaves and one of two means we had at our disposal to appease the white man.

Now, as ex-slaves, black men have more latitude to oppress black women, because the brothers no longer have to compete directly with the white man for control of black women's bodies. Now, the black man can assume the "master" role, and he can attempt to tyrannize black women. The black man may view the lesbian—who cannot be manipulated or seduced sexually by him—in much the same way the white slave master once viewed the black male slave, viz. as some perverse caricature of manhood threatening his position of dominance over the female body. This view, of course, is a "neurotic illusion" imposed on black men by the dictates of male supremacy, which the black man can never fulfill because he lacks the capital means and racial privilege.

Historically, the myth in the Black world is that there are only two free people in the United States, the white man and the Black woman. The myth was established by the Black man in the long period of his frustration when he longed to be free to have the material and social advantages of his oppressor, the white man. On examination of the myth this so-called freedom was based on the sexual prerogatives taken by the white man on the Black female. It was fantasied by the Black man that she enjoyed it.[3]

While lesbian-feminism does threaten the black man's predatory control of black women, its goal as a political ideology and philosophy is not to take the black man's or any man's position on top.

Black lesbians who do work within "by-for-about-black-people" groups or organizations either pass as "straight" or relegate our lesbianism to the so-called "private" sphere. The more male-dominated or black-nationalist-bourgeois the organization or group, the more resistant to change, and thus, the more homophobic and antifeminist. In these sectors, we learn to keep a low profile.

In 1979, at the annual conference of a regional chapter of the National Black Social Workers, the national director of that body was given a standing ovation for the following remarks:

> Homosexuals are even accorded minority status now. . . . And white women, too. And some of you black women who call yourselves feminists will be sitting up in meetings with the same white women who will be stealing your men on the sly.

This type of indictment of women's revolution and implicitly of lesbian liberation is voiced throughout the bourgeois black (male) movement. But this is the insidious nature of male supremacy. While the black man may consider racism his primary oppression, he is hard put to recognize that sexism is inextricably bound up with the racism the black woman must suffer, nor can he see that no women (or men for that matter) will be liberated from the original "master-slave" relationship, viz. that between men and women, until we are all liberated from the false premise of heterosexual superiority. This corrupted, predatory relationship between men and women is the foundation of the master-slave relationship between white and black people in the United States.

The tactic many black men use to intimidate black women from embracing feminism is to reduce the conflicts between white women and black women to a "tug-o'-war" for the black penis. And since the black lesbian, as stated previously, is not interested in his penis, she undermines the black man's only source of power over her, viz. his heterosexuality. Black lesbians and all black women involved in the struggle for liberation must resist this manipulation and seduction.

The black dyke, like every dyke in America, is everywhere—in the home, in the street, on the welfare, unemployment and social security rolls, raising children, working in factories, in the armed forces, on television, in the public school system, in all the professions, going to college or graduate school, in middle-management, et. al. The black dyke, like every other non-white and working class and poor woman in America, has not suffered the luxury, privilege, or oppression of being dependent on men, even though our male counterparts have been present, have shared our lives, work and struggle, and, in addition have undermined our "human dignity" along the way, like most men in patriarchy, the imperialist family of man. But we could never depend on them "to take care of us" on their resources alone—and, of course, it is another "neurotic illusion" imposed on our fathers, brothers, lovers, husbands that they are supposed to "take care of us" because we are women. Translate: "to take care of us" equals "to control us." Our brothers', fathers', lovers', husbands' only power is their manhood. And unless manhood is somehow embellished by white skin and generations of private wealth, it has little currency in racist, capitalist patriarchy. The black man, for example, is accorded native elite or colonial guard or vigilante status over black women in imperialist patriarchy. He is an overseer for the slave master. Because of his maleness he is given access to certain privileges, e.g., employment, education, a car, life insurance, a house, some nice vines. He is usually a rabid heterosexual. He is, since emancipation, allowed to raise a "legitimate" family, allowed to have his piece of turf, viz. his wife and children. That is as far as his dictatorship extends, for if his wife decides that she wants to leave that home for whatever reason, he does not have the power or resources to seduce her otherwise, if she is determined to throw off the benign or malicious yoke of dependency. The ruling class white man on the other hand, has always had the power to count women among his pool of low-wage labor, his means of production. Most recently, he has "allowed" women the right to sue for divorce, to apply for AFDC, and to be neocolonized.

Traditionally, poor black men and women who banded together and stayed together and raised children together did not have the luxury to cultivate dependence among the members of their families. So, the black dyke, like most black women, has been conditioned to be self-sufficient, i.e., not dependent on men. For me personally, the conditioning to be self-sufficient and the predominance of female role models in my life are the roots of my lesbianism. Before I became a lesbian, I often wondered why I was expected to give up, avoid, and trivialize the recognition and encouragement I felt from women in order to pursue the tenuous business of heterosexuality. And I am not unique.

As political lesbians, i.e., lesbians who are resisting the prevailing culture's attempts to keep us invisible and powerless, we must become more visible (particularly black and other lesbians of color) to our sisters hidden in their various closets, locked in prisons of self-hate and ambiguity, afraid to take the ancient act of woman-bonding beyond the sexual, the private, the personal. I am not trying to reify lesbianism or feminism. I am trying to point out that lesbian-feminism has the potential of reversing and transforming a major component in the system of women's oppression, viz. predatory heterosexuality. If radical lesbian-feminism purports an antiracist, anticlassist, anti–woman-hating vision of bonding as mutual, reciprocal, as infinitely negotiable, as freedom from antiquated gender prescriptions and proscriptions, *then all people struggling to transform the character of relationships in this culture have something to learn from lesbians.*

The woman who takes a woman lover lives dangerously in patriarchy. And woe betide her even more if she chooses as her lover a woman who is not of her race. The silence among lesbian-feminists regarding the issue of lesbian relationships between black and white women in America is caused by none other than the centuries-old taboo and laws in the United States against relationships between people of color and those of the Caucasian race. Speaking heterosexually, the laws and taboos were a reflection of the patriarchal slave master's attempts to control his property via controlling his lineage through the institution of monogamy (for women only) and justified the taboos and laws with the argument that purity of the Caucasian race must by preserved (as well as its supremacy). However, we know that his racist and racialist laws and taboos did not apply to him in terms of the black slave woman just as his classist laws and taboos regarding the relationship between the ruling class and the indentured servants did not apply to him in terms of the white woman servant he chose to rape. The offspring of any unions between the white ruling class slave master and the black slave woman or white woman indentured servant could not legally inherit their white or ruling class sire's property or name, just their mother's condition of servitude.

The taboo against black and white people relating at any other level than master-slave, superior-inferior has been propounded in America to keep black women and men and white women and men, who share a common oppression at the hands of the ruling class white man, from organizing against that common oppression. We, as black lesbians, must vehemently resist being bound by the white man's racist, sexist laws, which have endangered potential intimacy of any kind between whites and blacks.

It cannot be presumed that black lesbians involved in love, work, and social relationships with white lesbians do so out of self-hate and denial of our racial-cultural heritage, identities, and oppression. Why should a woman's commitment to the struggle be questioned or accepted on the basis of her lover's or comrade's skin color? White lesbians engaged likewise with black lesbians or any lesbians of color cannot be assumed to be acting out of some perverse, guilt-ridden racialist desire.

I personally am tired of going to events, conferences, workshops, planning sessions that involve a coming together of black and other lesbians of color for political or even social reasons and listening to black lesbians relegate feminism to white women, castigate black women who propose forming coalitions with predominantly white feminist groups, minimize the white woman's oppression and exaggerate her power, and then finally judge that a black lesbian's commitment to the liberation of black women is dubious because she does not sleep with a black woman. All of us have to accept or reject allies on the basis of politics not on the specious basis of skin color. *Have not black people suffered betrayal from our own people?*

Yes, black women's experiences of misogyny are different from white women's. However, they all add up to how the patriarchal slave master decided to oppress us. We both fought each other for his favor, approval, and protection. Such is the effect of imperialist, heterosexist patriarchy. Shulamith Firestone, in the essay, "Racism: the Sexism of the Family of Man," purports this analysis of the relationship between white and black women:

> How do the women of this racial Triangle feel about each other? Divide and conquer: Both women have grown hostile to each other, white women feeling contempt for the "sluts" with no morals, black women feeling envy for the pampered "powder puffs." The black woman is jealous of the white woman's legitimacy, privilege, and comfort, but she also feels deep contempt. . . . Similarly the white woman's contempt for the black woman is mixed with envy: for the black woman's greater sexual license, for her gutsiness, for her freedom from the marriage bind. For after all, the black woman is not under the thumb of a man, but is pretty much her own boss to come and go, to leave the house, to work (much as it is degrading work) or to be "shiftless." What the white woman doesn't know is that the black woman, not under the thumb of one man, can now be squashed by all. There is no alternative for either of them than the choice between being public or private property, but because each still believes that the other is getting away with something both can be fooled into mis-channeling their frustration onto each other rather than onto the real enemy, "The Man."[4]

Though her statement of the choices black and white women have under patriarchy in America has merit, Firestone analyzes only a specific relationship, i.e., between the ruling class white woman and slave or ex-slave black woman.

Because of her whiteness, the white woman of all classes has been accorded, as the black man has because of his maleness, certain privileges in racist patriarchy, e.g., indentured servitude as opposed to enslavement, exclusive right to public assistance until the 1960s, "legitimate" offspring, and (if married into the middle/upper class) the luxury to live on her husband's income, etc.

The black woman, having neither maleness nor whiteness, has always had her heterosexuality, which white men and black men have manipulated by force and at will. Further, she, like all poor people, has had her labor, which the white capitalist man has also taken and exploited at will. These capabilities have allowed black women minimal access to the crumbs thrown at black men and white women. So, when the black woman and the white woman become lovers, we bring that history and all those questions to the relationship, as well as other people's problems with the relationship. The taboo against intimacy between white and black people has been internalized by us and simultaneously defied by us. If we, as lesbian-feminists, defy the taboo, then we begin to transform the history of relationships between black women and white women.

In her essay, "Disloyal to Civilization: Feminism, Racism, Gynephobia," Adrienne Rich calls for feminists to attend to the complexities of the relationship between black and white women in the United States. Rich queries:

> What caricatures of bloodless fragility and broiling sensuality still imprint our psyches, and where did we receive these imprintings? What happened between the several thousand northern white women and southern black women who together taught in the schools founded under Reconstruction by the Freedmen's Bureau, side by side braving the Ku Klux Klan harassment, terrorism, and the hostility of white communities?[5]

So, all of us would do well to stop fighting each other for our space at the bottom, because there ain't no more room. We have spent so much time hating ourselves. Time to love ourselves. And that, for all lesbians, as lovers, as comrades, as freedom fighters, is the final resistance.

## Notes

1. Grahn, Judy. "The Common Woman," *The Work of a Common Woman*. Diana Press. Oakland, 1978, p. 67.

2. Rich, Adrienne, *On Lies, Secrets, and Silence: Selected Prose 1966–1978*. W.W. Norton. New York, 1979, p. 225.

3. Robinson, Pat and Group, "Poor Black Women's Study Papers by Poor Black Women of Mount Vernon, New York," in T. Cade (ed). *The Black Woman: An Anthology*. New American Library. New York. 1970. p. 194.

4. Firestone, Shulamith, *The Dialectic of Sex: The Case for Feminist Revolution*. Bantam Books, New York, 1972, p. 113.

5. Rich, op. cit., p. 298.

# Womanist

## Alice Walker

### 1983

**Womanist 1.** From *womanish*. (Opp. of "girlish," i.e., frivolous, irresponsible, not serious.) A black feminist or feminist of color. From the black folk expression of mothers to female children, "You acting womanish," i.e., like a woman. Usually referring to outrageous, audacious, courageous or *willful* behavior. Wanting to know more and in greater depth than is considered "good" for one. Interested in grown-up doings. Acting grown up. Being grown up. Interchangeable with another black folk expression: "You trying to be grown." Responsible. In charge. *Serious.*

**2.** *Also:* A woman who loves other women, sexually and/or nonsexually. Appreciates and prefers women's culture, women's emotional flexibility (values tears as natural counterbalance of laughter), and women's strength. Sometimes loves individual men, sexually and/or nonsexually. Committed to survival and wholeness of entire people, male *and* female. Not a separatist, except periodically, for health. Traditionally universalist, as in: "Mama, why are we brown, pink, and yellow, and our cousins are white, beige, and black?" Ans.: "Well, you know the colored race is just like a flower garden, with every color flower represented." Traditionally capable, as in: "Mama, I'm walking to Canada and I'm taking you and a bunch of other slaves with me." Reply: "It wouldn't be the first time."

**3.** Loves music. Loves dance. Loves the moon. *Loves* the Spirit. Loves love and food and roundness. Loves struggle. *Loves* the Folk. Loves herself. *Regardless.*

**4.** Womanist is to feminist as purple to lavender.

# The Uses of Anger
## Women Responding to Racism[1]

*Audre Lorde*

1984

*Racism.* The belief in the inherent superiority of one race over all others and thereby the right to dominance, manifest and implied.

*Women respond to racism.* My response to racism is anger. I have lived with that anger, ignoring it, feeding upon it, learning to use it before it laid my visions to waste, for most of my life. Once I did it in silence, afraid of the weight. My fear of anger taught me nothing. Your fear of that anger will teach you nothing, also.

Women responding to racism means women responding to anger; the anger of exclusion, of unquestioned privilege, of racial distortions, of silence, ill-use, stereotyping, defensiveness, misnaming, betrayal, and co-optation.

My anger is a response to racist attitudes and to the actions and presumptions that arise out of those attitudes. If your dealings with other women reflect those attitudes, then my anger and your attendant fears are spotlights that can be used for growth in the same way I have used learning to express anger for my growth. But for corrective surgery, not guilt. Guilt and defensiveness are bricks in a wall against which we all flounder; they serve none of our futures.

Because I do not want this to become a theoretical discussion, I am going to give a few examples of interchanges between women that illustrate these points. In the interest of time, I am going to cut them short. I want you to know there were many more.

For example:

— I speak out of direct and particular anger at an academic conference, and a white woman says, "Tell me how you feel but don't say it too harshly or I cannot hear you." But is it my manner that keeps her from hearing, or the threat of a message that her life may change?

— The Women's Studies Program of a southern university invites a Black woman to read following a weeklong forum on Black and white women.

"What has this week given to you?" I ask. The most vocal white woman says, "I think I've gotten a lot. I feel Black women really understand me a lot better now; they have a better idea of where I'm coming from." As if understanding her lay at the core of the racist problem.

— After fifteen years of a women's movement which professes to address the life concerns and possible futures of all women, I still hear, on campus after campus, "How can we address the issues of racism? No women of Color attended." Or, the other side of that statement, "We have no one in our department equipped to teach their work." In other words, racism is a Black women's problem, a problem of women of Color, and only we can discuss it.

— After I read from my work entitled "Poems for Women in Rage,"[2] a white woman asks me: "Are you going to do anything with how we can deal directly with *our* anger? I feel it's so important." I ask, "How do you use *your* rage?" And then I have to turn away from the blank look in her eyes, before she can invite me to participate in her own annihilation. I do not exist to feel her anger for her.

— White women are beginning to examine their relationships to Black women, yet often I hear them wanting only to deal with little colored children across the roads of childhood, the beloved nursemaid, the occasional second-grade classmate—those tender memories of what was once mysterious and intriguing or neutral. You avoid the childhood assumptions formed by the raucous laughter at Rastus and Alfalfa, the acute message of your mommy's handkerchief spread upon the park bench because I had just been sitting there, the indelible and dehumanizing portraits of Amos 'n Andy and your daddy's humorous bedtime stories.

— I wheel my two-year-old daughter in a shopping cart through a supermarket in Eastchester in 1967, and a little white girl riding past in her mother's cart calls out excitedly, "Oh, look, Mommy, a baby maid!" And your mother shushes you, but she does not correct you. And so fifteen years later, at a conference on racism, you can still find that story humorous. But I hear your laughter is full of terror and dis-ease.

— A white academic welcomes the appearance of a collection by non-Black women of Color.[3] "It allows me to deal with racism without dealing with the harshness of Black women," she says to me.

— At an international cultural gathering of women, a well-known white American woman poet interrupts the reading of the work of women of Color to read her own poem, and then dashes off to an "important panel."

If women in the academy truly want a dialogue about racism, it will require recognizing the needs and the living contexts of other women. When an academic woman says, "I can't afford it," she may mean she is making a choice about how to spend her available money. But when a woman on welfare says, "I can't afford it," she means she is surviving on an amount of money that was barely subsistence in 1972, and she often does not have enough to eat. Yet the National Women's Studies Association here in 1981 holds a conference in which it commits itself to responding to racism, yet refuses to waive the registration fee for poor women and women of Color who wished to present and conduct workshops. This has made it impossible for many women of Color—for instance, Wilmette Brown, of Black Women for Wages for Housework—to participate in this conference. Is this to be merely another case of the academy discussing life within the closed circuits of the academy?

To the white women present who recognize these attitudes as familiar, but most of all, to all my sisters of Color who live and survive thousands of such encounters —to my sisters of Color who like me still tremble their rage under harness, or who sometimes question the expression of our rage as useless and disruptive (the two most popular accusations) —I want to speak about anger, my anger, and what I have learned from my travels through its dominions.

*Everything can be used / except what is wasteful / (you will need / to remember this when you are accused of destruction.)*[4]

Every woman has a well-stocked arsenal of anger potentially useful against those oppressions, personal and institutional, which brought that anger into being. Focused with precision it can become a powerful source of energy serving progress and change. And when I speak of change, I do not mean a simple switch of positions or a temporary lessening of tensions, nor the ability to smile or feel good. I am speaking of a basic and radical alteration in those assumptions underlining our lives.

I have seen situations where white women hear a racist remark, resent what has been said, become filled with fury, and remain silent because they are afraid. That unexpressed anger lies within them like an undetonated device, usually to be hurled at the first woman of Color who talks about racism.

But anger expressed and translated into action in the service of our vision and our future is a liberating and strengthening act of clarification, for it is in the painful process of this translation that we identify who are our allies with whom we have grave differences, and who are our genuine enemies.

Anger is loaded with information and energy. When I speak of women of Color, I do not only mean Black women. The woman of Color who is not Black and who charges me with rendering her invisible by assuming that her struggles with racism are identical with my own has something to tell me that I had better learn from, lest we both waste ourselves fighting the truths between us. If I participate, knowingly or otherwise, in my sister's oppression and she calls me on it, to answer her anger with my own only blankets the substance of our exchange with reaction. It wastes energy. And yes, it is very difficult to stand still and to listen to another woman's voice delineate an agony I do not share, or one to which I myself have contributed.

In this place we speak removed from the more blatant reminders of our embattlement as women. This need not blind us to the size and complexities of the forces mounting against us and all that is most human within our environment. We are not here as women examining racism in a political and social vacuum. We operate in the teeth of a system for which racism and sexism are primary, established, and necessary props of profit. Women responding to racism is a topic so dangerous that when the local media attempt to discredit this conference they choose to focus upon the provision of lesbian housing as a diversionary device —as if the *Hartford Courant* dare not mention the topic chosen for discussion here, racism, lest it become apparent that women are in fact attempting to examine and to alter all the repressive conditions of our lives.

Mainstream communication does not want women, particularly white women, responding to racism. It wants racism to be accepted as an immutable given in the fabric of your existence, like evening time or the common cold.

So we are working in a context of opposition and threat, the cause of which is certainly not the angers which lie between us, but rather that virulent hatred leveled against all women, people of Color, lesbians and gay men, poor people —against all of us who are seeking to examine the particulars of our lives as we resist our oppressions, moving toward coalition and effective action.

Any discussion among women about racism must include the recognition and the use of anger. This discussion must be direct and creative because it is crucial. We cannot allow our fear of anger to deflect us nor seduce us into settling for anything less than the hard work of excavating honesty; we must be quite serious about the choice of this topic and the angers entwined within it because, rest assured, our opponents are quite serious about their hatred of us and of what we are trying to do here.

And while we scrutinize the often painful face of each other's anger, please remember that it is not our anger which makes me caution you to lock your doors at night and not to wander the streets of Hartford alone. It is the hatred which lurks in those streets, that urge to destroy us all if we truly work for change rather than merely indulge in academic rhetoric.

This hatred and our anger are very different. Hatred is the fury of those who do not share our goals, and its object is death and destruction. Anger is a grief of distortions between peers, and its object is change. But our time is getting shorter. We have been raised to view any difference other than sex as a reason for destruction, and for Black women and white women to face each other's angers without denial or immobility or silence or guilt is in itself a heretical and generative idea. It implies peers meeting upon a common basis to examine difference, and to alter those distortions which history has created around our difference. For it is those distortions which separate us. And we must ask ourselves: Who profits from all this?

Women of Color in America have grown up within a symphony of anger, at being silenced, at being unchosen, at knowing that when we survive, it is in spite of a world that takes for granted our lack of humanness, and which hates our very existence outside of its service. And I say *symphony* rather than *cacophony* because we have had to learn to orchestrate those furies so that they do not tear us apart. We have had to learn to move through them and use them for strength and force and insight within our daily lives. Those of us who did not learn this difficult lesson did not survive. And part of my anger is always libation for my fallen sisters.

Anger is an appropriate reaction to racist attitudes, as is fury when the actions arising from those attitudes do not change. To those women here who fear the anger of women of Color more than their own unscrutinized racist attitudes, I ask: Is the anger of women of Color more threatening than the woman-hatred that tinges all aspects of our lives?

It is not the anger of other women that will destroy us but our refusals to stand still, to listen to its rhythms, to learn within it, to move beyond the manner of presentation to the substance, to tap that anger as an important source of empowerment.

I cannot hide my anger to spare you guilt, nor hurt feelings, nor answering anger; for to do so insults and trivializes all our efforts. Guilt is not a response to anger; it is a response to one's own actions or lack of action. If it leads to change then it can be useful, since it is then no longer guilt but the beginning of knowledge. Yet all too often, guilt is just another name for impotence, for defensiveness destructive of communication; it becomes a device to protect ignorance and the continuation of things the way they are, the ultimate protection for changelessness.

Most women have not developed tools for facing anger constructively. Consciousness raising groups in the past, largely white, dealt with how to express anger, usually at the world of men. And these groups were made up of white women who shared the terms of their oppressions. There was usually little attempt to articulate the genuine differences between women, such as those of race, color, age, class, and sexual identity. There was no apparent need at that time to examine the contradictions of self, woman as oppressor. There was work on expressing anger, but very little on anger directed against each other. No tools were developed to deal with other women's anger except to avoid it, deflect it, or flee from it under a blanket of guilt.

I have no creative use for guilt, yours or my own. Guilt is only another way of avoiding informed action, of buying time out of the pressing need to make clear choices, out of the approaching storm that can feed the earth as well as bend the trees. If I speak to you in anger, at least I have spoken to you: I have not put a gun to your head and shot you down in the street; I have not looked at your bleeding sister's body and asked, "What did she do to deserve it?" This was the reaction of two white women to Mary Church Terrell's telling of the lynching of a pregnant Black woman whose baby was then torn from her body. That was in 1921, and Alice Paul had just refused to publicly endorse the enforcement of the Nineteenth Amendment for all women—by refusing to endorse the inclusion of women of Color, although we had worked to help bring about that amendment.

The angers between women will not kill us if we can articulate them with precision, if we listen to the content of what is said with at least as much intensity as we defend ourselves against the manner of saying. When we turn from anger we turn from insight, saying we will accept only the designs already known, deadly and safely familiar. I have tried to learn my anger's usefulness to me, as well as its limitations.

For women raised to fear, too often anger threatens annihilation. In the male construct of brute force, we were taught that our lives depended upon the good will of patriarchal power. The anger of others was to be avoided at all costs because there was nothing to be learned from it but pain, a judgment that we had been bad girls, come up lacking, not done what we were supposed to do. And if we accept our powerlessness, then of course any anger can destroy us.

But the strength of women lies in recognizing differences between us as creative, and in standing up to those distortions which we inherited without blame, but which are now ours to alter. The angers of women can transform difference through insight into power. For anger between peers births change, not destruction, and the discomfort and sense of loss it often causes is not fatal, but a sign of growth.

My response to racism is anger. That anger has eaten clefts into my living only when it remained unspoken, useless to anyone. It has also served me in classrooms without light or learning, where the work and history of Black women was less than a vapor. It has served me as fire in the ice zone of uncomprehending eyes of white women who see in my experience and the experience of my people only new reasons for fear or guilt. And my anger is no excuse for not dealing with your blindness, no reason to withdraw from the results of your own actions.

When women of Color speak out of the anger that laces so many of our contacts with white women, we are often told that we are "creating a mood of hopelessness," "preventing white women from getting past guilt," or "standing in the way of trusting communication and action." All these quotes come directly from letters to me from members of this organization within the last two years. One woman wrote, "Because you are Black and Lesbian, you seem to speak with the moral authority of suffering." Yes, I am Black and Lesbian, and what you hear in my voice is fury, not suffering. Anger, not moral authority. There is a difference.

To turn aside from the anger of Black women with excuses or the pretexts of intimidation is to award no one power—it is merely another way of preserving racial blindness, the power of unaddressed privilege, unbreached, intact. Guilt is only another form of objectification. Oppressed peoples are always being asked to stretch a little more, to bridge the gap between blindness and humanity. Black women are expected to use our anger only in the service of other people's salvation or learning. But that time is over. My anger has meant pain to me but it has also meant survival, and before I give it up I'm going to be sure that there is something at least as powerful to replace it on the road to clarity.

What woman here is so enamored of her own oppression that she cannot see her heel print upon another woman's face? What woman's terms of oppression have become precious and necessary to her as a ticket into the fold of the righteous, away from the cold winds of self-scrutiny?

I am a lesbian woman of Color whose children eat regularly because I work in a university. If their full bellies make me fail to recognize my commonality with a woman of Color whose children do not eat because she cannot find work, or who has no children because her insides are rotted from home abortions and sterilization; if I fail to recognize the lesbian who chooses not to have children, the woman who remains closeted because her homophobic community is her only life support, the woman who chooses silence instead of another death, the woman who is terrified lest my anger trigger the explosion of hers; if I fail to recognize them as other faces of myself, then I am contributing not only to each of their oppressions but also to my own, and the anger which stands between us then must be used for clarity and mutual empowerment, not for evasion by guilt or for further separation. I am not free while any woman is unfree, even when her shackles are very different from my own. And I am not free as long as one person of Color remains chained. Nor is any one of you.

I speak here as a woman of Color who is not bent upon destruction, but upon survival. No woman is responsible for altering the psyche of her oppressor, even when that psyche is embodied in another woman. I have suckled the wolf's lip of anger and I have used it for illumination, laughter, protection, fire in places where there was no light, no food, no sisters, no quarter. We are not goddesses or matriarchs or edifices of divine forgiveness; we are not fiery fingers of judgment or instruments of flagellation; we are women forced back always upon our woman's power. We have learned to use anger as we have learned to use the dead flesh of animals, and bruised, battered, and changing, we have survived and grown and, in Angela Wilson's words, we *are* moving on. With or without uncolored women. We use whatever strengths we have fought for, including anger, to help define and fashion a world where all our sisters can grow, where our children can love, and where the power of touching and meeting another woman's difference and wonder will eventually transcend the need for destruction.

For it is not the anger of Black women which is dripping down over this globe like a diseased liquid. It is not my anger that launches rockets, spends over sixty thousand dollars a second on missiles and other agents of war and death, slaughters children in cities, stockpiles nerve gas and chemical bombs, sodomizes our daughters and our earth. It is not the anger of Black woman which corrodes into blind, dehumanizing power, bent upon the annihilation of us all unless we meet it with what we have: our power to examine and to redefine the terms upon which we will live and work; our power to envision and to reconstruct, anger by painful anger, stone upon heavy stone, a future of pollinating difference and the earth to support our choices.

We welcome all women who can meet us, face to face, beyond objectification and beyond guilt.

### Notes

1. Keynote presentation at the National Women's Studies Association Conference, Storrs, Connecticut, June 1981.

2. One poem from this series is included in *Chosen Poems: Old and New* (W.W. Norton and Company, New York, 1982), pp. 105–108.

3. *This Bridge Called My Back: Writings by Radical Women of Color* edited by Cherríe Moraga and Gloria Anzaldua (Kitchen Table: Women of Color Press, New York, 1984), first published in 1981.

4. From "For Each of You," first published in *From A Land Where Other People Live* (Broadside Press, Detroit, 1973), and collected in *Chosen Poems: Old and New* (W.W. Norton and Company, New York, 1982), p. 42.

## Black Women
### Shaping Feminist Theory

*bell hooks*

1984

Feminism in the United States has never emerged from the women who are most victimized by sexist oppression; women who are daily beaten down, mentally, physically, and spiritually— women who are powerless to change their condition in life. They are a silent majority. A mark of their victimization is that they accept their lot in life without visible question, without organized protest, without collective anger or rage. Betty Friedan's *The Feminine Mystique*[1] is still heralded as having paved the way for contemporary feminist movement—it was written as if these women did not exist. Friedan's famous phrase, "the problem that has no name," often quoted to describe the condition of women in this society, actually referred to the plight of a select group of college-educated, middle and upper class, married white women—housewives bored with leisure, with the home, with children, with buying products, who wanted more out of life. Friedan concludes her first chapter by stating: "We can no longer ignore that voice within women that says: 'I want something more than my husband and my children and my house.'" That "more" she defined as careers. She did not discuss who would be called in to take care of the children and maintain the home if more women like herself were freed from their house labor and given equal access with white men to the professions. She did not speak of the needs of women without men, without children, without homes. She ignored the existence of all nonwhite women and poor white women. She did not tell readers whether it was more fulfilling to be a maid, a babysitter, a factory worker, a clerk, or a prostitute, than to be a leisure class housewife.

She made her plight and the plight of white women like herself synonymous with a condition affecting all American women. In so doing, she deflected attention away from her classism, her racism, her sexist attitudes towards the masses of American women. In the context of her book, Friedan makes clear that the women she saw as victimized by sexism were college-educated, white women who were compelled by sexist conditioning to remain in the home. She contends:

> It is urgent to understand how the very condition of being a housewife can create a sense of emptiness, nonexistence, nothingness in women. There are aspects of the housewife role that make it almost impossible for a woman of adult intelligence to retain a sense of human identity, the firm core of self or "I" without which a human being, man or woman, is not truly alive. For women of ability, in America today, I am convinced that there is something about the housewife state itself that is dangerous.[2]

Specific problems and dilemmas of leisure class white housewives were real concerns that merited consideration and change but they were not the pressing political concerns of masses of women. Masses of women were concerned about economic survival, ethnic and racial discrimination, etc. When Friedan wrote *The Feminine Mystique*, more than one third of all women were in the work force. Although many women longed to be house-wives, only women with leisure time and money could actually shape their identities on the model of the feminine mystique. They were women who, in Friedan's words, were "told by the most advanced thinkers of our time to go back and live their lives as if they were Noras, restricted to the doll's house by Victorian prejudices."[3]

From her early writing, it appears that Friedan never wondered whether or not the plight of college-educated, white housewives was an adequate reference point by which to gauge the impact of sexism or sexist oppression on the lives of women in American society. Nor did she move beyond her own life experience to acquire an expanded perspective on the lives of women in the United States. I say this not to discredit her work. It remains a useful discussion of the impact of sexist discrimination on a select group of women. Examined from a different perspective, it can also be seen as a case study of narcissism, insensitivity, sentimentality, and self-indulgence which reaches its peak when Friedan, in a chapter titled "Progressive Dehuman-ization," makes a comparison between the psychological effects of isolation on white housewives and the impact of confinement on the self-concept of prisoners in Nazi concentration camps.[4]

Friedan was a principal shaper of contemporary feminist thought. Sig-nificantly, the one-dimensional perspective on women's reality presented in her book became a marked feature of the contemporary feminist move-ment. Like Friedan before them, white women who dominate feminist dis-course today rarely question whether or not their perspective on women's reality is true to the lived experiences of women as a collective group. Nor are they aware of the extent to which their perspectives reflect race and class biases, although there has been a greater awareness of biases in recent years. Racism abounds in the writings of white feminists, reinforcing white supremacy and negating the possibility that women will bond politically across ethnic and racial boundaries. Past feminist refusal to draw attention to and attack racial hierarchies suppressed the link between race and class. Yet class structure in American society has been shaped by the racial politic of white supremacy; it is only by analyzing racism and its function in capitalist society that a thorough understanding of class relationships can emerge. Class struggle is inextricably bound to the struggle to end racism. Urging women to explore the full implication of class in an early essay, "The Last Straw," Rita Mae Brown explained:

> Class is much more than Marx's definition of relationship to the means of production. Class involves your behavior, your basic assumptions about life. Your experience (determined by your class) validates those assumptions, how you are taught to behave, what you expect from yourself and from others, your concept of a future, how you understand problems and solve them, how you think, feel, act. It is these behavioral patterns that middle class women resist recognizing although they may be perfectly willing to accept class in Marxist terms, a neat trick that helps them avoid really dealing with class behavior and changing that behavior in themselves. It is these behavioral patterns which must be recognized, understood, and changed.[5]

White women who dominate feminist discourse, who for the most part make and articulate feminist theory, have little or no understanding of white supremacy as a racial politic, of the psychological impact of class, of their political status within a racist, sexist, capitalist state.

It is this lack of awareness that, for example, leads Leah Fritz to write in *Dreamers and Dealers*, a discussion of the current women's movement published in 1979:

> Women's suffering under sexist tyranny is a common bond among all women, transcending the particulars of the different forms that tyranny takes. *Suffering cannot be measured and compared quantitatively.* Is the enforced idleness and vacuity of a "rich" woman, which leads her to madness and/or suicide, greater or less than the suffering of a poor woman who barely survives on welfare but retains somehow her spirit? There is no way to measure such difference, but should these two women survey each other without the screen of patriarchal class, they may find a commonality in the fact that they are both oppressed, both miserable.[6]

Fritz's statement is another example of wishful thinking, as well as the conscious mystification of social divisions between women, that has characterized much feminist expression. While it is evident that many women suffer from sexist tyranny, there is little indication that this forges "a common bond among all women." There is much evidence substantiating the reality that race and class identity creates differences in quality of life, social status, and lifestyle that take precedence over the common experience women share—differences which are rarely transcended. The motives of materially privileged, educated, white women with a variety of career and lifestyle options available to them must be questioned when they insist that "suffering cannot be measured." Fritz is by no means the first white feminist to make this statement. It is a statement that I have never heard a poor woman of any race make. Although there is much I would take issue with in Benjamin Barber's critique of the women's movement, *Liberating Feminism*, I agree with his assertion:

> Suffering is not necessarily a fixed and universal experience that can be measured by a single rod: it is related to situations, needs, and aspirations. But there must be some historical and political parameters for the use of the term so that political priorities can be established and different forms and degrees of suffering can be given the most attention.[7]

A central tenet of modern feminist thought has been the assertion that "all women are oppressed." This assertion implies that women share a common lot, that factors like class, race, religion, sexual preference, etc. do not create a diversity of experience that determines the extent to which sexism will be an oppressive force in the lives of individual women. Sexism as a system of domination is institutionalized but it has never determined in an absolute way the fate of all women in this society. Being oppressed means the *absence of choices*. It is the primary point of contact between the oppressed and the oppressor. Many women in this society do have choices (as inadequate as they are), therefore exploitation and discrimination are words that more accurately describe the lot of women collectively in the United States. Many women do not join organized resistance against sexism precisely because sexism has not meant an absolute lack of choices. They may know they are discriminated against on the basis of sex, but they do not equate this with oppression. Under capitalism, patriarchy is structured so that sexism restricts women's behavior in some realms even as freedom from limitations is allowed in other spheres. The absence of extreme restrictions leads many women to ignore the areas in which they are exploited or discriminated against; it may even lead them to imagine that no women are oppressed.

There are oppressed women in the United States, and it is both appro-priate and necessary that we speak against such oppression. French feminist Christine Delphy makes the point in her essay, "For a Materialist Femi-nism," that the use of the term oppression is important because it places feminist struggle in a radical political framework:

> The rebirth of feminism coincided with the use of the term "oppression." The ruling ideology, i.e., common sense, daily speech, does not speak about oppression but about a "feminine condition." It refers back to a naturalist explanation: to a constraint of nature, exterior reality out of reach and not modifiable by human action. The term "oppression," on the contrary, refers back to a choice, an explanation, a situation that is political. "Oppression" and "social oppression" are therefore synonyms or rather social oppression is a redundancy: the notion of a political origin, i.e., social, is an integral part of the concept of oppression.[8]

However, feminist emphasis on "common oppression" in the United States was less a strategy for politicization than an appropriation by conservative and liberal women of a radical political vocabulary that masked the extent to which they shaped the movement so that it addressed and promoted their class interests.

Although the impulse towards unity and empathy that informed the notion of common oppression was directed at building solidarity, slogans like "organize around your own oppression" provided the excuse many privileged women needed to ignore the differences between their social status and the status of masses of women. It was a mark of race and class privilege, as well as the expression of freedom from the many constraints sexism places on working class women, that middle class white women were able to make their interests the primary focus of feminist movement and employ a rhetoric of commonality that made their condition synony-mous with "oppression." Who was there to demand a change in vocabu-lary? What other group of women in the United States had the same access to universities, publishing houses, mass media, money? Had middle class black women begun a movement in which they had labeled themselves "oppressed," no one would have taken them seriously. Had they established public forums and given speeches about their "oppression," they would have been criticized and attacked from all sides. This was not the case with white bourgeois feminists for they could appeal to a large audience of women, like themselves, who were eager to change their lot in life. Their isolation from women of other class and race groups provided no immediate comparative base by which to test their assumptions of common oppression.

Initially, radical participants in the women's movement demanded that women penetrate that isolation and create a space for contact. Anthologies like *Liberation Now, Women's Liberation: Blueprint for the Future, Class and Feminism, Radical Feminism*, and *Sisterhood Is Powerful*, all published in the early 1970s, contain articles that attempted to address a wide audience of women, an audience that was not exclusively white, middle class, college-educated, and adult (many have articles on teenagers). Sookie Stambler articulated this radical spirit in her introduction to *Women's Liberation: Blueprint for the Future*:

> Movement women have always been turned off by the media's necessity to create celebrities and superstars. This goes against our basic philosophy. We cannot relate to women in our ranks towering over us with prestige and fame. We are not struggling for the benefit of the one woman or for one group of women. We are dealing with issues that concern all women.[9]

These sentiments, shared by many feminists early in the movement, were not sustained. As more and more women acquired prestige, fame, or money from feminist writings or from gains from feminist movement for equality in the workforce, individual opportunism undermined appeals for collective struggle. Women who were not opposed to patriarchy, capitalism, classism, or racism labeled themselves "feminist." Their expectations were varied. Privileged women wanted social equality with men of their class; some women wanted equal pay for equal work; others wanted an alternative lifestyle. Many of these legitimate concerns were easily co-opted by the ruling capitalist patriarchy. French feminist Antoinette Fouque states:

> The actions proposed by the feminist groups are spectacular, provoking. But provocation only brings to light a certain number of social contradictions. It does not reveal radical contradictions within society. The feminists claim that they do not seek equality with men, but their practice proves the contrary to be true. Feminists are a bourgeois avant-garde that maintains, in an inverted form, the dominant values. Inversion does not facilitate the passage to another kind of structure. Reformism suits everyone! Bourgeois order, capitalism, phallocentrism are ready to integrate as many feminists as will be necessary. Since these women are becoming men, in the end it will only mean a few more men. The difference between the sexes is not whether one does or doesn't have a penis, it is whether or not one is an integral part of a phallic masculine economy.[10]

Feminists in the United States are aware of the contradictions. Carol Ehrlich makes the point in her essay, "The Unhappy Marriage of Marxism and Feminism: Can It Be Saved?" that "feminism seems more and more to have taken on a blind, safe, nonrevolutionary outlook" as "feminist radicalism loses ground to bourgeois feminism," stressing that "we cannot let this continue":

> Women need to know (and are increasingly prevented from finding out) that feminism is *not* about dressing for success, or becoming a corporate executive, or gaining elective office; it is *not* being able to share a two career marriage and take skiing vacations and spend huge amounts of time with your husband and two lovely children because you have a domestic worker who makes all this possible for you, but who hasn't the time or money to do it for herself; it is *not* opening a Women's Bank, or spending a weekend in an expensive workshop that guarantees to teach you how to become assertive (but not aggressive); it is most emphatically *not* about becoming a police detective or CIA agent or marine corps general.
>
> But if these distorted images of feminism have more reality than ours do, it is partly our own fault. We have not worked as hard as we should have at providing clear and meaningful alternative analyses which relate to people's lives, and at providing active, accessible groups in which to work.[11]

It is no accident that feminist struggle has been so easily co-opted to serve the interests of conservative and liberal feminists since feminism in the United States has so far been a bourgeois ideology. Zillah Eisenstein discusses the liberal roots of North American feminism in *The Radical Future of Liberal Feminism*, explaining in the introduction:

> One of the major contributions to be found in this study is the role of the ideology of liberal individualism in the construction of feminist theory. Today's feminists either do not discuss a theory of individuality or they unself-consciously adopt the competitive, atomistic ideology of liberal individualism. There is much confusion on this issue in the feminist theory we discuss here. Until a conscious differentiation is made between a theory of individuality that recognizes the importance of the individual within the social collectivity and the ideology of individualism that assumes a competitive view of the individual, there will not be a full accounting of what a feminist theory of liberation must look like in our Western society.[12]

The ideology of "competitive, atomistic liberal individualism" has permeated feminist thought to such an extent that it undermines the potential radicalism of feminist struggle. The usurpation of feminism by bourgeois women to support their class interests has been to a very grave extent justified by feminist theory as it has so far been conceived. (For example, the ideology of "common oppression.") Any movement to resist the co-optation of feminist struggle must begin by introducing a different feminist perspective—a new theory—one that is not informed by the ideology of liberal individualism.

The exclusionary practices of women who dominate feminist discourse have made it practically impossible for new and varied theories to emerge. Feminism has its party line and women who feel a need for a different strategy, a different foundation, often find themselves ostracized and silenced. Criticisms of or alternatives to established feminist ideas are not encouraged, e.g., recent controversies about expanding feminist discussions of sexuality. Yet groups of women who feel excluded from feminist discourse and praxis can make a place for themselves only if they first create, via critiques, an awareness of the factors that alienate them. Many individual white women found in the women's movement a liberatory solution to personal dilemmas. Having directly benefited from the movement, they are less inclined to criticize it or to engage in rigorous examination of its structure than those who feel it has not had a revolutionary impact on their lives or the lives of masses of women in our society. Nonwhite women who feel affirmed within the current structure of feminist movement (even though they may form autonomous groups) seem to also feel that their definitions of the party line, whether on the issue of black feminism or on other issues, is the only legitimate discourse. Rather than encourage a diversity of voices, critical dialogue, and controversy, they, like some white women, seek to stifle dissent. As activists and writers whose work is widely known, they act as if they are best able to judge whether other women's voices should be heard. Susan Griffin warns against this overall tendency towards dogmatism in her essay "The Way of All Ideology":

> . . . when a theory is transformed into an ideology, it begins to destroy the self and self-knowledge. Originally born of feeling, it pretends to float above and around feeling. Above sensation. It organizes experience according to itself, without touching experience. By virtue of being itself, it is supposed to know. To invoke the name of this ideology is to confer truthfulness. No one can tell it anything new. Experience ceases to surprise it, inform it, transform it. It is annoyed by any detail which does not fit into its world view. Begun as a cry against the denial of truth, now it denies any truth which does not fit into its scheme. Begun as a way to restore one's sense of reality, now it attempts to discipline real people, to remake natural beings after its own image. All that it fails to explain it records as its enemy. Begun as a theory of liberation, it is threatened by new theories of liberation; it builds a prison for the mind.[13]

We resist hegemonic dominance of feminist thought by insisting that it is a theory in the making, that we must necessarily criticize, question, re-examine, and explore new possibilities. My persistent critique has been informed by my status as a member of an oppressed group, experience of sexist exploitation and discrimination, and the sense that prevailing feminist analysis has not been the force shaping my feminist consciousness. This is true for many women. There are white women who had never considered resisting male dominance until the feminist movement created an awareness that they could and should. My awareness of feminist struggle was stimulated by social circumstance. Growing up in a Southern, black, father-dominated, working class household, I experienced (as did my mother, my sisters, and my brother) varying degrees of patriarchal tyranny and it made me angry—it made us all angry. Anger led me to question the politics of male dominance and enabled me to resist sexist socialization. Frequently, white feminists act as if black women did not know sexist oppression existed until they voiced feminist sentiment. They believe they are providing black women with "the" analysis and "the" program for liberation. They do not understand, cannot even imagine, that black women, as well as other groups of women who live daily in oppressive situations, often acquire an awareness of patriarchal politics from their lived experience, just as they develop strategies of resistance (even though they may not resist on a sustained or organized basis).

These black women observed white feminist focus on male tyranny and women's oppression as if it were a "new" revelation and felt such a focus had little impact on their lives. To them it was just another indication of the privileged living conditions of middle and upper class white women that they would need a theory to inform them that they were "oppressed." The implication being that people who are truly oppressed know it even though they may not be engaged in organized resistance or are unable to articulate in written form the nature of their oppression. These black women saw nothing liberatory in party line analyses of women's oppression. Neither the fact that black women have not organized collectively in huge numbers around the issues of "feminism" (many of us do not know or use the term) nor the fact that we have not had access to the machinery of power that would allow us to share our analyses or theories about gender with the American public negate its presence in our lives or place us in a position of dependency in relationship to those white and nonwhite feminists who address a larger audience.

The understanding I had by age thirteen of patriarchal politics created in me expectations of the feminist movement that were quite different from those of young, middle class, white women. When I entered my first women's studies class at Stanford University in the early 1970s, white women were reveling in the joy of being together—to them it was an important, momentous occasion. I had not known a life where women had not been together, where women had not helped, protected, and loved one another deeply. I had not known white women who were ignorant of the impact of race and class on their social status and consciousness (Southern white women often have a more realistic perspective on racism and classism than white women in other areas of the United States). I did not feel sympathetic to white peers who maintained that I could not expect them to have knowledge of or understand the life experiences of black women. Despite my background (living in racially segregated communities) I knew about the lives of white women, and certainly no white women lived in our neighborhood, attended our schools, or worked in our homes.

When I participated in feminist groups, I found that white women adopted a condescending attitude towards me and other nonwhite participants. The condescension they directed at black women was one of the means they employed to remind us that the women's movement was "theirs"— that we were able to participate because they allowed it, even encouraged it; after all, we were needed to legitimate the process. They did not see us as equals. They did not treat us as equals. And though they expected us to provide first hand accounts of black experience, they felt it was their role to decide if these experiences were authentic. Frequently, college-educated black women (even those from poor and working class backgrounds) were dismissed as mere imitators. Our presence in movement activities did not count, as white women were convinced that "real" blackness meant speaking the patois of poor black people, being uneducated, streetwise, and a variety of other stereotypes. If we dared to criticize the movement or to assume responsibility for reshaping feminist ideas and introducing new ideas, our voices were tuned out, dismissed, silenced. We could be heard only if our statements echoed the sentiments of the dominant discourse.

Attempts by white feminists to silence black women are rarely written about. All too often they have taken place in conference rooms, classrooms, or the privacy of cozy living room settings, where one lone black woman faces the racist hostility of a group of white women. From the time the women's liberation movement began, individual black women went to groups. Many never returned after a first meeting. Anita Cornwall is correct in "Three for the Price of One: Notes from a Gay Black Feminist," when she states, ". . . sadly enough, fear of encountering racism seems to be one of the main reasons that so many black womyn refuse to join the women's movement."[14] Recent focus on the issue of racism has generated discourse but has had little impact on the behavior of white feminists towards black women. Often the white women who are busy publishing papers and books on "unlearning racism" remain patronizing and condescending when they relate to black women. This is not surprising given that frequently their discourse is aimed solely in the direction of a white audience and the focus solely on changing attitudes rather than addressing racism in a historical and political context. They make us the "objects" of their privileged discourse on race. As "objects," we remain unequals, inferiors. Even though they may be sincerely concerned about racism, their methodology suggests they are not yet free of the type of paternalism endemic to white supremacist ideology. Some of these women place themselves in the position of "authorities" who must mediate communication between racist white women (naturally they see themselves as having come to terms with their racism) and angry black women whom they believe are incapable of rational discourse. Of course, the system of racism, classism, and educational elitism remains intact if they are to maintain their authoritative positions.

In 1981, I enrolled in a graduate class on feminist theory where we were given a course reading list that had writings by white women and men, one black man, but no material by or about black, Native American Indian, Hispanic, or Asian women. When I criticized this oversight, white women directed an anger and hostility at me that was so intense I found it difficult to attend the class. When I suggested that the purpose of this collective anger was to create an atmosphere in which it would be psychologically unbearable for me to speak in class discussions or even attend class, I was told that they were not angry. *I* was the one who was angry. Weeks after class ended, I received an open letter from one white female student acknowledging her anger and expressing regret for her attacks. She wrote:

> I didn't know you. You were black. In class after a while I noticed myself, that I would always be the one to respond to whatever you said. And usually it was to contradict. Not that the argument was always about racism by any means. But I think the hidden logic was that if I could prove you wrong about one thing, then you might not be right about anything at all.

And in another paragraph:

> I said in class one day that there were some people less entrapped than others by Plato's picture of the world. I said I thought we, after fifteen years of education, courtesy of the ruling class, might be more entrapped than others who had not received a start in life so close to the heart of the monster. My classmate, once a close friend, sister, colleague, has not spoken to me since then. I think the possibility that we were not the best spokespeople for all women made her fear for her self-worth and for her PhD.

Often in situations where white feminists aggressively attacked individual black women, they saw themselves as the ones who were under attack, who were the victims. During a heated discussion with another white female student in a racially mixed women's group I had organized, I was told that she had heard how I had "wiped out" people in the feminist theory class, that she was afraid of being "wiped out" too. I reminded her that I was one person speaking to a large group of angry, aggressive people; I was hardly dominating the situation. It was I who left the class in tears, not any of the people I had supposedly "wiped out."

Racist stereotypes of the strong, superhuman black woman are operative myths in the minds of many white women, allowing them to ignore the extent to which black women are likely to be victimized in this society and the role white women may play in the maintenance and perpetuation of that victimization. In Lillian Hellman's autobiographical work *Pentimento*, she writes, "All my life, beginning at birth, I have taken orders from black women, wanting them and resenting them, being superstitious the few times I disobeyed." The black women Hellman describes worked in her household as family servants and their status was never that of an equal. Even as a child, she was always in the dominant position as they questioned, advised, or guided her; they were free to exercise these rights because she or another white authority figure allowed it. Hellman places power in the hands of these black women rather than acknowledge her own power over them; hence she mystifies the true nature of their relationship. By projecting onto black women a mythical power and strength, white women both promote a false image of themselves as powerless, passive victims and deflect attention away from their aggressiveness, their power (however limited in a white supremacist, male-dominated state), their willingness to dominate and control others. These unacknowledged aspects of the social status of many white women prevent them from transcending racism and limit the scope of their understanding of women's overall social status in the United States.

Privileged feminists have largely been unable to speak to, with, and for diverse groups of women because they either do not understand fully the inter-relatedness of sex, race, and class oppression or refuse to take this inter-relatedness seriously. Feminist analyses of woman's lot tend to focus exclusively on gender and do not provide a solid foundation on which to construct feminist theory. They reflect the dominant tendency in Western patriarchal minds to mystify woman's reality by insisting that gender is the sole determinant of woman's fate. Certainly it has been easier for women who do not experience race or class oppression to focus exclusively on gender. Although socialist feminists focus on class and gender, they tend to dismiss race or they make a point of acknowledging that race is important and then proceed to offer an analysis in which race is not considered.

As a group, black women are in an unusual position in this society, for not only are we collectively at the bottom of the occupational ladder, but our overall social status is lower than that of any other group. Occupying such a position, we bear the brunt of sexist, racist, and classist oppression. At the same time, we are the group that has not been socialized to assume the role of exploiter/oppressor in that we are allowed no institutionalized "other" that we can exploit or oppress. (Children do not represent an institutionalized other even though they may be oppressed by parents.) White women and black men have it both ways. They can act as oppressor or be oppressed. Black men may be victimized by racism, but sexism allows them to act as exploiters and oppressors of women. White women may be victimized by sexism, but racism enables them to act as exploiters and oppressors of black people. Both groups have led liberation movements that favor their interests and support the continued oppression of other groups. Black male sexism has undermined struggles to eradicate racism just as white female racism undermines feminist struggle. As long as these two groups or any group defines liberation as gaining social equality with ruling class white men, they have a vested interest in the continued exploitation and oppression of others.

Black women with no institutionalized "other" that we may discriminate against, exploit, or oppress often have a lived experience that directly challenges the prevailing classist, sexist, racist social structure and its concomitant ideology. This lived experience may shape our consciousness in such a way that our world view differs from those who have a degree of privilege (however relative within the existing system). It is essential for continued feminist struggle that black women recognize the special vantage point our marginality gives us and make use of this perspective to criticize the dominant racist, classist, sexist hegemony as well as to envision and create a counter-hegemony. I am suggesting that we have a central role to play in the making of feminist theory and a contribution to offer that is unique and valuable. The formation of a liberatory feminist theory and praxis is a collective responsibility, one that must be shared. Though I criticize aspects of feminist movement as we have known it so far, a critique which is sometimes harsh and unrelenting, I do so not in an attempt to diminish feminist struggle but to enrich, to share in the work of making a liberatory ideology and a liberatory movement.

## Notes

1. Although *The Feminine Mystique* has been criticized and even attacked from various fronts I call attention to it again because certain biased premises about the nature of woman's social status put forth initially in this text continue to shape the tenor and direction of feminist movement.

2. Betty Friedan, *The Feminine Mystique*, p. 15.

3. Friedan, p. 32.

4. Friedan, "Progressive Dehumanization," p. 305

5. Rita Mae Brown, "The Last Straw," in *Class and Feminism*, p. 15.

6. Leah Fritz, *Dreamers and Dealers*, p. 51.

7. Benjamin Barber, *Liberating Feminism*, p. 30.

8. Christine Delphy, "For a Materialist Feminism," p. 211. A fuller discussion of Christine Delphy's perspective may be found in the collected essays of her work *Close to Home*.

9. Sookie Stambler, *Women's Liberation: Blueprint for The Future*, p. 9.

10. Antoinette Fouque, "Warnings," in *New French Feminists*, pp. 117–118.

11. Carol Ehrlich, "The Unhappy Marriage of Marxism and Feminism: Can It Be Saved?," p. 130.

12. Zillah Eisenstein, *The Radical Future of Liberal Feminism*, p.5.

13. Susan Griffin, "The Way of All Ideology," *Signs*, Spring 1982, p. 648.

14. Anita Cornwell, "Three for the Price of One: Notes from a Gay Black Feminist," in *Lavender Culture*, p. 471.

## African American Women in Defense of Ourselves[1]

*Elsa Barkley Brown, Deborah K. King, and Barbara Ransby*

1991

As women of African descent, we are deeply troubled by the recent nomination, confirmation and seating of Clarence Thomas as an Associate Justice of the U.S. Supreme Court. We know that the presence of Clarence Thomas on the Court will be continually used to divert attention from historic struggles for social justice through suggestions that the presence of a Black man on the Supreme Court constitutes an assurance that the rights of African Americans will be protected. Clarence Thomas's public record is ample evidence this will not be true. Further, the consolidation of a conservative majority on the Supreme Court seriously endangers the rights of all women, poor and working-class people and the elderly. The seating of Clarence Thomas is an affront not only to African-American women and men, but to all people concerned with social justice.

We are particularly outraged by the racist and sexist treatment of Professor Anita Hill, an African American woman who was maligned and castigated for daring to speak publicly of her own experience of sexual abuse. The malicious defamation of Professor Hill insulted all women of African descent and sent a dangerous message to any woman who might contemplate a sexual harassment complaint. We speak here because we recognize that the media are now portraying the Black community as prepared to tolerate both the dismantling of affirmative action and the evil of sexual harassment in order to have any Black man on the Supreme Court. We want to make clear that the media have ignored or distorted many African American voices. We will not be silenced. Many have erroneously portrayed the allegations against Clarence Thomas as an issue of either gender or race. As women of African descent, we understand sexual harassment as both. We further understand that Clarence Thomas outrageously manipulated the legacy of lynching in order to shelter himself from Anita Hill's allegations. To deflect attention away from the reality of sexual abuse in African American women's lives, he trivialized and misrepresented this painful part of African American people's history. This country, which has a long legacy of racism and sexism, has never taken the sexual abuse of Black women seriously. Throughout U.S. history Black women have been sexually stereotyped as immoral, insatiable, perverse; the initiators in all sexual contacts—abusive or otherwise. The common assumption in legal proceedings as well as in the larger society has been that Black women cannot be raped or otherwise sexually abused. As Anita Hill's experience demonstrates, Black women who speak of these matters are not likely to be believed.

In 1991, we cannot tolerate this type of dismissal of any one Black woman's experience or this attack upon our collective character without protest, outrage, and resistance. As women of African descent, we express our vehement opposition to the policies represented by the placement of Clarence Thomas on the Supreme Court. The Bush administration, having obstructed the passage of civil rights legislation, impeded the extension of unemployment compensation, cut student aid and dismantled social welfare programs, has continually demonstrated that it is not operating in our best interests. Nor is this appointee. We pledge ourselves to continue to speak out in defense of one another, in defense of the African American community and against those who are hostile to social justice no matter what color they are. No one will speak for us but ourselves.

### Notes

1. This statement ran as an ad on Sunday, November 17, 1991 in the *New York Times* with 1603 signatures of Black women. It also appeared in six Black newspapers: the *Atlanta Inquirer*, the *Chicago Defender*, the *City Sun*, (New York City), the *Spotlight* (Washington D.C.), the *Los Angeles Sentinel*, and the *Sun-Reporter* (San Francisco). The cost of the ads was more than $50,000 and was raised by Black women and their allies in a few short weeks after Anita Hill's testimony before the Senate Judiciary Committee on October 11, 1991.

## A Black Man's Place in
## Black Feminist Criticism

*Michael Awkward*

1995

Many essays by male and female scholars devoted to exploring the subject of male critics' place in feminism generally agree about the uses and usefulness of the autobiographical male "I." Such essays suggest that citing the male critical self reflects a response to (apparent) self-difference, an exploration of the disparities between the masculine's antagonistic position in feminist discourse on the one hand and, on the other, the desire of the individual male critic to represent his difference with and from the traditional androcentric perspectives of his gender and culture. Put another way, in male feminist acts, to identify the writing self as biologically male is to emphasize the desire not to be ideologically male; it is to explore the process of rejecting the phallocentric perspectives by which men traditionally have justified the subjugation of women.[1]

In what strikes me as a particularly suggestive theoretical formulation, Joseph Boone articulates his sense of the goals of such male feminist autobiographical acts:

> In exposing the latent multiplicity and difference in the word "me(n)," we can perhaps open up a space within the discourse of feminism where a male feminist voice can have something to say beyond impossibilities and apologies and unresolved ire. Indeed, if the male feminist can discover a position *from which* to speak that neither elides the importance of feminism to his work nor ignores the specificity of his gender, his voice may also find that it no longer exists as an abstraction . . . but that it in fact inhabits a body: its own sexual/textual body.[2]

Because of an awareness that androcentric perspectives are learned, are transmitted by means of specific sociocultural practices in such effective ways that they come to appear natural, male feminists such as Boone believe that, through an informed investigation of androcentric and feminist ideologies, individual men can work to resist the lure of the normatively masculine. That resistance for the aspiring male feminist requires, he says, exposing "the latent multiplicity and difference in the word 'men,'" in other words, disrupting both ideologies' unproblematized perceptions of mono- lithic and/or normative maleness (as villainous, antagonistic "other" for feminism, and, for androcentricism, powerful, domineering patriarch). At this early stage of male feminism's development, to speak self-consciously— autobiographically—is to explore, implicity or explicitly, why and how the individual male experience (the "me" in men) has diverged from, has cre- ated possibilities for a rejection of, the androcentric norm.

And while there is not yet agreement as to what constitutes an identifi- ably male feminist act of criticism or about the usefulness of such acts for the general advancement of the feminist project, at least one possible expla- nation for a male critic's self-referential discourse is that it is a response to palpable mistrust—emanating from some female participants in feminism and perhaps from the writing male subject himself—about his motives. A skeptical strand of opinion with regard to male feminism is represented by Alice Jardine's "Men in Feminism: Odor di Uomo or Compagnons de Route?" Having determined that the most useful measure of an adequately feminist text is its "*inscription of struggle*—even of *pain*"—an inscription of a struggle against patriarchy which Jardine finds absent from most male feminist acts, perhaps because "the historical fact that is the oppression of women [is] . . . one of their favorite blind spots"—she admits to some confusion as to the motivations for males' willing participation: "Why . . . would men want to be in feminism if it's about struggle? What do men want to be in—in pain?"[3]

In addition to seeking to cure its blindness where the history of female oppression is concerned, a male feminism must explore the motivations for its participation in what we might call, in keeping with Jardine's formula- tions, a discourse of (en)gendered pain. If one of the goals of male feminist self-referentiality is to demonstrate to females that individual males can indeed serve as allies in efforts to undermine androcentric power—and it seems that this is invariably the case—the necessary trust cannot be gained by insisting that motivation as such does not represent a crucial area that must be carefully negotiated. For example, I accept as accurate and, indeed, reflective of my own situation Andrew Ross's assertion that "there are those [men] for whom the facticity of feminism, for the most part, goes without saying . . . , who are young enough for feminism to have been a primary component of their intellectual formation."[4] However, in discussions whose apparent function is a foregrounding of both obstacles to and possibilities of a male feminism, men's relation(s) to the discourse can never go "without saying"; for the foreseeable future at least, this relation needs necessarily to be rigorously and judiciously theorized, and grounded explicitly in the experiential realm of the writing male subject.

But no matter how illuminating and exemplary one finds self-referential inscriptions of a male feminist critical self, if current views of the impossibility of a consistently truthful autobiographical act are correct, there are difficulties implicit in any such attempt to situate or inscribe that male self. Because, as recent theorizing on the subject of autobiography has demonstrated, acts of discursive self-rendering unavoidably involve the creation of an idealized version of a unified or unifiable self, we can be certain only of the fact that the autobiographical impulse yields but some of the truths of the male feminist critic's experiences.[5] As is also the case for female participants, a male can never possess or be able to tell the whole truth and nothing but the truth about his relationship to feminist discourse and praxis.

But while autobiographical criticism, like the genre of autobiography itself, is poised tenuously between the poles of closure and disclosure, between representation and re-presentation, between a lived life and an invented one, I believe that even in the recoverable half-truths of my life are some of the materials that have shaped my perceptions, my beliefs, the self or selves that I bring to the interpretive act. In these half-truths is the source of my desire both to inscribe a black male feminism and to inscribe myself as a self-consciously racialized version of what Jardine considers a potentially oxymoronic entity—"male feminist"—whose literal, if not ideological or performative "blackness" is indisputable, and whose adequacy vis-à-vis feminism others must determine. By examining discussions of the phenomenon of the male feminist—that is to say, by reading male and female explorations of men's places in feminist criticism—and exploring responses of others to my own professional and personal relationships to feminism, I will identify autobiographically and textually grounded sources for my belief that while gendered difference might be said to complicate the prospect of a non-phallocentric black male feminism, it does not render such a project impossible.

At the outset, I acknowledge that mine is a necessary participation with regard to black feminist criticism in the half-invention, half-perception which, in Houston Baker's compelling formulation, represents every scholar's relationship to cultural criticism.[6] Such an acknowledgment is not intended to indicate that my male relationship to feminism is that of an illegitimate child, as it were. Rather, it is meant to suggest, like Elizabeth Weed's insistence on "the impossibility" of both men's and women's "relationship to feminism," my belief that while feminism represents a complex, sometimes self-contradictory "utopian vision" which no one can fully possess, a biological male can "develop political, theoretical [and, more generally, interpretive] strategies" which, though at most perhaps half-true to all that feminist ideologies are, nevertheless can assist in a movement toward actualizing the goals of feminism.[7]

I have been forced to think in especially serious ways about my own relationship to feminist criticism since I completed the first drafts of *Inspiring Influences*, my study of Afro-American women novelists.[8] I have questioned neither the explanatory power of feminism nor the essential importance of developing models adequate to the analysis of black female-authored texts, as my book—in harmony, I believe, with the black feminist project concerned with recovering and uncovering an Afro-American female literary tradition—attempts to provide on a limited scale. Instead, I have been confronted with suspicion about my gendered suitability for the task of explicating Afro-American women's texts, suspicion which has been manifested in the form of both specific responses to my project and general inquiries within literary studies into the phenomenon of the male feminist.

For example, a white female reader of the manuscript asserted—with undisguised surprise—that my work was "so feminist" and asked how I'd managed to offer such ideologically informed readings. Another scholar, a black feminist literary critic, recorded with no discernible hesitation her unease with my "male readings" of the texts of Zora Neale Hurston, Toni Morrison, Gloria Naylor, and Alice Walker. I wondered about the possibility of my being simultaneously "so feminist" and not so feminist (i.e., so "male"), about the meanings of these terms both for these scholars and for the larger interpretive communities in which they participate. Consequently, in what was perhaps initially an act of psychic self-protection, I began to formulate questions for which I still have found no consistently satisfactory answers. Were the differences in the readers' perceptions of the ideological adequacy of my study a function of their own views of feminist criticism, a product, in other words, of the differences not simply *within me* but *within feminism itself*? And if the differences within feminism are so significant, could I possibly satisfy everybody with "legitimate" interests in the texts of Hurston et al. by means of my own appropriated versions of black feminist discourse, my unavoidably half-true myth of what that discourse is, means, and does? Should my myth of feminism and its mobilization in critical texts be considered naturally less analytically compelling than that of a female scholar simply as a function of my biological maleness? And how could what I took to be a useful self-reflexivity avoid becoming a debilitating inquiry into a process that has come to seem for me, if not "natural," as Cary Nelson views his relationship to feminism, at least *necessary*?[9]

Compelled, and, to be frank, disturbed by such questions, I searched for answers in others' words, others' work. I purchased a copy of *Men in Feminism*, a collection which examines the possibility of men's participation as "comrades" (to use Toni Morrison's term) in feminist criticism and theory. Gratified by the appearance of such a volume, I became dismayed upon reading the editors' introductory remarks, which noted their difficulty in "locating intellectuals, who, having shown interest in the question, would offer, for instance, a gay or a black perspective on the problem."[10] While a self-consciously "gay . . . perspective" does find its way into the collection, the insights of nonwhite males and females are conspicuously absent.[11]

Even more troubling for me than the absence of black voices or, for that matter, of general inquiries into the effects of racial, cultural, and class differences on males' relationship to feminism, was the sense shared by many contributors of insurmountable obstacles to male feminism. In fact, the first essay, Stephen Heath's "Male Feminism," begins by insisting that "men's relation to feminism is an impossible one."[12] For me, Heath's formulations are insightful and provocative, if not always persuasive, as when he claims: "This is, I believe, the most any man can do today: to learn and so to try to write and talk or act in response to feminism, and so to try not in any way to be antifeminist, supportive of the old oppressive structures. Any more, any notion of writing a feminist book or being a feminist, is a myth, a male imaginary with the reality of appropriation and domination right behind."[13] Is male participation in feminism restricted to being either appropriative and domineering or not antifeminist? Must we necessarily agree with Heath and others who claim that men cannot be feminists? To put the matter differently, is gender really an adequate determinant of "class" position?

Despite the poststructuralist tenor of Heath's work generally and of many of his perspectives here, his is an easily problematized essentialist claim—that, in effect, biology determines destiny and, therefore, one's relationship to feminist ideology, that womanhood allows one to become feminist at the same time that manhood necessarily denies that status to men. And while Heath embraces its notions of history as a narrative of male "appropriation and domination" of gendered others, he appears resistant at this point in his discourse to evidence of a powerful feminist institutional *present* and *presence*. I believe that we must acknowledge that feminism represents, at least in areas of the American academy, an incomparably productive, influential, and resilient ideology and institution that men, no matter how cunning, duplicitous, or culturally powerful, will neither control nor overthrow in the foreseeable future, one whose perspectives have proved and might continue to prove convincing even to biological males. In surveying the potential implications of the participation of biological men in feminism, we must therefore be honest about feminism's current persuasiveness and indomitability, about its clarifying, transformative potential, and about the fact that the corruptive possibility of both the purposefully treacherous and the only half-convinced male is, for today at least, slight indeed. Surely it is neither naive, presumptuous, nor premature to suggest that feminism as ideology and reading strategy has assumed a position of exegetical and institutional strength capable of withstanding even the most energetically masculinist acts of subversion.

Below I want to focus specifically on the question of a black male feminism. Rather than seeing it as an impossibility or as a subtle new manifestation of and attempt at androcentric domination, I want to show that certain instances of afrocentric feminism provide Afro-American men with an invaluable means of rewriting—of *re-vis(ion)ing*—our selves, our history and literary tradition, and our future.

Few would deny that black feminist literary criticism is an oppositional discourse constituted in large part as a response against black male participation in the subjugation of Afro-American women. From Barbara Smith's castigation of black male critics for their "virulently sexist. . . treatment" of black women writers and her insistence that they are "hampered by an inability to comprehend Black women's experience in sexual as well as racial terms" to Michele Wallace's characterization of the "black male Afro-Americanists who make pivotal use of Hurston's work" as "a gang," Afro-American men are generally perceived as non-allied others of black feminist discourse.[14] And, as is evident in Wallace's figuration of male Hurston scholars as intraracial street warriors, they are viewed at times as always already damned and unredeemable, even when they appear to take black women's writing seriously. We—I—must accept the fact that black male investigations informed by feminist principles, including this one, may never be good enough or ideologically correct enough for some black women who are feminists.

This sense of an unredeemable black male critic/reader is in stark contrast to perspectives offered in such texts as Sherley Anne Williams's "Some Implications of Womanist Theory." In her essay, she embraces Alice Walker's term "womanist"—which, according to Williams, connotes a commitment "to the survival and wholeness of an entire people, female and male, as well as a valorization of women's works in all their varieties and multitudes"—because she considers the black feminist project to be separatist in "its tendency to see not only a distinct black female culture but to see that culture as a separate cultural form" from "the facticity of Afro-American life."[15]

I believe that a black male feminism, whatever its connections to critical theory or its specific areas of concern, can profit immensely from what
female feminists have to say about male participation. For example, Valerie
Smith's suggestion in "Gender and Afro-Americanist Literary Theory and
Criticism" that "Black male critics and theorists might explore the nature of
the contradictions that arise when they undertake black feminist projects"[16]
seems to me quite useful, as does Alice Jardine's advice to male feminists.
Speaking for white female feminists, Jardine addresses white males who
consider themselves to be feminists: "We do not want you to *mimic* us, to
become the same as us; we don't want your pathos or your guilt: and we
don't even want your admiration (even if it's nice to get it once in a while).
What we want, I would even say what we need, is your *work*. We need you to
get down to serious work. And like all serious work, that involves struggle
and pain."[17] The womanist theoretical project that has been adopted by Williams, Smith, and others provides aspiring Afro-American male feminists
with a useful model for the type of self-exploration that Smith and Jardine
advocate. What Williams terms "womanist theory" is especially suggestive
for Afro-American men because, while it calls for feminist discussions of
black women's texts and for critiques of black androcentricism, womanism
foregrounds a general black psychic health as a primary objective. Williams
argues that "what is needed is a thoroughgoing examination of male images
in the works of black male writers"; her womanism, then, aims at "ending the separatist tendency in Afro-American criticism," at leading black
feminism away from "the same hole The Brother has dug for himself—narcissism, isolation, inarticulation, obscurity," at the creation and/or continuation of black "community and dialogue."[18]

If a black man is to become a useful contributor to black feminism, he
must, as Boone argues, "discover a position *from which* to speak that neither
elides the importance of feminism to his work nor ignores the specificity of
his gender." However multiply split we perceive the subject to be, however
deeply felt our sense of "maleness" and "femaleness" as social constructions,
however heightened our sense of the historical consequences and current
dangers of black androcentricism, a black male feminism cannot contribute
to the continuation and expansion of the black feminist project by being so
identified against or out of touch with itself as to fail to be both self-reflective and at least minimally self-interested. A black male feminist self-reflec-
tivity of the type I have in mind necessarily would include examination of
both the benefits and the dangers of a situatedness in feminist discourse.
The self-interestedness of a black male feminist would be manifested in part
by his concern with exploring a man's place. Clearly if convincing mimicry
of female-authored concerns and interpretive strategies—speaking *like* a

female feminist—is not in and of itself an appropriate goal for aspiring male participants, then a male feminism necessarily must explore males' various situations in the contexts and texts of history and the present.

Perhaps the most difficult task for a black male feminist is striking a workable balance between male self-inquiry/interest and an adequately feminist critique of patriarchy. To this point, especially in response to the commercial and critical success of contemporary Afro-American women's literature, scores of black men have proved unsuccessful in this regard. As black feminist critics such as Valerie Smith and Deborah McDowell have argued, the contemporary moment of black feminist literature has been greeted by many Afro-American males with hostility, self-interested mis-representation, and a lack of honest intellectual introspection. In "Reading Family Matters," a useful discussion for black male feminism primarily as an exploration of what such a discourse ought not do and be, McDowell speaks of widely circulated androcentric male analyses of Afro-American feminist texts by writers such as Toni Morrison and Alice Walker:

> Critics leading the debate [about the representation of black men in black women's texts] have lumped all black women writers together and have focused on one tiny aspect of their immensely complex and diverse project—the image of black men—despite the fact that, if we can claim a center for these texts, it is located in the complexities of black female subjectivity and experience. In other words, though black women writers have made black women the subjects of their own fam-ily stories, these male readers/critics are attempting to usurp that place for themselves and place it at the center of critical inquiry.[19]

Although I do not believe that "the image of black men" is as microscopic an element in Afro-American women's texts as McDowell claims, I agree with her about the reprehensible nature of unabashed androcentricism found in formulations she cites by such writers as Robert Staples, Mel Watkins, and Darryl Pinckney. Nevertheless, in relation to the potential development of a black male feminism, I am troubled by what appears to be a surprisingly explicit determination to protect turf. In their unwillingness to grant that exploration of how Afro-American males are delineated by contemporary black female novelists is a legitimate concern that might produce illuminat-ing analyses, McDowell's formulations echo in unfortunate ways those of antifeminist male critics, white and black, who consider feminism to be an unredeemably myopic and unyielding interpretive strategy incapable of offering subtle readings of canonical, largely male-authored texts. Despite the circulation of reprehensibly masculinist responses to Afro-American women's literature, black feminist literary critics do not best serve the discourses that concern them by setting into motion homeostatic maneuvers intended to devalue all forms of inquiry except for those they hold to be most valuable (in this particular case, a female-authored scholarship that emphasizes Afro-American women's writings of black female subjectivity). If the Afro-American women's literary project is indeed "immensely complex and diverse," as McDowell claims, bringing to bear other angles of vision, including antipatriarchal male ones, can assist in analyzing aspects of that complexity.

While the views of Staples and others are clearly problematic, those problems do not arise specifically from their efforts to place males "at the center of critical inquiry" any more than feminism is implicitly flawed because it insists, in some of its manifestations, on a gynocritical foregrounding of representations of women. Rather, these problems appear to result from the fact that the particular readers who produce these perspectives do not seem sufficiently to be, in Toril Moi's titular phrase, "men against patriarchy."[20] Certainly, in an age when both gender studies and Afro-American women's literature have achieved a degree of legitimacy within the academy and outside of it, it is unreasonable for black women either to demand that black men not be concerned with the ways in which they are depicted by Afro-American women writers, or to see that concern as intrinsically troubling in feminist terms. If female feminist calls for a non-mimicking male feminism are indeed persuasive, then black men will have very little of substance to say about contemporary Afro-American women's literature, especially if we are also to consider as transgressive any attention to figurations of black manhood. It seems to me that the most black females in feminism can insist upon in this regard is that examinations which focus on male characters treat the complexity of contemporary Afro-American women novelists' delineations of black manhood with an antipatriarchal seriousness which the essays McDowell cites clearly lack.

From my perspective, what is potentially most valuable about the development of black male feminism is not its capacity to reproduce black feminism as practiced by black females who focus primarily on "the complexities of black female subjectivity and experience."[21] Rather, its potential value lies in the possibility that, in being antipatriarchal and as self-inquiring about their relationship(s) to feminism as Afro-American women have been, black men can expand the range and utilization of feminist inquiry and explore other fruitful applications for feminist perspectives, including such topics as obstacles to a black male feminist project itself and new figurations of "family matters" and black male sexuality.

For the purpose of theorizing about a black male feminism, perhaps the most provocative, enlightening, and inviting moment in feminist or in "womanist" scholarship occurs in Hortense Spillers's "Mama's Baby, Papa's Maybe: An American Grammar Book." Indeed, Spillers's essay represents a fruitful starting point for new, potentially nonpatriarchal figurations of family and of black males' relationship to the female. Toward the end of this illuminating theoretical text, which concerns itself with slavery's debilitating effects on the Afro-American family's constitution, Spillers envisions black male identity formation as a process whose movement toward successful resolution seems to require a serious engagement of black feminist principles and perspectives. Spillers asserts that as a result of those specific familial patterns which functioned during American slavery and beyond and "removed the African-American male not so much from sight as from *mimetic* view as a partner in the prevailing social fiction of the Father's name, the Father's law," the African-American male "has been touched . . . by the *mother, handed* by her in ways that he cannot escape." Because of separation from traditional American paternal name and law, "the black American male embodies the *only* American community of males which has had the specific occasion to learn *who* the female is within itself. . . . It is the heritage of the *mother* that the African-American male must regain as an aspect of his own personhood—the power of 'yes' to the 'female' within."[22]

Rather than seeing the "female" strictly as other for the Afro-American male, Spillers's afrocentric revisioning of psychoanalytic theory insists that we consider it an important aspect of the repressed in the black male self.[23] Employing Spillers's analyses as a starting point, we might regard Afro-American males' potential "in-ness" vis-à-vis feminism not, as Paul Smith insists in *Men in Feminism*, as a representation of male heterosexual desires to penetrate and violate female spaces[24] but rather as an acknowledgment of what Spillers considers the distinctive nature of the Afro-American male's connection to the "female." If Afro-American males are ever to have anything to say about or to black feminism beyond the types of reflex-action devaluations and diatribes about divisiveness that critics such as McDowell and Valerie Smith rightly decry, the investigative process of which womanist acts by Spillers and Williams speak is indispensable. Such a process, if pursued in an intellectually rigorous manner, offers a means by which black men can participate usefully in and contribute productively to the black feminist project.

Black womanism demands neither the erasure of the black gendered other's subjectivity, as have male movements to regain a putatively lost Afro-American manhood, nor the relegation of males to prone, domestic, or other limiting positions. What it does require, if it is indeed to become an ideology with widespread cultural impact, is a recognition on the part of both black females and males of the nature of the gendered inequities that have marked our past and present, and a resolute commitment to work for change. In that sense, black feminist criticism has not only created a space for an informed Afro-American male participation, but it heartily welcomes—in fact, insists upon—the joint participation of black males and females as *comrades,* to invoke, with a difference, this paper's epigraphic reference to *Sula.*

Reading "Mama's Baby, Papa's Maybe" was of special importance to me in part because it helped me to clarify and articulate my belief that my relationship to feminism need not mark me necessarily as a debilitatingly split subject. The source of that relationship can only be traced autobiographically, if at all. Having been raised by a mother who, like too many women of too many generations, was the victim of male physical and psychological brutality—a brutality which, according to my mother, resulted in large part from my father's frustrations about his inability to partake in what Spillers calls masculinity's "prevailing social fiction"—my earliest stories, my familial narratives, as it were, figured "maleness" in quite troubling terms. My mother told me horrific stories, one of which I was, in a sense, immediately involved in: my father—who left us before I was one year old and whom I never knew—kicked her in the stomach when my fetal presence swelled her body, because he believed she'd been unfaithful to him and that I was only "maybe" his baby.

As a youth, I pondered this and other such stories often and deeply, in part because of the pain I knew these incidents caused my mother, in part because, as someone without a consistent male familial role model, I actively sought a way to achieve a gendered self-definition. As one for whom maleness as manifested in the surrounding inner city culture seemed to be represented only by violence, familial abandonment, and the certainty of imprisonment, I found that I was able to define myself with regard to my gender primarily in oppositional ways. I had internalized the cautionary intent of my mother's narratives, which also served as her dearest wish for me: that I not grow up to be like my father, that I not adopt the definitions of "maleness" represented by his example and in the culture generally. Because the scars of male brutality were visibly etched—literally marked, as it were—on my mother's flesh and on her psyche, "maleness," as figured both in her stories and in my environment, seemed to me not to be a viable mimetic option. I grew up, then, not always sure of what or who I was with respect to prevailing social definitions of gender but generally quite painfully aware of what I could not become.

In order to begin to understand who my mother was, perhaps also who my father was, what "maleness" was and what extra-biological relationship

I could hope to have to it, I needed answers that my mother was unable to provide. I found little of value in the black masculinist discourse of the time, which spoke endlessly of the dehumanization and castration of the Afro-American male by white men and black women—our central social narrative for too long—for this rhetoric seemed simplistic and unself-consciously concerned with justifying domestic violence and other forms of black male brutality.

Afro-American women's literature, to which I was introduced along with black feminism in 1977 as a sophomore at Brandeis University, helped me move toward a comprehension of the world, of aspects of my mother's life, and of what a man against patriarchy could be and do. These discourses provided me with answers, nowhere else available, to what had been largely unresolvable mysteries. I work within the paradigm of black feminist literary criticism because it explains elements of the world about which I care most deeply. I write and read what and as I do because I am incapable of escaping the meanings of my mother's narratives for my own life, because the pain and, in the fact of their enunciation to the next generation, the sense of hope for better days that characterizes these familial texts are illuminatingly explored in many narratives by black women. Afro-American women's literature has given me parts of myself that—incapable of a (biological) "fatherly reprieve"—I would not otherwise have had.

I have decided that it is ultimately irrelevant whether these autobiographical facts, which, of course, are not, and can never be, the whole story, are deemed by others sufficient to permit me to call myself "feminist." Like Toril Moi, I have come to believe that "the important thing for men is not to spend their time worrying about definitions and essences ('am I *really* a feminist?'), but to take up a recognizable anti-patriarchal position."[25] What is most important to me is that my work contribute, in however small a way, to the project whose goal is the dismantling of the phallocentric rule by which black females and, I am sure, countless other Afro-American sons have been injuriously "touched."

My indebtedness to Spillers's and other womanist perspectives is, then, great indeed, as is my sense of their potential as illuminating moments for a newborn—or not-yet-born—black male feminist discourse. But to utilize these perspectives requires that we be more inquiring than Spillers is in her formulations, not in envisioning liberating possibilities of an acknowledgment of the "female" within the black community and the male subject, but in noting potential dangers inherent in such an attempted adoption by historically brutalized Afro-American men whose relationship to a repressed "female" is not painstakingly (re)defined.

Clearly, more thinking is necessary not only about what the female within is but about what it can be said to represent for black males, as well as serious analysis of useful means and methods of interacting with a repressed female interiority and subject. Spillers's theorizing does not perform this task, in part because it has other, more compelling interests and emphases—among which is the righting/(re)writing of definitions of "woman" so that they will reflect Afro-American women's particular, historically conditioned "female social subject" status—but a black male feminism must be especially focused on exploring such issues if it is to mobilize Spillers's suggestive remarks as a means of developing a fuller understanding of the complex formulations of black manhood found in many texts and contexts, including Afro-American women's narratives.

I want to build briefly on Spillers's provocative theorizing about the Afro-American male's maturational process and situation on American shores. To this end, I will look at an illuminating moment in Toni Morrison's *Sula*, a text that is, to my mind, not only an unparalleled Afro-American woman's writing of the complexities of black female subjectivity and experience but also of black males' relationship to the female within as a consequence of their limited access to "the prevailing social fiction" of masculinity. In this novel, the difficulty of negotiating the spaces between black male lack and black female presence is plainly manifested in such figures as the undifferentiatable Deweys; BoyBoy, whose name, in contrast to most of the authorial designations in *Sula*, speaks unambiguously for him; and Jude, whose difficulty in assuming the mantle of male provider leads him to view his union with Nel as that which "would make one Jude."[26]

The response of Plum, the most tragic of *Sula's* unsuccessful negotiators of the so-called white man's world, vividly represents for me some of the contemporary dangers of black male "in-ness" vis-à-vis the "female." Despite a childhood which included "float[ing] in a constant swaddle of love and affection" and his mother's intention to follow the Father's law by bequeathing "everything" to him (38), Plum appears incapable of embracing hegemonic notions of masculinity. Instead, he returns from World War I spiritually fractured but, unlike a similarly devastated Shadrack, lacking the imaginative wherewithal to begin to theorize or ritualize a new relationship to his world. He turns to drugs as a method of anesthetizing himself from the horrors of his devastation and, in his mother's view, seeks to compel her resumption of familiar/familial patterns of caretaking. In the following passage, Eva explains to Hannah her perception of Plum's desires, as well as the motivation for her participation in what amounts to an act of infanticide:

When he came back from that war he wanted to git back in. After all that carryin' on, just gettin' him out and keepin' him alive, he wanted to crawl back in my womb and well. . . . I ain't got the room no more even if he could do it. There wasn't space for him in my womb. And he was crawlin' back. Being helpless and thinking baby thoughts and dreaming baby dreams and messing up his pants again and smiling all the time. I had room enough in my heart, but not in my womb, got no more. I birthed him once. I couldn't do it again. He was growed, a big old thing. Godhavemercy, I couldn't birth him twice. . . . A big man can't be a baby all wrapped up inside his mamma no more; he suffocate. I done everything I could to make him leave me and go on and live and be a man but he wouldn't and I had to keep him out so I just thought of a way he could die like a man not all scrunched up inside my womb, but like a man. (62)[27]

What is significant about this passage for an analysis of the possibilities of a non-oppressive black male relationship to feminism—to female experience characterized by a refusal to be subjugated to androcentric desires—is its suggestiveness for our understanding of the obstacles to a revised male view of the repressed "female," obstacles which result in large part from black males' relative social powerlessness. If black feminism is persuasive in its analysis of the limitations of Afro-American masculinist ideology, emphasizing as it does achievement of black manhood at the expense of black female subjectivity, and if we can best describe an overwhelming number of Africa's American male descendants as males-in-crisis, the question a black male feminism must ask itself is, On what basis, according to what ideological perspective, can an Afro-American heterosexual male ground his notions of the female? Beyond its heterosexual dimension, can the "female" truly come to represent for a traditional black male-in-crisis more than a protective maternal womb from which he seeks to be "birthed" again? Can it serve as more than a site on which to find relief from or locate frustrations caused by an inability to achieve putatively normative American male socioeconomic status? If embracing normative masculinity requires an escape from the protection and life-sustaining aspects symbolized by maternal umbilical cords and apron strings and an achievement of an economic situation wherein the male provides domestic space and material sustenance for his dependents (including "his woman"), black manhood generally is, like Plum, in desperate trouble. And if, as has often been the case, a black female can be seen by an Afro-American male-in-crisis only if she has been emptied of subjectivity and selfhood, if she becomes visible for the male only when she is subsumed by male desire(s), then the types of refiguration and redefinition of black male subjectivity and engagement with the "female" central to Spillers's formulations are highly unlikely.

This question of seeing and not seeing, of the male gaze's erasure and recreation of the female, is crucial to *Sula's* general thematics. It seems to me that in all of her novels Morrison's figuration of black female subjectivity is largely incomprehensible without some serious attention both to her representation of black manhood and to her exploration of the relationships between socially constructed gendered (and racial) positions. To return explicitly to the case of Eva: What Eva fears, what appears to be a self-interested motivation for her killing of her intended male heir, is that Plum's pitiful, infantile state has the potential to reduce *her* to a static female function of self-sacrificing mother, which, according to Bottom legend, had already provoked her decision to lose a leg in order to collect insurance money with which to provide for her children. Having personally lost so much already, Eva chooses, instead of sacrificing other essential parts of herself, to take the life of her self-described male heir. And if Plum dies "like a man" in Eva's estimation, his achievement of manhood has nothing to do with an assumption of traditional masculine traits, nothing to do with strength, courage, and a refusal to cry in the face of death. Instead, that achievement results from Eva's creation of conditions that have become essential components of her definition of manhood: death forces him to "leave" her and to "keep . . . out" of her womb. It would appear that manhood is defined here not as presence as typically represented in Western thought, but—by and for Eva at least—as liberating (domestic and uterine) absence.

One of the intentions of this chapter is to suggest that feminism represents a fruitful and potentially not oppressive means of reconceptualizing, of figuratively birthing twice, the black male subject. But, as a close reading of the aforementioned passage from Sula suggests, interactions between men and women motivated by male self-interest such as necessarily characterizes an aspect of male participation in feminism are fraught with possible dangers for the biological/ideological female body of an enactment of or a capitulation to hegemonic male power. Indeed, if it is the case that, as Spillers has argued in another context, "the woman who stays in man's company keeps alive the possibility of having, one day, an unwanted guest, or the guest, deciding to 'hump the hostess,' whose intentions turn homicidal," then male proximity to feminism generally creates the threat of a specifically masculinist violation.[28] If, as I noted earlier, the dangers of a hegemonic, heterosexual Euro-American male's "in-ness" vis-à-vis feminism include (sexualized) penetration and domination, then those associated with a heterosexual black male's interactions with the ideological female body are at least doubled, and potentially involve an envisioning of the black female body as self-sacrificingly maternal or self-sacrificingly sexual. Because of a general lack of access to the full force of hegemonic male power, Afro-American men could see in increasingly influential black female texts not only serious challenges to black male fictions of the self but also an appropriate location for masculine desires for control of the types of valuable resources that the discourses of black womanhood currently represent.

But a rigorous, conscientious black male feminism need not give in to traditional patriarchal desires for control and erasure of the female. To be of any sustained value to the feminist project, a discourse must provide illuminating and persuasive readings of gender as it is constituted for blacks in America and sophisticated, informed, contentious critiques of phallocentric practices in an effort to redefine our notions of black male and female textuality and subjectivity. And in its differences from black feminist texts that are produced by individual Afro-American women, a black male feminism must be both rigorous in engaging these texts and self-reflective enough to avoid, at all costs, the types of patronizing, marginalizing gestures that have traditionally characterized Afro-American male intellectuals' response to black womanhood. What a black male feminism must strive for, above all else, is to envision and enact the possibilities signaled by the differences feminism has exposed and created. In black feminist criticism, being an Afro-American male does not mean attempting to invade an/other political body like a lascivious soul snatcher or striving to erase its essence in order to replace it with one's own myth of what the discourse should be. Such a position for black men means, above all else, an acknowledgment and celebration of the incontrovertible fact that "the Father's law" is no longer the only law of the land.

## Notes

1. Joseph Boone's and Gerald MacLean's essays in *Gender and Theory* assume that the foregrounding of gendered subjectivity is essential to the production of a male feminist critical practice. Consequently, in an effort to articulate his perspectives on the possibilities of a male feminist discourse, Boone shares with us professional secrets—he writes of his disagreement with the male-authored essays in Alice Jardine and Paul Smith's *Men and Feminism,* and of being excluded, because of his gender, from a Harvard feminist group discussion of Elaine Showalter's "Critical Cross-Dressing." And MacLean's essay discloses painfully personal information about his difficult relationship with his mother, his unsatisfying experience with psychoanalysis, and an incident of marital violence.

2. Joseph Boone, "Of Me(n) and Feminism: Who(se) is the Sex That Writes?" in *Gender and Theory,* 158–80. Here and below, I quote from p. 159. For my purposes, Boone's remarks are suggestive despite their use of language that might seem to mark them as a heterosexualization of men's participation in feminism ("open up a space," "discover a position"). I believe that Boone's passage implies less about any desire for domination on his part than it does about the pervasiveness in our language of terms which have ac-

quired sexual connotations and, consequently, demonstrates the virtual unavoidability of using a discourse of penetration to describe interactions between males and females. But it also appears to reflect a sense of frustration motivated by Boone's knowledge that while feminism has had a tremendous impact on his thinking about the world he inhabits, many feminists do not see a place in their discourse for him or other like-minded males. In order to make such a place for himself, violation and transgression seem to Boone to be unavoidable.

3. Alice Jardine, "Men in Feminism: Odor di Uomo or Compagnons de Route?" in *Men in Feminism*, 58.

4. Andrew Ross, "No Question of Silence," in *Men in Feminism*, 86.

5. See Georges Poulet, "Criticism and the Experience of Interiority," in *Reader-Response Criticism: From Formalism to Post-Structuralism*, ed. Jane P. Tompkins (Baltimore: Johns Hopkins University Press, 1980), 41–49.

6. Houston A. Baker, Jr., *Afro-American Poetics*, 8.

7. Elizabeth Weed, "A Man's Place," in *Men in Feminism*, 75.

8. Michael Awkward, *Inspiring Influences: Tradition, Revision, and Afro-American Women's Novels* (New York: Columbia University Press, 1989).

9. About his relationship to feminism, Nelson writes: "Feminism is part of my social and intellectual life, has been so for many years, and so, to the extent that writing is ever 'natural,' it is natural that I write about feminism" (153). Nelson's "Men, Feminism: The Materiality of Discourse" (*Men in Feminism*, 153–72) is, in my estimation, a model for self-referential male feminist inquiries that assume—or, at the very least, seek to demonstrate—a useful place for males in the discourse of feminism.

10. Jardine and Smith, *Men in Feminism*, vii–viii.

11. See Craig Owens, "Outlaws: Gay Men in Feminism," in *Men in Feminism*, 219–32. It is hard to believe that Jardine and Smith's difficulty reflected a lack of interest among Afro-Americans in exploring the relationship of men to black feminism. A number of texts give evidence of interest in "the problem": the 1979 *Black Scholar* special issue devoted to investigating black feminism as manifested primarily in Ntozake Shange's *for colored girls* and Michele Wallace's *Black Macho and the Myth of the Superwoman*; Mel Watkins, "Sexism, Racism, and Black Women Writers," *New York Times Book Review*, June 15, 1986, p.1; Darryl Pinckney, "Black Victims, Black Villains," *New York Review of Books* 34 (January 29, 1987): 17–20; and essays by Valerie Smith and Deborah McDowell from which I draw below.

Jardine and Smith's difficulties might have stemmed from the facts that most of the men who had spoken publicly on the subject were open about their hostility to black feminism, and most of them did not speak the language of contemporary theory, a high academic idiom which demonstrates that the contributors to *Men in Feminism* are, despite significant differences among them, members of the same speech community.

12. Stephen Heath, "Male Feminism," *Men in Feminism*, 1.

13. Ibid., 9.

14. Barbara Smith, "Toward a Black Feminist Criticism," 173, 172; Michele Wallace, "Who Dat Say Dat When I Say Dat? Zora Neal Hurston Then and Now," *Village Voice Literary Supplement*, April 1988, p. 18.

15. Sherley Anne Williams, "Some Implications of Womanist Theory," *Callaloo* 9 (1986): 304.

16. Valerie Smith, "Gender and Afro-Americanist Literary Theory and Criticism," in *Speaking of Gender*, 68.

17. Jardine, "Men in Feminism," *Men in Feminism*, 60.

18. Williams, "Some Implications," 307.

19. Deborah McDowell, "Reading Family Matters," in *Changing Our Own Words: Essays on Criticism, Theory, and the Writing by Black Women,* ed. Cheryl Wall (New Brunswick: Rutgers University Press, 1989), 84.

20. Toril Moi, "Men against Patriarchy," in *Gender and Theory,* 181–88.

21. McDowell's views notwithstanding, constructions of black male and black female subjectivity are too obviously interrelated in black women's narratives for feminist criticism to profit in the long run from ignoring—or urging that others ignore—the important function that delineations of black male subjectivity play in these narratives' thematics. Certainly the threat of antifeminist male critical bias is not cause to erase or minimize the significance of black male characters in these writers' work.

22. Spillers, "Mama's Baby, Papa's Maybe: An American Grammar Book," 80.

23. In this sense, Spillers's perspectives complement those of Sherley Anne Williams, for the latter demands, in effect, that we consider the extent to which black male repression of the "female" results from an attempt to follow the letter of the white Father's law.

24. Paul Smith, "Men in Feminism: Men and Feminist Theory," *Men in Feminism,* 33.

25. Moi, "Men against Patriarchy," 184.

26. Toni Morrison, *Sula* (New York: Plume, 1973), 71. Subsequent references to this novel appear in the text in parentheses.

27. At least one other reading of Eva's murder of her son is possible: as protection against the threat of incest. In a section of her explanation to Hannah—very little of which is contained in my textual citation of *Sula*—Eva discusses a dream she has had concerning Plum:

> I'd be laying here at night and he be downstairs in that room, but when I closed my eyes I'd see him . . . six feet tall smilin' and crawlin' up the stairs quietlike so I wouldn't hear and opening the door soft so I wouldn't hear and he'd be creepin' to the bed trying to spread my legs trying to get back up in my womb. He was a man, girl, a big old growed-up man. I didn't have that much room. I kept on dreaming it. Dreaming it and I knowed it was true. One night it wouldn't be no dream. It'd be true and I would have done it, would have let him if I'd've had the room but a big man can't be a baby all wrapped up inside his mamma no more; he suffocate. (72–73)

Morrison reverses to some extent the traditional dynamics of the most prevalent form of intergenerational incest. Instead of the male parent creeping to the bed and spreading the legs of his defenseless female child, in Eva's dream her man-child Plum is the active agent of violation. Eva's emphasis on Plum's immensity and her own uterus's size makes connections to incestuous creeping and spreading possible. It is not difficult to imagine, given Plum's constantly drugged state, that frustrations caused by an inability to re-insert his whole body into his mother's womb during what Eva views as an inevitable encounter might lead to a forced insertion of a part that "naturally" fits, his penis. At any rate, a reading of this scene that notes its use of language consistent with parent-child incest serves to ground what appear to be otherwise senseless fears on Eva's part concerning both the possible effects of Plum's desire for reentry into her uterine space and her own inability to deny her son access to that space ("I would have done it, would have let him").

28. Spillers, "Black, White, and in Color, or Learning How to Paint: Toward an Intramural Protocol of Reading."

# I CALL MY NAME

# Womanist Theology
## Black Women's Experience as a Source for Doing Theology, with Special Reference to Christology

*Jacquelyn Grant*

1986

## I. Introduction

This paper is an exploration into the experiences of Black Women for the purpose of providing alternative sources for doing theology.

Black theology and other third world theologies of liberation have shown through their challenge of the methodologies of classical theologies that experience of the dominant culture has been the invisible crucible for theologizing. They have demonstrated that theology is not unrelated to socio-political realities of existence, and that historically it has been used to maintain the social and political advantages of the status quo. The portrayal of the universal God was such that an affirmation of this God meant a simultaneous negation of all others' cultural perceptions of the divinity, as well as a negation of those very cultures. Nowhere was this more clear than in the area of Christian foreign missions where conversion to Christianity implicitly meant deculturalization and acceptance of the western value system on the part of Asians, Africans, and Latin Americans. Upon conversion, one had to withdraw from indigenous ways of imaging the divine reality and embrace foreign, western ways, which often served to undergird oppressive religious, social and political structures.

This is true not only in the foreign missions field but also in the western world; it is reflected in the ways in which oppressors deal with oppressed people within their own territory. We see this with respect to third world people in the first world context as well as with respect to women.

An illustration emerging out of Black theology and Feminist theology will make the point. Theologians in both these theological camps propose an alternative understanding, for example, of Christian love.

James Cone in an early work makes a distinction between a nonthreatening love of many Christians and the radical love of Jesus which demands justice.

There is no place in Christian theology for sentimental love—love without risk or cost. Love demands all, the whole of one's being. Thus, for the black [person] to believe the Word of God about [God's] love revealed in Christ, he/she must be prepared to meet head-on the sentimental "Christian" love of whites, which would make him/her a nonperson.[1]

Cone insists that one cannot practice Christian love and at the same time practice racism. He argues:

It seems that whites forget about the necessary interrelatedness of love, justice, and power when they encounter Black people. Love becomes emotional and sentimental. This sentimental, condescending love accounts for their desire to "help" by relieving the physical pains of the suffering blacks so they can satisfy their own religious piety and keep the poor powerless. But the new blacks, redeemed in Christ, must refuse their "help" and demand that blacks be confronted as persons. They must say to whites that authentic love is not "help," not giving Christmas baskets, but working for political, social, and economic justice, which always means a redistribution of power. It is a kind of power which enables the blacks to fight their own battles and thus keep their dignity. "Powerlessness breeds a race of beggars."[2]

Black people do not need a love which functions contrary to the establishment of Black personhood. This understanding of love was just recently affirmed by Black theologians (lay and clergy, professional and nonprofessional) in Southern Africa in their challenge to the church through *The Kairos Document*. They cautioned, "we must also remember that the most loving thing we can do for both the oppressed and for our enemies who are oppressors is to eliminate the oppression, remove the tyrants from power and establish a just government for the common good of all the people."[3] Here, love is not defined in the interest of those who wish to maintain the present status quo. But it is defined from the point of view of those on the underside of history—the victims of the oppressors' power.

In a similar vein, feminists challenge traditional understandings of love. Valerie Saiving Goldstein expresses her suspicions of traditional theological works in the following way:

I am no longer certain as I once was that, when theologians speak of "man," they are using the word in its generic sense. It is, after all, a well-known fact that theology has been written almost exclusively by men. This alone should put us on guard, especially since contemporary theologians constantly remind us that one of man's strongest temptations is to identify his own limited perspective with universal truth.[4]

Lifting up the Christian notion of sin and love, Goldstein suggests that it would be equally unsatisfactory to impose universal understanding on those concepts. The identification of these notions with self-assertion and selflessness respectively, functions differently in masculine experience and feminine experience. She explains further:

> Contemporary theological doctrines of love have, I believe, been con-structed primarily upon the basis of masculine experience and thus view the human condition from the male standpoint. Consequently, these doctrines do not provide an adequate interpretation of the situa-tion of women—nor, for that matter, of men, especially in light of cer-tain fundamental changes now taking place in our society.[5]

Because of their feminine character, for women love takes the form of nur-turing, supporting, and servicing their families. Consequently, if a woman believes:

> the theologians, she will try to strangle other impulses in herself. She will believe that, having chosen marriage and children and thus being face to face with the needs of her family for love, refreshment, and for-giveness, she has no right to ask anything for herself but must submit without qualification to the strictly feminine role.[6]

For women too, the issue is one of personhood—are women to deny who they are in order to be saved?

Goldstein then argues that when experience in theology is scrutinized, we will discover that because it has been synonymous with masculine expe-rience, it is inadequate to deal with the situation of women.

In other words, Black theologians and feminist theologians have argued that the universalism classical theologians attempt to uphold represents merely the particular experiences of the dominant culture. Blacks identify that experience as White experience; and women identify it as male experi-ence. The question then is, if universalism is the criterion for valid theology, how is such a universalism achieved?

What I will be exploring here is how Black women's experiences can provide some insights into this question. In doing so, Black women not only join Blacks and feminists in their challenge of theology but they also provide an internal critique for Black men as well as for White women. In this paper, I will focus primarily upon Black women's experience as related to the development of feminist theology. (In a rather limited way, I have addressed the issue of Black women's experiences and Black theology in an article entitled "Black Theology and The Black Woman."[7] That subject certainly has not been exhausted, and shall be treated in more substantive ways in the future.)

But here I am interested in engaging feminist theology with reference to its constructive efficacy for Black women, given the peculiarities of their experiences. The results will be the beginning of a theology from a Black woman's perspective with special reference to Christology.

In order to create a common starting point, let's begin with a synopsis of the basic tenets of feminist theology. First, feminist theology seeks to develop a *wholistic theology*. Feminist theology rejects the traditional forms of oppressive and one-sided, male-dominated theologies which arise out of patriarchal religion(s).[8] Women have begun to see that their continuous oppression in the church and society has its basis in these patriarchal religion(s). Historically, the theologies of religions have emerged out of the experiences of men, making the theologies representative thereof. Because humanity comprises both men and women, feminist theologians seek to develop a more holistic perspective in theology.

Second, in seeking to produce a wholistic perspective in theology, feminist theologians call for the *eradication of social/sexual dualisms* in human existence, which are inherent in patriarchy. A patriarchy is characterized by male-domination and female submission and subordination. In such a society, men are considered strong, intelligent, rational, and aggressive; women are considered weak, irrational, and docile.

A third function of feminist theology is to *conceptualize new and positive images of women*. Throughout history, including the history of theology, women have been portrayed in negative ways. They have been the sources of evil (snakes), authors of trickery (witches), and stimulants (therefore causes) for the sexual perversions of men (temptresses and prostitutes). These negative images must be changed to reflect reality.

Finally, Feminist theology must *evaluate male articulated understandings of the Christian faith*. Doctrines developed in a system of patriarchy merely perpetuate patriarchal structures. As the patriarchal theological system is challenged, so are the doctrines, e.g., God, Jesus Christ, the Fall, and the Church.

## II. Emerging Black Feminist Perspective

It has been argued by many Blacks that the women's liberation movement is a White middle-class movement. Therefore, it is believed to be totally irrelevant to the situation of Black women since the majority of them are not middle-class.

Brenda Eichelberger gives several reasons for Black women's noninvolvement in feminist causes. Among them are such things as class differences, the lack of Black women's knowledge about the real issues involved and the suspicion that the middle-class White women's movement is divisive to the Black community that claims prior allegiance.[9] In spite of these and other negative responses to the White women's liberation movement, there has been a growing feminist consciousness among many Black women and some Black men. This consciousness is coupled by the increased willingness of Black women to undertake an independent analysis of sexism, thereby creating an emerging Black perspective on feminism. Black feminism grows out of Black women's tridimensional reality of race/sex/class. It holds that full human liberation cannot be achieved simply by the elimination of any one form of oppression. Consequently, real liberation must be "broad in the concrete";[10] it must be based upon a multidimensional analysis.

Recent writings by secular Black feminists have challenged White feminist analysis and Black race analysis, particularly by introducing data from Black women's experience that has been historically ignored by White feminists and Black male liberationists.

In only a few of these articles do Black women employ only a gender analysis to treat Black women's reality. Whereas Ntozake Shange focuses chiefly upon sexism, Michele Wallace, like Alice Walker, presumes that White racism has had an adverse effect upon the Black community in a way that confuses and reinforces the already existing sexism. Sharon Harley, Rosalyn Terborg-Penn, Paula Giddings, and Gloria Wade-Gayles all recognize the inclusiveness of the oppressive reality of Black women as they endure racism, sexism and economic oppression. Barbara Smith, Gloria Hull, bell hooks, and Angela Y. Davis particularly explore the implications of this tridimensional oppression of Black women. In so doing, Black women have either articulated Black feminist perspectives or developed grounds for doing so.[11] These perspectives, however, have not led to the resolution of tensions between Black women and White women, and they even have brought to the forefront some tensions between Black women and Black men.

On the contrary, the possibly irreparable nature of these tensions is implied in Walker's suggestion that the experience of being a Black woman or a White woman is so different that another word is required to describe the liberative efforts of Black women. Her suggestion that the word "womanist" is more appropriate for Black women is derived from the sense of the word as it is used in Black communities:

Womanist, from *womanish*. (Opp. of "girlish," i.e., frivolous, irresponsible, not serious). A black feminist or feminist of color. From the black folk expression of mothers to female children, "You acting womanish," i.e., like a woman. Usually referring to outrageous, audacious, coura- geous or *willful* behavior. Wanting to know more and in greater depth than is considered "good" for one. Interest in grown-up doings. Act- ing grown up. Being grown up. Interchangeable with another black folk expression: "You trying to be grown." Responsible. In charge. *Serious.*[12]

Womanists were Sojourner Truth, Jarena Lee, Amanda Berry Smith, Ida B. Wells, Mary Church Terrell, Mary McCloud Bethune and countless oth- ers not remembered in any historical study. A womanist then is a strong Black woman who has sometimes been mislabeled as a domineering cas- trating matriarch. A womanist is one who has developed survival strategies in spite of the oppression of her race and sex in order to save her family and her people. Walker's womanist notation suggests not "the feminist," but the active struggle of Black women that makes them who they are. For some Black women that may involve being feminine as traditionally defined, and for others it involves being masculine as stereotypically defined. In any case, womanist means being and acting out who you are and interpreting the reality for yourself. In other words, Black women speak out for them- selves. As a Black feminist critic Barbara Christian explains, referring to Audre Lorde's poem about the deadly consequence of silence, Black women must speak up and answer in order to validate their own experience. This is important even if only to ourselves. It is to the womanist tradition that Black women must appeal for the doing of theology.

### III. The Beginnings of a Womanist Theology with Special Reference to Christology

Womanist theology begins with the experiences of Black women as its point of departure. This experience includes not only Black women's activities in the larger society but also in the churches, and reveals that Black women have often rejected the oppressive structure in the church as well.

These experiences provide a context significant for doing theology. Those experiences had been and continue to be defined by racism, sexism, and classism and therefore offer a unique opportunity and a new challenge for developing a relevant perspective in the theological enterprise. This per- spective in theology which I am calling womanist theology draws upon the life and experiences of some Black women who have created meaningful interpretations of the Christian faith.

Black women must do theology out of their tridimensional experience of racism/sexism/classism. To ignore any aspect of this experience is to deny the holistic and integrated reality of Black womanhood. When Black women say that God is on the side of the oppressed, we mean that God is in solidarity with the struggles of those on the underside of humanity, those whose lives are bent and broken from the many levels of assault perpetrated against them.

In a chapter entitled "Black Women: Shaping Feminist Theory," hooks elaborates on the interrelationship of the threefold oppressive reality of Black women and shows some of the weaknesses of White feminist theory. Challenging the racist and classist assumptions of White feminism, hooks writes:

> Racism abounds in the writings of white feminists, reinforcing white supremacy and negating the possibility that women will bond politically across ethnic and racial boundaries. Past feminist refusal to draw attention to and attack racial hierarchy suppressed the link between race and class. Yet class structure in American society has been shaped by the racial politics of white supremacy.[13]

This means that Black women, because of oppression determined by race and their subjugation as women, make up a disproportionately high percentage of the poor and working classes. However, the fact that Black women are a subjugated group even within the Black community and the White women's community does not mean that they are alone in their oppression within those communities. In the women's community poor White women are discriminated against, and in the Black community, poor Black men are marginalized. This suggests that classism, as well as racism and sexism, has a life of its own. Consequently, simply addressing racism and sexism is inadequate to bring about total liberation. Even though there are dimensions of class which are not directly related to race or sex, classism impacts Black women in a peculiar way which results in the fact that they are most often on the bottom of the social and economic ladder. For Black women doing theology, to ignore classism would mean that their theology is no different from any other bourgeois theology. It would be meaningless to the majority of Black women, who are themselves poor. This means that addressing only issues relevant to middle-class women or Blacks will simply not do. The daily struggles of poor Black women must serve as the gauge for the verification of the claims of womanist theology. Anna Julia Cooper makes a relevant point:

> Women's wrongs are thus indissolubly linked with all undefended woes, and the acquirement of her "rights" will mean the supremacy of triumph of all right over might, the supremacy of the moral forces of reason, and justice, and love in the government of the nations of earth.[14]

Black women's experience must be affirmed as the crucible for doing womanist theology. It is the context in which we must decide theological questions. More specifically, it is within the context of this experience that Black women read the Bible. A (brief) look at Black women's use of the Bible indicates how it is their experiences that determine relevant questions for them.

## III. The Bible in the Womanist Tradition

Theological investigation into the experiences of Christian Black women reveals that Black women considered the Bible to be a major source of religious validation in their lives. Though Black women's relationship with God preceded their introduction to the Bible, this Bible gave some content to their God-consciousness.[15] The source for Black women's understanding of God has been twofold: first, God's revelation directly to them, and second, God's revelation as witnessed in the Bible and as read and heard in the context of their experience. The understanding of God as creator, sustainer, comforter, and liberator took on life as they agonized over their pain and celebrated the hope that as God delivered the Israelites, they would be delivered as well. The God of the Old and New Testament became real in the consciousness of oppressed Black women. Of the use of the Bible, Fannie Barrier Williams quite aptly said:

> Though the Bible was not an open book to the Negro before emancipation, thousands of the enslaved men and women of the negro race learned more than was taught to them. Thousands of them realized the deeper meanings, the sweeter consolations and the spiritual awakenings that are part of the religious experiences of all Christians.[16]

In other words, though Black people in general and Black women in particular were politically impotent, religiously controlled, they were able to appropriate certain themes of the Bible which spoke to their reality. For example, Jarena Lee, a nineteenth century Black woman preacher in the African Methodist Episcopal Church, constantly emphasized the theme "Life and Liberty" in her sermons which were always biblically based. This interplay of scripture and experience was exercised even more expressly by many other Black women. An ex-slave woman revealed that when her experience negated certain oppressive interpretations of the Bible given by white preachers, she, through engaging the biblical message for herself, rejected them. Consequently, she also dismissed white preachers who distorted the message in order to maintain slavery. Her grandson, Howard Thurman, speaks of her use of the Bible in this way:

"During the days of slavery," she said, "the master's minister would occasionally hold services for the slaves. Always the white minister used as his text something from Paul. 'Slaves be obedient to them that are your masters . . . as unto Christ.' Then he would go on to show how, if we were good and happy slaves, God would bless us. I promised my Maker that if I ever learned to read and if freedom ever came, I would not read that part of the Bible."[17]

What we see here is perhaps more than a mere rejection of a White preacher's interpretation of the Bible: it is an exercise in internal critique of the Bible. The liberating message of the gospel is seen as overagainst the oppressive elements in the Bible.

The truth which the Bible brought was undeniable, though perception of it was often distorted in order to support the monstrous system of oppression. Sarcastically responding to this tendency, Fannie Barrier Williams admonished, "do not open the Bible too wide." Biblical interpretation, realized Williams, a non-theologically trained person, had at its basis the prior agenda of White America. She therefore argued:

Religion, like every other force in America, was first used as an instrument and servant of slavery. All attempts to Christianize the negro were limited by the important fact that he was property of [a] valuable and peculiar sort, and that the property value must not be disturbed, even if his soul were lost. If Christianity could make the negro docile, domestic and less an independent and fighting savage, let it be preached to that extent and no further.[18]

Such false, pernicious, demoralizing gospel could only be preached if the Bible was not opened wide enough, lest one see the liberating message of Jesus as summarized in Luke 4:18. The Bible must be read and interpreted in the light of Black women's own oppression and God's revelation within that context. A womanist must, like Sojourner Truth, "compare the teachings of the Bible with the witness" in them.[19]

To do womanist theology, then, we must read and hear the Bible and engage it within the context of our own experience. This is the only way that it can make sense to people who are oppressed. Black women of the past did not hesitate in doing this and we must do no less.

## IV. Jesus in the Womanist Tradition

Having opened the Bible wider than many White people, Black people, in general, and Black women in particular, found a Jesus who they could claim and whose claim for them was one of affirmation of dignity and self-respect.

In the experience of Black people, Jesus was "all things."[20] Chief among these however was the belief in Jesus as the divine co-sufferer, who empowers them in situations of oppression. For Christian Black women in the past, Jesus was their central frame of reference. They identified with Jesus because they believed that Jesus identified with them. As Jesus was persecuted and made to suffer undeservedly, so were they. His suffering culminated in the crucifixion. Their crucifixion included rapes, husbands being castrated (literally and metaphorically), babies being sold, and other cruel and often murderous treatments. But Jesus' suffering was not the suffering of a mere human, for Jesus was understood to be God incarnate. As Harold Carter observed of Black prayers in general, there was no difference made between the persons of the Trinity, Jesus, God, or the Holy Spirit. All of these proper names for God were used interchangeably in prayer language. Thus, Jesus was the one who speaks the world into creation. He was the power behind the Church.[21] Black women's affirmation of Jesus as God meant that White people were not God. One old slave woman clearly demonstrates this as she prayed:

> Dear Massa Jesus, we all uns beg Ooner [you] come make us a call dis yere day. We is nutting but poor Etiopian women and people ain't tink much 'bout we. We ain't trust any of dem great high people for come to we church, but do' you is de one great Massa, great too much dan Massa Linkum, you ain't shame to care for we African people.[22]

Implicit in the description "nothing but poor Black women" and what follows is the awareness of the public devaluation of Black women. But in spite of that Jesus is presented as a confidant who could be trusted while White people could not be trusted. This women affirmed the contribution of Abraham Lincoln to the emancipation of Blacks, but rejected Mr. Lincoln as her real or ultimate master. Quite a contrast to the master's (slave owner's) perception of his/herself.

This slave woman did not hesitate to identify her struggle and pain with those of Jesus. In fact, the common struggle made her know that Jesus would respond to her beck and call.

> Come to we, dear Massa Jesus. De sun, he hot too much, de road am dat long and boggy (sandy) and we ain't got no buggy for send and fetch Ooner. But Massa, you 'member how you walked dat hard walk up Calvary and ain't weary but tink about we all dat way. We know you ain't weary for to come to we. We pick out de torns, de prickles, de brier, de backsliding' and de quarrel and de sin out of you path so dey shan't hurt Ooner pierce feet no more.[23]

The reference to "no buggy" to send for Jesus brings to mind the limited material possessions of pre– and post–Civil War Blacks. In her speech, "Ain't I a Woman," Sojourner Truth distinguished between White women's and Black women's experiences by emphasizing that Black women were not helped into carriages as were White women.[24] In the prayer, this woman speaks of that reality wherein most Blacks didn't even have carriages or buggies. For had she owned one, certainly she'd send it to fetch Jesus. Here we see the concern for the comfort of the suffering Jesus. Jesus suffers when we sin—when we backslide or when we quarrel. But still Jesus is identified with her plight. Note that Jesus went to the cross with this Black woman on his mind. He was thinking about her and all others like her. So totally dedicated to the poor, the weak, the downtrodden, the outcast, that in this Black woman's faith, Jesus would never be too tired to come. As she is truly among the people at the bottom of humanity, she can make things comfortable for Jesus even though she may have nothing to give him—no water, no food—but she can give tears and love. She continues:

> Come to we, dear Massa Jesus. We all uns ain't got no good cool water for give you when you thirsty. You know, Massa, de drought so long, and the well so low, ain't nutting but mud to drink. But we gwine to take de 'munion cup and fill it wid de tear of repentance, and love clean out of we heart. Dat all we hab to gib you, good Massa.[25]

The material or physical deprivation experienced by this woman did not reduce her desire to give Jesus the best. Being a Black woman in the American society meant essentially being poor, with no buggy, and no good cool water. Life for Black women was indeed bad, hot, and at best muddy. Note that there is no hint that their condition results from some divine intention. Now, whereas I am not prepared to say that this same woman or any others in that church the next day would have been engaged in political praxis by joining such movements as Nat Turner's rebellion or Denmark Vesey's revolt, it is clear that her perspective was such that the social, political, and economic orders were believed to be sinful and against the will of the real master, Jesus.

For Black women, the role of Jesus unraveled as they encountered him in their experience as one who empowers the weak. In this vein, Jesus was such a central part of Sojourner Truth's life that all of her sermons made him the starting point. When asked by a preacher if the source of her preaching was the Bible, she responded "No honey, can't preach from de Bible—can't read a letter."[26] Then she explained, "When I preaches, I has jest one text to preach from, an' I always preaches from this one. My text is, 'When I found Jesus!' "[27] In this sermon Sojourner Truth recounts the events and struggles of life from the time her parents were brought from Africa and sold "up an' down, an' hither an' yon . . ."[28] to the time that she met Jesus within the context of her struggles for dignity of Black people and women. Her encounter with Jesus brought such joy that she became overwhelmed with love and praise:

> Praise, praise, praise to the Lord! An' I begun to feel such a love in my soul as I never felt before—love to all creatures. An' then, all of a sudden, it stopped, an' I said, Dar's de white folks that have abused you, an' beat you, and an' abused your people—think o' them! But then there came another rush of love through my soul, an' I cried out loud—'Lord, I can love even de white folks!'[29]

This love was not a sentimental, passive love. It was a tough, active love that empowered her to fight more fiercely for the freedom of her people. For the rest of her life she continued speaking at abolition and women's rights gatherings, and condemned the horrors of oppression.

## V. The Womanist Traditions and Christological Reflections

More than anyone, Black theologians have captured the essence of the significance of Jesus in the lives of Black people, which to an extent includes Black women. They all hold that the Jesus of history is important for understanding who he was and his significance for us today. By and large they have affirmed that this Jesus is the Christ, that is, God incarnate. They have argued that in the light of our experience, Jesus meant freedom.[30] They have maintained that Jesus means freedom from the sociopsychological, psychocultural, economic, and political oppression of Black people. In other words, Jesus is a political messiah.[31] "To free [humans] from bondage was Jesus' own definition of his ministry."[32] This meant that as Jesus identified with the lowly of his day, he now identifies with the lowly of this day, who in the American context are Black people. The identification is so real that Jesus Christ in fact becomes Black. It is important to note that Jesus' blackness is not a result of the ideological distortion of a few Black thinkers, but a result of careful Christological investigation. James Cone examines the sources of Christology and concludes that Jesus is Black because "Jesus was a Jew." He explains:

> It is on the basis of the soteriological meaning of the particularity of his Jewishness that theology must affirm the Christological significance of Jesus' present blackness. He is black because he was a Jew. The affirmation of the Black Christ can be understood when the significance of his past Jewishness is related dialetically to the significance of his present

blackness. On the other hand, the Jewishness of Jesus located him in the context of the Exodus, thereby connecting his appearance in Palestine with God's liberation of oppressed Israelites from Egypt. Unless Jesus were truly from Jewish ancestry, it would make little theological sense to say that he is the fulfillment of God's covenant with Israel. But on the other hand, the blackness of Jesus brings out the soteriological meaning of his Jewishness for our contemporary situation when Jesus' person is understood in the context of the cross and resurrection. Without negating the divine election of Israel, the Cross and resurrection are Yahweh's fulfillment of his original intention for Israel. . . .[33]

The condition of Black people today reflects the cross of Jesus. Yet the resurrection brings the hope that liberation from oppression is immanent. The resurrected Black Christ signifies this hope.

Cone further argues that this Christological title, "The Black Christ," is not validated by its universality, but in fact by its particularity. Its significance lies in whether or not the Christological title "points to God's universal will to liberate particular oppressed people from inhumanity."[34] These particular oppressed peoples to which Cone refers are characterized in Jesus' parable on the Last Judgment as "the least." "The least in America are literally and symbolically present in Black people."[35] This notion of "the least" is attractive because it descriptively locates the condition of Black women. "The least" are those people who have no water to give, but offer what they have, as the old slave woman cited above says in her prayer. Black women's experience in general is such a reality. Their tridimensional reality renders their particular situation a complex one. One could say that not only are they the oppressed of the oppressed, but their situation represents "the particular within the particular."

But is this just another situation that takes us deeper into the abyss of theological relativity? I would argue that it is not, because it is in the context of Black women's experience where the particular connects up with the universal. By this I mean that in each of the three dynamics of oppression, Black women share in the reality of a broader community. They share race suffering with Black men; with White women and other Third World women, they are victims of sexism; and with poor Blacks and Whites, and other Third World peoples, especially women, they are disproportionately poor. To speak of Black women's tridimensional reality, therefore, is not to speak of Black women exclusively, for there is an implied universality which connects them with others.

Likewise, with Jesus Christ, there was an implied universality which made him identify with others—the poor, the woman, the stranger. To affirm Jesus' solidarity with the "least of the people" is not an exercise in

romanticized contentment with one's oppressed status in life. For as the resurrection signified that there is more to life than the cross of Jesus Christ,
for Black women this affirmation signifies that their tridimensional oppressive existence is not the end but merely represents the context in which a
particular people struggle to experience hope and liberation. Jesus Christ
thus represents a three-fold significance; first he identifies with the "little
people," Black women, where they are; second, he affirms the basic humanity of these, "the least"; and third, he inspires active hope in the struggle for
resurrected, liberated existence.

To locate the Christ in Black people is a radical and necessary step, but
understanding of Black women's reality challenges us to go further. Christ
among the least must also mean Christ in the community of Black women.
William Eichelberger was able to recognize this as he further particularized the significance of the Blackness of Jesus by locating Christ in Black
women's community. He was able to see Christ not only as Black male but
also Black female.

> God, in revealing Himself and His attributes from time to time in
> His creaturely existence, has exercised His freedom to formalize His
> appearance in a variety of ways. . . . God revealed Himself at a point
> in the past as Jesus the Christ a Black male. My reasons for affirming
> the Blackness of Jesus of Nazareth are much different from that of the
> white apologist....God wanted to identify with that segment of man-
> kind which had suffered most, and is still suffering. . . . I am constrained
> to believe that God in our times has updated His form of revelation to
> western society. It is my feeling that God is now manifesting Himself,
> and has been for over 450 years, in the form of the Black American
> Woman as mother, as wife, as nourisher, sustainer and preserver of life,
> the Suffering Servant who is despised and rejected by men, a personal-
> ity of sorrow who is acquainted with grief. The Black Woman has borne
> our griefs and carried our sorrows. She has been wounded because of
> American white society's transgressions and bruised by white iniqui-
> ties. It appears that she may be the instrumentality through whom God
> will make us whole.[36]

Granted, Eichelberger's categories for God and woman are very traditional.
Nevertheless, the significance of his thought is that he is able to conceive of
the Divine reality as other than a Black male messianic figure.

Even though Black women have been able to transcend some of the
oppressive tendencies of White male (and Black male) articulated theologies, careful study reveals that some traditional symbols are inadequate for
us today. The Christ understood as the stranger, the outcast, the hungry,
the weak, the poor, makes the traditional male Christ (Black and White)

less significant. Even our sisters of the past had some suspicions about the effects of a male image of the divine, for they did challenge the oppressive use of it in the church's theology. In so doing, they were able to move from a traditional oppressive Christology, with respect to women, to an egalitarian Christology. This kind of equalitarian Christology was operative in Jarena Lee's argument for the right of women to preach. She argued "... the Savior died for the woman as well as the man."[37] The crucifixion was for universal salvation, not just for male salvation or, as we may extend the argument to include, not just for White salvation. Because of this, Christ came and died, no less for the woman as for the man, no less for Blacks as for Whites. For Lee, this was not an academic issue, but one with practical ramification:

> If the man may preach, because the Savior died for him, why not the woman? Seeing he died for her also. Is he not a whole Savior, instead of half one? as those who hold it wrong for a woman to preach, would seem to make it appear.[38]

Lee correctly perceives that there is an ontological issue at stake. If Jesus Christ were a Savior of men then it is true the maleness of Christ would be paramount.[39] But if Christ is a Savior of all, then it is the humanity—the wholeness—of Christ which is significant.

Sojourner was aware of the same tendency of some scholars and church leaders to link the maleness of Jesus and the sin of Eve with the status of women, and she challenged this notion in her famed speech "Ain't I a Woman?"

> Then that little man in black there, he says women can't have as much rights as men, 'cause Christ wasn't a woman! Where did your Christ come from? Where did your Christ come from? From God and a woman. Man had nothing to do with Him.
>
> If the first woman God ever made was strong enough to turn the world upside down alone, these women together ought to be able to turn it back, and get it right side up again! And now they is asking to do it, the men better let them.[40]

I would argue, as suggested by both Lee and Sojourner, that the significance of Christ is not his maleness, but his humanity. The most significant events of Jesus Christ were the life and ministry, the crucifixion, and the resurrection. The significance of these events, in one sense, is that in them the absolute becomes concrete. God becomes concrete not only in the man Jesus, for he was crucified, but in the lives of those who will accept the challenge of the risen Savior—the Christ. For Lee, this meant that women could preach; for Sojourner it meant that women could possibly save the world;

for me, it means today, this Christ, found in the experience of Black women, is a Black woman.

## VI. Conclusion

I have argued that Black women's tridimensional reality provides a fertile context for articulating a theological perspective which is wholistic in scope and liberating in nature. The theology is potentially wholistic because the experience out of which it emerges is totally interconnected with other experiences. It is potentially liberating because it rests not on one single issue that could be considered only a middle-class issue relevant to one group of people, but it is multifaceted. Thus, the possibility for wholistic theology is more likely. Feminist theology as presently developed is limited by virtue of the experience base for feminist theology. That is, when feminists say that experience is the crucible for doing [feminist] theology, they usually mean White women's experience. With few exceptions, feminist thinkers do their analysis primarily, and in some circles exclusively based on the notion that because sexism is the longest and most universal form of oppression, it should claim priority.[41]

Black women, by and large, have not held this assumption. Many have claimed that because of the pervasiveness of racism, and because of its defining character for Black life in general, racism is most important. Though Sojourner Truth never did develop a sophisticated social analysis she was aware of the fact that she (and her people) were poor because she was Black, and perhaps poorer because she was woman. I say "perhaps" simply because in the slave economy one could argue that there was relatively little distinction between the property status of slaves by virtue of gender; women were no less property than men. As property, they were a part of the material distributed, rather than participants in the inequitable (system of) material distribution. Thus as indicated above in the Black woman's prayer, material possessions of Blacks were limited. In a sense one could say that by virtue of one's race, one was slave and by virtue of that status one was poor.

Still as we see the issues today, class distinctions which have emerged even in the Black community, and sex differences, which have taken on new forms of institutionalization, must be addressed. For liberation to become a reality, race, sex, and class must be deliberately confronted. Interconnected as they are, they all impinge greatly on the lives of Black women. Overwhelming as are these realities, Black women do not feel defeated. For as Jarena Lee observed, the hope of the struggle is based on the faith that Jesus died (and was raised) for the woman as well as the man. This realization gave inspiration for the struggle. Black women today inside and outside of the church still bring an optimistic spirit as reflected in the conclusion of Maya Angelou's poem, "Still I rise:"

> Out of the hut of history's shame
> I rise
> Up from a past that's rooted in pain
> I rise
> I'm a Black ocean, leaping and wide,
> Welling and swelling, I bear in the tide
> Leaving behind nights of terror and fear
> I rise
> Into a daybreak that's wondrously clear
> I rise
> Bringing the gifts that my ancestors gave
> I am the dream and the hope of the slave.
> I rise.
> I rise.
> I rise.[42]

## Notes

1. James H. Cone, *Black Theology and Black Power* (New York: Seabury Press, 1969), pp. 53–54.

2. Ibid., 54–54.

3. The Kairos Theologians, *The Kairos Document: Challenge to the Church,* 2d ed. (Braarufontein, South Africa: Skotaville Publishers, 1985; repr. Grand Rapids, Michigan: Eerdmans Publishing Co., 1986), pp. 24–25.

4. Valerie Saiving Goldstein, "The Human Situation of a Feminine," *The Journal of Religion* 40 (April 1960): 100.

5. Ibid.

6. Ibid.

7. Jacquelyn Grant, "Black Theology and The Black Woman" in *Black Theology: A Documentary History, 1966–1979,* eds. Gayraud S. Wilmore and James H. Cone (New York: Orbis Books, 1979):418–433.

8. See Sheila D. Collins, *A Different Heaven and Earth: A Feminist Perspective on Religion* (Valley Forge, Penna.: Judson Press, 1974); Mary Daley, *Beyond God the Father: Toward a Philosophy of Women's Liberation* (Boston: Beacon Press, 1973); Mary Daley, *The Church and the Second Sex: With a New Feminist Post Christian Introduction by the Author* (New York: Harper. and Colophon, 1975).

9. Brenda Eichelberger, "Voice of Black Feminism," *Quest: A Feminist Quarterly* III (Spring, 1977):16–23.

10. This phrase is used by Anna Julia Cooper, *A Voice From the South* (Xenia, Ohio: Aldine Publishing House, 1852; repr. Westport, Conn.: Negro Universities Press, 1969), cited by bell hooks, *Ain't I A Woman: Black Women and Feminism* (Boston: South End Press, 1981), pp. 193–194. I use it here to characterize Black women's experience. To be concerned about Black women's issues is to be *concrete.* Yet because of their intercon-

nectedness with Black men (racism), White women (sexism) and the poor (classism), it is also to be, at the same time, concerned with broad issues.

11. See Ntozake Shange, *For Colored Girls Who Have Considered Suicide When the Rainbow is Enuf* (New York: Macmillan Publishing Co., Inc., 1975); Michele Wallace, *Black Macho and the Myth of the Superwoman* (New York: Dial Press, 1978); Alice Walker, *The Color Purple* (New York: Harcourt, Brace, and Jovanovich Publishers, 1982); and *In Search of Our Mothers' Gardens* (Harcourt, Brace, and Jovanovich Publishers, 1983); Sharon Harley and Rosalyn Terborg-Penn, eds., *Afro-American Women* (New York: Kennikat Press, 1978); Paula Giddings, *When and Where I Enter* (New York: William Morrow and Company, Inc., 1984); Gloria Wade-Grayles, *No Crystal Stair: Visions of Race and Sex in Black Women's Fiction* (New York: Pilgrims Press, 1984); bell hooks, *Feminist Theory: From Margin to Center* (Boston: South End Press, 1984); Gloria Hull, Patricia Scott, and Barbara Smith, *All the Women Are White, All the Blacks Are Men, But Some of Us Are Brave* (New York: The Feminist Press, 1982); Angela Y. Davis, *Women, Race, and Class* (New York: Vintage Books, 1981).

12. Walker, *In Search of Our Mothers' Gardens*, p. xi.

13. hooks, *Feminist Theory*, p. 3.

14. Cooper, *A Voice from The South*, p. 91

15. Cecil Wayne Cone, *Identity Crisis In Black Theology* (Nashville, Tenn.: African Methodist Episcopal Church Press, 1975), passim, especially chapter III.

16. Bert James Lowenberg and Ruth Bogin eds., *Black Women in Nineteenth-Century American Life: Their Words, Their Thoughts, Their Feelings* (University Park, Penn: The Pennsylvania State University Press, 1976), p. 267.

17. Howard Thurman, *Jesus and the Disinherited* (Nashville: Abingdon Press, 1949), pp. 30–31.

18. Lowenberg and Bogin, *Black Women in Nineteenth-Century*, p. 265.

19. Olive Gilbert, *Sojourner Truth: Narrative and Book of Life.* (1850 and 1875; repr. Chicago: Johnson Publishing Co., 1970), p. 83.

20. Harold A. Carter, *The Prayer Tradition of Black People* (Valley Forge: Judson Press, 1976), p. 50. Carter, in referring to traditional Black prayer in general, states that Jesus was revealed as one who "was all one needs!"

21. Ibid.

22. Ibid., p. 49.

23. Ibid.

24. Sojourner Truth, "Ain't I A Woman?" in Mariam Schneir, ed. *Feminism: The Essential Historical Writings* (New York: Vintage Books, 1972).

25. Carter, *The Prayer Tradition*, p. 49.

26. Gilbert, *Book of Life*, p. 118.

27. Ibid., p. 119.

28. Ibid.

29. Ibid.

30. James Deotis Roberts, *A Black Political Theology* (Philadelphia: Westminster Press, 1974), p. 138. See especially chapter 5. See also Noel Leo Erskine, *Decolonizing Theology: A Caribbean Perspective* (New York: Orbis Books, 1980), p. 125.

31. Roberts, *A Black Political* Theology, p. 133.

32. Albert Cleage, *The Black Messiah* (New York: Sheed and Ward, 1969):92.

33. James H. Cone, *God of the Oppressed* (New York: Seabury Press, 1975), p. 134.

34. Ibid., p. 135.

35. Ibid., p. 136.

36. William Eichelberger, "Reflections on the Person and Personality of the Black Messiah," *The Black Church* II (n.d.): 54.

37. Jarena Lee, *The Life and Religious Experiences and Journal of Mrs. Jarena Lee: A Colored Lady Giving an Account of Her Call to Preach* (Philadelphia, Penna.: n.p., 1836), pp. 15–16.

38. Ibid., 16.

39. There is no evidence to suggest that Black women debated the significance of the maleness of Jesus. The fact is that Jesus Christ was a real, crucial figure in their lives. However, recent feminist scholarship has been important in showing the relation between the maleness of Christ and the oppression of women.

40. Truth, "Ain't I A Woman," in *Feminism*, ed. by Schneir, p. 94.

41. This question is explored further in Jacquelyn Grant, "The Development and Limitation of Feminist Theology: Toward an engagement of black women's religious experience and white women's religious experience" (Ph.D. diss., Union Theological Seminary, New York, 1985).

42. Maya Angelou, *And Still I Rise* (New York: Random House, 1978), p. 42.

## But Who Do You Really Belong To—
## Black Studies or Women's Studies?

*Barbara Christian*

1989

            I entitled my paper "But Who Do You Really Belong to—Black Studies or Women's Studies?" because in the last decade I, and many of my sisters, have been asked that question, not so often in words as in the social gestures and roles demanded of us in Black Studies and Women's Studies, both marginal institutions in the universities. When we black women scholars who came out of the sixties see each other, we inevitably discuss that question and even though we know the correct answer is "Both Black Studies and Women's Studies," the realities of a university process belie such a pat response.

There is another reason for my title. Not so long ago, one of the graduate women of color on my campus came to me in tears because she'd been directly asked that question. Her rage, her frustration at her integrity being questioned, her awareness that she was being characterized as marginal to these already marginalized university programs caused her to doubt whether she could endure being a feminist scholar of color. Fragmentation, dilution, the need to continually defend one's existence, she thought, would be her fate.

Her outburst was not the first I've heard (nor do I expect it to be the last) from younger women who I'd hoped would continue the work we'd begun. Inevitably I am left with a quickening sense of my own rage and a question about whether our point of view can be articulated in the halls of academe. But this piece is not about the sexism and racism that exist in the university and are kept in place to some extent by the very structures within which we attempt to critique the university. I am sure we all know that. I know we've also heard many times that Third World Women often fall between the cracks, between the two categories, minorities and women. This brief paper is focused more on *how* we fall between the cracks, what conflicts of choice we have, and what possibilities for action, are open to us. My analysis is rooted not only in my own personal history and experience but also in the experiences of some of my peers with whom I have discussed this issue.

And my aim is to raise these issues in the woman's community in general, and in Afro-American studies and literary circles in particular, in order to enlarge our understanding of the experience of trying to be a feminist scholar of color in America.

As many of you know, I've spent much of my adult life studying the literature of black women. Yes—there was a particular moment in time when I asked myself the question—Where am I in the literature? The first time I asked, Where am I in British and American literature? Where was the black, the colonized, the racially oppressed woman? What have we said? The second time, some years later, I looked for my place in Afro-American literatures. Where am I?—the girl, the woman, the sexual female, the abused woman. What have we said?

I doubt I would have asked these "obvious" questions when I did, if the social context had not provided me with a psychologically exciting though not necessarily safe space within which to ask them. The words, gestures, music of the fifties and sixties, the Black movement and the seventies' women's movement suggested the power and the richness of these previously neglected literatures. Not only were my personal moments significant, but that they were *two* different moments rather than *one* is an indication of the complexity of the American social context. The first moment did not cancel out the need for the second. Yet there seemed to be a conflict of choice and possibility that feminist scholars sometimes experience, for Afro-American Studies, Ethnic Studies, and Women's Studies, the institutions which grew out of political movements of the sixties and seventies, are themselves sometimes in conflict.

So the specific ways in which these two institutions evolved on specific campuses, the sequence in which they developed, the extent to which one was more successful than the other in maneuvering campus bureaucracy, and the faculty of each institution—all these factors affect the choices black feminist scholars make about their home and their proper alliance. We, or more precisely the *singular one* that we usually are, often become a kind of bridge between Afro-American Studies, Women's Studies, and even a traditional discipline. There is often a black feminist scholar on one university campus who is one-third in Afro-American Studies, one-third in Women's Studies, and one-third in English, let's say, or who is situated in one of these departments with the understanding that she is the liaison person between the three. The one who we are is usually the *only woman* in Black Studies, the *only person of color* in Women's Studies, or in one's traditional department. It is not that we fall between the cracks but that we are the filler for too many cracks. What that kind of fragmentation can do to one's time is obvious. Not always so obvious is the possible effects such fragmentation or ''bridging'' (depending on your point of view) might have on one's scholarly foci and intentions.

Many of us chose to be black feminist scholars because we believed ideas could help to effect social change and that the university, though imperfect, *was* a place where ideas are important. Many of us entered academe not only because we liked doing research and teaching but because we believed the study of black and Third World Women would necessarily involve a critique of existing structures. We reasoned that since black and Third World Women occupied that vortex at which race, sex, and class interact, and since we had been excluded from academic life for so long, the university had itself lost out. It had lost a source of energy from the world it purported to contemplate. We thought our presence in academia would be a galvanizing one. However, many of us were not prepared for the exclusive ways in which the categories of race, class, and gender are studied, the way the very definitions of these concepts imply that women of color do not exist.

The scholar who explores questions of race within the context of different disciplines often sees gender as a wrinkle on the group fabric, as if people do not always come in two sexes. The woman scholar often sees race or class questions as somehow diluting rather than strengthening a feminist approach, as if men and women do not usually belong to a particular ethnic group and do not belong to or aspire to belong to a particular class. Each sees the other's subject as "deviant" in his or her field. Race, of course, usually refers to nonwhite; gender, of course, to non-male —the "nots" and "nos" indicate deviations from a pure field. That black feminist scholars bridge two, sometimes three, fields immediately suggests the inaccuracy of viewing these categories as pure and exclusive. Such abstractions negatively affect our work because they limit our possible perspective. For example, I have seen studies of Toni Morrison from an exclusively Afro-American perspective, from an exclusively "woman's" perspective, and from an exclusively "literary" perspective. So exclusive are these treatments that someone who did not know that Morrison was a black, female writer would not know that these papers were all about the same writer's work. How to satisfy the "pure" demands of any of these three areas, or what is more common, how not to be perceived as merely marginal to any of these three areas, as mere icing on the real cake, can be devastating for the black feminist scholar and can result in paralysis, in a sense of alienation, in the feeling that one is in a position of always validating oneself, that one must subscribe to reigning concerns of others. As one black feminist scholar said to me recently, instead of having to deal with the term "universal," we now have to contend with "theory" and with the pure categories of Gender, Race, and Class upon which it relies.

Increasingly, the term "theory" has come to represent to some of us the co-optation of these marginal points of view by academic language. By theory, let me hasten to add, I mean the tendency towards gross generalizations about culture, language, literature, and gender; theory also suggests the tendency towards philosophical and abstract logic in which some American academic circles have been engaging for the last few years. Activism has been reduced to that moment when one produces a theory that can be understood by only a few others in the world. As was the case in the sixties, standards of excellence are again the reason for exclusivity—thus the irrelevance of people who are not in one's very specific field—for there is no reason why any others should understand the ideas that might affect their lives. Scholarly focus and intentions have shifted even for marginal groups like Afro-American Studies and Women's Studies from the need for social transformation that implies some responsibility to constituencies outside academe to the scholar's need for validation within academic situations.

There are scholars, I hear, who produce feminist theory, and there are those of us, I guess, who practice feminist theory. Among the latter are usually listed women of color. Theory, in other words, occupies a different space from the study of the intersection of class/race/gender which the study of American women of color implies. It is so much easier, though, to make general statements about WOMEN in the abstract or BLACKS in the abstract than it is to make general statements about, let's say, poor black women who may be from the North, South, East, or West, from an extended or nuclear family, which is why the concrete theorizing one finds in narratives is so appealing to me. Theory is precisely the problem upon which a black feminist scholar stumbles. Having been excluded so many times from so many camps, we are I think, particularly attuned to the dangers of the abstract generalization. It may be why the concrete theorizing we find in our literature is so appealing even to those of us in the social sciences. And, frankly, I find the narrative theorizing of say a Toni Morrison or an Alice Walker to be far more dynamic, significant, and useful than the majority of lit crit theory being published today. Most of us barely know our own literature exists, yet we often feel compelled to create "smart" categories within which to contain it, as if it were a completed object we are contemplating rather than engaging in a live intellectual process.

Another area of concern for women scholars of color is a tension between cultural style and ideological position. Most Ethnic Studies and Afro-American Studies programs, for example, either avoid issues about lesbianism or are downright hostile to them. That is an ideological conflict that feminist scholars often face in an Ethnic Studies or Afro-American Studies frame of reference. Women scholars of color often experience discomfort with the cultural style of Women's Studies, with its language, its modes of maneuvering, its assumptions about goals. *We must,* for example, be concerned about the men of our cultural groups, and that concern affects our understanding and articulation of feminist issues. For example, it is important to me that black men in America have been just as fetishized as sex objects as women have been. And that realization affects my critique of gender issues. Yet I and most of my sisters who are concerned about the relationship between men and women in our group would not replace the word "feminist" with "gender" as so many Women's Studies institutions are doing today so that men will feel more comfortable about the research on women. One of my colleagues pointed out:

> I've worked with black men all my life, sometimes in rage, sometimes in harmony. I understand that terrain. But it is only recently that I've begun working with white women, who after all until recently were conceptualized as part of the problem rather than part of any solution. I'm still learning to read their style which often spells "white" to me rather than "women."

Trust, then, is another issue that affects the choices we make. Who can we trust if we are to help ourselves? Lately, as both Ethnic Studies and Women's Studies programs purge themselves, in order to fit into the more conservative scheme of the eighties, I have heard many a young feminist scholar of color speak more confidently of the traditional department as the place where one might be safest. What such a tendency will mean for the development of a Third World feminist approach is not hard to predict.

Our problem is that we do not have a "home really fitted to our needs," for the study of women of color is itself a critique of Afro-American Studies and Women's Studies, yet these groups are hardly powerful institutions in the university and their validity is still in question. Consequently, even though we are often perceived as "asides" in these groups, we are in the unenviable position of having to protect them, since they are usually the only groups that even acknowledge our existence.

Barbara Smith has proposed a solution to the homelessness we experience—Black Women's Studies Institutes. Frankly I do not see this solution as a viable one, given the political tone of the country and the way in which the few women scholars of color who are secure enough to engage in such an experiment are scattered all over the country. But more importantly, such units would bypass the central issue—the inappropriateness of studying gender, race, and class as pure categories.

It is this challenge that I see as one exciting possibility for women scholars of color, a possibility that has developed out of the conflict of choices we face. It is, I think, the great contribution we can make to scholarship, despite the fragmented situations with which we must contend. How strong and well-wrought our critique will be depends, I think, on the number and quality of young women scholars of color who will be inclined to pursue this perspective and who will be hired in Afro-American Studies and Women's Studies Programs. It is why I think this issue must receive as much discussion and analysis as we can give it so that a student such as the one I mentioned at the beginning of the paper will see that she is central to a great intellectual challenge. Her work may help substantially to change the way we study ourselves. Rather than being marginal to the concerns of Afro-American Studies and Women's Studies, the woman scholar of color must work toward redefinition of traditional categories.

# Revisiting "What's in a Name?"
## Exploring the Contours of
## Africana Womanist Tought

*Nikol G. Alexander-Floyd
and Evelyn M. Simien*

2006

Neither an outgrowth nor an addendum to feminism, *Africana Womanism* is not Black feminism, African feminism, or Walker's womanism that some Africana women have come to embrace. *Africana Womanism* is an ideology created and designed for all women of African descent. It is grounded in African culture, and[,] therefore, it necessarily focuses on the unique experiences, struggles, needs, and desires of Africana women. It critically addresses the dynamics of the conflict between the mainstream feminist, the Black feminist, the African feminist, and the Africana womanist. The conclusion is that *Africana Womanism* and its agenda are unique and separate from both White feminism and Black feminism, and[,] moreover, to the extent of naming in particular, Africana Womanism differs from African feminism. (emphasis in original)

Clenora Hudson-Weems,
*Africana Womanism*

## Introduction

Although Africana womanism is a growing academic and political identification, scholars have yet to adequately explore its relationship to Black feminism. Current interest in whether various types of Black women's intellectual production should be named womanism or Black feminism mirrors the pre-occupation with questions of individual versus group identity and crosscutting versus consensus issues that take place within Black civil society today. While some scholars conflate womanism and Black feminism, others insist the two are inherently incompatible. The uncertainty and controversy surrounding naming practices reflect a concern with differences among individual Black women who wish to emphasize the primacy of their racial identity, particularly nationalists,[1] and others who do not. At the

Reprinted from *Frontiers: a Journal of Women Studies*, volume 27, number 1 (2006) by permission of the University of Nebraska Press. Copyright © 2006 by Frontiers Editorial Collective.

heart of this debate, which involves such Black women intellectuals as Patricia Hill Collins, Alice Walker, and Clenora Hudson-Weems, is a struggle to authoritatively name a political identity for Black women: Black feminism, womanism, or Africana womanism.[2] Such a question forces Black academics, intellectuals, and activists to reconsider long-standing notions of race loyalty and the hierarchy of interests within Black communities relative to the prioritization of race, class, and gender.[3]

Notably, Black feminist sociologist Patricia Hill Collins addresses the above set of concerns by arguing that the controversy over naming is a political distraction. In her book, *Fighting Words*, Collins discusses the various meanings and uses of the terms Black feminism and womanism.[4] While she recognizes that womanism's affiliation with nationalism exaggerates out-group differences and minimizes in-group variation by assuming a stable and homogenous racial group identity, she also acknowledges that Black feminism's connection with women's liberation, domestically and globally, cultivates its rejection on the grounds that feminism is perceived as a for-Whites-only affair. More important, she argues that the politics of naming and the controversy that follows it draw critical attention away from the very circumstances that limit the life chances of Black women and undermine the struggle to overcome racist and sexist oppression.

Rather than focus our attention on the politics of naming and individual labels that often polarize rather than unify grassroots activists, Collins suggests that Black women academicians bypass the debate by concentrating on matters of practical concern. She suggests that this dialogue is largely elitist, since discussions about feminism and womanism often occur within academic spaces—colleges and universities—away from nonelite actors.[5] By asserting that we should sidestep the politics of naming to deal with real world issues, however, Collins underestimates the importance and political implications of such an exercise as naming.

In this essay, we carefully examine the key tenets underpinning Africana womanism. Africana womanism contrasts sharply with Black feminisms and womanisms, offering a unique read of the political world as it relates to identity. Challenging the theoretical and historical foundations of Africana womanism, we argue that the master narrative and characteristics upon which it is based ignore and distort Black feminist thought and history, fail to join theory with practice, and depend on an ahistoric, monolithic view of African cultures.[6] For the purpose of this study, we concentrate on second-wave Black feminism as conceived by the Combahee River Collective and theorized by Patricia Hill Collins, among others, and on Africana womanism as posited by Clenora Hudson-Weems.[7] It is important to note that we do not profess to offer an exhaustive treatment of Africana womanism; rather, we examine and respond to its major tenets as conceived by Clenora Hudson-Weems, its lead theorist, in an effort to bring greater critical attention to and discussion of this significant political theory amongst feminists across disciplinary boundaries.

## Defining the Core: Key Tenets of Africana Womanism

Clenora Hudson-Weems's *Africana Womanism: Reclaiming Ourselves* is perhaps the best articulation of antisexist theory to emerge from a nationalist, Afrocentric thinker.[8] It has been received favorably at gatherings of the National Council of Black Studies (the oldest and leading Black studies organization), and several parts of the book have been published in such leading Black studies journals as the *Journal of Black Studies* and the *Western Journal of Black Studies*, the latter by invitation of the founding editor, Talmadge Anderson. Several Black studies notables have also endorsed the book. C. Eric Lincoln, an esteemed scholar well known for his work on Black nationalism, noted that "Hudson-Weems' *Africana Womanism* sent unaccustomed shock waves through the domain of popular thinking about feminism and established her as an independent thinker, unafraid to unsettle settled opinion;" Charles V. Hamilton, Black political scientist and co-author of the Black nationalist classic, *Black Power*, opined, "This work [*Africana Womanism*] is indeed a triumph. It is a product that not only must be read, but more important, be studied;" Robert L. Harris, Jr., former director of the Africana Studies and Research Center at Cornell University, dubbed *Africana Womanism* a "remarkable book" that would bring much needed "healing . . . for men and women of African ancestry and ultimately for all caring men and women."[9] Finally, a special issue paying homage to Hudson-Weems's scholarly work was published in the *Western Journal of Black Studies*. As its name and institutional bases of support suggest, *Africana Womanism* falls solidly within the Afrocentric tradition.

In the following section, we offer a general overview of the book by outlining the key tenets (or characteristics) of Africana womanism that for Hudson-Weems define the "Agenda for Africana womanism."[10] These characteristics total eighteen and are as follows: self-naming, self-definition, role flexibility, family-centeredness, struggling with males against oppression, adaptability, Black female sisterhood, wholeness, authenticity, strength, male compatibility, respect, recognition, respect for elders, ambition, mothering, nurturing, and spirituality. While Hudson-Weems refers to these characteristics as "distinct and diverse,"[11] for purposes of analytical clarity and systematic organization, we identify three salient themes—agency, alliances, and attributes—by which to classify them.

The first theme, agency, is achieved through self-naming and self-definition. In African culture, self-naming or "nommo" is important because it is in "the correct naming of a thing that it comes into existence."[12] Drawing on the work of Lerone Bennett, Jr., Daphne Williams Ntiri notes in the introduction to *Africana Womanism* that "Naming is too critical an act to be left in the hands of the dominant group" and Black people have "an increasing need for self-naming, self-defining and self-identity."[13] In African culture, self-definition serves as the basis for collective action and individual identity.[14] It is the means by which people of African descent can assert their own vision of their reality in opposition to that of the dominant culture.[15] Africana womanism is therefore deemed the most authentic (or accurate) label for women of African descent concerned with patriarchy, as it resonates with the historical and cultural experiences of the constituency that it aims to serve.[16]

The second theme, alliances, includes family-centeredness, wholeness, authenticity, flexible role-playing, adaptability, political alignment with Black men, and "genuine sisterhood" with Black women. The first five—family-centeredness, wholeness, authenticity, flexible role-playing, and adaptability—speak to Black women's commitment to family. According to Hudson-Weems, while "the mainstream feminist is self-centered or female-centered, interested in self-realization and personal gratification," Africana womanists are family-centered and community-centered, interested in collective outcomes and group achievement.[17] Sexism is an important problem, but not one that supersedes racism.[18] From slavery on, Black women have been deprived of the material circumstances to "stay at home." Nonetheless, they are spiritually connected to the home.[19] As with self-naming and self-definition, the emphasis on family is rooted in African culture. Whereas "wholeness ([or] completeness)" dictates that she put family first, but not to the neglect of career, "authenticity ([or] cultural connection)" is achieved to the extent that her identity is African-based.[20] The Africana woman then values family as part of her African heritage.

Flexible role-playing and adaptability are just as important elements of family-centeredness. According to Hudson-Weems, racism dictated that Black women and men assume unconventional gender roles. Historically, Black women have had to work outside of the home and their men have assumed greater homemaking responsibilities than is typical in the dominant culture. Because the Black woman has always had flexible gender roles, the mainstream feminist goal of dismantling traditional roles is, at best, inapplicable and, at worst, irrelevant to them. The goal of mainstream feminism is problematic for Black women because, even though circumstances have not supported their adoption of traditional gender roles, they continue to recognize some elements as ideal.[21] With regard to adaptability, the Africana womanist does not recognize a need for a "separate space" as does the mainstream, White feminist. While Virginia Woolf called for a separate space, ideally away from home, to support and nurture female creativity, the Black woman has had no such luxury. Despite this fact, however, she has been adaptable or resilient enough to be creative and proactive.[22]

The second theme, alliances, is achieved through political alignment with Black men and "genuine sisterhood" with Black women. While the mainstream feminist sees men as independent from and opposed to their cause for equality,[23] the Africana womanist sees herself fighting "in concert with males" against Black oppression.[24] The Africana womanist also shares an important "bond" with Black women in genuine sisterhood.[25] Black women share the same experience of oppression and can empathize with each other's lot in life.[26] By identifying the sisterhood as "genuine," Hudson-Weems implicitly contrasts it with the superficial articulations of sisterhood widely discussed in mainstream feminist discourse.[27]

The third and final theme, attributes of Africana womanists, includes strength, male compatibility, respect, recognition, respect for elders, ambition, mothering, nurturing, and spirituality. Black women have always exhibited psychological and physical strength, especially during the slave era when Black women had to endure the separation of their families.[28] The Africana womanist also seeks "positive male companionship" and sees it as vital to family and the mutual survival of Black men and women.[29] Some men abandon women, but many who are good husbands and fathers do not get recognized as such.[30] For Hudson-Weems, the bond between Black men and Black women is important to perpetuating the race. Every Black woman wants a man, "a special somebody to fill a void in her life, one who makes her complete."[31]

Respect, ambition, mothering, nurturing, and spirituality are also vital to Africana womanism. Respect and recognition are what Africana womanists require so that they can have healthy respect for themselves and in turn relate well with other people.[32] A lack of "self-love" can lead to Black women allowing others to treat them with disrespect. Internalizing White beauty standards can diminish Black women's self-esteem. Gender oppression is a reality for Black women, to be sure. It does not trump class or race, however. Hudson-Weems explains, "Sexism is clearly not the most critical issue for the Africana womanist. Unquestionably, the salient phenomenon that plagues the Africana community is poverty, in which racism plays a major part. . . ."[33] In addition to requiring respect and recognition for herself, the Africana womanist has and affirms a deep love, admiration, and respect for elders or older members of the Black community and prizes their wisdom and guidance. This, too, is an aspect of African culture.[34] Also, [Africana women] have a strong drive to succeed and create ways to gain the "space" they need.[35] "It may be in a tiny room, or a closet, or it may be in the wee hours. Whatever the case, the Africana woman, with ingenuity, provides herself with whatever is necessary for her creative energies to soar."[36] Africana womanists are mothers both to their children and "the entire Africana family."[37] Unlike many white, mainstream feminists, the Africana womanist comes from a tradition that values mothering and nurturing.[38] Finally, the Africana womanist believes in a "higher power."[39] In African religious cosmology, the natural and spiritual worlds are intertwined.[40]

### Examining the Uninterrogated Assumptions of Africana Womanism

We assess the theory of Africana womanism by exposing and challenging several uninterrogated assumptions upon which it is founded. We first begin by examining the primary and overarching assumption concerning the master narrative of Africana womanism. We then proceed to examine the main assumptions associated with the three themes discussed above—agency, alliances, and attributes. We respond to Hudson-Weems's primary claims by providing a more nuanced understanding of Black feminism.

Hudson-Weems argues that Black feminism is a derivative of White feminism. In *Africana Womanism*, she writes: "Feminism, a term conceptualized and adopted by White women, involves an agenda that was *designed to meet the needs and demands of that particular group*. For this reason, it is quite plausible for White women to identify with feminism and the feminist movement (emphasis in original)."[41] Here Hudson-Weems directly characterizes feminism as an inherently "White" politics. Like other Afrocentric theorists, Hudson-Weems believes that theory—both its naming and contours—should be culturally grounded or "centered" and clearly identified with people of African descent.[42] Her characterization of feminism as a White theory, grounded in the experiences of white women, serves one purpose: to disqualify it as a legitimate political theory for Black women. This perspective constitutes a popular master narrative that both ignores and distorts parts of feminist history in general and Black feminist history in particular. This master narrative reduces the women's liberation movement to a spontaneous, emotional eruption of angry White women who were bored suburban housewives. It both trivializes and discounts the problem of sexism and the varied political responses to it. Although Hudson-Weems correctly identifies racism in the mainstream feminist movement, the master narrative underlying Africana womanism uses White feminism as its primary point of reference and neglects the unique contributions of Black feminists in critiquing White feminists' racism. Such treatment reinforces prevailing notions of the women's liberation movement—that feminism is the cultural property of White women and that Black women who support its tenets are less authentically Black—and deprives readers of a much more complex and nuanced history.

Black feminists have leveled a wide range of criticisms at the racism of white feminists. The now famous Combahee River Collective Statement, for example, lambastes both the Black liberation and women's liberation movements for their inattention to the ways in which various aspects of identity—race, class, gender, and sexuality—are inseparable and must be addressed in tandem.[43] In her classic piece, "Double Jeopardy: To Be Black and Female," Frances Beale argues that White women's groups are middle-class and do not have an antiracist, anticapitalist ideology, as do many Black women activists.[44] She writes, "If the white groups do not realize that they are in fact fighting capitalism and racism, we do not have common bonds . . . we cannot unite with them around common grievances or even discuss these groups in a serious manner because they're completely irrelevant to the Black struggle."[45] Similarly, critiquing White feminists' focus on White female subjugation, Black lesbian feminist poet Audre Lorde maintained, "As white women ignore their built-in privilege of whiteness and define woman in terms of their own experience alone, then women of color become 'other,' the outsider whose experience and tradition is too 'alien' to comprehend."[46] In her classic work, *When and Where I Enter*, Paula Giddings cogently argues that the alliances between Black and White women were strained, and suggests that the Equal Rights Amendment failed because the National Organization of Women did not address the concerns of poor, working-class, and Black women.[47]

Still other Black feminists, from Deborah King and Evelyn Brooks Higginbotham through bell hooks and [Patricia J. Williams], have explored the related ideas of "double jeopardy" and the "metalanguage of race," of writing "from margin to center," and theorizing as an "outsider," making creative use of their marginal status as women of African descent and providing a trenchant critique of White feminist racism.[48] The perspectives of these scholars were, of course, echoed by other women of color feminists, such as Gloria Anzaldúa, who criticized White feminists and argued that their history, struggles, and issues were distinct from that of White women.[49] In fact, these scholars, along with postmodern and poststructuralist feminists—such as Judith Butler and Joan Scott—as well as third world feminists—such as Chandra T. Mohanty and Aihwa Ong—were instrumental in deconstructing the category "women," or the notion of an "essential" identity for women.[50]

In light of this extensive body of scholarly literature, the representation of feminism that Hudson-Weems provides is an ahistorical caricature. Black feminists were among the first to recognize the racism of the women's liberation movement, an observation that disrupts the master narrative, which suggests Black feminists uncritically adopted a White feminist ideology.[51] Black feminism is not a carbon copy of White feminism. It is merely one school of thought or category for feminist analyses.

Feminist scholars have long pointed out that it is necessary to think of a plurality of feminisms and emphasize the diversity of women's experiences. Robyn Warhol and Diane Price Herndl, for instance, maintain that feminism is not "a monolithic, prescriptive, conformist stance—that . . . is singular."[52] Similarly, Rosemarie Tong contends that feminism has a rich and complex history.[53] Given the array of labels used to characterize feminist thinkers from liberal to radical, and Marxist-socialist to postmodern, it is fair to say that not all feminists think alike, as their perspectives, approaches, and frameworks differ.[54] Terms such as these mark the dynamic interplay of feminist theory and politics to date. More recently, in *Separate Roads to Feminism*, Benita Roth demonstrates that contrary to conventional wisdom, Black and Chicana feminisms were not derivatives of White second wave feminism, but developed at the same time as other feminisms of the era, having their own institutional networks and unique theoretical perspectives and contributions.[55] Taken together, the work of these scholars suggests that to speak of feminism as a monolithic entity or as the sole preserve of White women is historically inaccurate.

The theme of agency, which focuses on self-naming and self-definition, reflects a broader effort on the part of Hudson-Weems to articulate one collective voice for Africana womanists and set forth an agenda other Black women might follow. Hudson-Weems emphasizes the importance of "nommo" (self-naming) and of Black women taking charge of their life circumstances (self-definition). Black feminists have always been attuned to these objectives. In terms of the former, the Combahee River Collective provides the starkest example. The Collective derived its name from the first armed struggle led by a woman in the United States—that is, Harriet

Tubman.[56] As this suggests, Black feminists have always assumed a proactive stance in translating their theories into meaningful action.

While Africana womanist theory is clearly outlined, the agenda for Africana womanists remains rather limited, for Hudson-Weems fails to merge theory with practice. Assuming she wishes to compete in the ideological marketplace amid Black feminists and other womanists, she must go beyond promulgating Africana womanist theory and translate her ideas to mass political behavior. That is to say, Hudson-Weems must determine ways in which her agenda might be put into practice through resistance strategies, institutional or organizational networks, and grassroots activism. Hudson-Weems might expand her vision and take the discussion a step further by considering the extent to which Africana womanist theory shapes, or at least informs, active participation in politics. Otherwise, Africana womanism will have little prescriptive utility for those confronting systematic oppression—namely, women of African descent.

In sharp contrast, Black feminist theorists have already made their intellectual pursuits available to nonelite actors via various grassroots organizations and professional networks. Take, for instance, the Combahee River Collective that reached the source of many race problems by supporting Black family life via rape crisis centers and health care workshops that provided services to working mothers. The Collective worked on a range of issues and projects that focused on sterilization abuse, abortion rights, battered women, rape, and child welfare.

Since then, Black feminists have signed petitions, staged mass rallies and protest demonstrations, testified before the court of public opinion, and hosted educational workshops on college campuses. During the highly publicized confirmation hearings for Supreme Court nominee Clarence Thomas, for instance, Black feminists published a statement in support of Anita Hill that appeared November 17, 1991, in the *New York Times* and six Black newspapers.[57] Black feminists also launched an antirape campaign against the appeals case of Mike Tyson, which involved obtaining signatures in support of a full-page ad that appeared April 15–21, 1993, in the *St. Louis American* and included educational workshops, radio interviews, and television appearances, as well as flyers and mailings debunking racist and sexist myths about rape.[58] In this collective protest against rape, Black feminist organizers relied on mobilizing strategies to recruit male and female supporters through preexisting social networks.[59]

Working in this way, Black feminists participated in a process that wedded Black feminist theory with political behavior. Such political activism attests to the lengths at which Black feminists are willing to resist White patriarchal power aimed at their families and communities. Perhaps this is why Barbara Smith avers that "Black feminism is, on every level, organic to Black experience" when she recalls her reluctance to work with White, mainstream feminists exclusively on gender (and not race or class) oppression.[60]

The theme of alliances, which focuses on family- and community-centeredness, working with Black men against oppression, and Black female sisterhood, is addressed by Black feminists as well. The characteristics associated with the second theme are troublesome, because, since Hudson–Weems uses White, mainstream feminism as the point of comparison, she fails to account for the contributions of Black feminists and therefore fails to live up to her stated goal of developing a community for all Black women. Recall that Hudson–Weems sees family and community as the central focus of Africana womanism. Where the mainstream, White feminist is focused on self, promoting the cause of other women, and upsetting traditional gender roles in the family, Africana womanists are focused on family and the advancement of Black communities and are largely comfortable with traditional gender roles, although they have generally not been able to fulfill such roles because of the impact of racism.

Various elements of her critique hold true for White, mainstream feminists. White feminists, for example, did advocate for greater workplace participation for "women," a goal that was inapplicable to Black women who have always had high workforce participation. Likewise, different feminists have also identified men antagonistically, even arguing that women should separate themselves from them personally and politically.[61] Still, when one takes a close look at Black feminist thought, these assumptions do not hold.

While Black feminists join with others in critiquing patriarchy, they have developed a range of assessments and understand family as an important mechanism of survival. In her classic piece, "Reflections on the Black Woman's Role in the Community of Slaves," Angela Y. Davis remarks that Black women's role in the family provided a primary means of survival for Black people and was indeed a form of resistance.[62] Similarly, Black British feminist Hazel Carby points out that there are significant differences in the meaning of family, patriarchy, and reproduction for Black and White feminists.[63] She states:

> We would not wish to deny that the family can be a source of oppression for us [Black women] but we also wish to examine how the black family has functioned as a prime source of resistance to oppression. We need to recognize that during slavery, periods of colonialism and under the present authoritarian state, the black family has been a site of political and cultural resistance to racism.[64]

Even Black feminist bell hooks, who continues to present a consistent critique of patriarchy, draws a distinction between "dominator" and benign
forms of patriarchy.[65] While she sees patriarchal families as a traditional
source of confinement for Black women, she recognizes distinctions in
the types of patriarchal, two-parent homes. In the end, although Hudson-
Weems states that Black families have been and are important for Black
communities, this argument is only a departure from some dominant forms
of White feminism. Black feminists have been critical, but not dismissive, of
this important institution.

Contrary to what Hudson-Weems's analysis would suggest, Black feminists do, in fact, value community interests and advancement. By developing
an integrated analysis of gender, race, class, and sexuality, they have articulated a much broader definition of community than Africana womanism
permits. Hudson-Weems maintains that feminism centers on sexual difference as the key category of political analysis. She avers that Africana men
and women share what Angela Y. Davis would call a "deformed equality of
equal oppression" that has generated a stable and homogenous racial group
identity.[66] Far from being adversarial with Black men, Africana womanists
are allies in the fight against racism. Racism and class inequality are the two
most pressing concerns of Africana people because racism, unlike sexism,
is a "human" problem.[67] Race and class, in that order, supersede gender.
This is epitomized, for Hudson-Weems, in an anecdote by one woman who
claims that "from so many feet away, her race was noticed; as she got into
closer proximity, her class was detected; but that it was not until she got in
the door that her sex was known."[68] The ordering of race, then class, and
then gender, as well as its complete disavowal of feminism, distinguishes
Africana womanism from other antisexist political theories.

Black feminists, on the other hand, maintain that African American
women "don't have the luxury of choosing to fight only one battle," because
they contend with many burdens.[69] Moreover, these various aspects of
identity cannot be treated as separate or distinct.[70] As the Combahee River
Collective explains, "We believe that sexual politics under patriarchy is as
pervasive in black women's lives as are the politics of class and race. We also
often find it difficult to separate race from class from sex oppression because
in our lives they are most often experienced simultaneously."[71] Critical race
theorist Kimberlé Crenshaw explains that "Neither Black liberationist politics nor feminist theory can ignore the intersectional experiences of those
whom the movements claim as their respective constituents. In order to
include Black women, both movements must distance themselves from earlier approaches in which experiences are relevant only when they are related

to certain clearly identifiable causes. . . ."[72] Unlike Hudson-Weems, Black feminists reject the notion that one can separate and therefore rank race, class, and gender in that order. Also, contrary to Hudson-Weems, Black feminists like those of the Combahee River Collective and Patricia Hill Collins affirm the humanity and political interests of Black lesbians within the broader Black political agenda and, in doing so, fashion a more expansive definition of community. In this sense, most Black feminists support a political approach that addresses the complex matrix of domination.

In reality, Black feminists do not advocate separation from Black men, and argue that Black feminists must work with Black men against oppression and create feminist solidarity and community with Black women as well. As the members of the Combahee River Collective report, many Black feminists were involved with Black men in the struggle against racist oppression and were drawn to developing feminism in part because of the sexism they experienced in antiracist organizations.[73] Nevertheless, the Collective affirmed the desire and necessity of working with Black men. They write that, "Although we are feminists and lesbians, we feel solidarity with progressive black men and do not advocate the fractionalization that white women who are separatists demand."[74] They echo Hudson-Weems in her contention that the dire predicament of racist assault against Black people requires Black men and women to work together; more specifically, they note, "Our situation as black people necessitates that we have solidarity around the fact of race, which white women of course do not need to have with white men. . . . We struggle together with black men against racism, while we also struggle with black men about sexism."[75] In a similar vein, Black feminist Patricia Hill Collins posits that while Black women maintain organizations that focus on women's issues, they do so as a basis for coalition building and to pursue a humanist agenda.[76] Indeed, Black feminists consistently recognize the need for Black men and women to work together politically. Members of the Combahee River Collective, for instance, built a functional sisterhood with other Black women in fighting oppression, but they did so with an understanding that their political efforts would also include an alliance with Black men.

Through the characteristics associated with the third theme, attributes, Clenora Hudson-Weems posits an essential, Black female subject. These characteristics—strength, male compatibility, respect, recognition, respect for elders, ambition, mothering, nurturing, and spirituality—are all necessary to have a vital and authentic Black female identity. Hudson-Weems argues that these characteristics are all derived from African culture. The power of these characteristics is that, taken together, they, along with the characteristics associated with agency and alliances, represent a litmus test for identifying those women who are or who are not sufficiently Black and Afrocentric. Those who remain loyal to the race affirm, adopt, and/or exhibit the attributes of the Africana womanist.

Significantly, Hudson-Weems positions herself as a loyal race woman not only by emphasizing these attributes but also by asserting the primacy of race over class and (most especially) gender. She asserts that Black women who adopt the term "feminist," even if they insert the adjective "Black," are at best confused and at worst betrayers of the race. Hudson-Weems goes on to explain how most in Black communities view Black feminists:

> [T]hey [i.e., Africana women and men] hold to the opinion that those Africana women who embrace the feminist movement are mere assimilationists or sellouts who, in the final analysis, have no true commitment to their culture or their people, particularly as it relates to the historical and current collective struggle of Africana men and women.[77]

She argues, moreover, that many Black feminists embrace feminism out of "either naiveté about the history and ramifications of feminism or on negative experiences with Africana men."[78] Duped into adopting an "alien framework,"[79] Black feminists join White women in deeming gender the "most critical [factor] in [Black women's] quest for empowerment and selfhood."[80]

Through her characterization of Black feminists as sell-outs or assimilationists, Hudson-Weems implicitly establishes herself as a sophisticated and knowledgeable woman. Where Black feminists, according to Hudson-Weems, are "naïve" about historical realities, she understands that racism, unlike sexism, is a threat to Black female and male survival. In addition to being loyal, politically sophisticated, and knowledgeable, Clenora Hudson-Weems (as Africana womanist) presents herself as empathetic, being concerned about the plight of Black men and the entire Black community. Unlike a number of Black feminists, she does not believe "that all or most Africana men are less worthy than women."[81] Interestingly, in the end, although Clenora Hudson-Weems promotes "true sisterhood" among Black women and bemoans competition among Black women and the emotional violence this is said to generate,[82] her theory of Africana womanism rests on a derisive and divisive differentiation between the type of women who are Africana womanists and those who are Black or African feminists as well as womanists. The Black feminine ideal that Clenora Hudson-Weems projects for herself through Africana womanism is a model she hopes other Black women will be inspired to adopt.

Like other Afrocentrists, Clenora Hudson-Weems develops a theory that is based on a static, transhistorical view of African culture and identity. By transhistorical we mean that Hudson-Weems's theory of Africana womanism assumes a composite African culture that remains largely untouched by the forces of history, context, and contact with other cultures. Barbara Ransby reminds us that "neither African-Americans nor Africans have created their own history insulated from the larger evolution of world history."[83] Indigenous African peoples exhibit a vast array of cultural differences in kinship, political structures, language, and economic systems. Africa is "an immense, diverse, and complex continent."[84] Africans have also been affected by interaction through wars and exchange with other African cultures, as well as with colonialism and neocolonialism. Hudson-Weems's theory, however, assumes African culture is unified, monolithic, and fixed. The fact that it is multifaceted and shifting undermines the authenticating function African culture has for her theory of Africana womanism.

Africana womanism is a type of standpoint theory that fails to account for the diversity of Black women's experiences, even while claiming a special right for Africana womanists to speak for Black women. Standpoint theory, as developed by feminists like Nancy Hartsock and Patricia Hill Collins, maintains that women in general and Black women in particular occupy a certain status or standpoint that affords them, in Collins's words, a unique "angle of vision."[85] This angle of vision allows them to see and understand the true nature of their oppression. Standpoint theory has been criticized, however, because it fails to account for the multiplicity of Black women's lives. Black feminist historian E. Frances White, for instance, argues, "although Collins recognizes the importance of discussing class, she seems unable to keep class as a variable throughout her analysis."[86] White further criticizes Collins for suggesting that the most racially, economically, and sexually marginalized Black women are also the most authentic.[87]

Similarly, Hudson-Weems insists that the authentic, loyal, and conscious Africana womanist possesses the only true voice of Black women. Africana womanism does not recognize the diversity of Black women. Instead it creates and legitimizes a single, all-encompassing identity for Black women across the Diaspora. The background and experiences of Black women are such that they are afforded a unique standpoint and political interests. Those who fall outside its purview, the inauthentic Black feminist or womanist, have no epistemic privilege or special position from which they can know or speak to Black women's realities. The projection of Africana womanists as loyal and authentic, then, affirms an essential Black female subject.

## Africana Womanist Literary Theory Reconsidered

While *Africana Womanist: Reclaiming Ourselves* is her best known and seminal work, Hudson-Weems has extended her theory of Africana womanism in a more recently published book, *Africana Womanist Literary Theory*.[88] In it she applies Africana womanist philosophy, including the eighteen key characteristics, to an assessment of contemporary Black feminists, historical figures, and fiction and nonfiction by Black women. She takes to task those who have ignored her work, even suggesting that some have wrongly used her work without attribution. She also develops her analysis of sexism by dealing more broadly with male-female relationships. The foundational concepts of Africana womanism, however, appear largely unchanged. We focus on two unique and compelling aspects of her latest work, namely, her treatment of Black feminists and the concept of complementarity at the heart of her discussion of Black male-female relationships.

Hudson-Weems presents a scathing critique of contemporary Black feminists—Patricia Hill Collins, bell hooks, and Elizabeth Higginbotham. She argues that they have either willfully ignored or appropriated her work.[89] She notes that Patricia Hill Collins "inaccurately asserts that 'No term currently exists that adequately represents the substance of what diverse groups of black women alternately call womanism and black feminism' (Collins 17)."[90] As she explains, "The truth of the matter is that the so-called nonexistent term to which Collins refers had already been articulated years before in *Africana Womanism*, which was, at the time of her article, in its third revised edition."[91]

She further claims that Black feminists "duplicate" her work on Africana womanism, which is "distinguishable only, for the most part, by misnaming."[92] For example, in her 1992 classic piece "African-American Women's History and the Metalanguage of Race," Evelyn Brooks Higginbotham calls feminists to incorporate racial analysis into their assessment of power, something done by Africana womanists long before.[93] Likewise, Hudson-Weems states that bell hooks makes an unrealistic claim in arguing that feminists should bring Black women "from margin to center," and that hooks later adopts characteristics of Africana womanism in her work.[94]

The above analysis by Hudson-Weems excludes the body of Black feminist literature that either predates or disrupts her theory. First, it is difficult for Hudson-Weems to claim ownership of the idea that race should figure more prominently in the analysis of gender when the point Higginbotham explored in her classic piece was merely an extension of earlier arguments set forth by Black feminists in the 1970s. It can be argued that race, along with class and gender, always figured prominently in Black feminist analyses of White, patriarchal power. Second, it is just as difficult for Hudson-Weems to claim Africana womanism as a culturally based paradigm when she traces her concept of Africana Womanism to Sojourner Truth's "Ain't I a Woman?" speech. In her 1993 biography, historian Nell Painter established that a White woman suffragist, Frances Gage, published a grossly distorted version of Sojourner Truth's "Ain't I a Woman?" speech.[95] Nonetheless, Hudson-Weems continues to cite Truth as a "pre-Africana womanist" and Gage's version of the speech as a founding document for Africana womanist theory. This is significant because Hudson-Weems stresses the need for Black feminist scholars to create their own culturally based paradigms and theoretical frameworks so as not to duplicate the duplicate—that is, copy White feminists who have replicated Black women's political activism for their own interests.[96] By continuing to use Truth's speech "Ain't I a Woman?" as a legitimating reference, Hudson-Weems arguably patterns Africana womanism after Eurocentric feminism. In light of her own critiques, it is ironic that Hudson-Weems ignores the scholarship that establishes a timeline for Black feminist thought that predates her work and undermines the key premise of her texts.

Clearly, Hudson-Weems's use of Sojourner Truth has implications for the politics of naming. Such an iconic figure has come to represent distinct political philosophies—namely, Africana womanism and Black feminism. To date, Truth's powerful, magnetic personality in addition to her ability to articulate deeply held grievances has been subject to rigorous scholarly investigation. While the work of Nell Painter should have put the symbolic Sojourner Truth dependent-upon-Gage's text to rest, scholars (like Hudson-Weems) continue to invoke this legend for the purpose of legitimizing their knowledge claims. Current interest in whether Sojourner Truth represents an Africana womanist or Black feminist speaks to the question of whether such concepts of identity are inherently incompatible and highlight the contestability of what is taken as historical fact. At the heart of this debate is a struggle to authoritatively name a political identity for Black women: Black feminism or Africana womanism. Both the uncertainty and controversy surrounding naming practices force Black academics, intellectuals, and activists to reconsider long-standing notions of race loyalty and the hierarchy of interests within Black communities relative to the prioritization of race, class, and gender. At the same time, the politics of naming demonstrates two things: the heterogeneity between and among Black women—those who wish to emphasize the primacy of their racial identity and others who do not—and the function of self-definition in developing critical social theory.

Hudson-Weems condemns sexism in the Black community, but the male-female complementarity she recommends is not authentically African as she suggests, and actually affirms Western standards of gender relations. To her credit, Hudson-Weems strongly argues against men battering women and womanizing, and other aspects of gender inequality. She states, "The fact remains that while the number one obstacle to success for Africana people is racism, the problem of sexism in our community continues to rear its ugly head. . . ."[97] Her solution is complementarity, or a view of relationships that sees men and women as equals who fulfill different yet complementary or balancing roles. This concept, a mainstay of Afrocentric politics, simplifies the nature of gender relations in Africa. Most African Americans came from West African cultures, which were diverse in their sexual practices.[98] Some African cultures supported transgenderal unions where women could marry with one taking the role of the "husband."[99] These relationships may not involve sex but are nevertheless indicative of the pliability of gender constructs.[100] Polygamy, or a family relationship where a male has several wives, is also present in African cultures. In another vein, African scholar Oyeronke Oyewumi argues that Yoruba culture does not even operate through gender at all, focusing rather on social distinctions based on seniority based on age differences.[101] Hudson-Weems's insistence that patriarchal, two-parent families are the ideal, authentically African option for male-female relations sidesteps the diversity of African history and practices, and asserts a standard for family structure not exclusive to, but arguably most associated with, the West.

## Conclusion

In this essay, we have examined the major tenets underpinning Africana womanism. Arguing that the master narrative upon which it is based at once ignores and distorts Black feminist thought and praxis, we provide an important corrective to Africana womanism—an area of scholarly research that has garnered support from the most prominent wing of Black or Africana studies (that is, nationalists). By so doing, we enable readers to acquire a more in-depth, complex, and accurate understanding of Africana womanism in relationship to Black feminism.

Far from being revolutionary, Africana womanism is an accomodationist politics that effectively thwarts critique of sexism in Black communities. In this case, accomodationist politics refers to an adjustment of Black women's goal of fighting sexism in light of potential resistance from others in Black communities. More specifically, Africana womanism serves a disciplining function by providing an abbreviated or limited antisexist politics palatable to detractors of feminism. To the extent that Black women who adopt Africana womanism can press antisexist claims, they do so in a way that emphasizes race loyalty and homogeneity within Black communities. Africana womanism thereby establishes the Black woman's place within a particular ideological corridor in the academy and beyond.

Given the absence of a large-scale, antisexist political movement within Black communities today, one might wonder why debates between and among Black women intellectuals matter. They matter in a number of ways, most especially in terms of the implications of these debates for coalition politics and legitimizing competing political worldviews. While effective political action demands some consensus of opinion in identifying political problems and solutions, the debate between these various camps (Black feminists, womanists, and Africana womanists) comes with the terrain as scholars pursue issue identification and articulation. Lack of consensus and divergent interests that naturally splinter groups is endemic to the process of building antisexist theory and engaging in meaningful praxis. Although most Black feminists forthrightly critique sexism in Black communities and are not necessarily averse to multiracial coalitions, the same cannot be said for Africana womanists. These debates also reflect the ongoing struggle to identify Black women's political interests and to claim a right to speak on behalf of Black women.

Black antisexist thought is complex and multifaceted. Over time, it has evolved and taken varied forms. Both Africana womanist and Black feminist theory continue to develop in terms of their breadth and complexity. Insufficient attention, however, has been given to investigating these divergent ideological dispositions and competing interests. In light of this, the project at hand fills a void in the literature and paves the way for additional research to explore the complexity of Black antisexist political thought in more detail.

## Notes

1. As Wahneema Lubiano explains, "Black nationalism in its broadest sense is a sign, an analytic, describing a range of historically manifested ideas about black American possibilities that include any or all of the following: racial solidarity, cultural specificity, religious, economic, and political separatism. . . . It is particularized as a constantly reinvented and reinventing discourse that generally opposes the Eurocentrism of the U.S. state, but neither historically nor contemporaneously depends upon a consistent or complete opposition to Eurocentrism. . . . In fact, one consistent black feminist critique of black nationalist ideology is that it insufficiently breaks with patriarchal modes of economic, political, cultural (especially familial), and social circulations of power

that mimic Euro-American modes and circulations." Wahneema Lubiano, "Standing in for the State: Black Nationalism and 'Writing' the Black Subject," in *Is It Nation Time?: Contemporary Essays on Black Power and Black Nationalism,* ed. Eddie S. Glaude, Jr. (Chicago: University of Chicago Press, 2002), 157.

2. For a discussion of Hudson-Weems's approach to these issues, see Clenora Hudson-Weems, "Africana Womanism: An Historical, Global Perspective for Women of African Descent," in *Call and Response: The Riverside Anthology of the African American Literary Tradition,* ed. Patricia Liggins Hill (Boston: Houghton Mifflin, 1998), 1812–1815.

3. For a discussion of the concept of "intersectionality" regarding race, class, and gender, see Kimberlé Crenshaw, "Demarginalizing the Intersection of Race and Sex: A Black Feminist Critique of Antidiscrimination Doctrine, Feminist Theory, and Antiracist Politics," in *Feminism and Politics,* ed. Anne Phillips (New York: Oxford University Press, 1998), 314–343. For a contrasting view of race, class, and gender as "mutually constitutive" categories, see Anne McClintock, *Imperial Leather: Race, Gender, and Sexuality in the Colonial Contest* (New York: Routledge, 1995); Leela Fernandes, *Producing Workers: The Politics of Gender, Class, and Culture in the Calcutta Jute Mills* (Philadelphia: University of Pennsylvania Press, 1997); Rose M. Harris, "Signifying Race and Gender: Discursive Strategies in Feminist Theory and Politics" (PhD diss., Rutgers, 1999); and Nikol G. Alexander-Floyd, "Interdisciplinarity, Black Politics, and the Million Man March: A Case Study," in *An Introduction to Interdisciplinary Studies,* ed. Michael Herndon (Dubuque, IA: Kendall/Hunt Publishing, 2004) 90–110.

4. Patricia Hill Collins, "What's In a Name?: Womanism, Black Feminism, and Beyond," *Black Scholar* 26, no. 1 (1996): 9–17.

5. Ibid., 15.

6. Master narratives or "'stories' . . . are discrete narratives focused on describing or explaining a particular phenomenon," and create "'imaginaries'" that create "communities and individuals." Sanford Schram and Philip Neisser, eds., *Tales of the State: Narrative in Contemporary U.S. Politics and Public Policy* (Lanham, MD: Rowman & Littlefield, 1997), 4. We describe and discuss the master narrative upon which womanism depends later in this text.

7. Patricia Hill Collins, *Black Feminist Thought* (New York: Routledge, 2000); Clenora Hudson-Weems, *Africana Womanism: Reclaiming Ourselves* (Troy, MI: Bedford Publishers, 1993). While the scope and focus of this article does not permit a full account of these distinct forms so as to render an exact typology, we note that Black feminist thought encompasses revolutionary or radical, critical race feminism, third wave, liberal, and nationalist varieties. Helen A. Neville and Jennifer Hamer, "We Make Freedom: An Exploration of Revolutionary Black Feminism," *Journal of Black Studies* 31, no. 4 (2001): 437–461; Adrienne Katherine Wing, ed. *Critical Race Feminism: A Reader* (New York: New York University Press, 1997); and Kimberly Springer, "Third Wave Black Feminism?" *Signs* 27, no. 4 (2002): 1059–1082. Similarly, womanist thought encompasses "traditional" or secular womanism, liberal Christian womanism, orthodox Christian womanism, and Afrocentric womanist perspectives. For a foundational and secular definition of womanism, see Alice Walker, *In Search of Our Mothers' Gardens* (New York: Harcourt Brace, 1983). While most attribute the term "womanism" to Alice Walker, there is some controversy about the origins of this term. See Rufus Burow, "Enter Womanist Theology and Ethics," *The Western Journal of Black Studies* 22, no. 1 (1988): 19–29. For examples of liberal, orthodox Christian womanism, and Afrocentric womanism, respectively, see Katie Geneva Cannon, *Katie's Canon: Womanism and the Soul of the Black Community* (Lexington, NY: Continuum Publishing Company, 1995); Cheryl Townsend Gilkes, *If It Wasn't for the Women: Black Women's Experience and*

*Womanist Culture in Church and Community* (Maryknoll, NY: Orbis Books, 2001); and Hudson-Weems, *Africana Womanism*.

8. Although Hudson-Weems sees her theory as generally applicable to people of African descent everywhere, her work is decidedly nationalist and most likely finds its audience in nationalist circles. The constructs she uses, for instance, like nommo and male-female complementarity, are popular among Afrocentric nationalists, and the theorists she uses for support and which she engages, like Maulana Karenga, Molefi Asante, and Julia Hare, are also nationalists. The venues in which she publishes and circulates professionally are nationalist as well. The audience for her work, as a practical matter, then is most likely nationalists.

9. Hudson-Weems, *Africana Womanism*, iv.

10. Ibid., 55.

11. Ibid.

12. Barbara Christian, as quoted in Ibid., 55.

13. Ibid., 2.

14. Ibid., 57.

15. Ibid., 57–58.

16. Ibid., 55.

17. Ibid., 58.

18. Ibid.

19. Ibid., 59–61.

20. Ibid., 69.

21. Ibid., 63–65.

22. Ibid.

23. Ibid., 61.

24. Ibid.

25. Ibid., 65.

26. Ibid.

27. Ibid.

28. Ibid., 66.

29. Ibid., 66–67.

30. Ibid., 67.

31. Ibid.

32. Ibid., 68.

33. Ibid.

34. Ibid. 70.

35. Ibid., 71–72.

36. Ibid., 72.

37. Ibid., 73.

38. Ibid., 72–73.

39. Ibid., 69.

40. Ibid., 70.

41. Ibid., 21.

42. Molefi Asante, *Afrocentricity* (Trenton, NJ: Africa World Press, 1988).

43. The Combahee River Collective, "A Black Feminist Statement," in *All the Women Are White, All the Blacks Are Men, But Some of Us Are Brave: Black Women's Studies*, ed. Gloria T. Hull, Patricia Bell Scott, and Barbara Smith (New York: The Feminist Press, 1982), 13–22.

44. Frances Beale, "Double Jeopardy: To Be Black and Female," in *Words of Fire: An Anthology of African-American Feminist Thought,* ed. Beverly Guy-Sheftall (New York: The New Press, 1995), 153.

45. Ibid.

46. Audre Lorde, "Age, Race, Class, and Sex: Women Redefining Difference," in *Words of Fire: An Anthology of African-American Feminist Thought,* ed. Beverly Guy-Sheftall (New York: The New Press, 1995), 286.

47. Bonnie Thornton Dill, "When and Where I Enter. . . : The Impact of Black Women on Race and Sex in America; Labor of Love, Labor of Sorrow: Black Women, Work, and the Family from Slavery to Present," *Signs* 11, no. 4 (1986): 799.

48. Deborah King, "Multiple Jeopardy, Multiple Consciousness: The Context of Black Feminist Ideology," *Signs* 14, no. 1 (1988): 42–72; Evelyn Brooks Higginbotham, "African American Women's History and the Metalanguage of Race," *Signs* 17, no. 2 (1992):251–274; bell hooks *Feminist Theory: From Margin to Center* (Boston: South End Press, 1984); Patricia J. Williams, *The Alchemy of Race and Rights* (Boston: Harvard University Press, 1991).

49. Gloria Anzaldúa, "La Consciencia de la Mestiza/Towards a New Consciousness," *Borderlands/La Frontera: The New Mestiza* (New York: Aunt Lute Books, 1999), 99–113.

50. Judith Butler, *Gender Trouble: Feminism and the Subversion of Identity* (New York: Routledge, 1990); Joan Scott, "Deconstructing Equality-versus-Difference: Or, the Uses of Poststructuralist Theory for Feminism," *Feminist Studies* 14, no. 1 (1988): 32–50; Chandra Mohanty, "Under Western Eyes: Feminist Scholarship and Colonial Discourses," in *Feminism Without Borders: Decolonizing Theory, Practicing Solidarity* (Durham: Duke University Press, 2003), 17–42; Aihwa Ong, "Colonialism and Modernity: Feminist Representations of Women in Non-Western Societies," *Inscriptions* 3, no. 4 (1988): 79–93; Susan J. Carroll and Debra J. Liebowitz, "Introduction: New Challenges, New Questions, New Direction." In *Women and American Politics: New Questions, New Directions,* ed. Susan J. Carroll (Oxford: Oxford University Press, 2003), 1–29.

51. Benita Roth, *Separate Roads to Feminism: Black, Chicana, and White Feminist Movements in America's Second Wave* (New York: Cambridge University Press, 2004).

52. Robyn R. Warhol and Diane Price Herndl, eds., *Feminisms: An Anthology of Literary Theory and Criticism* (New Brunswick, NJ: Rutgers University Press, 1997), ix.

53. Rosemarie P. Tong, *Feminist Thought: A More Comprehensive Introduction* (Boulder: Westview Press, 1998), 1–2.

54. Ibid.

55. Roth, *Separate Roads to Feminism.*

56. Duchess Harris, "From the Kennedy Commission to the Combahee River Collective: Black Feminist Organizing, 1960–80," in *Sisters in the Struggle: African American Woman in the Civil Rights-Black Power Movement,* ed. Bettye Collier-Thomas and V. P. Franklin (New York: New York University Press, 2001), 294.

57. Aaronette M. White, "Talking Feminist, Talking Black: Micromobilization Processes in a Collective Protest Against Rape," *Gender and Society* 13, no. 1 (1999): 83.

58. Ibid., 80.

59. Ibid., 92.

60. Barbara Smith, *Home Girls: A Black Feminist Anthology* (New York: Kitchen Table Woman of Color Press, 1983), xxiii.

61. Alison M. Jagger and Paula S. Rothenberg, *Feminist Frameworks* (New York: McGraw-Hill, 1984), 383–84.

62. Angela Y. Davis, "Reflections on the Black Woman's Role in the Community of Slaves," in *Words of Fire*, ed. Guy-Sheftall (New York: The New Press, 1995), 205.

63. Hazel V. Carby, "White Woman Listen!: Black Feminism and the Boundaries of Sisterhood," in *Black British Feminism*, ed. Heidi Safia Mirza (New York: Routledge, 1997), 46.

64. Ibid.

65. bell hooks, *We Real Cool* (New York: Routledge, 2004), 4.

66. Davis, "Reflections on the Black Woman's Role in the Community of Slaves."

67. Ibid., 25–30.

68. Ibid., 41.

69. Tamara Jones, "Building Effective Black Feminist Organizations." *Souls* 2, no. 4 (2000): 56.

70. Evelyn M. Simien, "Gender Differences in Attitudes toward Black Feminism Among African Americans," *Political Science Quarterly* 119, no. 2 (2004): 315–338.

71. The Combahee River Collective, "A Black Feminist Statement," 16.

72. Kimberlé Crenshaw, "Demarginalizing the Intersection of Race and Sex: A Black Feminist Critique of Antidiscrimination Doctrine, Feminist Theory, and Antiracist Politics," in *Feminism and Politics*, ed. Anne Phillips (Oxford: Oxford University Press, 1998), 334.

73. The Combahee River Collective, "A Black Feminist Statement," 14.

74. Ibid., 16.

75. Ibid.

76. Collins, *Black Feminist Thought*, 38–43.

77. Hudson-Weems, *Africana Womanism*, 26.

78. Ibid., 27.

79. Ibid.

80. Ibid., 26.

81. Ibid., 28.

82. Clenora Hudson-Weems, "Africana Womanism: The Flip Side of a Coin," *The Western Journal of Black Studies* 25, no. 3 (2001): 137

83. Barbara Ransby, "Afrocentrism, Cultural Nationalism, and the Problem with Essentialist Definitions of Race, Gender, and Sexuality," in *Dispatches from the Ebony Tower: Intellectuals Confront the African American Experience*, ed. Manning Marable (New York: Columbia University Press, 2000), 217.

84. Ibid., 218.

85. Collins, *Black Feminist Thought*, 35.

86. E. Frances White, *Dark Continent of Our Bodies: Black Feminism and the Politics of Respectability* (Philadelphia: Temple University Press, 2001), 148.

87. Ibid., 149.

88. Clenora Hudson-Weems, *Africana Womanist Literary Theory* (Trenton, NJ: Africa World Press, 2004).

89. Ibid., 5.

90. Ibid.

91. Ibid.

92. Ibid.

93. Ibid.

94. Ibid.

95. See Nell Painter, *Sojourner Truth: A Life, A Symbol* (New York: W.W. Norton, 1996), 164–178. Contrary to what is represented in Gage's speech, for instance, Truth

did not have thirteen children, did not speak with a Southern dialect, and never uttered "Ain't I a woman?" the question which is famously attributed to her. Gage penned her recounting of the speech twelve years after the event, likely from memory, and in response to an essay published by Harriet Beecher Stowe. This, of course, casts further doubt on the historical accuracy of the speech.

96. Hudson-Weems, "Africana Womanism: An Historical, Global Perspective for Women of African Descent," 1814.

97. Hudson-Weems, *Africana Womanist Literary Theory*, 93.

98. Johnetta B. Cole and Beverly Guy-Sheftall, *Gender Talk: The Struggle for Women's Equality in African American Communities* (New York: Ballantine Books, 2003), 162.

99. Ibid., 163.

100. Ibid.

101. Oyeronke Oyewumi, "De-confounding Gender: Feminist Theorizing and Western Culture, a Comment on Hawkesworth's 'Confounding Gender,'" *Signs* 23, no. 4 (1998): 1049–1062.

## Must I Be Womanist?

*Monica A. Coleman*
2006

### Early Influences: Black Feminist and Womanist

I'm a black female religious scholar, but I'm not sure I'm a womanist. I was a black feminist before I heard of "womanist." I discovered black feminists in college when studying the black arts movements of the 1970s. I identified black feminism with the 1970s—black power, poetry, literature, and defiance. In my eyes, black feminists were radical, fire-eating, justice-loving, law-defying women. Later in my college career, I came to the term *womanist* through literature. While writing a paper on *Their Eyes Were Watching God*, I read Alice Walker's essays about recovering Zora Neale Hurston. I appreciated and related to Walker's quest for a role model: "I write all the things I *should have* been able to read."[1]

I later learned of the womanist movement in religious scholarship. While looking for religious themes in black women's writings, I came across Katie G. Cannon's *Black Womanist Ethics* (1988).[2] It was the first time I read about black women's literature from the perspective of a religious scholar. As a result of Cannon's work and that of other womanists, I never once doubted that I could have a place in religious scholarship. I never felt the pain that no one was talking about my experience, my literature, or my role models. I know that the first generation of womanist religious scholars worked hard to create a world where a young woman could have this kind of experience. They gave me *the experience they wanted to have; the experience they should have been able to have*. For this, I am grateful beyond words, and I think of them as my godmothers. They mothered me into the academic study of God.

As I have met the women whose work I read, I know them as more than writers and scholars. They are passionate people of faith, dedicated teachers, gentle and encouraging mentors, and weary but joyful trailblazers. I can't imagine what kind of scholar I would be, what kind of woman I would be, if I had not encountered Walker, Cannon, and Renita Weems, and encountered them *before* William Faulkner, Reinhold Niebuhr, and Walter Brueggemann.

I tell these stories as more than personal narrative. I believe that I am one of a number of black female scholars who do not know the world or the discipline of religious studies without the influence of feminist and womanist religious scholarship. I question my identity as womanist because I've also been shaped by black feminists, and I believe that I'm part of a generation of women who have grown up (intellectually) during a time that takes womanism as a given.

## Not a Womanist: Critiques and Black Feminist Leanings

I'm not sure I'm a womanist. In her definition, Walker describes *womanist* as "a black feminist or feminist of color."[3] But I've long sensed a difference between the two—or at least in the way the two movements have developed. There are those who identify specifically as "womanist": Cannon, Delores Williams, Emilie Townes, and Jacquelyn Grant. And there are some people who call themselves "black feminist" but not "womanist": Angela Y. Davis, Beverly Guy-Sheftall, bell hooks, Audre Lorde, and Barbara Smith. I haven't been able to put my finger on the precise nature of this difference, but I have some intimations.

When I read Walker's definition, I feel at home, but the trajectory of womanist religious scholarship has left me in a house without enough furniture. There are not enough chairs, couches, or beds for me or many of the black women I know and love. It isn't a place where we can be who we are in some of the most important ways we live—sexually, spiritually, or politically. I've been dissatisfied by the heteronormativity of womanist religious scholarship. Walker clearly states that a womanist "loves other women sexually and/or nonsexually." I think it no coincidence that Walker references sexual love before nonsexual love, and that this phrase falls before her reference to loving men. Walker gives a primacy to the sexual love between women, something that womanists have often failed to do.

Womanist religious scholars have done very little to address the theological, spiritual, and religious experiences of black lesbians (and gays). More than ten years ago, womanist theologian Renee Hill critiqued her colleagues for their failure to address the issue of lesbianism: "Christian women have failed to recognize heterosexism and homophobia as points of oppression that need to be resisted if *all* Black women (straight, lesbian and bisexual) are to have liberation and a sense of their own power."[4] On the one hand, womanist theologians have long been willing to add heterosexism to the matrix of oppressive forces that affect the lives of black women (in addition to racism, sexism, and classism).[5] In fact, Kelly Brown Douglas does this as early as *The Black Christ* (1994) and gives it greater attention in her later book *Sexuality and the Black Church* (1999).[6] To her credit, Douglas writes about the entire purview of black sexuality and the black church, and other womanists actively teach about heterosexism and homophobia.[7] I'm not sure which is more disappointing though—that no womanist wrote more than a few paragraphs about homosexuality until the twenty-first century, or that Douglas connects the church's need to address homosexuality with the HIV/AIDS crisis in the black community.[8]

Generally, however, womanist religious scholarship is typified by a silence about homosexuality. At times the silence is obvious and deafening. Womanists reference Audre Lorde's discussion of the erotic as power without discussing Lorde's personal expression of the erotic. Womanists discuss Baby Suggs's sermon in Toni Morrison's *Beloved*'s Clearing without including the perhaps-sexual relationship in Morrison's *Sula*.[9] Womanists frequently cite Celie and Shug's conversation about God in Walker's *The Color Purple*, while omitting the passionate love Celie finds in Shug's arms.[10] Without giving detailed attention to the issue of sexual orientation, womanists paint a picture of black women as sisters, other-mothers, girlfriends, and loving church mothers, when there is much more to the picture. Douglas asserts that this silence is part of the overall taboo of discussing sexuality within the black community.[11] Karen Baker-Fletcher is more direct: "I suspect that for many [womanists, our silence about homosexuality] is for the same reason that many gays and lesbians hesitate to come out of the closet: fear of losing a job, of being thrown out of church, ostracized in the community."[12] The silence is understandable, but it quickly becomes complicity.

This silence is particularly disturbing given the fact that black lesbians were so active and vocal in the development of black feminism. In the Combahee River Collective's black feminist statement of 1977, the authors repeatedly refer to the collaboration among "black feminists and lesbians."[13] In "The Failure to Transform: Homophobia in the Black Community" (1983), Cheryl Clarke harshly criticizes black female scholars for their homophobic silence: "Like her black male counterpart, the black woman intellectual is afraid to relinquish heterosexual privilege." Clarke insists that the black community address homophobia, not because of HIV/AIDS or to fight oppression, but because "ain't lesbians women too?"[14] Self-identified black feminists spoke out about the issue of heterosexism more than twenty years before womanist religious scholars did.

Black female ethicist Cheryl Sanders readily, and appropriately, I believe, divorces herself from the label "womanist," because she refuses to "affirm

and/or advocate homosexual practices."[15] For this reason, she argues, no
Christian should embrace the label "womanist." In many ways, I agree. If
one is not willing to openly, forthrightly, and consistently critique heterosexism and homophobia with the same fervor as the critique of sexism, racism, and classism, then perhaps one should not be a "womanist."

As noted earlier, I also feel that womanist religious scholarship has not
done well in reflecting the religious pluralism of black women's faith associations. When Walker writes that a womanist "loves the Spirit," womanist
religious scholars seem to have read, "loves the Christian Spirit." I cannot
fault womanists for being true to their own faith declarations, which often
are Christian. In fact, womanist religious scholars have done a wonderful
job at transforming the church from within. Marcia Riggs analyzes sexism
within black churches in *Plenty Good Room* (2003). Cheryl Townsend Gilkes reminds the black church of its historical and contemporary dependence
on black women in *If It Wasn't for the Women* (2001). In *Time for Honor*,
Delores Carpenter writes extensively on the often-inequitable experiences
of black female clergy in comparison with their male counterparts.[16] Many
womanists maintain a commitment to write for both the church and the
academy: Renita Weems, Cheryl Kirk-Duggan, and Karen Baker-Fletcher
immediately come to mind. Where others may have, and some have, given
up on the church's ability to include and value the voices and leadership of
women, Christian womanists cling to their faith and the ground of this faith
with a tenacity that is second to none.

In this process, however, womanists have often assumed that black
women's religious experiences are Christian. Sanders's earlier comment
reveals both the assertion of a particular kind of Christianity and the
assumption that womanist religious scholars always reference Christianity. Baker-Fletcher notes that womanists have often followed the pattern
of "black Christian women" who tend to "conflate God (Creator), Jesus,
and Holy Spirit during the ordinary, everyday eloquent prayers in homes,
churches, and gatherings."[17] Without clarifying the theological difference
between God and Jesus, womanists are incapable of speaking to the many
black women who do not identify as Christian (or Christians with low
Christologies). Intentionally or not, womanists have created a Christian
hegemonic discourse within the field.

This Christocentric discourse leaves womanist religious scholarship
without a language for many black women's religious experiences. How,
for example, might a womanist interpret the strength Tina Turner finds in
Buddhism and the role her faith played in helping her to leave a violent relationship? More important, how would a womanist describe Walker's "born-
again pagan" spirituality?[18] Few womanist scholars have dared to describe

black women's spirituality when a womanist is one who "loves nature" or "loves the universe."[19] I find this aspect of womanist religious scholarship particularly painful, because the Christian assumption does not speak to the multifaith nature of my own spirituality and scholarship.

Black feminists have been more willing to consider non-Christian religions. As a Lucumi priestess[20] and voodoo researcher, Luisah Teish describes "woman-oriented magical practices" in the early black feminist anthology *Home Girls* (1983).[21] Teish connects New Orleans voodoo and the leadership of Marie LaVeau and her female descendants to African women and black feminism, asserting that the religious practices "can be used to harness power and direct it toward social change."[22] In 1981, black feminist Sabrina Sojourner described black men and women's departure from the church into goddess religions. Acknowledging that some white feminists are well known for their rejection of Christianity (Mary Daly, Starhawk, and Carol Christ come to mind), Sojourner highlighted the goddess heritage of black women.[23] In fact, the anthology with the most diverse representation of black women's spirituality was compiled by a self-identified black feminist: Gloria Wade-Gayles's *My Soul Is a Witness* (1995).[24]

Womanist religious scholarship has taken few strong political stances. This is not to say that womanist religious scholarship is apolitical. Womanist scholars have excavated and analyzed the politics of African American women in history. Riggs includes political leaders such as Fannie Lou Hamer, Mary Church Terrell, and Shirley Chisholm as "prophetic voices" in her 1997 anthology *Can I Get a Witness?*[25] Townes examines the moral fervor and influence of Ida Wells-Barnett's antilynching campaign in *Womanist Justice, Womanist Hope* (1993).[26] In *Witnessing and Testifying* (2003), Rosetta E. Ross discusses the moral and religious fiber of the work of several African American female activists.[27] Williams, Grant, and Douglas have given sustained attention to the ways that slavery and white racism shaped the particular religious experiences of black women. Most womanists have not, however, connected black women's historic beliefs with the rationale for why one should continue to believe the same things in today's postmodern pluralistic context. Thus, they have been more descriptive than proscriptive and have tackled few issues of contemporary politics.

Some womanists have, nevertheless, engaged current affairs. Kirk-Duggan's work on violence discusses black women's experiences with sexual, domestic, and gang violence and the complicity of religion.[28] Baker-Fletcher's *Sisters of Dust, Sisters of Spirit* (1998) draws the church's attention to issues of environmental racism.[29] Townes's *Breaking the Fine Rain of Death* (1998) eloquently describes the health-care crises in the African American community.[30] These works connect black women's (Christian) spirituality to important crises and their correlative public-policy issues. They raise the consciousness of both ecclesial and academic communities, and offer suggestions for next steps. I am, however, still disappointed that few womanist religious scholars, nonethicists in particular, will boldly state, "One *ought* to believe X" or "One *should* interpret the text in Y way" because this (womanist) perspective has uncovered an important and crucial insight.

This critique brings up the larger issue of the scope of womanist religious scholarship. The descriptive nature of womanist religious scholarship suggests that it is of black women, by black women, for black women. If so, is the academic contribution any greater than telling white folk what we already know about our own spirituality? Is a book a piece of womanist religious scholarship if the author identifies herself as a womanist but makes no reference to the particular experiences of black women? Or is a work womanist because it draws on the work of womanist religious scholars? Does drawing from the experiences of black women make something womanist? Can womanists make religious assertions for all people? Or have womanists shied so far away from the universalism of white men's experiences that they are reluctant to expand the insights from black women's experiences to a more universal audience?

Perhaps it is the political edge that draws me toward the label "black feminist." The word *feminist* still conjures images of the commitments I express on a daily basis—issues around music, love, and teaching. Johnnetta Cole and Beverly Guy-Sheftall boldly critique the misogyny of hip-hop culture.[31] In her work, bell hooks writes candidly of men, women, love, and sex.[32] I turn to Patricia Hill Collins every semester to check my feminist pedagogy.[33] To put it in anecdotal terms, when I tell my black male friends that I'm a womanist, they think of me as a black churchwoman, which I sometimes am. When I tell them that I am a black feminist, they get a little uneasy, because they start to wonder if I'm aligned with lesbians, if I'm going to question their power, and if I'm going to call God "She"—all of which I also do. I find the word *feminist*, whether modified by *black* or not, to have the disruptive effect that I want.

In her 1996 essay "What's in a Name? Womanism, Black Feminism, and Beyond," Patricia Hill Collins writes about the schisms between "womanists" and "black feminists." She notes that Walker's definition highlights the existing heterogeneity within black social and political thought—the same heterogeneity that exists among black women. Collins chastises the scholars who self-identify as womanist and "carefully select the parts that agree with their world-view and reject the rest," and calls womanists to distinguish between using the word *womanist* to "describe black women's historical responses" and using it to "delineate an ethical or ideal vision."[34]

Collins also talks about the connotation of being a black feminist. Black feminists are associated with an advocacy of the economic, political, marital, and health rights of women around the globe. One more readily thinks of black feminists as entering into conversation with white feminists, lesbians, and politics in general. Still, Collins wonders how black feminists will contend with the issues of difference, deconstruction, and individualism that typify feminism. Do they, she asks, limit their ability to communicate with black religious traditions that may have theological or biblical contestations with an embrace of homosexuality? I agree with Collins on all points. Womanist religious scholarship makes me feel that I am grounded in my own history. But black feminism makes me feel global and political. They both have shortcomings.

## Must Be Womanist: The Branding of "Womanist"

I'm a black female religious scholar. On the academic job market, that means I'm also a womanist. As I approached both the job market and the writing of my dissertation, I found that my colleagues and superiors had an often-stated assumption not only that I was familiar with womanist theology but also that I was committed to writing womanist theology. The assumption is that all black women in the academic study of religion are womanists. Sadly enough, it is almost a marketable necessity. Whatever my academic proficiencies, interviewing committees always ask, "Can you teach black and womanist theology?" This fact became clear: if I wanted to get a job, I had better identify as a womanist, and do it quickly. The theme continues as I prepare to publish revisions of my dissertation. The word *womanist* should appear in the title, I am told. That way, editors say, people can find the book when they do a word search and the publishers know how to identify the book.

I give these personal sketches as examples of the commodification and commercialization of the term *womanist* within the academic study of religion. I cannot imagine that the first womanists ever dreamed that this would happen. After all, as Cannon says, so many of them had to fight just to prove that black women were a legitimate subject/object of study in the field of religion.[35] As womanist religious scholars grew from the initial triumvirate (Cannon, Grant, and Weems) to a second and third generation of black female religious scholars, the term *womanist* was inserted and generally accepted as a significant field of study. One dare not study liberation theologies or feminist theologies without mention of womanist theology. For this, there is cause célébre. But has this progress forced all black female religious scholars into the rubric of "womanist"?

The academy's religion market does not bear sole responsibility for the branding of "womanist." Black female religious scholars use the word *womanist* to identify a support network, Listserv, and programmatic section at local and national meetings of the American Academy of Religion. The term *womanist* was originally created to engender freedom: Walker chose the word because it was "more reflective of black women's culture, especially Southern culture."[36] She liked "the feel, the fit, the sound" of the word.[37] I don't always feel or fit into "womanist." As I choose a name for myself, I commit treason against someone—either the womanists who mentored me into religion or the black feminists who raised my consciousness, employed me, and encouraged my writing.[38]

Just as the field of womanist religious scholarship has grown in convergence with and departure from Walker's life and definition, so the term *womanist* may now be larger than the women who initially claimed it. Can womanists reclaim the term? Do they even want to? Is this commercialization a sign of advancement? Or have hierarchical (often white and male) entities co-opted it, as yet another way to brand and classify black women and our thoughts? If this is the case, womanism has not had the revolutionary effect of its black feminist roots. Perhaps the realistic need for job security tempers the fire of the revolution.

## More Womanists: A Third Wave?

I'm a black female religious scholar, and I've been strongly influenced by both black feminism and womanist religious scholarship. In *Introducing Black Theology of Liberation* (1999), Dwight Hopkins identifies a first generation and second generation of black theologians, applauding the womanists for challenging the sexism of their male elders in black theology.[39] But Hopkins does not classify my generation of black female religious scholars.

What would it mean to discuss a third generation of black religious scholarship? Perhaps black religious scholarship is experiencing something similar to feminism's third wave. Third-wave feminism is the name given to an eclectic group of young feminists with diverse issues and strategies of addressing injustice in contemporary society. It is easier to describe *who* the third wave is than *what* the third wave is. Third-wave feminists are the generation of women and men who came of age in the 1970s and 1980s. Third wavers are the "first generation for whom feminism has been entwined in the fabric of [their] lives."[40] Yet third-wave feminists believe that theirs is better identified as a political generation.[41] That is, membership in the third wave is determined not simply by age or birth rite but by affiliation with similar issues and politics.[42] Third wavers represent diverse issues as they break away from the definitive stance of the previous generation. Some will eschew the problems and terms of their forebears. Others will want to claim them and change their meaning. Third-wave feminists are individualistic and communitarian, academics, activists and stay-at-home moms, knitters and athletes, bitches, dykes, and ladies. Third wavers want to live out the rights for which the second generation fought.

Acknowledging a third wave within black religious scholarship may allow for the reclamation of religious heritage and terminology. I have colleagues who refuse to be called "womanist," preferring instead "black feminist," because they do not want to be associated with what they see as the shortcomings of womanist religious scholarship. I also have a cadre of friends who still want to own the label "womanist" and bring it back to its roots in Walker's definition and writings. Some black female religious scholars still want to be called "womanist" as they broaden the field. Three examples come to mind: Dianne Stewart, who works with Caribbean religions; Tracey Hucks, who works on African traditional religions; and Debra Mubashshir Majeed, who works in Islam. Still others want to qualify their womanist associations. Baker-Fletcher has claimed the label "Walker-womanist" as she articulates her convergences with and departures from Alice Walker's expressed spirituality.[43]

The idea of a third wave of black religious scholarship could lead to a redefinition of womanist religious scholarship. Such naming has room for Randall Bailey, who is currently calling himself a "womanist sympathizer."[44] This kind of womanism could include Darnise C. Martin's work with African American new-thought religions, Irene Monroe's black lesbian commitments, and my decidedly Whiteheadian process theology. This terminology may give my wave of black female religious scholars a reason to call ourselves "womanist." We would be grateful for the work of the earlier generations, and, given the relative youth of this theological movement, we can be rather excited that there is a third wave *already*. We can identify ourselves as male and female, Christian, Muslim, pagan, new-thought, Buddhist, and Ifa. We can call ourselves academics and activists and ministers, priests, nuns, and *iyalorishas*.[45] We will be straight, lesbian, and bisexual, faithful and humanist. We knit, make jewelry, sing, write poetry, and dance. We run two miles a day, lift weights, and climb rocks. Some of us may be southerners, Christians, and members of the NAACP. Others of us may be northerners, Dutch, South Africans, Black Nationalists, or Greens. This wave can reserve the right to, in fact relish in the opportunity to, challenge the assumptions of those who have come before.

This wave may tackle some of the issues that the second wave missed: bisexuality, colorism and standards of beauty,[46] eating disorders and obesity,

class realities (after all, if we're writing books, we can't be too far down on
the class scale), mental health, progressive Christianity, paganism, indigenous spirituality, and participation in other world religions—like Baha'i
and Buddhism. These are the issues I want to read about. Then again, there
could be other options. We might need to keep the distinction between
"black feminist" and "womanist" to connote our commitments, putting on
the mask of "womanist" when it's time to get that job. It could be time for
new words, or a modifier for "womanist." Or maybe we'll find that the term
*womanist* has had its run, and it is time for a new term altogether.

## Notes

1. Alice Walker, "Saving the Life That Is Your Own: The Importance of Models in
the Artist's Life," in *In Search of Our Mothers' Gardens: Womanist Prose* (San Diego:
Harcourt Brace Jovanovich, 1983), 13. See also Zora Neale Hurston, *Their Eyes Were
Watching God* (Philadelphia: Lippincott, 1937).

2. Katie G. Cannon, *Black Womanist Ethics* (Atlanta: Scholars Press, 1988).

3. All references to Walker's definition are found in Walker, *In Search of Our Mothers'
Gardens,* xi–xii.

4. Renee Leslie Hill, "Who Are We for Each Other? Sexism, Sexuality and Womanist
Theology," in *Black Theology: A Documentary History,* 2nd ed., vol. 2, *1980–1992,* ed.
James H. Cone and Gayraud S. Wilmore (Maryknoll, NY: Orbis, 1993), 346.

5. Delores S. Williams, "A Womanist Perspective on Sin," in *A Troubling in My Soul:
Womanist Perspectives on Evil and Suffering,* Bishop Henry NcNeal Studies in North
American Black Religion 8 (Maryknoll, NY: Orbis, 1993), 146–47; Toinette M. Eugene,
"'Swing Low, Sweet Chariot!' : A Womanist Response to Sexual Violence and Abuse," in
*Violence against Women and Children: A Christian Theological Sourcebook,* ed. Carol J.
Adams and Marie M. Fortune (New York: Continuum, 1995), 189.

6. Kelly Brown Douglas, *The Black Christ,* Bishop Henry McNeal Studies in North
American Black Religion 9 (Maryknoll, NY: Orbis, 1994), 101; Kelly Brown Douglas,
*Sexuality and the Black Church: A Womanist Perspective* (Maryknoll, NY: Orbis, 1999).

7. See interviews with Jacquelyn Grant, Emilie M. Townes, Kelly Brown Douglas, and
M. Shawn Copeland in Gary David Comstock, *A Whosoever Church: Welcoming Les-
bians and Gay Men into African American Congregations* (Louisville, KY: Westminster
John Knox, 2001).

8. Douglas, *Sexuality and the Black Church,* 1–3. Douglas acknowledges that there is
no direct correlation between homosexuality and HIV/AIDS; nevertheless, she uses the
HIV/AIDS crisis as a personal and institutional entrée into the discussion of homophobia in the black community (3).

9. Toni Morrison, *Beloved: A Novel* (New York: Knopf, 1987); Toni Morrison, *Sula*
(New York: Knopf, 1973).

10. Alice Walker, *The Color Purple* (New York: Washington Square, 1982); Cheryl
Clarke makes a similar critique in "The Failure to Transform: Homophobia in the Black
Community," in *Home Girls: A Black Feminist Anthology,* ed. Barbara Smith (New York:
Kitchen Table, 1983), 203–5.

11. Kelly Brown Douglas, "Daring to Speak: Womanist Theology and Black Sexuality," in *Embracing the Spirit: Womanist Perspectives on Hope, Salvation, and Transformation*, ed. Emilie M. Townes (Maryknoll, NY: Orbis, 1998), 236–37.

12. Karen Baker-Fletcher in Karen Baker-Fletcher and Garth Kasimu Baker-Fletcher, *My Sister, My Brother: Womanist and Xodus God-Talk* (Maryknoll, NY: Orbis, 1997), 259.

13. The Combahee River Collective, "Black Feminist Statement," in *All the Women Are White, All the Blacks Are Men, But Some of Us Are Brave: Black Women's Studies,* ed. Gloria T. Hull, Patricia Bell-Scott, and Barbara Smith (New York: Feminist Press, 1982), 13–22.

14. Clarke, "Failure to Transform," 205.

15. Cheryl J. Sanders, "Christian Ethics and Theology in Womanist Perspective," *Journal of Feminist Studies in Religion* 5, no. 2 (Fall 1989): 90.

16. Marcia Y. Riggs, *Plenty Good Room: Women versus Male Power* in *the Black Church* (Cleveland: Pilgrim, 2003); Cheryl Townsend Gilkes, *"If It Wasn't for the Women . . .":* *Black Women's Experience and Culture in Church and Community* (Maryknoll, NY: Orbis, 2001); Delores C. Carpenter, *Time for Honor: A Portrait of African American Clergywomen* (St. Louis: Chalice, 2001).

17. Karen Baker-Fletcher in Baker-Fletcher and Baker-Fletcher, *My Sister, My Brother,* 31.

18. Alice Walker, "The River: Honoring the Difficult," in *The Same River Twice: Honoring the Difficult; A Meditation on Life, Spirit. Art, and the Making of the Film "The Color Purple" Ten Years Later* (New York: Scribner, 1996), 25.

19. Only two womanists have ventured close: Karen Baker-Fletcher, in *Sisters of Dust, Sisters of Spirit: Womanist Wordings on God and Creation* (Minneapolis: Fortress, 1998), and Barbara A. Holmes, in *Race and the Cosmos: An Invitation to View the World Differently* (Harrisburg, PA: Trinity Press International, 2002).

20. Lucumi is a West African Yoruba-based religion closely related to Santeria.

21. Luisah Teish, "Women's Spirituality: A Household Act," in Smith, *Home Girls,* 333.

22. Ibid.

23. Sabrina Sojourner, "From the House of Yemanja: The Goddess Heritage of Black Women," in *The Politics of Women's Spirituality: Essays on the Rise of Spiritual Power within the Feminist Movement,* ed. Charlene Spretnak (Garden City, NY: Anchor, 1982), 57–63.

24. Gloria Wade-Gayles, ed., *My Soul Is a Witness: African-American Women's Spirituality* (Boston: Beacon, 1995).

25. Marcia Y. Riggs, ed., *Can I Get a Witness? Prophetic Religious Voices of African American Women* (Maryknoll, NY: Orbis, 1997).

26. Emilie M. Townes, *Womanist Justice, Womanist Hope* (Atlanta: Scholars Press, 1993).

27. Rosetta E. Ross, *Witnessing and Testifying: Black Women, Religion, and Civil Rights* (Minneapolis: Fortress, 2003).

28. Cheryl A. Kirk-Duggan, *Refiner's Fire: A Religious Engagement with Violence* (Minneapolis: Augsburg Fortress, 2000) and *Misbegotten Anguish: A Theology and Ethics of Violence* (St. Louis: Chalice, 2002). I do not include Traci C. West's *Wounds of the Spirit: Black Women, Violence, and Resistance Ethics* (New York: New York University Press, 1999) here, because West intentionally identifies herself as a "black feminist."

29. Baker-Fletcher, *Sisters of Dust.*

30. Emilie M. Townes, *Breaking the Fine Rain of Death: African American Health Issues and a Womanist Ethic of Care* (New York: Continuum, 1998). I want to note that this work is not very christocentric and is open to non-Christian interpretation and use.

31. Johnnetta Betsch Cole and Beverly Guy-Sheftall, *Gender Talk: The Struggle for Women's Equality in African American Communities* (New York: One World/ Ballantine, 2003), 182–215.

32. bell hooks, *All About Love: New Visions* (New York: Perennial Currents, 2001).

33. Patricia Hill Collins, *Black Feminist Thought: Knowledge, Consciousness, and the Politics of Empowerment* (New York: Routledge, 1991).

34. Patricia Hill Collins, "What's in a Name? Womanism, Black Feminism, and Beyond," *Black Scholar26*, no. 1 (Winter–Spring 1996): 16.

35. Katie G. Cannon, "Katie's Canon: Womanism and the Soul of the Black Community" (Women in Ministry and Justice Lecture Series, Bennett College for Women, Greensboro, NC, March 2005).

36. Alice Walker, "Audre's Voice," in *Anything We Love Can Be Saved: A Writer's Activism* (New York: Random House, 1997), 80.

37. David Bradley, "Alice Walker: Telling the Black Women's Story," *New York Times Magazine*, January 8, 1984, 25–37.

38. Here I am referring to my employment at Bennett College for Women, where self-identified black feminist Johnnetta B. Cole is the president; and to my meeting with Gloria Wade-Gayles at the Southern Writers' Festival (July 1998).

39. Dwight N. Hopkins, *Introducing Black Theology of Liberation* (Maryknoll, NY: Orbis, 1999).

40. Barbara Findlen, introduction to *Listen Up: Voices from the Next Feminist Generation* (Seattle: Seal Press, 1995), xii.

41. Nancy Whittier, "Turning It Over: Personnel Change in the Columbus, Ohio, Women's Movement, 1969–1984," in *Feminist Organizations: Harvest of the New Women's Movement,* ed. Myra Marx and Patricia Yancey Martin (Philadelphia: Temple University Press, 1995), 180.

42. Rita Alfonso and Jo Trigilio, "Surfing the Third Wave: A Dialogue between Two Third Wave Feminists," *Hypatia: A Journal of Feminist Philosophy* 12, no. 3 (Summer 1997): 7–16.

43. Karen Baker-Fletcher, "Womanist Passion," in *The Passion of the Lord: African American Reflections,* ed. James A. Noel and Matthew V. Johnson (Minneapolis: Augsburg Fortress, 2005), 125–36.

44. Randall C. Bailey, lecture at the annual meeting of the Society for the Study of Black Religion (Louisville Theological Seminary, Louisville, KY, March 11, 2005).

45. Ifa is a system of divination among the Yoruba of West Africa. Many African Americans refer to the practice of traditional Yoruba religion with the term *Ifa. Iyalorishas* are priestesses in this tradition.

46. "Colorism" is another aspect of black experiences that Alice Walker references in the definition of *womanist:* "Well, you know the colored race is just like a flower garden, with every color flower represented." See note 3.

# When Fighting Words Are Not Enough
## The Gendered Content of Afrocentrism

*Patricia Hill Collins*

1998

In American higher education, Afrocentrism generates some curious contradictions. On the one hand, many African American intellectuals staunchly support Afrocentrism, contending that its commitment to centering scholarship on people of African descent, its treatment of Black people as subjects rather than objects of history, its valorization of Blackness, and its attempts to speak to and not simply about Black people throughout the Black diaspora provide African-Americans with a much-needed corrective to existing scholarship on race (Karenga 1978, 1982, 1988, 1990; Turner 1984; Asante 1987, 1990; Welsing 1991). Other respected African American academics disagree. Defining Afrocentrism as an ideology or dogma, they claim that it romanticizes the African and rural African American past while ignoring social issues in the urban Black present; suppresses heterogeneity among Black people in search of an elusive racial solidarity; forwards a problematic definition of Blackness as an essential, innate quality of a general ancestral connection to Africa; and remains male-centered and heterosexist (West 1993; hooks 1990, 103–13; Gilroy 1992, 1993; White 1990; Marable 1993; Gates 1992a; Ransby and Matthews 1993).[1]

Beyond these academic disagreements, Afrocentrism has a broader history and meaning. As one of several Black nationalist projects in the United States in the late twentieth century (Van Deburg 1992), Afrocentrism simultaneously represents and shapes Black political aspirations for freedom and justice. Much social theory rarely considers Black audiences except as markers of difference. In contrast, Afrocentrism speaks primarily to Black people by "centering" on their experiences and concerns. In a climate of postmodern criticism in which rhetoric of decentering holds sway, any discourse that "centers" on anything may seem hopelessly flawed. However, Black frustration within a new politics of containment provides one explanation why African Americans seem more willing to accept Afrocentrism and other Black nationalist philosophies during a period when academics increasingly view nationalisms of all sorts with disdain. The resurgence of African American interest in Black nationalism in the 1980s and 1990s may be a direct result of an increasingly conservative political climate in the United States, the deteriorating economic base in African American communities resulting from changes in global capitalism, and the persistence of an increasingly sophisticated racial segregation (Massey and Denton 1993; Squires 1994).

Because Afrocentrism aims to influence the thinking and behavior of Black people outside academia, it participates in controversies unlike those affecting other discourses. Unlike most other academic discourses, Afrocentrism received substantial media coverage in the 1990s, most of it negative and centered on two themes. One concerned the inroads of Afrocentrism into the curricular offerings of urban public schools. Schools populated by predominantly African American poor children that had been written off by everyone found themselves the center of attention when they tried to institute "Afrocentric" curricula. Another area of controversy surrounded the claim by some Afrocentrists that ancient Egypt not only constituted an African civilization but that it shaped subsequent European classical civilizations. This media controversy, in part, helped to narrow understandings of *Afrocentrism* from its broader meaning as "Black consciousness." *Afrocentrism* increasingly described the "authentic" Afrocentrist garbed in traditional African attire. Nevertheless, despite the negative treatment in the popular press of both Afrocentric curricula and claims of African origins of civilization, *Afrocentrism* as synonymous with "Black consciousness" remains meaningful to Black youth (see, e.g., the autobiography of hip-hop artist Sister Souljah [1994]), to many African American academics, and to African Americans of diverse economic classes and genders in ways that social theories deemed more respected and more prestigious within higher education have yet to accomplish. I have found African American college students receptive to "Afrocentric" course offerings, symposia, and programs. As part of a larger contingent of Black youth who see the devastation affecting their communities, many see Afrocentrism as the only critical social theory interested in addressing social problems of this magnitude (Lusane 1993).

The institutional placement of many Black intellectuals in higher education may also contribute to the persistence of Black nationalism generally and Afrocentrism in particular as one guiding interpretive framework for Black studies scholarship.[2] Despite considerable media attention to selected Black public intellectuals, most African Americans in higher education experience far less privilege. For this group, Black studies programs have been vital. As Black studies initiatives proliferated at historically White universities in the United States, less celebrated African American academics gained a crucial institutional niche that allowed them to become Black studies professionals, many within Black studies programs and departments. Moreover, the placement of Black academics in historically White institutions meant that such thinkers routinely encountered the residual effects of scientific racism that viewed Blacks as objects of knowledge in sociology, psychology, history, and other academic disciplines (Gould 1981; McKee 1993; Tucker 1994). With limited power to change these institutions, many Black thinkers turned inward toward the task of creating cultural communities that might provide them and their students solace on what were often hostile White campuses. Afrocentrism flourishes in these spaces.[3]

Given Afrocentrism's distinctive political and intellectual ties to Black nationalism, a deep-seated belief in the promise of Afrocentrism by many everyday African Americans cannot be analyzed away as "false consciousness." This would only aggravate existing divisions between Black academics and African Americans outside the academy, as well as growing divisions among Black intellectuals within higher education. Much more is at stake than merely questions of the logical consistency or empirical merit of Afrocentrism. As with Black nationalist philosophies in general, the appeal of having a "Black consciousness" or being "Afrocentric" lies, in part, in the ability of Afrocentrism to mean different things to different African Americans. Rather than trying to define Afrocentrism precisely or, worse yet, elevating one form of Afrocentrism over another and proclaiming it "correct," a more intriguing and useful approach lies in identifying the diverse ways in which African Americans employ Afrocentrism as a system of meaning.

In this chapter, I confine my analysis to Afrocentrism as critical social theory within higher education. As critical social theory, Afrocentrism aims to theorize about social issues confronting Black people with an eye toward fostering economic and social justice. Rather than establishing a taxonomic framework designed to classify Afrocentric scholars (see, e.g., Darlene Clark Hine's useful discussion of Afrocentrism as one of three paradigms operating within Black Studies [1992]), I examine selected "orienting strategies" (Wagner 1992) that frame the practice of Afrocentrism as critical social theory. As the progeny of a Black cultural nationalism that has been institutionalized within higher education, Afrocentrism adamantly claims to "fight the words" of traditional racist discourse. It aims to construct an oppositional social theory grounded in a "fighting words" paradigm. How effectively is Afrocentrism as critical social theory fulfilling this objective?

Although a variety of themes lend themselves to analyzing the oppositional nature of Afrocentrism, among them economic class, heterosexism, and religion, gender offers a particularly useful lens. Gender operates as a

central yet largely unexamined tenet of most nationalist projects, whether
the nationalism is forwarded by dominant groups in defense of institutionalized racism, colonialism, or imperialism, or by groups such as African
Americans who use nationalist aspirations to challenge hierarchical power
relations (Yuval-Davis 1997). Although mainstream media portray Afrocentrism as a monolithic, static doctrine, Afrocentric intellectual production remains decidedly heterogeneous and incorporates diverse perspectives
on a range of topics, including gender (Adler et al., 1991; Petrie et al., 1991).
Despite this heterogeneity among individual scholars, neither Afrocentric
intellectual production overall nor Afrocentrism in the academy has shown
a sustained interest in gender. Neither the specific experiences of African
American women caused by gender oppression nor gender as a major category of analysis framing the experiences of both Black women and Black
men has received sustained attention. Thus, Afrocentric treatment of gender might shed light on the challenges confronting critical social theories
that embrace "fighting words" paradigms.

## From Black Cultural Nationalism to Afrocentrism

Evaluating the effectiveness of Afrocentrism as critical social theory involves
examining the gender politics in the version of Black cultural nationalism
that emerged during the Black Power Movement in the 1960s and early
1970s. Although Black nationalist movements have a long history in the
United States (see, e.g., Pinckney 1976; Moses 1978; and Franklin 1992,
1995), Black cultural nationalism was the political and intellectual predecessor of contemporary Afrocentrism in the academy. For African Americans, the 1960s represented a period of rising expectations about Black
equality coupled with a growing realization that change would not come
easily. The hopes generated by successful decolonization movements in
Africa and the dismantling of de jure segregation in the United States stood
in stark contrast to the seeming permanence of poverty and powerlessness
plaguing Black urban communities. Disenchantment with civil rights, seen
as an outmoded solution, led many younger African Americans to Black
nationalism and the search for a heroic national identity or "Blackness" that
could serve as the basis for a reenergized political activism. Black cultural
nationalism emerged in these social conditions and found its expression
in the Black Arts movement guided by a Black Aesthetic (Gayle 1971; Van
Deburg 1992).

In contrast to other Black nationalist projects, Black cultural nationalism concerns itself with both evaluating Western treatment of Black culture
as deviant (see, e.g., Gossett 1963; Jordan 1968; Gould 1981; Goldberg 1993;

and McKee 1993) and constructing new analyses of the Black experience. Social-science scholarship on race typically sees Black culture in the United States in one of two ways. On the one hand, African American contributions to mainstream culture have been deracialized and considered simply "American" or "universal." On the other hand, dimensions of African American culture that have resisted absorption and remain distinctive are either neglected or dismissed as deviant (Crenshaw 1993). Consider the differential treatment afforded to jazz and Black English in dominant discourse. Despite their shared roots in African-derived philosophical frameworks—their expressiveness, improvisation, rootedness in dialogue, and valuing of individual sound or "voice"—dominant scholarship identifies jazz as the only "classical" music produced in the United States and routinely derogates Black language. Ignoring and minimizing the African origins and African American practitioners of jazz, this approach effectively deracializes a major dimension of American culture. In contrast, when assessing Black language, dominant scholarship interprets the same African-derived characteristics as pathologies that retard African Americans' social advancement (Smitherman 1977). The "Blackness" that created jazz remains ignored, yet the same "Blackness" that generates Black English is maligned.

Based on the premise that Black people make up a cultural nation, Black cultural nationalism aims to reconstruct Black consciousness by replacing prevailing ideas about race with analyses that place the interests and needs of African people at the center of any discussion (Asante 1987; 1990). For African Americans, reclaiming Black culture involves identifying dimensions of an "authentic" Black culture that distinguish it from European-derived worldviews. Reconstructing Black history by locating the mythic past and the origins of the nation or the people (see, e.g., Diop 1974) is intended to build pride and commitment to the nation. These elements allegedly can be used to organize the Black consciousness of people of African descent as a "chosen people." Identifying the unique and heroic elements of the national culture, in this case, Black culture, ideally enables members of the group to fight for the nation (Fanon 1963; Karenga 1978).[4]

Four guiding principles or domain assumptions framed the Black Aesthetic of Black cultural nationalism (Gayle 1971; Dubey 1994). First, in the absence of any substantive African American participation in sociology and other academic disciplines, social-science approaches had long viewed Black culture as "primitive," inferior, and deviant. In response to this scientific racism, the Black Aesthetic aimed to reconstruct a positive, philosophically distinct Black culture. Central to this reconstructed culture lay the thesis of "soul" interpreted as a condensed expression of the unconscious energy of the Black experience. Soul could not be acquired—one was born with it or one wasn't. Soul or essential Blackness was naturalized, and true believers either believed it existed or discounted it altogether. Thus, the concept of soul aimed to name the essential, authentic, and positive quality of Blackness (Rainwater 1970).

A second guiding principle of the Black Aesthetic involved reclaiming Black identity via this reconstructed Black culture. For African Americans, institutionalized racism had severed this link between authentic Black identity and an affirming Black culture to create a "psychology of oppression" (Baldwin 1980). Internalized oppression substituted this authentic identity expressed via solidarity with the Black community, with an identity constructed on premises of scientific racism that deemed Black people intellectually and morally inferior. As a step toward recovering their identity and subjectivity, Black people needed to undergo a conversion experience of "Nigrescence" from "Negro" to "Black" (Cross 1971). Completing a four-stage transformation—preencounter, encounter with Whites, immersion in Black culture, and internalization of a new Black identity—distinguished "Negroes" mesmerized by Whiteness from authentic Black people prepared to participate in liberation struggles (Fanon 1967; Cross 1971; Nobles 1972).

A third assumption concerned the significance of maintaining racial solidarity grounded in a distinctive notion of Black community. Race became family, racial family meant community, and Black community symbolized the "imagined community" of nation (Anderson 1983). Reconstructing Black culture and grounding it in a family model of community organization gave newly "Black" people a home, a family to which they were linked by ties of blood. This stance reinforced the bonds of consanguinity, or blood ties, characterizing the racial family with the sense of political obligation that accompanies blood ties. Family metaphors and their unspoken assumptions about gender permeated Black nationalist discourse of this period. For example, Yosef Ben-Jochannan's influential volume positing African influence on European civilization was entitled *Black Man of the Nile and His Family* (1972). Family ties of consanguinity demand absolute submission because they are built not on political or social issues but on simple belonging (Appiah 1992).

Finally, when nurtured by this unified Black community relating as family, this newfound Black identity would stimulate a new politics for African Americans. African Americans in touch with their essential Blackness would be more willing to serve the Black nation, defined as a large, imagined Black community. This ethic of service to Black families, Black communities, and the Black nation, one wherein Black people would function as "brothers" and "sisters," emerged from the conversion experience of immersion in Black culture, reclaiming Black identity via racial solidarity.[5]

In the 1980s, Molefi Asante, Maulana Ron Karenga, and other African American intellectuals basically imported these four principles into Black studies programs and departments and recast them as premises of Afrocentrism in the academy. Yet as each core theme traveled into the academy, it received a distinctive treatment reflecting the new politics of containment characterizing the 1980s and 1990s. The bulk of contemporary Afrocentric intellectual production, particularly that housed in Black studies programs, emphasizes the first core theme of the Black Aesthetic. Such scholarship explores the distinguishing features of Black culture through identifying the distinctive elements of an Afrocentric worldview (Karenga 1982; Asante 1987, 1991; Myers 1988).[6] Even though the term *soul* disappeared and was replaced by the search for the "essence" of Blackness, Afrocentrism retained this focus on opposing social-scientific constructions of Black culture as deviant. Recasting Black culture through an essentially Black and often celebratory corrective lens, African history (Diop 1974), philosophies (Serequeberhan 1991), religions (Mbiti 1969; Zahan 1979), and social systems (Thompson 1983) all generated new interest. The assumption guiding much of this research was that Black culture had an essential core. Uncovering the philosophical foundations of a distinctive African-centered, Black, or Afrocentric worldview expressed differently throughout the Black diaspora would provide a new Afrocentric context for examining Black community organization (Herskovits 1990; Holloway 1990).

Building on the search for "soul" in the Black Arts movement, Afrocentric scholarship posited several distinguishing features of "essential Blackness." These features were a distinctive relationship of the Black individual to the Black community that fosters a connected definition of self (Myers 1988); a concern for harmony as a fundamental principle of community organization whereby individuals find their worth in relationship to a community, to nature, and to some supreme idea or being (Asante 1987); a relationship between the spiritual and material aspects of being wherein material life is not privileged over spirituality (Richards 1990); and a cyclical rather than linear conception of time, change, and human agency whereby individuals see their connectedness to all life and whereby the appearance of phenomena always change while the underlying essence remains basically unchanged (Richards 1980).

Efforts to verify how these key elements of the African philosophical tradition shaped African-influenced cultures throughout the Diaspora also stimulated scholarship on "classical" African civilizations (Asante and Asante 1990; Holloway 1990). Investigations of the roots of Black culture parallel efforts to reclaim Black history by empirically verifying how the elements of an African philosophical tradition have shaped Black history and, in some versions, Western civilization itself (Diop 1974; Bernal 1987; Brodhead 1987). This component has led to an increased interest in African civilizations and cultures, especially the study of ancient Egypt. Because Egypt was perceived as the original "Black" civilization serving as the philosophical foundation for all subsequent societies formed by people of African descent, interest in ancient Egypt or Kemet increased (Asante 1990; Karenga 1990).

Identifying elements of a distinctive Afrocentric worldview created the conceptual space for scholars to begin the painstaking task of reinterpreting a range of social institutions in Black civil society. Black family studies represent one area in which Afrocentric interpretations have challenged social-science assumptions of Black family deviance, especially in female-headed households (Sudarkasa 1981; Dickerson 1995). Studies of Black religious expression and spirituality make up another important area of scholarship on Black culture (Sobel 1979; Mitchell and Lewter 1986; Hood 1994). Black cultural production, especially music, dance, the visual arts, and literature, constitutes yet another area of important reinterpretation (Cone 1972; Thompson 1983; Asante and Asante 1990). Finally, Black language has benefited greatly from establishing a new normative center that is derived from African societies (Smitherman 1977).

Despite these contributions of thirty years of Afrocentric scholarship aimed at addressing more than 150 years of scientific racism, the definition of culture currently shaping much Afrocentric intellectual production runs the risk of limiting its effectiveness. Black cultural nationalism in the 1950s and 1960s was inspired by the use of culture in actual and not *imagined* national liberation struggles. As a result, the definitions of culture forwarded by thinkers such as Amilcar Cabral (1973) and Frantz Fanon (1963) differ markedly from those of today. These and other Black nationalist thinkers saw culture as dynamic and changing, a complex network of social practices that determine positions of domination, equality, and subordination (San Juan 1992). The close links that ideas and actions had in political struggle fostered a particular view of praxis grounded in a constantly tested Black culture.

In contrast, contemporary Afrocentric constructions of Black culture replaced this dynamic self-reflexivity with an a priori set of cultural norms culled from the belief systems of selected African societies. These norms are often used as yardsticks for assessing normative qualities of Black culture (Asante 1990). Afrocentric preoccupation with forwarding "positive" views of Black culture stems from efforts to extract it from the uniformly "negative" constructions long permeating Western scholarship and popular culture. However, as Michele Wallace observes, "Focus on good and bad images may be more fundamentally connected to the western metaphysical dualism that is the philosophical underpinning of racist and sexist domination than with radical efforts to reconceptualize black cultural identities" (1990, 19). Ironically, this type of thinking reifies the notion of a fundamentally good, essential Blackness increasingly submerged by an encroaching and inherently bad Whiteness. From this perspective, essential Blackness has much to offer an intellectually and spiritually bankrupt White world that has little of value (see, e.g., Welsing 1991).

Reconstituting Black identity, the second core theme of the Black Aesthetic, remains a less focused goal, yet unstated assumptions about identity permeate Afrocentric intellectual production. Work in Black psychology demonstrates efforts to use the core elements of Black culture to assist African Americans in dealing with racial oppression. As prominent Afrocentrist Na'im Akbar observes, "We now know that psychology is not only what the European behavioral scientists have taught. We have a new grasp on the concept that Africans view the world differently" (1991, 36). Substantial scholarship aims to redefine a new basis for viewing African American identity and personality (Baldwin 1990; Myers 1988; Akbar 1989; White and Parham 1990).[7]

As is the situation with Black culture, reconstructing Black identity faces its own set of challenges. In some cases, constructing a normative Black identity easily slips into attempting to describe the ideal, normative, and "authentic" Black person. The search for the "authentic" Black person as evidenced in the glorification of "pure" African biological heritage; the displacement of an essential Blackness from sight to sound by viewing orality, rhythm, and "soul" as the source of Blackness; listing of components of the "normative" Black personality that can be used to measure African American mental health; the belief that a Black essence or "soul" exists that is distinctive to Black people and that only Blacks can access—all have been accused of being instances of Black essentialism (hooks 1990, 103–13; Dyson 1992). In essence, this approach to identity construes Black culture as a package of insulated traits possessed in varying degrees by Black individuals and then uses these traits to assess Black mental health.

Although designed to oppose scientific racism, Afrocentric definitions of culture and identity inadvertently rely on assumptions resembling those of positivist science. For example, positivist science claims that its tools can accurately depict reality. Within scientific contexts of justification, empiricism and rationality constitute tools that uncover the "truth" of social phenomena. Afrocentric views of culture and identity share this belief in a truth that is waiting to be discovered by the science of Afrocentrism. This theme of the embeddedness of Afrocentrism in scientific assumptions concerning culture and identity has had a deep impact on Black cultural criticism. African American writers whose work seems to challenge dimensions of essential Blackness depicted as "truth" often encounter censure. For example, criticisms of Alice Walker's novels *The Color Purple* (1982) and *Possessing the Secret of Joy* (1992) often challenged Walker's accuracy in portraying the Black experience. Even though Walker never claimed that she was trying to "represent" or "depict" the Black experience, holding her work to this standard allowed for its dismissal.

In contrast to the treatment of culture and identity, the two remaining themes of racial solidarity and the ethic of service are treated less as areas of scholarly investigation and more as unquestioned rules that regulate relationships among professionals in some Black studies programs. Much less attention has been paid to examining the actual and potential mechanisms by which African Americans create racial solidarity and/or engage in community service in Black civil society. Instead, Black-on-Black surveillance seems designed to ensure that racial solidarity and an ethic of service as articles of faith are observed. On some college campuses, maintaining racial solidarity at all costs often degenerates into policing the borders of who is authentically "Black." At times, this posture has proved extremely costly. For example, during the confirmation hearings of now Supreme Court Justice Clarence Thomas, conservative Republicans manipulated this automatic invocation of racial solidarity to their own advantage. Many African Americans made the misguided assumption that, once on the bench, Thomas would demonstrate his racial loyalty by expressing an ethic of service to the Black community.

The lack of attention within Afrocentrism to current political and economic issues may stem, in part, from academic norms. Such standards support apolitical scholarship on culture, especially when displaced to a distant and safe past, while eschewing more contentious contemporary African American political realities. Molefi Asante has been producing Afrocentric arguments for years. When his work was deemed politically ineffective, he was left alone. But Asante's work became the center of controversy when it began to be used in shaping school programs in Milwaukee, Detroit, and Portland, Oregon. Only then was it publicly censured. Afrocentric analyses that suggest that psychological freedom must precede concrete political action also uphold academic assumptions. Treatments of Black identity, when confined to analyses of poor Black self-esteem and the need for more role models, represent another safe topic. Unfree minds limit Black participation in both racial solidarity and an ethic of service. The solution: fix the mind. These approaches sever analyses of culture and identity internal to African American civil society from political challenges such as racial segregation and surveillance that originate outside Black communities. In other words, not only are culture and politics severed—a shrinking of the notion of praxis—but also the meaning of each becomes changed as a result of this separation. Thus, restricting Black intellectual activity to the terrain of culture and psychology may signal yet another strategy of co-optation characterizing the new politics of containment (Winant 1994). As Barbara Ransby and Tracye Matthews point out, "The Afrocentric prescription for progress is predicated upon the notion that the main problems confronting the African American community and diaspora at this historical juncture are internal to the Black community itself. The problems are defined as cultural, behavioral and psychological, not as political, economic or structural. In other words—our problem is us" (1993, 59).

Comparing the power relations confronting Black cultural nationalism in the 1960s to those facing Afrocentrism in the 1990s sheds light on the contrasting views of culture deployed by both. The Black Arts movement of the 1960s clearly reflects a stance of "strategic essentialism" (Spivak 1993, 1–25) whereby an essentialist Black culture played a pivotal role in Black nationalist struggles. However, intellectuals from that era recognized that national culture can become problematic for liberation struggles if the moment of "strategic essentialism" hardens into dogma. Cabral (1973), Fanon (1967), and others never meant Black essentialism to be the organizing principle of Black social organization. Instead, they saw culture as one tool essential for political liberation.

The question for African Americans concerns whether we are still in such a historical moment. Will producing a national culture of Blackness yield political results similar to those characterizing earlier historical periods? More important, who benefits from Black essentialist positions that appear unable to generate theoretically compelling arguments for political practice? In a paper appropriately entitled "Afro-Kitsch," the film critic Manthia Diawara scathingly alludes to the political limitations of some versions of Afrocentrism:

> Until Afrocentricity learns the language of black people in Detroit, Lingala in Zaire, and Bambara in Mali, and grounds itself in the material conditions of the people in question, it is nothing but a kitsch of blackness. It is nothing but an imitation of a discourse of liberation. Afrocentric academics fix blackness by reducing it to Egypt and *kente* cloth. Hence, like Judaism, Christianity, and Islam, Afrocentric social theory has become a religion, a camp movement, where one can find refuge from the material realities of being black in Washington, D.C., London, or Nairobi. (1992, 289)

As currently constructed, some dimensions of Afrocentrism seem designed to soothe their advocates comfortably ensconced in teaching and research positions in higher education. Their value as critical social theory seems much more questionable.

## Gender and the Black Aesthetic

As the discussion in chapter I of African American women and Black civil society suggests, Afrocentric domain assumptions of culture, identity, solidarity, and service have markedly different implications for African American men and women. These differences stem in large part from the Afrocentric reliance on Black Aesthetic notions of community, which in turn rely on mainstream views of family. As in nationalist movements globally, women and gender have proscribed functions (Yuval-Davis 1997). Using the experiences of selected White middle-class families as normative, 1960s gender ideology posited that "normal" families maintained a dichotomous split between the public sphere of the political economy, reserved for men, and the private sphere of family relegated to women. These nuclear families in which benevolent male authority ruled, with women assuming their proper, natural roles as wives and mothers, reproduced appropriate gender roles for men and women (Andersen 1991; Thorne 1992). Within this interpretive framework, strong African American women in Black families and Black civil society were labeled deviant (Zinn 1989; Coontz 1992). Moreover, the seemingly flawed gender roles in African American families fostered a slew of problems, among them Black poverty, criminality, poor school performance, and adolescent childbearing. In other words, by not reflecting dominant gender ideology, Black families reproduced a Black cultural deviance that in turn fostered Black economic class disadvantage (Collins 1989).

Despite writings of Black feminists disputing these views (see, e.g., essays in Toni Cade Bambara's *The Black Woman* [1970]), in the absence of a Black feminist political movement, these views were incorporated into Black cultural nationalist agendas. Autobiographies of Black women activists from the Black Power era describe the sexism in Black cultural nationalist organizations. For example, Elaine Brown (1992), a former leader of the Black Panther Party for Self-Defense, describes the sexism in this revolutionary Black nationalist organization. Brown identifies similar practices in US, a Black cultural nationalist movement led by Maulana Ron Karenga, the creator of Kwanzaa and a figure closely associated with Black studies in higher education. Echoing Brown, Angela Davis (1974) also reports elements of sexism in Karenga's Black cultural nationalist organization. Brown, Davis, and other, less prominent Black women assumed a particular place in Black cultural nationalist efforts to reconstruct authentic Black culture, reconstitute Black identity, foster racial solidarity, and institute an ethic of service to the Black community. Although Black cultural nationalism staunchly opposed racial oppression, it ironically incorporated dominant ideologies about White and Black gender roles into its domain assumptions. Consider the following passage, quoted at length, from Imamu Amiri Baraka, in 1970 a prominent Black cultural nationalist in the United States. In his article entitled "Black Woman," Baraka offers an especially concise example of the gender ideology that permeated Black cultural nationalism:

> We do not believe in "equality" of men and women. . . . We could never be equals . . . nature has not provided thus . . . But this means that we will complement each other, that you, who I call my house, because there is no house without a man and his wife, are the single element in the universe that perfectly completes my essence. You are essential, to the development of any life in the house, because you are that house's completion. When we say complement, completes, we mean that we have certain functions which are more natural to us, and you have certain graces that are yours alone. We say that a Black woman must first be able to inspire her man, then she must be able to teach our children, and contribute to the social development of the nation. How do you inspire Black Man? By being the conscious rising essence of Blackness . . . By race, by identity, and by action. You inspire Black Man by being Black Woman. By being the nation, as the house, the smallest example of how the nation should be. So you are my "house," I live in you, and together we have a house, and that must be the microcosm, by example, of the entire Black nation. Our nation is our selves (1970, 8).[8]

Although participants in Black nationalist projects certainly differed in their adherence to these beliefs, in its bold assertion of typically more diffuse assumptions, Baraka's rendition remains unusual and therefore useful. The significance of this passage lies in its particularly concise statement of the gender ideology permeating 1960s Black cultural nationalism. Moreover, it illuminates how key ideas about gender framed subsequent assumptions of Afrocentrism. Four areas are of special significance. They are the importance attached to controlling Black women's reproduction and sexuality; the significance of Black mothers in passing on Black culture; the notion of complementary gender roles as points of departure in constructing Black masculinity and Black femininity; and the symbolic association of Black women with the nation.

First, since women are the only group who can biologically reproduce the population of Black families, communities, or nations, regulating Black women's reproduction becomes central to nationalist aspirations. Controlling biological reproduction to produce more of one's own "people" or, depending on political and economic policy, more or fewer of an outsider group's "people" typifies nationalist philosophies generally and Black nationalist philosophies in particular (Yuval-Davis 1997). Responding in large part to eugenicist, scientific, and public policies long leveled against Black people and others deemed socially undesirable (Davis 1981, 202–21; Haller 1984; Kevles 1985; Duster 1990), Black nationalist projects claim that without sufficient population there can be no Black individuals whose identities are in question. Without population, the Black nation ceases to exist. Within this intellectual and political context, Black nationalist projects of the 1960s often opposed contraceptive and reproductive services for African American women. Viewing such services as genocide, they argued that because family planning services were largely White-run, such services represented a continuation of long-standing eugenics policies targeted toward Blacks. In a climate of medical experimentation on Blacks typified by the then-in-progress Tuskegee syphilis experiment (see e.g., Jones 1993), claims of government-initiated efforts to eliminate the Black population appeared highly plausible. However, although the Black nationalist phrase "have a baby for the nation" made good political rhetoric, it failed to address the issue of who would care for the population born. Despite their analyses, Black nationalist groups often found themselves at odds with the African American women left to raise the future warriors of the nation with few resources. These women often viewed the denial of reproductive services quite differently.

Controlling Black women's biological reproduction raises an accompanying issue of who would control Black women's sexuality. Assumptions about Black women's sexuality central to relations of ruling also influence Black nationalist projects (Collins 1990). For example, Baraka's passage mirrors dominant gender ideology that divides women into two opposed categories: the virginal, married, good girls, contrasted to the sexually promiscuous, immoral, unmarried bad girls. Within this oppositional difference, good girls are sexually active only within the context of marriage and family. In contrast, bad girls represent the sexualized woman, who lacks the protection of marriage and whose sexuality renders her deviant. Within this context, African American women who embody the "conscious rising essence of Blackness" are to be protected, revered, and seen as good women, whereas those who fall outside of this union with a Black man garner less favor. This model legitimates Black women's sexuality only in relation to Black men, yet it offers no parallel legitimation of Black male sexuality in relation to attachment to Black women. Moreover, statements such as "a

Black woman must first be able to inspire her man" suggest that the primary utility of Black women's sexuality lies in inspiring her Black man in the privacy of their home.

Controlling Black women's sexuality simultaneously addresses another issue of great concern within Black nationalist projects. By reversing the color hierarchy of White supremacist beliefs that derogate darkness, Black becomes beautiful. If "the blacker the berry the sweeter the juice" typifies standards of Black beauty and moral authority, Black women remain far superior to White women and other women of color in their ability to produce the authentic Black bodies that this ideology requires. Moreover, keeping the race biologically "Black" and pure directs attention to policing Black women's sexuality. Black women who sleep with "the enemy" place the Black families, Black communities, and the Black nation at risk, for this choice perpetuates the bastardization of the Black race. As mothers of the race, Black women need to be good girls, and good girls do not sleep around. Within a sexual double standard, Black women become mothers of the nation while Black men serve as warriors in the revolution. As warriors, they maintain the right to sleep with, own, and, in some cases rape the women of the alien nation, in this case, White women, while receiving praise for these actions (see e.g., Eldridge Cleaver's *Soul on Ice* [1968]). This ideological framework constrains Black women and Black men differently, with patterns of choices made by actual African American women and men reflecting their struggles with this unstated yet powerful gender subtext of reproduction and sexuality within Black cultural nationalism.

The significance of African American women as mothers in passing on Black culture also constitutes a significant feature of Black nationalist projects. Within nationalist philosophies, the people of a nation not only exist as a measurable, quantifiable population but also represent a group occupying and/or dispersed from a homeland and possessing a national culture symbolic of the nation (Anthias and Yuval-Davis 1992). Since nationalism remains closely associated with notions of self-determination over territory and homeland, Black women, by virtue of their association with land, family, and homes, become keepers of the family, home, community, and nation (Collins 1998a and forthcoming 1998b). For example, Baraka notes that the collective self-determination of a people is expressed through building a "nation" composed of "houses." These houses form a microcosm for the nation as a whole. Thus, the family becomes the approved, natural site where Black culture and racial identity are reproduced. Viewing families as the building blocks of nations, in conjunction with identifying women's actions as more central to the family's well-being and functioning within the house and community than men's, elevates Black women's responsibilities as mothers in certain ways. Since women typically carry the burden of child-care responsibilities within African American households, conceptualizing family as intricately linked with both community and nation effectively joins women's activity in socializing the young in individual households to that of transmitting the symbols, meanings, and culture of the Black nation itself. Viewing African American women as moral mothers or keepers of the "nation," Baraka argues that Black women must be able to "teach our children and contribute to the social development of the nation." Maintaining elements of culture such as language, ways of living, and cultural values of a people is essential to the continuation of the national group. Through their activities as mothers, Black women reproduce authentic Black culture, in this case, the positive qualities that would ensure the loyalty of members of the national group. Thus, Black women's highest accomplishment becomes inspiring Black men and keeping "house," the building block of the nation.

With so much vested in glorifying the mother, Black women who fail to fulfill these functions can face only censure. A distinction can be made between those women who uphold the values of the nation but do not adhere to them and those women who, by refusing protection, challenge the premises of the system. Within this framework, Black gays, Black lesbians, and Black women who embrace feminism all become suspect, because each group in its own way challenges the centrality of motherhood for Black families, communities, and ultimately the Black nation. The homophobia in Black cultural nationalism seems linked to the belief that maintaining a conservative gender ideology is essential for Black families, communities, and the Black nation. As Henry Louis Gates Jr. points out, although the ideology of Black nationalism does not have any unique claim on homophobia, "it is an almost obsessive motif that runs through the major authors of the black aesthetic and the Black Power movements. In short, national identity became sexualized in the sixties in such a way as to engender a curious subterraneous connection between homophobia and nationalism" (1992b, 79). Overall, those Black women who fail to have children or who reject the gender politics of the heterosexist nuclear family face being labeled racial traitors or lesbians.

As Baraka points out, Black women's actions as mothers, although extremely important, remain secondary to the objective of "inspiring their men." Thus, Black women's partnership with Black men via gender-appropriate nation-building endeavors constitutes a third key idea about gender. The thesis of the complementarity of men and women working in partnership in building strong Black families and communities functions as a deep root in Black cultural nationalism. In this discourse, complementarity symbolizes equality, so that the revered Black mother role complements the benevolent yet warriorlike father. But although equality and complementarity are related, they are not the same. Baraka flatly states that African American men and women can never be equal. By this, he endorses natural, separate identities for men and women that parallel the notion of natural, complementary identities for Blacks and Whites. This notion of gender complementarity dovetails with an ethic of service in which Black women and men exhibit racial solidarity by submerging their individual needs, goals, and concerns to those of the Black community as a collectivity. Theoretically, all sacrifice so that racial solidarity can be maintained. But in actual everyday life, African American women typically sacrifice more.

Not only are Black women supposed to reproduce the population of the new nation and pass on national culture but, within the confines of gender complementarity, they also are expected to serve as symbols of the national family or national culture to be protected and preserved. Symbols of American nationalism, such as Mom, God, the flag, and apple pie, are deeply gendered images. They revolve around a nexus of traditional nuclear family values with a nurturing mother at the center under the protection of a supportive husband/father/good citizen and watched over by a powerful male God. Although Black cultural nationalism alters the symbols of the nation through the creation of a Black liberation flag, a Black value system, and Black holidays such as Kwanzaa, it simultaneously imports the notion of women as symbolic of the nation. Tactics such as referring to Africa as "Mother Africa" and identifying it as the mythical homeland of Black people scattered throughout the Black Diaspora promote gender-specific images. Within Black cultural nationalism, as its "conscious, rising essence," only certain Black women symbolize the nation "by race, by identity, and by action." In this sense, Black women become defined as "keepers of the race" both literally and symbolically.

Black community, race, and nation understood through the rubric of family thus become constructed on certain notions of gender that, although not as explicit as Baraka's rendition, depend on African American women's and men's adhering to a particular gender ideology. Black women's contributions remain both biological—as mother, she physically produces the children for the nation as well as provides sexual services for male warriors—and symbolic or cultural—as mother, she socializes Black children for the nation through exemplary role modeling of authentic Black femininity. In contrast, Black men claim masculinity by protecting their households, their communities, and their nation, as symbolized by their Black women.

The dangers here for African American women become clear. If protecting Black women becomes conflated with the construction of Black manhood, any woman who is seen as unworthy of this protection becomes a threat to the entire community and is thus open to group censure. It is one thing to refuse to have a baby for the nation and yet to support the importance of that activity. It is quite another to reject the role itself as part of the heterosexual nuclear family under Black male leadership. The actions of an individual woman are far less threatening than what her rebellion symbolizes to the entire community.

## Gender and Afrocentrism

The guiding principles of Afrocentrism reflect Black cultural nationalism's emphases on reconstructing Black culture, reconstituting Black identity, using racial solidarity to build Black community, and fostering an ethic of service to Black community development. More important, the unexamined yet powerful gender ideology of Black cultural nationalism concerning reproduction, motherhood, gender complementarity, and Black women's symbolic association with nationalist aspirations is also present in the fighting words stance of Afrocentrism.

Most commonly, discussions of Black culture operating within Afrocentric domain assumptions exclude gender altogether and discuss Black "people." In some versions, the phrase "the Black man" stands as proxy for Black people. However, in far too many cases, "the Black man" really refers to men, suggesting that the experiences of Black men adequately represent those of African Americans overall. This approach both renders the distinctive experiences of African American women invisible and reinforces the notion that if Black women are not explicitly discussed, then the discourse itself lacks a gendered analysis. Thus, although it may appear that Black women in particular and a gendered analysis in general remain absent from efforts to reconstruct Black culture and Black identity, Black women's absence and invisibility structure the very terms of the argument advanced.

Another approach to Black culture consists of incorporating the work of a few clearly exceptional Black women, but only if these Black women worthies do not challenge preexisting Afrocentric assumptions. For example, Harriet Tubman is routinely portrayed as the "Moses of her people" because she meets a standard of greatness derived from male experience, namely, military leadership in warfare. Women whose accomplishments seem to advance the dual goals of furthering the development of a positive Black culture and fostering positive Black identities without challenging prescribed gender roles within Black communities also garner the status afforded to Black women worthies. In some cases, only part of the African American woman can be claimed—her nationalist part is embraced, but any feminist, socialist, antiheterosexist ideas that challenge Afrocentric domain assumptions are conveniently omitted. For example, Mary McLeod Bethune's contributions to Black civil society by founding a college for Black youth, if they are mentioned at all, remain more prominent than her contributions as a skilled negotiator within Franklin Delano Roosevelt's "kitchen cabinet." Her community development activities reinforce norms of Black motherhood within Black civil society, whereas her participation in the public sphere challenges views that such activities are best left to African American men. Even the most radical Black women worthies may have trouble recognizing themselves within the Afrocentric canon. Despite Angela Davis's socialist-feminist, antiracist political analysis, reconfiguring her image as the essence of a 1960s-style "authentic" Black woman—signified by presenting Davis as wearing a large "natural" hairstyle—effectively recasts her complex political activism in terms of a more simplistic cultural nationalist framework. As Davis herself notes, "It is both humiliating and humbling to discover that a single generation after the events that constructed me as a public personality, I am remembered as a hairdo. It is humiliating because it reduces a politics of liberation to a politics of fashion" (1994, 37).

In response to the obvious exclusion of Black women in analyses of Black culture, some Afrocentric scholarship tries to present African American women's experiences as equal and complementary to those of African American men. Responding to earlier patterns of the exclusion and marginalization of African American women, Black women scholars in particular aim to correct the Afrocentric record by highlighting Black women's activities in shaping Black culture and history. Although volumes such as *Women in Africa and the African Diaspora* (Terborg-Penn et al. 1987) foster Black women's visibility within Afrocentrism and work within the assumptions of complementarity, they disrupt gender ideology relegating Black women exclusively to home and family, because they highlight Black women's activities in Black civil society. In this volume exploring Black women's resistance in African, Caribbean, and African American societies, several authors suggest that Black women's activities have not been confined to the so-called private or domestic sphere. Works such as this create conceptual space to investigate how African American men and women both have been central to the creation and continuation of Black culture in the areas of religion, music, language, and families. This focus on Black women's complementary contributions to Black culture challenges views of Black culture as male-created and male-defined. For example, by demonstrating Black women's contributions to the creation and continuation of Black culture, Bernice Johnson Reagon's work on Black women as cultural workers (1987) deepens Afrocentric analyses of Black culture. Similarly, Niara Sudarkasa's reconceptualization of African women's gender activities (1981) provides a much needed perspective for understanding African American women.

The outpouring of works by contemporary Black women writers in the United States can be seen as an initial corrective to the male bias in African American literature. On the one hand, by focusing on different yet equally important themes permeating Black civil society, such writers illustrate complementarity and demonstrate solidarity with Black men (Tate 1983). For example, anthropologist and novelist Zora Neale Hurston writes of Black life and culture—contact with Whites does not figure into her greatest work, *Their Eyes Were Watching God* (1978). In contrast, Richard Wright, Hurston's contemporary, writes about interracial interaction, primarily among men. Hers is affirmation, his is protest. Both offer valid approaches to African American experience, for Black affirmation and protest against White domination can be seen as complementary parts of the same process (Jordan 1981). Yet one has traditionally been elevated above the other as superior. Reclaiming the ideas of Hurston and other Black women writers redresses these long-standing imbalances.

On the other hand, African American women writers' treatment of reproduction, sexuality, and motherhood definitely breaks with the Black cultural nationalist idealized gender ideology of men as warriors and women as nurturers. Black women writers' works are revealing on this point, primarily because, unlike social scientists or historians, fiction writers encounter fewer requirements to depict reality and instead can explore its contested nature. For example, Alice Walker's fiction has long been criticized because, although it invokes traditional Black culture, it simultaneously refuses to valorize that culture's construction of gender. Like Walker, other African American women writers increasingly eschew uniformly positive treatment of Black culture and instead situate themselves within the space created by Black nationalist discourse to rework some of the themes of that discourse (Dubey 1994).

Despite its appeal in reinforcing long-standing norms of racial solidarity, the hypothesis of gender complementarity can be applied only to selected topics. Far more attention has been paid to positing areas of Black women's equality with Black men in an imagined ancient African past than to exploring gender complementarity within either contemporary Black civil society in the United States or contemporary African societies. For example, in her popular and controversial volume *The Isis Papers: The Keys to the Colors* (1991), Frances Cress Welsing claims that the Black classical civilization of Kemet fostered a gender complementarity whereby women and men were essentially equal. Her argument suggests that prior to European-installed institutionalized racism, Africans in Kemet lived an idyllic life. Ransby and Matthews disagree, claiming that "the great African past which we are told we need to recreate is also a patriarchal past in which men and women knew their respective place. These unequal gender roles are then redefined euphemistically as 'complementary' rather than relationships of subordination and domination" (1993, 59). Historical settings of African antiquity appear to be more amenable to this type of reinterpretation than contemporary African American civil society. This is because historical analyses of this nature cannot be easily disproved, and because applying similar arguments to contemporary conditions would generate a storm of protest. Reactions such as those of the historian E. Frances White, who notes, "the ideology of complementarity and collective family continues to work against the liberation of black women" (1990, 75), would surely arise. Given these caveats, locating complementarity in the distant past represents a wise decision.

In responding to sustained Black feminist criticisms from Toni Cade Bambara (1970) through E. Frances White (1990), more recent Afrocentric scholarship acknowledges the significance of gender but relegates it as secondary to the more pressing cause of fighting racism. Working within the assumptions of gender complementarity, scholars such as Molefi Asante (1987; 1990), Linda Jane Myers (1988), and Haki Madhubuti (1990a; 1990b) acknowledge differences in male and female experiences but minimize the effects of gender oppression in the lives of both Black women and Black men. Lip service is paid to Black women, but gender as a major category of analysis can be ignored. For example, in *Kemet, Afrocentricity and Knowledge*, widely acknowledged as a central text in contemporary Afrocentrism, Asante advises his readers to incorporate gender as a principal cosmological issue in Afrocentric inquiry. Afrocentric researchers must be cognizant of "sexist language, terminology, and perspectives," counsels Asante, and should investigate the "historic impact and achievement of women within the African community" (1990, 9). Asante further advises his readers to "examine the roles women have played in liberating Africans and others from oppression, resisting the imposition of sexist repression and subjugation, and exercising economic and political authority" (10). Asante's advice is especially odd, given that he makes little mention of gender in this volume despite his advice that it be taken seriously. Eschewing intersectional analyses of race, class, and gender, this approach assumes that only Black women are affected by gender, that Black women's political activism should be analyzed solely within the Black nationalist race as family framework, and that sexism is something that exists *outside* this racial family. As a result, gender has little explanatory power.

Including Black women worthies, incorporating material on Black women, and investigating Black women's experiences within assumptions of gender complementarity all expand the knowledge base about Black women. Given the sorry history of social-science scholarship on African Americans in general and Black women in particular, Afrocentric efforts, however flawed, can serve a purpose. Unfortunately, however, these correctives typically fail to challenge how gender influences the domain assumptions of Afrocentrism concerning culture, identity, solidarity, and service. They reinforce notions of Black women as people who curiously escaped the effects of sexism. Within these constraints and in the absence of any sustained interest in intersectional analyses of race, class, and gender, certain dimensions of Black women's experiences in the United States cannot be adequately addressed. Reconceptualizations of rape, violence, and the overarching structure of sexual politics (Davis 1981; Hall 1983; hooks 1990); of Black women's political activism and resistance outside traditional family models (Gilkes 1983b, 1988, 1994; Terborg-Penn 1986); of the relationships between work and family for both Black women and Black men (Higginbotham 1983, 1994; Dill 1988a, 1988b); of reproductive rights issues such as access to family planning services, and Black women's rights of choice(Davis 1981); of homophobia and its impact on Black identity, families, and communities (Smith 1983; Lorde 1984); and of the ways race, class, and gender interlock in framing Black women's poverty (Brewer 1988; Omolade 1994) are all topics currently explored in Black feminist thought that are routinely neglected by those working exclusively within Afrocentric domain assumptions.

Despite its contributions, Afrocentrism as critical social theory remains unable to address the inherently problematic stance toward gender that plagued the Black Arts movement. The Black Arts movement did contain the seeds for a quite different gender ideology. For example, the first groundbreaking book of contemporary Black feminist theory, Toni Cade Bambara's edited volume *The Black Woman*, published in 1970, contains several essays by Black women whose feminist ideology developed in large part within the context of Black nationalist struggle. Despite this resource, Afrocentric scholarship conveniently ignores these Black feminist analyses, choosing instead to incorporate a conservative gender analysis. Moreover, because the Black Arts movement catalyzed not only Afrocentrism but also a Black feminist movement in the 1970s and 1980s (Dubey 1994), the failure of Afrocentrism to examine its own gendered ideology represents a profound missed opportunity. Unfortunately, as a discourse following both the Black cultural nationalism of the 1960s and 1970s and Black feminist analyses of the 1970s and 1980s, contemporary Afrocentrism seems to have taken only one to heart.

## How Oppositional Is Afrocentrism?

On the surface, developing Afrocentrism as critical social theory appears to be relatively straightforward. Afrocentric thinkers should simply identify the most problematic elements of established scholarship on race, criticize these components, and construct alternatives to them. However, this uncomplicated, reactive posture generates additional problems. As African American writer James Baldwin once observed, "You cannot escape the pathology of a country in which you're born. You can resist it, you can react to it, you can do all kinds of things, but you're trapped in it" (Baldwin and Mead 1971, 24). In the case of Afrocentrism, merely reacting duplicates the binary thinking that divides social reality into White oppressors and Black oppressed. Presenting only two groups distorts both groups' experiences and fails to recognize how the two categories gain meaning from one another.

Notions of White oppressors and Black oppressed also rely on the same gender ideology. Feminist critiques remind us that Afrocentrism confronts a positivist science that is not just overtly racist but deeply sexist as well (Keller 1985; Hubbard 1990; Fausto-Sterling 1992; Harding 1986, 1991). Despite its trenchant critique of scientific racism, Afrocentrism turns a blind eye toward the sexist bias of that same science. Afrocentrism may "resist" and "react" to the premises of racial scholarship, yet it remains "trapped" in its premises concerning gender. Thus, although Afrocentrism assumes a "fighting words" posture in response to institutionalized racism, on a deeper level the nature of its critique inadvertently supports the intellectual frameworks that legitimate hierarchical power relations.

In the context of scientific racism, the very existence of Afrocentrism as an avowedly antiracist project speaks to its oppositional intent. Because the guiding principles of Afrocentrism have been formed largely within the domain assumptions of a science it opposes, it remains limited as critical social theory, as its treatment of gender illustrates. Since the predominantly male practitioners of Afrocentrism experience Western science as "fighting words," in response they generate "fighting words" of their own. Without grounding their analyses in more complex notions of culture and society that deconstruct all binary thinking, Afrocentric countermyths can reinforce the very categories they aim to oppose. For example, reclassifying Kemet as "Black" does little to challenge the cognitive frameworks that juxtapose civilization to primitivism (White 1987). Reversing the value attached to the color symbolism legitimated by scientific racism leaves the system itself intact—only the colors of the players have changed.

Unfortunately, for African Americans in search of antiracist critical social theory grounded in lived Black experience, Black nationalist projects such as Afrocentrism often appear to be the only game in town. Afrocentrism seems increasingly effective in attracting those segments of Black civil society who, for a variety of reasons, see little hope that racial integration can solve economic and social injustices. Given the racial polarization in the United States, Afrocentric reliance on Black essentialism may not be as misplaced as a *political* strategy as some Black public intellectuals believe. Afrocentric discourse that treats Blackness as a free-floating, ahistorical essence expressed differently at different historical moments provides continuity with the past and gives members of communities so constructed an identity and purpose that provide guidance for the future. In this sense, criticisms that Afrocentrism remains riddled with troublesome essentialist thinking that harms both women and men, especially when advanced by Black intellectuals who have minimal current contact with racial segregation, typically fall on deaf ears. Despite the limitations of Afrocentrism as critical social theory, its strong pro-Black posture, combined with its masculinist thrust, contributes to its popularity among many African Americans. The Nation of Islam, a competing Black nationalist project, has long recognized the effectiveness of us/them binary thinking as a strategy for mobilizing African Americans. Few of the estimated eight hundred thousand Black men and their female supporters who attended the 1995 Million Man March in Washington, D.C., expressed concern about Black essentialism and its purported suppression of differences among Black people. They were there in a show of unity. If Black academics in the United States tried to organize a rally of that magnitude, how many African Americans would attend? Moreover, in a climate in which hate speech escalates and racial violence targeted toward African Americans gains strength from the resurgence of scientific racism resurrected by the far right, essentialist thinking continues to enjoy widespread success at mobilizing large numbers of Whites in defense of White privilege. In a situation in which, for example, thirty-two southern Black churches in the United States experienced arson fires in an eighteen-month period preceding the 1996 presidential campaign, Black essentialism may be the best defense against White essentialism. While intellectuals in academia deconstruct everything, including their own leftist politics, little remains on which to construct a new politics capable of responding to unemployment, police brutality, teen violence, adolescent childbearing, AIDS, and other social issues of pressing concern to African Americans.

Black people in the United States need critical social theory that provides leadership and hope in the face of these troublesome conditions. In this sense, the distinctive and fundamental contribution of Afrocentrism may be one that, as of yet, other theories cannot match. Philosopher Cornel West suggests that nihilism, or the feeling that life has no meaning, constitutes a new, fundamental threat to African American existence: "Nihilism is not overcome by arguments or analysis; it is tamed by love and care. Any disease of the soul must be conquered by a turning of one's soul. This turning is done by one's own affirmation of one's worth—an affirmation fueled by the concern of others. This is why a love ethic must be at the center of a politics of conversion" (1993, 19). West may have touched upon why, despite its problematic treatment of gender, economic class, and sexuality, Afrocentrism remains important to both Black men and Black women. In a climate of institutionalized racism that valorizes Whiteness, Afrocentrism offers an affirmation of Blackness, a love ethic directed toward Black people. In this sense, it reaches out to everyday African American women and men in ways lost to even the best antiracist, feminist, Marxist, or postmodern academic social theories. Whereas sociology provides knowledge and postmodernism stresses tools of critique, Afrocentrism offers hope.

Despite this essential contribution, the fighting words of Afrocentrism appear increasingly ineffective in both changing the academy and guiding Black political activism. Exclusivity in the name of nation building eventually fails. Fear of dissent undermines the creativity that must lie at the heart of truthful, sustained, and meaningful struggle. An Afrocentrism that remains analytically self-critical of its own ideas, practices, and practitioners could seriously engage questions of gender, economic class, nation, and sexuality. By situating itself in dynamic versus essentialist definitions of Black culture, such a revitalized Afrocentrism might manage to craft an elusive racial solidarity simultaneously sensitive to Black heterogeneity and difference and prepared to engage in principled coalitions. Until that day, domination is domination, no matter who is doing it. Any critical social theory that counsels African American women or any other group to be silent and step back in the name of an ill-defined unity hurts Black women, cheats African American communities of the best talent and leadership, and ultimately impoverishes us all.

## Notes

1. Molefi Asante's volume *The Afrocentric Idea* (1987) is most often credited with introducing the term *Afrocentrism*. Both Asante's *Kemet, Afrocentricity, and Knowledge* (1990) and Maulana Karenga's *Introduction to Black Studies* (1982) are considered "instructional and model texts that focus on theory, methods, and disciplinary location of Africology" (Conyers 1995, 15). For an overview of Afrocentrism written by an insider, see Kershaw (1992). For an outsider's overview that succinctly summarizes its scope and practices, see Marable (1993), especially pp. 119–22. Marable makes a distinction between "scholarly" and "vulgar" Afrocentrism, viewing thinkers such as Asante as "scholarly" and media figures associated with political issues as "vulgar." Marable does

not simply juxtapose "scholarly" and "vulgar" as positive and negative variations but also critiques inconsistencies in "scholarly" Afrocentrism. Ransby and Matthews (1993) also discuss the resurgence of Black cultural nationalism in African American communities. They link Afrocentrism to interest in Malcolm X and rap music within hip-hop culture.

2. Darlene Clark Hine (1992) classifies Black studies scholarship in three paradigmatic orientations, namely, the traditionalist, feminist, and Afrocentrist. Individual scholars often cannot be easily classified within one orientation and may move among all three. Hine argues that Black studies practitioners reflect diverse racial backgrounds and can be found across a range of academic disciplines. However, although Black studies unite in house practitioners of all three paradigms, the Afrocentrist paradigm is found almost exclusively within Black studies programs and departments. Hine's view differs from other taxonomies. For examples, see essays in Talmadge Anderson's volume (1990), especially the introductory essay "Black Studies: Overview and Theoretical Perspective."

3. For contrasting interpretations of the history of Black studies programs in higher education, see Huggins (1985), especially his discussion "Separatism—Black Cultural Nationalism" (45–46), and Conyers (1995). Former Black Panther Elaine Brown (1992) provides a political analysis of Maulana Karenga's Black cultural nationalism and its impact on Black studies formation at UCLA. Henry Louis Gates Jr. (1992b) offers an interesting comparison between the different paths taken by Black studies and women's studies and their impact on Black women's studies. Gates notes that the Black Arts movement of the 1960s generated Black studies but did not have an impact on the traditional university curriculum. In contrast, White women in the academy and the women's studies programs they created have influenced the general curriculum and in turn are part of the revitalization of Black women's studies.

Accounting for the appeal of Afrocentrism to some Black academics in higher education is another issue. Describing the relationship of British Black social workers to their clients, Paul Gilroy speculates about how the contradictory location of Blacks working on behalf of Black issues in White-supported institutional settings heightens the appeal of Black consciousness approaches such as Afrocentrism to this constituency: "It is possible to see the invocation of racial identity and culture in the mystic forms of kinship and blood characteristic of cultural nationalism as the means with which black professionals in these institutions have sought to justify the special quality of their relationship with their black clients. These ideas provide a superficially coherent ideological reply to the contradictory position black professionals occupy" (1987, 66–67). In short, Afrocentrism may provide a mechanism for remaining ideologically connected to Black civil society when practitioners find themselves distanced by being in White-controlled institutions.

4. In this effort, Black cultural nationalism is not an aberration but instead shows parallels to other groups expressing comparable nationalist aspirations. Analyzing Chicano nationalism, theorist Genero M. Padilla observes, "What we see repeated again and again, whether it be in nineteenth-century Hungary or Czechoslovakia, the Irish nationalist movement, the African anti-colonial uprisings, or even the French Canadian autonomy drive . . . is a close relationship between a people's desire to determine their own political fortunes and their passion to report their own cultural myths, a vital psychic component of national identity which gives energy and purpose to their political struggle" (1989, 113). Black cultural nationalism aims to give a similar purpose to Black political struggle, namely, the purpose of self-definition and self-determination.

As Padilla points out, "Without heroic dreams and cultural symbols of mythic proportion . . .the material aims of a nationalist movement may lack the spiritual center which sustains struggle" (114).

5. For an analysis and a historical context for this approach and its ties to prior racial analyses, see Appiah (1992). The chapter "Ethnophilosophy and Its Critics" is especially useful, particularly Appiah's critique of Diop (101) and the links between Pan-Africanism and Black cultural nationalism.

6. Invoking African-derived frameworks to explain and interpret Black life and culture originated much earlier (Herskovits 1990). For example, William E. B. Du Bois's work on the Negro-American family (1969) explicitly addressed the African origins of such family life. Du Bois's situation illustrates how political factors have shaped the contours of Afrocentrism. Du Bois could not find a position as an academician and turned to political activism as the primary orientation for his intellectual production. As a result, although he may have pursued Afrocentric scholarship had he been able to find the resources to do so, he turned to political activism outside academia (Broderick 1974; Green and Driver 1978). Thus, the issue is less the longevity of Afrocentrism as a theoretical orientation guiding scholarship and more the lack of institutional resources available for the development of Afrocentrism.

7. For representative scholarship in Black psychology, see articles by Wade Nobles, Na'im Akbar, and William E. Cross, among others, in the special issue "Psychological Nigrescence" of the *Consulting Psychologist* (1989). Also, the *Journal of Black Psychology* routinely examines issues of Black identity.

8. Baraka has since gone through substantial changes of political philosophy. Smitherman reports that Baraka had the following reaction to the 1995 Million Man March on Washington: "Some Blacks, such as 1960s activist and writer Amiri Baraka, took issue with the March because it did not include women. Baraka remarked that if he were going to war, he wouldn't leave half the army at home" (1996, 105).

# BODY AND SOUL

## The Last Taboo

*Paula Giddings*
1992

The agonizing ordeal of the Clarence Thomas nomination should have taught us a valuable lesson: racial solidarity is not always the same as racial loyalty. This is especially true, it seems to me, in a postsegregation era in which solidarity so often requires suppressing information about any African American of standing regardless of their political views or character flaws. Anita Hill's intervention in the proceedings should have told us that when those views or flaws are also sexist, such solidarity can be especially destructive to the community.

As the messenger for this relatively new idea, Anita Hill earned the antipathy of large segments of the African American community. More at issue than her truthfulness—or Clarence Thomas's character or politics—was whether she *should* have testified against another black person, especially a black man, who was just a hairsbreadth away from the Supreme Court. Of course, Anita Hill was not the only black person who testified against the nomination of Clarence Thomas, nor even the only woman to do so. But the nature of her complaint went further. It forced a mandate on gender: "the cultural definition of behavior defined as appropriate to the sexes in a given society at a given time," to borrow historian Gerda Lerner's definition. For many what was *inappropriate* was that a black woman's commitment to a gender issue superseded what was largely perceived as racial solidarity. Still others, I think, reacted to an even greater taboo, perhaps the last and most deeply set one. This was to disclose not only a gender but a sexual discourse, unmediated by the question of racism. What Hill reported to the world was a black-on-black sexual crime involving a man of influence in the mainstream community.

The issues of gender and sexuality have been made so painful to us in our history that we have largely hidden them from ourselves, much less the glaring eye of the television camera. Consequently, they remain largely unresolved. I am convinced that Anita Hill, by introducing the issues in a way that could not be ignored, offered the possibility of a modern discourse on these issues that have tremendous, even lifesaving import for us.

I

It is our historical experience that has shaped or, perhaps more accurately, misshaped the sex/gender issues and discourse in our community. That history was broached by Clarence Thomas himself when he used the most remembered phrase of the hearings: "high-tech lynching." Thus, he evoked the image of the sexually laden nineteenth-century lynching—often announced several days in advance to assure a crowd—after which the body was hung, often burned, mutilated, and body parts, including genitals, were fought over for souvenirs. These were low-tech lynchings. Interestingly, it was almost exactly a century ago, in 1892, when the number of African Americans being lynched, 241, reached a peak after steadily escalating since the decade before. Then the epidemic of mob murder against blacks continued with impunity because of the perception that black men, no longer constrained by the "civilizing influence" of slavery, had regressed to a primitive state and were routinely raping white women. At that time "rape, and the rumors of rape [were] a kind of acceptable folk pornography in the Bible Belt," observed historian Jacquelyn Dowd Hall.

Although Thomas's application of this phenomenon to his own situation was highly questionable, even ironic, in one way he was substantially correct. Now, as a century ago, white men, regardless of their own moral standing, still exercise the power to judge blacks on the basis of their perceived sexuality. However, what many failed to take into account with Thomas's evocation was that it was a black woman, Ida B. Wells, who initiated the nation's first antilynching campaign. For lynching was also a woman's issue: it had as much to do with ideas of gender as it had with race.

Often overlooked is the fact that black men were thought capable of these sexual crimes *because* of the lascivious character of the women of the race in a time when women were considered the foundation of a group's morality. Black men raped, it was widely believed, because black men's mothers, wives, sisters, and daughters were seen as "morally obtuse," "openly licentious," and had "no immorality in doing what nature prompts," as Harvard-educated Phillip A. Bruce, brother-in-law of writer Thomas Nelson Page, observed in his influential *Plantation Negro as Freeman* (1889). As one offer of proof, the author noted that black women never complained about being raped by black men. Other observers such as the following southern female writer to the popular periodical The Independent confirmed:

> Degeneracy is apt to show most in the weaker individuals of any race; so
> negro women evidence more nearly the popular idea of total depravity
> than the men do. They are so nearly lacking in virtue that the color of a

negro woman's skin is generally taken (and quite correctly) as a guarantee of her immorality. . . . And they are evidently the chief instruments of the degradation of the men of their race. . . . I sometimes read of a virtuous negro woman, hear of them, but the idea is absolutely inconceivable to me. . . . I cannot imagine such a creation as a virtuous black woman.

The status of black women had been dramatically etched into the annals of science earlier in the century. It was in fact personified in the figure of a single South African woman by the name of Sara Bartmann, aka the "Hottentot Venus." In 1810, when England was in the throes of debate about the slave trade, Ms. Bartmann was first exhibited in London "to the public in a manner offensive to decency," according to observers at the time (Gilman 1985).

What made Ms. Bartmann such a subject of interest was the extraordinary size and shape of her buttocks, which served as a displacement of the fascination with female genitalia at the time. Sara Bartmann was displayed for five years, until she died, in Paris, at the age of twenty-five. Her degradation by what was defined as science and civilization did not end there. An autopsy was performed, preparing her genitalia "in such a way as to allow one to see the nature of the labia." Her organs were studied and reported upon by Dr. George Cuvier in 1817, coolly comparing Ms. Bartmann's genitalia with that of orangutans. Her sexual organs were then given to the Musée de l' Homme in Paris—where they are still on display.

Sara Bartmann's sexual parts, her genitalia and her buttocks, serve as the central image for the black female throughout the nineteenth century, concludes Gilman. It was also the image, he notes, that served as an icon for black sexuality throughout the century.

It is no coincidence that Sara Bartmann became a spectacle in a period when the British were debating the prohibition of slavery. As historian Barbara Fields and others have pointed out, there, as in North America, race took on a new significance when questions arose about the entitlement of nonenslaved blacks to partake of the fruits of Western liberty and citizenship. In North America, Euro-Americans had to resolve the contradictions between their own struggle for political freedom and that of the black men and women they still enslaved. This contradiction was resolved (by both pro- and antislavery whites) by racialism: ascribing certain inherited characteristics to blacks, characteristics that made them unworthy of the benefits of first-class citizenship. At the core of those characteristics was the projection of the dark side of sexuality, now literally embodied by black females. The use of a broad racial tarbrush, in turn, meant looking at race through the veneer of ideology: an institutionalized set of beliefs through which one interprets social reality. By the nineteenth century, then, race had become an ideology, and a basis of that ideology had become sexual difference. If there was a need for racialism in the late eighteenth century, it became an absolute necessity by the late nineteenth century, when lynching reached its peak. For after the Civil War, the Thirteenth, Fourteenth and Fifteenth amendments granted freedmen suffrage and black men and women many of the privileges of citizenship. In a state like Mississippi, which had some of the strongest black political organizations of any state, this translated into the kind of empowerment that saw, in the 1870s, two black men serve as U.S. senators, and blacks as secretaries of state and education, among other high offices. Throughout the South, especially, there was also dramatic evidence of African Americans gaining an economic foothold as the numbers of black-owned businesses and black landowners increased.

Additionally, unprecedented numbers of African American men and women were attending both predominantly white and predominantly black colleges, and aspiring to professional positions deemed out of reach just a generation before. This was even true of black women. By the 1880s the first black women were passing state bar exams to become attorneys, and were the first women of any race to practice medicine in the South. By the turn of the century, Booker T. Washington's National Business League reported that there were "160 Black female physicians, seven dentists, ten lawyers, 164 ministers, assorted journalists, writers, artists, 1,185 musicians and teachers of music and 13,525 school instructors." The period saw a virtual renaissance among black women artists and writers. The Philadelphia-born sculptor Meta Warwick Fuller was under the tutelage of Auguste Rodin; Frances Ellen Harper and Pauline Hopkins published two of the earliest novels by black women; Oberlin-educated Anna Julia Cooper published *A Voice from the South* (1892), a treatise on race and feminism that anticipated much of the later work of W. E. B. Du Bois; and journalist Ida B. Wells, in 1889, was elected as the first woman secretary of the Afro-American Press Association.

Ironically, such achievements within a generation of slavery did not inspire an ideology of racial equality but one of racial difference, the latter being required to maintain white supremacy. That difference would be largely based on perceptions of sexual difference, and as noted before, the foundation of sexual difference lay in attitudes about black women.

## II

By the late nineteenth century, however, difference would be characterized at its most dualistic: as binary opposition—not just in terms of race and sexuality but of gender and class as well. Such oppositions were effective means of social control at a time when the country was losing its socio-sexual mooring in the face of radical and fundamental changes driven (like now) by a technological revolution. For if the late twentieth century was shaped by advances like the computer, the late nineteenth was adjusting itself around innovations such as the typewriter, the gasoline-driven car, the internal-combustion airplane, the sewing machine, the incandescent light, the phonograph, and the radio. Such innovations bring on new systems of marketing and financing them, and thus new possibilities of wealth, as the late nineteenth century emergence of the Rockefellers, Morgans, Du Ponts, and Carnegies attest. In addition, new corporate cultures increased urbanization, made sex outside of the family more possible and contributed to the increased commodification of sex in forms of pornography and brothels, as it became more associated with pleasure rather than merely reproduction. At the same time, money and the labor-saving devices allowed middle-class women to spend less time doing domestic housework and more time seeking education and reform outside of the home. Add to this growing numbers of immigrants from eastern and southern Europe, the increasing disparity between the haves and the have-nots (by 1890, the poorest one-half of families received one-fifth of all wages and salaries), labor unrest and unemployment that reached 30 percent in some years during the decade, and the need for control becomes obvious. That control was effectively handled through creating categories of difference through binary opposition. For example, maleness was defined by its opposition to femaleness; whiteness by its opposition to blackness. The same dualism applied to the concepts of civilization and primitivity, purity and pollutedness, goodness and evil, public and private. The nineteenth century paradigm regarding sexuality tied all of these oppositions together, which operated to the detriment of blacks and women in general, and black women in particular.

For example, in the late nineteenth century, men were believed to have a particularly rapacious sexual drive that had to be controlled. The last thing needed at home was a woman who had the same sexual drive that men had; what was needed was in binary opposition to perceived male sexuality. What was needed was a woman who did not tempt, and was thus synonymous with "good." And so, although in another period women were thought to have strong, even the more ungovernable, sexual drives, by the late nineteenth century, they were thought to have hardly any libido at all. Furthermore, female sexuality was now considered pathological (Gilman 1985). That meant, of course, that good women did not have erotic feelings, and those who might have had inappropriate urges were recommended to see physicians like J. Marion Sims or Robert Battey, who employed radical gynecological surgery, including clitorectomies, to "correct" masturbation and other forms of sexual passion (D'Emilio, Freedman 1988). Such severe methods were necessary to sustain diametrically opposed identities to "bad" women: lower-class women, and especially black women.

Economically lower-class women fell under the "bad" column by virtue of the fact that they worked outside the home and thus were uninsulated from the sexual aggression of the society. Certainly, it was the former group of women who made up the growing numbers of prostitutes, a label that could fall even on women more drawn to casual sex than to remuneration, and were of great interest to scientists as well as white middle-class female reformers and repressed men. With Sara Bartmann as a model and basis of comparison, their sexual organs were studied, codified, and preserved in jars. Anthropologists such as Cesare Lombrosco, coauthor of the major study of prostitution in the late nineteenth century, *The Prostitute and the Normal Woman* (1893), wrote that the source of their passion and pathology lay in the labia, which reflected a more primitive structure than their upper-class counterparts. One of Lombrosco's students, Abele de Blasio, focused on the buttocks. His specialty was steatopygia (excessive fat on the buttocks), which was also deemed to be a special characteristic of whores— and, of course, black women. They would represent the very root of female eroticism, immorality, and disease.

In the medical metaphors of the day, the sexual organs of sexual women were not only hotbeds of moral pathology, but of disease. In the nineteenth century the great fear was of a sexually transmitted disease that was spreading among the population, was incurable, and after invading the body, disfigured and decomposed it in stages. The name of the disease was syphilis and it was the era's metaphor for the retribution of sexual sin. Despite evidence to the contrary, it was seen as a disease that affected not only persons but groups perceived as both licentious and deviant. Prostitutes of course fell into this category, but it did not seem to affect business. Science even abandoned long held views to accommodate the paradigm. Formerly, it was believed that Christopher Columbus's sailors had introduced the disease to Europe. Now the new wisdom traced it to a form of leprosy that had long been present in Africa and had spread into Europe during the Middle Ages. At the wellspring of this plague were the genital organs of black women (Gilman 1985).

As the epitome of the immorality, pathology, and impurity of the age, black women were seen in dualistic opposition to their upper-class, pure, and passionless white sisters. It was this binary opposition of women (black men's sex drives were not seen as inherently different than those of white men, only less controlled) that was the linchpin of race, class, and even gender difference. It was this opposition, furthermore, that also led to lynching. For it was the white women's qualities, so profoundly missing in black women, that made black men find white women irresistible, and "strangely alluring and seductive," in the words of Phillip Bruce.

### III

Categorizing women through binary opposition had a devastating impact. Even the relatively privileged middle-class white women were subjected to the sexual tyrannies of the age. The opposition of public, a male sphere, and private, a female one, led to conclusions that imprisoned women in the home. The eminent Harvard-trained physician Dr. Edward Clarke, for example, wrote in his influential book *Sex in Education* (1873) that education could ruin a woman's sexual organs. Ideas about male sexual irrepressibility in opposition to women's passionlessness were largely responsible for the fact that "rape in marriage was no crime, nor even generally disapproved," "wife-beating was only marginally criminal," and "incest was common enough to require skepticism that it was tabooed," according to historians Linda Gordon and Ellen Carol DuBois (1983). Women would have to untangle and rework paradigms in order to protect themselves and, as DuBois and Gordon note, exercise their right to enjoy the pleasure of sex. Toward this end, white feminists began challenging the oppositional frameworks concerning the sexuality of men and women. For example, Dr. Elizabeth Blackwell, a physician, offered the startling counteropinion that men and women had equal sexual urges, thus providing a rationale for consensual sex in marriage—and for "free lovers" outside of marriage as well. They also regulated the torrent of male sexuality by insisting that women should only be required to have sex when they wanted to get pregnant. Called "voluntary motherhood," it was a "brilliant" tactic, says Gordon, for it "insinuated a rejection of male sexual domination into a politics of defending and improving motherhood." And at a time when they still had little power or even identity outside of the home, women disdained abortion and contraception, insisting—in a world of depersonalized sex—on maintaining the link between sexual intercourse and reproduction. Consequently, say the authors, the principle of marital mutuality and women's right to say no was established among white middle-class couples in the late nineteenth century. This is perhaps evidenced by the fact that although birth-control methods were not widely approved, the birthrate among white native-born women declined by 1900 to an average of 3.54—50 percent below the level of the previous century!

Despite their enlightened views on such issues as a single standard of sexuality for men and women, as well as others, white feminists fell short on issues like nonmarital rape, probably because of its interracial implications. Although they could bring themselves to counter gender oppositions, those which involved race, and to a lesser extent class, seemed to be beyond their reach. This would be left to black feminists like Ida B. Wells and others who constantly challenged the dualism between good and bad, black and white, and its implications especially as it affected African American women.

Ida Wells simply turned this paradigm on its head, with her own empirical evidence gathered from her investigation of the circumstances of 728 lynchings that had taken place over the previous decade. Her meticulously documented findings would not only challenge the assumption of rape—which also exonerated black women to a significant extent—but also included findings about the lynching of black women as well as their sexual exploitation at the hands of whites. It was black women who needed protection, Wells insisted, as "the rape of helpless Negro g irls and women, which began in slavery days, still continued without reproof from church, state, or press," thus changing their representation to that of victims. Her most dramatic challenge to the paradigm, of course, was her questioning of the passionless purity of southern white women. There were interracial liaisons between black men and white women, Wells published in her findings, but they were consensual and often initiated by white women. In May of 1892, Wells would publish the editorial that got her exiled from the South: "If Southern white men are not careful . . . ," she challenged, "a conclusion will be reached which will be damaging to the moral reputation of their women" (Wells, *On Lynchings* [New York: Arno Press, 1969]). Wells, perhaps the first leader to broach the subject of black sexual oppression after slavery, had now completely challenged the period's assumptions. Black men weren't rapists, white men were; black women weren't doing what "nature prompted," White women were; Wells's framework actually rescued both black and white women from their dehumanized objectification.

When, in reaction to Wells's ideas, the president of the Missouri Press Association, John Jacks, wrote a letter calling all black women "prostitutes, thieves and liars," it was the proverbial straw for nascent regional clubs to come together under a national umbrella in 1896. "Read the letter carefully, and use it discriminately" (it was "too indecent for publication"), challenged Boston activist and editor Josephine St. Pierre Ruffin, and "decide if it be not the time to stand before the world and declare ourselves and our principles." Formed as the National Association for Colored Women (NACW), with a membership that would reach 50,000 by 1916, it would act not only as a means to realize suffrage, education, and community development, but the vessel through which black women challenged, in public, the beliefs that were getting black men lynched and black women raped and exploited. Sexual exploitation was so pervasive that it drove black women north in search of safer climes. "It is a significant and shameful fact that I am constantly in receipt of letters from still unprotected women in the South," complained the nineteenth century Chicago activist Fannie Barrier Williams, "begging me to find employment for their daughters . . . to save them from going into the homes of the South as servants as there is nothing to save them from dishonor and degradation." In 1893, before the predominantly white Congress of Representative Women, Williams challenged that black women shouldn't be disparaged but protected, adding that "I do not want to disturb the serenity of this conference by suggesting why this protection is needed and the kind of man against whom it is needed."

## IV

Nevertheless, despite their extraordinary boldness in bringing this issue before the white public, black women activists were precluded from presenting another kind of critique, one which was also important. The brutal concept of binary opposition prevented them from a frank public discourse concerning intraracial gender relations and sexuality, with which white feminists had been relatively successful. This void was a potentially life-threatening one in a time of adjustment to nonslavery; a time when gender roles, altered first by slavery and then by rapid social and economic changes, were in chaos; a time when the sexuality of both black men and women had to have been twisted by sexism and racism, and now by numbing poverty. Ghettos were congealing, families were in disarray, domestic violence was on the increase, cocaine and alcohol were being abused, and venereal diseases were increasing at an alarming rate. But in this social Darwinistic environment, where blacks were judged harshly, even murderously, by their perceived difference from the white middle-class ideal, where it was believed that the poor deserved to be poor because of moral and character flaws, where a man, as Wells reported, could be lynched under the pretense of beating his wife, how could there be a public discourse about such things? How was one going to explain the higher rates of venereal disease such as syphilis among blacks? And how was one to explain before a hostile white public that the higher rates of infant mortality were largely due to children inheriting "enfeebled constitutions and congenital diseases, inherited from parents suffering from the effects of sexual immorality and debauchery" (25), as an 1897 report, *Proceedings of the Second Conference for the Study of Problems Concerning Negro City Life*, under the general direction of W. E. B. Du Bois, then at Atlanta University, stated?

Publicly voicing such concerns in a society defined by binary opposition could leave blacks in general and black women in particular vulnerable to the violent whims of whites. It is no wonder that the issues of intraracial sexuality and gender have long been tabooed in public discourse. At the same time, not voicing these concerns has left the community, especially women, bereft of the help and protection so needed. As an anonymous black woman writer, one of the few who dared break the silence of intraracial sexuality, wrote to the *Independent* in 1904, "We poor colored wage-earners of the South are fighting a terrible battle, on the one hand, we are assailed by white men, and on the other hand, we are assailed by Black men who should be our natural protectors." There are sexist backlashes within our community, too.

For black women, the accumulated effects of assault and the inability to "eradicate negative social and sexual images of their womanhood" had "powerful ideological consequences," concludes historian Darlene Hine. To protect themselves, she observes, black women created what she calls "a culture of dissemblance." Hine defines this as "the behavior and attitudes of Black women that created the appearance of openness and disclosure but actually shielded the truth of their inner lives and selves from their oppressors" (292)—and I would add, even from ourselves. This is the reason, I think, why we have not forced such sex/gender discourses, seen primarily as disclosures, in our community. It is why feminist issues, though not women's rights issues, are more problematic for us. Not only is feminism specifically associated with our historic binary opposites—middle-class white women—it demands an analysis of sexual issues. This is why to break through the silence and traditional sense of racial solidarity is such a controversial act for us. This, in turn, largely accounts for the vitriol earned by those who indicate a public discourse on sexuality in their work, such as Alice Walker in *The Color Purple* or Ntozake Shange in *For Colored Girls.* . . . I think these traditional notions are also the reason why Anita Hill's appearance was so controversial in the black community. Those who publicly supported her, namely black scholars and the National Coalition of 100 Black Women—formed in 1970 when the women's movement was making an impact—were those in touch with gender issues and their role in the needed transformation of our institutions and communities. This is the window black women writers have pointed toward but that Anita Hill, in her first-person, clear, unswervingly direct testimony before the public, has actually opened. It was an act of great inner courage and conviction, to turn back the veil of our Du Boisian double consciousness. It was an act that provided clarity about our new status in the late twentieth century.

## V

There would be some that would argue that that status is no more empowered than it was a hundred years ago, thus requiring that we use the same strategies of solidarity. There is no question that, in some ways, the essential aspects of racism and sexism still affect us. This was evident in the statement "African American Women in Defense of Ourselves," first appearing in the *New York Times* as a paid ad on November 17, 1991 signed by 1,603 black women, most of them scholars, in response to the treatment of Anita Hill during the hearings. Insisting that the "malicious defamation of Professor Hill insulted all women of African American descent," it concluded that "throughout U.S. history, Black women have been stereotyped as immoral, insatiable, perverse; the initiators in all sexual contacts—abusive or otherwise. . . . As Anita Hill's experience demonstrates, Black women who speak of these matters are not likely to be believed. . . ." The words sound very much like those that led women to organize the NACW almost exactly a century ago, and in fact, the similar conditions that previously made us want to wrap ourselves in that protective skin have come back around with a vengeance. Certainly, the late twentieth century, with its dislocating technological revolution, rapacious moneymaking, excesses of sex, guilt and consumption, and incurable diseases viewed as Old Testament warnings should give us pause. For when such a confluence occurs, there are cultural reflexes to create categories of difference, including sexual difference, with all of its murderous Willie Horton, Bensonhurst, David Duke, and Central Park gang-rape implications. And although we may have passed the era that could take a Hottentot Venus seriously, we cannot rest assured that advances in science will save us from such folly. That respectable journals would make connections between green monkeys and African women, for example, or trace the origin of AIDS to African prostitutes—the polluted sexual organs of black women—reveals our continued vulnerability to racist ideology. It tells us that concepts of racial difference (in this situation, sexual practices) can still be used as weapons of degradation, and that the idea of difference turns on sexuality, and sexuality, in this culture, is loaded with concepts of race, gender, and class. This explains in part why the backlashes against women, black and nonblack, as well as race, carry a virulence that goes beyond the fear of competition or the sharing of power once so handily monopolized by others.

On the other hand, there have been some fundamental dramatic changes, largely realized by our own struggle for equality and empowerment, that allow us, in fact demand, a new strategy. For although racism still exists, our situation has changed since the sixties in spite of it. It has changed because of two interrelated developments: the sexual revolution and de jure deseg-regation. They are interrelated because sex was the principle around which wholesale segregation and discrimination was organized with the ultimate objective of preventing intermarriage (D'Emilio, Freedman 1988). The sexual revolution, however, separated sexuality from reproduction, and so diluted the ideas about purity—moral, racial, and physical.

Both desegregation and the sexual revolution make dissemblance and suppression in the name of racial solidarity anachronistic, for they were prescribed to divert perceptions of difference, based on sexual difference between black women and white. Despite the tenacity about ideas of dif-ference, recent sociopolitical developments—further codified by feminist theory as well as black studies—make binary opposition as a sole indicator of meaning passé.

In the meantime, increasing sexual aggression, including date rape on col-lege campuses that tend to be underreported by black women; the number of "children having children," the plague of domestic violence, the breakup of families, and the spread of fatal venereal disease among African Ameri-cans at a time when we have more "rights" than ever before, tells us that gender issues are just as important—if not more so—in the black commu-nity as racial issues have always been. More than ever before it is essential that we advance a discourse on sexuality that is liberating for those who engage in it and truncating to the souls of those who don't. As Naima Major, former director of the National Black Women's Health Project (NBWHP)—one of the few black institutions that regularly engages in sexuality issues—said to me, most of the black women she sees "seem to cut themselves off at the waist," even when they are coming to talk specifically about sexuality.

This is particularly alarming in view of the fact that we are in a sexu-ally aggressive era, one where sex is commodified and often depersonal-ized, especially for young women. Their worlds were the subject of a study of adolescents aged fifteen to seventeen, conducted by Pat McPherson and Michelle Fine, and their observations were disturbing. From the sto-ries of these young women, the authors surmised that their generation is more likely to "be aware of, witness to, and victim of" male sexual abuse among both peers and family. Their sexual experiences with peers are not characterized by learning the meaning or enjoyment of sex, or even mak-ing choices about engaging in it, but in protecting themselves from what is viewed (as in the past) as the irrepressible sexual drives of the men in their lives. A black adolescent in this interracial group spoke about not her own sexual preferences but the need to satisfy, indeed mollify, men quickly through fellatio so that the evening could end early, and hassle-free. And the authors noted that female adolescents also protect themselves by suppressing signs of their gender: by becoming "one of the boys" through not only dress, but through even misogynist behavior and attitudes. These are issues that were addressed a century ago, under similar sociosexual conditions, but the solutions have not been passed on through families or social institutions. We must begin to do it.

The analysis of how sex/gender systems apply to us in the 1990s becomes urgent when we see that *58 percent* of black women beyond the age of eighteen *never* use any form of birth control, according to a 1991 study conducted by the National Council of Negro Women (NCNW). Yet only 1 percent of those women said that they wanted to get pregnant, and only 2 percent said that they did not know how to use birth control. Does this finding indicate ambivalence about separating sexuality from reproduction despite not wanting a child? Does it indicate the desire, however sublimated, to become pregnant? Or, as I suspect, is the finding a reflection of the fact that their male partners look down on birth control?

One thing we know, there seems to be what one might call a cult of motherhood in our community. How else might one interpret the finding of journalist Leon Dash in his book *When Children Want Children* (1988), that nearly a fourth of all unmarried teenage mothers intentionally become pregnant? What does motherhood mean to these youngsters? The ability to exercise maternal authority in lieu of other avenues of self-esteem and empowerment; rebellion against the depersonalization of sex; or perhaps, as a century ago, does this finding represent the effort to control male sexuality? The answers to these questions are important, as the babies of teenagers are more apt to be underweight and thus have learning and other physical disabilities. There is also tragedy in another statistic: 48 percent of the teenagers who intentionally got pregnant later regretted their decision.

Even college students, according to a report by the Black Women's Health Project, indicated a conflict about delaying childbearing in the face of "women's traditional and proper role as mother"—"indeed as a respected 'matriarch' in a community beset by failing family structures." Of course, there is also male pressure insinuated in some of these findings. The college students said that they felt intense pressure from male partners who wanted to be fathers—one of the few avenues toward manhood?—as well as from cultural and religious leaders not to have abortions. Although one has to respect religious and/or moral views about this, you have to wonder if young women are making rational, informed decisions about these things—lives depend on it.

Another issue not engaged adequately is one that Leon Dash discovered after hours of interviews with teenagers over the course of an entire year—

the time it takes to get beyond their personal dissemblance strategies. Many of the motives behind sexual decisions—for better sometimes, but often for worse—were shaped by the fact that their families had a tremendous amount of sexual abuse within them, sometimes traced through two, three, or more generations. Ironically, Dash's decision to publicly reveal such information caused more consternation among self-conscious middle-class blacks than the dire implications of the information itself.

If all of this sounds very nineteenth century, there is a reason for it. Black men and women have not had their own sexual revolution—the one we couldn't have before. We need a discourse that will help us understand modern ideas about gender and sex/gender systems, about male privilege, and about power relations; about the oppressive implications of pornography—something even at least one Harvard professor seems not to understand.

In our considerations of Anita Hill, it is important to understand that she spoke not of a physical transgression on the part of Clarence Thomas, but a verbal one masked in pornographic language. Pornography, "a fantasy salvation that inspires non-fantasy acts of punishment for uppity females," as one historian put it, speaks specifically to power relations between men and women. For African Americans these relations remain unanalyzed in the light of the empowerment of black male elites like those represented by Thomas, who, since the seventies, have emerged as gatekeepers for the upward mobility of all blacks in the newly accessible corporate, political, academic and business spheres of influence. It is men, not women, who control the sociosexual and professional relationships in the black community. Among other notions that must be dispensed with is the weak male/strong female patriarchal paradigm that clouds so much of our thinking about ourselves.

Implicit in Hill's testimony is the challenge to transcend a past that once protected but now twists the deepest sense of ourselves and our identities. The silences and dissemblance in the name of a misguided solidarity must end. A modern and transformative discourse must begin. Anita Hill has broken through. Let us follow.

## Notes

In this essay, Gerda Lerner's definition of gender can be found in *The Creation of Patriarchy* (New York: Oxford University Press, 1987). Secondary sources regarding Phillip A. Bruce can be found in *The Black Family in Slavery and Freedom, 1750–1925* by Herbert G. Gutman (New York: Pantheon, 1976); and Jacquelyn Dowd Hall explores lynching and rape in *Revolt Against Chivalry: Jessie Daniel Ames and the Women's Campaign Against Lynching* (New York: Columbia University Press, 1971). The issue of the

*Independent* referred to is dated March 17, 1904; and explications of Sara Bartmann, the Hottentot Venus, can be found in Sander L. Gilman's essay "Black Bodies, White Bodies: Toward an Iconography of Female Sexuality in Late Nineteenth-Century Art, Medicine and Literature," published in Henry Louis Gates, ed., *"Race," Writing and Difference* (Chicago: University of Chicago Press, 1985, 1986). Analysis of sexuality during different periods in American history can be found in John D'Emilio and Estelle Freedman, *Intimate Matters: The History of Sexuality in America* (New York: Harper & Row, 1988). Discussions of the National Association of Colored Women, black women's status in the nineteenth century and Fannie B. Williams's and Ida B. Wells's antilynching campaign can be found in *When and Where I Enter: The Impact of Black Women on Race and Sex in America* (New York: Morrow, 1984). The article by Barbara Fields is entitled "Ideology and Race in American History" and is found in J. Kousser and James M. McPherson, eds., *Race, Region and Reconstruction* (New York: Oxford University Press, 1982). The references to Gordon and DuBois are found in Ellen DuBois and Linda Gordon, "Seeking Ecstasy on the Battlefield: Danger and Pleasure in Nineteenth Century Feminist Sexual Thought," in *Feminist Studies,* vol. 9., no. 1 (Spring) 1983. The quote by Anna Julia Cooper is in her *Voice from the South* (1893), reprinted by Negro Universities Press (New York) in 1969, pp.68–69. The report cited under the direction of W. E. B. Du Bois, about blacks' health and sexuality in the late nineteenth century, is entitled *Proceedings of the Second Conference for the Study of Problems Concerning Negro City Life,* originally published by Atlanta University Publications. See vol. I, reprinted by Octagon Books, 1968. The explanation of the culture of dissemblance is found in Darlene Clark Hine, "Rape and the Inner Lives of Black Women in the Middle West: Preliminary Thoughts on the Culture of Dissemblance," in Ellen Carol DuBois and Vicki L. Ruiz, eds., *Unequal Sisters: A Multicultural Reader in U.S. Women's History* (New York: Routledge, 1990). The study on contemporary adolescents is "Hungry for an Us: Our Girl Group Talks About Sexual and Racial Identities," by Pat Macpherson and Michelle Fine. It will be published in Janice M. Irvine, ed., *Sexual Cultures: Adolescence, Community and the Construction of Identity* (Philadelphia: Temple University Press, 1993). The women-of-color study was underwritten by the National Council of Negro Women with the Communications Consortium Media Center and is entitled "Women of Color Reproductive Health Poll," August 29, 1991. The book in which Leon Dash published his findings on pregnant teenagers is entitled *When Children Want Children: The Urban Crisis of Teenage Childbearing* (New York: Morrow, 1989). The report issued in 1991 by the National Black Women's Health Project is entitled "Report: Reproductive Health Program of the National Black Women's Health Project."

# Phallus(ies) of Interpretation
## Toward Engendering the
## Black Critical "I"

*Ann duCille*

1993

*"'Love, Oh, love, Oh careless love.' That's the story. It's in the songs. It's in the books. And everybody knows it. . . . The only problem is that the story almost everybody knows is almost totally false."*[1]

Writing in *Ebony* in August of 1981, black historian Lerone Bennett, Jr., accused contemporary black writers of creating "a new literature based on the premise that Black America is a vast emotionless wasteland of hustlin' men and maimed women." As Bennett heard and read them, lines and lyrics about ceaseless sex and heedless love, like those immortalized by Bessie Smith in "Careless Love" and by Robert Hayden in "Homage to the Empress of the Blues," his tribute to Bessie, have helped construct a false history of tortuous gender relations among African Americans.[2] Such lyrics, like a great deal of modern black literature, in Bennett's view, tell a story of a "Black love deficit" almost entirely false. "As a matter of hard historical fact," he wrote, "the true story of Black love—love colored by, love *blackened* by the Black experience—is the exact opposite of the traditional myth." The "true story," as Bennett told it, is that "Black men and women—despite slavery, despite segregation, despite everything—created a modern love song in life and art that is the loveliest thing dreamed or sung this side of the seas" (32).

Bennett's "true story"—what black feminist critic Deborah McDowell might call his black family romance[3]—is seductive. It affirms what many of us (us being here African American men and women) would like to believe about our past and the possibilities for our future *together*. But, as Bennett argued in his essay, the story of an all-enduring black love is a plot many modern-day African American writers have rejected in favor of what he is hardly alone in labeling literary gender bating and male bashing.

Bennett named no one in particular in his generic indictment of artists who have gotten the story wrong, but throughout the past two decades, scores of other black male scholars and critics have pointed accusing fingers at such black women writers as Alice Walker, Toni Morrison, Gayl Jones, Ntozake Shange, and, most recently, Terry McMillan. These writers are chief among the many black women artists charged not only with histori-cal inaccuracy but with racial infidelity as well—with in effect putting their gender before their race, their (white) feminism before their black family—and inventing historical fictions that serve a feminist rather than a black nationalist agenda.

Indeed, for black women, membership (real or assumed[4]) in the sis-terhood of feminists is in some circles an unpardonable sin punishable by excommunication, if not from the race, certainly from the ranks of those who have authored the sacred texts of the race's canon. As one pair of critics put it: black feminists have drawn "a simplistic sex line in society" that has put them "on the wrong side of some fundamental questions"[5]—questions which presumably have more to do with race than with gender. One can be black *or* a woman, but claiming both identities places one on shaky familial ground, outside the black family romance.

In the minds or, more important, in the *critiques* of influential black men of letters such as critic Addison Gayle and poet/novelist Ishmael Reed, contemporary black women authors have not only miswritten the romance, they have slandered black men in the process of inventing their own feminist fictions. As McDowell notes in her incisive reading of this dubious battle of the sexes, while "female readers see an implicit affirmation of *black women*," many male readers see "a programmatic assault on black men" (75–76). What is for female writers like Alice Walker a commitment "to exploring the oppressions, the insanities, the loyalties, and the triumphs of black women," is for male readers like Gayle and Reed "a hatchet job" directed viciously against black men or a libel campaign akin to "the kind of propaganda spread by the Ku Klux Klan and the American Nazi party."[6] What for black women is an effort to write themselves into history is for Gayle and Reed a malicious form of myth-making that holds black men, black love, and black history hostage to a portrait of the past too painful to be anything but a lie. Addison Gayle has spoken in a particularly telling way to this nagging question of historical truth: "If we look at [Alice Walker's] work in history," he said in an interview with Roseann P. Bell, "particularly if there is any great deal of accuracy in her portrayal of Black men, then we're in more trouble than I thought we were, *and I thought we were okay*" (214).

In calling up these critiques, charges, and counter charges, I do not want merely to resurrect ancient arguments that pit black men and women

against each other or simply to retrace ground already ably covered by scholars such as Deborah McDowell and Calvin Hernton,[7] who has also analyzed this text-based battle of the sexes. Nor in placing in opposition black
women writers and black male critics do I mean to imply that male readers
have been singularly disdainful of the "feminist fictions" of contemporary
black women writers or that only male readers have offered such criticism.[8]
Rather, what I hope to do in this essay is to explore from a slightly different angle some of the problematic, gender-loaded assumptions and racial
imperatives that underpin many male-authored critiques of black women's
fiction: (1) that there is an essential black experience; (2) that there is an
absolute historical truth; (3) that art absolutely must tell the truth; (4) that
black men and women in America are "okay" in their erotic relations with
one another. I want to examine the different conceptions of *I* and *You—Self*
and *Other*—that are at stake in a race-conscious, gender-bound criticism in
which "black is beautiful" is the only "truth"—the sole story (or maybe *soul*
story)—we are allowed to tell.

Because art is invention, "truth" is generally held to be a false standard
by which to evaluate a writer's work. This should be the case whether the
issue is Alice Walker's representation of black men or Spike Lee's treatment
of black women. Yet, as I argue in this essay, this is precisely the leap of
faith that critics of African American literature continue to make. Texts are
transparent documents that must tell the truth as I know it. Failure to tell
*my* truth not only invalidates the text, it also discredits, de-authorizes, and
on occasion deracializes the writer. Truth, however, like beauty, is in the eye
and perhaps the experience of the beholder.

The beholder metaphor suggests a problematic of the gaze—of power
and perspective—worth pursuing. It invites us to question the authority of
the critical *I* to constitute the *Other* it beholds, even in the midst of reading
the *Other's* celebration of its own subjectivity. As black men and women, our
racial alterity makes us always-already other—always-already beheld—but
what happens when blacks read each other, when the beheld becomes the
beholder, when black men read black women reading black men? How does
a black male reader constitute himself as the center of seeing in a female-
authored text? Must the beheld always be constituted in terms of her difference from the beholder? Is it possible for the male *I* to read the female text
of others without reinscribing hierarchies of one kind or another, without
in effect de-authorizing and even deracializing the female beheld?

While I generally shy away from efforts to define distinctly male and
female ways of knowing, in this essay I want to take the risk of gender essentialism and codify this great divide as a battle between colliding and collud-
ing subjectivities, between male and female stories, between phallocentric

and gynocentric "truths." The collisions of gender I address in this essay are all the more difficult to tease out, it seems to me, because of the collusions of race—the shared racial alterity—that historically have made it hard to be at once black and woman.

While I readily acknowledge that my own readings of history and literature are colored by my indivisible blackwomaness, this essay is not intended as a black feminist manifesto or as an attack on male critics, on masculinism, on phallocentrism, or on what Elaine Showalter calls "phallic criticism": masculinist criticism which focuses on the phallus as principal signifier and on man as principal referent. I come in effect to praise Caesar, not to bury him—to legitimize phallic criticism, not to condemn it. Phallocentrism and masculinism have become for the most part loaded terms—pejoratives—whose invocation often makes men jumpy in the same way accusations of racism tend to make white people defensive. My own use of the terms, however, is practical rather than pejorative or metaphoric. It is based on my belief that as scholars, as critics, as intellectuals, we need to be up front about the roles that sex and gender, as well as race and culture, play in shaping our interpretive strategies. As I argue throughout this essay, we need to engender the critical *I*, "who reads here"—to use Houston Baker's phrase—and call masculinist, as well as feminist, criticism by its rightful name.

As I also argue, an important step in this naming ceremony is surrendering the myth that our shared racial alterity—our common American experience of slavery, institutionalized racism, and discrimination—makes black men and women "brothers under the skin," who are at heart "okay" with each other. "The enemy is not Black men," Addison Gayle has said. "The enemy is not Black men, not Black women, it's this country" (Bell 214). While I can hardly quarrel with the point that both black men and black women have been victims of American racism, the "we're okay" rendition of African American history carries with it a decidedly masculine bias that factors out the sexism which has indeed made some black men the enemy.

If we didn't know it or refused to see it before, we have only to look as far as Anita Hill and Clarence Thomas to see that black men and women in America are no more "okay" than the patriarchal system that has reared us. Our dis-ease is embedded in what Michele Wallace describes as our almost deliberate ignorance about the sexual politics, power relations, and social pathology that have both defined and been defined by our experience in this country.[9] While there may be an advantage for black men in whitewashing "black love" into the "loveliest thing dreamed or sung this side of the seas," many contemporary black female writers realize that for women the costs of sustaining such myths are continued harassment, brutalization, insanity, suicide, or even death.

Long before the Thomas/Hill hearings declared to the world the degree to which black men and women in America are not okay, black women had ceased to sing the lovely little love song that Bennett and Gayle would have us all claim as the true story of black America. In singing a different tune, writers such as Walker, Morrison, and Jones have committed what phallic criticism necessarily reads as racial heresy. They have broken with what I call the "discourse of deference"—a nationalistic, masculinist ideology of uplift, which has historically demanded female deference in the cause of empowering the race by elevating its men.

As McDowell and others have demonstrated, this is precisely the charge Mel Watkins levels against Jones, Shange, and Walker in his infamous review in the *New York Times*. "[T]hose black women writers who have chosen black men as the target have set themselves outside of a tradition as old as black American literature itself," he asserts. "They have, in effect, put themselves at odds with what seems to be an unspoken but almost universally accepted covenant among black writers."[10]

Watkins suggests, in other words, that in naming as oppressors black men as well as white, black women novelists are acting outside black history, writing outside the racial fold, the colored community. But Watkins's community is first and foremost the world of men. Since he acknowledges in the same article that until recently the most acclaimed black fiction writers were men, the ancient tradition to which he refers is not, it seems to me, a "universally accepted covenant," but an understanding among men—a kind of gentlemen's agreement, as it were, that suborns female silence in the name of racial empowerment.

In a perhaps more theoretically sophisticated, though ultimately no less male-identified, reading, W. Lawrence Hogue attributes this break with history and tradition to the influence of what he calls "the feminist discourse" of the sixties on the work of black women writers like Alice Walker. Rooting his analysis in Foucault's concept of discursive formation, Hogue argues that Walker's first novel *The Third Life of Grange Copeland* (1970)—along with other feminist texts such as Jones's *Corregidora* (1975) and *Eva's Man* (1976) and Morrison's *The Bluest Eye* (1970) and *Sula* (1973)—necessarily invents its own African American historical myths in order to validate its feminist assumptions about women's reality and existence. While he praises the novel for its attempt to show how the powers and pressures of white patriarchy cause black men "bruised and beaten by the system" to batter and abuse their wives and children, he also argues that the novel manipulates certain historical "facts" to meet its feminist ideologeme.[11] For while

*The Third Life* indeed indicts the system, it also holds black men culpable for their own allegiance to and reinscription of the patriarchal values that reduce black women to mules of the world. While the Copeland men blame the white man for their own behavior ("white folks just don't let nobody *feel* like doing right"), the text blames as well black men's complicity in replicating an overarching system of domination.

Hogue, I think, makes the right theoretical move in acknowledging feminist fiction as invention. Unfortunately, however, this theoretical move is not fully realized in practice, for he ultimately treats the discursive strategies and emplotments he attributes to Walker, Jones, Morrison, et al., as if they are unique to feminist fiction rather than properties of textual production more generally. Novels like *The Third Life*, he argues, are completely silent about the thousands of black men who refused to be dehumanized by a dehumanizing system—men who "maintained their humanity, their integrity, and their sanity by turning honestly and genuinely to the church and Christianity"—men who "openly and vehemently defied the system, even at the expense of their own lives" (104–05).

As examples of such heroic black men, Hogue offers Ernest Gaines's characters Ned Douglass and Jimmy Aaron from *The Autobiography of Miss Jane Pittman* (1971) and Marcus Payne from *Of Love and Dust* (1967). Like Aaron and Douglass, Marcus Payne, Hogue writes, "refuses to accept the constrictions of the system. He strikes out against it and meets his death" (105). It seems from these and other similar examples that Hogue actually wants black women novelists to write Ernest Gaines's stories rather than their own. Like Bennett and Gayle, he seems ultimately to believe in a set of true historical "facts" that male writers such as Ernest Gaines have presented with greater fidelity to *the* African American experience than black women novelists.

Moreover, in the discursive formation of his own argument, Hogue transforms important textual "facts" and omits significant, telling details. He does not mention, for example, that Marcus Payne strikes out against the system in somewhat the same fashion as Alice Walker's character Brownfield Copeland—with his penis—by sleeping with the white boss's white wife. Seemingly following the advice of Eldrige Cleaver, Ernest Gaines has created in Marcus Payne a character who fucks the white man by fucking his wife, a character who in effect uses his own tool to dismantle the master's house and is destroyed in the process.

Though far less caustic than the condemnations of Watkins, Gayle, and Reed, Hogue's analysis has inscribed in it precisely the gender blind spots and biases I want to illuminate in this essay. His reading of *The Third Life* and other feminist texts is dependent on his reading of such male-authored and authorized novels as *The Autobiography of Miss Jane Pittman* and *Of Love and Dust*. Here as elsewhere, the work of contemporary black women writers is evaluated in terms of its difference from the work of men—from the true history, from the normative master narrative. Curiously enough, however, this would-be normative narrative is based on an understanding of the past so inherently masculine—so subliminally rooted in the phallus—that sleeping with the white overseer's wife is read completely unself-consciously as a revolutionary act. Put another way, in this decidedly male-centered reading of African American literature and history, penile erection is equated with political insurrection.

The difference between Hogue's sense of history and heroism and Walker's is a critical difference—a critical difference that may cut to the core of the controversy over male and female texts, masculinist and feminist readings. It may be that at the heart of this controversy lie not only different notions of truth, art, and history, but very different readings of the phallus and the penis. What Houston Baker reads as the cosmic force of the black phallus in *Invisible Man*, for example, Toni Morrison exposes as the black penis that rapes and impregnates a twelve-year-old girl in *The Bluest Eye*. What for Ellison is symbolic action, is for Morrison a father's rape of his daughter. What for Baker is an aristocratic procreativity turned inward, is in Morrison's novel "a bolt of desire [that] ran down [Cholly Breelove's] genitals, giving it length." What Baker calls "outgoing phallic energy," Morrison names inbreeding lust, a lust bordered by politeness that makes a father want to fuck his daughter—tenderly. "But the tenderness would not hold," Morrison writes in parodic undertones, which at least one male critic has mistaken for sympathy.[12] "The tightness of her vagina was more than he could bear. His soul seemed to slip down to his guts and fly out into her, and the gigantic thrust he made into her then provoked the only sound she made—a hollow suck of air in the back of her throat."[13]

It is interesting to note—and perhaps telling for my argument—that Baker repeatedly uses the term phallus—as Lacanian signifier, as originator of meaning—when he is talking about the action of the penis, a word that never appears in his extended reading of the Trueblood Incident. As he himself has argued elsewhere: "The PHALLUS is, of course, to be distinguished from the penis. The PHALLUS is not a material object but a signifier of the Father, or, better, of the Father's LAW."[14] Morrison's portrait of incest complicates what it seems to me both Ellison and Baker have oversimplified. It reminds us that signifier and signified are not so easily separable. For while the phallus may not be a material object, its action, its "phallic energy," its "Father LAW" are not immaterial—certainly not to Matty Lou Trueblood, Pecola Breedlove, and other objects of its power.

Baker's reading, like Ellison's narrative, erases the penis that rapes and impregnates the daughter as it privileges the phallus that fathers and rules what Baker describes as "the entire clan or tribe, of Afro-America." Baker's interpretation is, in perhaps the most literal sense possible, phallic criticism. But again, my motive in labeling it such is not to denigrate it but to denature it, to localize it, to wrest it of the illusion of universality and objectivity and to acknowledge that it, like feminist criticism, is situational, vested with a variety of imperatives.

The effort to denature phallic criticism or masculinist criticism must make an important second move, however—one that resists polarizing the interpretive process along easily drawn gender lines. For I do not mean to imply that only men do such readings or that such readings are the only kind male critics do. I would be remiss if I did not point out, for example, that one of the sharpest critiques of the gender biases of both Ellison's novel and Baker's reading has come from black male scholar Michael Awkward. Calling *The Bluest Eye* a "purposefully feminist revision" of Ellison's masculinist reading of incest, Awkward writes: "Baker's essay mirrors the strategies by which Trueblood (and Trueblood's creator) validates male perceptions of incest while, at the same time, silencing the female voice or relegating it to the evaluative periphery."[15]

In prose, in poetry, in song, modern black women artists speak, write, and sing through such silences. Complementing and by all means challenging male perspectives with their own, they offer up different and often difficult tunes—somebody-done-somebody-wrong-songs that not only indict as oppressors black men as well as white, but that also identify love of men as the root of women's oppression.

Zora Neale Hurston's character Nanny makes such an identification in *Their Eyes Were Watching God* (1937). "'Dat's de very prong all us black women gits hung on,'" she tells her granddaughter Janie. "'Dis love! Dat's just whut's got us uh pullin' and uh haulin' and sweatin' and doin' from can't see in de mornin' till can't see at night.'"[16] In placing these words in her character's mouth—in identifying "dis love" as a potentially devastating force in the lives of black women—Hurston gave voice to a concern that reverberates throughout modern African American women's fiction. From Jessie Fauset and Nella Larsen writing in the 1920s to Alice Walker and Toni Morrison writing in the 1990s, black women novelists have been consistently concerned with exploring on paper what Hortense Spillers calls "the politics of intimacy"[17] and with confronting the consequences, burdens, and mixed blessings of love, men, and marriage in the lives of African American women.

But Hurston is also signifying, I think. For the prong on which women are impaled is not just simply "dis love" but "dat penis"—the domain of dominating power. At least one of my male colleagues has accused me of over-reading in making this claim. "'Dis love,'" he insists, "is just love." I remain convinced, however, that this sexual double entendre, like so many others in *Their Eyes*, is Hurston's invention, not mine. Part of what catches women up, Hurston seems to me to say, is not just their penchant for confusing and conflating sex and love, love and marriage, dream and truth, but their tendency to measure manliness by the same yardstick as men, to believe like men in the power vested in the penis.

Janie's implicit understanding of penile power is made explicit when she calls Joe out, as it were—when she finally responds in kind (and then some) to his harassment. After years of verbal and physical abuse, Janie delivers an ultimately fatal blow to her big-voiced husband's power source by telling him publicly that all he is is a big voice. To Joe's taunt that she "ain't no young gal no mo'" she replies:

> "Naw, Ah ain't no young gal no mo' but den Ah ain't no old woman neither. Ah reckon Ah looks mah age too. But Ah'm uh woman every inch of me, and Ah know it. Dat's uh whole lot more'n you kin say. You big-bellies around here and puts out a lot of brag, but 'tain't no thin' to it but your big voice. . . . When you pull down yo' britches, you look lak de change uh life." (122–23)

So saying, Janie announces to his male subjects that the mighty Mayor Joe Starks is sexually inadequate, that he can't get it up, that he's not enough man for "every inch" of woman she still is. It is significant, of course, that Janie reckons her sexuality by the male measurement of inches and signifies to all present that Joe's shriveled penis doesn't stand up. Hers is a series of well-placed punches that land below the belt, that not only rob Joe of "his illusion of irresistible maleness," but that metaphorically *feminize* him by linking his impotence to female menopause—"de change uh life." In the wake of Janie's words, Joe's "vanity bled like a flood." It is a bloodletting—a symbolic castration—that ultimately ends in the mayor's death.

Like Janie, Mem Copeland, Brownfield's brutalized wife in *The Third Life*, eventually effects a shift in the balance of power within her marriage by attacking her husband below the belt with a shotgun strategically aimed at his genitals. Thrusting the "cool hard gun barrel down between his thighs," Mem for a moment acts outside the submissive role she has accepted for nine years. "'To think,'" she tells Brownfield at gunpoint, "'I put myself to the trouble of wanting to git married to you. . . . And just think how many times I done got my head beat by you just so you could feel a little bit like a man.'"[18] Wielding the shotgun (described as smooth and black and big) like a penis and threatening to shoot her husband's balls off if he doesn't abide by *her* rules, Mem negotiates a better life for herself and her family. She moves them out of their rat-infested country shack into a city house, "a 'mansion' of four sheet-rocked rooms" (102). The jobs she finds for herself and for Brownfield bring a sense of progress and new-found, if short-lived, prosperity to the Copeland household.

"If he had done any of it himself," the text tells us, "if he had insisted on the move, he might not have resisted the comfort" Mem's ingenuity brings the family (103). But instead Brownfield's bruised manhood flares tragically, and he plots to destroy his wife by using her own female body against her, twice impregnating her in a deliberate, calculated attempt to undermine her already fragile health. Mem's shotgun was a great equalizer, but ultimately Brownfield's penis proves the more powerful weapon. "'[Y]ou thought I fucked you 'cause I wanted it,'" he says to Mem in bitter triumph. "'Your trouble is you just never learned how not to git pregnant'" (107). Some radical feminist readers might argue that in surrendering to heterosexual desire—in sleeping with her husband—Mem, in effect, collaborates with her own assassin. For, not content with nearly impregnating her to death, Brownfield eventually shoots and kills Mem with a shotgun. Patriarchy in this text is indeed black as well as white, and its penile oppression is lethal.

Toni Morrison gives a similarly oppressive, though less physically violent, face to patriarchy in *Song of Solomon*. And, like Hurston and Walker, she locates the source of man's abusive power between his legs. "You have never picked up anything heavier than your own feet or solved a problem harder than fourth-grade arithmetic," her character Lena says to her brother Milkman. "Where do you get the *right* to decide our lives? I'll tell you where," she continues. "From that hog's gut that hangs down between your legs."[19] As a parting shot at her brother and the value system and gender codes that have made his male life of greater value than her female one, Lena says: "You are a sad, pitiful, stupid, selfish, hateful man. I hope your little hog's gut stands you in good stead, and that you take good care of it, because you don't have anything else." Her message to Milkman resembles Janie's message to Joe. While this verbal assault on male genitalia does not kill or castrate, it does send Milkman Dead on a search that eventually brings him into a different quality of manhood.

Like Hurston and Walker, Morrison places the penis under scrutiny, at once acknowledging and problematizing its power. If dominative male power, as these writers suggest, is indeed located below the belt, disempowering men means not simply placing the penis under scrutiny, but under erasure. This is precisely the action the title character takes in Gayl Jones's highly controversial second novel *Eva's Man*.

After a month as "the willing prisoner of Davis Carter's love"[20]—to use one critic's characterization—Eva Medina Canada first poisons the man who has held her "captive" and then mutilates his dead body by severing his penis with her teeth:

> I opened his trousers and played with his penis. My mouth, my teeth, my tongue went inside his trousers. I raised blood. . . . I got back on the bed and squeezed his dick in my teeth. I bit down hard . . .
> I got the silk handkerchief he used to wipe me after we made love, and wrapped his penis in it. I laid it back inside his trousers, zipped him up.[21]

Davis becomes for Eva an *Everyman*, and as such he is made to atone for the sins of a myriad of men (and an eight-year-old boy with a dirty popsicle stick) who have sexually abused her throughout her life. Here, too, however, it is not simply men who are under attack but the penis.

Coming on the heels of *Corregidora* the year before, the publication of *Eva's Man* in 1976 set off a hue and cry of foul among many black male critics, for whom Davis Carter's mutilated member is evidently more than just phallus, more than simply signifier. While the specter of a bloody, gnawed, dismembered member is surely horrifying for all audiences, it is, I suspect, particularly so for male readers whose connection to the severed organ is more than metaphorical. Yet there is more at issue in the negative critical reception of *Eva's Man* than mere castration anxiety, just as there is more at stake in the controversy over the feminist text than just negative portrayals of black men. Black men do not necessarily fare so well in such sacred, male-authored texts as *Native Son*, *Go Tell It on the Mountain*, and *Invisible Man*. Yet these novels continue to be championed by some of the same critics who have condemned *Eva's Man*. Moreover, the castration of the protagonist in Invisible Man is acknowledged and accepted as symbolic in a way that Davis Turner's castration is not, even though for all its graphic language it, too, I would argue, is metaphoric. What is actually at stake, it seems to me, are all the larger questions: Who holds the power? Who owns the black body? Who can tell the black story? Who can write the true black history? Who gets to say "I'm okay"? Who gets to sing the true blues? All of these larger questions are played out *masterfully* in Jones's first novel *Corregidora*.

*Corregidora* is literally and figuratively a blues novel; or, more specifically, in its treatment of erotic coupling and the marital relation, *Corregidora* is what I call "dearly beloved blues"—my name for a particular variety of prose, poetry, and song that focuses (often as a lament) on the problems of married life.[22] On the literal level, the text tells the story of blues singer Ursula "Ursa" Corregidora, the last in a long line of black women haunted and emotionally burdened by history—by a legacy of rape, incest, and patriarchal psychosexual abuse, passed down through four generations like a sacred family heirloom. The novel recounts the passions and pains of Ursa's brief marriage in 1947 to Mutt Thomas—their breakup after just four months of trying to work through and around Mutt's inability to accept Ursa's need to sing the blues—and the couple's eventual reunion twenty-two years later. In a figurative sense, the blues are the extended metaphor around which Jones works the magic of her text—the medium she uses to enable Ursa to tell her story.

Ursa is the great granddaughter of an unspeakably evil Portuguese slavemaster named Corregidora who prostituted and impregnated the women he owned, including his own daughter, Ursa's grandmother. Despite the unspeakable nature of Corregidora's crimes and the destruction of all record of those crimes, precisely the task with which Ursa, like her mother, grandmother, and great grandmother before her, has been entrusted is to *speak* Corregidora's evil: to "make generations" that bear witness to his cruelty and his abuses.

After a drunken Mutt causes Ursa to fall down a flight of stairs, she loses the child she is carrying and is forced to have a hysterectomy, leaving her physically unable to make generations. Her inability to live up to the charge of her mother and grandmothers is only part of her problem, however—only part of the difficulty Ursa has in loving Mutt or Tadpole (the cafe owner she marries briefly) or Cat or Jeffy (women friends who represent the perhaps intriguing but frightening possibility of lesbian love). Corregidora's larger problem lies in the contradiction and dishonesty inherent in Great Gram's charge to her to "make generations." Making generations, as Janice Harris has pointed out, means making love; but making love for the purpose of making human evidence turns what should be an act of love into an act of historical vengeance. As Harris says of this crippling contradiction: "The goal of lovemaking subverts the act; the end denies the means."[23]

What Ursula must ultimately face is not only the crippling contradiction inherent in Great Gram's charge, but the emotional ambivalence that underpins it: a tangle of mixed emotions and conflicting subjectivities that were no doubt present in a great many sexual liaisons between master and slave, owner and property. The question Ursa must confront in her own life is the question only her father Martin has had the courage to ask of her grandmothers: "How much was hate for Corregidora and how much was love?"

When at the end of the novel, a forty-seven-year-old Ursula is reunited with Mutt Thomas after a separation of twenty-two years, she asks herself the same question. "'You never would suck it,'" Mutt says to Ursa, as she takes his penis in her mouth. "'You never would suck it when I wanted you to. Oh, baby . . . I didn't think you would do this for me'" (184). At a moment in which she holds Mutt delicately suspended between pleasure and pain, Ursa understands what it was her great grandmother did to the man who owned her that made him hate her one minute and unable to get her out of his mind the next. "It had to be sexual . . . it had to be something sexual that Great Gram did to Corregidora." In this moment of understanding—in "a split second of hate and love"—Ursa realizes as well that she could kill Mutt: "'I could kill you,'" she says (though it is unclear whether this is thought or spoken, for in the next line we are told "'He came and I swallowed.'"). Love and hate for him, like Great Gram's love and hate for Corregidora, are so intimately intertwined that even or, perhaps, *especially* at the moment of giving intense sexual pleasure, *she could kill him.*

Unlike the psychosexually tormented heroine of *Eva's Man*, Ursa does not kill Mutt; she does not bite off his penis, as Eva does, or break the skin, as she imagines her great grandmother did. Instead, she swallows Mutt's semen in a sexual act that will not make generations, an act which can be read metaphorically as swallowing the past—not forgetting it, as Mutt would wish, but taking it inside as an act of reconciliation rather than carrying it outside as a weapon of revenge. The act of fellatio, then, particularly the swallowing, suggests a loosening of the bonds of history that have kept Ursa yoked to Corregidora; it signals Ursa's acceptance of the past, as Jones herself has said, as "an aspect of her own character, identity and present history."[24]

Melvin Dixon[25] suggests, however, that the climax of the novel is, in fact, an act of vengeance. "Ursa avenges herself on Mutt," he argues, "by performing fellatio on him—an act that places her in control of herself and Mutt." The mouth of the blues singer becomes, in Dixon's words, "an instrument of direct sexual power."[26] This is a possible and certainly popular reading, one a number of critics have endorsed, one the text surely invites. In such a reading, performing fellatio is said to empower the female because of her potential to disempower—to dismember—her male partner with a bite. I wonder if this empowerment isn't illusory, however, if the penis isn't, in this instance, indeed dematerialized as phallus. Just how long would a live specimen lie passive—recline (or sit) powerless—while his penis was being bitten off?

Jones elides this question in *Corregidora* by making the assault a fantasy, a theory, and in *Eva's Man* by having Eva poison Davis before she dismembers him. Critics, for the most part, have elided the question altogether. One exception is Richard Barksdale, who is so intent on making his case for female mandibular empowerment (Mother JAW as a counterpoint to Father LAW) that he goes so far as to rewrite Jones's novel so that "during an act of fellatio [Eva] mutilates her lover and *leaves him to bleed to death*" (402, my emphasis).

In any case, if *Corregidora's* poetic closure can be read as an act of revenge and empowerment, perhaps it can also be read as suggesting female submission and surrender. Ursa's mouth doesn't become a powerful instrument through the act of fellatio; it has always been a powerful instrument. In singing the blues—singing her mama's songs and her own—she has used her mouth as her mother and grandmothers used their wombs. She has, in effect, made generations in song; her survival has depended on her voice; she has sung "because it was something [she] had to do" (3). With her "hard voice,"—powerful, potent, penetrating like a penis, a voice so hard it "hurts you and makes you still want to listen," Ursa has both participated in and perpetuated an oral tradition. Her final act of oral *sexual* reconciliation may also be an act of self-silencing—an act in which Ursa's hard voice is not simply softened but quite literally silenced by Mutt's penis. I wonder: will Ursa still sing the blues in the morning and, if so, whose blues will they be?

I wonder also about the ideology of empowerment at work here. It troubles me that so many of our critical discussions about *Corregidora* define reconciliation and what Dixon calls "successful coupling" in terms of empowerment—who has power over whom sexually. Moreover, the role which so many critics (especially male critics) see as empowering the female—the privilege of "performing fellatio on" the man who for most of the novel has been more patriarch than partner—seems to me to confirm Ursa in precisely the role Mutt has wanted for her all along: as "his woman," as the instrument of his pleasure. The novel's climax can be read as a reconciliation certainly, but it also can be read as male sexual gratification: Ursa finally does *for him* what she would not do before. Mutt acknowledges as much himself: "'You never would suck it when I wanted you to,'" he says to Ursa, as she goes to work between his legs. "'I didn't think *you would do this for me*'" (my emphasis). Mutt cums, Ursa succumbs.

The question of power and pleasure becomes even more complex if we consider it in terms of both *Corregidora* and *Eva's Man*. Eva achieves the climax with Elvira Moody, her woman cellmate, that Ursa does not with Mutt. Yet, the latter is read as the successful coupling. Mutt's pleasure is expressed: "'Oh, baby.'" "He came and I swallowed." Ursa's is assumed (or perhaps consumed). Yet, it is this encounter that Melvin Dixon describes as the more active lovemaking—the better side of "the unrelenting violence, emotional silence, and passive disharmony in *Eva's Man*" (117).

"'Tell me when it feels sweet,'" Elvira says to Eva in the final moments of *Eva's Man*. "'Tell me when it feels sweet, honey.'" "I leaned back, squeezing her face between my legs," Eva says, "and told her, '*Now*'" (177, my emphasis). Eva, as Dixon reads her, allows herself to be seduced by Elvira Moody, "passively receiv[ing] her in the act of cunnilingus," unlike Ursa who, through the act of fellatio, "brings Mutt within the orbit of her physical control." I would argue, however, that the language of the encounter is hardly passive. Eva squeezes Elvira's face between her legs and *speaks* her own pleasure—"'Now'"—in a way she has not done before. Dixon's otherwise sensitive and provocative reading ultimately privileges the male principle, implying that it is better for a woman to give pleasure to a man than to take it with another woman. Throughout the novel, Eva has been "trapped in the prison of her own emotions," but will she remain there, trapped in her own silence, "forever singing solo," as Dixon suggests? "'*Now*'" . . . I'm not so sure.

The novel ends in an ambiguity whose possibilities are both beautiful and ugly. Elvira Moody may be just another in a long line of men and women who abuse Eva, who take advantage of her. Or, as Ann Allen Shockley suggests, she may do no more in the novel than provide "a background litany of on-going seduction,"[27]—a seduction to which Eva finally submits simply because there is no man around, because she can't keep knocking Elvira out of bed. But when read in light of the fellatio with which *Corregidora* closes, the cunnilingus that brings Eva (and *Eva's Man*) to climax may suggest something else entirely. It may suggest a way off the prong "dat all us black women gits hung on": not *necessarily* lesbian sexuality, but definitely paying less attention to male gratification and more to our own, to our own pleasure and our own pain. In other words: making ourselves the subjects of our own stories, our own lives.

Perhaps this is what has been difficult for many black male readers to accept: seeing themselves depicted as something other than the heroes of *their* women's lives, seeing the black penis portrayed as something other than the royally paternal black phallus. They have misread the refusal of a certain kind of male behavior as a rejection of black men. Such a misreading seems to me to underpin Addison Gayle's critique not of Gayl Jones's work, but of her. Protesting that black women novelists only write about black men as "white folks' Toms" or "brutes a la *Corregidora*," Gayle suggests that "if Gayl Jones believes that Black men are what she says they are, she ought to get a white man" (Bell 214–15). So saying, Gayle shifts the venue of literary criticism from the written fictions of the text to the assumed facts of the author's life, while at the same time questioning the writer's allegiance to the race she betrayed with her pen.

In appraisals like Gayles's, the beholder exceeds his authority as reader. He extrapolates a universal real—"all black men"—from the particular fiction—"a black man" or "some black men." At the same time, he denigrates the woman writer by assigning to her the attitudes, problems, proclivities, and conflicts of her characters, thus denying her the courtesy of a creative imagination.

In general, black women writers have weathered well the storms of criticism that their fictions have stirred up. But Gayl Jones, by her own admission, has been made "extremely 'double conscious'" by criticisms which, as she says (likely referring to Gayle, in particular), "suggest that the fictional invention must imply something about the personal relationships or the way I think 'black men are.'"[28] While she has not been completely silenced by such interpretive phallus(ies), the kind of vitriolic, overly personalized censure her first two novels received in certain circles has altered the course of her writing, particularly its attention to sexuality. "I had to force myself to go ahead with such scenes in *The Stone Dragon*," she says, "because they belonged there, but they're not as graphic and they don't use the same kind of vocabulary (that was true of the characters) of *Eva's Man* and *Corregidora*." Though she, like Walker, remains committed to exploring relationships between men and women, in most of her later work Jones either changes the race or gender of her antagonists or avoids sexual scenes altogether.

That Gayl Jones (or any other writer) would feel called upon to change the race, gender, or actions of her characters because some readers are unable, as she says, to "see beyond those details of erotic consciousness to other meanings" seems to me a travesty of both the creative and the critical process. It is a move which makes literary criticism an act of violence that ironically reinscribes the same oppressive, patriarchal attitudes the literature refracts.

### Conclusion

Ishmael Reed, articulating the sentiments of many black male readers, has asked black women writers why they always feel the need to castrate the black man?[29] Perhaps the answer or, at least, one answer may be because, like the mountain, sexism is there. The novel and other literary forms have given black women a forum for exploring the oppression, insanities, sorrows, joys, and triumphs of women's lives and for transforming those experiences into art.

Clifford Geertz has suggested that all art forms render ordinary, everyday experience comprehensible.[30] Using Geertz's theory to explain the persistence of rape fantasies in white women's romantic fiction, Janice Radway has argued that "the romance's preoccupation with male brutality is an attempt to understand the meaning of an event that has become almost unavoidable in the real world."[31] Writing rape into the romance, then, Radway suggests, is a way for women to work through and deal with the misogynistic attitudes that are so deeply embedded in our society. A similar claim can be made for both the preoccupation with the politics of sexuality and the attention to male violence and penile oppression in the novels of writers such as Morrison, Walker, and Jones. Their fictions are not about doing a hatchet job on black men as mates, but about claiming women as the authors of their own lives rather than as objects of desire in a truth-as-I-know-it/I'm-okay-we're-okay history of blacks in America that is actually the "truths" of men.

Like a number of black male critics, Darryl Pinckney resists the effort to supplement male "truths" with female perceptions. He protests that in *The Color Purple*, "the black men are seen at a distance . . . entirely from the point of view of women."[32] From whose perspective should male characters in a woman-authored text be seen? From whose point of view is Ernest Gaines's Miss Jane Pittman seen or Bessie in *Native Son* or Matty Lou True-blood in *Invisible Man*? Is a literature or a criticism utterly without (gender) perspective—without male or female perceptions—possible? In the realm of African American literary studies, both the texts and the interpretations of black men often have been treated as if they were indeed without such perspective—without male perceptions. They have been treated simply as *the truth*, like Bennett's true story of Black love.

Readings are never neutral. All criticisms are local, situational. My own critical interpretations, as I have acknowledged, are always-already colored by my race and my gender, by my blackness and my feminism. I readily (some might say too readily) label what I do "black feminist criticism." Masculinist criticism needs to be similarly willing to acknowledge and label itself and its biases. But what the field needs is not only more truth in advertising, as it were, but more introspection—more internal critique. For all of us—masculinists, feminists, womanists—the challenge of our critical practice is to see both inside and outside our own assumptions. Texts have a way of becoming what we say they are. But what's at stake is not just the fidelity we owe to the books we read, but the way we do our jobs, our own intellectual integrity. Many black male scholars have accused contemporary black women writers of wielding words like a sword, even as they have done so themselves. It remains to be seen whether the woman writer's sword is mightier than the pen is.

## Notes

1. Lerone Bennett, Jr., "The Roots of Black Love," *Ebony* (August 1981): 31.

2. Bennett exempts such writers as Paul Laurence Dunbar and such musicians as John Coltrane and the Commodores (all male) whom he sees as contributing to "the vitality of the Black love tradition" with poems like "When Malindy Sings" and songs like "Soul Eyes" and "Once, Twice, Three Times a Lady," all of which position black women not as active agents in history but as objects of male desire. "Careless Love," to which Bennett alludes in his essay, is an old folk song which Bessie Smith made famous. Poet Robert Hayden incorporates lyrics from "Careless Love" into his poetic tribute to Smith, "Homage to the Empress of the Blues," writing "Faithless Love/Twotiming Love Oh Love Oh Careless Aggravating Love." Bennett may be referring to Hayden's poem as well as to the song itself. Interestingly enough, Zora Neale Hurston also incorporates lyrics from this "old, old ballad" in her last novel, *Seraph on the Suwanee* (1948).

3. See McDowell's essay "Family Matters," in *Changing Our Own Words: Essays on Criticism, Theory, and Writing by Black Women*, ed. Cheryl Wall (New Brunswick, NJ: Rutgers University Press, 1989). Drawing on reviews and articles published primarily in the white literary media and popular press, McDowell brilliantly analyzes the often vitriolic responses that the fictions of writers like Walker, Morrison, and Jones have inspired from black male critics such as Mel Watkins and Darryl Pinckney. Part of the problem, McDowell points out, is that African American history has been written (by men) as a black family romance in which black men battle not their women but the oppressive forces of white racism. In representing black male abuse within the family, black women writers are writing outside the family, against the family romance.

4. A number of black women writers labelled "feminists" by some of their black male critics—Gayl Jones, for example—have not so identified themselves.

5. Don Alexander and Christine Wright, "Race, Sex and Class: The Clash over *The Color Purple*," *Women and Revolution* 34 (Spring 1988): 20.

6. "Interview with Alice Walker," in *Interviews with Black Writers*, ed. John O'Brien (New York: Liveright, 1973): 192; Roseann P. Bell, "Judgment: Addison Gayle," in *Sturdy Black Bridges: Visions of Black Women in Literature* (Garden City, NY: Anchor Books, 1979): 214; Ishmael Reed, *New Amsterdam News* (January–February, 1987). Quoted by Don Alexander and Christine Wright in "Race, Sex and Class: The Clash over *The Color Purple*," *Women and Revolution* 34 (Spring 1988): 20.

7. See Calvin C. Hernton, *The Sexual Mountain and Black Women Writers: Adventures in Sex, Literature and Real Life* (New York: Doubleday, 1987).

8. As it has gained in popularity both in and outside the academy, black women's literature has acquired many champions among black male scholars. Some of the work of some of these male critics presents a problem of a kind slightly different from the one I address in this essay. Rather than denigrating feminism and its fictions, this criticism announces itself as feminist discourse, even as it remains primarily male-identified. It is also worth noting that several black feminist critics—Barbara Smith, Ann Allen Shockley, and Jewelle Gomez, for example—have been severely critical of what they read as either the silence about or the negative representation of lesbians in the fiction of such writers as Gayl Jones and Gloria Naylor.

9. See Michele Wallace, *Black Macho and the Myth of the Superwoman* (New York: Warner Books, 1978).

10. Mel Watkins, "Sexism, Racism and Black Women Writers," *New York Times Book Review* (15 June 1986): 36.

11. W. Lawrence Hogue, "History, the Feminist Discourse, and *The Third Life of Grange Copeland*," chapter 5 in his book *Discourse and the Other* (Durham: Duke University Press, 1986): 86–106.

12. See Watkins, p. 35. While Watkins criticizes other black women writers for their negative portraits of black male brutality, he praises Morrison for her "subtle, intelligent prose," which he suggests directs our sympathies away from the actual horror of the rape to the swirl of emotions that motivate Cholly's actions.

13. Toni Morrison, *The Bluest Eye* (New York: Washington Square Press, 1970): 128–29. See also Houston A. Baker, Jr., *Blues, Ideology, and Afro-American Literature: A Vernacular Theory* (Chicago: University of Chicago Press, 1984): 177–88.

14. Houston A. Baker, Jr., *Workings of the Spirit: The Poetics of Afro-American Women's Writing* (Chicago: University of Chicago Press, 1991).

15. Michael Awkward, *Inspiriting Influences: Tradition, Revision, and Afro-American Women's Novels* (New York: Columbia University Press, 1989): 82–83.

16. Zora Neale Hurston, *Their Eyes Were Watching God,* 1937, reprint with a foreword by Sherley Anne Williams (Urbana: University of Illinois Press, 1978): 41.

17. See Hortense Spillers, "The Politics of Intimacy: A Discussion," in *Sturdy Black Bridges,* 87–106.

18. Alice Walker, *The Third Life of Grange Copeland* (New York: Harcourt Brace Jovanovich, 1970): 94.

19. Toni Morrison, *Song of Solomon* (New York: New American Library, 1977): 217.

20. Richard K. Barksdale, "Castration Symbolism in Recent Black American Fiction," *CLA Journal* 29 (June 1986): 403.

21. Gayl Jones, *Eva's Man* (New York: Random House, 1976): 128–29.

22. My coinage of the term "dearly beloved blues" was inspired by Alice Walker's short story "Roselily," in which she interweaves the title character's thoughts as she is married to a Black Muslim with the words of the minister conducting the ceremony. From the simple but significant details that occupy Roselily's thoughts as the minister speaks— "ropes," "chains," "handcuffs," and "the stiff severity of [the groom's] plain black suit"— we know that this will not be a happy marriage. Also alluding to Walker, Gayl Jones calls male/female relationships of the kind she deals with in *Corregidora* "blues relationships," coming out of a "tradition of 'love and trouble.'" See Alice Walker, "Roselily," in *In Love and Trouble: Stories of Black Women* (New York: Harcourt Brace Jovanovich, 1973): 3; "Gayl Jones: An Interview," *Chant of Saints: A Gathering of Afro-American Literature, Art, and Scholarship,* Michael S. Harper and Robert Stepto, eds. (Urbana: University of Illinois Press, 1979): 360.

23. Janice Harris, "Gayl Jones' *Corregidora, Frontiers* 3 (1981): 2.

24. Charles H. Rowell, "Interview with Gayl Jones," *Callaloo* 5 (October 1982): 45.

25. I cannot invoke Melvin Dixon without noting with sadness and regret his untimely passing in October of 1992. Melvin, Gayl Jones, and I were all graduate students together at Brown University in the early seventies. How remarkable it seems to me as I write this that our paths should cross textually in this way twenty years later.

26. Melvin Dixon, *Ride Out the Wilderness: Geography and Identity in Afro-American Literature* (Chicago: University of Illinois Press, 1987): 112.

27. Ann Allen Shockley, "The Black Lesbian in American Literature," in *Home Girls: A Black Feminist Anthology,* ed. Barbara Smith (New York: Women of Color Press, 1983): 89.

28. Rowell, 46–47.

29. See Reed's novel *Reckless Eyeballing,* among other sources.

30. Clifford Geertz, "Notes on the Balinese Cockfight," chapter in *The Interpretation of Culture* (New York: Basic Books, 1973): 443. Geertz writes: "Like any art form . . . the cockfight renders ordinary, everyday experience comprehensible by presenting it in terms of acts and objects which have had their practical consequences removed and been reduced . . . to the level of sheer appearances, where their meaning can be more powerfully articulated and more easily perceived."

31. Janice A. Radway, *Reading the Romance: Women, Patriarchy, and Popular Literature* (Chapel Hill: University of North Carolina Press, 1984): 71.

32. Darryl Pinckney, "Black Victims, Black Villains," *New York Review of Books* (19 January 1987): 18.

# Race, Gender, and the Prison Industrial Complex
## California and Beyond

*Angela Y. Davis and*
*Cassandra Shaylor*

2001

### Women's Rights as Human Rights

A central achievement of the 1995 United Nations Fourth World Conference on Women in Beijing was the emphatic articulation of women's rights as human rights. In specifically identifying violence against women in both public and private life as an assault against women's human rights, the Beijing Conference helped to deepen awareness of violence against women on a global scale. Yet, even with this increasing attention, the violence linked to women's prisons remains obscured by the social invisibility of the prison. There, violence takes the form of medical neglect, sexual abuse, lack of reproductive control, loss of parental rights, denial of legal rights and remedies, the devastating effects of isolation, and, of course, arbitrary discipline.

Recent reports by international human rights organizations have begun to address the invisibility of women prisoners and to highlight the severity of the violence they experience. For example, Human Rights Watch and Amnesty International have specifically focused on the widespread problem of sexual abuse in United States' prisons. In 1999 the United Nations Special Rapporteur on Violence Against Women issued a report on her findings—which were even more disturbing than prison activists had predicted—from visits to eight women's prisons in the U.S. In general, although international human rights standards rarely have been applied within the context of the U.S., particularly in the legal arena, UN documents (such as the *International Covenant on Civil and Political Rights* and the *Standard Minimum Rules for the Treatment of Prisoners*) have been used productively by activists to underscore the gravity of human rights violations in women's prisons.

### The Prison Industrial Complex

As prison populations have soared in the United States, the conventional assumption that increased levels of crime are the cause has been widely contested. Activists and scholars who have tried to develop more nuanced understandings of the punishment process—and especially racism's role—have deployed the concept of the "prison industrial complex" to point out that the proliferation of prisons and prisoners is more clearly linked to larger economic and political structures and ideologies than to individual criminal conduct and efforts to curb "crime." Indeed, vast numbers of corporations with global markets rely on prisons as an important source of profit and thus have acquired clandestine stakes in the continued expansion of the prison system. Because the overwhelming majority of U.S. prisoners are from racially marginalized communities, corporate stakes in an expanding apparatus of punishment necessarily rely on and promote old as well as new structures of racism.

Women especially have been hurt by these developments. Although women comprise a relatively small percentage of the entire prison population, they constitute, nevertheless, the fastest growing segment of prisoners. There are now more women in prison in the State of California alone than there were in the United States as a whole in 1970 (Currie 1998). Because race is a major factor in determining who goes to prison and who does not, the groups most rapidly increasing in number are black, Latina, Asian-American, and indigenous women.

Globalization of capitalism has precipitated the decline of the welfare state in industrialized countries, such as the U.S. and Britain, and has brought about structural adjustment in the countries of the southern region. As social programs in the U.S. have been drastically curtailed, imprisonment has simultaneously become the most self-evident response to many of the social problems previously addressed by institutions such as Aid to Families with Dependent Children (AFDC). In other words, in the era of the disestablishment of social programs that have historically served poor communities, and at a time when affirmative action programs are being dismantled and resources for education and health are declining, imprisonment functions as the default solution. Especially for women of color, who are hardest hit by the withdrawing of social resources and their replacement with imprisonment, these draconian strategies—ever longer prison sentences for offenses that are often petty—tend to reproduce and, indeed, exacerbate the very problems they purport to solve.

There is an ironic but telling similarity between the economic impact of the prison industrial complex and that of the military industrial complex, with which it shares important structural features. Both systems simultaneously produce vast profits and social destruction. What is beneficial to the corporations, politicians, and state entities involved in these systems brings blight and death to poor and racially marginalized communities throughout the world. In the case of the prison industrial complex, the transformation of imprisoned bodies of color into consumers and/or producers of an immense range of commodities effectively transforms public funds into profit, leaving little in the way of social assistance to bolster the efforts of women and men who want to overcome barriers erected by poverty and racism. For example, when women who spend many years in prison are released, instead of jobs, housing, health care, and education, they are offered a small amount of release money, which covers little more than a bus ride and two nights in an inexpensive hotel. In the "free world," they are haunted by the stigma of imprisonment, which renders it extremely difficult for a "felon" to find a job. Thus they are inevitably tracked back into a prison system that in this era of the prison industrial complex has entirely dispensed with even a semblance of rehabilitation.

The emergence of a prison industrial complex means that whatever rehabilitative potential the prison may have previously possessed (as implied by the bizarre persistence of the term "corrections") is negated. Instead, the contemporary economics of imprisonment privilege the profitability of punishment at the expense of human education and transformation. State budgets increasingly are consumed by the costs of building and maintaining prisons, while monies dedicated to sustaining and improving communities are slashed. A glaring example of the misplaced financial investment in punishment is the decreasing state support for public education; for example, in California in 1995 the budget for prisons exceeded that for higher education.

Corporations are intimately linked to prison systems in both the public and the private sector. The trend toward privatization is only one manifestation of a growing involvement of corporations in the punishment process. While a myopic focus on private prisons in activist campaigns may tend to legitimate public prisons by default, placing this development within the context of a far-reaching prison industrial complex can enhance our understanding of the contemporary punishment industry. In the U.S., there are currently twenty-six for-profit prison corporations that operate approximately 150 facilities in twenty-eight states (Dyer 2000). The largest of these companies, Corrections Corporations of America (CCA) and Wackenhut, control 76.4 percent of the private prison market globally. While CCA is headquartered in Nashville, Tennessee, its largest shareholder is Sodexho Marriott, the multi-national headquartered in Paris, which provides catering services at many U.S. colleges and universities. Currently, CCA, Wackenhut and the other smaller private prison companies together bring in $1.5 to 2 billion a year (Dyer 2000).

Though private prisons represent a fairly small proportion of prisons in the U.S., the privatization model is quickly becoming the primary mode of organizing punishment in many other countries (Sudbury 2000).[1] These companies have tried to take advantage of the expanding population of women prisoners, both in the U.S. and globally. In 1996, the first private women's prison was established by CCA in Melbourne, Australia. The government of Victoria

> adopted the U.S. model of privatization in which financing, design, construction, and ownership of the prison are awarded to one contractor and the government pays them back for construction over twenty years. This means that it is virtually impossible to remove the contractor because that contractor owns the prison (George 1999, 190).

However, to understand the reach of the prison industrial complex, it is not enough to evoke the looming power of the private prison business. Of course, by definition, those companies court the state inside and outside the U.S. for the purpose of obtaining prison contracts. They thus bring punishment and profit into a menacing embrace. Still, this is only the most visible dimension of the prison industrial complex, and it should not lead us to ignore the more comprehensive corporatization that is a feature of contemporary punishment. As compared to earlier historical eras, the prison economy is no longer a small, identifiable and containable set of markets. Many corporations, whose names are highly recognizable by "free-world" consumers, have discovered new possibilities for expansion by selling their products to correctional facilities.

> In the 1990s, the variety of corporations making money from prisons is truly dizzying, ranging from Dial Soap to Famous Amos cookies, from AT&T to health-care providers. . . . In 1995 Dial Soap sold $100,000 worth of its product to the New York City jail system alone. . . . When VitaPro Foods of Montreal, Canada, contracted to supply inmates in the State of Texas with its soy-based meat substitute, the contract was worth $34 million a year (Dyer 2000, 14).

The point here is that even if private prison companies were prohibited—an unlikely prospect, indeed—the prison industrial complex and its many strategies for profit would remain intact.

Moreover, it is not only the private prison— CCA and Wackenhut in particular—that gets reproduced along the circuits of global capital and insinuates itself into the lives of poor people in various parts of the world. Connections between corporations and public prisons, similar to those in the U.S., are currently emerging throughout the world and are being reinforced by the contemporary idea, widely promoted by the U.S., that imprisonment is a social panacea. The most obvious effects of these ideas and practices on women can be seen in the extraordinary numbers of women arrested and imprisoned on drug charges throughout the world. The U.S.-instigated "war on drugs" has disproportionately claimed women as its victims inside the U.S., but also elsewhere in Europe, South America, the Caribbean, Asia, and Africa (Stern 1998). In what can be seen as the penal equivalent of ambulance chasing, architectural firms, construction companies, and other corporations are helping to create new women's prisons throughout the world.

## Race, Gender, and the Prison Industrial Complex

Activist opposition to the prison industrial complex has insisted on an understanding of the ways racist structures and assumptions facilitate the expansion of an extremely profitable prison system, in turn helping to reinforce racist social stratification. This racism is always gendered, and imprisonment practices that are conventionally considered to be "neutral"—such as sentencing, punishment regimes, and health care—differ in relation to the ways race, gender, and sexuality intersect.[2]

The women most likely to be found in U.S. prisons are black, Latina, Asian American, and Native American women. In 1998, one out of every 109 women in the U.S. was under the control of the criminal justice system (Greenfeld and Snell 1999). But where these women are located within the system differs according to their race: while about two-thirds of women on probation are white, two-thirds of women in prison are women of color. An African American woman is eight times more likely to go to prison than a white woman; a Latina woman is four times more likely. African American women make up the largest percentage of women in state prisons (48 percent) and federal detention centers (35 percent), even though they are only approximately 13 percent of the general population (Greenfeld and Snell 1999). As the population of Latinas in the U.S. grows, so does their number in prisons. In California, for example, though Latinas comprise 13 percent of the general population, they make up around 25 percent of women in prison (*Characteristics of Population in California State Prisons* 2000). Though there is no official data maintained on the numbers of Native American women in prison, numerous studies document that they are arrested at a higher rate than whites and face discrimination at all levels of the criminal justice system (Ross 1998).

Given the way in which U.S. government statistics fail to specify racial categories other than "white," "black," and "Hispanic" (figures regarding women who self-identify as Native American, Vietnamese, Filipina, Pacific Islander, or as from any other racially marginalized community, are consolidated into a category of "other"), it is difficult to provide precise numbers of women from these groups in prison (Greenfeld and Snell 2000). However, advocates for women prisoners report that the numbers of Asian women, including Vietnamese, Filipinas, and Pacific Islanders, are growing in women's prisons.[3]

The vast increase in the numbers of women of color in U.S. prisons has everything to do with the "war on drugs." Two African American women serving long federal sentences on questionable drug charges— Kemba Smith and Dorothy Gaines—were pardoned by President Bill Clinton during his last days in office. In the cases of both Smith, who received a twenty-four-and-a-half year sentence, and Gaines, whose sentence was nineteen years and seven months, their sole link to drug trafficking was their involvement with men who were accused traffickers (Newsome 2000).

Considering only the federal system, between 1990 and 1996, 84 percent of the increase in imprisoned women (2,057) was drug-related. In the entire complex of U.S. prisons and jails, drug-related convictions are largely to blame for the fact that black women are imprisoned at rates that are twice as high as their male counterparts and three times the rate of white women (Bush-Baskette 1999, 220). Harsh sentencing laws, such as mandatory minimums attached to drug convictions and "three strikes" laws, which can result in a life sentence for a relatively minor drug offense, have created a trap door through which too many women of color have fallen into the ranks of disposable populations.

## Violence Against Women in Prison

Dorothy Gaines and Kemba Smith were fortunate, but they are only two of the women incarcerated during the Clinton years, during which more women than ever were sentenced to prison. What happens to the vast numbers of women behind walls? In the first place, contrary to international human rights standards, imprisonment means much more than just a loss of freedom. Women's prisons are located on a continuum of violence that extends from the official practices of the state to the spaces of intimate relationships. Both public and private incarnations of this violence are largely hidden from public view. But while domestic violence increasingly is an issue of concern in public life, the violence of imprisonment rarely is discussed. Prisons are places within which violence occurs on a routine and constant basis; the functioning of the prison depends upon it. The threat of violence emanating from prison hierarchies is so ubiquitous and unpredictable that some women have pointed out the striking structural similarities between the experiences of imprisonment and battering relationships (Chevigny 1999).

Though many women prisoners have indeed experienced intimate violence, the profile of "the woman prisoner" tends to imply that this victimization in the "free world" is the cause of imprisonment. Such a simplistic causal link fails to recognize the complex set of factors related to the social and political legitimation of violence against women, emphasizing *domestic* violence at the expense of an understanding of state violence—both in the "free world" and in the world of prison.

Violence in prison is directed at the psyche as well as the body. Increasingly, prisons in the U.S. are becoming a primary response to mental illness among poor people. The institutionalization of mentally ill people, historically, has been used more often against women than against men. However, for women who do not enter prison with mental problems, extended imprisonment is sure to create them. According to Penal Reform International,

> [l]ong term prisoners may develop mental and psychic disturbances by imprisonment itself and by being cut off from their families. Mental problems also arise and may become chronic in big prisons, where there is much overcrowding; where there are few activities; where prisoners have to stay a long time in their cells in daytime. . . (*Making Standards Work* 1995, 95–96).

Thus, this organization interprets the *Standard Minimum Rules for the Treatment of Prisoners* (SMR) as not only proscribing the incarceration of mentally ill persons in prisons but as also calling for compassionate care by medical, psychological, and custodial staff of those who suffer mental and emotional problems as a consequence of imprisonment.

Most women in prison experience some degree of depression or post-traumatic stress disorder. Very often they are neither diagnosed nor treated, with injurious consequences for their mental health in and out of prison. Many women report that if they ask for counseling they are offered psychotropic medications instead. Despite legal challenges, prison regimes construct prisoners who suffer the effects of institutionalization as "sick" and in need of treatment with psychotropic drugs (Kupers 2000). Historically, this "medicalization model" has been most widely used against women (Dobash 1986).

As technologies of imprisonment become increasingly repressive and practices of isolation become increasingly routine, mentally ill women often are placed in solitary confinement, which can only exacerbate their condition. Moreover, women prisoners with significant mental illnesses frequently do not seek treatment because they fear harsh procedures (such as being placed in a "strip cell" if they say they are suicidal) and/or over-medication with psychotropic drugs. While women who have mental health concerns are mistreated, women with serious physical conditions often are labeled mentally ill in order to preempt their complaints—sometimes with grave consequences.[4]

## Medical Neglect

At the historic legislative hearings recently conducted inside California women's prisons,[5] prisoner Gloria Broxton declared: "They don't have the right to take my life because they thought I was worthless. I didn't come here to do my death sentence. I did a stupid thing, but I should not have to pay for it with my life" (*Truth to Power* 2000).[6] As Broxton's words indicate, she would probably not be dying of endometrial cancer today had she been granted earlier treatment. Violence is promoted by prison regimes, which also divest prisoners of the agency to contest them. The most salient example of this habitual violence is the lack of access to decent health care—in prison, medical neglect can result in death. Widely accepted interpretations of UN documents, such as the *Convention Against Torture, and Other Cruel, Inhuman or Degrading Treatment or Punishment*, and the *International Covenant on Civil and Political Rights* (Articles 6.1 and 7), and the *Standard Minimum Rules for the Treatment of Prisoners*, emphasize the importance of health care in prisons. "The level of health care in prison and medication should be at least equivalent to that in the outside community. It is a consequence of the government's responsibility for people deprived of their liberty and thus fully dependent on state authority" (*Making Standards Work* 1995, 71).

Women in California prisons overwhelmingly have identified lack of access to medical information and treatment as their primary concern. At the hearings on conditions in women's prisons in California, witnesses reported that they often waited months to see a doctor and weeks for prescriptions to be refilled. For women with heart disease, diabetes, asthma, cancer, seizures, and HIV/AIDS, such delays in medication can cause serious medical complications or premature death. For example, Sherrie Chapman, an African American woman imprisoned at the California Institution for Women, testified about extreme delays in treatment that led to the development of a terminal condition. Chapman sought diagnosis of breast lumps for ten years and was denied access to medical care. By the time she received treatment, she was subjected to a double mastectomy, and ten months later a hysterectomy. Despite the fact that at the time of the hearings her cancer had metastasized to her head and neck, she consistently was denied adequate pain management. As she testified: "I can't just go to the doctor and ask for help without being looked at and thought of as a manipulator, a drug seeker" (*Truth to Power* 2000). Her requests for a compassionate release—in order to live with her mother until she dies—have been denied, and she will likely die in prison.

Tragically, all too often medical neglect in prison results in premature death. As Beverly Henry, a prisoner peer educator, testified:

> I have seen women die on my yard, women that I was very close to and women that I knew. If I could see that the whites of their eyes were as yellow as a caution sign, why couldn't somebody else? I watched a woman's waist grow from approximately 27 inches to 67 inches because her liver was cirrhoted [a sign of advanced liver failure]. She could not wear shoes, she looked nine months pregnant, and every day she asked me: "Am I gonna die here? Am I gonna die here? Do you think this is what is gonna happen to me?" And she died. And there was nothing we could do about it. And I know that something could have been done (*Truth to Power* 2000).

During an eight-week period at the end of 2000, nine women did, in fact, die in the Central California Women's Facility (CCWF) in Chowchilla, California. Though these women died of a variety of illnesses, all of their deaths were in some way attributable to severe medical neglect on the part of the prison.[7] One of these women was Pamela Coffey, a forty-six-year-old African American woman who complained of a mass on her side and swelling in her abdomen for several months but was denied medical treatment. On the night she died, she complained of extreme abdominal pain, swelling in her face and mouth, and numbness in her legs. Her roommates called for medical help, but for three hours no one came. She collapsed on the bathroom floor in her cell, and when a Medical Technical Assistant (MTA)—a guard with minimal medical training—finally arrived, he failed to examine her or to call for medical help. He left the cell, and Coffey's condition deteriorated. Her cellmates again called for help, but by the time the MTA arrived thirty minutes later, Coffey was dead. Prison staff then left her body in the cell for over an hour, further traumatizing her cellmates. Pamela Coffey's death exemplifies the severe medical neglect many women prisoners face, as well as the punishment all women are subjected to in an environment in which medical neglect is rampant. Many women are forced to watch other women deteriorate and sometimes die, and as a result must live in fear that they or someone they care about will be next.

Following the deaths, prison officials attempted to further criminalize the women who died by claiming that their deaths were attributable to illicit drug use in prison, despite the fact that there was no evidence to support such a claim. Prison administrators thus easily relied on widely circulating stereotypes of women prisoners as drug addicts—stereotypes fueled by the "war on drugs"—to demonize women who died as a result of medical neglect. Prison staff also instituted a new practice of treating the cell of a woman who called for medical help after hours as a "crime scene," which meant searching all of the women, upending the cell, and seizing property. Such a practice serves to make women fearful of calling for help because they or their cellmates will be punished. All of the women who died at CCWF were determined to have died of "natural" causes. Given that these premature deaths were preventable, they cannot be considered to be "natural." On the other hand, given that women prisoners are systematically denied appropriate health care leading to the development of serious illnesses and premature death, medical neglect and death in prison have become, sadly, all too "natural."

Women prisoners are consistently accused of malingering, and medical staff often use intimidation to dissuade them from seeking treatment. In order to complain about inadequate medical care, women must first file written grievances with the staff person with whom they have a problem. In other words, the recipient of the complaint is the only person who ostensibly can provide them with the care they need. Because there is only one doctor on each prison yard, women prisoners have told outside advocates that they rarely complain in order to avoid retaliation and the denial of treatment altogether. This process clearly violates the spirit of Rule thirty-six of the SMR, which encourages prison authorities to make confidential channels available to prisoners who decide to make complaints.[8]

Beyond the ongoing epidemic of medical neglect of individual women prisoners, prisons also operate to create and exacerbate public health crises such as Hepatitis C Virus (HCV) and HIV. Lack of treatment and callous disregard for individual women's lives is even more frightening within the context of such massive infectious epidemics. HIV rates are at least ten times higher among prisoners than among people outside of prison, and the rate is higher among women prisoners than men (DeGroot, Hammett, and Scheib 1996). HCV has reached epidemic levels in California prisons—the California Department of Corrections estimates that 40 percent of the prison population is infected (Steinberg 2000). Because the Department of Corrections regularly fails to test women for HCV or to provide information about prevention, advocates for women prisoners believe the numbers to be considerably higher. Not only is there a dearth of access to treatment but also to information about prevention. Women report that when they request to be tested for communicable diseases, they often do not get the results, even if they test positive. By virtue of this medical neglect, the prison promotes the spread of these diseases both inside prison and in the communities outside of prison to which women go when they are released.

Medical neglect in prison reflects and extends the lower value society places on the provision of preventative care and treatment to poor women of color outside of the prison. The abuse of women prisoners through medical neglect recapitulates a long history of inadequate health care for women, particularly women of color, which is often explicitly justified by sexist and racist ideologies.

### Reproductive Rights

Reproductive health care in prisons is equally informed by these ideologies and often equally abysmal. Pregnant women are provided limited pre-natal care, and in several U.S. jurisdictions, women are shackled during labor (Amnesty International 2001). Women prisoners wait months, and sometimes years, to receive routine gynecological examinations that protect against the development of serious health conditions.[9] For some women, these delays, combined with a consistent failure of prison medical staff to address treatable conditions early, result in the development of serious reproductive health problems. Theresa Lopez, a young Latina in her twenties, developed and died of cervical cancer, a condition that is easily treatable in its early stages, because prison medical staff failed to provide her with basic medical treatment.[10]

In an interview with community activists recording women prisoners' oral histories, Davara Campbell described the politics of reproductive health in prisons:

> In the 1970s I was suffering severe menstrual cramps and a tilted uterus. As a young woman in the criminal justice system serving a life sentence complicated by medical female "disorders" and subject to misdiagnoses by questionable, unprofessional, unethical medical personnel, it was recommended I have a hysterectomy. I was maybe twenty-years-old. Having some enlightenment about genocide, I felt that the prospect of my being able to have a family was being threatened, so I escaped from prison to have a child. I had a son. He is now 28 years old, and I have four grandchildren who I would not have if I had given up my rights. Any imposition upon reproductive rights is an injustice against the well-being of family units—the rights of women, children, and grandchildren, or the promise of the future (Campbell 1999).

As this account highlights, gynecological and reproductive health services in prisons are inadequate at best, dangerous and life-threatening at worst. Inside prisons, women are subject to substandard gynecological care that sometimes results in loss of reproductive capacity or leads to premature death. Often this inadequate care amounts to practices of sterilization, as Campbell's analysis highlights. The use of sterilization as a "solution" to women's gynecological problems resonates with racist practices that women of color in the U.S. have experienced historically.

In the contemporary efforts to justify the abolition of welfare, continuing accusations of over-reproduction directed at African American and Latina single mothers legitimize differential claims to reproductive rights. Racist ideologies circulating outside prisons then enable the kinds of assaults on women's reproductive capacities inside prisons that are reminiscent of earlier historical eras, such as the forced sterilization of Puerto Rican and Native American women and forced reproduction of enslaved black women. Thus prisons operate as sites where those reproductive rights putatively guaranteed to women in the "free world" are often systematically ignored, especially where women of color are concerned.

Gynecology is one of the most problematic areas in prison health care. Historical connections with racist gynecological practices continue to live on within the prison environment. More generally, to say that imprisonment deleteriously affects the health of women is clearly a criticism of health care in women's prisons, conditions that have been abundantly documented by legal and human rights organizations. But it is also to raise questions about the inertia that appears to prevent significant change in health care conditions, even when there is acknowledgment that such change is necessary. Why, for example, do accusations of sexual abuse continue to hover around medical regimes in women's prisons? Why have women prisoners complained for many decades about the difficulty of gaining access to skilled medical personnel? One of the ways to answer these questions is to look at the prison as a receptacle for obsolete practices—a site where certain practices, even when discredited in the larger society, acquire a second life.

There are children and families left behind in the "free world" on whom the imprisonment of women undoubtedly has a devastating impact. Almost 80 percent of women in prison have children for whom they were the primary caretakers before their imprisonment (Belknap 1996). The removal of a significant number of women of color, coupled with the alarming rates of incarceration for their male counterparts, has a disabling effect on the ability of poor communities to support families, whatever their constellation. When mothers are arrested, children are often placed in foster care and, in line with new laws, such as the Adoption and Safe Families Act of 1997, many are streamlined into adoption. All ties with birth mothers and extended families are thus systematically severed. In many instances, this process tracks children into juvenile detention centers and from there into adult prisons. For women who are reunited with their children upon release, the challenges for them are amplified by new welfare reform guidelines that prevent a former prisoner from receiving public benefits, including housing assistance. When previously imprisoned women are divested of their rights to social services—a move related to the political disenfranchisement of former prisoners in many states—they are effectively tracked back into the prison system. This is one of the modes of reproduction of the prison industrial complex.

## Sexual Harassment and Abuse

The development of putatively "feminist" campaigns by prison administrators has had deleterious consequences for women in prison. The assumption that formal gender equality inevitably leads to better conditions for women is contradicted by the recent pattern of modeling the architecture, regimes and staff of women's prisons after the men's counterparts. The current tendency, for example, is to place gun towers in women's maximum-security units in order to render them equal to similar men's units. The hiring of male custodial staff, who have visual access at all times to women's cells—even when they are changing clothes—and to the showers, creates a climate that invites sexual abuse. In U.S. women's prisons, the ratio of male to female corrections staff is often two to one and sometimes three to one. Though this disproportion alone does not inevitably lead to abuse, the administration and culture of the prison creates an environment in which sexual abuse thrives.

Partly as a result of these increasingly repressive models, and partly because of the rampant sexist and racist ideologies that support and sustain women's prisons, routine sexual abuse and harassment amount to a veritable climate of terror. Among the many abuses women prisoners have identified are inappropriate pat searches (male guards pat searching and groping women), illegal strip searches (male guards observing strip searches of women), constant lewd comments and gestures, violations of their right to privacy (male guards watching women in showers and toilets), and in some instances, sexual assault and rape (UN Special Rapporteur on Violence Against Women 1999, 12–14).

According to international human rights standards, the rape of a woman in custody is an act of torture. Furthermore, violations of rights to privacy and preservation of human dignity are protected by the *International Covenant on Civil and Political Rights*. Recent studies by human rights organizations have confirmed that these international standards are routinely violated in U.S. prisons. Human Rights Watch, for example, found that sexual abuse is often related to perceived sexual orientations of prisoners (Human Rights Watch 1996, 2). Sexual abuse is also frequently linked to medical practices. Many women in California prisons have indicated that they avoid much-needed medical treatment because male doctors can force them to submit to inappropriate pelvic examinations regardless of their symptoms (Nightline 1999). However, only a small proportion of sexually harassed women report these incidents to prison authorities, not only because staff perpetrators are rarely disciplined but also because they themselves may suffer retaliation.

Sexual harassment and abuse are also linked to the new technologies of imprisonment. For example, the rapidly proliferating "supermax units," which isolate prisoners in individual cells for twenty-three out of twenty-four hours a day, render women even more vulnerable to sexual assault and harassment. In a legal interview, Regina Johnson, a thirty-six-year-old African American woman in the Security Housing Unit at Valley State Prison for Women in Chowchilla, California, reported being required to expose her breasts to a male guard in order to obtain necessary hygiene supplies (Johnson 1998).

"Cell extractions," a practice linked to the "supermax," involve subduing a prisoner, usually by means of restraints, and performing a strip-search before removing her from her cell. The involvement of male guards—although female guards also participate—especially imbues cell extractions with a very real potential for sexual abuse.

In the State of Arizona, the sheriff in Maricopa County has installed video cameras in the women's holding and search cells in the county jail; he broadcasts live footage of women in these cells on the internet. Though such prurient monitoring is unacceptable in any detention setting, it is particularly disturbing in the jail setting because many of these women are pretrial detainees who have not been found guilty of any crime and, therefore, presumably are not yet to be subjected to any form of punishment.

## Policing Sexuality

Such sexual harassment of women, in the guise of being "tough on crime," illustrates the myriad ways in which prisons attempt to control women and their sexuality through sexual violence. In the sexualized environment of the prison, prison guards and staff learn not to fear sanctions for being sexually abusive to women. At the same time, women's sexuality, both inside and outside of prison, is policed and punished. A significant number of women enter the prison system as a direct result of the criminalization of sexual practices. Laws against sex work in most United States' jurisdictions result in the arrest and conviction of thousands of poor women. Sex workers most often arrested work the streets, as opposed to working in organized environments such as brothels, parlors, or escort services. Street workers, who are disproportionately women of color, are most likely to land in jail. In several states, there is now a charge of "felony prostitution" for sex workers with a known HIV-positive status, carrying a mandatory minimum sentence of four years. The criminalization of sex work creates a cycle of imprisonment: women are arrested, sentenced to jail time and often charged heavy fines and court fees, which then force them back onto the streets only to be arrested again.

Such criminalization of women's sexuality begins at a young age; girls are now the fastest growing population in the juvenile justice system. Most often these girls are arrested for "status offenses," which include truancy, underage drinking, breaking curfew, running away, and prostitution. Boys are less likely to be arrested for similar behavior, reflecting an obvious gender bias, but race determines which girls will actually end up in juvenile hall. As in the prison system, communities of color are represented disproportionately in juvenile justice systems. Almost half of girls in juvenile detention in the United States are African American and 13 percent are Latina. While seven out of ten cases involving white girls are dropped, only three out of ten cases involving African American girls are dismissed (American Bar Association and National Bar Association 2001). This increasing imprisonment of girls occurs despite the fact that the juvenile crime rate, particularly violent crime, has continued to decline since 1994 (American Bar Association and National Bar Association 2001). The targeting of girls of color for imprisonment in juvenile detention is a precursor to their later entrapment in women's prisons, because a majority of women in prison first entered the prison system as girls.

The anxieties about women's sexualities that circulate outside of the prison, and often lead to women's criminalization, are exacerbated and foregrounded within the prison. Guards and staff sexualize the space of the prison through their abuse of women, and in so doing not only cast women prisoners as criminal but also as sexually available.

At least since the publication of Rose Giallombardo's *Society of Women: A Study of a Women's Prison* (1966), the most salient characteristic of women's prisons is assumed to be women's intimate and sexual involvement with each other. Yet the ideological presumption of heterosexuality is policed more systematically than in the free world. Women's prisons have rules against "homosecting"—a term used within prisons to refer to same-sex sexual practices among prisoners. The racism and sexism associated with prison regimes intersect in the construction of women of color as hyper-deviant, and the addition of hetereosexism means that lesbians of color face a triple jeopardy. A Latina lesbian couple at Valley State Prison for Women reported in a legal interview that masculine-identified prisoners are targeted for verbal harassment and sometime physical assault by male guards, while their feminine-identified partners are sexually harassed by those same guards (Mendoza and Garcia 1998). This gendered form of harassment exemplifies the ways in which gender identity is rigidly policed inside prisons.

## Women's Prisons and Anti-Immigrant Campaigns

Women immigrants to the United States are policed and punished in myriad ways. Racist and xenophobic campaigns against immigrant communities, which particularly target people from Mexico and Central America (and increasingly people from Asian countries), have contributed to the criminalization of immigrants, the militarization of the U.S.-Mexico border, and the build-up of the Immigration and Naturalization Service (INS) as an arm of the prison system.

The INS has shifted its focus from providing services to immigrants seeking refuge in the U.S. to enforcement and detention of individuals labeled "illegal aliens," thus establishing itself as a significant component of the prison industrial complex. In many cases, immigrants choose to travel to the United States in order to escape economic dislocation produced by global corporations (often U.S.-headquartered) in their own countries. The profit potential of INS detention centers mirrors that of state and federal prisons both for corporations and for state institutions. For example, the INS rents space in public and private prisons, as well as county jails, often paying twice what the state government would pay for the same beds (Welch 2000).

Immigrant rights and human rights organizations have documented conditions in INS detention facilities that violate basic human rights: detention of immigrants for inordinately long periods, sometimes years; denial of basic medical treatment; and forcing immigrants to sleep on cell floors. (American Civil Liberties Union 1993; Human Rights Watch 2000). Furthermore, the INS practice of purchasing space for detainees in state systems often means that detainees are placed in state prisons and jails that already face lawsuits over poor conditions. In New Orleans Parish Prison in Louisiana, for example, women detainees are housed in a jail that is being sued for sexual abuse of women prisoners (Welch 2000).

Beyond warehousing immigrants for the INS, state and federal prisons in the U.S. independently play a significant role in criminalizing and punishing women from other countries. In federal prisons, for example, approximately 30 percent of prisoners are foreign nationals (Federal Bureau of Prisons 2001), many of whom are in prison for extremely long sentences as a result of the "war on drugs." Many of these women face deportation upon conclusion of their prison sentence.

As a consequence of the Illegal Immigration Reform and Immigrant Responsibility Act of 1996, immigrants who have criminal convictions have been deported systematically. This law added offenses that are considered misdemeanors in many states to the list of "Aggravated Felonies," for which immigrants face mandatory deportation. Further, the law enabled the INS to use convictions from years before to justify deportation, and it eliminated the ability of judges to review the actions of the INS. As a result of this law, many women are separated permanently from their families in the U.S. and effectively are exiled to a country of origin to which they have no ties.

In states with larger immigrant populations, prisoners in the state system often confront dilemmas produced by the intersection of xenophobia and criminalization. In California, for example, Sylvia Rodriguez was dying in prison of metastasized cancer, but if legal advocates were able to secure a compassionate release for her, she would face deportation.[11] She was sixty-seven years old and had moved to the U.S. from the Philippines when she was nine years old. She knew no one in her country of origin and was suffering from a terminal illness, but the INS would not guarantee that they would allow her to go home to be with her family before she died. In the process of fighting for her release, she died in state custody.

## Legal Challenges to Women's Imprisonment

Over the past thirty years, prisoners have faced the steady erosion of laws that ostensibly protect them against the abuses of the punishment system. The Supreme Court of the United States has systematically dismantled civil rights protections for prisoners, making it virtually impossible for prisoners to demonstrate that their mistreatment violates the Eighth Amendment to the U.S. Constitution, a provision that is supposed to protect against "cruel and unusual punishment." In addition to court decisions that detrimentally impact prisoners' access to justice, the U.S. Congress has also undermined legal protections for prisoners. In 1996, with little opposition, the legislature passed the Prison Litigation Reform Act (PLRA), which creates almost insurmountable legal barriers to prisoners and their advocates seeking remedies in court.

One of the most difficult provisions of the PLRA requires a prisoner to "exhaust available administrative remedies" before seeking assistance from a court. This requirement fails to acknowledge how systematically the prison denies prisoners agency and basic human rights. Indeed, it establishes a double-bind for the women who must fulfill it. The PLRA states that if there is any procedure in place, however flawed, a prisoner must prove that she has fulfilled the requirements of that procedure. In California, for example, a woman must first file a grievance form with the person with whom she has a complaint (e.g., the guard who sexually assaulted her or the doctor on whom she relies for treatment) and then pursue the complaint up several levels of review. Many women report that they never see the complaint again after they submit it at the first level. Others have described guards tearing up the complaints in their faces. But regardless of how fruitless the process may be, and considering that it ultimately most often fails, the fact remains that a woman cannot take a complaint to court without completing the procedure.

This process encapsulates and perpetuates the abuse of women inside. As the space of the prison becomes increasingly repressive, prison litigation "reform" only acts to obscure human and legal rights violations in prison, exacerbate the suffering of women inside, and facilitate the expansion of the prison industrial complex. As a result, women in prison in the U.S., the so-called "free" world, are neither free nor able to pursue legal remedies deemed basic and necessary human rights by international standards.

## Organizing for Change

Despite the significant obstacles encountered by those who want to challenge conditions of their confinement, especially through traditional legal methods, women prisoners find many ways to meaningfully organize and contest the injustices of imprisonment. In many states, women prisoners organize formal or informal peer networks that provide information and support on a wide range of issues, including health care prevention and treatment, child custody, labor conditions, and legal rights. In New York, women at Bedford Hills Correctional Facility organized a program called AIDS Counseling and Education (ACE), which provides prevention and treatment education and support to women in prison about HIV and AIDS. In California, peer educators have organized against the spread of HIV and HCV in prison and have provided health care information about a variety of medical conditions. Women prisoners have also filed individual and class action lawsuits demanding protection of their legal and human rights. In Washington, D.C., Massachusetts, and Michigan, for example, women successfully organized lawsuits challenging systemic sexual abuses in state prisons. The Legislative Hearings in October 2000 marked the first time in the history of California that proceedings were conducted inside women's prisons with prisoners serving as the primary witnesses. Approximately twenty women testified at two institutions on medical neglect, sexual assault, battered women's issues, and separation from their children and families. As a result of this testimony, two bills were introduced in the California legislature that will potentially have a far-reaching impact on health care in California prisons.

Advocates for women in prison are increasingly locating their efforts to ameliorate conditions of confinement within the frame of a broader resistance to the prison industrial complex. Human rights instruments are deployed to emphasize the systematic denial of human rights further exacerbated by the contemporary corporatization of punishment. However, the strategic goal of this work is not to create better prisons but rather to abolish prisons insofar as they function as a default solution for a vast range of social problems that need to be addressed by other institutions. It is within this context that the most far-reaching challenges are emerging to the racism that has been bolstered by the expansion of prisons. In California, for example, a number of groups work collaboratively to develop more radical approaches of working with and for women in prison. Justice Now is an organization that actively contests violence against women in prison and its connections to the prison industrial complex by training students, family members, and community members to provide direct services to women prisoners in California in conjunction with community-based education, media, and policy campaigns. The California Coalition for Women Prisoners organizes activist campaigns with and for women prisoners to raise awareness about inhumane conditions and advocate for positive changes. Legal Services for Prisoners with Children provides civil legal services to women prisoners, support to prisoner family members, and it also organizes in the communities from which prisoners come. California Prison Focus investigates and exposes human rights violations in California prisons, in particular those in Security Housing Units and supermax prisons. Critical Resistance (CR) builds national campaigns framed by analyses of the prison industrial complex that foreground the intersections of race, gender, and class. In the course of these campaigns, CR encourages people to envision social landscapes where ubiquitous state punishment will have been replaced by free education, health care, and drug rehabilitation, as well as affordable housing and jobs.

While national campaigns are rapidly advancing in the U.S., the World Conference Against Racism, Racial Discrimination, Xenophobia, and Related Intolerance provides a major opportunity to learn from and share experiences with organizations in other parts of the world. Greater emphasis must be placed on the global reach of the prison industrial complex and the further proliferation of the gendered racism it encourages. It is especially important that the punishment industry be seen as a significant component of the developing global political economy. An overarching recommendation for action thus calls for international networking among organizations that acknowledge the link between prisons and racism and that locate the important work of providing services to imprisoned women within a strong anticorporate and antiracist framework.

Further recommendations for action include the decriminalization of drug use and the establishment of free drug rehabilitation programs that are not tied to criminal justice agencies and procedures. This would drastically decrease the number of women in prison. In conjunction with these decarceration strategies, local and transnational campaigns to prevent the construction of new public and private prisons are also necessary. Legislation is needed that makes state and federal governments, as well as individual perpetrators, responsible for sexual abuse and harassment of women prisoners. In line with human rights standards, women's reproductive and family rights must be guaranteed. This means that civilian boards with enforcement powers should be established to review and act upon the grievances of women prisoners, especially those involving medical neglect, arbitrary discipline, and sexual abuse. In general, more widespread education and media campaigns are needed to expand and deepen awareness of the central role women's prisons play throughout the world in perpetuating misogyny, poverty, and racism.

## Notes

This essay was prepared as a contribution to the report presented by the Women of Color Resource Center, Berkeley, Calif., U.S.A. to the United Nations World Conference Against Racism, Racial Discrimination, Xenophobia, and Related Intolerance, held on 31 August–7 September 2001, in Durban, South Africa.

1. Julia Sudbury offers an analysis of the growing trend toward privatization of prisons in England in particular.

2. For a discussion of intersectional analysis, see Kimberlé Crenshaw, "Mapping the Margins: Intersectionality, Identity Politics, and Violence Against Women of Color."

3. Interview with Cynthia Chander, Co-Director, Justice Now, May 25, 2001; Interview with Heidi Strupp, Legal Assistant, Legal Services for Prisoners with Children, June 1, 2001.

4. For example, Jody Fitzgerald recently died at the Central California Women's Facility. In legal interviews with staff of Legal Services for Prisoners with Children, several women prisoners testified that prison staff ignored Ms. Fitzgerald's serious physical symptoms—claiming they were "all in her head"— and sent her to a psychiatric unit where she subsequently died.

5. Legislative hearings were conducted at Valley State Prison for Women on October 11, 2000, and at California Institution for Women on October 12, 2000. Twenty women provided testimony about medical neglect, sexual abuse and harassment, separation from their children and communities, and criminalization of battered women.

6. The contributions of women prisoners to this report were drawn from a number of sources: public testimony at legislative hearings; legal interviews with attorneys at Justice Now and Legal Services for Prisoners with Children; and oral histories recorded by community activists Cynthia Chandler and Carol Kingery. Names of women prisoners are used only when they offered public testimony or when they gave explicit permission for their names to be used. Otherwise the authors have assigned pseudonyms to protect their privacy.

7. Based on extensive interviews with women prisoners, reviews of medical records, and reports of outside doctors, legal advocates at Justice Now and Legal Services for Prisoners with Children concluded that all of the deaths of women at CCWF were attributable to medical neglect in one form or another.

8. See the discussion of prisoners' complaints machinery in *Making Standards Work* 1995, 37–40.

9. Legal interviews conducted by lawyers at Justice Now and Legal Services for Prisoners with Children with hundreds of women at Valley State Prison for Women, Central California Women's Facility and California Institution for Women reveal a pattern and practice of extreme neglect of women's reproductive health in prisons.

10. Theresa Lopez was a client of Justice Now who was granted compassionate release a few days before she died.

11. Ms. Rodriquez was a client of Justice Now.

## Works Cited

ABC News. 1999. *Crime & Punishment: Women in Prison: Medical Care.* Nightline. 2 November.

ACE Program. 1998. *Breaking the Walls of Silence: AIDS and Women in a New York State Maximum Security Prison.* Woodstock, NY: The Overlook Press.

American Bar Association (ABA) and National Bar Association (NBA). 2001. *Justice by Gender: The Lack of Appropriate Prevention, Diversion and Treatment Alternatives for Girls in the Juvenile Justice System.* Washington, D.C.: ABA and NBA.

American Civil Liberties Union Immigrant Rights Project (ACLU). 1993. *Justice Detained: Conditions at the Varick Street Immigration Detention Center.* New York: ACLU.

Amnesty International. 1999. *"Not Part of My Sentence": Violations of the Human Rights of Women in Custody.* New York: Amnesty International.

Belknap, Joanne. 1996. *The Invisible Woman: Gender, Crime, and Justice.* Belmont, CA: Wadsworth Publishing Company.

Bush-Baskette, Stephanie R. 1999. "The 'War on Drugs': A War Against Women?" In *Harsh Punishment: International Experiences of Women's Imprisonment,* edited by Sandy Cook and Susanne Davies. Boston: Northeastern University Press.

California Department of Corrections. *Monthly Ethnicity Population Report.* November 2000. www.cdc.state.ca.us/reports/montheth.htm.

Campbell, Davara. 1999. Unpublished interview on file with Justice Now. Central California Women's Facility. 16 July.

Chevigny, Bell. 1999. *Doing Time: Twenty-Five Years of Prison Writing.* New York: Arcade Publishing.

Cook, Sandy and Susanne Davies, eds. 1999. *Harsh Punishment: International Experiences of Women's Imprisonment*. Boston: Northeastern University Press.

Crenshaw, Kimberlé. 1995. "Mapping the Margins: Intersectionality, Identity Politics, and Violence Against Women of Color." In *Critical Race Theory: The Key Writings that Formed the Movement*, edited by Kimberlé Crenshaw, Neil Gotanda, Gary Peller, and Kendall Thomas. New York: The New Press.

Currie, Elliot. 1998. *Crime and Punishment in America*. New York: Metropolitan Books, Henry Holt and Company.

De Groot, A., T. Hammett, and R. Scheib. "Barriers to Care of HIV-Infected Inmates: A Public Health Concern," *The AIDS Reader*, May/June 1996.

Department of Corrections Services Division. 2000. *Characteristics of Population in California State Prisons By Institution*. Offender Information Services Branch. Estimates and Statistical Analysis Section, Data Analysis Unit, 30 June. Sacramento, CA.

Dobash, Russel P., R. Emerson Dobash, and Sue Gutteridge. 1986. *The Imprisonment of Women*. Oxford: Basil Blackwell.

Dyer, Joel. 2000. *The Perpetual Prisoner Machine: How America Profits from Crime*. Boulder, CO: Westview Press.

Federal Bureau of Prisons. 2001. *Quick Facts: April 2001*. http://www.bop.gov./facto598. html#Citizenship. 1 June.

Garcia, Maria and Gina Mendoza. 1998. Legal Interview. Valley State Prison for Women. 20 October.

George, Amanda. 1999. "The New Prison Culture: Making Millions from Misery." In *Harsh Punishment: International Experiences of Women's Imprisonment*, edited by Sandy Cook and Susanne Davies, 211–29. Boston: Northeastern University Press.

Giallombardo, Rose. 1966. *Society of Women: A Study of a Women's Prison*. New York: John Wiley.

Greenfeld, L.A. and T. Snell. 1999. "Women Offenders." *Bureau of Justice Statistics Special Report*. Washington, D.C.: U.S. Department of Justice.

Human Rights Watch. 2000. *Letter to INS Commissioner Doris Meissner*. New York: Human Rights Watch.

Human Rights Watch. 1998. *Locked Away: Immigration Detainees in Jails in the United States*. New York: Human Rights Watch.

Human Rights Watch. 1996. *All Too Familiar: Sexual Abuse of Women in U.S. State Prisons*. New York: Human Rights Watch.

Johnson, Regina. 1998. Legal Interview. Valley State Prison for Women. 3 March.

Kupers, Terry. 2000. *Prison Madness: The Mental Health Crisis Behind Bars and What We Must Do About It*. San Francisco: Jossey-Bass.

Live Jail-Cam. 2001. 23 May. http://www.crime.com.

Newsome, Melba. 2000. "Hard Time." *Essence Magazine* 31, no, 5:146–50, 210–14.

*Nightline*. 1999. "Crime and Punishment: Women in Prison: Medical Care." ABC News, 2 November.

Penal Reform International. 1995. *Making Standards Work: An International Handbook on Good Prison Practice*. The Hague: P.R.I.

Ross, Luana. 1998. *Inventing the Savage; The Social Construction of Native American Criminality*. Austin: University of Texas Press.

Steinberg, Susann. Deputy Director of Health Care Services Division, California Department of Corrections. 2000. Meeting with prisoner advocates. California Department of Corrections, Sacramento, CA. 10 October.

Stern, Vivien. 1998. *A Sin Against the Future: Imprisonment in the World*. Boston: Northeastern University Press.

Sudbury, Julia. 2000. "Transatlantic Visions: Resisting the Globalization of Mass Incar-
    ceration." *Social Justice* 27, no. 3:133–49.
*Truth to Power: Women Testify at Legislative Hearings.* 2000. Excerpts from Legislative
    Hearings on Women in Prison at Valley State Prison for Women, 11 October, and
    California Institution for Women, 12 October. Produced by Women in Prison Emer-
    gency Network. 40 min. Videocassette.
UN Special Rapporteur on Violence Against Women. 1999. *Report of the mission to the
    United States of America on the issue of violence against women in state and federal
    prisons.* New York: United Nations Economic and Social Council.
Welch, Michael. "The Role of Immigration and Naturalization Service in the Prison-
    Industrial Complex." *Social Justice* 27, no. 3:73–88.

## "Don't Let Nobody Bother Yo' Principle"
The Sexual Economy of
American Slavery

*Adrienne Davis*

2002

Many . . . young women are afraid to speak, let alone write. When I witness their fear, their silences, I know no woman has written enough.
—bell hooks, *Remembered Rapture*

### Personal Statement

I was an Afro-American studies major in college. Yes, *Afro-American* studies, so you can imagine this was the 1980s. Not the hard-edged black studies of the 1970s or the gentle chicness of African American or Africana studies in the 1990s. Afro-American. Language situates us in time and politics.

The two events that remain most impressed upon my mind from college occurred in the course of pursuing my major. I was a student of black feminist theorist bell hooks, Gloria Watkins, who taught courses in literature, specializing in fiction by black women. For Gloria, as we called the woman, and her classes into which we crowded, the rigorous study of literature yielded the greatest gift of all: mastery of language, the fundamental Western tool of self-articulation and representation. The students of all races who "took Gloria" learned how, through language, one acquires a voice, thus demanding recognition by others. Through these linguistic eruptions into existence, people achieve subjectivity, agency, humanity. Her courses, unable to contain the student excitement over the possibilities that language suggested for our agency, spilled over into her office. There, she encouraged black undergraduate women to use the study of literature to reclaim our sexuality, our lives, to realize that in a world structured to deny our humanity, we had choices, options. Through language, we could represent, and thus reclaim, our intimate selves.

This conversation, which continued over the course of two years, was punctuated by a moment when Toni Morrison came to campus to speak. Post-*Sula* and *The Bluest Eye*, pre-*Beloved* and *Paradise*, she talked about the paucity of language to describe the horror of American slavery. What language can we use to represent human bondage, to describe the conversion of humans into property, to capture the experience of being possessed or, even more grimly perhaps, of *possessing* another? The emptiness of language to describe the process of enslavement mirrors the void of slavery in the nation's memory.

Yet slavery, like our sexuality, lies continually at the periphery of our consciousness; eluding representation, it hovers over us. It disrupts our lives with unpredictable eruptions. Mimicking the American conspiracy of silence around slavery, black women often avoid speaking of sex and intimacy. But in its repression, black women continually create images, representations, which we then either embody in flat unidimensional cartoons of "respectable good girls" or reject, thereby risking sanction by our sisters. Without language, slavery and black women's sexuality each remains unspeakable—repressed, yet ever present.

Comprehending and filling the linguistic vacuums around slavery and black women's sexuality are directly linked to the project of this book: representing black women's work. What I now realize, as a scholar and a woman with her own sexual battlegrounds to conquer, is how the unspeakability of slavery contains the seeds of the unspeakability, for black women, of our own sexuality. As I say in my essay, the economy of American slavery systematically expropriated black women's sexuality and reproductive capacity for white pleasure and profit. As their descendants, we continue to suffer from the silence. The failure of language to document and archive the sexual abuse of reproductive exploitation of enslaved women is the origin of the absence of language to articulate for contemporary black women sexual identities that are empowering, fulfilling, and joyous.

In much of my professional adult life, through my research and my writing, I have tried to restore and engage that voice, to offer myself and other black women a voice sketched through history and law. My essay in this volume tries to combine and, to an extent, reconcile those two defining moments from a decade ago in my life when Toni Morrison and bell hooks urged me and other black women students to see that understanding both history and ourselves lay in mastering language and its mysteries. Without a vocabulary to describe slavery, contemporary black women have been without a voice to describe and confront the history of sexual and reproductive expropriation and exploitation that slavery entailed. In my essay, I propose to label slavery as a "sexual economy," hoping that this may give us the tools we need to excavate black women's history, document our exploitation, and archive our resistance. We can use this vocabulary to understand our collective sexual histories and then confront our choices, realizing that each of us makes different ones.

Toni Morrison and bell hooks were right, without language we can't represent; without representation, we can't imagine; without imagination, we can't comprehend; without comprehension, we can't move forward.

Beyond the backbreaking, soul-savaging labor that all enslaved people performed, American slavery extracted from black women another form of "work" that remains almost inarticulable in its horror: reproducing the slave workforce through giving birth and serving as forced sexual labor to countless men of all races. The political economy of slavery systematically expropriated black women's sexuality and reproductive capacity for white pleasure and profit. Yet what discourse has confronted and accused this national horror? What documents record its effects on enslaved women? In the face of this unspeakable work, chroniclers of American history have all but erased its existence. This essay attempts to initiate the beginnings of just such a conversation by naming the world of these legal conflicts a "sexual economy."

Voice and vocabulary are vitally important in antiracist and antisexist politics. Vocabulary is much more than grammatical choice, as represented in debates as diverse as the validity of Ebonics and whether "sex worker" or "prostitute" is the better word. Word choices represent political views of the world, especially when describing the topic of this book: work. We may need new terms, such as "sexual economy," to capture that history and reality and begin a discourse of national confrontation and, ultimately, of personal reconciliation.

This essay examines two cases in which enslaved black women's sexuality was at the heart of the dispute. It starts with an 1806 Virginia case in which two enslaved women used slavery's rules of reproduction and race to argue that they were not legally black and hence should be set free. The second case, an 1859 Mississippi case, involved the rape of an enslaved girl. I use these cases to investigate some of the primary legal doctrines that enabled elite white men to extract forced sexual and reproductive labor from enslaved women. Taken together, these cases and rules reveal how law and markets of the antebellum South seized enslaved women's intimate lives, converting private relations of sex and reproduction into political and economic relations. This interplay of sex and markets leads me to name this world a sexual political economy.

The idea of a "sexual economy of slavery" may seem odd on first impression. We divide our economic relationships in the workplace from our intimate, family interactions. We view these relations as taking place in two segregated spheres: the market and our intimate lives. It is in this latter space that we feel enabled to make our decisions, conduct our lives, love our own families. We may experience dissonances when sex and economics are jux-taposed. In addition, many of us imagine slavery as an institution of racial hierarchies, not gender hierarchies. But the cases and rules I will examine expose a different relationship between sex and markets for enslaved black women. In the process, they expose the brutal gender subordination that slavery entailed.

One quick caveat: slavery varied from region to region and slaveholder to slaveholder. It also evolved and mutated during its 250-odd years. I use two cases from two significantly different regions and periods (Virginia in 1806 and Mississippi in 1859). I do not mean to suggest that these cases are representative of slavery. However, I use them because individually and taken together they raise intriguing questions about the central and distinc-tive role that black women's sexuality and reproductive capacity played in the southern political economy.[1]

## A Life of Labor: Production and Reproduction

When we think of enslavement, we think of labor. Recent studies of enslaved women have shown that they labored no less than enslaved men. As activ-ist-scholar Angela Davis put it, "As slaves, compulsory labor overshadowed every other aspect of women's existence. It would seem, therefore, that the starting point for any exploration of Black women's lives under slavery would be an appraisal of their role as workers."[2] Historian Jacqueline Jones discovered that "in the 1850s at least 90 percent of all female slaves over sixteen years of age labored more than 261 days per year, eleven to thirteen hours each day."[3]

But the labor that slavery compelled of enslaved women was distinct from the way others worked in two ways. First, unlike white women, they performed the same work as men, while also doing the domestic work typi-cally reserved for women, free and enslaved. In the middle of the nineteenth century, seven-eighths of enslaved people, regardless of sex, were field work-ers.[4] In 1800, when the Santee Canal was built in North Carolina, enslaved women constituted 50 percent of the construction crew.[5] Deborah Gray White notes: "[I]t appears that [enslaved women] did a variety of heavy and dirty labor, work which was also done by men. In 1853, Frederick Olmsted saw South Carolina slaves of both sexes carting manure on their heads to the cotton fields where they spread it with their hands between the ridges in which cotton was planted. In Fayetteville, North Carolina, he noticed that women not only hoed and shoveled but they also cut down trees and drew wood."[6] Thus, enslaved women performed much of the same productive labor done by men who shared their race and status as slaves.[7] Jones notes that while the form of *extracting* their labor differed from that of a free labor system, the content of what enslaved men did could be analogized at some level to the work that all men did on farms, including in New England and on smaller southern farms.[8] This was not so for enslaved women, whose labor differed markedly from that performed by white women.

In colonial American society, privileged white women rarely worked in the fields. Occasionally, white female indentured servants were forced to work in the fields as punishment for misdeeds, but this was not a common practice. In the eyes of colonial white Americans, only debased and degraded members of the female sex labored in the fields. And any white woman forced by circumstances to work in the fields was regarded as unworthy of the title "woman."[9] Historians caution us not to overstate the point: there was gender differentiation in enslaved men's and women's labor.[10] Still, enslaved women did not perform gender-segregated labor nearly to the same extent that white women did.[11]

Performance by enslaved women of conventionally male work distinguished their labor from that of black men, white women, and white men. Enslaved men, and free whites of both sexes, worked in accord with gender roles. In fact, when enslaved men were assigned "women's work," it was often for the specific purpose of humiliation or discipline.[12] And historians Nell Painter and Chris Tomlins reinforce the intriguing point that, for those white women who did work in the fields, the reality of their daily lives departed from the rhetoric of white femininity.[13] The existence of this disjuncture in the lives of many working white women stemmed from the cultural and racialized importance of rigid gender roles. "[W]hile white women's field labor challenged gender roles, African women's field labor *confirmed* racial roles. Enslaved African women's substitution for white women field workers (occurring far earlier than the late 17th/early 18th century 'transition to slavery' would suggest) then increased opportunities for white women's participation in household formation, stabilizing white culture with an approximation of 'good wife' domesticity."[14] Within a society that enforced strict adherence to sex roles, only enslaved women were compelled to labor consistently across gender boundaries. This aspect of their physical work is one of the distinguishing features of their experience.

But slavery's political economy forced enslaved women to labor in a second way that was not required of any other group. As the remainder of this essay shows, enslaved women, and only enslaved women, were forced to perform sexual and reproductive labor to satisfy the economic, political, and personal interests of white men of the elite class. Even more so than crossing gender boundaries in physical labor, this second distinguishing feature of their experience under slavery foregrounds their gender and demonstrates how embedded their sexuality was in slavery's economic markets.

In an 1806 case, *Hudgins v. Wrights*, two enslaved women, Hannah and her unnamed daughter, sued for their freedom.[15] They alleged the wrongful enslavement of the woman who was, respectively, their mother and grandmother, Butterwood Nan. Let me consider in some detail the arguments of both Hannah and her daughter (the plaintiffs) and the man claiming to be their master (the defendant). Ultimately, Hannah and her daughter's freedom turned on how the law decided to characterize Butterwood Nan's reproduction.

The defendant, who claimed ownership of Hannah and her daughter, did so based on a fundamental rule of slavery: *partus sequitur ventrem*, Latin for "the child follows the mother." Under this law, adopted in every enslaving state, children inherited their status as enslaved or free from their mothers. This rule dictated that enslaved women gave birth to enslaved children and free women gave birth to free children. Accordingly, the slaveholder argued that because the ancestral matriarch, Butterwood Nan, had been enslaved, her daughter Hannah had inherited her enslaved status and subsequently passed it on to her own daughter, akin almost to tainted blood.

As early as 1662, Virginia adopted the rule that enslaved black women gave birth to enslaved children.[16] By the time of the founding of our democratic nation, all of the enslaving states dictated that enslaved black women gave birth to enslaved children, regardless of the father's status or race. As one judge said, "The father of a slave is unknown to our law."[17] This is a striking conclusion, given the general patriarchal and patrilineal nature of antebellum Anglo-American law. But, it is not a surprising one, given the direction of the political economy and wealth holding. Historians agree that "land and slaves became the two great vehicles through which slaveholders realized their ambitions of fortune . . . . The usefulness of land increased in proportion to the availability of black slaves."[18] Peter Kolchin documents the need for growing numbers of forced laborers as early as the colonial period: "Cultivating [tobacco and rice], however, required labor; in an environment where land was plentiful and people few, the amount of tobacco or rice one could grow depended on the number of laborers one could command."[19] Of course, the United States was not alone in basing its economy on black slave labor. It did distinguish itself, however, in how it met the ongoing need to replenish its workforce.

Other New World slave systems continued to kidnap Africans through the international slave trade to meet their labor needs. Varying combinations of higher ratios of men to women, low fertility rates, and extreme mortality rates meant that natural reproduction did not sustain the enslaved populations of Latin America and the Caribbean. The demography of these slave societies stood in stark contrast to the United States slave system. One "unquestionable—indeed unique—mark of slavery in the southern states was the natural increase of the slave population. In all other slave societies of the New World, the slave population failed to reproduce itself and was sustained or increased only by constant injections of new slaves from Africa."[20] This had striking demographic effects. "Jamaica, Cuba, and Haiti each imported many more slaves than the whole of the North American mainland. Yet, in stark contrast, by 1825 the southern states of the United States had the largest slave population of any country in the New World, amounting to well over one-third of the total."[21] Thus, the rule that children's status followed their mothers' was a foundational one for our economy. It converted enslaved women's reproductive capacity into market capital to serve economic interests. In the United States, it was enslaved women who reproduced the workforce.

Thus, childbearing by enslaved women created economic value independent of the physical, productive labor they performed. Southern legal rules harnessed black reproductive capacity for market purposes, extracting from it the profits one might expect from a factory or livestock. According to historian James Oakes, "The distinguishing function of slaves in the South's market economy was to serve not only as a labor supply but also as capital assets."[22] Law and markets operated synthetically in converting black reproductive capacity into capital creation. Slaveholders used the same logic of reproductive profits to get courts to void sales of enslaved women who couldn't bear children.[23] Functionally, reproductive relations were market relations of incredible economic significance. In its centrality to the political economy, enslaved women's reproduction was arguably the most valuable labor performed in the entire economy.

Thus, when the slaveholder in *Hudgins* invoked the rule that a child inherits its status from its mother, he was drawing on a foundational cultural assumption. Slaveholders owned all of the offspring of women they enslaved. The legal rule had immense economic and political significance for antebellum culture. Not only did slaves constitute the overwhelming proportion of the southern labor force, but this rule meant that it was a workforce that reproduced itself. Enslaved women gave birth to enslaved children and did so in a system that set considerable economic importance on this fact.

One of the nation's earliest and most prominent leaders, President Thomas Jefferson, personally proclaimed the unique, dual value of an enslaved workforce. Jefferson, who enslaved more than 144 people, said, "'I consider a woman who brings a child every two years as more profitable than the best man on the farm; what she produces is an addition to capital.'"[24] The value of short-term productive labor, such as that provided by the male slaves, or by the female slaves when viewed as mere field hands, "disappeared in mere consumption."[25] In keeping with this, Jefferson instructed his plantation manager to monitor the overseers and ensure that they were encouraging female slave reproduction, the source of his wealth. Repeated references to enslaved females' fertility in advertisements and negotiations for sales indicate that Jefferson was not alone in his sentiments.[26]

The secretary of the treasury and president of Georgia Cotton Planters Association estimated that a slaveholder's workforce would double every fifteen years through the process of normal reproduction.[27] Slavery scholar Deborah Gray White estimates that 5 to 6 percent of profit came from the increase of slaves due to reproduction.[28] Indeed, many members of the planting aristocracy owed their success to initial large gifts or inheritances of enslaved persons from their families.[29] Gray White notes, "Many farmers made their first investment not in a male slave, but in a young childbearing woman."[30] As one judge stated: "With us, nothing is so usual as to advance children by gifts of slaves. They stand with us, instead of money."[31] Historian Cheryl Ann Cody found that one of the men she studied "acquired slaves, once his estate was well established in the 1790s, primarily to give his sons their economic start rather than to expand his own labor force."[32]

Finally, southern judges drew analogies to rules governing livestock. Owners of female animals also got legal possession of their offspring. Should there be any doubt that southern whites grasped this analogy, one South Carolina judge declared that "the young of slaves . . . stand on the same footing as other animals."[33] Meanwhile a famous observer of the American South, Frederick Olmsted, concluded from his travels that "a slave woman is commonly esteemed least for her working qualities, most for those qualities which give value to a brood mare."[34]

The date of the case, 1806, is significant. The United States Constitution provided that no enslaved people could be imported (legally) from abroad after 1808.[35] Yet the expanding economies of the Deep South required larger and larger workforces. In 1806, Old South slave states, such as Virginia, were poised to take over the (legal) international slave trade with a domestic trade in slaves.[36] With enormous profits from reproduction anticipated, rules determining status became more crucial than ever.[37]

Therefore, the slaveholder in *Hudgins* drew upon the strong cultural expectation that personal economic profit would and should stem from an enslaved woman's childbearing. His lawyers cast his case as a question of "rights of *property*, those rules which have been established, are not to be departed from, because *freedom* is in question."[38] In other words, white economic rights trumped black liberty rights.[39]

Against this American backdrop of property rights in people, how could Hannah and her daughter have possibly responded? One would assume that the force of this law and custom would have dictated the outcome of the case: the law would side with the slaveholder, declaring him to be the legal owner of Hannah and her daughter. But, as central as these property rights were in the slaveholding South, they were countered by another, equally fundamental tenet of slavery, the rules of race. Hannah and her daughter argued that they could not be enslaved because, by law, they were *legally not black*.

Under Virginia law, only people of African descent could be enslaved.[40] Proving membership in the Native American or white races constituted a legal defense to slavery. Southern law dictated that blacks were presumptively slaves, while whites and Native Americans were presumptively free.[41] Judge Roane stated the law in *Hudgins*: "In the case of a person visibly appearing to be a negro, the presumption is, in this country, that he is a slave, and it is incumbent on him to make out his right to freedom: but in the case of a person visibly appearing to be a white man, or an Indian, the presumption is that he is free, and it is necessary for his adversary to shew that he is a slave."[42] Accordingly, Hannah and her daughter claimed that Butterwood Nan was Native American and therefore illegally enslaved. If Butterwood Nan had been wrongfully enslaved, then as a free woman she could not have transmitted any enslaved status to her daughter Hannah, who, in turn, could not transmit it to her own daughter. In a fascinating instance of valuing white racial privilege over white wealth, the laws of race trumped the law that enslaved the children of female slaves. From within this legal box of race and status, Hannah and her daughter asserted the only legal argument that could win their freedom, their own nonblackness.

The plaintiffs' argument rested on gender as well as racial rules of slavery. Mother and daughter claimed their freedom through Butterwood Nan. To counter this, the slaveholder argued that Nan was, in fact, black and that it was her sexual partner who was Native American. Therefore, the non-black (and legally free) ancestor was male. The establishment of nonblack ancestry had to be done through the maternal line to a female ancestor to be grounds for a claim of wrongful enslavement. Strikingly, within this deeply patriarchal culture, neither the father's race nor his status was relevant to the legal inquiry.[43] Free black men who took up with enslaved women fathered children who were enslaved by law. Moreover, showing white ancestry through one's father's side, indeed, showing that one's father was white, was no defense to enslavement. As noted before, by American law, the child of an enslaved black mother had no father. An enslaved woman who was black could not alter the status of her children through selecting either a free black or a white sexual partner.

Even more brutally, because the race of the father did not alter the status of an enslaved black woman's child, tens of thousands of white men were able to sexually abuse and coerce individual enslaved women without the risk that the women would bear children whose legal status would be affected in any way by their own. Such a child would not be construed by law as white or free, but as black and the father's slave.

Within what we now understand to be an absurd system, the assertions of both the slaveholder and the women he claimed as his property raise fascinating questions. Was Butterwood Nan exempted from the rule by virtue of being Native American? Had she lived her entire life held illegally as a slave? Were Hannah and her daughter free or enslaved? The arguments of both sides illustrate the centrality of enslaved women's reproduction to the political economy and culture of American slavery.

Let me finally reveal the outcome of the case. Judge Roane decided: "No testimony can be more complete and conclusive than that which exists in this cause to shew that *Hannah* had every appearance of an Indian. That *appearance* . . . will suffice for the claim of her posterity, unless it is opposed by counter-evidence shewing that some *female* ancester [*sic*] of her's [*sic*] was a negro slave, or that she or some female ancestor, was *lawfully* an Indian slave."[44] The court never described Butterwood Nan's appearance. Most likely she was deceased or had been sold out of the area and away from her family. But because Hannah and her daughter did not look black, they were presumptively free. The burden was on the slaveholder to prove that Butterwood Nan had been legally enslaved. He failed to do so. Hannah and her daughter went free.

Hannah's successful efforts to seek a racial exemption from slavery's status classifications left intact legal assumptions that relegated the overwhelming majority of blacks to enslavement. So, is this a case to be celebrated? Condemned? How do we evaluate the efforts of Hannah and her daughter to escape from the grip of *partus sequitur ventrem*? Their lawyer started his argument before the court, "This is not a common case of mere *blacks* suing for their freedom."[45] Looking backwards from the twenty-first century, should we blame Hannah for seeking her family's freedom with such arguments? What other argument could she make within a racial logic that drew a legal equivalent between blackness and enslavement? What else could Hannah argue, except that she was not black?

Earlier, this essay identified black women's deployment across the conventional sexual division of labor as one of the things that distinguished their lives from those of other groups. The physical labor of enslaved women differed from white women's work both absolutely and relative to the work done by enslaved men. The case of Hannah and her daughter exposes a second, more brutal way that the economic roles that slavery assigned enslaved women distinguished their labor from other groups. White men and black men (free and enslaved) could father children either free or enslaved, and white women could give birth only to free children.[46] Laws of race and gender merged with *partus sequitur ventrem*'s status classifications to condemn the wombs of enslaved black women. This is a point about race and gender: only black women could give birth to enslaved children, and every black woman who was enslaved and gave birth did so to an enslaved child. In other words, the class that reproduced the workforce was limited to black women.[47] It is this terrorizing aspect of enslaved women's lives that also distinguished their role in the political economy from that of black men, white women, and white men. At labor in the fields and in labor in the birthing bed—the enslaved woman was both a mode of production and a mode of reproduction.

I turn now from reproductive relations to sexual relations. Like reproduction, from a contemporary perspective, many of us tend to think of sexual relationships as intimate, noneconomic relationships. But, again like reproduction, enslaved women's sexuality played an essential role in the antebellum political economy. If the rule of *partus sequitur ventrem* reflected the southern investment in enslaved women's reproductive capacity, then the law of rape reveals the interests, economic and political, in their sexuality.

### Pleasure, Profit, and Punishment: Sexual Exploitation of Enslaved Women

In Mississippi in 1859, an enslaved man was accused of raping an unnamed enslaved girl, under ten years old.[48] Convicted at trial, the defendant, named only as George, appealed to the Mississippi Supreme Court. The lawyer representing him argued: "The crime of rape does not exist in this State between African slaves. Our laws recognize no marital rights as between slaves; their sexual intercourse is left to be regulated by their owners. The regulations of law, as to the white race, on the subject of sexual intercourse, do not and cannot, for obvious reasons, apply to slaves; their intercourse is promiscuous, and the violation of a female slave by a male slave would be a mere assault and battery."[49] Influential legal commentator Thomas Cobb agreed: "The violation of the person of a female slave, carries with it no other punishment than the damages which the master may recover for the trespass upon his property."[50] This meant that an enslaved woman's master could prosecute her rape as a crime against his property, but the state would not prosecute her rape as a crime against her person. The court agreed and overturned George's conviction. Nearly every southern court that ruled on rape and enslaved women followed this ruling.[51] As Carolyn Pitt Jones, a student, succinctly summarized it, within slavery's sexual subtext, the female slave was an extralegal creature who could not use the law to protect herself.[52]

It would be folly to overgeneralize about a society's sexual norms based solely on its laws of rape. But criminal laws of rape define the boundaries of sexual access to bodies, especially women's and children's.[53] And the doctrine in *George v. State* shows how white institutions, including law, created and legitimized black women's sexual vulnerability. The refusal of law to protect enslaved women from rape institutionalized access to their bodies. Their exclusion from rape doctrine enabled their sexuality to be seized for multiple purposes.

First, slaveholders could force the relations they had with enslaved women as their laborers beyond the economic arena and into the sexual one without significant social disruption. Not only productive labor and reproduction could be demanded of enslaved women, but sexual gratification as well. The refusal of law to recognize sexual crimes against enslaved women enabled masters to compel sex.

"Since the white male could rape the black female who did not willingly respond to his demands, passive submission on the part of the enslaved black women cannot be seen as complicity. Those women who did not willingly respond to the sexual overture of masters and overseers were brutalized and punished. Any show of resistance on the part of enslaved females increased the determination of white owners eager to demonstrate their power."[54] Sexual relations were part and parcel of what women were expected to do as members of an enslaved workforce.

Under this theory of law, and on a brutal daily basis, enslaved women's sexuality was under the direct control of men in the slaveholding class. But it is important to note that sexual abuse of enslaved women was not limited to white men in slaveholding families. This group comprised only a small percentage of whites in the South. Other men, poorer, nonslaveholding whites and black men, took advantage of enslaved women's sexual vulnerability. Overseers frequently sexually assaulted or coerced enslaved women. In addition, a slaveholder could compel an enslaved woman to have sexual relations with his friends or to "initiate" a son or younger nephew, much as he might hire her out for her productive labor. In the alternative, he might by his silence authorize sexual access for men related to him by blood or economics. In short, law granted masters not only economic and political authority, but sexual authority as well.

Sadly, there is a need for intraracial as well as interracial critiques of sexual abuse. Recall that the case of *George v. State* involved the rape of a ten-year-old enslaved girl by an enslaved man. This may be one of the reasons the case was ever prosecuted. While certainly many black men of this era respected black women's sexual integrity and rights over their own bodies even in the absence of legal dictates to do so, others did not. Black women's sexual vulnerability was created and legitimized by white institutions of law and social power, but black men as well as white took advantage of it. Intraracial sexual abuse of black women surely has a different social meaning and significance than their abuse by white men. But that should not preclude our investigating what that different meaning is, and why some black men and not others took advantage of their sisters.[55]

Second, some white slaveholders embraced the sexual exploitation of enslaved women to defend slavery against abolitionists who charged sexual abuse as one of the evils of slavery. According to Chancellor Harper, a judge: "And can it be doubted that this purity [of the white woman] is caused by, and is a compensation for, the evils resulting from the existence of an enslaved class of more relaxed morals? . . . I do not hesitate to say that the intercourse which takes place with enslaved females is less depraving in its effects than when it is carried on with females of their own caste. . . . [The white man] feels that he is connecting him with one of an inferior and servile caste, and there is something of degradation in the act. The intercourse is generally casual; he does not make her habitually an associate, and is less likely to receive any taint from her habits and manners."[56] Southern white men openly justified their exploitation of enslaved women as resulting in the better treatment of white women. The same sexual norms that protected (white) female chastity with vigilance and brutality (sometimes directed at the women themselves) construed enslaved women as perpetual "outlets."[57] Elite white women, represented as delicate and often asexual, found their own sexual relations closely guarded and monitored by these same men. "Whereas the lady was deprived of her sexuality, the black woman was defined by hers."[58] Sexual access to enslaved women was central in the creation and maintenance of this repressive ideology of white femininity. Black enslaved women were therefore excluded from, yet essential to, the gender ideology of white masculinity and femininity.

Third, sexual abuse of enslaved women must be understood as an exercise of political power as well as sexual license. Contemporary feminists have demonstrated that rape entails power relations as much as sexual relations. Men rape women not only for personal pleasure, but to discipline women into conforming to certain behaviors: to achieve women's submissiveness in personal relationships or adherence to conservative dress codes or to dictate physical activity, i.e., where and when women feel safe. Slavery offers a primary and stark example of the power relations embedded in forced sexual relations.

An enslaved woman might be sexually punished for any number of perceived or actual offenses. Forced sex reminded an enslaved woman of her powerlessness in the hands of her master or his agent, the overseer. It functioned to humiliate her and demonstrate that the legal system had given control over her body to the man who enslaved her. Angela Y. Davis offers the following characterization: "Rape was a weapon of domination, a weapon of repression, whose covert goal was to extinguish slave women's will to resist, and in the process, to demoralize their men."[59] Rape under slavery was an extremely powerful tool of disciplining women workers.[60]

In addition, rape helped to maintain racial hierarchy by reminding black women and men of black men's subordinate status to white men. As noted, a hallmark of southern antebellum culture was the protection of female chastity by male family members. An enslaved man who sought to do the same risked his life and that of the woman. "Clearly the master hoped that once the black man was struck by his manifest inability to rescue his women from sexual assaults of the master, he would begin to experience deep-seated doubts about his ability to resist at all."[61] Rape of enslaved women demoralized the entire black community. Law thus endorsed the use of sexual power as a mechanism of labor, racial, and gender control.

Finally, in addition to serving antebellum interests of pleasure and politics, enslaved women's sexuality was a source of economic profits for those inclined to reap them. Historians have identified an active market in enslaved women for prostitution, called the "Fancy Trade." "Slaves selected for their grace, beauty and light skins were shipped to the 'fancy-girl markets' of New Orleans and other cities. At a time when prime field hands sold for $1,600, a 'fancy girl' brought $5,000. Some ended up in bordellos, but the majority became the mistresses of wealthy planters, gamblers, or businessmen."[62] Sex might be extracted from any enslaved woman or girl. However, an enslaved woman sold primarily for sex commanded a higher price than other enslaved women.[63] The market assigned economic value directly related to sexual attractiveness. The seller reaped as extra profit the market's valuation of their sexuality, whether in skin color, hair, or whatever the buyer happened to personally value as erotic. As Brenda Stevenson incisively puts it, "What, after all, could be more valuable than a woman of 'white' complexion who could be bought as one's private 'sex slave'?"[64] To accommodate these buyers and ensure that they were getting what they expected, fancy-girl traders might allow the buyer to "inspect" his proposed purchase alone. At this juncture, sexual abuse and economic profits brutally collided.

The appearance of enslaved women as explicit sexual commodities in markets illuminates yet another way in which the South profited from enslaved women's sexuality. The fancy-girl trade offers perhaps the most vivid image of how enslaved women's sexual relations were integrally tied to market relations in the antebellum political economy. Many historians now acknowledge that white men used enslaved women for sexual gratification. But with the above analysis I have tried to point out the nuances of their sexual labor. At the southern antebellum juncture of sex and markets, enslaved women were sexually exploited for a variety of purposes: pleasure, politics, punishment, as well as profit. In addition, as I have described earlier, slavery replenished its workforce through black women. This convergence of sexual and reproductive relations with market and political relations is what leads me to name slavery a sexual political economy.

## A Sexual Economy

A political economy is characterized in some part by how wealth is defined, who owns it, and who creates it. In their descriptions of expected profits, ways to maximize yield, and transmissions of wealth between generations, elite members of antebellum society characterized enslaved women's reproductive capacity in the language of capital assets. Judges, cabinet members, and at least one president declared the economic value of enslaved women's childbearing capacity. This reproduction was integral to the plantation economy, which required a steady flow of cheap, largely unskilled labor. Hence black reproduction yielded economic profits, creating value for the slaveholding class. Enslaved black women gave birth to white wealth.

A political economy is also characterized by the interests it prioritizes and how those are served. White men established enslaved women as sexual outlets, forcing them to perform sexual labor. In the process, their sexuality could be exploited to reinforce gender conventions among elite whites and to defend slavery against northern charges. In addition, enslaved women could be sexually terrorized in order to coerce economic work or quell political resistance. Their exploitation could also be used to discipline enslaved men. Finally, as the fancy-girl trade illustrates, economic profits were to be made in slavery's sexual markets. Pleasure, punishment, politics, and profit: once laws of rape authorized elite white male legal and economic control over enslaved women's sexuality, their sexuality could be manipulated to serve any number of interests.

Taken together, *Hudgins v. Wrights* and *George v. State* show how law extracted and markets expected dual labor from enslaved women. Like enslaved men, they were coerced into performing grueling physical productive labor. But they were also compelled to do sexual and reproductive labor required of no other group. This suggests the need for attention to gender to fully understand the economics and effects of U.S. enslavement. Economists of slavery have characterized the political economy of slavery as a system in which blacks transferred millions of dollars of uncompensated labor to white slaveholders. "[Slavery] directly enriched those who bought, sold, transported, financed, bred, leased, and managed slaves in agriculture. But it was also important in other sectors, including mining, transportation, manufacturing, and public works—roads, dams, canals, levees, railroads, clearing land—and so on."[65] Wealth not only was transferred from blacks to whites, as scholars have noted, but, in addition, was transferred from black women to white men. Hence, the economics of slavery were gendered as well as racialized.

In addition, the economic impact of its sexual exploitation distinguishes the antebellum South from other enslaving systems. Other slave societies entailed sexual and reproductive exploitation.[66] Indeed, some cultures enslaved primarily women (and children). In this sense, they were more gendered than U.S. slavery with its relatively equal sex ratios. But, what I have tried to show in this essay is the extent to which enslaved women's sexual and reproductive labor was an integral and critical part of the economic and political viability of the South. One measure of slavery is how central or peripheral it is to the immediate economic functioning of the society. People might be enslaved to serve primarily as servants, political officials, soldiers, wives, or concubines.[67] Enslavement in the United States stands in stark contrast to all of these. David Brion Davis elaborates the relationship of slavery to the U.S. market economy: "No slave system in history was quite like that of the West Indies and the Southern states of America. Marked off from the free population by racial and cultural differences, for the most part deprived of the hope of manumission, the Negro slave also found his life regimented in a highly organized system that was geared to maximize production for a market economy."[68] Enslaved women both labored in and reproduced this workforce. I have also shown how their sexual exploitation was inextricably tied not only to economic viability but also to maintaining and defending the social order, ranging from pleasure to punishment to politics. In sum, slavery's legal and cultural institutions systematically made enslaved women's reproductive and sexual capacity available to serve any number of political and economic interests of elite white men. For all these reasons, I name the antebellum South a sexual political economy. Rules of race, rape, gender, and *partus sequitur ventrem* formed the legal core of slavery's sexual economy.

What, then, do we gain from viewing slavery as a sexual economy? I would suggest three things. One purpose in labeling the antebellum South a sexual economy is to draw attention to the extent to which slavery drew distinctions on the basis of sex as well as race. It was a gendered and sexualized as well as a racial institution. Or, in the language of subordination, a language that may more aptly characterize slavery's brutal hierarchies, American slavery, while obviously racially supremacist, was also fundamentally a system of gender supremacy. Designating it as a sexual economy draws attention to its axes of male power as well as racial power, thereby shedding light on the lives and exploitation of both enslaved women and enslaved men.

Viewing slavery through the sexual economy lens also suggests insights about the very nature of gender itself. "Masculine" and "feminine" mean different things in different races, classes, and ethnicities. Sexual roles and norms evolve over time and across cultural boundaries. Enslaved women offer an early, dramatic example of the political, cultural, economic, and violent forces that can shape gender. Angela Davis offers an excellent description of the manipulation of enslaved women's gender: "Expediency governed the slaveholders' posture toward female slaves: when it was profitable to exploit them as if they were men, they were regarded, in effect, as genderless, but when they could be exploited, punished and repressed in ways suited only for women they were locked into their exclusively female roles."[69] Jacqueline Jones concurs: "The master took a more crudely opportunistic approach toward the labor of slave women, revealing the interaction (and at times conflict) between notions of women qua 'equal' black workers and women qua unequal reproducers."[70] Against the feminine delicacy and chastity ascribed to most white women in this society, enslaved women were clearly gendered differently. They were gendered as masculine when performing conventionally male work or suffering the same brutal physical discipline as enslaved men. But an enslaved woman might have her sexuality or childbearing capacity seized for pleasure, profit, or punishment at any moment, suffering rape or giving birth to white wealth. She was male when convenient and horrifically female when needed. In this sense, she was "gendered to the ground," as legal feminist theorist Catharine MacKinnon would say.[71] Comprehending gender as brutally malleable may uncover deeply buried historical facts.

Finally, seeing slavery in this way challenges the way we divide the intimate from the economic. For enslaved women, sexual and reproductive relations were economic and market relations.[72] While their family lives and personal relationships offered some solace from the daily brutality of slavery, white men could invade this sphere at will, abusing women sexually or reproductively. Excellent work by historians Darlene Clark Hine and Nell Painter invites our attention to the ongoing sociological and psychological effects of slavery's sexual economy. Clark Hine makes the powerful argument that all of these manipulations and abuses of sexuality were primary factors in shaping cultures of resistance in southern black women. Dissemblance, flight northward, and most tragically, violence targeted at their own bodies were tactics black women employed.[73] And Painter argues that because sexual abuse of enslaved women was woven into the fabric of southern households and families, its cultural, sociological, and psychological effects reached far beyond enslaved females or even the larger enslaved and black communities.[74]

In the black community too often we still view sexuality as something to be kept private and not spoken about. Black women's magazines are filled with stories of the trauma and loss of self-esteem this repression causes. Perhaps understanding black women's sexual history as something under public control for so long can help us to see the inherently political nature of our sexuality.[75] For black women to reclaim our sexuality, our intimate selves, from all of the people and forces who would seek to expropriate it, regulate it, define it, and confine it, we must first become comfortable speaking about it. The language of the sexual economy may help in this process.

To summarize, enslaved black women shared the world of productive labor with white men, black men, and white women but also inhabited a separate world of compelled sexual and reproductive labor. By understanding American slavery as a sexual economy in which black women's reproduction and sexuality were appropriated for any number of white economic and political interests, we can see more clearly how slavery was a deeply gendered and sexualized institution in which there was a constant interplay between black sexuality and white economic profits. Such an understanding collapses the distinctions we draw between sex and work, families and markets, also showing how this distinction was itself largely under male control. It also enables us to see more clearly the institutions, including law, that slavery erected, institutions that systematically made enslaved women's reproductive and sexual capacity available for sale and consumption.

## Afterword: Reclaiming Ourselves

Grandma Baby said people look down on her because she had eight children with different men. Colored people and white people both look down on her for that. Slaves not supposed to have pleasurable feelings on their own; their bodies not supposed to be like that, but they have to have as many children as they can to please whoever owned them. Still, they were not supposed to have pleasure deep down. She said for me not to listen to that. That I should always listen to my body and love it.

—Toni Morrison, *Beloved*

Beyond the brutal exploitation and abuse of the slave economy, black women have reclaimed productive work as something that can be fulfilling and affirming. But much of the labor that slavery extracted from women in the enslaved workforce was sexual and reproductive. Toni Morrison's Pulitzer Prize–winning novel, *Beloved*, is a story about a black woman who is thoroughly brutalized and haunted by the sexual economy of slavery described above. Morrison poetically renders her character's exhausting struggle to reclaim herself, and her family, from the terror of her past.

Have we, today, fully reclaimed our own intimate lives from that horror? What are the ongoing effects of slavery's systemic expropriation of black women's reproduction and sexuality for market and political purposes? How does the sexual economy of slavery continue to affect the policing of black women's sexuality? From current national debates about welfare reform to local debates within the black community about sexual aggression by black men against black women, our intimate lives cannot be tidily defined as and confined to a private space. This essay has used cases and legal doctrine that document and record the real lives and experiences of black women who were enslaved, not only for academic insight, but to enable us to combat the effects of sexual economies, past and present.

## Notes

The title of this essay comes from Minnie Folkes, a former Virginia slave. Her full statement was, "Don't let nobody bother yo' principle, 'cause dat wuz all yo' had." John Blassingame, *The Slave Community: Plantation Life in the Antebellum South* (New York and Oxford: Oxford University Press, 1972), 163

1. On the specificity of slavery, see Peter J. Parish, *Slavery: History and Historians* (New York: Harper and Row, 1989), 3–6, 97–112.

2. Angela Y. Davis, *Women, Race, and Class* (New York: Random House, 1983), 5. Leslie Schwalm's study of enslaved women on South Carolina rice plantations also reinforces this point. Leslie A. Schwalm, *A Hard Fight for We: Women's Transition from Slavery to Freedom in South Carolina* (Urbana: University of Illinois Press, 1997), 19–46.

3. Jacqueline Jones, *Labor of Love, Labor of Sorrow: Black Women, Work, and the Family from Slavery to the Present* (New York: Basic Books, 1985), 18.

4. Davis, *Women, Race, and Class*, 5.

5. Ibid., 10.

6. Deborah Gray White, "Female Slaves: Sex Roles and Status in the Antebellum Plantation South," in *Half Sisters of History: Southern Women and the American Past*, ed. Catherine Clinton (Durham, N.C.: Duke University Press, 1994), 56, 59.

7. See also Brenda E. Stevenson, *Life in Black and White: Family and Community in the Slave South* (New York: Oxford University Press, 1996), 159, 187–192; Schwalm, *A Hard Fight for We*, 19–23; Carole Shammas, "Black Women's Work and the Evolution of Plantation Society in Virginia," *Labor History* 5 (1985): 5–6.

8. Jones, *Labor of Love, Labor of Sorrow*, 12. Brenda Stevenson notes that this was not the case in many African tribes. Stevenson, *Life in Black and White*, 171 (under sexual division of labor in many African tribes, men did not perform agricultural labor, which was considered women's work).

9. bell hooks, *Ain't I a Woman: Black Women and Feminism* (Boston: South End Press,1981), 22.

10. For instance, Deborah Gray White warns: "[I]t would be a mistake to say that there was no differentiation of field labor on southern farms and plantations. . . .Yet the exceptions to the rule were so numerous as to make a mockery of it." Gray White, "Female Slaves," 59–60 (emphasis added). In addition, "Pregnant women, and sometimes women breastfeeding infants, were usually given less physically demanding work." Ibid., 60 (footnote omitted). See also, Ira Berlin, *Many Thousands Gone: The First Two Centuries of Slavery in North America* (Cambridge, Mass.: Belknap Press of Harvard University Press, 1998), 56,135,168 (describing the evolution of sexual division of labor); Stevenson, *Life in Black and White*, 192–193.

11. See hooks, *Ain't I a Woman*, 22–23. Ira Berlin notes, "Only rarely—for the very young and the very old—did household labor occupy slave women on a full-time basis." See also Berlin, *Many Thousands Gone*, 168, 270–271, 311–312; Eugene D. Genovese, *Roll, Jordan, Roll: The World the Slaves Made* (New York: Pantheon Books, 1972), 495; Schwalm, *A Hard Fight for We*, 19–28.

12. See, e.g., Peter Kolchin, *American Slavery: 1619–1877* (New York: Hill and Wang, 1993), 121–122 (describing one slaveholder who used this tactic).

13. Nell Irvin Painter, "Soul Murder and Slavery: Toward a Fully Loaded Cost Accounting," in *U.S. History as Women's History: Feminist Essays,* ed. Linda Kerber et al. (Chapel Hill: University of North Carolina Press, 1995), 125, 142; Chris Tomlins, "Why Wait for Industrialism? Work, Legal Culture, and the Example of Early America," *Labor History* 40 (February 1999): 5.

14. See Tomlins, "Why Wait for Industrialism?" 32.

15. *Hudgins v Wrights*, 11 Va. (1 Hen. and M.) 134 (1806).

16. Act XII, 2 Laws of Virginia 170 (Hening 1823) (enacted 1662). For further discussion of this rule in Virginia, see Karen A. Getman, "Note, Sexual Control in the Slaveholding South: The Implementation and Maintenance of a Racial Caste System," *Harvard Women's Law Journal* 7 (1984): 115, 130–132; A. Leon Higginbotham Jr. and Barbara K. Kopytoff, "Racial Purity and Interracial Sex in the Law of Colonial and Antebellum Virginia," *Georgetown Law Journal* 77 (1989): 1967, 1970–1975; hooks, *Ain't I a Woman*, 39–44; Wilbert E. Moore, "Slave Law and the Social Structure," *Journal of Negro History* 26 (1941): 171, 184–191 (intriguing early discussion about definitions of enslavement).

17. *Frazier v Spear,* 5 Ky. (2 Bibb) 385, 386 (1811).

18. James Oakes, *The Ruling Race: A History of American Slaveholders* (New York: Knopf, 1982), 73.

19. Kolchin, *American Slavery*, 6–7.

20. Parish, *Slavery*, 23. "[T]he North American mainland was one of the smallest importers of slaves from Africa, and yet became the home of the largest slave population in the Western hemisphere." Ibid., 112, see also 16. See also Albert J. Raboteau, *Slave Re-*

ligion: *The "Invisible Institution" in the Antebellum South* (New York: Oxford University Press, 1978), 91. Slavery in the United States was not static, however, and at times failed to reproduce by natural increase. See, e.g., Berlin, *Many Thousands Gone*, 149 (through most of the eighteenth century, the slave population in the low country did not naturally reproduce); Parish, *Slavery*, 16 ("the first generation of slaves did not even reproduce their own population, let alone produce a natural increase").

21. Parish, *Slavery*, 12 (footnote omitted).

22. Oakes, *The Ruling Race*, 26.

23. Margaret Burnham discusses such cases in her excellent article on the legal treatment of enslaved families, Margaret A. Burnham, "An Impossible Marriage: Slave Law and Family Law," *Law and Inequality* (1987): 187,198–199.

24. Letter from Thomas Jefferson to Joel Yancy (17 January 1819), reprinted in *Thomas Jefferson's Farm Book: With Commentary and Relevant Extracts from Other Writings*, ed. Edwin Morris Betts (Princeton: American Philosophical Society, Princeton University Press, 1953). 42, 43.

25. Ibid.

26. Stevenson, *Life in Black and White*, 245.

27. Herbert G. Gutman, *The Black Family in Slavery and Freedom, 1750–1925* (New York: Pantheon Books, 1976), 76.

28. Deborah Gray White, *Ar'n't I a Woman? Female Slaves in the Plantation South* (New York: Norton, 1985), 177 n. 22. She describes the economics in excellent detail. Ibid., 67–70.

29. In 1818, one southerner wrote: "For a young man, just commencing life the best stock, in which he can invest Capital, is, I think, negro Stock . . .; negroes will yield a much larger income than any Bank dividend." Oakes, *The Ruling Race*, 73. Quoted in Leslie Howard Owens, *This Species of Property: Slave Life and Culture in the Old South* (New York: Oxford University Press, 1976), 16. Similarly, an uncle advised his young nephew: "Get as many young negro women as you can. Get as many cows as you can. . . . It is the greatest country for an increase that I have ever saw in my life. I have been hear [sic] six years and I have had fifteen negro children born and last year three more young negro women commenced breeding which added seven born last year and five of them is living and doing well." Oakes, *The Ruling Race*, 74 (quoting Alva Fitzpatrick to Phillips Fitzpatrick, Aug. 20, 1849, Fitzpatrick Papers, University of North Carolina, Chapel Hill, N.C.).

30. Gray White, *Ar'n't I a Woman?*, 67–70.

31. *Jones v Mason*, 22 Va. (1 Rand.) 577, n. 1 (Aug. 1827) (Carr, J., concurring).

32. Cheryl Ann Cody, "Naming, Kinship, and Estate Dispersal: Notes on Slave Family Life on a South Carolina Plantation, 1786 to 1833," in *Black Women in United States History: From Colonial Times through the Present*, ed. Darlene Clark Hine (New York: Carlson Publishing, 1990), 242.

33. *M'Vaughters v Elder*, 4 S.C.L. (2 Brev.) 307, 314 (1809). See also Parish, *Slavery*, 80 (describing a South Carolina planter who registered the births of enslaved children and of colts, naming the horses' sires but not the slaves' fathers).

34. Gray White, *Ar'n't I a Woman?* 177 n. 22 (quoting *DeBow's Review* 30 [1857]: 74, which is quoting Frederick Olmsted, *The Cotton Kingdom*, ed. David Freeman Hawke [Indianapolis: Bobbs-Merrill, 1971], 12, 72.)

35. U.S. Constitution, art. I, § 9, cl. 1.

36. See, e.g., August Meier and Elliott Rudwick, *From Plantation to Ghetto*, 3rd ed. (New York: Hill and Wang, 1976), 40–41 (describing the role of the United States in

ongoing illegal trade). On the slave trade generally, see Philip D. Curtin, *The Atlantic Slave Trade: A Census* (Madison: University of Wisconsin Press, 1969); Herbert S. Klein, *The Middle Passage: Comparative Studies in the Atlantic Slave Trade* (Princeton, N.J.: Princeton University Press, 1978); Stanley L. Engerman and Joseph E. Inikori, eds., *The Atlantic Slave Trade: Effects on Economies, Societies, and Peoples in Africa, the Americas, and Europe* (Durham, N.C.: Duke University Press, 1992). On the domestic slave trade see, e.g., Stevenson, *Life in Black and White,* 175–176; Walter Johnson, *Soul by Soul: Life Inside the Antebellum Slave Market* (Cambridge, Mass.: Harvard University Press, 1999); Michael Tadman, *Speculators and Slaves: Masters, Traders, and Slaves in the Old South* (Madison: University of Wisconsin Press, 1989); see also Parish, *Slavery,* 56–57 (summarizing the debate over extent and effects of domestic slave trade).

37. The scope, design, and profitability of breeding enslaved females remains deeply contested among historians. See Parish, *Slavery,* 63 n. 33; Richard Sutch, "The Breeding of Slaves for Sale and the Westward Expansion of Slavery, 1850–1860," in *Race and Slavery in the Western Hemisphere: Quantitative Studies,* ed. Stanley L. Engerman and Eugene D. Genovese (Princeton, N.J.: Princeton University Press, 1975); Richard G. Lowe and Randolph B. Campbell, "The Slave Breeding Hypothesis: A Demographic Comment on the 'Buying and Selling' States," *Journal of Southern History* 42 (1976): 401–412.

38. *Hudgins v Wrights,* 11 Va. (1 Hen. and M.), 136 (italics in original).

39. The *Hudgins* ruling suggests a different outcome when the contest is between white economic versus *white* liberty interests. See *Hudgins v Wrights,* 11 Va. (1 Hen. and M.), 140–141. For further discussion of this point, see Adrienne D. Davis, "Identity Notes Part One: Playing in the Light," *American University Law Review* 45 (1996): 695, 702–707.

40. Native Americans could be enslaved in Virginia only during a certain period of time, and whites could not be enslaved at all.

41. In an earlier essay, I joined other commentators in arguing that the decision in the case exemplifies the role of law in shaping the existence and meaning of racial categories, such as black, white, and Native American, in the U.S. law that protected those who were not black from being enslaved. One of the judges, for instance, said, "The distinguishing characteristics of the different species of the human race are so visibly marked, that those species may be readily discriminated from each other by mere inspection only." *Hudgins v Wrights,* 11 Va. (1 Hen. and M.), 141. The essay calls this assignment of race based on visual appearance a "scopic" determination of race, which it contrasts with assignments based on ancestry or genealogy. While many slave laws protected white economic interests, I argue that *Hudgins's* scopic rule of racial classification identified a second legally protected interest, the white liberty interest. Not surprisingly, under such a rule, the definition of "black" itself became a matter of legal contestation. See, e.g. Davis, "Identity Notes Part One," 702–711; see also Ariela J. Gross, "Litigating Whiteness: Trials of Racial Determination in the Nineteenth-Century South" *Yale Law Journal* 108 (1998): 109; Higginbotham and Kopytoff, "Racial Purity and Interracial Sex," 1975–1988.

42. *Hudgins v Wrights,* 11 Va. (1 Hen. and M.), 141 (italics in original).

43. See *Frazier v Spear,* 5 Ky. (2 Bibb) 385, 386 (1811).

44. *Hudgins v Wrights,* 11 Va. (1 Hen. and M.), 142 (italics in original).

45. *Hudgins v Wrights,* 11 Va. (1 Hen. and M.), 135 (italics in original).

46. At various points, white women, too, suffered regulations not unlike those suffered by enslaved black women. At times, white women giving birth to children deemed to be black could be sold into indentured servitude, and their children could be indentured.

If an indentured white woman had a child, it could extend the period of her own inden-ture (the child would be indentured until an adult, as well). In one extreme iteration, in 1664, Maryland enslaved white women marrying enslaved men for the lifetime of the husband, enslaving also any children. This law was repealed due to fear of its abuse by white masters seeking to extend white female servants' period of service. See, e.g., James Hugo Johnston, *Race Relations in Virginia and Miscegenation in the South: 1776–1860* (Amherst: University of Massachusetts Press, 1970); 172–179; Thomas D. Morris, *South-ern Slavery and the Law: 1619–1860* (Chapel Hill: University of North Carolina Press, 1996), 23; Martha Hodes, *White Women, Black Men: Illicit Sex in the Nineteenth-Century South* (New Haven: Yale University Press, 1997), 24–25.

47. Darlene Clark Hine concurs: "Slave women were expected to serve a dual function in this system and therefore suffered a dual oppression. They constituted an important and necessary part of the work force and they were, through their child-bearing func-tion, the one group most responsible for the size and indeed the maintenance of the slave labor pool." Darlene Clark Hine, "Female Slave Resistance: The Economics of Sex," in *Hine Sight: Black Women and the Re-Construction of American History,* ed. Darlene Clark Hine (New York: Carlson Publishing, 1994) 27, 34.

48. *State v George,* 37 Miss. 316 (1859).

49. Ibid., 317.

50. Thomas Cobb, *An Inquiry into the Law of Negro Slavery in the United States of America* (Philadelphia: T. & J. W. Johnson and Co.; Savannah, Ga.: W. T. Williams, 1858), § 107.

51. See, e.g., Higginbotham and Kopytoff, "Racial Purity and Interracial Sex"; Morris, *Southern Slavery and the Law,* 304–307.

52. Carolyn Pitt Jones, "Litigating Reparations for African-American Female Victims of Coerced/Uninformed Sterilization and Coerced/Uninformed Norplant Implanta-tion," 1999, 41 (memorandum written for class, on file with author).

53. "Serious prohibitions of rape strengthen the bargaining power of the weaker sex-ual player by making the stronger obtain consent from the weaker rather than force the sexual transaction. The various possible incarnations of rape—stranger rape, statutory rape, marital rape, acquaintance rape, and rape by abuse of familial or professional au-thority—mark the boundaries of one person forcibly claiming access to another's body without their consent and accordingly are central in setting the terms of such consent. . . . The law governing forcible rape also reflects the core beliefs of a society about the role of sexual access." Linda R. Hirshman and Jane E. Larson, *Hard Bargains: The Politics of Sex* (New York: Oxford University Press, 1998), 6.

54. hooks, *Ain't I a Woman,* 25–26.

55. Brenda Stevenson, for instance, describes a variety of factors that may have led some enslaved men to sexually objectify enslaved women. Stevenson, *Life in Black and White,* 242–243.

56. Genovese, *Roll, Jordan, Roll,* 420, quoting Robert Goodloe Harper, *Cotton Is King and Pro-Slavery Arguments,* ed. E. N. Elliott (New York: Vintage Books, 1976), 44–45, 61. See also Painter, "Soul Murder and Slavery," 142 (describing the complex reasoning of apologists defending the sexual norms of slavery).

57. Darlene Clark Hine notes: "Another major aspect of black women under slavery took the form of the white master's consciously constructed view of black female sexual-ity. This construct, which was designed to justify his own sexual passion toward her, also blamed the female slave for the sexual exploitation she experienced at the hands of her master." Hine, "Female Slave Resistance," 28.

58. Katherine Fishburn, *Women in Popular Culture: A Reference Guide* (Westport, Conn.: Greenwood Press, 1982), 10–11.

59. Davis, *Women, Race, and Class,* 23–24.

60. Enslaved men may have been sexually victimized for similar purposes; this topic is underexplored in the literature. For discussion, see Painter, "Soul Murder and Slavery," 137–138; Stevenson, *Life in Black and White,* 181,195–196. Judith Kelleher Schafer discusses the sexual torture of an enslaved boy in "Sexual Cruelty to Slaves: The Unreported Case of *Humphreys v. Utz" Chicago-Kent Law Review* 68 (1993): 1313. In *Beloved,* Toni Morrison alludes to sexual abuse of black men on the chain gang. Toni Morrison, *Beloved* (New York: Knopf, 1987), 107–108.

61. Angela Y. Davis, "Reflections on the Black Woman's Role in the Community of Slaves," in *The Angela Y. Davis Reader,* ed. Joy James (Malden, Mass.: Blackwell, 1998) 111, 124 (originally published in *The Black Scholar* 3/4 [1971]: 3,13); see also Stevenson, *Life in Black and White,* 240.

62. Dorothy Sterling, ed., *We Are Your Sisters: Black Women in the Nineteenth Century* (New York: W. W. Norton, 1984), 27. Deborah Gray White notes that the cities of New Orleans, Charleston, St. Louis, and Lexington seem to have been the centers of the trade. Gray White, *Ar'n't I a Woman?* 37. One trader insisted on separating a mother and daughter, speculating that when the daughter was a few years older, "there were men enough in New Orleans who would give five thousand dollars for such an extra handsome, fancy piece as Emily would be." Ibid., 38 (quoting Solomon Northrup, "Twelve Years a Slave: Narrative of Solomon Northrup," in *Puttin' on Ole Massa,* ed. Gilbert Osofsky [New York: Harper and Row, 1969], 268). See also Frederic Bancroft, *Slave Trading in the Old South* (1931; reprint, Columbia: University of South Carolina Press, 1996), 57,102,131, 328–330, in reprint; Stevenson, *Life in Black and White,* 180–181, 239.

63. "Only 'fancy' women commanded higher prices than skilled male slaves. . . . Joe Bruin of the Alexandria firm of Bruin and Hill placed Emily Russell, a beautiful mulatto whom he planned to sell as a prostitute in New Orleans, on the market for $1800. Bruin and Hill realized the profit that could be garnered from the 'fancy girl' market and often purchased females in Virginia and Maryland for that purpose." Stevenson, *Life in Black and White,* 180. This item appeared in a southern newspaper: "A slave woman is advertised to be sold in St. Louis who is so surpassingly beautiful that $5,000 has already been offered for her, at private sale, and refused." Bancroft, *Slave Trading in the Old South,* 329, see also 329–333. See also Kenneth M. Stampp, *The Peculiar Institution: Slavery in the Antebellum South* (New York: Knopf, 1956), 259.

64. Stevenson, *Life in Black and White,* 180.

65. Richard F. America, *Paying the Social Debt: What White America Owes Black America* (Westport, Conn.: Praeger, 1993), 6.

66. Orlando Patterson, *Slavery and Social Death: A Comparative Study* (Cambridge, Mass.: Harvard University Press.,1982), 50, 229, 230, 261.

67. See, e.g., Kolchin, *American Slavery,* 4. The sexual labor of enslaved women in the United States differed from sexual exploitation in other societies. The South was practically alone among slave systems in denying and prohibiting any legal recognition of women who built sexual families with their masters. See, e.g., Patterson, *Slavery and Social Death,* 231–232, 260–261.

68. David Brion Davis, *The Problem of Slavery in Western Culture* (Ithaca, N.Y.: Cornell University Press, 1966), 60.

69. Davis, *Women, Race, and Class,* 6.

70. Jones, *Labor of Love, Labor of Sorrow,* 12.

71. Catharine A. MacKinnon, *Feminism Unmodified: Discourses on Life and Law* (Cambridge, Mass.: Harvard University Press, 1987), 173; Catharine A. MacKinnon, *Toward a Feminist Theory of the State* (Cambridge, Mass.: Harvard University Press, 1989), 183,198.

72. "When the profitability of slaves as capital became that great, as it did very early on, the market economy came to intrude deeply into the most intimate of human relationships." Oakes, *The Ruling Race,* 26.

73. "Rape and the threat of rape influenced the development of a culture of dissemblance among southern black women" in the late nineteenth and early twentieth centuries. Darlene Dark Hine, "Rape and the Inner Lives of Black Women: Thoughts on the Culture of Dissemblance," in *Hine Sight,* ed. Hine, 37. She continues, "Black women as a rule developed a politics of silence, and adhered to a cult of secrecy, a culture of dissemblance, to protect the sanctity of the inner aspects of their lives." Ibid., 41. She also makes the case that "the most common, and certainly the most compelling, motive for running, fleeing, or migrating was a desire to retain or claim some control of their own sexual beings and the children they bore." Ibid., 40–41. In addition, Hine argues that enslaved women understood their own sexual economic value and used that to resist slavery; "When they resisted sexual exploitation through such means as sexual abstention, abortion, and infanticide, they were, at the same time, rejecting their vital economic function as breeders. . . . The female slave, through her sexual resistance, attacked the very assumptions upon which the slave order was constructed and maintained. Resistance to sexual exploitation therefore had major political and economic implications." Hine, "Female Slave Resistance," 34. See also Stevenson, *Life in Black and White,* 245–246.

74. In two path-breaking essays, Painter argues that historians have failed to approach sexual abuse in the context of interracial households as families and enslaved women as workers and hence have missed critical psychological effects that spanned all of southern society. Nell Irvin Painter, "Of *Lily,* Linda Brent, and Freud: A Non-Exceptionalist Approach to Race, Class, and Gender in the Slave South," in *Half Sisters of History: Southern Women and the American Past,* ed. Catherine Clinton (Durham, N.C.: Duke University Press, 1994), 93; Painter, "Soul Murder and Slavery," 126–128.

75. Darlene Clark Hine puts it powerfully: "The fundamental tensions between black women and the rest of the society—especially white men, white women, and to a lesser extent, black men—involved a multifaceted struggle to determine who would control black women's productive and reproductive capacities and their sexuality. At stake for black women caught up in this ever evolving, constantly shifting, but relentless war was the acquisition of personal autonomy and economic liberation." Hine, "Rape and the Inner Lives of Black Women, 41.

## Punks, Bulldaggers, and Welfare Queens
### The Radical Potential of Queer Politics?

*Cathy J. Cohen*

2005

On the eve of finishing this essay, my attention is focused not on how to rework the conclusion (as it should be) but instead on the news stories of alleged racism at Gay Men's Health Crisis (GMHC). It seems that three black board members of this largest and oldest AIDS organization in the world have resigned over their perceived subservient position on the GMHC board. Billy E. Jones, former head of the New York City Health and Hospitals Corporation and one of the board members who quit, was quoted in the *New York Times* as saying that "much work needs to be done at GMHC to make it truly inclusive and welcoming of diversity. . . . It is also clear that such work will be a great struggle. I am resigning because I do not choose to engage in such struggle at GMHC, but rather prefer to fight for the needs of those ravaged by H.I.V."[1]

This incident raises mixed emotions for me, for it points to the continuing practice of racism that many of us experience on a daily basis in lesbian and gay communities. But, just as disturbing, it also highlights the limits of a lesbian and gay political agenda based on a civil rights strategy, where assimilation into, and replication of, dominant institutions are the goals. Many of us continue to search for a new political direction and agenda, one that does not focus on integration into dominant structures but instead seeks to transform the basic fabric and hierarchies that allow systems of oppression to persist and operate efficiently. For some of us, such a challenge to traditional gay and lesbian politics was offered by the idea of queer politics. Here we had a potential movement of young antiassimilationist activists committed to challenging the very way that people understand and respond to sexuality. These activists promised to engage in struggles that would disrupt dominant norms of sexuality, radically transforming politics in lesbian, gay, bisexual, and transgendered communities.

Despite the possibility invested in the idea of queerness and the practice of queer politics, I argue here that a truly radical or transformative politics has not resulted from queer activism. In many instances, instead of destabilizing the assumed categories and binaries of sexual identity, queer politics has served to reinforce simple dichotomies between the heterosexual and everything "queer." An understanding of the ways in which power informs and constitutes privileged and marginalized subjects on both sides of this dichotomy has been left unexamined.

I query in this essay whether there are lessons to be learned from queer activism that can help us construct a new politics. I envision a politics where one's relation to power, and not some homogenized identity, is privileged in determining one's political comrades. I am talking about a politics where the nonnormative and marginal position of punks, bulldaggers, and welfare queens, for example, is the basis for progressive transformative coalition work. Thus, if any truly radical potential is to be found in the idea of queerness and the practice of queer politics, it would seem to be located in its ability to create a space in opposition to dominant norms, a space where transformational political work can begin.

### The Emergence of Queer Politics and a New Politics of Transformation

Theorists and activists alike generally agree that it was not until the early 1990s that the term "queer" began to be used with any regularity.[2] This term would come to denote not only an emerging politics but also a new cohort of academics working in programs primarily in the humanities centered around social and cultural criticism.[3] Individuals such as Judith Butler, Eve Sedgwick, Teresa de Lauretis, Diana Fuss, and Michael Warner produced what are now thought of as the first canonical works of "queer theory." Working from a variety of postmodernist and poststructuralist theoretical perspectives, these scholars focused on identifying and contesting the discursive and cultural markers found within both dominant and marginal identities and institutions that prescribe and reify "heterogendered" understandings and behavior.[4] These theorists presented a different conceptualization of sexuality, one that sought to replace socially named and presumably stable categories of sexual expression with a new fluid movement among and between forms of sexual behavior.[5]

Through its conception of a wide continuum of sexual possibilities, queer theory stands in direct contrast to the normalizing tendencies of hegemonic sexuality rooted in ideas of static, stable sexual identities and behaviors. In queer theorizing, the sexual subject is understood to be constructed and contained by multiple practices of categorization and regulation that systematically marginalize and oppress those subjects thereby defined as deviant and "other." And, at its best, queer theory focuses on and makes central not only the socially constructed nature of sexuality and sexual categories but also the varying degrees and multiple sites of power distributed within all categories of sexuality, including the normative category of heterosexuality.

It was in the early 1990s, however, that the postmodern theory being produced in the academy (later to be recategorized as queer theory) found its most direct interaction with the real-life politics of lesbian, gay, bisexual, and transgendered activists. Frustrated with what was perceived to be the scientific "de-gaying" and assimilationist tendencies of AIDS activism, with their invisibility in the more traditional civil rights politics of lesbian and gay organizations, and with increasing legal and physical attacks against lesbian and gay community members, a new generation of activists began the process of building a more confrontational political formation, which they labeled "queer politics."[6] Queer politics, represented most notoriously in the actions of the group Queer Nation, is understood as an "in your face" politics of a younger generation. Through action and analysis these individuals seek to make "queer" function as more than just an abbreviation for lesbian, gay, bisexual, and transgendered. Similar to queer theory, the queer politics articulated and pursued by these activists first and foremost recognizes and encourages the fluidity and movement of people's sexual lives. In queer politics sexual expression is something that always entails the possibility of change, movement, redefinition, and subversive performance— from year to year, from partner to partner, from day to day, and even from act to act. In addition to highlighting the instability of sexual categories and sexual subjects, queer activists also directly challenge the multiple practices and vehicles of power that render them invisible and at risk. However, what seems to make queer activists unique, at this particular moment, is their willingness to confront normalizing power by emphasizing and exaggerating their own antinormative characteristics and nonstable behavior. Joshua Gamson, in "Must Identity Movements Self-Destruct? A Queer Dilemma," writes that queer activism and theory pose the challenge of a form of organizing in which, far from inhibiting accomplishments, the *destabilization* of collective identity is itself a goal and accomplishment of collective action. The assumption that stable collective identities are necessary for collective action is turned on its head by queerness, and the question becomes: When and how are stable collective identities necessary for social action and social change? Secure boundaries and stabilized identities are necessary not in general, but in the specific, a point social movement theory seems currently to miss.[7]

Thus queer politics, much like queer theory, is often perceived as standing in opposition, or in contrast, to the category-based identity politics of traditional lesbian and gay activism. And for those of us who find ourselves on the margins, operating through multiple identities and thus not fully served or recognized through traditional single-identity-based politics, theoretical conceptualizations of queerness hold great political promise. For many of us, the label "queer" symbolizes an acknowledgment that through our existence and everyday survival we embody sustained and multi-sited resistance to systems (based on dominant constructions of race and gender) that seek to normalize our sexuality, exploit our labor, and constrain our visibility. At the intersection of oppression and resistance lies the radical potential of queerness to challenge and bring together all those deemed marginal and all those committed to liberatory politics.

The problem, however, with such a conceptualization and expectation of queer identity and politics is that in its present form queer politics has not emerged as an encompassing challenge to systems of domination and oppression, especially those normalizing processes embedded in heteronormativity. By "heteronormativity" I mean both those localized practices and those centralized institutions that legitimize and privilege heterosexuality and heterosexual relationships as fundamental and "natural" within society. I raise the subject of heteronormativity because it is this normalizing practice/power that has most often been the focus of queer politics.[8]

The inability of queer politics to effectively challenge heteronormativity rests, in part, on the fact that despite a surrounding discourse that highlights the destabilization and even deconstruction of sexual categories, queer politics has often been built around a simple dichotomy between those deemed queer and those deemed heterosexual. Whether in the infamous "I Hate Straights" publication or in queer kiss-ins at malls and straight dance clubs, very near the surface in queer political action is an uncomplicated understanding of power as it is encoded in sexual categories: all heterosexuals are represented as dominant and controlling and all queers are understood as marginalized and invisible. Thus, even in the name of destabilization, some queer activists have begun to prioritize sexuality as the primary frame through which they pursue their politics.[9] Undoubtedly, within different contexts various characteristics of our total being—for example, race, gender, class, sexuality—are highlighted or called on to make sense of a particular situation. However, my concern is centered on those individuals who consistently activate only one characteristic of their identity, or a single perspective of consciousness, to organize their politics, rejecting any recognition of the multiple and intersecting systems of power that largely dictate our life chances.

The focus of this essay is the disjuncture, evident in queer politics, between an articulated commitment to promoting an understanding of sexuality that rejects the idea of static, monolithic, bounded categories, on the one hand, and political practices structured around binary conceptions of sexuality and power, on the other. Specifically, I am concerned with those manifestations of queer politics in which the capital and advantage invested in a range of sexual categories are disregarded and, as a result, narrow and homogenized political identities are reproduced that inhibit the radical potential of queer politics. It is my contention that queer activists who evoke a single-oppression framework misrepresent the distribution of power within and outside of gay, lesbian, bisexual, and transgendered communities, and therefore limit the comprehensive and transformational character of queer politics.

Recognizing the limits of current conceptions of queer identities and queer politics, I am interested in examining the concept of "queer" in order to think about how we might construct a new political identity that is truly liberating, transformative, and inclusive of all those who stand on the outside of the dominant constructed norm of state-sanctioned white middle- and upper-class heterosexuality.[10] Such a broadened understanding of queerness must be based on an intersectional analysis that recognizes how numerous systems of oppression interact to regulate and police the lives of most people. Black lesbian, bisexual, and heterosexual feminist authors such as Kimberlé Crenshaw, Barbara Ransby, Angela Davis, Cheryl Clarke, and Audre Lorde have repeatedly emphasized in their writing the intersectional workings of oppression. And it is just such an understanding of the interlocking systems of domination that is noted in the opening paragraph of the now famous black feminist statement by the Combahee River Collective: "The most general statement of our politics at the present time would be that we are actively committed to struggling against racial, sexual, heterosexual, and class oppression and see as our particular task the development of *integrated* analysis and practice based upon the fact that the major systems of oppression are interlocking. The synthesis of these oppressions creates the conditions of our lives. As Black women we see Black feminism as the logical political movement to combat the manifold and simultaneous oppressions that all women of color face."[11] This analysis of an individual's place in the world, which focuses on the intersection of systems of oppression, is informed by a consciousness that undoubtedly grows from the lived experience of existing within and resisting multiple and connected practices of domination and normalization. Just such a lived experience and analysis have determined much of the progressive and expansive nature of the politics emanating from people of color—people who are both inside and outside of lesbian and gay communities.

However, beyond a mere recognition of the intersection of oppressions there must also be an understanding of the ways our multiple identities work to limit the entitlement and status that some receive from obeying a heterosexual imperative. For instance, how would queer activists understand politically the lives of women (particularly women of color) on welfare, who may fit into the category of heterosexual but whose sexual choices are not perceived as normal, moral, or worthy of state support? Further, how do queer activists understand and relate politically to those whose same-sex sexual identities position them within the category of queer, but who hold other identities based on class, race, and/or gender categories that provide them with membership in and the resources of dominant institutions and groups?

Thus, inherent in our new politics must be a commitment to Left analysis and politics. Black feminists as well as other marginalized and progressive scholars and activists have long argued that any political response to the multilayered oppression that most of us experience must be rooted in a Left understanding of our political, economic, social, and cultural institutions. Fundamentally, a Left framework makes central the interdependency among multiple systems of domination. Such a perspective also ensures that while activists should rightly be concerned with forms of discursive and cultural coercion, we also recognize and confront the more direct and concrete forms of exploitation and violence rooted in state-regulated institutions and economic systems. The "Statement of Purpose" from the first Dialogue on the Lesbian and Gay Left comments specifically on the role of interlocking systems of oppression in the lives of gays and lesbians: "By leftist we mean people who understand the struggle for lesbian and gay liberation to be integrally tied to struggles against class oppression, racism and sexism. While we might use different political labels, we share a commitment to a fundamental transformation of the economic, political and social structures of society."[12]

A Left framework of politics, unlike civil rights or liberal frameworks, brings into focus the systematic relationship among forms of domination, where the creation and maintenance of exploited, subservient, marginalized classes is a necessary part of, at the very least, the economic configuration. For example, Urvashi Vaid in *Virtual Equality* writes of the limits of civil rights strategies in confronting systemic homophobia: "Civil rights do not change the social order in dramatic ways; they change only the privileges of the group asserting those rights. Civil rights strategies do not challenge the moral and antisexual underpinnings of homophobia, because homophobia does not originate in our lack of full civil equality. Rather, homophobia arises from the nature and construction of the political, legal, economic, sexual, racial and family systems within which we live."[13] Proceeding from the starting point of a system-based Left analysis, strategies built on the possibility of incorporation and assimilation are exposed as simply expanding and making accessible the status quo for more privileged members of marginal groups, while the most vulnerable in our communities continue to be stigmatized and oppressed.

It is important to note, however, that while Left theorists tend to provide a more structural analysis of oppression and exploitation, many of these theorists and activists have also been homophobic and heterosexist in their approach to or avoidance of the topics of sexuality and heteronormativity. For example, Robin Podolsky, in "Sacrificing Queers and Other 'Proletarian' Artifacts," writes that quite often on the Left lesbian and gay sexuality and desire have been characterized as "more to do with personal happiness and sexual pleasure than with the 'material basis' of procreation—we were considered self-indulgent distractions from struggle . . . [an example of] 'bourgeois decadence.'"[14] This contradiction between a stated Left analysis and an adherence to heteronormativity has probably been most dramatically identified in the writing of several feminist authors. I need only refer to Adrienne Rich's well-known article "Compulsory Heterosexuality and Lesbian Existence" as a poignant critique of the white, middle-class heterosexual standard running through significant parts of feminist analysis and actions.[15] The same adherence to a heterosexual norm can be found in the writing of self-identified black Left intellectuals such as Cornel West and Michael Eric Dyson. Thus, while these writers have learned to make reference— sparingly—to lesbian, gay, bisexual, and transgendered segments of black communities, they continue to foreground black heterosexuality and masculinity as the central unit of analysis in their writing—and most recently in their politics: witness their participation in the Million Man March.

This history of Left organizing and the Left's visible absence from any serious and sustained response to the AIDS epidemic have provoked many lesbian, gay, bisexual, and transgendered people to question the relevance of this political configuration to the needs of our communities. Recognizing that reservations of this type are real and should be noted, I still hold that a left-rooted analysis that emphasizes economic exploitation and class structure, culture, and the systemic nature of power provides a framework of politics that is especially effective in representing and challenging the numerous sites and systems of oppression. Further, the Left-centered approach that I embrace is one that designates sexuality and struggles against sexual normalization as central to the politics of all marginal communities.

## The Root of Queer Politics:
## Challenging Heteronormativity?

In his introduction to *Fear of a Queer Planet: Queer Politics and Social Theory*, Michael Warner asks the question, "What do queers want?" He suggests that the goals of queers and their politics extend beyond the sexual arena to the acknowledgment of their lives, struggles, and complete existence; that is, that queers want to be represented and included fully in Left political analysis and American culture. What queers want is thus to be a part of the social, economic, and political restructuring of this society; as Warner writes, queers want to have queer experience and politics "taken as starting points rather than as footnotes" in the social theories and political agendas of the Left. He contends that it has been the absence or invisibility of lived queer experience that has marked or constrained much of Left social and political theories and that has "posited and naturalized a heterosexual society" in such theories. The concerns and emerging politics of queer activists, as formulated by Warner and others interested in understanding the implications of the idea of queerness, are focused on highlighting queer presence and destroying heteronormativity not only in the larger dominant society but also in extant spaces, theories, and sites of resistance, presumably on the Left. He suggests that those embracing the label of "queer" understand the need to challenge the assumption of heteronormativity in every aspect of their existence: "Every person who comes to a queer self-understanding knows in one way or another that her stigmatization is connected with gender, the family, notions of individual freedom, the state, public speech, consumption and desire, nature and culture, maturation, reproductive politics, racial and national fantasy, class identity, truth and trust, censorship, intimate life and social display, terror and violence, health care, and deep cultural norms about the bearing of the body. Being queer means fighting about these issues all the time, locally and piecemeal but always with consequences."[16]

Independent of the fact that few of us could find ourselves in such a grandiose description of queer consciousness, I believe that Warner's description points to the fact that in the roots of a lived "queer" existence are experiences with domination, and in particular heteronormativity, that form the basis for genuine transformational politics. In using the term "transformational" I mean a politics that does not search for opportunities to integrate into dominant institutions and normative social relationships but instead pursues a political agenda that seeks to change values, definitions, and laws that make these institutions and relationships oppressive.

Queer activists experiencing displacement both within and outside of lesbian and gay communities rebuff what they deem the assimilationist practices and policies of more established lesbian and gay organizations. These organizers and activists reject cultural norms of acceptable sexual behavior and identification and instead embrace political strategies that promote self-definition and full expression. Members of the Chicago-based group Queers United Against Straight-Acting Homosexuals (QUASH) state just such a position in the article "Assimilation Is Killing Us: Fight for a Queer United Front" published in their newsletter, *Why I Hated the March on Washington*:

> Assimilation is killing us. We are falling into a trap. Some of us adopt an apologetic stance, stating "that's just the way I am" (read: "I'd be straight if I could"). Others pattern their behavior in such a way as to mimic heterosexual society so as to minimize the glaring differences between us and them. No matter how much [money] you make, fucking your lover is still illegal in nearly half of the states. Getting a corporate job, a fierce car and a condo does not protect you from dying of AIDS or getting your head bashed in by neo-Nazis. The myth of assimilation must be shattered.
>     . . . Fuck the heterosexual, nuclear family. Let's make families which promote sexual choices and liberation rather than sexual oppression. We must learn from the legacy of resistance that is ours: a legacy which shows that empowerment comes through grassroots activism, not mainstream politics, a legacy which shows that real change occurs when we are inclusive, not exclusive.[17]

At the very heart of queer politics, at least as it is formulated by QUASH, is a fundamental challenge to the heteronormativity—the privilege, power, and normative status invested in heterosexuality—of the dominant society.

It is in their fundamental challenge to a systemic process of domination and exclusion, with a specific focus on heteronormativity, that queer activists and queer theorists are tied to and rooted in a tradition of political struggle most often identified with people of color and other marginal groups. For example, activists of color have, through many historical periods, questioned their formal and informal inclusion and power in prevailing social categories. Through just such a process of challenging their centrality to lesbian and gay politics in particular, and lesbian and gay communities more generally, lesbian, gay, bisexual, and transgendered people of color advanced debates over who and what would be represented as "truly gay." As Steven Seidman reminds us in "Identity and Politics in a 'Postmodern' Gay Culture: Some Historical and Conceptual Notes," beyond the general framing provided by postmodern queer theory, gay and lesbian (and now queer) politics owes much of its impetus to the politics of people of color and other marginalized members of lesbian and gay communities. "Specifically, I make the case that postmodern strains in gay thinking and politics have their immediate social origin in recent developments in the gay culture. In the reaction by people of color, third-world-identified gays, poor and working class gays, and sex rebels to the ethnic/essentialist model of identity and community that achieved dominance in the lesbian and gay cultures of the 1970s, I locate the social basis for a rethinking of identity and politics."[18] Through the demands of lesbian, gay, bisexual, and transgendered people of color as well as others who did not see themselves or their numerous communities in the more narrowly constructed politics of white gays and lesbians, the contestation took shape over who and what type of issues would be represented in lesbian and gay politics and in larger community discourse.

While a number of similarities and connections between the politics of lesbians, gay men, bisexuals, and transgendered people of color during the 1970s and 1980s and queer activists of today clearly exist, the present-day rendition of this politics has deviated significantly from its legacy. Specifically, while both political efforts include as a focus of their work the radicalization and/or expansion of traditional lesbian and gay politics, the politics of lesbian, gay, bisexual, and transgendered people of color have been and continue to be much broader in terms of its understanding of transformational politics.

The politics of lesbian, gay, bisexual, and transgendered people of color has often been guided by the type of radical intersectional Left analysis that I detailed earlier. Thus, while the politics of lesbian, gay, bisexual, and transgendered activists of color might recognize heteronormativity as a primary system of power structuring our lives, it understands that heteronormativity interacts with institutional racism, patriarchy, and class exploitation to define us in numerous ways as marginal and oppressed subjects.[19] And it is this constructed subservient position that allows our sisters and brothers to be used either as surplus labor in an advanced capitalist structure and/ or seen as expendable, denied resources, and thus locked into correctional institutions across the country. While heterosexual privilege negatively impacts and constrains the lived experience of "queers" of color, so too do racism, classism, and sexism.

In contrast to the Left intersectional analysis that has structured much of the politics of "queers" of color, the basis of the politics of some white queer activists and organizations has come dangerously close to a single oppression model. In experiencing "deviant" sexuality as the prominent characteristic of their marginalization, these activists begin to envision the world in terms of a "hetero/queer" divide. Using the framework of queer theory in which heteronormativity is identified as a system of regulation and normalization, some queer activists map the power and entitlement of normative heterosexuality onto the bodies of all heterosexuals. Further, these activists naively characterize as powerless all of those who exist under the category of "queer." Thus, in the process of conceptualizing a decentered identity of queerness meant to embrace those who stand on the outside of heteronormativity, a monolithic understanding of heterosexuality and queerness has come to dominate the political imagination and actions of many queer activists.

This reconstruction of a binary divide between heterosexuals and queers, while discernible in many of the actions of Queer Nation, is probably most evident in the manifesto "I Hate Straights." Written by an anonymous group of queers and distributed at gay pride parades in New York and Chicago in 1990, the declaration begins:

> I have friends. Some of them are straight.
>
> Year after year, I see my straight friends. I want to see how they are doing, to add newness to our long and complicated histories, to experience some continuity.
>
> Year after year I continue to realize that the facts of my life are irrelevant to them and that I am only half listened to, that I am an appendage to the doings of a greater world, a world of power and privilege, of the laws of installation, a world of exclusion. "That's not true," argue my straight friends. There is the one certainty in the politics of power: those left out of it beg for inclusion, while the insiders claim that they already are. Men do it to women, whites do it to blacks, and everyone does it to queers.
>
> . . . *The main dividing line, both conscious and unconscious, is procreation . . . and that magic word—Family* [emphasis added].[20]

Screaming out from this manifesto is an analysis that places not heteronormativity but heterosexuality as the central "dividing line" between those who would be dominant and those who are oppressed. Nowhere in this essay is there recognition that "nonnormative" procreation patterns and family structures of people who are labeled heterosexual have also been used to regulate and exclude them. Instead, the authors declare, "Go tell them [straights] to go away until they have spent a month walking hand in hand in public with someone of the same sex. After they survive that, then you'll hear what they have to say about queer anger. Otherwise, tell them to shut up and listen." For these activists, the power of heterosexuality is the focus, and queer anger the means of queer politics. Missing from this equation is any attention to, or acknowledgment of, the ways in which identities of race, class, and/or gender either enhance or mute the marginalization of queers, on the one hand, and the power of heterosexuals, on the other.

The fact that this essay is written about and out of queer anger is undoubtedly part of the rationale for its defense.[21] But I question the degree to which we should read this piece as just an aberrational diatribe against straights motivated by intense queer anger. While anger is clearly a motivating factor for such writing, we should also understand this action to represent an analysis and politics structured around the simple dichotomy of straight and queer. We know, for instance, that similar positions have been put forth in other anonymously published, publicly distributed manifestos. For example, in the document *Queers Read This*, the authors write, "Don't be fooled, straight people own the world and the only reason you have been spared is you're smart, lucky or a fighter. Straight people have a privilege that allows them to do whatever they please and fuck without fear." They continue by stating, "Straight people are your enemy."

Even within this document, which seems to exemplify the narrowness of queer conceptions, there is a surprising glimpse at a more enlightened Left intersectional understanding of what queerness might mean. As the authors state, for instance, "being queer is not about a right to privacy; it is about the freedom to be public, to just be who we are. It means every day fighting oppression; homophobia, racism, misogyny, the bigotry of religious hypocrites and our own self-hatred." Evident in this one document are the inherent tensions and dilemmas that many queer activists currently encounter: How does one implement in real political struggle a decentered political identity that is not constituted by a process of seemingly reductive "othering"?

The process of ignoring or at least downplaying queers' varying relationships to power is evident not only in the writings of queer activists, but also in the political actions pursued by queer organizations. I question the ability of political actions such as mall invasions (pursued by groups such as the Queer Shopping Network in New York and the Suburban Homosexual Outreach Program [SHOP] in San Francisco) to address the fact that queers exist in different social locations. Lauren Berlant and Elizabeth Freeman describe mall invasion projects as an attempt to take "the relatively bounded spectacle of the urban pride parade to the ambient pleasures of the shopping mall. 'Mall visibility actions' thus conjoin the spectacular lure of the parade with Hare Krishna–style conversion and proselytizing techniques. Stepping into malls in hair-gelled splendor, holding hands and handing out fliers, the queer auxiliaries produce an 'invasion' that conveys a different message. 'We're here, we're queer, you're going shopping.'"[22] The activity of entering or "invading" the shopping mall on the part of queer nationals is clearly one of attempted subversion. Intended by their visible presence in this clearly coded heterosexual family economic mecca is a disruption of the agreed-on segregation between the allowable spaces for queer "deviant" culture and the rest of the "naturalized" world. Left unchallenged in such an action, however, are the myriad ways, besides the enforcement of normative sexuality, in which some queers feel alienated and excluded from the space of the mall. Where does the mall as an institution of consumer culture and relative economic privilege play into this analysis? How does this action account for the varying economic relationships that queers have to consumer culture? If you are a poor or working-class queer the exclusion and alienation you experience when entering the mall may not be limited to the normative sexual codes associated with the mall but rather may also be centered on the assumed economic status of those shopping in suburban malls. If you are a queer of color your exclusion from the mall may, in part, be rooted in racial norms and stereotypes that construct you as a threatening subject every time you enter this economic institution. Queer activists must confront a question that haunts most political organizing: How do we put into politics a broad and inclusive Left analysis that can actually engage and mobilize individuals with intersecting identities?

Clearly, there will be those critics who will claim that I am asking too much from any political organization. Demands that every aspect of oppression and regulation be addressed in each political act seem and indeed are unreasonable. However, I make the critique of queer mall invasions neither to stop such events nor to suggest that each oppression be dealt with by this one political action. Instead, I raise these concerns to emphasize the ways in which varying relations to power exist not only among heterosexuals but also among those who label themselves queer.

In its current rendition, queer politics is coded with class, gender, and race privilege, and may have lost its potential to be a politically expedient organizing tool for addressing the needs—and mobilizing the bodies—of people of color. As some queer theorists and activists call for the destruction of stable sexual categories—for example, moving instead toward a more fluid understanding of sexual behavior—left unspoken is the class privilege that allows for such fluidity. Class or material privilege is a cornerstone of much of queer politics and theory as they exist today. Queer theorizing that calls for the elimination of fixed categories of sexual identity seems to ignore the ways in which some traditional social identities and communal ties can, in fact, be important to one's survival. Further, a queer politics that demonizes all heterosexuals discounts the relationships—especially those based on shared experiences of marginalization—that exist between gays and straights, particularly in communities of color.

Queers who operate out of a political culture of individualism assume a material independence that allows them to disregard historically or culturally recognized categories and communities or, at the very least, to move fluidly among them without ever establishing permanent relationships or identities within them. However, I and many other lesbian and gay people of color, as well as poor and working-class lesbians and gay men, do not have such material independence. Because of my multiple identities, which locate me and other "queer" people of color at the margins in this country, my material advancement, my physical protection, and my emotional well-being are constantly threatened. In those stable categories and named communities whose histories have been structured by shared resistance to oppression, I find relative degrees of safety and security.

Let me emphasize again that the safety I feel is relative to other threats and is clearly not static or constant. For in those named communities I also find versions of domination and normalization being replicated and employed as more privileged/assimilated marginal group members use their associations with dominant institutions and resources to regulate and police the activities of other marginal group members. Any lesbian, gay, bisexual, or transgendered person of color who has experienced exclusion from indigenous institutions, such as the exclusion many openly gay black men have encountered from some black churches responding to AIDS, recognizes that even within marginal groups there are normative rules determining community membership and power. However, in spite of the unequal power relationships located in marginal communities, I am still not interested in disassociating politically from those communities, for queerness, as it is currently constructed, offers no viable political alternative since it invites us to put forth a political agenda that makes invisible the prominence of race, class, and to varying degrees gender in determining the life chances of those on both sides of the hetero/queer divide.

So despite the roots of queer politics in the struggles of "queer" people of color, despite the calls for highlighting categories that have sought to regulate and control black bodies like my own, and despite the attempts at decentralized grassroots activism in some queer political organizations, there still exist—for some, like myself—great misgivings about current constructions of the term "queer." Personally speaking, I do not consider myself a "queer" activist or, for that matter, a "queer" anything. This is not because I do not consider myself an activist; in fact, I hold my political work to be one of the most important contributions I make to all of my communities. But like other lesbian, gay, bisexual, and transgendered activists of color, I find the label "queer" fraught with unspoken assumptions that inhibit the radical political potential of this category.

The alienation, or at least discomfort, that many activists and theorists of color have with current conceptions of queerness is evidenced, in part, by the minimal numbers of theorists of color who engage in the process of theorizing about the concept. Further, the sparse numbers of people of color who participate in "queer" political organizations might also be read as a sign of discomfort with the term. Most important, my confidence in making such a claim of distance and uneasiness with the term "queer" on the part of many people of color comes from my interactions with other lesbian, gay, bisexual, and transgendered people of color who repeatedly express their interpretation of "queer" as a term rooted in class, race, and gender privilege. For us, "queer" is a politics based on narrow sexual dichotomies that make no room either for the analysis of oppression of those we might categorize as heterosexual, or for the privilege of those who operate as "queer." As black lesbian activist and writer Barbara Smith argues in "Queer Politics: Where's the Revolution?": "Unlike the early lesbian and gay movement, which had both ideological and practical links to the left, black activism, and feminism, today's 'queer' politicos seem to operate in a historical and ideological vacuum. 'Queer' activists focus on 'queer' issues, and racism, sexual oppression and economic exploitation do not qualify, despite the fact that the majority of 'queers' are people of color, female or working class. . . . Building unified, ongoing coalitions that challenge the system and ultimately prepare a way for revolutionary change simply isn't what 'queer' activists have in mind."[23] It is this narrow understanding of the idea of queer that negates its use in fundamentally reorienting the politics and privilege of lesbian and gay politics as well as more generally moving or transforming the politics of the Left. Despite its liberatory claim to stand in opposition to static categories of oppression, queer politics and much of queer theory seem in fact to be static in the understanding of race, class, and gender and their roles in how heteronormativity regulates sexual behavior and identities. Distinctions between the status and the acceptance of different individuals categorized under the label of "heterosexual" thus go unexplored.

I emphasize here the marginalized position of some who embrace heterosexual identities not because I want to lead any great crusade to understand more fully the plight of "the heterosexual." Rather, I recognize the potential for shared resistance with such individuals. This potential is especially relevant not only for coalitional work but for a shared analysis, from my vantage point, to "queer" people of color. Again, in my call for coalition work across sexual categories, I do not want to suggest that same-sex political struggles have not, independently, played an essential and distinct role in the liberatory politics and social movements of marginal people. My concern, instead, is with any political analysis or theory that collapses our understanding of power into a single continuum of evaluation.

Through a brief review of some of the ways in which nonnormative heterosexuality has been controlled and regulated through the state and systems of marginalization, we may be reminded that differentials in power exist within all socially named categories. And through such recognition we may begin to envision a new political formation in which one's relation to dominant power serves as the basis of unity for radical coalition work in the twenty-first century.

### Heterosexuals On the (Out)side of Heteronormativity

In the text following I want to return to the question of a monolithic understanding of heterosexuality. I believe that through this issue we can begin to think critically about the components of a radical politics built not exclusively on identities but rather on identities as they are invested with varying degrees of normative power. Thus, fundamental to my concern about the current structure and future agenda of queer politics is the unchallenged assumption of a uniform heteronormativity from which all heterosexuals benefit. I want again to be clear that there are, in fact, some who identify themselves as queer activists who do acknowledge relative degrees of power, along with heterosexual access to that power, even evoking the term "straight queers": "Queer means to fuck with gender. There are straight queers, bi queers, tranny queers, lez queers, fag queers, SM queers, fisting queers in every single street in this apathetic country of ours."[24]

Despite such sporadic insight, much of the politics of queer activists has been structured around the dichotomy of straight versus everything else, assuming a monolithic experience of heterosexual privilege for all those identified publicly with heterosexuality. A similar reductive dichotomy between men and women has consistently reemerged in the writing and actions of some feminists. And only through the demands, the actions, and the writing of many "feminists" and/or lesbians of color have those women who stand outside the norm of white, middle-class, legalized heterosexuality begun to see their lives, needs, and bodies represented in feminist theory.[25] In a similar manner lesbian, gay, bisexual, and transgendered people of color have increasingly taken on the responsibility for at the very least complicating and most often challenging reductive notions of heteronormativity articulated by queer activists and scholars.[26]

If we follow such examples, complicating our understanding of both heteronormativity and queerness, we move one step closer to building the progressive coalition politics that many of us desire. Specifically, if we pay attention to both historical and current examples of heterosexual relationships that have been prohibited, stigmatized, and generally repressed, we may begin to identify those spaces of shared or similar oppression and resistance that provide a basis for radical coalition work. Further, we may begin to answer certain questions: In narrowly positing a dichotomy of heterosexual privilege and queer oppression under which we all exist, are we negating a basis of political unity that could serve to strengthen many communities and movements seeking justice and societal transformation? How do we use the relative degrees of ostracism that all sexual/cultural "deviants" experience to build a basis of unity for broader coalition and movement work?

A little history (as a political scientist a little history is all I can offer) might be helpful here in trying to sort out the various ways that heterosexuality, especially as it has intersected with race, has been defined and experienced by different groups of people. Such information should also help to underscore the fact that many of the roots of heteronormativity are in white-supremacist ideologies that sought (and continue) to use the state and its regulation of sexuality, in particular through the institution of heterosexual marriage, to designate which individuals were truly "fit" for the full rights and privileges of citizenship. For example, the prohibition of marriages between black women and men imprisoned in the slave system was a component of many slave codes enacted during the seventeenth and eighteenth centuries. M. G. Smith, in his article on the structure of slave economic systems, succinctly states: "As property slaves were prohibited from forming legal relationships or marriages which would interfere with and restrict their owner's property rights."[27] Herbert Gutman, in *The Black Family in Slavery and Freedom*, 1750–1925, elaborates on the ideology of slave societies that denied the legal sanctioning of marriages between slaves, and further reasoned that blacks had no conception of family.[28]

> The *Nation* identified sexual restraint, civil marriage, and family stability with civilization itself.
> Such mid-nineteenth-century class and sexual beliefs reinforced racial beliefs about Afro-Americans. As slaves, after all, their marriages had not been sanctioned by the civil laws and therefore "the sexual passion" went unrestrained. . . . Many white abolitionists denied the slaves a family life or even, often, a family consciousness because for them [the whites] the family had its origins in and had to be upheld by the civil law.[29]

Thus it was not the promotion of marriage or heterosexuality per se that served as the standard or motivation of most slave societies. Instead, marriage and heterosexuality, as viewed through the lenses of profit and domination and the ideology of white supremacy, were reconfigured to justify the exploitation and regulation of black bodies, even those presumably engaged in heterosexual behavior. It was this system of state-sanctioned, white male, upper-class heterosexual domination that forced these presumably black heterosexual men and women to endure a history of rape, lynching, and other forms of physical and mental terrorism. In this way, marginal group members lacking power and privilege although engaged in heterosexual behavior have often found themselves defined as outside the norms and values of dominant society. This position has most often resulted in the suppression or negation of their legal, social, and physical relationships and rights.

In addition to the prohibition of marriage between slaves, A. Leon Higginbotham Jr., in *The Matter of Color: Race and the American Legal Process: The Colonial Period*, writes of the legal restrictions barring interracial marriages. He reminds us that the essential core of the American legal tradition was the preservation of the white race. The "mixing" of the races was to be strictly prohibited in early colonial laws. The regulation of interracial heterosexual relationships, however, should not be understood as exclusively relegated to the seventeenth, eighteenth, and nineteenth centuries. In fact, Higginbotham informs us that the final law prohibiting miscegenation (the "interbreeding" or marrying of individuals from different "races" that was actually meant to inhibit the "tainting" of the white race) was not repealed until 1967: "Colonial anxiety about interracial sexual activity cannot be attributed solely to seventeenth-century values, for it was not until 1967 that the United States Supreme Court finally declared unconstitutional those statutes prohibiting interracial marriages. The Supreme Court waited thirteen years after its *Brown* decision dealing with desegregation of schools before, in *Loving v. Virginia*, it agreed to consider the issue of interracial marriages."[30]

It is this pattern of regulating the behavior and denigrating the identities of those heterosexuals on the outside of heteronormative privilege—in particular those perceived as threatening systems of white supremacy, male domination, and capitalist advancement—that I want to highlight here. An understanding of the ways in which heteronormativity works to support and reinforce institutional racism, patriarchy, and class exploitation must therefore be a part of how we problematize current constructions of heterosexuality. As I stated previously, I am not suggesting that those involved in publicly identifiable heterosexual behavior do not receive political, economic, and social advantages, especially in comparison to the experiences of some lesbian, transgendered, gay, and bisexual individuals. But the equation linking identity and behavior to power is not as linear and clear as some queer theorists and activists would have us believe.

A more recent example of regulated nonnormative heterosexuality is located in the debates and rhetoric regarding the "underclass" and the destruction of the welfare system. The stigmatization and demonization of single mothers, teen mothers, and, primarily, poor women of color dependent on state assistance has had a long and suspicious presence in American "intellectual" and political history. It was in 1965 that Daniel Patrick Moynihan released his "study" titled *The Negro Family: The Case for National Action*, which would eventually come to be known simply as the Moynihan report. In this document the author points to the "pathologies" increasingly evident in so-called Negro families, notably the destructive nature of Negro family formations. Indeed, the introduction argues that "the fundamental problem in which this is most clearly the case is that of family structure. The evidence—not final, but powerfully persuasive—is that the Negro family in urban ghettos is crumbling. A middle-class group has managed to save itself, but for vast numbers of the unskilled, poorly educated, urban working-class the fabric of conventional social relationships has all but disintegrated." Later in the document Moynihan goes on to describe the crisis and pathologies facing the Negro family structure as being generated by the increasing number of households headed by single females, the increasing number of "illegitimate" births, and, of course, increasing welfare dependency: "In essence, the Negro community has been forced into a matriarchal structure, which because it is so out of line with the rest of the American society seriously retards the progress of the group as a whole and imposes a crushing burden on the Negro male and, in consequence, on a great many Negro women as well. . . . In a word, most Negro youth are in danger of being caught up in the tangle of pathology that affects their world, and probably a majority are so entrapped. . . . Obviously, not every instance of social pathology afflicting the Negro community can be traced to the weakness of family structure. . . . Nonetheless, at the center of the tangle of pathology is the weakness of the family structure."[31]

It is not the nonheterosexist behavior of these black men and women that is under fire but rather the perceived nonnormative sexual behavior and family structures of these individuals, whom many queer activists— without regard to the impact of race, class, or gender—would designate as part of the heterosexist establishment or those mighty "straights they hate." Over the last thirty years the demonization of poor women, engaged in nonnormative heterosexual relationships, has continued under the auspices of scholarship on the "underclass." Adolph L. Reed, in "The 'Underclass' as Myth and Symbol: The Poverty of Discourse about Poverty," discusses the gendered and racist nature of much of this literature, in which poor women, often black and Latina, are portrayed as unable to control their sexual impulses and eventual reproductive decisions; unable to raise their children with the right moral fiber; unable to find "gainful" employment to support themselves and their "illegitimate children"; and of course unable to manage "effectively" the minimal assistance provided by the state. Reed writes,

> The underclass notion may receive the greatest ideological boost from its gendered imagery and relation to gender politics. As I noted in a critique of Wilson's *The Truly Disadvantaged*, "family" is an intrinsically ideological category. The rhetoric of "disorganization," "disintegration," "deterioration" reifies one type of living arrangement—the ideal type of the bourgeois nuclear family—as outside history, nearly as though it were decreed by natural law. But—as I asked earlier—why exactly is out-of-wedlock birth pathological? Why is the female-headed household an indicator of disorganization and pathology? Does that stigma attach to all such households—even, say, a divorced executive who is a custodial mother? If not, what are the criteria for assigning it? The short answer is race and class bias inflected through a distinctively gendered view of the world.[32]

In this same discourse of the "underclass," young black men engaged in "reckless" heterosexual behavior are represented as irresponsible baby factories, unable to control or restrain their "sexual passion" (to borrow a term from the seventeenth century). And, unfortunately, often it has been the work of professed liberals like William Julius Wilson, in his book *The Truly Disadvantaged*, that, while not using the word "pathologies," has substantiated in its own tentative way the conservative dichotomy between the deserving working poor and the lazy, Cadillac-driving, steak-eating, welfare queens of Ronald Reagan's imagination.[33] Again, I raise this point to remind us of the numerous ways that sexuality and sexual deviance from a prescribed norm have been used to demonize and to oppress various segments of the population, even some classified under the label "heterosexual."

The policies of politicians and the actions of law enforcement officials have reinforced, in much more devastating ways, the distinctions between acceptable forms of heterosexual expression and those to be regulated—increasingly through incarceration. This move toward the disallowance of some forms of heterosexual expression and reproductive choice can be seen in the practice of prosecuting pregnant women suspected of using drugs—nearly 80 percent of all women prosecuted are women of color; through the forced sterilization of Puerto Rican and Native American women; and through the state-dictated use of Norplant by women answering to the criminal justice system and by women receiving state assistance.[34] Further, it is the "nonnormative" children of many of these nonnormative women that Newt Gingrich would place in orphanages. This is the same Newt Gingrich who, despite his clear disdain for gay and lesbian "lifestyles," has invited lesbians and gay men into the Republican Party but made no such offer to the women on welfare discussed above. Who, we might ask, is truly on the outside of heteronormative power? Maybe most of us?

## Conclusion: Destabalization and Radical Coalition Work

While the points I make above may, in fact, seem interesting or troubling or both, we might ask what does it have to do with the question of the future of queer politics? It is my argument, as I stated earlier, that one of the great failings of queer theory and especially queer politics has been their inability to incorporate into analysis of the world and strategies for political mobilization the roles that race, class, and gender play in defining people's differing relations to dominant and normalizing power. I present this essay as the beginning of a much longer and protracted struggle to acknowledge and delineate the distribution of power within and outside of queer communities. This is a discussion of how to build a politics organized not merely by reductive categories of straight and queer, but organized instead around a more intersectional analysis of who and what the enemy is and where our potential allies can be found. This analysis seeks to make clear the privilege and power embedded in the categorizations of, on the one hand, an upstanding, "morally correct," white, state-authorized, middle-class male heterosexual, and on the other, a culturally deficient, materially bankrupt, state-dependent *heterosexual* woman of color, who is found most often in our urban centers (those that haven't been gentrified), on magazine covers, and on the evening news.

I contend, therefore, that the radical potential of queer politics, or any liberatory movement, rests on its ability to advance strategically oriented political identities arising from a more nuanced understanding of power. One of the most difficult tasks in such an endeavor (and there are many) is not to forsake the complexities of both how power is structured and how we might think about the coalitions we create. Far too often movements revert to a position in which membership and joint political work are based on a necessarily similar history of oppression—but this is too much like identity politics.[35] Instead, I am suggesting here that the process of movement building be rooted not in our shared history or identity but in our shared marginal relationship to dominant power that normalizes, legitimizes, and privileges.

We must, therefore, start our political work from the recognition that multiple systems of oppression are in operation and that these systems use institutionalized categories and identities to regulate and socialize. We must also understand that power and access to dominant resources are distributed across the boundaries of "het" and "queer" that we construct. A model of queer politics that simply pits the grand "heterosexuals" against all those oppressed "queers" is ineffectual as the basis for action in a political environment dominated by Newt Gingrich, the Christian Right, and the recurring ideology of white supremacy. As we stand on the verge of watching those in power dismantle the welfare system through a process of demonizing the poor and young—primarily poor and young women of color, many of whom have existed for their entire lives outside the white, middle-class heterosexual norm—we have to ask if these women do not fit into society's categories of marginal, deviant, and "queer." As we watch the explosion of prison construction and the disproportionate incarceration rates of young men and women of color, often as part of the economic development of poor white rural communities, we have to ask if these individuals do not fit society's definition of "queer" and expendable.

I am not proposing a political strategy that homogenizes and glorifies the experience of poor heterosexual people of color. In fact, in calling for a more expansive Left political identity and formation I do not seek to erase the specific historical relation between the stigma of "queer" and the sexual activity of gay men, lesbians, bisexuals, and transgendered individuals. And in no way do I intend or desire to equate the experiences of marginal heterosexual women and men to the lived experiences of queers. There is no doubt that heterosexuality, even for those heterosexuals who stand outside the norms of heteronormativity, results in some form of privilege and feelings of supremacy. I need only recount the times when other women of color, more economically vulnerable than myself, expressed superiority and some feelings of disgust when they realized that the nice young professor (me) was "that way."

However, in recognizing the distinct history of oppression that lesbian, gay, bisexual, and transgendered people have confronted and challenged, I am not willing to embrace every queer as my marginalized political ally. In the same way, I do not assume that shared racial, gender, and/or class position or identity guarantees or produces similar political commitments. Thus, identities and communities, while important to this strategy, must be complicated and destabilized through a recognition of the multiple social positions and relations to dominant power found within any one category or identity. Kimberlé Crenshaw, in "Mapping the Margins: Intersectionality, Identity Politics, and Violence against Women of Color," suggests that such a project use the idea of intersectionality to reconceptualize or problematize the identities and communities that are "home" to us. She demands that we challenge those identities that seem like home by acknowledging the other parts of our identities that are excluded: "With identity thus reconceptualized [through a recognition of intersectionality], it may be easier to understand the need to summon up the courage to challenge groups that are after all, in one sense, 'home' to us, in the name of the parts of us that are not made at home. . . . The most one could expect is that we will dare to speak against internal exclusions and marginalizations, that we might call attention to how the identity of 'the group' has been centered on the intersectional identities of a few. . . . Through an awareness of intersectionality, we can better acknowledge and ground the differences among us and negotiate the means by which these differences will find expression in constructing group politics."[36] In the same ways that we account for the varying privilege to be gained by a heterosexual identity, we must also pay attention to the privilege that some queers receive from being white, male, and upper class. Only through recognizing the many manifestations of power, across and within categories, can we truly begin to build a movement based on one's politics and not exclusively on one's identity.

I want to be clear here that what I am calling for is the destabilization and not the destruction or abandonment of identity categories.[37] We must reject a queer politics that seems to ignore in its analysis of the usefulness of traditionally named categories the roles of identity and community as paths to survival, using shared experiences of oppression and resistance to build indigenous resources, shape consciousness, and act collectively. Instead, I would suggest that it is the multiplicity and interconnectedness of our identities that provide the most promising avenue for the *destabilization and radical politicalization* of these same categories.

This is not an easy path to pursue because most often it requires building a political analysis and political strategies around the most marginal members of our society, some of whom look like us but many of whom do not. Most often, this will mean rooting our struggle in, and addressing the needs of, communities of color, and it will mean highlighting the intersectionality of one's race, class, gender, and sexuality and the relative power and privilege that one receives from being a man and/or being white and/or being middle class and/or being heterosexual. This challenge is a particularly daunting one because so much of our political consciousness has been built around simple dichotomies such as powerful/powerless; oppressor/victim; enemy/comrade. It is difficult to feel safe and secure in those spaces where both one's relative privilege and experiences with marginalization are understood to shape a commitment to radical politics. However, as Bernice Johnson Reagon so aptly put it in her essay, "Coalition Politics: Turning the Century," "if you feel the strain, you may be doing some good work."[38]

And while this is a daunting challenge and an uncomfortable position, those who have taken it up have not only survived but succeeded in
their efforts. For example, both the needle exchange and prison projects
pursued through the auspices of ACT-UP New York point to the possibilities and difficulties involved in principled transformative coalition work.
In each project individuals from numerous identities—heterosexual, gay,
poor, wealthy, white, black, Latino—came together to challenge dominant
constructions of who should be allowed care and who deserved it. No particular identity exclusively determined the shared political commitments
of these activists; instead their similar positions, as marginalized subjects
relative to the state—made clear through the government's lack of response
to AIDS—formed the basis of this political unity.

In the prison project, it was the contention of activists that the government, which denied even wealthy gay men access to drugs to combat
HIV and AIDS, must be regarded as the same source of power that denied
incarcerated men and women access to basic health care, including those
drugs and conditions needed to combat these diseases. The coalition work
that this group engaged in involved a range of people, from formerly incarcerated individuals to heterosexual men and women of color to those we
might deem privileged white lesbians and gay men. And this same group of
people who came together to protest the conditions of incarcerated people
with AIDS also showed up at public events to challenge the homophobia
that guided the government's and the biomedical industries' response to
this epidemic. The political work of this group of individuals was undoubtedly informed by the public identities they embraced, but these were identities that they further acknowledged as complicated by intersectionality
and placed within a political framework where their shared experience as
marginal, nonnormative subjects could be foregrounded. Douglas Crimp,
in his essay "Right On, Girlfriend!," suggests that through political work
our identities become remade and must therefore be understood as relational. Describing such a transformation in the identities of queer activists
engaged in, and prosecuted for, needle exchange work, Crimp writes: "But
once engaged in the struggle to end the crisis, these queers' identities were
no longer the same. It's not that 'queer' doesn't any longer encompass their
sexual practices; it does, but it also entails a *relation* between those practices
and other circumstances that make very different people vulnerable both
to HIV infection and to the stigma, discrimination, and neglect that have
characterized the societal and governmental response to the constituencies
most affected by the AIDS epidemic."[39]

The radical potential of those of us on the outside of heteronormativity
rests in our understanding that we need not base our politics in the dissolu-

tion of all categories and communities, but rather that we instead need to work toward the destabilization and remaking of our identities. Difference, in and of itself—even that difference designated through named categories—is not the problem. Instead it is the power invested in certain identity categories and the idea that bounded categories are not to be transgressed that serve as the basis of domination and control. The reconceptualization not only of the content of identity categories but of the intersectional nature of identities themselves, must become part of our political practice. We must thus begin to link our intersectional analysis of power with concrete coalitional work. In real terms this means identifying political struggles such as the needle exchange and prison projects of ACT-UP that transgress the boundaries of identity to highlight, in this case, both the repressive power of the state and the normalizing power evident within both dominant and marginal communities. This type of principled coalition work is also being pursued in a more modest fashion by the Policy Institute of the National Gay and Lesbian Task Force. Recently, the staff at the task force distributed position papers not only on the topics of gay marriages and gays in the military but also on right-wing attacks against welfare and affirmative action. Here we have political work based in the knowledge that the rhetoric and accusations of nonnormativity that Newt Gingrich and others on the Right launch against women on welfare closely resemble the attacks of nonnormativity mounted against gays, lesbians, bisexuals, and transgendered individuals. Again it is the marginalized relation to power, experienced by both of these groups—and I do not mean to suggest that the groups are mutually exclusive—that frames the possibility for transformative coalition work. This prospect diminishes when we do not recognize and deal with the reality that the intersecting identities that gay people embody—in terms of race, class, and gender privilege—put some of us on Gingrich's side of the welfare struggle (e.g., Log Cabin Republicans). And in a similar manner a woman's dependence on state financial assistance in no way secures her position as one supportive of gay rights and/or liberation. While a marginal identity undoubtedly increases the prospects of shared consciousness, only an articulation and commitment to mutual support can truly be the test of unity when pursuing transformational politics.

Finally, I realize here that I have been short on specifics when trying to describe how we move concretely toward a transformational coalition politics among marginalized subjects. The best I can do in response is to offer this discussion as a starting point for reassessing the shape of queer, lesbian, gay, bisexual, and transgendered politics as we begin the twenty-first century. A reconceptualization of the politics of marginal groups allows us not only to privilege the specific lived experience of distinct communities, but also to search for those interconnected sites of resistance from which we can wage broader political struggles. Only by recognizing the link between the ideological, social, political, and economic marginalization of punks, bulldaggers, and welfare queens can we begin to develop political analyses and political strategies effective in confronting the linked yet varied sites of power in this country. Such a project is important because it provides a framework from which the difficult work of coalition politics can begin. And it is in these complicated and contradictory spaces that the liberatory and Left politics that so many of us work for is located.

## Notes

I would like to thank Mark Blasius, Nan Boyd, Ed Cohen, Carolyn Dinshaw, Jeff Edwards, Licia Fiol-Matta, Joshua Gamson, Lynne Huffer, Tamara Jones, Carla Kaplan, Ntanya Lee, Ira Livingston, and Barbara Ransby for their comments on various versions of this essay.

1. David W. Dunlap, "Three Black Members Quit AIDS Organization Board," *New York Times,* January 11,1996, B2.

2. The very general chronology of queer theory and queer politics referred to throughout this essay is not meant to indicate the definitive historical development of each phenomenon. Instead the dates are used to provide the reader with a general frame of reference. See Steven Epstein, "A Queer Encounter: Sociology and the Study of Sexuality," *Sociology Theory* 12.2 (1994): 188–202, for a similar genealogy of queer theory and queer politics.

3. Donald Morton, "The Politics of Queer Theory in the (Post)Modern Movement," *Genders* 17 (fall 1993): 121.

4. See Chrys Ingraham, "The Heterosexual Imaginary: Feminist Sociology and the Theories of Gender," *Sociological Theory* 12 (1994): 203–19, for a discussion of the heterogendered imaginary.

5. Arlene Stein and Kenneth Plummer, " 'I Can't Even Think Straight': 'Queer' Theory and the Missing Sexual Revolution in Sociology," *Sociological Theory* 12 (1994): 182.

6. Allan Bérubé and Jeffrey Escoffier, "Queer/Nation," *Out/look: National Lesbian and Gay Quarterly* 11 (winter 1991):12.

7. Joshua Gamson, "Must Identity Movements Self-Destruct? A Queer Dilemma," *Social Problems* 42 (1995): 403.

8. See Mark Blasius, *Gay and Lesbian Politics: Sexuality and the Emergence of a New Ethic,* (Philadelphia: Temple University Press, 1994), 19–20; and Michael Warner, ed., *Fear of a Queer Planet: Queer Politics and Social Theory* (Minneapolis: University of Minnesota Press, 1993), xxi–xxv.

9. I want to be clear that in this essay I am including the destruction of sexual categories as part of the agenda of queer politics. While a substantial segment of queer activists and theorists call for the destabilization of sexual categories, there are also those self-avowed queers who embrace a politics built around the deconstruction and/or elimination of sexual categories. For example, a number of my self-identified queer students engage in sexual behavior that most people would interpret as transgressive of sexual identities and categories. However, these students have repeatedly articulated a differ-

ent interpretation of their sexual behavior. They put forth an understanding that does not highlight their transgression of categories, but rather one that represents them as individuals who operate outside of categories and sexual identities altogether. They are sexual beings, given purely to desire, truly living sexual fluidity, and not constrained by any form of sexual categorization or identification. This interpretation seems at least one step removed from that held by people who embrace the fluidity of sexuality while still recognizing the political usefulness of categories or labels for certain sexual behavior and communities. One example of such people might be those women who identify as lesbians and who also acknowledge that sometimes they choose to sleep with men. These individuals exemplify the process of destabilization that I try to articulate within this essay. Even further removed from the queers who would do away with all sexual categories are those who also transgress what many consider to be categories of sexual behaviors while they publicly embrace one stable sexual identity (for example, those self-identified heterosexual men who sleep with other men sporadically and secretly).

10. I want to thank Mark Blasius for raising the argument that standing on the outside of heteronormativity is a bit of a misnomer, since as a dominant normalizing process it is a practice of regulation in which we are all implicated. However, despite this insight I will on occasion continue to use this phrasing while understanding the limits of its meaning.

11. The Combahee River Collective, "The Combahee River Collective Statement," in *Home Girls: A Black Feminist Anthology*, ed. Barbara Smith (New York: Kitchen Table: Women of Color Press, 1983), 272.

12. Dialogue on the Lesbian and Gay Left, "Statement of Purpose." Duncan Conference Center, Del Ray Beach, Florida, April 1993.

13. Urvashi Vaid, *Virtual Equality: The Mainstreaming of Gay and Lesbian Liberation* (New York: Anchor, 1995), 183.

14. Robin Podolsky, "Sacrificing Queers and Other 'Proletarian' Artifacts," *Radical America* 25.1 (January 1991): 54.

15. Adrienne Rich, "Compulsory Heterosexuality and Lesbian Existence," in *Powers of Desires: The Politics of Sexuality*, ed. Ann Snitow, Christine Stansell, and Sharon Thompson (New York: Monthly Review, 1983), 177–206.

16. Warner, *Fear of a Queer Planet*, vii, xiii.

17. Queers United Against Straight-Acting Homosexuals, "Assimilation Is Killing Us: Fight for a Queer United Front," *Why I Hated the March on Washington* (1993): 4.

18. Steven Seidman, "Identity and Politics in a 'Postmodern' Gay Culture," in Warner, ed., *Fear of a Queer Planet*, 106.

19. For a discussion of Left analysis and the limits of queer theory, see Rosemary Hennessy, "Queer Theory, Left Politics," *Rethinking Marxism* 17.3 [1994]: 85–111.

20. Queer Nation, "I Hate Straights" manifesto, New York, 1990.

21. Lauren Berlant and Elizabeth Freeman, "Queer Nationality," in Warner, ed., *Fear of a Queer Planet*, 200.

22. Berlant and Freeman, "Queer Nationality," 210.

23. Barbara Smith, "Queer Politics: Where's the Revolution?" *Nation* 257.1 (July 5, 1993): 13–14.

24. Anonymous, quoted in Mary McIntosh, "Queer Theory and the War of the Sexes," in Joseph Bistrow and Angelia R. Wilson, ed., *Activating Theory: Lesbian, Gay, Bisexual Politics* (London: Lawrence and Wishart, 1993), 31.

25. See Hazel Carby, *Reconstructing Womanhood: The Emergence of the Afro-American Woman Novelist* (New York: Oxford University Press, 1987); Patricia Hill Collins,

*Black Feminist Thought: Knowledge, Consciousness, and the Politics of Social Empowerment* (Boston: Unwin Hyman, 1990); bell hooks, *Feminist Theory: From Margin to Center* (Boston: South End, 1984).

26. See Jacqui Alexander, "Redefining Morality: The Postcolonial State and the Sexual Offences Bill of Trinidad and Tobago," in Chandra Talpade Mohanty, Ann Russo, and Lourdes Torres, eds., *Third World Women and the Politics of Feminism* (Bloomington: Indiana University Press, 1991), 133–152; Elias Farajaje-Jones, "Ain't I a Queer?," paper presented at the Creating Change Conference, National Gay and Lesbian Task Force, November 1995, Detroit; Audre Lorde, *Sister Outsider* (New York: Crossing Press, 1984); Cherríe Moraga and Gloria Anzaldúa, eds., *This Bridge Called My Back: Writings by Radical Women of Color* (New York: Kitchen Table; Women of Color Press, 1983); and Barbara Smith, *Home Girls: A Black Feminist Anthology* (New York: Kitchen Table Women of Color Press, 1983).

27. M. G. Smith, "Social Structure in the British Caribbean about 1820," *Social and Economic Studies* 1.4 (August 1953): 71.

28. Herbert G. Gutman, *The Black Family in Slavery and Freedom, 1750–1925* (New York: Vintage, 1976).

29. Ibid., 295.

30. A. Leon Higginbotham Jr., *In the Matter of Color: Race and the American Legal Process: The Colonial Period* (New York: Oxford University Press, 1978), 41.

31. Daniel Patrick Moynihan, *The Negro Family: The Case for National Action* (Washington, D.C.: Office of Planning and Research, U.S. Department of Labor, 1965), 29–30.

32. Adolph L. Reed Jr., "The 'Underclass' as Myth and Symbol: The Poverty of Discourse about Poverty," *Radical America* 24.1 (January 1990): 33–34.

33. William Julius Wilson, *The Truly Disadvantaged: The Inner City, the Under-class, and Public Policy* (Chicago: University of Chicago Press, 1987).

34. For an insightful discussion of the numerous methods used to regulate and control the sexual and reproductive choices of women, see Suzanne Shende, "Fighting the Violence against Our Sisters: Prosecution of Pregnant Women and the Coercive Use of Norplant," in *Women Transforming Politics: An Alternative Reader*, ed. Cathy Cohen, Kathleen Jones, and Jones Tronto (New York: New York University Press, 1997). 123–35.

35. See Shane Phelan, *Identity Politics: Lesbian Feminism and the Limits of Community* (Philadelphia: Temple University Press, 1989).

36. Kimberlé Williams Crenshaw, "Mapping the Margins: Intersectionality, Identity Politics, and Violence against Women of Color." *Stanford Law Review* 43 (1991): 1299.

37. See Tamara Jones, "Inside the Kaleidoscope: How the Construction of Black Gay and Lesbian Identities Inform Political Strategies" (unpublished essay, 1995) for an articulation of differences between the destabilization and the destruction of identity categories.

38. Bernice Johnson Reagon, "Coalition Politics: Turning the Century," in Smith, ed., *Home Girls*, 362.

39. Douglas Crimp, "Right On, Girlfriend!" in Warner, ed., *Fear of a Queer Planet*, 317–18.

## AIDS the Secret, Silent, Suffering Shame

*Evelynn M. Hammonds*

2005

The epidemic of HIV/AIDS in the United States has taken a huge toll on African American women. When I first wrote about the epidemic in 1987 an African American woman was thirteen times more likely to be infected with AIDS than a white woman. In 2004 that number has almost doubled such that in twenty-nine states today an African American woman is twenty-three times more likely to be infected with AIDS than a white woman.[1] In 1991, 20,000 women in the United States had been diagnosed with AIDS and the numbers of women infected was increasing rapidly—doubling every one to two years. In that year, AIDS was the leading cause of death for Black women in New York and New Jersey.[2] By 1992, the majority of women with AIDS (72 percent) were African American or Hispanic. Most of the African American women who contracted HIV did so primarily via their own drug-using practices and secondarily through heterosexual sex with infected men. By 2004, an estimated 67 percent of Black women with AIDS contracted the virus through heterosexual sex, a nearly 10 percent increase from a decade earlier. The switch in how African American women contract the virus is attributed to the increase in the numbers of African American men who are infected and are bisexual. At the same time it was already clear by 1992 that a significant number of African American women had acquired AIDS through heterosexual transmission. We also knew by 1989 that the social, political, and economic problems of the urban poor—racism, unemployment, poverty, drug abuse, prostitution, inadequate housing, poor education, poor access to health care and social services—provided the means for the virus to spread rapidly through African American communities. Yet, even as this stark background became more clear to scholars, researchers, activists, health care workers and service providers, women were by and large excluded from most of the biomedical and psychological research on AIDS.

The AIDS epidemic can be characterized in many ways—but I call it the 4S epidemic—Silence, Secrets, Suffering, and Shame. For historians of

American medicine, epidemics provide a lens for examining the social, cultural, and moral values that determine how societies respond to disease. The epidemic of HIV/AIDS has provided a singular event for the exploration of how Americans think about issues of sexuality, deviance, drug use/abuse, public health policy, the distribution of resources for health care, the conduct of clinical trials, and, of course, race, gender, masculinity, and femininity. These issues have been particularly acute in African American communities. Our long collective history of silence on these subjects is being shattered as AIDS spreads in our communities.

## AIDS and History

A historically informed discussion of AIDS has to consider the way in which social and political relations are mediated by disease, the way disease comes in and out of focus because of particular political and social circumstances, and the way in which differences within cultures and nations structure reactions to disease. The AIDS epidemic in the United States has never been, in my view, one epidemic but many, moving through space and time through the many diverse communities and regions of this country. As AIDS moved through these different groups and communities, responses to it were shaped by what had gone on before. As the impact of AIDS on gay communities occupied center stage, its effects on communities of color, and on women, remained hidden from view, waiting in the wings, so to speak, for their turn in the spotlight. These are the groups whose perceptions of risk have been profoundly shaped both by their perceived social distance from gay communities and by the restricted characterization of their connections to these communities. In reflecting on this epidemic of silence, secrets, suffering, and shame, the historical episode that provides the most meaningful historical insights for me is that of the epidemic of yellow fever in Philadelphia in 1793.

Let me briefly outline this epidemic for you. In early August, 1793, Philadelphia physicians were puzzling over isolated cases of a new disease marked by yellowing of the skin and vomiting of an unknown black substance. On August 19, the eminent physician Dr. Benjamin Rush, signer of the Declaration of Independence, proclaimed that yellow fever had returned to the city for the first time since 1762. Between August 19 and November 15, 1793, 10 to 15 percent of the estimated 45,000 Philadelphians perished, while another 20,000, including most government officials, simply fled. A committee of citizen volunteers remained in the city setting up a hospital, distributing food, clothes, and medicine to the poor, burying abandoned corpses, and cleaning up the city.

The yellow fever epidemic of 1793 provides an early example of the complex links between health and politics in American society. As the historians in the room know, the link between theology and medicine was still very strong in this period. While some believed that the cause of the disease was strictly medical, others saw it as God's punishment for the sins of the poor, or of immigrants. Some physicians even declared that blacks and West Indian immigrants were more immune than respectable white Philadelphians. There are many things we could discuss about this epidemic with respect to religious and political debates that shaped responses to yellow fever, but I want to just say a word about its impact on the poor, especially African Americans.[3]

Two African American men, Richard Allen and Absalom Jones, remained in Philadelphia during the epidemic and worked with Benjamin Rush to treat the victims of yellow fever. At the end of the epidemic they were charged with plundering and taking advantage of the sick and the dead. Their written response which was published in 1793 is an elegant rebuttal of this charge. Jones and Allen documented their journeys through the back alleys and basements of the city during the epidemic where they found many of the black citizens of the city suffering from yellow fever. "We have suffered equally with the whites, our distress has been very great, but much unknown to the white people. . . . [I]t is even to this day a generally received opinion, in this city, that our color was not so liable to the sickness as the whites. . . . The public was informed that in the West Indies and other places where this terrible malady had been, it was observed that the blacks were not affected with it. . . . Happy would it have been for you, and much more for us, if this observation had been verified by our experience."[4] These Black men appealed for recognition of their efforts, their personal sacrifice, and the suffering of their people. John Edgar Wideman, in his short story based on the Jones and Allen narrative, provides an apt reference for this essay. "To explain the fever we need no boatloads of refugees ragged and wracked with killing fevers bringing death to our shores. We have bred the affliction within our breasts. Each solitary heart contains all the world's tribes. . . . We are our ancestors and our children, neighbors and strangers to ourselves. Fever descends when the waters that connect us are clogged. The waters cannot come and go when we are shut off from one another, each in his frock coat, bonnet, apron, shop, shoes, skin, behind locks, doors, sealed faces, our blood grows thick and sluggish. . . . Fever is a drought consuming us from within."[5]

The epidemic of yellow fever revealed the way disease categories and views of the susceptible and the immune shaped and fragmented the notion of community along the axes of race and class. AIDS too carries with it this

capacity for fragmentation. This epidemic has revealed the fallacy of looking at gender, race, class, sexuality, and culture in terms of non-intersecting
categories, and it has also revealed the limitations of the categories and
divisions that govern our views of social life and sexual difference. What
Wideman recognized in his moving meditation on yellow fever was that
disease breaks down the ties that bind communities—and it is this breakdown of community by race, by class, by sexuality—that pathways for disease to spread are made. Thus the presence of disease and the refusal to help
those who are stricken—is a symbol of a loss of community. The pathways
for the spread of HIV/AIDS have been created by individual and institutional practices within and outside of African American communities. But
most importantly with respect to African American women HIV/AIDS has
revealed the ways in which our silence, our secrets, our suffering, and our
shame have made it impossible to conceive of community in terms that
would allow us to stop the spread of this disease.

I have experienced the silence, secrets, suffering, and shame that AIDS
has brought to African American communities in both personal and professional ways. Many of us have spent the last two decades playing the role of
that tragic Greek figure Cassandra, as Mindy Fullilove describes it, warning
our communities of the impending crisis that the epidemic of HIV/AIDS
would bring. Many of us start every talk just as I did today with an overview of the numbers of African American women infected with HIV/AIDs
over this period. For me as historian and early activist for AIDS programs
for African Americans in Boston, I often found myself in the early nineties
in rooms full of white men and some white women trying to explain why
the models used to chart the impact of this epidemic were wrong because
they could not capture what was happening to Black people and specifically
Black women. The usual response of those at such meetings was silence.
They argued that there was no data on what was happening to Black men
and women with AIDS, or they would suggest that the sample size was too
small for analysis; or they would point out that the epidemic was different
among those people who used and abused drugs; or most significantly they
would shake their heads and say "but race is not a factor in the spread of
AIDS." And the profound differences between affluent white gay men sitting at the table fighting for attention and resources and the absent poor
black women was palpable.

Then I would usually leave such meetings and go to another meeting in
the basement of a Black church or in the conference room of a community
health center and talk to Black people about the numbers and how they
were creeping up; and about how many people they knew were dying. As
I would leave these meetings people who had been silent throughout my

presentation would whisper to me about people they knew who were sick and dying; or they would tell me a story about how hard it was to get help in the emergency room at a Harvard-affiliated hospital; or about how many sick Black people were being rejected by their churches. Such information was always whispered passed on to me as if it were a secret that we had to guard and protect from the ears of those who would use the information to further hurt Black people rather than help them.

I came face to face with the suffering that people with AIDs experienced for the first time in those days as I sat in a hospital room in St. Vincent's hospital in New York City on Christmas Day, keeping company with a dear friend whose brother lay in a bed before us dying of AIDS. Earlier in the day we had traveled to Queens to pick up Christmas dinner for this man from his mother who told us she just couldn't find the time to come all the way into Manhattan on Christmas Day to see her son. I will never forget the look on his face when we told him that his mother would not be coming to visit him that day—his last Christmas. In the next months I watched as more and more African American women came to meetings about AIDS. They were angry at the men who gave them the virus; they were angry at themselves for using drugs; they were sick with worry about their children and what would happen to them if they couldn't get into drug treatment programs; they were scared about how the disease was ravaging their bodies.

I can remember a beautiful summer day in Long Beach, California, during a gay pride celebration. I had offered to help my friend Dr. Vickie Mays hand out leaflets to African American men and women along the parade route. The leaflet advertised a hotline for folks to call in to if they had questions about AIDS. Throughout the day the African American men and women we approached looked at us with scorn and anger as they read the leaflet. Many angrily asked us, "Why are you giving this to me? Do I look like I have AIDS? Do I look like I'm gay?" In most instances there was nothing we could say to convince them that what we offered was not blame but help and perhaps hope.

At the time I was working on my doctorate in the history of science and medicine, and I had less and less time to spend as an AIDS activist. Yet I watched as the epidemic changed. Many of my friends continued to advocate African American women as the fight against AIDS changed from the grassroots activism of groups like ACT-UP and Boston's Multicultural AIDS Coalition to a full blown infrastructure—international conferences were held every year; new medical journals appeared devoted solely to AIDS; nurses, clinical social workers, public health experts, medical research-ers, and newly formed community-based organizations all had their own perspective on the epidemic as they vied for increasing amounts of federal funds. A new category of expert was created out of these efforts: the AIDS worker. These AIDS workers began to draw a more complete picture of the details and contours of the AIDS epidemic as it affected African American women. As AIDS work itself became more and more fragmented, the work being done to address the situation for African American women broadened, and we began to learn the depths to which the disease had struck within our communities. Yet the critical problem was that the plight of African American women never took center stage in mainstream efforts to control the epidemic.

Many AIDS activists and researchers have stories like mine. What did we learn from the stories, the surveys, the interviews, the counseling sessions, the clinical trials? We learned that as late as 1990, many Black women still did not perceive themselves to be at risk from the disease. There were few media representations of them in public health prevention materials, and those that were shown almost universally couched Black women as being incapable of controlling their own lives in the face of AIDS. We knew that many of the African American women with AIDS were adolescents who knew little about contraception nor how to use it with male partners who were often in an older age cohort. While the official public health message emphasized abstinence, we knew that many poor Black women couldn't afford abstinence. We found out that little was known about condom use in Black communities. All the AIDS reduction advice to Black women in the early 1990s asked women to change their behavior as if their behavior did not have a social context.[6] And none of that advice emphasized that the numbers of African American women with AIDS was surely going to increase if behaviors did not change. And the numbers did increase.

We learned some things that we already knew—that a disproportionate number of HIV-positive Black women are poor living in deteriorating urban environments. We learned that they were often the sole supporter of themselves and their children. These women faced tragedies associated with impoverished living: inadequate housing, poor health, violence, isolation, discrimination, and substance abuse that pre-dated their HIV-infection. We learned that many of these women were at a greater risk for HIV infection because of the sexual and drug-using behaviors of the men they were involved with. We learned that many poor African American women and those who are not poor were struggling with a sex-ratio imbalance—a shortage of suitable male partners that has taken a psychological toll on their sense of self-esteem and leads them to practice unsafe sexual behaviors. We are beginning to learn about the serious and complicated effects on Black women and their children of the high numbers of African American men who are now or have been in prison. On the positive side, we are learning a great deal more about the strategies for survival that Black women employ in order to minimize the stigma associated with AIDS, drug use, and homosexuality. These strategies include denial but not only denial. These strategies also include practices to maintain a sense of dignity and control over one's life and to find pleasure in sexual expression. With respect to denial we are learning that African American women learn to practice denial around these issues in multiple venues including the church. In sum, we are also learning about the complex ways in which Black women and men are creating, sustaining, and justifying sexual practices that are born out of their social context.

The social context that African American women live in is not the same as that experienced by white Americans—it is different. As Dorie Gilbert has noted, "For the past two decades, prevention programs have been crippled by a lack of knowledge about the sociocultural context of the lives of African American women."[7] There has been a bit of fear, or rather hesitancy, or both, about exploring this social context on the part of African American health care professionals. The fear on the part of African American health professionals and some AIDS activists is, I think, that the different sexual practices, cultural values, desires of poor, but not only poor, Black women, will be seen by white medical and public health professionals as not simply different but inherently deviant. This fear that difference equals deviance is totally justified by even a cursory examination of the history of African Americans in this country. Nonetheless it is a fear that must be faced head on.

Many researchers and AIDS activists have called for new models for public health practices in order to deal with the AIDS crisis in African American communities. Some have argued that the trauma of AIDS has been so severe that we need to think about new ways of healing our communities, that is, ways to ". . . heal the kind of horizontal oppression that alienates gay and lesbian African Americans from their community, that creates violence in our communities, and that supports the systems by which Black men degrade Black women . . . in addition we have to find ways to help individuals heal through traumatic experiences, including the trauma experiences in decaying communities, while at the same time working to better those communities."[8] Others call for more programmatic approaches. They want funding for new investigations that would examine the role of social, interpersonal, and community contexts in risk taking and their possible role in risk reduction and funding for new research which would document and differentiate the many aspects of sexuality and sexual practices engaged in by African Americans. We have very little research on the relationship between identity and the disclosure of sexual orientation in different community contexts. We also must begin to study and outline the pathways of resilience in coping with stress and trauma so that those pathways and practices can be enhanced to support protective behaviors against HIV.[9] We know how much we need to develop more specific mental health interventions and access to mental health services within African American communities. This of course implies that there will be training for mental health professionals who must bring to their work an understanding of and respect for the strengths of African American women as well as skill in helping them tap into those strengths in order to resist AIDS.[10] This is a very extensive and comprehensive agenda that recognizes that the epidemic of HIV/AIDS in African American communities touches on every aspect of life especially for African American women. Yet in many respects these recommendations are couched in the language of public health and social science research. And as such they appeal for more federal funding for research and programs that researchers and activists believe will help African American communities overcome the AIDS crisis. There is little recognition in such appeals of how such funding will be obtained. What is needed to stop the spread of AIDS in African American communities is a comprehensive campaign against a disease that is simply unprecedented in the history of American public health.

## A Campaign to End AIDS

African American women have a long history of involvement in public health reform in the twentieth century. As Darlene Clark Hine, Vanessa Northington Gamble, Susan Smith, and other historians have shown, these efforts have ranged from building medical institutions in African American communities; to challenges by Black medical professionals to racism within medical, nursing, and public health organizations; to grass roots and community based efforts by sororities and religious organizations.[11] These efforts can be broadly characterized as universalist in their aims, innovative in their practices, and ultimately failing to effect structural change in the U.S. health care system.

For example, in her wonderful book *Sick and Tired of Being Sick and Tired: Black Women's Health Activism, 1890—1950*, historian Susan Smith documented the efforts of Black women to address the dire health needs of their people in the 1940s. In this period she notes that "Black health reform was gendered to the extent that men held most of the formal leadership positions and women did most of the grassroots organizing. In her words, "men led, but women organized."[12] Indeed Smith argues that there was a continuous, unbroken line of Black women's health activism since at least the 1890s. Black female professionals and community leaders formed the

backbone of the Black health movement and were central to the founding and maintenance of Black public health projects for the first half of the
twentieth century.

The Alpha Kappa Alpha (AKA) Mississippi Health project was started
in 1934 during the Depression to help Black folks who worked as sharecroppers on plantations in the region. In the Mississippi Delta area Black
people lived in dire poverty—housing consisted largely of small cabins with
dirt floors, no plumbing, and only outdoor privies. Malnutrition was a serious problem, because plantation owners did not want workers to spend
time away from cash crops to tend home gardens. Most food had to be
purchased at the plantation store, which offered only limited items—mostly
salt, sugar, grits, cornmeal, molasses, and fatback. Sharecroppers' difficulties were compounded by limited formal education and a political system
characterized by violence and intimidation. That a middle class African
American sorority would develop a health project for this region is worthy
of note. The project was an attempt on the part of these middle class women
to bridge the class gap since they recognized, in their words, ". . . there can
be no top—if the bottom is not solidly there." They wanted to demonstrate
concern *for* and their connection *to* the Black poor.[13]

The AKA set up clinics throughout the Mississippi delta region—they
gave physical examinations, vaccinations, nutrition and personal hygiene
information, clothing, food items, and treatments for malaria and venereal
disease, and dental services. They immunized over 15,000 children against
smallpox and diphtheria. Throughout this project the AKA volunteers
struggled with their class biases, while many gained a deeper insight and a
richer understanding of the life, needs, and outlook of the poor Black agricultural workers they helped.[14] The annual reports of the project that Smith
analyzed show that the women slowly developed a critique of the Southern
economic system, and they came to the conclusion that real change involved
altering the entire living and working environment of the sharecroppers. As
Dr. Dorothy Ferebee, head of the project, concluded, " [T]he Health project
revealed many significant findings, but none more important than the fact
the standard of health is indissolubly linked to all the socio-economic factors of living."[15] The AKA health project members saw clearly that poverty
was the primary factor underlying the poor health of the sharecroppers.
They concentrated their efforts on Black women and children, because they
believed that the only way to 'uplift the race' was by uplifting women and
children. They had no illusions that anyone else would advocate for Black
women and children except other Black women.

The Mississippi Health project ended in 1942 in large part because of
the restrictions on travel imposed as a result of World War II gas ration-

ing. The project's leaders also directed their efforts elsewhere. They realized that their voluntary efforts simply could not make a dent in the severe
and overwhelming health crisis that Black people faced. They needed more
funds, and more medical, nursing, and social service personnel. They tried
to convince the federal government to take over the work, but by and large
their efforts went unheeded. Support at the state level proved equally disappointing. Mary McLeod Bethune, then president of the National Council
of Negro Women along with Dorothy Ferebee, the head of the AKA Health
project, intensively lobbied federal agencies to address the health plight of
Black women and children. Predictably, they were not heard. But they continued to believe, based on their efforts, that Black women's interests would
not be represented in national health and welfare policy until Black women
themselves had the opportunity to construct and administer federal policy.
With characteristic candor, Bethune stated, "[T]he day has come now, not
tomorrow, but the day has come *now* for us, as Negro women, to be counted
among the women of this country who are making the plans and adminis-
tering the program to the people of America."[16]

Bethune, Ferebee, and the members of the AKA sorority and other Black
women's organizations could not move the federal government to make the
health care of poor Black women and children a priority. However, in a
limited way their efforts were successful. These women rejected Cassandra's
role of merely crying out for attention—they used the resources they had
to develop innovative and creative health programs for the Black poor in
the Mississippi Delta. However, the tragedy is that such efforts could not
be sustained.

It should not be surprising that their efforts could not be sustained. The
*only* successful public health campaigns in this country have been those
that enlisted the majority of Americans in a narrowly focused war against
disease that had a clear technical solution. The public health campaigns
against the most deadly childhood disease of the nineteenth and early
twentieth century, diphtheria, were successful because they engaged physicians, private businesses, philanthropic organizations, churches, and the
public in a battle against the disease. The goal of the campaigns was to make
sure that every child would be immunized against diphtheria. Immuniza-
tion was a straightforward technical solution that could protect children
from disease without confronting the structural issues that made some children more vulnerable to disease than others. The universalistic aims of such
campaigns convinced everyone that conquering disease served the public
good. The public in such campaigns was a unified one—not one that was
fragmented by class, race, or ethnicity. For the architects of these campaigns
the control and eradication of the disease was seen as a more important

goal than such divisions. The leaders of these campaigns met opposition from physicians, drug manufacturers, and insurance companies, yet they persevered and overcame that opposition, and they brought a deadly disease under control.[17]

The epidemic of HIV/AIDS emerged in a historical moment when the health care system in this country had shifted from a focus on infectious diseases like diphtheria to chronic diseases like cancer, from collective to individual responsibility for health, and from access and equity to cost containment and fiscal restraint. Where in the 1940s and 1950s our health care system was largely centralized, by the 1970s and 1980s this centralization was replaced by fragmentation and localization, which made responding to this disease in a unified way almost impossible.[18] While many people have lauded the public health activities that have successfully reduced the spread of AIDS among white gay men, these programs have not been successful in African American communities. Currently, federal funding for HIV/AIDS in the United States has been called a "quilt with many holes," because of the many barriers that still exist for minorities to get full access to HIV/AIDS treatment and support.[19]

As in other eras Black women are playing a large and diverse set of roles in confronting the AIDS epidemic—and they are doing so in the absence of institutions inside and outside of Black communities to address this difficult and growing health crisis. African American women have stepped into the breach created by the failure of these institutions. HIV/AIDS prevention in African American communities has faltered on many fronts—the failure of churches to address AIDS; the inability to deal with the stigma associated with the disease; the silence about sexuality, gender roles, and sexual practices; and the refusal of the U.S. government to make the epidemic in African American communities the focus of prevention and research efforts.

While we now have a federal office of minority health, including a national project called Healthy People 2010, which is ostensibly dedicated to ending health disparities and improving the health of all Americans, I would argue that such efforts fall far short of the kind of effort that is needed to fight HIV/AIDS. We have yet to witness a concerted, sustained public health campaign against HIV/AIDS in African American communities. The federal government has never promoted a public health campaign that addresses the structural and cultural issues that support and enable the spread of disease. The focus of the majority of federal efforts has largely been on technical solutions, e.g., to provide funds for vaccine development. Indeed the new public health that emerged in the twentieth century United States was premised on avoiding structural issues such as poverty and housing, and promoting reductionist approaches that focused on pathogens not people. In sum, AIDS researchers and activists must recognize that the federal government cannot and perhaps will not end the multifaceted, complex social and cultural crisis that is AIDS in African American communities.

## Conclusion

"They fancied themselves free," Camus wrote of the citizens of the town of Oran just before plague struck, "and no one will ever be free as long as there are pestilences."[20] Here in 2004, we have learned a great deal about HIV/AIDS and perhaps more about ourselves, as Camus reminded us. If the AIDS epidemic has revealed the fragmentation of our society and more importantly the breakdown of African American communities, then, in the end, to truly contain it, we must find the political will to make it whole. What is needed goes far beyond federal support of innovative and creative programs to reach and help individuals and their families. What is needed is a Civil Rights Movement organized around health as a right of citizenship. Poor African American women are not free when they cannot protect themselves and their families against disease, poverty, and urban decay. They are not free when sexual relationships must be conducted in a context of shame, mistrust and betrayal. None of us is free when we silently tolerate suffering among us. None of us is free when the expression of sexual desire is shaped by shame and stigma. As in the past, it is African American women who must take the lead in this effort. We need a massive grassroots movement that demands the right to health the way we demanded the right to vote in the 1960s. We need a movement that claims for the poorest, most vulnerable women in our society the right to gender and sexual justice. African American women must lead the effort to make all of our institutions accountable to us. There is only one way to end silence, secrets, shame, and suffering, and that it to act. Can we do this? I don't think we have any other choice. We must draw strength for this work from our own past—after all, African American women "specialize in the wholly impossible."[21]

## Notes

1. See Evelynn M. Hammonds, "Race, Sex, AIDS: The Construction of Other," *Radical America*, 1986 and Linda Villarosa, "AIDS Fears Grow for Black Women," *The New York Times*, March 5, 2004, p.A1.

2. Vickie M. Mays and Susan Cochran, "Issues in the Perception of AIDS Risk and Risk Reduction Activities by Black and Hispanic/Latina Women," *American Psychologist*, 43: 11, p. 949.

3. For a discussion of the yellow fever epidemic in Philadelphia see Martin Pernick, "Politics, Parties, and Pestilence: Epidemic Yellow Fever in Philadelphia and the Rise of

the First Party System," in J. Leavitt and R. Numbers, eds. *Sickness and Health in America* (Madison, WI: University of Wisconsin Press, 1978), pp. 241–258.

4. Absalom Jones and Richard Allen, "A Narrative of the Proceedings of the Black People, During the late Awful Calamity in Philadelphia, in the Year, 1793," in Dorothy Porter, ed. *Negro Protest Pamphlets* (New York: The Arno Press, 1969) pp. 12–13.

5. John Edgar Wideman, "Fever" in *Fever: Twelve Stories* (New York: Penguin Books, 1989) p. 132.

6. Cochran and Mays, Ibid.

7. Dorie J. Gilbert and Ednita M. Wright, *African American Women and HIV/AIDS: Critical Responses* (Westport, CT: Praeger Publishers, 2003) p. 21.

8. Ibid.

9. Vickie M. Mays, Susan D. Cochran, A. Zamudio, "HIV Prevention Research: Are We Meeting the Needs of African American Men Who Have Sex With Men?" *Journal of Black Psychology*, 30, no. 1, Feb. 2004 78–105.

10. Ibid.

11. See for example Darlene Clark Hine, *Black Women in White: Racial Conflict and Cooperation in the Nursing Profession, 1890–1915*(Bloomington: Indiana University Press, 1989), Vanessa Northington Gamble, *Making a Place for Ourselves: The Black Hospital Movement, 1920–1945* (Oxford: Oxford University Press, 1995), and Susan L. Smith, *Sick and Tired of Being Sick and Tired: Black Women's Health Activism in America, 1890–1950* (Philadelphia: University of Pennsylvania Press, 1995)

12. Ibid., p. 1.

13. Ibid., p. 151.

14. Ibid., p. 161.

15. Ibid.

16. Ibid., p. 164.

17. See Evelynn M. Hammonds, *Childhoods' Deadly Scourge: The Campaign to Control Diphtheria in New York City, 1880 to 1930* (Baltimore: The Johns Hopkins University Press, 2000)

18. See John Duffy, *The Sanitarians: A History of American Public Health* (Urbana: The University of Illinois Press, 1992) pp. 304–305.

19. "Financing HIV/AIDS: A Quilt with Many Holes" Henry J. Kaiser Foundation Report, May 2004.

20. Albert Camus quoted in Charles Rosenberg, "What is an Epidemic: AIDS in Historical Perspective," *Daedalus*, Spring, 1989, p.14.

21. See Darlene Clark Hine, L. Reed, and W. King eds., *We Specialize in the Wholly Impossible: A Reader in Black Women's History* (Brooklyn: Carlson Publishing Co. Inc., 1995)

# IV

# TO BE YOUNG, GIFTED, AND BLACK

# "What Has Happened Here":
The Politics of Difference in Women's
History and Feminist Politics

*Elsa Barkley Brown*

1992

My work is not traditional. I like it that way. If people tell me to turn my ends under, I'll leave them raggedy. If they tell me to make my stitches small and tight, I'll leave them loose. Sometimes you can trip over my stitches they're so big. You can always recognize the traditional quilters who come by and see my quilts. They sort of cringe. They fold their hands in front of them as if to protect themselves from the cold. When they come up to my work they think to themselves, "God, what has happened here–all these big crooked stitches." I appreciate these quilters. I admire their craft. But that's not my kind of work. I would like them to appreciate what I'm doing. They are quilters. But I am an artist. And I tell stories.

—Yvonne Wells, quoted in *Stitching Memories:*
*African American Story Quilts*

Questions of difference loom large in contemporary intellectual and political discussions. Although many women's historians and political activists understand the intellectual and political necessity, dare I say moral, intellectual, and political correctness, of recognizing the diversity of women's experiences, this recognition is often accompanied with the sad (or angry) lament that too much attention to difference disrupts the relatively successful struggle to produce and defend women's history and women's politics, necessary corollaries of a women's movement. Like the traditionalists who view Yvonne Wells's quilts,[1] many women's historians and feminist activists cringe at the big and loose rather than small and tight stitches that now seem to bind women's experiences. They seek a way to protect themselves and what they have created as women's history and women's politics, and they wonder despairingly, "'God, what has happened here.'" I do not say this facetiously; the fear that all this attention to the differences among women will leave us with only a void, a vacuum, or chaos is a serious concern. Such despair, I believe, is unnecessary, the product of having accepted the challenge to the specifics of our historical knowledge and political organizing while continuing to privilege a linear, symmetrical (some would say Western) way of thinking about history and politics themselves.

I am an optimist. It is an optimism born of reflecting on particular historical and cultural experiences. If I offer some elements of the cultural understandings underpinning those experiences as instructive at this juncture of our intellectual and political journey, it is because "culture, in the largest sense is, after all, a resource that provides the context in which [we] perceive [our] social world. Perceptions of alternatives in the social structure [can] take place only within a framework defined by the patterns and rhythms" of our particular cultural understandings. A rethinking of the cultural aesthetics that underlie women's history and women's politics are essential to what I perceive as the necessary rethinking of the intellectual and political aesthetics.[2]

And it is here that I think African American culture is instructive as a way of rethinking, of reshaping our thinking processes, our understandings of history and politics themselves. Like Yvonne Wells, Zora Neale Hurston—anthropologist, folklorist, playwright, and novelist—also addressed questions of cultural difference and, in the process, suggested ways of thinking about difference itself:

> Asymmetry is a definite feature of Negro art. . . . The sculpture and the carvings are full of this beauty and lack of symmetry. It is present in the literature, both prose and verse. . . . It is the lack of symmetry which makes Negro dancing so difficult for white dancers to learn. The abrupt and unexpected changes. The frequent change of key and time are evidences of this quality in music. . . . The presence of rhythm and lack of symmetry are paradoxical, but there they are. Both are present to a marked degree. There is always rhythm, but it is the rhythm of segments. Each unit has a rhythm of its own, but when the whole is assembled it is lacking in symmetry. But easily workable to a Negro who is accustomed to the break in going from one part to another, so that he adjusts himself to the new tempo.[3]

Wells and Hurston point to nonlinear ways of thinking about the world, of hearing multiple rhythms and thinking music not chaos, ways that challenge the notion that sufficient attention to difference leads to intellectual chaos, to political vacuum, or to intellectual and political void. Considering Wells's and Hurston's reflections on cultural difference might show us that it is precisely differences which are the path to a community of intellectual and political struggle.[4]

Also instructive is the work of Luisah Teish. In *Jambalaya: The Natural Woman's Book of Personal Charms and Practical Rituals*, she writes about going home to New Orleans for a visit and being met by her family at the airport: "Before I can get a good look in my mother's face, people begin arranging themselves in the car. They begin to talk gumbo ya ya, and it goes on for 12 days. . . . Gumbo ya ya is a creole term that means 'Everybody talks at once.'" It is through gumbo ya ya that Teish learns everything that has happened in her family and community and she conveys the essential information about herself to the group.[5] That is, it is through gumbo ya ya that Teish tells the history of her sojourn to her family and they tell theirs to her. They do this simultaneously because, in fact, their histories are joined—occurring simultaneously, in connection, in dialogue with each other. To relate their tales separately would be to obliterate that connection.

To some people listening to such a conversation, gumbo ya ya may sound like chaos. We may better be able to understand it as something other than confusion if we overlay it with jazz, for gumbo ya ya is the essence of a musical tradition where "the various voices in a piece of music may go their own ways but still be held together by their relationship to each other."[6] In jazz, for example, each member has to listen to what the other is doing and know how to respond while each is, at the same time, intent upon her own improvisation. It is in this context that jazz pianist Ojeda Penn has called jazz an expression of true democracy, for each person is allowed, in fact required, to be an individual, to go her or his own way, and yet to do so in concert with the group.[7]

History is also everybody talking at once, multiple rhythms being played simultaneously. The events and people we write about did not occur in isolation but in dialogue with a myriad of other people and events. In fact, at any given moment millions of people are all talking at once. As historians we try to isolate one conversation and to explore it, but the trick is then how to put that conversation in a context which makes evident its dialogue with so many others—how to make this one lyric stand alone and at the same time be in connection with all the other lyrics being sung.

Unfortunately, it seems to me, few historians are good jazz musicians; most of us write as if our training were in classical music. We require surrounding silence—of the audience, of all the instruments not singled out as the performers in this section, even often of any alternative visions than the composer's. That then makes it particularly problematic for historians when faced with trying to understand difference while holding on to an old score that has in many ways assumed that despite race, class, ethnicity, sexuality, and other differences, at core all women do have the same gender; that is, the rhythm is the same and the conductor can point out when it is time for each of us to play it. Those who would alter the score or insist on being able to keep their own beat simultaneously with the orchestrated one are not merely presenting a problem of the difficulty of constructing a framework that will allow for understanding the experiences of a variety of women but as importantly the problem of confronting the political implications of such a framework, not only for the women under study but also for the historians writing those studies.

I think we still operate at some basic levels here. This is an opinion which may not be widely shared among women's historians. For I am aware that there is a school of thought within women's history that believes that it, more than any other field of history, has incorporated that notable triumvirate—race, class, and gender-and has addressed difference. But my point is that recognizing and even including difference is, in and of itself, not enough. In fact, such recognition and inclusion may be precisely the way to avoid the challenges, to reaffirm the very traditional stances women's history sees itself as challenging, and to write a good classical score—silencing everyone else until the spotlight is on them but allowing them no interplay throughout the composition. We need to recognize not only differences but also the relational nature of those differences. Middle-class white women's lives are not just different from working-class white, Black, and Latina women's lives. It is important to recognize that middle-class women live the lives they do precisely because working-class women live the lives they do. White women and women of color not only live different lives but white women live the lives they do in large part because women of color live the ones they do.

Let me here grossly simplify two hundred years of Black and white women's history in the United States. Among the major changes we have seen has been the greater labor force participation of white middle-class women; the increasing movement of white middle-class women from the home to voluntary associations within the larger society to formal public political roles; the shift among Black women from agricultural labor to industrial, service, and clerical work; the emergence of Black working-class women from the kitchens of white women to jobs in the private sector; and the shift of middle-class Black women to jobs in the public sector. We could, and often do, set these experiences side by side, thus acknowledging the differences in the experiences of different women. And most often, whether stated or not, our acknowledgment of these differences leads us to recognize how Black women's life choices have been constrained by race—how race has shaped their lives. What we are less apt to acknowledge (that is, to make explicit and to analyze) is how white women's lives are also shaped by race.[8] Even less do I see any real recognition of the relational nature of these differences.

But white middle-class women moved from a primary concern with home and children to involvement in voluntary associations when they were able to have their homes and children cared for by the services—be they direct or indirect—of other women. White middle-class women have been able to move into the labor force in increasing numbers not just differ-ently from other women but precisely because of the different experience of other women and men. The growth in white women's participation in the labor force over the last two decades and the increased opportunities for managerial and professional positions for white women has accom-panied the U.S. transition from an industrial to a technological economy. This transition is grounded in the very deindustrialization and decentral-ization which has meant the export of capital to other parts of the world, where primarily people of color—many of them female—face overwhelm-ing exploitation from multinational corporations' industrial activities and the flight of business from urban (particularly inner-city) areas within the United States, and thus the tremendous rise in unemployment and under-employment among African American women and men.[9] It is precisely the connection between global industrial exploitation, rising unemployment, and underemployment in inner-city, largely minority communities, and the growth in opportunities for the middle-class (and especially white middle-class women) which are likely to go unexplored. The change in the economy has meant not only the growth of the highly publicized "high-technology" jobs but also the tremendous growth in distinctly "low-tech" service jobs. The increased labor force participation of white middle-class women has been accompanied, indeed made possible, by the increased availability out-side the home of services formerly provided inside the home—cleaning, food, health, and personal services. These jobs are disproportionately filled by women of color—African American, Latina, Asian American.[10] Middle-class Black women were hired to perform social service functions in the public sector at the same time that white middle-class women were moving from performing these functions, often as volunteer work, to better paid and higher status positions in the private sector.[11]

We are likely to acknowledge that white middle-class women have had a different experience from African American, Latina, Asian American, and Native American women; but the relation, the fact that these histories exist simultaneously, in dialogue with each other, is seldom apparent in the studies we do, not even in those studies that perceive themselves as deal-ing with the diverse experiences of women. The overwhelming tendency now, it appears to me, is to acknowledge and then ignore differences among women. Or, if we acknowledge a relationship between Black and white women's lives, it is likely to be only that African American women's lives are shaped by white women's but not the reverse. The effect of this is that acknowledging difference becomes a way of reinforcing the notion that the experiences of white middleclass women are the norm; all others become deviant—different from.

This reflects the fact that we have still to recognize that being a woman is, in fact, not extractable from the context in which one is a woman—that is, race, class, time, and place. We have still to recognize that all women do not have the same gender. In other words, we have yet to accept the fact that one cannot write adequately about the lives of white women in the United States *in any context* without acknowledging the way in which race shaped their lives. One important dimension of this would involve understanding the relationship between white women and white men as shaped by race. This speaks not just to the history we write but to the way we understand our own lives. And I believe it challenges women's history at its core, for it suggests that until women's historians adequately address difference and the causes for it, they have not and cannot adequately tell the history of even white middle-class women.

The objections to all of this take many forms but I would like to address two of them. First, the oft-repeated lament of the problems of too many identities; some raise this as a conceptual difficulty, others as a stylistic one. In either case, such a discussion reinforces the notion that women of color, ethnic women, and lesbians are deviant, not the norm. And it reinforces not just the way in which some histories are privileged but also the way in which some historians are privileged. In fact, in women's history difference means "not white middle-class heterosexual," thus renormalizing white middle-class heterosexual women's experiences. One result of this is that white middle-class heterosexual women do not often have to think about difference or to see themselves as "other."[12] Not only do people of color not have the luxury in this society of deciding whether to identify racially but historians writing about people of color also do not have the privilege of deciding whether to acknowledge, at least at some basic level, their multiple identities. No editor or publisher allows a piece on Black or Latina women to represent itself as being about "women." On the other hand, people who want to acknowledge that their pieces are about "white" women often have to struggle with editors to get that in their titles and consistently used throughout their pieces—the objection being it is unnecessary, superfluous, too wordy, awkward. Historians writing about heterosexual women seldom feel compelled to consistently establish that as part of their subjects' identity whereas historians writing about lesbian women must address sexuality. Does this imply that sexuality is only a factor in the lives of lesbian women, that is, that they are not only different from but deviant? These seem to me to be issues that historians cannot address separately from questions of the privilege some people have in this society and the way in which some historians have a vested interest in duplicating that privilege within historical constructions.

Another objection to the attention to difference is the fear, expressed in many ways, that we will in the process lose the "voice of gender."[13] This reifies the notion that all women have the same gender and requires that most women's voices be silenced and some privileged voice be given center stage. But that is not the only problem with this assumption for it also ignores the fact that gender does not have a voice; women and men do. They raise those voices constantly and simultaneously in concert, in dialogue with each other. Sometimes the effect may seem chaotic because they respond to each other in such ways; sometimes it may seem harmonic. But always it is polyrhythmic; never is it a solo or single composition.

Yet there is in the academy and society at large a continuing effort to uphold some old and presumably well-established literary and historical canon. Those bent on protecting such seem well trained in classical music; they stand on the stage and proudly proclaim: "We have written the score; we are conducting it; we will choose those who will play it without changing a chord; and everyone else should be silent." Unfortunately, much of the current lament among women's historians about the dangers, disruptiveness, and chaos of difference sounds much like this—reifying a classical score, composed and conducted this time by women.

This is not merely a question of whether one prefers jazz to classical music. Like most intellectual issues, this one, too, has real political consequences. We have merely to think about the events surrounding Anita Hill's fall 1991 testimony before the Senate Judiciary Committee. When Professor Hill testified, a number of women, individually and collectively, rallied to her support and to advance awareness of the issue of sexual harassment. Many of Hill's most visible supporters, however, ignored the fact that she is a Black woman, the thirteenth child of Oklahoma farmers, or treated these as merely descriptive or incidental matters.[14] The National Organization for Women, feminist legal scholar Catharine MacKinnon, and others spoke forcefully and eloquently about the reality of sexual harassment in women's lives, but in doing so often persisted in perpetuating a deracialized notion of women's experiences.[15] One wonders if many white feminists, especially, were not elated to have found an issue and a Black woman who could become a universal symbol, evidence of the common bonds of womanhood. Elevating Hill to such a status, however, required ignoring the racialized and class-specific histories of women's sexuality and stereotypes and our different histories of sexual harassment and sexual violence.[16]

In the end, I would argue, the ignoring of these racialized and class-specific histories became a political liability. Having constructed Anita Hill as a generic or universal woman with no race or class, and having developed an analysis of sexual harassment in which race and class were not central issues, many of Hill's supporters were unable to deal with the racialized and class-specific discussion when it emerged. This suggests how little our scholarship and politics has taught us about the construction of race in the United States, and I think this is connected to the failure to construct race as a significant factor in white women's experiences.[17] Once Clarence Thomas played the race card and a string of his female supporters raised the class issue, they had much of the public discussion to themselves.[18] Thomas and his supporters did not create a race and class context. They exploited it.

Thomas's analysis of Hill's charges and the committee hearings as "a modern day lynching based in white men's sexual stereotypes of black men hinge[d] on assuming that race should be considered only when thinking about his situation."[19] He, therefore, constructed himself as a Black man confronting a generic (read, for many people, "white" or "whitened") woman assisted by white men. "Thomas outrageously manipulated the legacy of lynching in order to shelter himself from Anita Hill's allegations"; by "trivializ[ing] and misrepresent[ing] this painful part of African American people's history," Thomas was able "to deflect attention away from the reality of sexual abuse in African American women's lives."[20] Such a strategy could only have been countered effectively by putting the experience of sexual harassment for Anita Hill in the context of her being a Black woman in the United States.[21]

Eleven years prior, Anita Hill embarked on her legal career. This was a woman who began her formal education before the Morris, Oklahoma, schools were integrated and who had gone on to graduate from one of the country's most elite law schools. When she confronted the sexual harassment, so painfully described in her testimony, the weight of how to handle these advances lay on Anita Hill not merely as "a woman or a Yale Law School graduate," but as "a young black woman, the daughter of Oklahoma farmers, whose family and community expected her to do well. It is essential to understand how this may have shaped both her experiences and her responses."[22] Hill's friend, Ellen Wells, herself the victim of sexual harassment on the job, explained much in her succinct statement before the committee: "You don't walk around carrying your burdens so that everyone can see them. You're supposed to carry that burden and try to make the best of it."[23]

Few Black women of Anita Hill's age and older grew up unaware of the frequency of sexual abuse as part of Black women's employment history. Many of us were painfully aware that one reason our families worked so hard to shield us from domestic and factory work was to shield us from sexual abuse. And we were aware that the choices many of our mothers made (or our fathers insisted upon) to forgo employment were in fact efforts to avoid abusive employment situations. Sexual harassment as a legal theory and a public discussion in white middle-class communities may be a late 1970s' phenomenon, but sexual harassment has been not only a widespread phenomenon of Black women's labor history but also the subject of widespread public and private discussion within Black communities.[24] From the late nineteenth century on, Black women and men spoke out about the frequency of sexual abuse of Black women laborers, the majority of whom were employed in domestic service.

In fact, it is hard to read the politics of Black communities, especially Black women's organizations, in the late nineteenth and early twentieth centuries, without recognizing this awareness of the reality of sexual harassment.[25] By the mid-twentieth century this was no longer as public a discussion in our communities as it had been in the late nineteenth and early twentieth centuries, but it was still a significant part of the private discussion and necessary socialization to being a Black female living in a racial and racist society.[26] A collective memory of sexual harassment runs deep in African American communities and many Black women, especially those born before the 1960s' civil rights movement, would likely recognize sexual harassment not as a singular experience but as part of a collective and common history.

Given the economic and racial circumstances, Black women understand from an early age that figuring out how to endure, survive, and move forward is an essential responsibility. As a newly minted, young, Black professional, the pride of one's family and community, the responsibility to do so would be even greater. You think "they endured and so should I." You think you are expected to represent success. How can you dash your family's and community's joy at your achievements and their hopes that education, mobility, and a good job would protect you?[27]

Analyses which offered as explanation of Hill's long silence only that it was representative of the common tendency of women to individualize the experience, to feel isolated, and therefore not to report such incidents assume in fact a lack of socialization around these issues or a socialization which leads women to see themselves as alone, unique in these experiences; and they miss the complexity of such experiences for differing women.[28] By complicating the discussion past singular explanations or in ways that truly explored the differential dimensions and expressions of power, one might have expanded the base of support—support not based on a commonality of experience but on a mobilization that precisely spoke to particularities and differences.

Anita Hill experienced sexual harassment not as a woman who had been harassed by a man but as a Black woman harassed by a Black man. Race is a factor in all cases of sexual abuse—inter- or intraracial—although it is usually only explored in the former. When white middle-class and upper-class men harass and abuse white women they are generally protected by white male privilege; when Black men harass and abuse white women they may be protected by male privilege, but they are as likely to be subject to racial hysteria; when Black men harass and abuse Black women they are often supported by racist stereotypes which assume different sexual norms and different female value among Black people.[29] I think we understand this only if we recognize that race is operative even when all the parties involved are white.

But, recognizing race as a factor in sexual harassment and sexual abuse requires us particularly to consider the consequences of the sexual history and sexual stereotypes of African Americans, especially African American women. "Throughout U.S. history Black women have been sexually stereotyped as immoral, insatiable, perverse; the initiators in all sexual contacts— abusive or otherwise." A result of such stereotyping as well as of the political, economic, and social privileges that resulted to white people (especially white men but also white women) from such stereotyping is that "the common assumption in legal proceedings as well as in the larger society has been that black women cannot be raped or otherwise sexually abused."[30] This has several effects. One is that Black women are most likely not to be believed if they speak of unwarranted sexual advances or are believed to have been willing or to have been the initiator. Both white and Black women have struggled throughout the nineteenth and twentieth centuries to gain control of their sexual selves. But while white elite women's sexual history has included the long effort to break down Victorian assumptions of sexuality and respectability in order to gain control of their sexual selves, Black women's sexual history has required the struggle to be accepted as respectable in an effort to gain control of their sexual selves.[31] Importantly, this has resulted in what Darlene Clark Hine has described as a culture of dissemblance—Black women's sexuality is often concealed, that is, Black women have had to learn to cover up all public suggestions of sexuality, even of sexual abuse. Black women, especially middle-class women, have learned to present a public image that never reveals their sexuality.[32]

Further, given the sexual stereotyping of Black men, a young Anita Hill may also have recognized that speaking of the particularities of Thomas's harassment of her had the potential to restigmatize the whole Black community—male and female. This is not merely, as some have suggested, about protecting Black men or being "dutiful daughters." Black women sought their own as well as the larger community's protection through the development of a politics of respectability.[33] Respectable behavior would not guarantee one's protection from sexual assault, but the absence of such was certain to reinforce racist notions of Black women's greater sexuality, availability, or immorality, as well as the racist notions of Black men's bestiality which were linked to that.

Thomas exploited these issues. Only a discussion which explored the differences and linkages in Black and white women's and working-class and middle-class women's struggles for control of their sexual selves could have effectively addressed his manipulation of race and class and addressed the fears that many Black people, especially women, had at the public discussion of what they perceived as an intraracial sexual issue. Dismissing or ignoring these concerns or imposing a universal feminist standard which ignores the differential consequences of public discourse will not help us build a political community around these issues.

Attending to the questions of race and class surrounding the Thomas hearings would have meant that we would not have had a linear story to tell. The story we did have would not have made good quick sound bites or simple slogans for it would have been far more complicated. But, in the end, I think, it would have spoken to more people's experiences and created a much broader base of understanding and support for issues of sexual harassment. Complicating it certainly would have allowed a fuller confrontation of the manipulation and exploitation of race and class on the part of Thomas and his supporters. The political liability here and the threat to creating a community of struggle came from *not* focusing on differences among women and not seriously addressing the race and class dimensions of power and sexual harassment. It would, of course, have been harder to argue that things would have been different if there were a woman on the committee.[34] But then many Black working-class women, having spent their days toiling in the homes of white elite women, understood that femaleness was no guarantee of support and mutuality. Uncomplicated discussions of universal women's experiences cannot address these realities. Race (and yes gender, too) is at once too simple an answer and at the same time a more complex answer than we have yet begun to make it.

The difficulty we have constructing this more complicated story is not merely a failure to deal with the specifics of race and class; the difficulty is also, I believe, in how we see history and politics—in an underlying focus on linear order and symmetry which makes us wary, fearing that layering multiple and asymmetrical stories will only result in chaos with no women's history or women's story to tell, that political community is a product of homogeneity, and that exploring too fully our differences will leave us void of any common ground on which to build a collective struggle. These are the ideas/assumptions which I want to encourage us to think past.

I suggest African American culture as a means to learning to think differently about history and politics. I do this not merely because these are cultural forms with which I am familiar and comfortable. Rather, I do this because there is a lot that those who are just confronting the necessity to be aware of differences can learn from those who have had always to be aware of such. Learning to think nonlinearly, asymmetrically, is, I believe, essential to our intellectual and political developments. A linear history will lead us to a linear politics and neither will serve us well in an asymmetrical world.

## Notes

This is a revised and expanded version of a paper that was presented at the American Historical Association in New York in December 1990 and published as "Polyrhythms and Improvisation: Lessons for Women's History," *History Workshop Journal* 31 (Spring 1991): 85–90. For thinking through the original paper and/or this expanded version with me, I thank Deborah Britzman, Carole Boyce Davies, Marilynn Desmond, Evelyn Nakano Glenn, Tera Hunter, Robin D.G. Kelley, Deborah K. King, Jerma Jackson, Leslie S. Rowland, Susan Sterrett, and the editors of *Feminist Studies*.

1. See *Stitching Memories: African American Story Quilts*, Gallery Guide, Eva Grudin, curator (Williamstown, Mass.: Williams College Museum of Art, 1989), 1.

2. Elsa Barkley Brown, "African American Women's Quilting: A Framework for Conceptualizing and Teaching African American Women's History," *Signs* 14 (Summer 1989): 925–26.

3. Zora Neale Hurston, "Characteristics of Negro Expression," in *Negro: An Anthology*, ed. Nancy Cunard (London: Wishart, 1934); reprinted in Zora Neale Hurston, *The Sanctified Church* (Berkeley, Calif.: Turtle Island Press, 1983), 54–55.

4. My thinking that communities of struggle are created out of and sustained by difference as much as similarity is, in part, the product of my research on southern urban African American communities in the late nineteenth and early twentieth centuries. See Elsa Barkley Brown, "Weaving Threads of Community: The Richmond Example" (Paper presented at the Southern Historical Association, Fifty-fourth Annual Meeting, Norfolk, Virginia, 12 Nov. 1988); and "'Not Alone to Build This Pile of Brick': Institution Building and Community in Richmond, Virginia" (Paper presented at The Age of Booker T. Washington: Conference in Honor of Louis Harlan, University of Maryland, College Park, May 1990).

5. Luisah Teish, *Jambalaya: The Natural Woman's Book of Personal Charms and Practical Rituals* (San Francisco: Harper & Row, 1985), 139–40.

6. Lawrence Levine, *Black Culture and Black Consciousness: Afro-American Folk Thought from Slavery to Freedom* (New York: Oxford University Press, 1977), 133.

7. Ojeda Penn, "Jazz: American Classical Music as a Philosophic and Symbolic Entity" (Faculty lecture series, Fifteenth Anniversary of African and African-American Studies Program, Emory University, Atlanta, Georgia, March 1986).

8. We need historical studies of white women in the United States comparable to the work begun by Alexander Saxton, David Roediger, Vron Ware, and Ann Laura Stoler—

work which takes seriously the study of the racial identity of white U.S. men and white European women and men. See, Alexander Saxton, *The Rise and Fall of the White Republic: Class Politics and Mass Culture in Nineteenth-Century America* (New York: Verso, 1990); David R. Roediger, *The Wages of Whiteness: Race and the Making of the American Working Class* (New York: Verso, 1991); Vron Ware, *Beyond the Pale: White Women, Racism, and History* (London: Verso, 1992); Ann Laura Stoler, "Carnal Knowledge and Imperial Power: Gender, Race, and Morality in Colonial Asia," in *Gender at the Crossroads of Knowledge: Feminist Anthropology in the Postmodern Era,* ed. Micaela di Leonardo (Berkeley: University of California Press, 1991), 51–101.

9. Linda Burnham, "Struggling to Make the Turn: Black Women and the Transition to a Post-Industrial Society" (Paper presented at "Survival and Resistance: Black Women in the Americas Symposium," Schomburg Center for Research in Black Culture, New York City, 9 June 1989).

10. Evelyn Nakano Glenn, "From Servitude to Service Work: Historical Continuities in the Racial Division of Reproductive Labor," *Signs* (Autumn 1992).

11. Social service work in the late nineteenth and early twentieth centuries was often performed as volunteer work by Black and white women. With the development of the welfare state, white middle-class women increasingly were able to perform these functions as paid employees of the state and social service agencies. After World War II, as white middle-class women increasingly moved into private sector jobs, Black women were able, for the first time in large numbers, to move out of domestic and industrial work into clerical and professional positions. But they did so principally through their employment in the public sector providing social service functions for Black clients under the pay and scrutiny of local, state, and federal governments. See Teresa L. Amott and Julie A. Matthaei, *Race, Gender, and Work: A Multicultural Economic History of Women in the United States* (Boston: South End Press, 1991); Linda Gordon, "Black and White Visions of Welfare: Women's Welfare Activism, 1890–1945," *Journal of American History* 78 (September 1991): 559–90; Elizabeth Higginbotham, "Employment for Professional Black Women in the Twentieth Century," Research Paper No. 3, Memphis State University Center for Research on Women, 1985.

12. One result of this is that women of color often come to stand for the "messiness" and "chaos" of history and politics much as an "aesthetic of uniformity" led the Radio City Music Hall Rockettes to perceive the addition of Black dancers to their chorus line as making "it ugly ('unaesthetic'), imbalanced ('nonuniform'), and sloppy ('imprecise')." See Patricia J. Williams's wonderful discussion in *The Alchemy of Race and Rights* (Cambridge: Harvard University Press, 1991), 116–18.

13. See, for example, "Editor's Notes," *Journal of Women's History* 1 (Winter 1990): 7.

14. The discussion which follows should not be read as a critique of Hill's testimony but rather of those who set themselves out as political and intellectual experts able to speak with authority on "women's issues." It is concerned with public discussion in mainstream media by those identifying themselves as feminist activists, primarily white. My focus on such is a reflection of the scope of this essay and is not intended to hold white women solely or even primarily responsible for the state of public discussion. For my analysis that addresses and critiques developments within the Black community and among Black organizations, see "Imaging Lynching: African American Communities, Collective Memory, and the Politics of Respectability," in *Reflections on Anita Hill: Race, Gender, and Power in the United States,* ed. Geneva Smitherman (Detroit: Wayne State University Press). Finally, I am not naive enough to think the conclusion of the Thomas confirmation process would have been different if these issues had been effec-

tively addressed. I do believe public discussion and political mobilization then and in the future could have been shaped differently by these discussions. Given that for two decades Black women have, according to almost all polls, supported feminist objectives in larger numbers than white women, I think we have to look to something other than Black women's reported antifeminism or privileging of race over gender for the answer to why an effective cross-race, cross-class political mobilization and discussion did not develop.

15. This is not to say that they did not acknowledge that Hill was Black or even, in Catharine MacKinnon's case, that "most of the women who have brought forward claims that have advanced the laws of sexual harassment have been black. Because racism is often sexualized, black women have been particularly clear in identifying this behavior as a violation of their civil rights." See *People*, 28 Oct. 1991, 49. It is to say that having acknowledged this, race is not a significant factor in the analysis of women's experience of sexual harassment. For a more extensive analysis of this and other issues raised in this essay, see "Imaging Lynching," and Elsa Barkley Brown, "Can We Get There from Here? The Contemporary Political Challenge to a Decade of Feminist Research and Politics." Paper prepared for "What Difference Does Difference Make? The Politics of Race, Class, and Gender Conference," Duke University-University of North Carolina Center for Research on Women, Chapel Hill, 31 May 1992.

16. For an analysis fully attuned to questions of race and class, see Kimberlé Crenshaw's participation in "Roundtable: Sexuality after Thomas/Hill," *Tikkun*, January/February 1992, 25–30. See also Crenshaw's analysis of Thomas's nomination pre-Anita Hill in "Roundtable: Doubting Thomas," *Tikkun*, September/October 1991, 23–30. It is useful to compare Crenshaw's analysis in the first with Ellen Willis's and in the latter with Catharine MacKinnon's.

17. In fact, race has been methodologically and theoretically written out of many analyses of sexual harassment. See, for example, the pioneering historical work of Mary Bularzik and the pioneering legal theory of Catharine MacKinnon. Bularzik is, quite appropriately, writing on white women and developing a discussion of the class dimension of sexual harassment; in the process, however, she offhandedly dismisses many Black women's understandings as false consciousness since they "often interpreted sexual harassment as racism, not sexism." See "Sexual Harassment at the Workplace: Historical Notes," *Radical America* 12 (July–August 1978); reprinted in *Workers' Struggles, Past and Present: A "Radical America" Reader,* ed. James Green (Philadelphia: Temple University Press, 1983), 117–35. MacKinnon acknowledges race as a factor only in cases involving persons of different races. See, for example, *Sexual Harassment of Working Women: A Case of Sex Discrimination* (New Haven: Yale University Press, 1979), 30–31. More importantly, her legal theory is built upon a notion of universal women and generic men which assumes that "men" are white and heterosexual.

Over time, women have been economically exploited, relegated to domestic slavery, used in denigrating entertainment, deprived of a voice and authentic culture, and disenfranchised and excluded from public life. Women, by contrast with comparable men, have systematically been subjected to physical insecurity; targeted for sexual denigration and violation; depersonalized and denigrated; deprived of respect, credibility, and resources; and silenced and denied public presence, voice, and representation of their interests. *Men as men have generally not had these things done to them; that is, men have had to be Black or gay (for instance) to have these things done to them as men.* See *Toward a Feminist Theory of the State* (Cambridge: Harvard University Press, 1989), 160 (emphasis mine).

18. Thomas did this most significantly in his dramatic calling up of the lynching issue and situating himself, for the first time in the hearings, as a Black man, and also in his efforts to portray Hill as a Black woman who felt inferior to and threatened by lighter skinned and white women. Those who testified for him [reinforced this position], most notably J.C. Alvarez, in her venomous references to Hill as a Black female Yale Law School graduate who, by Alvarez's account, could have gotten any job anywhere that she wanted. The following analysis, for reasons of space, addresses the manipulation of issues of race; for a more extensive analysis of the class issues, see my "Imaging Lynching," and "Can We Get There from Here?"

19. Letter to The Honorable Senators of the United States from African American Academic and Professional Women Who Oppose the Clarence Thomas Nomination, 15 Oct. 1991; "Official Statement to All Members of the United States Senate from African American Academic and Professional Women: A Petition to Reject the Clarence Thomas Nomination," 15 Oct. 1991; see also, "Official Statement to All Members of the United States Senate—A Petition of African-American Professors of Social Science and Law," 12 Oct. 1991; all in my possession.

20. "African American Women in Defense of Ourselves," Guest Editorial in *New York Amsterdam News,* 26 Oct. 1991 and Advertisement in *New York Times,* 17 Nov. 1991; San Francisco *Sun Reporter,* 20 Nov. 1991; *Capitol Spotlight* (Washington, D.C.), 21 Nov. 1991; *Los Angeles Sentinel,* 21 Nov. 1991; *Chicago Defender* 23 Nov. 1991; *Atlanta Inquirer,* 23 Nov. 1991; *Carolinian* (Raleigh, N.C.), 28 Nov. 1991.

21. The following discussion is not meant to speak for or analyze specifically Anita Hill's personal experience but to suggest the ways in which complicating the issues was essential to a discussion which would engage women from differing racial and class backgrounds.

22. "Official Statement to All Members of the United States Senate from African American Academic and Professional Women."

23. Ellen Wells, testimony before Senate Judiciary Committee, 13 Oct. 1991.

24. Mary Bularzik documents the longstanding recognition and discussion of sexual harassment of white working-class women but argues that white middle-class women were initially more reluctant to make public the sexual harassment that accompanied their employment. See "Sexual Harassment in the Workplace."

25. For public discussions of the connections between Black women's employment conditions and sexual abuse, see, for example, Maggie Lena Walker, "Traps for Women," Bethel A.M.E. Church, Richmond, Virginia, 15 Mar. 1925:

Poverty is a trap for *women,* and especially for our women; . . . When I walk along the avenue of our city and I see our own girls employed in the households of the whites, my heart aches with pain. Not that I cast a slur, or say one word against any kind of honest employment, yet when I see the good, pure, honest colored girl who is compelled to be a domestic in a white man's family–while I applaud the girl for her willingness to do honest work in order to be self supporting, and to help the mother and father who have toiled for her, yet, I tremble lest she should slip and fall a victim to some white man's lust.

See Maggie Lena Walker Papers, Maggie Lena Walker National Historical Site, Richmond, Virginia. See Black female domestic workers' own public accounts. For example: I lost my place because I refused to let the madam's husband kiss me. . . . I believe nearly all white men take, and expect to take, undue liberties with their colored female servants–not only the fathers, but in many cases the sons also. Those servants who rebel against such familiarity must either leave or expect a mighty hard time, if they stay. See

A Negro Nurse, "More Slavery at the South," *Independent* 72 (25 Jan. 1912): 197–98. Black club women such as Fannie Barrier Williams talked publicly of the letters they received from Black parents urging them to work to secure employment opportunities that would save their daughters from "going into the [white] homes of the South as servants." See "A Northern Negro's Autobiography," *Independent* 57 (14 July 1904): 96.

26. The primary persons continuing these discussions were, of course, domestic workers themselves. See, for example, "When maids would get together, they'd talk of it. ... They always had to fight off the woman's husband" in Florence Rice's interview with Gerda Lerner, quoted in *Black Women in White America: A Documentary History*, ed. Gerda Lerner (New York: Vintage Books, 1972), 275; or "nobody was sent out before you was told to be careful of the white man or his sons" in Elizabeth Clark-Lewis, " 'This Work Had a' End': The Transition from Live-In to Day Work," *Southern Women: The Intersection of Race, Class, and Gender*, Working Paper No. 2, Center for Research on Women, Memphis State University, 15. It was common practice for domestic workers to gather together to socialize and/or to provide support and advice regarding working conditions, survival strategies, and so on. Because many of these gatherings occurred in the workers' homes, they were often overheard if not participated in by the young people in the homes. See, for example, Bonnie Thornton Dill, " 'Making Your Job Good Yourself': Domestic Service and the Construction of Personal Dignity," in *Women and the Politics of Empowerment*, ed. Ann Bookman and Sandra Morgen (Philadelphia: Temple University Press, 1988), 33–52; Paule Marshall, "From the Poets in the Kitchen," *New York Times Book Review*, 9 Jan. 1983. Because the majority of Black women in the labor force up to 1960 were employed as domestic workers, a substantial number of African American women grew up with one or more family members who did domestic work and therefore were in frequent earshot of such conversations. In my own family a majority of my aunts and great-aunts were employed in either domestic or factory work. My mother, even though she had a college degree, when she took on paid employment to supplement the family income worked as a domestic or in a factory. For discussions of sexual abuse among Black women factory workers, see, for example, Beverly W. Jones, "Race, Sex, and Class: Black Female Tobacco Workers in Durham, North Carolina, 1920–1940, and the Development of Female Consciousness," *Feminist Studies* 10 (Fall 1984): 443–50. Robin D.G. Kelley suggests that the strategies adopted by Black female factory operatives to resist sexual harassment may have been passed down and developed out of domestic workers' experiences. " 'We Are Not What We Seem': Towards a Black Working-Class Infrapolitics in the Twentieth Century South" (unpublished paper cited by permission of the author).

27. These are obviously not just questions exclusive to African American women but suggest what may happen to any group of people when so few are able to succeed and what may happen when you see yourself, and are seen, as representing your community and not just yourself. I think of Chinua Achebe's protagonist in *A Man of the People*, of Alice Dunbar-Nelson's diary entries which reveal her awareness of her responsibility to maintain a particular image even when she had not the money to do so, and of Black male professionals employed in Richmond in the early twentieth century who told me of the difficulty they had making ends meet financially when their professional positions paid very little but their obligation to represent the potential for African American people's success meant that the Black community did not want them taking on second jobs as hotel waiters or janitors. All expressed an awareness that many people depended—not just financially but psychologically—on their success and a belief that they needed to portray success and hide all traces that mobility had not allowed them to escape the traps of any of the others.

28. See, for example, Catharine MacKinnon in "Hill's Accusations Ring True to a Legal Trailblazer," *Detroit Free Press,* 13 Oct. 1991, 6F.

29. One of the most egregious examples of the latter as related to this particular case can be seen in Orlando Patterson's argument that if Thomas said the things Hill charged he was merely engaging in a "down-home style of courting" which would have been "immediately recognizable" to Hill "and most women of Southern working-class backgrounds, white or black, especially the latter" but which would have been "completely out of the cultural frame of [the] white upper-middle-class work world" of the senators who would vote on his confirmation. See, "Race, Gender, and Liberal Fallacies," *New York Times,* 20 Oct. 1991, and the even more obnoxious defense of his position in *Reconstruction* 1, 4 (1992): 68–71, 75–77.

30. "African American Women in Defense of Ourselves." For a good discussion of the sexual stereotypes of African American women in the late nineteenth and early twentieth centuries, see Beverly Guy-Sheftall, *Daughters of Sorrow: Attitudes toward Black Women, 1880–1920* (Brooklyn: Carlson Publishing, 1990), esp. chaps. 3 and 4. See also Patricia Morton, *Disfigured Images: The Historical Assault on Afro-American Women* (New York: Praeger, 1991).

31. Crenshaw, "Roundtable: Sexuality after Thomas/Hill," 29.

32. Darlene Clark Hine, "Rape and the Culture of Dissemblance: Preliminary Thoughts on the Inner Lives of Black Midwestern Women," *Signs* 14 (Summer 1989): 912–20.

33. The implications of this are explored in my "Imaging Lynching."

34. This became a common argument during and in the days following the hearings; see, for example, Barbara Ehrenreich, "Women Would Have Known," *Time,* 21 Oct. 1991, 104.

# African Feminist Scholars in Women's Studies
## Negotiating Spaces of Dislocation and Transformation in the Study of Women

*Josephine Beoku-Betts and*
*Wairimū Ngarūiya Njambi*

2004

## Introduction

The past decade has witnessed the publication of numerous feminist writings on issues of identity and difference in the analysis of women's lives (Anzaldúa 1990, 2001; Collins 1990; hooks 2000; Imam 1997; Mama 1996; Mohanty 1991; Oyewumi 1997; Sandoval 2001). Previously, a homogenized notion of "women" was taken for granted, and the experience of white middle-class women was generalized to other categories of women, irrespective of race, ethnicity, class, sexual orientation, nationality, and cultural difference. This homogenization effectively ignored or dismissed the agency of historically marginalized groups of women whose modes of identity and self-definition did not fit into conventional discourses on gender. Feminist scholarship has more recently rethought this homogenization of women, and it has moved significantly toward a more complex analysis of women's differentiated lives, including those in the academic community.

In the academy, including women's studies, many feminists, particularly women of color, lesbians, and women with working-class backgrounds, have raised concerns about heterosexist, ethnocentric, and class-biased curricula; Eurocentric theoretical frameworks; applications of double standards; sexual harassment; unfair evaluations, unequal pay, bypassed promotions; negative images from both students and colleagues; tokenism; as well as pressure to fit into a male model of behavior and/or to sever oneself from one's race and ethnic and class identity prior to entering academe (Cordova 1998; Dews and Law 1995; Garcia 1997; Zinn et al. 1986).

These kinds of experiences can lead to feelings of exclusion and isolation, especially in academic contexts where women and minority scholars are few and lack academic and cultural support systems. It can also influence the degree to which such scholars become incorporated into departmental and student networking. M. Jacqui Alexander and Chandra Talpade Mohanty describe the emotional effects of these complex and often con-

flicting experiences as a "sense of alienation, dislocation, and marginalization, that often accompanies a racialized location within white institutions"
(1997: xiv). Edward W. Said (1999) describes this positioning as being "Out
of Place," while Patricia Hill Collins (1990) describes it as the "outsider
within."

Although these kinds of problems may be common among academic
women in general, it is also important to account for the distinctive ways in
which women of color, and African women scholars in particular, encounter
and negotiate such institutions. For example, some problems that African
women faculty face in academia are specific to the geographical, political,
racial, and cultural histories of the societies from which they originate, and
these issues stem partly from misrepresentations of African societies and
cultures. Assumptions about Africans include cultural "backwardness";
preconceived notions about the inability and incompetence of Africans
to teach American students; a persistent depiction of African accents and
styles and forms of spoken English as bad and inferior; and depictions of
African women as ignorant, exotic, and highly sexualized beings.

The ways in which women scholars of color perceive and experience
American academic institutions can vary tremendously and depend very
much on their already differentiated racial, sexual, cultural, and national
backgrounds. For example, the stereotyping of Asian immigrants as scien-
tifically and technically competent is directly associated with the notion of
brain drain. Gayatri Chakravorty Spivak suggests, "The Indian community
in the United States is the only coloured community which came in with the
brain drain" (1990: 61). This suggests that the experience of Indian women
in U.S. academic institutions, and the ways in which Americans perceive
and treat them, will be quite different from that of African women, who are
stereotyped as less intelligent as a result of the already unquestioned presumption of African backwardness (Beoku-Betts 2005, 2004).

In most cases the feeling of "being out of place" that these experiences
generate may not be recognized, understood, or acknowledged by those in
privileged positions unless they fit into the general pattern of already familiar problems such as those associated with gender, race, ethnicity, sexual
orientation, international status, class, and disability within the U.S. context.
Furthermore, insisting on the distinctiveness and seriousness of problems
that some women in the academy encounter might be dismissed as an exag-
geration. The experiences that women seem to have in common are often
given more weight at the cost of ignoring those that differentiate them.

This paper examines some of the problems and dilemmas that African
women scholars face in U.S. academic institutions: how such experiences
inform the nature of their relationships with colleagues and students, and

the pedagogical and resistance strategies that they practice. By reflecting on our own professional journeys as scholars of women's studies and sociology in various academic institutions in the United States, we are particularly interested in narrating our experiences as well as some of the ways in which we challenge and navigate situations that we encounter in our classrooms. Our perspectives and concerns are marked by our historical, educational, political, and cultural location as Africans (a Sierra Leonean and a Kenyan) and as feminists, as well as by our experience of living in the United States with our newly acquired identities as black women, and as third world immigrants. Additionally, our usage of the phrase "African women" is not intended to imply a unitary perspective or group that can be identified as such; as with "women of color" or "third world women," the phrase "African women" is employed here to emphasize a political constituency rather than a biological bond. For both of us, learning how to identify ourselves as Africans as opposed to Kenyan or Sierra Leonean has been largely shaped by our similar political struggles to name and resist oppressive conditions that we find in the U. S. academic environment. First we will discuss the history of our migration and dislocation, followed by theorization of academic and classroom (dis)locations. After that we will discuss some of the problematic ways in which some feminist discourses have represented African women, as well as ways in which we try to disrupt or challenge such representations in our own classrooms.

## Historicizing Our Migration and Dislocation

We both came to the United States, from Sierra Leone and Kenya, in the 1980s at different stages of our lives. One of us had completed her undergraduate and some graduate work in England and had taught for a number of years at the university level in Sierra Leone, before completing her PhD work in the United States. The other completed her undergraduate and graduate work in the United States. Our intellectual and political backgrounds are both rooted in colonial and postcolonial experiences and perspectives, and set the context for locating our engagement in third world feminist scholarship.

We both grew up knowing much more about British history and the history of the British in Africa, the geography of Europe, English literature, and British political and religious institutions than about Africa's history and institutions—a colonization legacy that affects the former colonies of Africa. As young women in newly independent countries, we were both surrounded by nationalist ideologies that instilled in us not only a sense of identity but perhaps also a naïve sense of political commitment to nation building. As such, whether through Christian church activities or Western forms of education, the idea of being educated was closely tied to the idea of serving to building our nations. But, as we both later learned (in part through our engagement with feminist practices), the nationalism in which we granted so much faith had very little interest in promoting gender equality.

As Geraldine Heng attests, "historically, almost without exception, feminism has arisen in the Third World in tandem with nationalist movements—whether in the form of anti-colonial/anti-imperialist struggles, national modernization and reform movements, or religious-nationalist/cultural-nationalist revivalism" (1997: 31). Yet in the case of Africa, Amina Mama (1996) points out that there were examples of African feminist consciousness prior to colonialism (Amina of Zazzau and Queen Zinga of Angola are famous instances). However, the imposition of Western colonialism and its interaction with existing African patriarchal structures disrupted the wider development of such practices. Against this background, a distinguishing feature of African women's involvement in nationalist struggles for independence in the 1950s was that issues of gender, race, ethnicity, and class relations were already integral to struggles in which women were engaged when compared to counterparts in the West, who only began to acknowledge the intersection of these issues in the 1980s (Ampofo et al. 2004; Lewis 2002). Nonetheless, the participation of African women in the construction of nation building has not guaranteed gender equality in peacetime. Yet because of their involvement in nationalist struggles, their political participation has often been used as a measure of progress toward political democracy. In this regard, Mama (1996) points out that it is ironic that postindependence governments have not made more viable efforts to involve women at the decision-making levels of politics, finance, and governance; now it is Western nations instead of colonial powers that are among the main forces pushing African governments to address themselves to the question of improving women's levels of participation.

Moving to the United States in the 1980s led us to a range of new dislocating and unfamiliar alienating experiences. The categorization of a racialized and gendered immigrant status created in us a sense of confusion regarding our new identities, including the dominant society's perception of these identities. For the first time, perhaps even more so than before, we developed a conscious political awareness of an outsider status that our new experience of being identified as black women, women of color, and third world immigrants reinforced heavily, in an undeniably racially defined society. As Molara Ogundipe-Leslie (1994), a Nigerian feminist scholar, points out, until she went abroad, she had never viewed herself as black or used this language to describe other African women. In her culture of origin, the question of one's identity and representation involved multiple and complex signifiers such as that of age, kinship, clan, ethnicity, class, and marital status, among others things, but never one's skin color. Similarly, Mohanty (2001) expresses the adjustment she had to make between the status of a foreign student and that of a student of color when she came to the United States. Being a foreign student entailed assumptions about her ability to speak American English, questions about where she first came from, and whether she had plans to return home at the end of her studies, as well as assumptions of exoticism regarding her South Asian background. She observed that being a student of color entailed racial identity, as it is defined and manifested in the social and political fabric of the United States. Inevitably, she saw the need to develop a sophisticated analytical and political awareness of the ways in which racism and sexism operate in structuring experiences of third world immigrants in the United States.

Such experiences have challenged us to learn how to navigate and subvert the kinds of conflicts and tensions involved in trying to claim an identity and a voice as an African, a black woman, a scholar, and a third world immigrant in the United States. While none of these identities are mutually exclusive, they each have provided us with a vision from which to view how our experiences have shaped and dislocated us in various institutions in which we have taught in the U.S. academy.

## Theorizing Academic and Classroom Dislocations

While African scholars play an important role in the production of diverse faculties on many college campuses throughout the United States, we do acknowledge that the role we play in the establishment of such diversity goals is in many ways problematic and must be identified. Regardless of whether we are labeled as African, international, third world, or immigrant, and regardless of our expertise in specific areas of study, we have come to learn that the presence of Africans in such institutions often operates as a mask to disguise the exclusion of African Americans. Faculty, students, administrators, alumni, and legislators are informed that an institution is making progress regarding the issue of diversity while little or no progress is made to include both African American faculty and students. African and Afro-Caribbean faculty tend to be seen as easy substitutes for African American faculty, a tendency that many African American scholars have criticized as an easy way out in addressing a complex racial history of marginalization. African and Afro-Caribbean faculty may even be preferred over African Americans, especially those among the latter who are perceived to be too vocal regarding racism. For example, immigrant women of color, as Alexander and Mohanty point out, are "(differently) less threatening than African American women to white women, who often preferred to deal with our 'foreignness' rather than our racialization in the United States. This, in turn, sometimes created divisive relations between us and African American feminists" (1997: xv). We see this as an important topic for scholarly discussion that has yet to be explored fully and honestly, particularly by African and Afro-Caribbean scholars whose academic benefits and gains are directly tied to the marginalization of African Americans. As scholars of women's studies, our solidarity and coalition with African American feminists must be forged with such kinds of racial history in mind.

Teaching offers a wide space for intellectual pursuit, growth, and transformation for both students and professors, and it is an important forum through which critical ideas are exchanged. At the same time, it is also a field of struggle in which certain serious tensions and battles are fought and managed. To be a black, African, woman professor is to be forced to constantly dispel doubts and anxieties on the part of students and faculty who have already conceptualized blackness, Africanness, and femaleness as markings of inferiority. Being a female African professor in an all-white classroom can create even more disheartening and alienating feelings. A number of white students who have never dealt with a black person, let alone an African woman, in a position of authority can have difficulty adjusting, and a number are often skeptical regarding the competency or the intellectual ability of such a professor.

Consider the following expressions on the first days of class by some white students that we have encountered over the years in various institutions in which we have taught: "Excuse me ma'am, I don't mean to offend you, but I had no idea you were going to be black"; "Am I in the right classroom?"; "Who wrote this syllabus?"; "To whom should I turn my assignment?"; "Why are we reading so many writings by black people?" Some students even feel the need to verify our assertions in the classroom by later seeking corroboration from white faculty members. And while some students may question our competency to teach certain mainstream courses, other students are much more sophisticated in the way they approach such a situation. For example, some students are quite eager to take our classes, and even declare at the end of the semester how much they have learned from us. They might even utilize knowledge gained from such courses to develop their research proposals. However, at the point of choosing a major advisor to direct their theses, they quickly ignore our presence and opt for a white faculty member. When some students ask us to be their thesis/dissertation advisors, often it is because we have been successful at performing what we call the ritual of convincing, that is, after we have finally convinced many such students who are interested in our areas of research and teaching that we are indeed intelligent enough to direct their theses/ dissertations, or white faculty ask them to consider working with us given our mutual research interests.

It is possible to characterize this problem by utilizing what African American feminists call the black nanny phenomenon, where the black nanny raised the masters' or colonizers' children but had no rights to discipline or to make important decisions that affected them. Within an all white academic setting, a similar phenomenon can be observed: the effect of being like a nanny who motivates young white scholars by parenting and nurturing their thesis or dissertation direction only to be abandoned when some students view whiteness as an important criteria in guiding students successfully; someone else gets the parenting credit despite our close involvement in these students' academic raising.

At other times, we are often invited to speak on issues such as race, ethnicity, or multiculturalism, or serve on a number of committees that are exclusively white, yet in need of tokens. This idea of tokenization is underscored in Gayatri Chakravorty Spivak's statement that "tokenization goes with ghettoization—when you are perceived as a token, you are also silenced in a certain way because, as you say, if you have been brought there it has been covered, they needn't worry about it anymore, you salve their conscience" (1990: 61). As tokens, we can speak but only in a specific manner. We are not supposed to generate any meaningful or intelligible perspectives on other issues but only the ones we are invited to represent. When we do choose to exploit our tokenization and speak about issues that we are supposedly not qualified to speak about, we ignite a shock wave that can be seen tumbling across the room. It reminds us of what African American feminists have always known and resisted: the unspoken and unwritten rule of speaking only when we are spoken to.

In other words, these kinds of experiences are not unique to African women. African American feminists-scholars such as bell hooks (1989), Patricia J. Williams (1991), Patricia Hill Collins (1990), Johnnetta Cole (1994), Adrianne Andrews (1993), Paula J. Giddings (1984), John B. Reid (1995), Afua Cooper (1995), and Yolanda Moses (1989), among others, have given us much insight regarding black women's experiences while teaching in predominantly white institutions, which point out the complex interrelationship of race, class, gender, and sexuality and the unique challenges that those who are marked black face in such situations. Most important, they have shown us how black women scholars fought tokenization and the stereotype of mammies of the academy, often pointing to the double edge of racism and sexism that greeted these women in the academy since the moment of their arrival to this enslaving society to the present. In his breathtaking essay on nineteenth-century Detroit's first black women teachers, Reid explains some of the challenges that confronted black women:

> After breaking the barriers, these teachers contradicted existing racial and sexual stereotypes by serving as symbols of black female competence at a time when the abilities of all black Americans were being called into question. The nineteenth century witnessed the progressive growth of scientific racism, which declared blacks inherently and permanently inferior . . . some whites considered black teachers to be inconsistent with their place in the racial hierarchy of the time. In this context, the act of teaching, especially the teaching of white students, contradicted assumptions about the intellectual ability of black people (1995: 310–11).

Besides overcoming the negative images of black competence, black women teachers had to find ways to overcome also the stereotypes of "the Mammy image" and "the Jezebel image." This is because, as Reid points out, "Dominant [white] culture discourse had divided black womanhood into good and bad stereotypes: the Mammy stereotype exemplifying the good, the sexually promiscuous and mean Jezebel exemplifying the bad" (1995, 311).

As Patricia J. Williams explains, although segregationist laws that dominated much of the past have been dismantled and are no longer formalized in legal matters today, the mentality that white equals good and black equals bad continues to play a significant role in the attitudes of many students. In her discussion of one Stanford law student's (Fred) reaction to the idea that Beethoven was black, Williams writes:

> When Fred's whole relationship to the music changed once he discovered that Beethoven was black, it made me think of how much my students' relationship to me is engineered by my being black; how much I am marginalized based on a hierarchy of perception, by my relation to definitional canons that exercise superhuman power in my life. When Beethoven is no longer übermensch, but real and really black, he falls to a place beneath contempt, for there is no racial midpoint between the polarities of adoration and aversion. When some first-year law students walk in and see that I am their contracts teacher, I have been told, their whole perception of law school changes (1991: 115).

In addition to such experiences that African American feminist scholars have eloquently documented, having unfamiliar or non-European accents and cultural backgrounds sometimes triggers a level of discomfort among many American students who associate such accents and backgrounds as a sign of ignorance. Such students do not see having a European accent and cultural background as a threat because it is consistent with a legacy of white superiority that enhances students' perceptions of professors' intellectual ability. At the same time, when these issues are discussed with some of our African male colleagues, they may recognize the racist element of such problems, but they sometimes fail to acknowledge the gender dynamics. As a result, racism may be given more weight at the cost of sexism. Perhaps this is because, as men, they are already situated within a patriarchal structure that treats their voices in the classroom as the presumed voice of authority.

## African Women and Feminist Discourses

Other troubling elements that we have encountered in some women's studies discourses involve the virtual exclusion or absence of African women as knowledge producers in relation to feminism. In such discourses African women are typically represented only as victims of oppressive and unchanging traditional practices. The following section will focus on how such perceptions of African women, as well as their subversion, can influence the production and transmission of knowledge about African women. Having been trained within a Western feminist epistemological tradition, the application of a universal notion of feminism has been rather unsettling for both of us—especially when applied to our own cultural and historical backgrounds. As some contemporary feminists-scholars have shown, this hegemonic tradition often ignores the varied ways in which feminism has been understood and practiced historically in different societal contexts. As Sharon Sievers (1992) points out, the globalized stereotype is that feminism has always been a Western experience, defined narrowly in terms of women's rights, opposition to maleness, and/or as advocating a radical separatism from masculinist society. From African feminist perspectives, however, the problem of this image is in dichotomized notions of public versus private, and the individual versus the collective.

The tendency to dichotomize social space into public and private spheres and according to gender does not adequately reflect the historical and cultural realities of African life practices. Biographical and oral histories of African women during nationalist struggles for independence show that women were not necessarily assigned to the private or even gender sphere as colonial gender ideologies perceived them to be. Women were able to exercise leadership in multiple contexts outside of the dominant Western influences, such as the European women's movement (Denzer 1995; Ngaiza and Koda 1991).

In many African contexts even the strict separation of female and male is open to question. In the case of gender analysis, African feminists (for instance, Amadiume 1987; Imam 1997; Oyewumi 1997) point out that in many African regions the concepts of gender, women, and masculinity and femininity are fluid and change over time. For example, there can be more than one gender associated with biological sex, as in the case of female husbands and male daughters among the Igbo of southeastern Nigeria (Amadiume 1987). Other examples include practices of woman-to-woman marriage in parts of Kenya, which in some contexts blurs female and male identities (Njambi and O'Brien 2000), and the *yan daudu* in Hausa culture, where men can adopt a feminized form of dress and mannerism and sometimes engage in homosexual relationships (Abdullahi 1983; Gaudio 1995).

Another troubling element underlying understandings and representations of feminism is the assumption of a global hierarchy of feminisms in which Western varieties are seen as superior while alternative versions, particularly from the third world, are viewed as inferior. Central to this assumption is the question of whether women's roles as political actors can be truly viewed as feminist. For example, Maxine Molyneux (1985) makes a distinction between strategic gender interests and practical gender interests in the analysis of women's politicized identity. Practical gender interests arise from the material conditions of women's position within a gendered division of labor and are usually a response to meeting the survival needs of their families. They do not generally involve a strategic goal such as fighting for women's emancipation or gender equality, which entails a particular level of consciousness that is viewed as real feminism according to Molyneux (1985). Practical gender interests are then viewed with some caution, because of the potential for both feminist and antifeminist political action (Gerson and Peiss 1985).

Such a dichotomy is of relevance to us because it allows us to understand how African women's experiences are located in some Western feminist discourses. Such dichotomies erase the importance of particular material, cultural, and historical conditions, and also what may be interpreted as multiple and interacting gender identities in African contexts. For example, in the context of marriage, Ogundipe-Leslie (1994) explains that African women are more than wives in their communities, and to understand the multiple facets of their identity and status we need to look into other roles and statuses they occupy, such as daughter, sister, mother, entrepreneur, political leader, and secret society member. In this sense, the conjugal relationship is just one aspect of the experience of women's lives in African societies. African feminist perspectives are therefore crucial to advancing feminist knowledge about the varied ways in which feminisms are under-stood and practiced in different social contexts.

The objectification of African women as powerless and voiceless vic-tims of oppressive and unchanging cultural practices is a recurring theme deeply embedded in many women's studies courses. On this point, Ayesha M. Imam and Amina Mama write:

> "African woman" is caricaturized as a limited series of stereotypes in many cases of social thought, with repetitive and oversimplified images underlying social science, much as they persist in literature—. The docile, obedient, village woman, custodian of culture; the simple peas-ant grinding millet outside the productive life of the community; the matriarch of the shrine and market place; the corrupt urban prostitutes: these are the stereotypes of much Africanist, Western feminist and male scholarship on African women, such as it is (1994: 82).

Mohanty (1991) points out that such negative and sensational stereotypes are examples of how the process of racialization and sexualization is used to consolidate particular relations of rule in the production of knowledge. By positioning African women as victims of poverty, illiteracy, or sexual oppression against European American women as educated, modern, and in control of their own lives and sexuality, the latter are privileged and used as the binary standard against which others are measured.

For example, much of Western feminists' discussion regarding female genital cutting (FGC) practices in Africa presents what appears at first glance to be an unproblematic critique of traditional mutilation and domi-nation of women under patriarchal regimes; the perception is that women and girls are genitally mutilated so that they may be rendered sexually sub-servient to men. Common sense in Western contexts suggests that if Afri-cans who perform such female genital mutilation (FGM) could only see beyond their cultural blinders of tradition, they surely would oppose such presumed barbarity. However, such a mentality is not only deeply rooted in the colonial period (when colonizers justified colonialism on the need to rescue indigenous women from indigenous men); it is also based on "sen-sationalistic images intended to help mobilize political action" (Kratz 1994, 342; Njambi 2004).

African feminist scholars are also critical of such practices that oppress women and do not condone or accept them as part of African culture regardless of the length of their historical existence (Imam 1997). How-ever, they rebuke Western feminists for failing to acknowledge the broader educational elements associated with such practices and silencing women's sexuality by ignoring traditions that empower and give women more rather than less control of their sexual and reproductive rights (Mama 1996, 47). By removing these heterogeneous practices from their varying contexts, Western critics erase the idea that particular practices are "each differently embedded in specific institutional and social structures" (Kratz 1994, 346). In discussing FGC practices in Mali, Assitan Diallo (2004) urges us to reject the simplistic notion of oppression in order to understand the social dimensions and complexities of practices such as magnonmaka (the practice of sexual pleasure enhancement or nuptial advisors) and bolokoli-kêla (practices of hindering women's sexuality). According to Diallo, "Western feminist scholars and activists who critique these practices view them as oppressing women's sexuality to benefit patriarchal cultural systems" (Arnfred 2004, 1). However, these critics are "neither interested nor motivated to find out whether the same society would also consider promoting women's sexual behaviour at some point in their life cycle" (Arnfred 2004, 1). For example, "in indigenous Malian structures, magnonmaka, as nuptial advisors, advise women on how to enhance their sexuality during the wedding period and beyond" (cited in Pereira 2003). In sum, Diallo argues that "there is a paradox and ambiguity in how society deals with female sexuality in Mali" and both magnonmaka and bolokoli-kêla are ingredients in prevailing norms and practices that enhance and hinder women's sexuality in this society (Arnfred 2004, 1).

## Subversive Classroom Strategies

We attempt in our classrooms to disrupt the normalized images of African women that many U.S. students carry with them, including those of victimhood and as lacking in intellect. For instance, in teaching about feminism, we make sure that students interrogate and challenge reductive and dichotomizing representations of African women in order to broaden the terms of definition, theoretical formulations, and scope of different historical locations in feminism. We draw on the writings of African feminists such as Ifi Amadiume (1987), Assitan Diallo (2004), Ayesha Imam (1997), Amina Mama (1996), Molara Ogundipe-Leslie (1994), Oyeronke Oyewumi (1997), Filomena Steady (1987), and Desiree Lewis (2002), among others, to help map out the history and contemporary understandings of feminist practices in Africa. Such feminists have urged us to be critical of Western mainstream feminists' assumptions of third world women's problems, which view African women as nothing more than victims of oppressive cultural practices. They have also cautioned that the feminist project must become more accountable and relevant to those about whom it theorizes. As Cheryl Johnson-Odim points out, women should be able to recognize themselves or their lives in theory, and theory must speak to an improvement in their concrete material and political conditions (2001, 114–15).

We challenge the reductive nature of Western perceptions of African cultural practices in our women's studies courses by introducing to students these kinds of texts that represent African women in their multiple and complexed situatedness, including their social agencies and particular perspectives (Ampofo et al. 2004; Diallo 2004; Njambi 2004; Imam 1997; Mama 1996). We incorporate African feminist journals such as *Feminist Africa*, *Jenda*, and the *CODESRIA Bulletin* in our teaching, and in the past two years we have introduced a study abroad program to Ghana that is specifically feminist in focus and puts various feminist voices and agencies at the center of the learning process. Such an approach is particularly important for us as African feminist scholars teaching in the United States as it represents an attempt to remake the normal in a way that depicts African women as integral to the knowledge production process.

We also now refuse to invest a significant amount of time resolving students' doubts regarding our intellectual abilities. Instead, we challenge students from the start of the semester to reflect on and confront the privileges that shape their classroom perceptions. In most of our classes, we spend time reading, discussing, and writing about the role and impacts of white privilege in academia and elsewhere. For instance, we include critical white studies texts "that seek to make whiteness visible, to analyze the nature of white privilege, and to offer suggestions for using that privilege in order to combat racism" (Rothenberg 2002). Such texts include, but are not limited to, "White Privilege: Unpacking the Invisible Knapsack," by Peggy McIntosh (2002); "White Women, Race Matters: The Social Construction of Whiteness," by Ruth Frankenberg (1997); "The Social Construction of Whiteness," by Martha R. Mahoney (1997); "Representations of Whiteness in the Black Imagination," by bell hooks (1998); *Playing in the Dark: Whiteness and the Literary Imagination*, by Toni Morrison (1992); and "White Privilege Shapes the U.S.," by Robert Jensen (1998), among others. We find that emphasizing such readings at the beginning of the semester helps students to reframe their perceptions of how practices of white privilege produce and maintain whiteness as the norm, in the classroom and larger society. Additionally, rather than only reading texts that scholars and/or feminists of color have written, we also emphasize texts that Euro-American scholars and/or white feminists have written, in order to help students see various ways in which some white critical scholars position themselves in their struggles against white privilege and as well the history of whiteness. Rather than breaking us, our experiences of being marginalized in the academy and in our classrooms provide us with necessary tools as African women scholars to act subversively.

At the end of the semester, many students convey to us or in their evaluation comments how they have been transformed by the experience. Some of the comments include statements such as "I learned so much about myself"; "It made me think, not much has ever made me think. I've had some ups and downs in here, but for the most part it has been a good learning experience"; "The breadth of material covered—although intense was very diverse and profound. I learned a lot"; "I learned a lot and my thinking has changed"; "I got introduced to many topics & ideas I didn't know before, learned to think in other ways"; "I loved having my eyes opened to the amount of inequality that still exists in today's society. . . . I loved this class! It gave me so much insight to my own life and surroundings, and exposed me to so many wonderful authors"; "I really enjoyed class discussion and the text 'White Critical Studies'"; and "I liked learning about everything from how science has constructed our views towards other cultures and races to actually realizing that science can never be objective."

## Conclusion

Although women professors share similar experiences in U.S. academic institutions, there are certain unique and complex contexts of struggle that women of color face. As we have shown, for many African women scholars, the experience of negotiating a self-defined space and voice for themselves is filled with struggle. Some of the problems and conflicts we explained are shared in common with other women academics generally, while some are shared specifically with women academics of color. Such women face problems and dilemmas that are more specific to their particular geographical, political, racial, cultural, and gendered histories. Negotiating solutions to such dilemmas and conflicts must be strategic and must be approached from multiple angles of vision. It is imperative that whatever strategies are imagined and implemented by African women scholars, such strategies must function to interrogate, challenge, and transform social contexts of unequal power relations and representations of marginalized communities, within the academy, the wider society of the United States, and the societies of origin of these scholars. We hope this paper will be a step in developing a stronger feminist pedagogy that embraces these challenges.

## Works Cited

Abdullahi, S. A. 1983. "Some Romances on the Role of Daud audu in Hausa Female Prostitution." Postgraduate Seminar, Department of Sociology. Kanu: Bayero University.

Alexander, M. Jacqui, and Chandra Talpade Mohanty. 1997. "Introduction: Genealogies, Legacies, Movements." In *Feminist Genealogies, Colonial Legacies, Democratic Futures,* ed. M. Jacqui Alexander and Chandra Talpade Mohanty, xiii–xlii. New York and London: Routledge.

Amadiume, Ifi. 1987. *Male Daughters, Female Husbands: Gender and Sex in an African Society.* London: Zed Books.

Ampofo, Akosua Adomako, Josephine Beoku-Betts, Wairimũ Ngarũiya Njambi, and Mary Osirim. 2004. "Women's and Gender Studies in English-Speaking Sub-Saharan Africa: A Review of Research in the Social Sciences." *Gender & Society* 18, no. 6: 685–714.

Andrews, Adrianne. 1993. "Balancing the Personal and Professional." In *Spirit, Space and Survival: African American Women in (White) Academe,* ed. Joy James and Ruth Farmer, 179–95. New York: Routledge.

Anzaldúa, Gloria, ed. 1990. *Making Face, Making Soul: Haciendo Caras, Creative and Critical Perspectives by Feminists of Color.* San Francisco, Calif: Aunt Lute Books.

———. 2001. "La Consciencia de la Mestiza/Towards a New Consciousness." In *Feminism and Race* (Oxford Readings in Feminism), ed. Kum-Kum Bhavnani, 93–107. Oxford and New York: Oxford University Press.

Arnfred, Signe, ed. 2004. *Rethinking Sexualities in Africa.* Uppsala, Sweden: Nordiska Afrikainstitutet.

Beoku-Betts, Josephine. 2004. "African Women Pursuing Graduate Studies in the Sciences: Racism, Gender Bias, and Third World Marginality." *National Women's Studies Association Journal* 16, no. 1:116–35.

———. 2005. "Western Perceptions of African Women in the Nineteenth and Early Twentieth Centuries." In *Readings in Gender in Africa,* ed. Andrea Cornwall, 20–25. Bloomington: Indiana University Press.

Cole, Johnnetta. 1994. Keynote Address. Black Women in the Academy Conference. Cambridge, Mass.: MIT. January.

Collins, Patricia Hill. 1990. *Black Feminist Thought: Knowledge, Consciousness, and the Politics of Empowerment.* Boston and London: Unwin Hyman.

Cooper, Afua. 1995. "The Search for Mary Bibb, Black Woman Teacher in Nineteenth-Century Canada West." In *We Specialize in the Wholly Impossible: A Reader in Black Women's History,* ed. Darlene Clark Hine, Wilma King, and Linda Reed, 171–85. Brooklyn, N.Y.: Carlson Publishing, Inc.

Cordova, T. 1998. "Power and Knowledge: Colonialism in the Academy." In *Living Chicana Theory,* ed. Carla Trujillo, 17–45. Berkeley, Calif.: Third Woman Press.

Denzer, Laray. 1995. *Constance Cummings-John: Memoirs of a Krio Leader.* Ibadan: Humanities Research Center.

Dews, C. L. Barney, and Carolyn Leste Law, eds. 1995. *This Fine Place So Far from Home: Voices of Academics from the Working Class.* Philadelphia: Temple University Press.

Diallo, Assitan. 2004. "Paradoxes of Female Sexuality in Mali: On the Practices of *Magnonmaka* and *Bolokoli-kêla.*" In *Rethinking Sexualities in Africa,* ed. Signe Arnfred, 173–94. Uppsala, Sweden: Nordiska Afrikainstitutet.

Frankenberg, Ruth. 1997. "White Women, Race Matters: The Social Construction of Whiteness." In *Critical White Studies: Looking Behind the Mirror,* ed. Richard Delgado and Jean Stefancic, 632–34. Philadelphia: Temple University Press.

Garcia, A. M, ed. 1997. *Chicana Feminist Thought: The Basic Historical Writings.* New York: Routledge.

Gaudio, Rudolf. 1995. "Pilgrims Transgress: Gender, Sexuality and the New Trans-Saharan Trade." Paper to Panel on Issues of Gender, Sexuality, and the Body in the Saharan Region. Orlando, Florida: Association of African Studies Meeting.

Gerson, J. M., and K. Peiss. 1985. "Boundaries, Negotiation, Consciousness: Reconceptualizing Gender Relations." *Social Problems* 32: 317–31.

Giddings, Paula. 1984. *When and Where I Enter: The Impact of Black Women on Race and Sex in America*. New York: William Morrow and Company.

Heng, Geraldine. 1997. "A Great Way to Fly: Nationalism, the State, and the Varieties of Third-World Feminism." In *Feminist Genealogies, Colonial Legacies, Democratic Futures*, ed. M. Jacqui Alexander and Chandra Talpade Mohanty, 30–45. New York and London: Routledge.

hooks, bell. 1989. *Talking Back: Thinking Feminist, Thinking Black*. Boston, Mass.: South End Press.

———. 1998. "Representations of Whiteness in the Black Imagination." In *Black On White*, ed. and intro. David R. Roediger. New York: Schocken Books.

———. 2000. *Feminist Theory: From Margin to Center*. Boston, Mass.: South End Press.

Imam, Ayesha. 1997. "Engendering African Social Sciences: An Introductory Essay." In *Engendering African Social Sciences* (Codesria Book Series), ed. Ayesha M. Imam, Amina Mama, and Fatou Sow, 1–30. Dakar: Conseil Pour Le Developement.

Imam, Ayesha M., and Amina Mama. 1994. "The Role of Academics in Limiting and Expanding Academic Freedom." In *Academic Freedom in Africa* (Codesria Book Series), ed. Mahmoud Mamdani, 73–107. Dakar: Conseil Pour Le Developement.

Jensen, Robert. 1998. "White Privilege Shapes the U.S." *Baltimore Sun*. 19 July.

Johnson-Odim, Cheryl. 1991. "Common Themes, Different Contexts: Third World Women and Feminism." In *Third World Women and the Politics of Feminism*, ed. C. T. Mohanty, A. Russo, and L. Torres, 314–27. Bloomington: Indiana University Press.

———. 2001. "Who's to Navigate and Who's to Steer? A Consideration of the Role of Theory in Feminist Struggle." In *Feminist Locations: Global and Local, Theory and Practice*, ed. Marianne Dekoven, 110–26. New Brunswick, N.J.: Rutgers University Press.

Kratz, Corinne A. 1994. *Affecting Performance: Meaning, Movement, and Experience in Okiek Women's Initiation*. Washington and London: Smithsonian Institution Press.

Lazreg, M. 1988. "Feminism and Difference: The Perils of Writing as a Woman on Women in Algeria." In *Conflicts in Feminism*, ed. Marianne Hirsch and Evelyn Fox Keller, 326–48. New York and London: Routledge.

Lewis, Desiree. 2002. "African Feminist Studies: 1980–2002." In *Gender and Women's Studies Africa*, http://www.gwafrica.org/knowledge/africa.

Mahoney, Martha R. 1997. "The Social Construction of Whiteness." In *Critical White Studies: Looking behind the Mirror*, ed. Richard Delgado and Jean Stefancic, 330–33. Philadelphia: Temple University Press.

Mama, Amina. 1995. *Beyond the Masks: Race, Gender, and Subjectivity*. New York and London: Routledge.

———. 1996. *Women's Studies and Studies of Women in Africa during the 1990s*. Working Paper Series Codesria Green Book. Dakar, Senegal: Codesria.

———. 1997. "Sheroes and Villians: Conceptualizing Colonial and Contemporary Violence against Women in Africa." In *Feminist Genealogies, Colonial Legacies, Democratic Futures*, ed. M. Jacqui Alexander and Chandra Mohanty, 46–62. New York and London: Routledge.

McIntosh, Peggy. 2002. "White Privilege: Unpacking the Invisible Knapsack." In *White Privilege: Essential Readings on the Other Side of Racism,* ed. Paula S. Rothenberg, 97–101. New York: Worth Publishers.

Mohanty, Chandra. 1991. "Under Western Eyes: Feminist Scholarship and Colonial Discourses." In *Third World Women and the Politics of Feminism,* ed. C. T. Mohanty, A. Russo, and L. Torres, 17–42. Bloomington: Indiana University Press.

Mohanty, Chandra Talpade. 2001. "Defining Genealogies: Feminist Reflections on Being South Asian in North America." In *Women's Lives: Multicultural Perspectives,* ed. G. Kirkand and M. Okazawa-Rey, 38–43. Mountain View, Calif.: Mayfield Publishing Company.

Molyneux, Maxine. 1985. "Mobilization without Emancipation? Women's Interests, the State, and Revolution in Nicaragua." *Feminist Studies* 11, no. 2: 227–54.

Morrison, Toni. 1992. *Playing in the Dark: Whiteness and the Literary Imagination.* Cambridge, Mass.: Harvard University Press.

Moses, Yolanda. 1989. *Black Women in Academe: Issues and Strategies.* Washington: Association of American Colleges.

Nayaran, U. 1997. *Dislocating Cultures: Identities, Traditions, and Third World Feminism.* London and New York: Routledge.

Ngaiza, M., and B. Koda. 1991. *The Unsung Heroines: Women's Life Histories from Tanzania.* Dar es Salaam: Research and Documentation Project.

Njambi, Wairimũ Ngarũiya. 2004. "Dualisms and Female Bodies in Representations of African Female Circumcision: A Feminist Critique." *Feminist Theory: An International Journal* 5, no. 3: 281–303.

Njambi, Wairimũ Ngarũiya, and William E. O'Brien. 2000. "Revisiting 'Woman-Woman Marriage': Notes on Gĩkũyũ Women." *NWSA Journal* 12, no. 1:1–23.

Ogundipe-Leslie, Molara. 1994. *Re-Creating Ourselves: African Women and Critical Transformation.* Trenton, N.J.: Africa World Press.

Oyewumi, Oyeronke. 1997. *The Invention of Women: Making an African Sense of Western Gender Discourses.* Minneapolis: University of Minnesota Press.

Pereira, Charmaine. 2003. "Where Angels Fear to Tread? Some Thoughts on Patricia McFadden's 'Sexual Pleasure as Feminist Choice.'" In *Feminist Africa,* no. 2. http://www.feministafrica.org/. Accessed July 2005.

Reid, John B. 1995. "'A Career to Build, a People to Serve, a Purpose to Accomplish': Race, Class, Gender, and Detroit's First Black Women Teachers, 1865–1916." In *We Specialize in the Wholly Impossible: A Reader in Black Women's History,* ed. Darlene Clark Hine, Wilma King, and Linda Reed, 303–20. Brooklyn, N.Y.: Carlson Publishing, Inc.

Rothenberg, Paula S. 2002. *White Privilege: Essential Readings on the Other Side of Racism.* New York: Worth Publishers.

Said, Edward W. 1999. *Out of Place: A Memoir.* New York: Alfred A. Knopf.

Sandoval, C. 2001. "U.S. Third World Feminism: The Theory and Method of Oppositional Consciousness in the Postmodern World." In *Feminism and Race* (Oxford Readings in Feminism), ed. Kum-Kum Bhavnani, 261–80. Oxford and New York: Oxford University Press.

Sievers, Sharon. 1992. "Six (or More) Feminists in Search of a Historian." In *Expanding the Boundaries of Women's History: Essays on Women in the Third World,* ed. C. Johnson-Odim and M. Strobel, 319–30. Bloomington: Indiana University Press.

Spivak, Gayatri Chakravorty. 1990. *The Post-Colonial Critic: Interviews, Strategies, Dialogues,* ed. Sarah Harasym. New York and London: Routledge.

Steady, Filomena. 1987. "African Feminism: A Worldwide Perspective." In *Women in Africa and the African Diaspora*, ed. R. Terborg-Penn, S. Harley, and A. Benton Rushing, 3–24.Washington, D.C.: Howard University Press.

Steyn, Melissa. 1998. "A New Agenda: Restructuring Feminism in South Africa." *Women's Studies International Forum* 21, no. 1: 41–52.

Williams, Patricia J. 1991. *The Alchemy of Race and Rights: A Diary of a Law Professor.* Cambridge, Mass.: Harvard University Press.

Zinn, Baca M., L. Weber Cannon, E. Higginbotham, and B. Thornton Dill. 1986. "The Costs of Exclusionary Practices in Women's Studies." *Signs* 11, no. 2: 290–303.

## Olympia's Maid
Reclaiming Black Female
Subjectivity

*Lorraine O'Grady*

2003

The female body in the West is not a unitary sign. Rather, like a coin, it has an obverse and a reverse: on the one side, it is white; on the other, nonwhite or, prototypically, black. The two bodies cannot be separated, nor can one body be understood in isolation from the other in the West's metaphoric construction of "woman." White is what woman is; not-white (and the stereotypes not-white gathers in) is what she had better not be. Even in an allegedly postmodern era, the not-white woman as well as the not-white man are symbolically and even theoretically excluded from sexual difference.[1] Their function continues to be, by their chiaroscuro, to cast the difference of white men and white women into sharper relief.

A kaleidoscope of not-white females, Asian, Native American, and African, have played distinct parts in the West's theater of sexual hierarchy. But it is the African female who, by virtue of color and feature and the extreme metaphors of enslavement, is at the outermost reaches of "otherness." Thus she subsumes all the roles of the not-white body.

The smiling, bare-breasted African maid, pictured so often in Victorian travel books and *National Geographic* magazine, got something more than a change of climate and scenery when she came here.

Sylvia Ardyn Boone, in her book *Radiance from the Waters* (1986), on the physical and metaphysical aspects of Mende feminine beauty, says of contemporary Mende: "Mende girls and women go topless in the village and farmhouse. Even in urban areas, girls are bare-breasted in the house: schoolgirls take off their dresses when they come home, and boarding students are most comfortable around the dormitories wearing only a wrapped skirt."[2]

What happened to the girl who was abducted from her village, then shipped here in chains? What happened to her descendents? Male-fantasy images on rap videos to the contrary, as a swimmer, in communal showers at public pools around the country, I have witnessed black girls and women of all classes showering and shampooing with their bathing suits *on*, while beside them their white sisters stand unabashedly stripped. Perhaps the progeny of that African maiden feel they must still protect themselves from the centuries-long assault that characterizes them, in the words of the *New York Times* ad placed by a group of African American women to protest the Clarence Thomas–Anita Hill hearings, as "immoral, insatiable, perverse; the initiators in all sexual contacts—abusive or otherwise."[3]

Perhaps they have internalized and are cooperating with the West's construction of not-white women as not-to-be-seen. How could they/we not be affected by that lingering structure of invisibility, enacted in the myriad codicils of daily life and still enforced by the images of both popular and high culture? How not get the message of what Judith Wilson calls "the legions of black servants who loom in the shadows of European and European-American aristocratic portraiture,"[4] of whom Laura, the professional model that Edouard Manet used for Olympia's maid, is in an odd way only the most famous example? Forget euphemisms. Forget "tonal contrast." We know what she is meant for: she is Jezebel *and* Mammy, prostitute and female eunuch, the two-in-one. When we're through with her inexhaustibly comforting breast, we can use her ceaselessly open cunt. And best of all, she is not a real person, only a robotic servant who is not permitted to make us feel guilty, to accuse us as does the slave in Toni Morrison's *Beloved* (1987). After she escapes from the room where she was imprisoned by a father and son, that outraged woman says: "You couldn't think up what them two done to me."[5] Olympia's maid, like all the other "peripheral Negroes,"[6] is a robot conveniently made to disappear into the background drapery.

To repeat: castrata and whore, not madonna and whore. Laura's place is outside what can be conceived of as woman. She is the chaos that must be excised, and it is her excision that stabilizes the West's construct of the female body, for the "femininity" of the white female body is ensured by assigning the not-white to a chaos safely removed from sight. Thus only the white body remains as the object of a voyeuristic, fetishizing male gaze. The not-white body has been made opaque by a blank stare, misperceived in the nether regions of TV.

It comes as no surprise, then, that the imagery of white female artists, including that of the feminist avant-garde, should surround the not-white female body with its own brand of erasure. Much work has been done by black feminist cultural critics (Hazel Carby and bell hooks come immediately to mind) that examines two successive white women's movements, built on the successes of two black revolutions, which clearly shows white women's inability to surrender white skin privilege even to form basic alliances.[7] But more than politics is at stake. A major structure of psychic definition would appear threatened were white women to acknowledge and embrace the sexuality of their not-white "others." How else explain the treatment by that women's movement icon, Judy Chicago's *Dinner Party* (1973–78), of Sojourner Truth, the lone black guest at the table? When thirty-six of thirty-nine places are set with versions of Chicago's famous "vagina" and recognizable slits have been given to such sex bombs as Queen Elizabeth I, Emily Dickinson, and Susan B. Anthony, what is one to think when Truth, the mother of four, receives the only plate inscribed with a face?[8] Certainly Hortense Spillers is justified in stating that "the excision of the genitalia here is a symbolic castration. By effacing the genitals, Chicago not only abrogates the disturbing sexuality of her subject, but also hopes to suggest that her sexual being did not exist to be denied in the first place."[9]

And yet, Michele Wallace is right to say, even as she laments further instances of the disempowerment of not-white women in her essay on *Privilege* (1990), Yvonne Rainer's latest film, that the left-feminist avant-garde "in foregrounding a political discourse on art and culture" has fostered a climate that makes it "hypothetically possible to publicly review and interrogate that very history of exclusion and racism."[10]

What alternative is there really—in creating a world sensitive to difference, a world where margins can become centers—to a cooperative effort between white women and women and men of color? But cooperation is predicated on sensitivity to differences among ourselves. As Nancy Hartsock has said, "We need to dissolve the false 'we' into its real multiplicity."[11] We must be willing to hear each other and to call each other by our "true-true name."[12]

To name ourselves rather than be named we must first see ourselves. For some of us this will not be easy. So long unmirrored in our true selves, we may have forgotten how we look. Nevertheless, we can't theorize in a void, we must have evidence. And we—I speak only for black women here—have barely begun to articulate our life experience. The heroic recuperative effort by our fiction and nonfiction writers sometimes feels stuck at the moment before the Emancipation Proclamation.[13] It is slow and it is painful. For at the end of every path we take, we find a body that is always already colonized. A body that has been raped, maimed, murdered—that is what we must give a healthy present.

It is no wonder that when Judith Wilson went in search of nineteenth-century nudes by black artists, she found only three statues of non-black children—Edmonia Lewis's *Poor Cupid*, 1876; her *Asleep* (1871); and one of the two children in her *Awake* (1872)[14] (though Wilson cautions that, given the limits of current scholarship, more nudes by nineteenth-century blacks may yet surface).[15] Indeed, according to Wilson, the nude, one of high art's favorite categories, has been avoided during most of "the 200-year history of fine art production by North American blacks."[16] Noting exceptions that only prove the rule, i.e., individual works by William H. Johnson and Francisco Lord in the 1930s and Eldzier Cortor's series of Sea Island nudes in the 1940s, she calls "the paucity of black nudes in U.S. black artistic production prior to 1960 . . . an unexamined problem in the history of Afro-American art."[17] And why use 1960 as a marker of change? Because, says Wilson, after that date there was a confluence of two different streams: the presence of more, and more aggressive, black fine artists such as Bob Thompson and Romare Bearden, and the political use of the nude as a symbol of "Black Is Beautiful," the sixties slogan of a programmatic effort to establish black ethnicity and achieve psychic transformation.[18]

Neither of these streams, however, begins to deal with what I am concerned with here: the reclamation of the body as a site of black female subjectivity. Wilson hints at part of the problem by subtitling a recent unpublished essay "Bearden's Use of Pornography." An exterior, pornographic view, however loving, will not do any more than will the emblematic "Queen of the Revolution." But though Wilson raises provisional questions about Bearden's montaging of the pornographic image, her concerns are those of the art historian, while mine must be those of the practitioner.[19] When, I ask, do we start to see images of the black female body by black women made as acts of auto-expression, the discrete stage that must immediately precede or occur simultaneously with acts of auto-critique? When, in other words, does the present begin?

Wilson and I agree that, in retrospect, the catalytic moment for the subjective black nude might well be Adrian Piper's *Food for the Spirit* (1971), a private loft performance in which Piper photographed her physical and metaphysical changes during a prolonged period of fasting and reading of Immanuel Kant's *Critique of Pure Reason*.[20] Piper's performance, unpublished and unanalyzed at the time (we did not have the access then that we do now), now seems a paradigm for the willingness to look, to get past embarrassment and retrieve the mutilated body, as Spillers warns we must if we are to gain the clearsightedness needed to overthrow hierarchical binaries: "Neither the shameface of the embarrassed, nor the not-looking-back of the self-assured is of much interest to us," Spillers writes, "and will not help at all if rigor is our dream."[21]

It is cruelly ironic, of course, that just as the need to establish our subjectivity in preface to theorizing our view of the world becomes most dire, the idea of subjectivity itself has become "problematized." But when we look to see just whose subjectivity has had the ground shifted out from under it in the tremors of postmodernism, we find (who else?) the one to whom Hartsock refers as "the transcendental voice of the Enlightenment" or, better yet, "He Who Theorizes."[22] Well, good riddance to him. We who are inching our way from the margins to the center cannot afford to take his problems or his truths for our own.

Though time may be running out for such seemingly marginal agendas as the establishment of black female subjectivity (the headlines remind us of this every day) and we may feel pressured to move fast, we must not be too conceptually hasty. This is a slow business, as our writers have found out. The work of recuperation continues. In a piece called *Seen* (1990) by the conceptual artist Renee Greene, two of our ancestresses most in need, Saartjie Baartman ("the Hottentot Venus") and Josephine Baker, have been "taken back." Each in her day (early nineteenth and twentieth century, respectively) was the most celebrated European exhibit of exotic flesh. Greene's piece invited the viewer to stand on a stage inscribed with information about the two and, through a "winkie" of eyes in the floor and a shadow screen mounted on the side, to experience how the originals must have felt, pinned and wriggling on the wall. The piece has important attributes: it is above all cool and smart. But from the perspective being discussed here— the establishment of subjectivity—because it is addressed more to the other than to the self and seems to deconstruct the subject just before it expresses it, it may not unearth enough new information.

The question of to whom work is addressed cannot be emphasized too strongly. In the 1970s, African American women novelists showed how great a leap in artistic maturity could be made simply by turning from their male peers' pattern of "explaining *it* to *them*," as Morrison once put it, to showing how it feels to *us*.[23]

Besides, pleading contains a special trap, as Gayatri Spivak noted in her discussion of the character Christophine in Jean Rhys's *Wide Sargasso Sea*: "No perspective *critical* of imperialism can turn the Other into a self, because the project of imperialism has always already historically refracted what might have been the absolutely Other into a domesticated Other that consolidates the imperialist self."[24] Critiquing *them* does not show who *you* are; it cannot turn you from an object into a subject of history.

The idea bears repeating: self-expression is not a stage that can be bypassed. It is a discrete moment that must precede or occur simultaneously with the deconstructive act. An example may be seen in the work of the painter Sandra Payne. In 1986, at the last show of the now legendary black avant-garde gallery Just Above Midtown in Soho, Payne presented untitled drawings of joyously sexual and sublimely spiritual nudes. The opening reception was one of those where people speak of everything but what is on the walls. We do not yet have the courage to look.

Understandably, Payne went into retreat. Three years later, she produced attenuated mask drawings that, without the hard edge of postmodernism, are a postmodern speech act in the dialogue of mask and masquerade. Without the earlier subjective nudes, she may not have arrived at them.

A year ago, as a performance artist in a crisis of the body (how to keep performing without making aging itself the subject of the work?), I opted for the safety of the wall with a show of photomontages. My choice of the nude was innocent and far from erotic; I wanted to employ a black self stripped of as many layers of acculturation as possible. The one piece in the show with explicitly represented sexuality, *The Clearing*, a diptych in which a black female engaged with a white male, was to me less about sex than it was about culture. It was not possible to remain innocent for long, however. I soon encountered an encyclopedia of problematics concerning the black body: age, weight, condition, not to mention hair texture, features, and skin tone. Especially skin tone. Any male and female side by side on the wall are technically married. How to arrange a quadriptych such as *Gaze*, composed of head and shoulder shots of differently hued black men and women? Should I marry the fair woman to the dark man? The dark woman to the fair man? What statements will I be making about difference if I give them mates matching in shade? What will I be saying about the history of class?

There was another problematic, as personal as it was cultural. Which maimed body would be best retrieved as the ground of my biographic experience? Young, or middle-aged? Jezebel, or Mammy? The woman I was, or the woman I am now? And, which body hue should I use to generalize my upper-middle-class West Indian–American experience? A black-skinned "ancestress," or the fairer-skinned product of rape? I hedged. In the end, I chose an African-British high-fashion model, London-born but with parents from Sierra Leone. For me, she conveyed important ambiguities: she was black-skinned, but her nude body retained the aura of years of preparation for runway work in Europe. In *The Strange Taxi: From Africa to Jamaica to Boston in 200 Years*, where the subject was hybridism itself, my literal ancestresses, who to some may have looked white, sprouted from a European mansion rolling on wheels down the African woman's back. Although they may have been controversial, I liked the questions those beautifully dressed, proudly erect, ca. World War I women raised, not least of which was how the products of rape could be so self-confident, so poised.

As I wrestled with ever shifting issues regarding which black woman to shoot, I came to understand and sympathize with Lorna Simpson's choice of a unified response in such montages as *Guarded Conditions* (1989), in which a brown-skinned woman in a shapeless white shift is shot from behind—with every aspect of subjectivity both bodily and facial occluded, except the need to cover up itself—and then multiplied. No doubt about it. This multiple woman showers and shampoos in her shift.

But, I tell myself, this cannot be the end. First we must acknowledge the complexity, and then we must surrender to it. Of course, there isn't any final answering of the question, "What happened to that maid when she was brought here?" There is only the process of answering it and the complementary process of allowing each answer to come to the dinner party on its own terms. Each of these processes is just beginning, but perhaps if both continue, the nature of the answers will begin to change and we will all be better off. For if the female body in the West is obverse and reverse, it will not be seen in its integrity—neither side will know itself—until the not-white body has mirrored herself fully.

## Postscript

The paragraphs above were drafted for delivery before a panel of the College Art Association early in 1992.[25] Rereading them, I can see to how great an extent they were limited by the panel's narrowly feminist brief. The topic assigned was "Can the naked female body effectively represent women's subjectivity in contemporary North American media culture, which regularly presents women's bodies as objects for a voyeuristic and fetishizing male gaze?"

I think I was invited because I was the only black female artist employing the nude anyone on the panel had heard of. I felt like the extra guest who's just spilt soup on the tablecloth when I had to reject the panel's premise. The black female's body needs less to be rescued from the masculine "gaze" than to be sprung from a historic script surrounding her with signification while at the same time, and not paradoxically, it erases her completely.

Still, I could perhaps have done a better job of clarifying "what it is I think I am doing anyway."[26] Whether I will it or not, as a black female artist my work is at the nexus of aggravated psychic and social forces as yet mostly uncharted. I could have explained my view, and shown the implications for my work, of the multiple tensions between contemporary art and critical theory, subjectivity and culture, modernism and postmodernism, and, especially for a black female, the problematic of psychoanalysis as a leitmotif through all of these.

I don't want to leave the impression that I am privileging representation of the body. On the contrary: though I agree, to alter a phrase of Merleau-Ponty, that every theory of subjectivity is ultimately a theory of the body,[27] for me the body is just one artistic question to which it is not necessarily the artistic answer.

My work in general deals with what Gayatri Spivak has called the "'winning back' of the position of the questioning subject."[28] To win back that position for the African American female will require balancing in mental solution a subversion of two objects which may appear superficially distinct: on the one hand, phallocentric theory; and on the other, the lived realities of Western imperialist history, for which all forms of that theory, including the most recent, function as willing or unwilling instruments.

It is no overstatement to say that the greatest barrier I/we face in winning back the questioning subject position is the West's continuing tradition of binary, "either:or" logic, a philosophic system that defines the body in opposition to the mind. Binaristic thought persists even in those contemporary disciplines to which black artists and theoreticians must look for allies. Whatever the theory of the moment, before we have had a chance to speak, we have always already been spoken and our bodies placed at the binary extreme, that is to say, on the "other" side of the colon. Whether the theory is Christianity or modernism, each of which scripts the body as all-nature, *our* bodies will be the most natural. If it is poststructuralism/postmodernism, which through a theoretical sleight of hand gives the illusion of having conquered binaries, by joining the once separated body and mind and then taking this "unified" subject, perversely called "fragmented," and designating it as all-culture, we can be sure it is *our* subjectivities that will be the most culturally determined. Of course, it is like whispering about the emperor's new clothes to remark that nature, the other half of the West's founding binary, is all the more powerfully present for having fallen through a theoretical trapdoor.

Almost as maddening as the theories themselves is the time lag that causes them to overlap in a crazy quilt of imbrication. There is never a moment when new theory definitively drives out old. Successive, contradictory ideas continue to exist synchronistically, and we never know where an attack will be coming from, or where to strike preemptively. Unless one understands that the only constant of these imbricated theories is the black body's location at the extreme, the following statements by some of our more interesting cultural theorists might appear inconsistent.

Not long ago, Kobena Mercer and Isaac Julien felt obliged to argue against the definition of the body as all-nature. After noting that "European culture has privileged sexuality as the essence of the self, the innermost core of one's 'personality,'" they went on to say: "This 'essentialist' view of sexuality . . . *already contains racism*. Historically, the European construction of sexuality coincides with the epoch of imperialism and the two interconnect. [It] is based on the idea that sex is the most basic form of naturalness which is therefore related to being *un*civilized or *against* civilization."[29]

Michele Wallace, on the other hand, recently found herself required to defend the black body against a hermeneutics of all-culture. "It is not often recognized," she commented, "that bodies and psyches of color have trajectories in excess of their socially and/or culturally constructed identities."[30] Her statement is another way of saying: now that we have "proved" the personal is political, it is time for us to reassert that the personal is not *just* political.

Wallace and Mercer and Julien are all forced to declare that subjectivity belongs to *both* nature *and* culture. It's true, "both:and" thinking is alien to the West. Not only is it considered primitive, it is now further tarred with the brush of a perceived connection to essentialism. For any argument that subjectivity is partly natural is assumed to be essentialist. But despite the currency of antiessentialist arguments, white feminists and theorists of color have no choice: they must develop critiques of white masculinist "either:or-ism," even if this puts them in the position of appearing to set essentialism up against antiessentialism. This inherent dilemma of the critique of binarism may be seen in Spivak's often amusing ducking and feinting. To justify apparent theoretical inconsistencies, Spivak once explained her position to an interviewer as follows: "Rather than define myself as specific rather than universal, I should see what in the universalizing discourse could be useful and then go on to see where that discourse meets its limits and its challenge within that field. I think we have to choose again strategically, not universal discourse but essentialist discourse. I think that since as a deconstructivist—see, I just took a label upon myself—I cannot in fact clean my hands and say, 'I'm specific.' In fact I must say I am an essentialist from time to time. There is, for example, the strategic choice of a genitalist essentialism in antisexist work today. How it relates to all of this other work I am talking about, I don't know, but *my search is not a search for coherence*."[31] Somebody say Amen.

If artists and theorists of color were to develop and sustain our critical flexibility, we could cause a permanent interruption in Western "either:or-ism." And we might find our project aided by that same problematic imbrication of theory, whose disjunctive layers could signal the persistence of an unsuspected "both:and-ism," hidden, yet alive at the subterranean levels of the West's constructs. Since we are forced to argue both that the body is more than nature, and *at the same time* to remonstrate that there is knowledge beyond language/culture, why not seize and elaborate the anomaly? In doing so, we might uncover tools of our own with which to dismantle the house of the master.[32]

Our project could begin with psychoanalysis, the often unacknowledged linchpin of Western (male) cultural theory. The contradictions currently surrounding this foundational theory indicate its shaky position. To a lay person, postmodernism seems to persist in language that opposes psychoanalysis to other forms of theoretical activity, making it a science or "truth" that is not culturally determined. Psychoanalysis's self-questioning often appears obtuse and self-justifying. The field is probably in trouble if Jacqueline Rose, a Lacanian psychologist of vision not unsympathetic to third world issues, can answer the question of psychoanalysis's universality as follows: "To say that psychoanalysis does not, or cannot, refer to non-European cultures, is to constitute those cultures in total 'otherness' or 'difference'; to say, or to try to demonstrate, that it can, is to constitute them as the 'same.' This is not to say that the question shouldn't be asked."[33]

The implication of such a statement is that no matter how many times you ask the question of the universality of psychoanalysis or how you pose it, you will not arrive at an answer. But the problem is not the concept of "the unanswerable question," which I find quite normal. The problem is the terms in which Rose frames the question in the first place: her continuing use of the totalizing opposition of "otherness" and "sameness" is the sign of an "either:or" logic that does not yet know its own name.

If the unconscious may be compared to that common reservoir of human sound from which different peoples have created differing languages, all of which are translated more or less easily, then how can any of the psyche's analogous products be said to constitute total "otherness" or "difference"? It's at this point that one wants, without being *too* petulant, to grab psychoanalysis by the shoulders and slap it back to a moment before Freud's Eros separated from Adler's "will-to-power," though such a moment may never have existed even theoretically. We need to send this field back to basics. The issue is not whether the unconscious is universal, or whether it has the meanings psychoanalysis attributes to it (it is, and it does), but rather that, in addition, it contains contradictory meanings, as well as some that are unforeseen by its current theory.

Meanwhile, psychoanalysis and its subdisciplines, including film criticism, continue having to work overtime to avoid the "others" of the West. Wallace has referred to "such superficially progressive discourses as feminist psychoanalytic film criticism which one can read for days on end without coming across any lucid reference to, or critique of, 'race.'"[34]

But that omission will soon be redressed. We are coming after them. In her most brilliant theoretical essay to date, "The Oppositional Gaze," bell hooks takes on white feminist film criticism directly.[35] And Gayatri Spivak brooks no quarter. She has declared that non-Western female subject constitution is the main challenge to psychoanalysis and counter-psychoanalysis and has said: "The limits of their theories are disclosed by an encounter with the materiality of that other of the West."[36]

For an artist of color, the problem is less the limits of psychoanalysis than its seeming binarial *rigidity*. Despite the field's seeming inability to emancipate itself from "either:or-ism," I hope its precepts are salvageable for the non-West. Psychoanalysis, after anthropology, will surely be the next great Western discipline to unravel, but I wouldn't want it to destruct completely. We don't have to reinvent that wheel. But to use it in our auto-expression and auto-critique, we will have to dislodge it from its narrow base in sexuality. One wonders if, even for Europeans, sexuality as the center or core of "personality" is an adequate dictum. Why does there have to be a "center:not-center" in the first place? Are we back at that old Freud–Adler crossroad? In Western ontology, why does somebody always have to win?

"Nature:culture," "body:mind," "sexuality:intellect," these binaries don't begin to cover what we "sense" about ourselves. If the world comes to us through our senses—and however qualified those are by culture, no one says culture determines *everything*—then even they may be more complicated than their psychoanalytic description. What about the sense of balance, of equilibrium? Of my personal *cogito*'s, a favorite is "I dance, therefore I think." I'm convinced that important, perhaps even the deepest, knowledge comes to me through movement, and that the opposition of materialism to idealism is just another of the West's binarial theorems.

I have not taken a scientific survey, but I suspect most African Americans who are not in the academy would laugh at the idea that their subjective lives were organized around the sex drive and would feel that "sexuality," a conceptual category that includes thinking about it as well as doing it, is something black people just don't have time for. This "common sense" is neatly appropriated for theory by Spillers in her statement: "Sexuality describes another type of discourse that splits the world between the 'West and the Rest of Us.'"[37]

Not that sex isn't important to these folks; it's just one center among many. For African American folk wisdom, the "self" revolves about a series of variable "centers," such as sex and food; family and community; and a spiritual life composed sometimes of God or the gods, at others of esthetics or style. And it's not only the folk who reject the concept of a unitary center of the "self." Black artists and theorists frequently refer to African Americans as "the first postmoderns." They have in mind a now agreed understanding that our inheritance from the motherland of pragmatic, "both:and" philosophic systems, combined with the historic discontinuities of our experience as black slaves in a white world, have caused us to construct subjectivities able to negotiate between "centers" that, at the least, are double.[38]

It is no wonder that the viability of psychoanalytic conventions has come into crisis. There is a gulf between Western and non-Western quotidian perceptions of sexual valence, and the question of how psychic differences come into effect when "cultural differences" are accompanied by real differences in power. These are matters for theoretical and clinical study. But for artists exploring and mapping black subjectivity, having to track the not-yet-known, an interesting question remains: Can psychoanalysis be made to triangulate nature and culture with "spirituality" (for lack of a better word) and thus incorporate a sense of its own limits? The discipline of art requires that we distinguish between the unconscious and the limits of its current theory, and that we remain alive to what may escape the net of theoretical description.

While we await an answer to the question, we must continue asserting the obvious. For example, when Elizabeth Hess, a white art critic, writes of Jean-Michel Basquiat's "dark, frantic figures" as follows, she misses the point: "There is never any one who is quite human, realized; the central figures are masks, hollow men. . . . It can be difficult to separate the girls from the boys in this work. *Pater* clearly has balls, but there's an asexualness throughout that is cold."[39] Words like "hot" and "cold" have the same relevance to Basquiat's figures as they do to classic African sculptures.

The space spirituality occupies in the African American unconscious is important to speculate upon, but I have to be clear. My own concern as an artist is to reclaim black female agency. Subjectivity for me will always be a social and not merely a spiritual quest.[40] To paraphrase Brecht, "It is a fighting subjectivity I have before me," one come into political consciousness.[41]

Neither the body nor the psyche is all-nature or all-culture, and there is a constant leakage of categories in individual experience. As Stuart Hall says of the relations between cultural theory and psychoanalysis, "Every attempt to translate the one smoothly into the other doesn't work; no attempt to do so can work. Culture is neither just the process of the unconscious writ large nor is the unconscious simply the internalisation of cultural processes through the subjective domain."[42]

One consequence of this incommensurability for my practice as an artist is that I must remain wary of theory. There have been no last words spoken on subjectivity. If what I suspect is true, that it contains a multiplicity of "centers" and all the boundaries are fluid, then most of what will interest me is occurring in the between-spaces. I don't have a prayer of locating these by prescriptively following theoretical programs. The one advantage art has over other methods of knowledge, and the reason I engage in it rather than some other activity for which my training and intelligence might be suited, is that, except for the theoretical sciences, it is the primary discipline where an exercise of calculated risk can regularly turn up what you had not been looking for. And if, as I believe, the most vital inheritance of contemporary art is a system for uncovering the unexpected, then programmatic art of any kind would be an oxymoron.

Why should I wish to surrender modernism's hard-won victories, including those of the Romantics and Surrealists, over classicism's rear-guard ecclesiastical and statist theories? Despite its "post-ness," postmodernism, with its privileging of mind over body and culture over nature, sometimes feels like a return to the one-dimensionality of the classic moment. That, more than any rapidity of contemporary sociocultural change and "fragmentation," may be why its products are so quickly desiccated.

Because I am concerned with the reclamation of black female subjectivity, I am obliged to leave open the question of modernism's demise. For one thing, there seems no way around the fact that the method of reclaiming subjectivity precisely mirrors modernism's description of the artistic process. Whatever else it may require, it needs an act of will to project the inside onto the outside long enough to see and take possession of it. But, though this process may appear superficially *retardataire* to some, repossessing black female subjectivity will have unforeseen results both for action and for inquiry.

I am not suggesting an abandonment of theory: whether we like it or not, we are in an era, postmodern or otherwise, in which no practitioner can afford to overlook the openings of deconstruction and other poststructural theories. But as Spivak has said with respect to politics, practice will inevitably norm the theory instead of being an example of indirect theoretical application: "Politics is assymetrical [sic]," Spivak says; "it is provisional, you have broken the theory, and that's the burden you carry when you become political."[43]

Art is, if anything, more asymmetrical than politics, and since artistic practice not only norms but, in many cases, self-consciously produces theory, the relation between art and critical theory is often problematic. Artists who are theoretically aware, in particular, have to guard against becoming too porous, too available to theory. When a well-intentioned critic like bell hooks says, "I believe much is going to come from the world of theory-making, as more black cultural critics enter the dialogue. As theory and criticism call for artists and audiences to shift their paradigms of how they see, we'll see the freeing up possibilities,"[44] my response must be: Thanks but no thanks, bell. I have to follow my own call.

Gayatri Spivak calls postmodernism "the new proper name of the West," and I agree. That is why for me, for now, the postmodern concept of *fragmentation*, which evokes the mirror of Western illusion shattered into inert shards, is less generative than the more "primitive" and active *multiplicity*. This is not, of course, the cynical *multi* of "multiculturalism," where the Others are multicultural and the Same is still the samo. Rather, paradoxically, it is the *multi* implied in the best of modernism's primitivist borrowings, for example in Surrealism, and figured in Éluard's poem: "Entre en moi toi ma multitude"/ Enter into me, you, my multitude.[45] This *multi* produces tension, as in the continuous equilibration of a *multiplicity of centers*, for which dance may be a brilliant form of training.

Stuart Hall has described the tensions that arise from the slippages between theory development and political practice and has spoken of the need to live with these disjunctions without making an effort to resolve them. He adds the further caveat that, in one's dedication to the search for "truth" and "a final stage," one invariably learns that meaning never arrives, being never arrives, we are always only becoming.[46]

Artists must operate under even more stringent limitations than political theorists in negotiating disjunctive centers. Flannery O'Connor, who in her essays on being a Catholic novelist in the Protestant South may have said most of what can be said about being a strange artist in an even stranger land, soon discovered that though an oppositional artist like herself could choose what to write, she could not choose what she could make live. "What the Southern Catholic writer is apt to find, when he descends within his imagination," she wrote, "is not Catholic life but the life of this region in which he is both native and alien. He discovers that the imagination is not free, but bound."[47] You must not give up, of course, but you may have to go below ground. It takes a strong and flexible will to work both with the script and against it at the same time.

Every artist is limited by what concrete circumstances have given her to see and think, and by what her psyche makes it possible to initiate. Not even abstract art can be made in a social or psychic vacuum. But the artist concerned with subjectivity is particularly constrained to stay alert to the tension of differences between the psychic and the social. It is her job to make possible that dynamism Jacqueline Rose has designated as "medium subjectivity" and to avert the perils of both the excessively personal and the overly theoretical.

The choice of *what* to work on sometimes feels to the artist like a walk through a mine field. With no failproof technology, you try to mince along with your psychic and social antennae swiveling. Given the ideas I have outlined here, on subjectivity and psychoanalysis, modernism and multiplicity, this is a situation in which the following modest words of Rose's could prove helpful: "I'm not posing what an ideal form of medium subjectivity might be; rather, I want to ask where are the flashpoints of the social and the psychic that are operating most forcefully at the moment."[48]

I would add to Rose's directive the following: the most interesting social flashpoint is always the one that triggers the most unexpected and suggestive psychic responses. This is because winning back the position of the questioning subject for the black female is a two-pronged goal. First, there must be provocations intense enough to lure aspects of her image from the depths to the surface of the mirror. And then, synchronously, there must be a probe for pressure points (which may or may not be the same as flashpoints). These are places where, when enough stress is applied, the black female's aspects can be reinserted into the social domain.

I have only shadowy premonitions of the images I will find in the mirror, and my perception of how successfully I can locate generalizable moments of social agency is necessarily vague. I have entered on this double path knowing in advance that as another African American woman said in a different context, it is more work than all of us together can accomplish in the boundaries of our collective lifetimes.[49] With so much to do in so little time, only the task's urgency is forcing me to stop long enough to try and clear a theoretical way for it.

## Notes

1. Hortense J. Spillers, "Interstices: A Small Drama of Words," in Carole S. Vance, ed., *Pleasure and Danger: Exploring Female Sexuality* (Boston: Routledge and Kegan Paul, 1984), p. 77.

2. Sylvia Ardyn Boone, *Radiance from the Waters: Ideals of Feminine Beauty in Mende Art* (New Haven: Yale University Press, 1986), p. 102.

3. "African American Women in Defense of Ourselves," advertisement, *New York Times*, Nov. 17, 1991, p. 53.

4. Judith Wilson, "Getting Down to Get Over: Romare Bearden's Use of Pornography and the Problem of the Black Female Body in Afro-U.S. Art," in *Black Popular Culture*, ed. Gina Dent (Seattle: Bay Press, 1992), p. 114.

5. Toni Morrison, *Beloved* (New York: Alfred A. Knopf, 1987), p. 119.

6. George Nelson Preston, quoted in Wilson, *Getting Down*, p. 114.

7. For an examination of the relationship of black women to the first white feminist movement, see Hazel V. Carby, *Reconstructing Womanhood: The Emergence of the Afro-American Woman Novelist* (New York: Oxford University Press, 1987), Chs. 1 and 5, and bell hooks, *Ain't I a Woman: Black Women and Feminism* (Boston: South End Press, 1981), *passim*. For insights into the problems of black women in the second white feminist movement, see Audre Lorde, "Age, Race, Class, and Sex: Women Redefining Difference," in Russell Ferguson, Martha Gever, Trinh T. Minh-ha, Cornel West eds., *Out There: Marginalization and Contemporary Cultures*, (New York: The New Museum

of Contemporary Art, 1990) and Bernice Johnson Reagon, "Coalition Politics: Turning the Century," in Barbara Smith, ed., *Home Girls: A Black Feminist Anthology* (New York: Kitchen Table: Women of Color Press, 1983). For problems of women of color in a white women's organization at the start of the third feminist movement, see Lorraine O'Grady on WAC, "Dada Meets Mama," *Artforum*, 31, 2 (Oct. 1992):11–12.

8. See Judy Chicago, *The Dinner Party: A Symbol of Our Heritage* (New York: Anchor / Doubleday, 1979).

9. Spillers, p. 78.

10. Michele Wallace, "Multiculturalism and Oppositionality," in *Afterimage* 19. 3 (Oct. 1991):7.

11. Nancy Hartsock, "Rethinking Modernism: Minority vs. Majority Theories," in *Cultural Critique* 7, special issue: "The Nature and Context of Minority Discourse II," edited by Abdul R. JanMohamed and David Lloyd, 204.

12. See the title story by Merle Hodge in Pamela Mordecai and Betty Wilson, eds., *Her True-True Name* (London: Heinemann Caribbean Writers Series, 1989), 196–202. This anthology is a collection of short stories and novel extracts by women writers from the English, French, and Spanish-speaking Caribbean.

13. The understanding that analysis of the contemporary situation of African-American women is dependent on the imaginative and intellectual retrieval of the black woman's experience under slavery is now so broadly shared that an impressive amount of writings have accumulated. In fiction, a small sampling might include, in addition to Morrision's *Beloved*, Margaret Walker, *Jubilee* (New York: Bantam, 1966); Octavia E. Butler, *Kindred* (1979; reprint, Boston: Beacon Press, 1988); Sherley A. Williams, *Dessa Rose* (New York: William Morrow, 1986); and Gloria Naylor, *Mama Day* (New York: Ticknor and Fields, 1988). For the testimony of slave women themselves, see Harriet A. Jacobs, edited by Jean Fagan Yellin, *Incidents in the Life of a Slave Girl* (Cambridge: Harvard University Press, 1987); *Six Women's Slave Narratives*, the Schomburg Library of Nineteenth Century Black Women Writers (New York: Oxford University Press, 1988); and Gerda Lerner, ed., *Black Women in White America: A Documentary History* (New York: Vintage Books, 1972). For a historical and sociological overview, see Deborah Gray White, *Ar'n't I a Woman? Female Slaves in the Plantation South* (New York: W.W. Norton, 1985).

14. Wilson, p. 121, note 13.

15. Ibid., p. 114.

16. Ibid.

17. Ibid.

18. Judith Wilson, telephone conversation with the author, Jan. 21, 1992.

19. Wilson, op. cit., pp. 116–18.

20. Adrian Piper, "Food for the Spirit, July 1971," in *High Performance* 13 (Spring 1981). This was the first chronicling of "Food" with accompanying images. The nude image from this performance first appeared in Piper's retrospective catalogue, Jane Farver. *Adrian Piper: Reflections 1967–87* (New York: Alternative Museum, April 18–May 30, 1987).

21. Hortense J. Spillers, "Mama's Baby, Papa's Maybe: An American Grammar Book," in *Diacritics* 17, 2 (Summer 1987): 68.

22. Hartsock, "Rethinking Modernism," pp. 196, 194.

23. Toni Morrison, in Charles Ruas, "Toni Morrison's Triumph," an interview in *Soho News*, March 11–17 1981, p. 12.

24. Gayatri Chakravorty Spivak, "Three Women's Texts and a Critique of Imperialism," in Henry Louis Gates Jr., ed., *"Race," Writing, and Difference* (Chicago: University of Chicago Press, 1986), p. 272.

25. "Carnal Knowing: Sexuality and Subjectivity in Representing Women's Bodies," a panel of the College Art Association, 80th Annual Conference, Chicago, February 15, 1992.

26. A riff on Barbara Christian's title, "But What Do We Think We're Doing Anyway: The State of Black Feminist Criticism(s)," in Cheryl A. Wall, ed., *Changing Our Own Words: Essays on Criticism, Theory, and Writing by Black Women* (New Brunswick, NJ: Rutgers University Press, 1989), which is itself a riff on Gloria T. Hull's title, "What It Is I Think She's Doing Anyhow: A Reading of Toni Cade Bambara's *The Salt Eaters*," in Smith, *Home Girls*, which is in turn a riff on Toni Cade Bambara's autobiographical essay, "What It Is I Think I'm Doing Anyhow," in Janet Sternberg, ed., *The Writer on Her Work* (New York: W.W. Norton, 1980).

27. "But by thus remaking contact with the body, and with the world, we shall also discover ourselves, since, perceiving as we do with our body, the body is a natural self and, as it were, the subject of perception." Quoted by Edward R. Levine, unpublished paper delivered at College Art Association, 80th Annual Conference, Chicago, February 13, 1992.

28. Gayatri Chakravorty Spivak, "Strategy, Identity, Writing," in *The Post-Colonial Critic: Interviews, Strategies, Dialogues*, ed. Sarah Harasym (New York: Routledge, 1990), p. 42.

29. Kobena Mercer and Isaac Julien, "Race, Sexual Politics and Black Masculinity: A Dossier," in Rowena Chapman and Jonathan Rutherford, eds., *Male Order: Unwrapping Masculinity* (London: Lawrence & Wishart, 1987), pp. 106–7.

30. Wallace, op. cit., p. 7.

31. Spivak, "Criticism, Feminism, and The Institution," in *The Post-Colonial Critic* [see note 28], p. 11 (italics mine).

32. See the oft-quoted phrase, "For the master's tools will never dismantle the master's house," in Lorde, "Age, Race," p. 287.

33. Jacqueline Rose, "Sexuality and Vision, Some Questions," in Hal Foster, ed., *Vision and Visuality*, Dia Art Foundation, Discussions in Contemporary Culture no. 2 (Seattle: Bay Press, 1988), p. 130.

34. Wallace, op. cit., p. 7.

35. bell hooks, *Black Looks: Race and Representation* (Boston: South End Press, 1992), pp. 115–31.

36. Spivak, op. cit., p. 11.

37. Spillers, "Interstices," p. 79.

38. See the famous description of African-American "double-consciousness" in W.E.B. DuBois, *The Souls of Black Folk* (New York: New American Library, 1982), p. 45.

39. Elizabeth Hess, "Black Teeth: Who Was Jean-Michel Basquiat and Why Did He Die?" *Village Voice*, November 3, 1992, p. 104.

40. "The expressionist quest for immediacy is taken up in the belief that there exists a content beyond convention, a reality beyond representation. Because this quest is spiritual not social, it tends to project metaphysical oppositions (rather than articulate political positions); it tends, that is, to stay within the antagonistic realm of the Imaginary." Hal Foster, *Recodings: Art, Spectacle, Cultural Politics* (Seattle: Bay Press, 1985), p. 63.

41. Teresa de Lauretis, *Feminist Studies/Critical Studies* (Bloomington: Indiana University Press, 1986), p. 17.

42. Stuart Hall, "Theoretical Legacies," in Lawrence Grossberg, Cary Nelson, Paula Treichler eds., *Cultural Studies*, (New York: Routledge, 1992), p. 291.

43. Spivak, op. cit., p. 47.

44. bell hooks, interviewed by Lisa Jones, "Rebel without a Pause," in the *Voice Literary Supplement*, Oct. 1992, p. 10.

45. Paul Éluard, quoted in Mary Ann Caws, *The Poetry of Dada and Surrealism: Aragon, Breton, Tzara, Éluard, and Desnos* (Princeton: Princeton University Press, 1970), p. 167.

46. Hall, *passim.*

47. Flannery O'Connor, *Mystery and Manners: Occasional Prose*, selected and edited by Sally and Robert Fitzgerald (New York: Farrar, Straus & Giroux, 1961), p. 197.

48. Rose, op. cit., p. 129.

49. Deborah E., McDowell, "Boundaries," in Houston A. Baker Jr. and Patricia Redmond, eds., *Afro-American Literary Study in the 1990s* (Chicago: University of Chicago Press, 1989), p. 70.

## That the Mothers May Soar and the Daughters May Know Their Names:
### A Retrospecitve of Black Feminist Literary Criticism

*Farah Jasmine Griffin*

2007

All segments of the literary world—whether establishment, progressive, Black, female, or lesbian—do not know, or at least act as if they do not know, that Black women writers and Black lesbian writers exist. . . . Black women's existence, experience, and culture and the brutally complex systems of oppression which shape these are in the "real world" of white and/or male consciousness beneath consideration, invisible, unknown.

—Barbara Smith, 1977, 25

Within and around the modern academy, racial and gender alterity has become a hot commodity that has claimed black women as its principal signifier. . . . Why have we—black women—become the subjected subjects of so much contemporary scholarly investigation, the peasants under glass of intellectual inquiry in the 1990s?

—Ann duCille, 1994, 591

The span of time that separates these two statements by preeminent critics gave birth to a rich and varied body of literature that seeks to uncover, explore, analyze, and theorize the lives and works of (primarily North American) black women. Consequently, Barbara Smith's (1977) lament that black women were invisible as subjects of scholarly attention was certainly not true by the time Ann duCille (1994) published her essay. This was largely due to the efforts of a small but significant cadre of black women writers and scholars. The ventures of these pioneering critics proved to be so successful that black men and white women also began to study the works of black women writers. Even so, given the continued existence of racial and gender hierarchies as well as the systems of power that undergird them, there was still cause for concern. As duCille saw it, although black women's texts gained a great deal of popularity, the black women scholars who pioneered the study of these texts were becoming less and less visible—not only as members of university faculties but also in the footnotes of a voluminous scholarship devoted to black women's writing.

While it is impossible to provide a critical review of all the work that falls under the rubric of black feminist theory or criticism, this essay will consider key moments in the development of the field and its institutionalization in the academy as well as provide an assessment of its current state and modestly look toward its future.[1] First, a word about nomenclature: although much of the early writing by black feminist critics focused on the works of U.S. black writers, I have chosen to use the term *black feminist criticism* instead of *African American feminist criticism*. It is under the rubric of black feminist criticism that scholars have challenged one another to develop a more expansive understanding of the term. While we have not always lived up to such an inclusive critical practice, I do believe it is worth striving for.

Indeed, by the mid-1990s black feminist literary studies was one of the most intellectually exciting and fruitful developments in American literary criticism. Today many scholars and critics continue to contribute to and expand the field. Nonetheless, black feminist criticism (as well as women's studies and African American studies) has experienced a backlash from both the left and the right. The overall assault on multiculturalism and political correctness as well as those critiques that fault the field for being a bastion of identity politics and essentialism have targeted black feminist criticism and challenged its adequacy as a mode of critical analysis. Interestingly, it is quite likely that the latter critique of essentialism was made possible by the very terms and successes of black feminist literary critics who were among the first to call attention to the constructed nature of racial and gender identity.

## That the Mothers May Soar

The 1970s were a heady time for the development of African American women's literature. But this productivity did not emerge in a historical and political vacuum. Historian Darlene Clark Hine notes, "In the 1970s and 1980s black women searched for their place in the politics of race and gender" (1998, 201). As has been remarked a number of times, the development of African American women's literature and the criticism it spawned were a direct response to the masculinist bias of the civil rights and especially the black power and black arts movements (see Dubey 1994). Just as important, it was also a response to the feminist movement's tendency to normalize the experiences of middle-class white women as equivalent for all women. In both instances, black women found themselves lost in the cracks, as *black people* were gendered male, and *women* most often meant white women. Although the gender politics of the civil rights, black power, and black arts movements have often been critiqued harshly, those movements actually contributed a number of voices to what would become black feminism. Toni Cade, Alice Walker, Angela Y. Davis, June Jordan, and Audre Lorde were all actively engaged in the struggles of the 1960s. Some, like Walker, were involved in the women's rights movement as well.

What began as internal debates within the women's and black power movements would provide the basis for the literature that followed. The foundational text of an emerging black women's studies is *The Black Woman: An Anthology*, edited by Cade (1970). Although that volume does not contain literary criticism, it does contain poetry, short stories, essays, and critical analysis by an emerging generation of black women thinkers. The text is not addressed to an academic audience but instead to a diverse variety of black women readers. The editor of and contributors to the volume saw the book as a tool in the liberation of black people; they also sought to give voice to a politicized and articulate generation of black women writers. Consequently, the text itself is not necessarily a feminist document; instead it holds a myriad of opinions about the status and place of black women in the black freedom movement, in the women's rights movement, and in American society at large. As such, it is one of the first multigeneric texts to center the experiences, concerns, and, most important, voices of black women. Finally, the anthology contains works by women who would become central to the literary renaissance that followed its publication: Cade (not yet Bambara), Walker, Lorde, and Paule Marshall, to name just a few.

*The Black Woman* opened a decade that witnessed an explosion in black women's creative writing. The year 1970 presented readers with Maya Angelou's *I Know Why the Caged Bird Sings*, Mari Evans's *I Am a Black Woman*, Toni Morrison's *The Bluest Eye*, and Walker's *The Third Life of Grange Copeland*. These writers continued to produce throughout the decade, and Gayl Jones, Ntozake Shange, Michele Wallace, and Jordan joined them. Shange's play *for colored girls who have considered suicide when the rainbow is enuf* (the second play by a black woman to reach the Broadway stage, in 1976) and Wallace's *Black Macho and the Myth of the Superwoman* (1978) set off firestorms of controversy. These writers published in genres as diverse as the novel, drama, poetry, and autobiography; in so doing they openly challenged any notion of the black community as a monolith of like ideologies, politics, and standpoints. They produced powerful narratives that focused on black women's lives and that dared to expose the conflicts between black men and women. Some, such as Morrison, Walker, and Wallace, became important literary and cultural critics as well. Certainly this generation of black women writers was not the first: Zora Neale Hurston, Ann Petry, Gwendolyn Brooks, Sarah Wright, and others preceded them.

Yet the atmosphere created by the political and social movements of the 1960s produced a context in which these writers could find an interested, informed, and astute audience.

In the late 1970s black women critics both within and outside the academy began to construct a critical discourse and a body of work that attended to the specificities of this new renaissance. Just as the political and social contexts of the early 1970s gave rise to a movement of black women writers, so too did this period witness the emergence of black feminist criticism. As with the creative writers, many of the first black feminist literary critics had been politically involved with the social movements of the 1960s and 1970s. As the creative works gained more visibility, popularity, and in some cases notoriety, black feminist intellectuals began to formally study black women's history and literature. As early as 1972, Mary Helen Washington published "The Black Woman's Search for Identity: Zora Neale Hurston's Work" in *Black World*. In fact, *Black World* published a number of essays by African American women critics on black women's fiction and an issue devoted to Hurston.[2] Significantly, as critics began to construct a tradition of black women's writing, they turned to Hurston as an important literary foremother. Hurston was significant to these younger critics not only because her work focused on black women but also because of the way that work had been treated by Richard Wright and the critical establishment that followed him. In search of her own literary ancestors, Walker discovered Hurston. At that time, most of Hurston's books, with the exception of *Mules and Men*, were out of print. The stories of a generation of young black women intellectuals sharing photocopies of her novel *Their Eyes Were Watching God*, passing it around as if it were contraband, are by now legendary. *Their Eyes Were Watching God*, which had been out of print for thirty years, was republished and soon became a staple in college and university literature classes. But Walker's most significant critical intervention came in the form of her essays about Hurston. In March 1975 Walker published the essay "In Search of Zora Neale Hurston" in *Ms.* magazine. During this time Robert Hemenway published *Zora Neale Hurston: A Literary Biography* (1977), and, as noted above, Washington published important critical essays on Hurston.[3]

However, it was Walker who emerged as Hurston's most influential champion. Walker wrote a number of important essays about Hurston, placed a marker on her grave, and edited a collection of her writing, *I Love Myself When I Am Laughing . . . and Then Again When I Am Looking Mean and Impressive* (Hurston 1979). By privileging Hurston's use of black English, black folk culture, and the black South, Walker created a tradition that originated with Hurston and that led directly to her own work. Her

important collection of essays *In Search of Our Mothers' Gardens* (Walker
1983a) contained another highly influential essay, "Zora Neale Hurston: A
Cautionary Tale and a Partisan View" (Walker 1983b). In addition to turning our attention to Hurston and others, that collection also introduced
the term *womanist*, which Walker famously defines as a black feminist who
loves women (sometimes sexually) and who is committed to the welfare
of black people. Furthermore, a womanist is not a separatist, "except periodically, for health" (1983a, xi). Walker derived the term from the African
American folk term *womanish*, often used to describe a young girl who is
bold, precocious, and curious. For a number of black women activists, artists, and intellectuals who identified feminism and the feminist movement
with the concerns and goals of white women, Walker's term provided an
adequate naming. Black women theologians concerned with race and gender also took up the term to describe their own practices: black womanist
theology. Interestingly, a number of Afrocentric black women critics chose
to call their practice "Africana Womanism" (Hudson-Weems 1993) even
though the black nationalist politics of their intellectual project differed
greatly from Walker's own.[4] *In Search of Our Mothers' Gardens* also contains
a number of other essays that helped shape the direction of black feminist
criticism. Finally, the collection demonstrates the major intellectual tasks
of early black feminist critics. The first of these tasks was archaeological:
In order to construct a tradition that led to contemporary writers such
as Morrison and Walker, critics charged themselves with locating, teaching, and writing about earlier "lost" works by African American women.[5]
Second, they created a critical vocabulary and framework for discussing
works by African American women. Third, they theorized that body of
work as well as the critical practices of black feminist critics. The boundaries between these tasks are porous and flexible. Much of the early theorizing
about black women's writings came in the form of introductions to reis-
sued works. Washington's important anthologies *Black-Eyed Susans: Classic
Stories by and about Black Women* (1975), *Midnight Birds: Stories by Contemporary Black Women Writers* (1980), and *Invented Lives: Narratives of
Black Women, 1860–1960* (1987) not only reintroduced a number of black
women writers but also served to posit the themes, structures, and concerns
that held them together—and began to theorize the contours of that tradition. Similarly, Deborah McDowell's (1986) introduction to Nella Larsen's
Harlem Renaissance novels *Quicksand and Passing* reclaimed these novels
from a critical history that dismissed them or that read them only through
the lens of race. McDowell also provided an alternative feminist reading
that made the works relevant to contemporary readers and students. Beacon Press's Black Women Writers Series is but one example of where one

might find prefaces and introductions by scholars such as Frances Smith Foster and Hazel Carby.

Just as scholars rediscovered Hurston, so too did they begin to uncover works by her contemporaries and her literary forebears. Following his discovery of Harriet Wilson's novel *Our Nig*, the influential literary critic Henry Louis Gates Jr. served as the general editor for the Schomburg Library of Nineteenth-Century Black Women Writers—a forty-volume set. Once *Our Nig* was republished, it shifted our notion of literary history; prior to its publication, most scholars had cited Frances Ellen Watkins Harper's *Iola Leroy* as the first novel written by an African American woman. Although Gates's efforts made a number of important texts available, it was the hard work of feminist critics that helped situate them historically and provide frameworks for reading them. Foster, in *Written by Herself: Literary Production by African American Women, 1746–1892* (1993), and Claudia Tate, in *Domestic Allegories of Political Desire: The Black Heroine's Text at the Turn of the Century* (1992), both historicized and theorized these works. Foster helped bring our attention to the works of nineteenth-century African American women writers, especially Harper. Tate's earlier collection of interviews with contemporary black women writers, *Black Women Writers at Work* (1983), joined Evans's *Black Women Writers (1950–1980): A Critical Evaluation* (1984) as an important document of the black woman's literary renaissance of the 1970s and 1980s. In her critical work, Tate reaches back to locate earlier black women writers, and in *Domestic Allegories of Political Desire: The Black Heroine's Text at the Turn of the Century* (1992) she takes on the marriage plot in black women's fiction and argues that it constitutes a domestic allegory about the political ambitions of black people following emancipation and Reconstruction. Similarly, Carla Peterson's 1995 *"Doers of the Word": African American Women Speakers and Writers in the North (1830–1880)* focuses on northern black women's intellectual and political culture.

It is important to note that even as these critics constructed tradition they did so knowing that they were positing a construct. Hortense Spillers writes: "Traditions are not born. They are made. We would add that they are not, like objects of nature, here to stay, but survive as *created social events* only to the extent that an audience cares to intersect them" (1985: 250).

## But What Do We Think We're Doing Anyway

At the same time that a new generation of black women critics and writers were discovering earlier writers and using their work to help establish a tradition of black women writing in the United States, African American

women activists also founded a number of black feminist political organizations. The most famous of these is the Combahee River Collective; its
fame is less a result of its greater activism than of the fact that the collective
left an eloquent written document, "A Black Feminist Statement" (1977).
This political group of Boston-based black feminists, founded in 1974,
issued its famous manifesto at the same time that one of its founding members, Smith, published the first explicit statement of black feminist criticism, "Toward a Black Feminist Criticism" (1977). In both documents we
find early efforts to define black feminism. The writers of "A Black Feminist
Statement" put forth the following:

> Above all else, our politics initially sprang from the shared belief that
> Black women are inherently valuable, that our liberation is a necessity
> not as an adjunct to somebody else's but because of our need as human
> persons for autonomy. . . . We believe that sexual politics under patriar-
> chy is as pervasive in Black women's lives as are the politics of class and
> race. We also often find it difficult to separate race from class from sex
> oppression because in our lives they are most often experienced simul-
> taneously. . . . Although we are feminists and lesbians, we feel solidarity
> with progressive Black men and do not advocate the factionalization
> that white women who are separatists demand. Our situation as Black
> people necessitates that we have solidarity around the fact of race. . . .
> We struggle together with Black men against racism, while we also
> struggle with Black men about sexism (The Combahee River Collective
> 1977: 204).

There are a number of things worth noting here. From the beginning, black
feminists have been committed to the freedom of all people, especially black
people. Black feminists have always seen their struggle as part of, indeed a
necessary component of, the larger black freedom struggle. The black feminist critical practice that emerged from this politics finds its articulation in
Smith's essay. For Smith, black feminist criticism plays an important role
in making black women's literature "recognizable" (1977, 26) in that it provides a "non-hostile and perceptive analysis of works written" (27) by black
women. Although a number of black women were engaged in creating a
critical discourse around African American women's writing, Smith's essay
established the notion of black feminist literary criticism. Since its publication, the essay has been reprinted in a number of anthologies; it was also
issued as one in a series of pamphlets published by Smith's Kitchen Table
Press, one of the institutional formations of black feminism. "Toward a
Black Feminist Criticism" seeks to make explicit connections between "the
politics of Black women's lives, what we write about and our situation as
artists" (Smith 1977, 26). Smith's essay first outlines the stereotypical rac-

ist and misogynist representations of black women and then demonstrates the need for black feminist criticism. Finally, and most controversially, she posits a reading of Morrison's *Sula* as a lesbian text. Smith argues, "a Black feminist approach to literature that embodies the realization that the politics of sex as well as the politics of race and class are crucially interlocking factors in the works of Black women writers is an absolute necessity" (Smith 1977, 27–28). And she insists that because of shared political, social, and economic experience, black women writers also share thematic, stylistic, and aesthetic conceptions and approaches.

One need only chart the reception of Smith's essay in the years since its publication to derive a sense of the development of and challenges to black feminist criticism, for her essay spawned an intertextual debate and dialogue that became central to the field. In 1980, McDowell built on and challenged Smith's conception of black feminist criticism. McDowell's essay "New Directions for Black Feminist Criticism" (1980) marked black feminism's move into the academy. This move began to yield a body of academically sophisticated works; although much of this work was no longer directly grounded in overt political struggle, these critics never lost sight of the political implications of their work. This is evident in Washington's observation that "what we have to recognize is that the creation of the fiction of tradition is a matter of power, not justice, and that that power has always been in the hands of men—mostly white but some black" (1994, 444). Implicit in this sentence is the understanding that the fights over canons and curricula were in fact struggles for power. The academy became yet another location, another site in the centuries-long battle against white supremacy and patriarchy. And the creation of a tradition of black women's writing, though itself a construction, was but a necessary tool in this struggle. From the beginning black feminist critics knew that literary traditions were not organic but were constructed with a mindful understanding of cultural politics. Carby, Barbara Christian, Beverly Guy-Sheftall, bell hooks, Nellie McKay, Valerie Smith, Spillers, Eleanor Traylor, Gloria Wade-Gayles, Cheryl Wall, and Sherley Ann Williams are but a few of the architects of black feminist criticism in the 1980s.[6] While Traylor, Wade-Gayles, and Guy-Sheftall labored in historically black institutions, the others entered elite white institutions in unprecedented (though still small) numbers; they sought to assist in the widespread transformation of the humanities taking place at the time. Along with black women historians and sociologists, they greatly influenced their disciplines even if they did so from the margins. The move into the academy sometimes marked a shift from a focus on the social and political to the more linguistic and literary.

In "New Directions for Black Feminist Criticism" McDowell writes: "Unfortunately, Black feminist scholarship has been decidedly more practical than theoretical, and the theories developed thus far have often lacked sophistication and have been marred by slogans, rhetoric, and idealism" (1980, 154). Here McDowell echoes the critique of African American literary criticism launched by her contemporaries, Gates and Robert Stepto. McDowell challenged Smith to provide greater specificity in defining a lesbian aesthetic as well as less reductive understandings of the tradition of black women's writings. (Ironically, although McDowell accuses Smith of oversimplifying, obscuring, and stripping lesbianism of its explanatory power, one of McDowell's most insightful and original essays would read the lesbian subtexts in Larsen's novels.) "New Directions" also calls on black feminist critics to consider "the specific language of Black women's literature, to describe the ways Black women writers employ literary devices in a distinct way, and to compare the way Black women writers create their own mythic structures" (McDowell 1980, 158). In other words, she challenges critics of African American women's writing to engage in more rigorous study of the literary nature of black women's writing and in so doing to demonstrate the artistic sophistication of these texts. Interestingly, when McDowell republished this essay in her collection *"The Changing Same": Black Women, Literature, Criticism, and Theory* (1995), she added a response or postscript where she reiterates or reconsiders a number of points. Of her criticism of the ideological dimension of Smith's essay, she writes, "I was fairly harsh in my judgment. I faulted [Smith] for allowing ideology to inform critical analysis, but now I know there is no criticism without ideology" (McDowell 1995, 23).

By the time Carby published her influential *Reconstructing Womanhood: The Emergence of the Afro-American Woman Novelist* (1987a), black feminist critics had succeeded in constructing a tradition of black women's writing from throughout the nineteenth and twentieth centuries. (Barbara Christian's important *Black Women Novelists* was published in 1980.) Carby provides a materialist analysis of writings by nineteenth-century African American women in order to demonstrate how they engaged in a process of reconstructing notions of womanhood and in so doing laid the groundwork for the forms of black feminism that emerged in the late twentieth century. However, Carby argues against the notion of tradition and encourages a move away from the focus on experience or bonds between critic and novelists as a basis for critical practice. She argues that a "reliance on a common or shared experience is essentialist and ahistorical" (1987b, 16).

In *Reconstructing Womanhood* Carby addresses Smith and McDowell by asserting that black feminist criticism should be "regarded critically as a problem, not a solution, as a sign that should be interrogated, a locus of contradictions" (1987a, 15). She argues that the turn toward formalism often ignored the ways that black women writers saw themselves as engaging in and helping shape political discourse through their fiction. Furthermore, in the closing chapter of *Reconstructing Womanhood*, "Quicksands of Representation," Carby argues that locating the tradition in the figure of Hurston privileges the South and the folk tradition of that region over and against texts that focus on the experiences of the urban, migrant, and working-class populations. In this way, Carby joined Gloria Naylor, who proclaimed Petry, a writer of urban fiction, as her own literary foremother.

Although Carby's critique greatly influenced the direction of black feminist criticism, others still argued in favor of an identifiable black women's literary tradition. Michael Awkward explains that his own project in *Inspiriting Influences: Tradition, Revision, and Afro-American Women's Novels* (1989) is "to demonstrate, with reference to a small segment of the Afro-American woman's literary corpus, the accuracy of Smith's claim that 'black women writers constitute an identifiable literary tradition'" (Awkward 1989, 13).

A number of critics took up Carby's notion of black feminist criticism as "a problem, not a solution, as a sign that should be interrogated, a locus of contradictions" (1987a, 15). As such, by the early 1990s we began to witness challenges to the very notion of black feminist criticism as it had been conceived by Smith and other early critics. These challenges took many forms (see Fuss 1989; Baker 1991). In 1993, Deborah G. Chay published an extensive critique of Smith's essay. In "Rereading Barbara Smith: Black Feminist Criticism and the Category of Experience," Chay criticizes Smith for a "debilitating reliance on experience" (1993, 639) as well as for her ability to rightly protest black women's political positions while failing to "theorize their transformation" (639). Furthermore, Chay claims, those black feminist critics who built on and critiqued Smith's essay articulate black feminist critical practice "as a tradition" but fail to "theorize the positions taken within that tradition" (648). According to Chay, these critics have failed to account for how the field "is itself constituted and transformed" (648). (It seems that Carby's work does in fact seek to do this.) Ultimately, Chay urges black feminist critics to point to the ways that their "differentiation cannot be maintained" (649) and in so doing to demonstrate the continuing importance of their critical project.

In *Black Women, Writing and Identity: Migrations of the Subject* (1994), Carole Boyce Davies offered another challenge even as she helped redefine the field. She writes, "Black feminist criticism began as a subversion and counterarticulation to the terms of both Black and feminist criticism. But its limitation, so far, is that it is almost wholly located in African American women's experiences" (1994, 31). Davies argues that the variety of black women's writing globally and the diversity of languages in which black women write call for black feminist criticism to have "a consciousness of tentativeness and incompletion" (32) at its center. For Davies, "Black women's writing . . . should be read as a series of boundary crossings and not as a fixed, geographical, ethnically or nationally bound category of writing. In cross-cultural, transnational, translocal, diasporic perspectives this reworking of the grounds of 'Black Women's Writing' redefines identity away from exclusion and marginality" (4).

The primary arguments in *Black Women, Writing and Identity* appear in the two-volume collection of essays *Moving Beyond Boundaries: International Dimensions of Black Women's Writings* (1995) and *Moving Beyond Boundaries: Black Women's Diasporas* (1995). Both volumes argue for a geographically broad conception of black feminist criticism. It should also be noted that even before the publication of Davies's books, Karla Holloway used black feminist analysis to read texts across national, indeed, continental boundaries. Her *Moorings and Metaphors: Figures of Culture and Gender in Black Women's Literature* (1992) focuses on works by African American and West African women writers.

By the end of the decade, inspired by the work of black feminist and critical race theorist Kimberlé Crenshaw, Valerie Smith argued in *Not Just Race, Not Just Gender: Black Feminist Readings* (1998) that black feminist criticism provided a mode of reading that took account of the "intersections of constructions of race, gender, class and sexuality" (xiii). Smith seeks to uncover the way that the dominance of one of these categories often masks the others and serves to hide the interconnections among them. Smith does not limit her attention to texts produced by black women. She writes: "Black feminism is not a biologically grounded positionality . . . black feminism provides strategies of reading simultaneity . . . black feminist inquiry is a site of critique that challenges monolithic notions of Americaness, womanhood, blackness, or for that matter, black womanhood" (xv). Here Smith begins to lead us out of the sometimes debilitating maze created by critiques of essentialism.

In *Black Women, Identity, and Cultural Theory: (Un)becoming the Subject* (2004), Kevin Everod Quashie continues this line of argument and actually seeks to rescue Barbara Smith's "Toward a Black Feminist Criticism." Quashie argues, "Whatever Smith's errors of overstatement, whatever presumptuous integrity she ascribes to the dalliance between one black female subject and another, her statement's usefulness is not mutilated. Nor is the larger case I am making: that Black women's cultural expressions are encountering and grappling with poststructuralist terms and, in doing so, are articulating their own poststructure, their own guiding principles of the subject's becoming and undoing" (5). In other words, Quashie articulates what black feminists have known—that race and gender identities have always been socially constructed, that black feminists' project is one of developing an alternative subjectivity to the one that has been imposed on them in order to challenge and dismantle the ideological structures that undergird their oppression.

Many of the articles and essays cited above first appeared in anthologies and volumes sparked by a number of conferences and workshops where black feminist critics gathered to debate, discuss, and define the field of black women's literature. While critics engaged in the important work of defining the role of the black feminist critic and the parameters of her intellectual process, they also located texts, constructed a tradition (and in some cases contested tradition), and analyzed and theorized that body of work. Mae Gwendolyn Henderson and Spillers are among the most influential critics/theorists. Henderson's original "Speaking in Tongues: Dialogics, Dialectics, and the Black Woman Writer's Literary Tradition" (1989) combined the linguistic theory of Mikhail Bakhtin with the black vernacular practice of speaking in tongues (glossalia) in her discussion of black women's texts and the role of the black feminist critic. Although Houston Baker's theorizing of the blues (1984) and Gates's use of "signifying" (1988) have gained much deserved attention for their efforts to use the black vernacular to help theorize African American writings, Henderson's lesser-known essay joins them in this project, but unlike the work of her two colleagues, gender is central to her analysis.

As did Henderson, Spillers places gender in the center of her theories of black literature. In a series of important essays, Spillers influenced not only the fields of black women's literary studies but also the broader fields of African American studies, women's studies, and psychoanalytic criticism. Lindon Barrett, himself a brilliant theorist of African American literature, writes:

> Hortense Spillers stages a confrontation between race and psychoanalysis, noting that psychoanalytic approaches are oddly absent from the leading critical paradigms of African American literary studies. Defining psychoanalysis in terms of its interests in locating "interior intersubjectivity," Spillers begins to detail its diacritical relation to race by arguing that the primary template for psychoanalysis is sexuality in its apparently necessary relation to concealment, whereas the primary symbolics of race and racialization rest on visibility, in matters understood ideally to be so plain as to be beyond concealment. This

diacriticism persists further, Spillers argues, since race is conceptualized as a collective enterprise, whereas psychoanalysis focuses on the individual. She contends that race insinuates itself within ethnicities as an evacuated psychic space, an aporia that, more fully considered, discloses the concept of race as a cultural construct. The analytic curiosity is the means by which this point of evacuation supplies, nonetheless, fundamental content for psychic organization.[7] (Barrett 2005)

As Spillers sees it, of course, the psychoanalytic opens up the possibility to speak on all these levels. For many of us, Spillers rescued the psychoanalytic from the depoliticized, ahistorical realm into which we had placed it. In "'All the Things You Could Be by Now if Sigmund Freud's Wife Was Your Mother': Psychoanalysis and Race" (1996) and elsewhere, Spillers has argued that the psychoanalytic leads to "greater self-consciousness, a self-critical capacity in your relationship to others" (Haslett 1998). It is not something that is private and personal but a distinction "between the 'one' and the 'individual'"—individual in relationship to property and early modern capital and one as having been "put in place . . . by language, by one's relationship to the social" (Haslett 1998). Spillers sees the psychoanalytic as a way of getting to a more complex black subjectivity, not simply that which is created by oppression, domination, violence, and economic exploitation, powerful as these forces are, but subjectivity that is created by agency.

Spillers's work has greatly influenced an entire generation of critics and theorists, and it, along with the work of other black feminist literary critics, has helped produce works that reread African American cultural history and literature from perspectives informed by black feminism. Sharon Holland's *Raising the Dead: Readings of Death and (Black) Subjectivity* (2000), Elizabeth Alexander's *The Black Interior* (2004a), Saidiya Hartman's *Scenes of Subjection: Terror, Slavery, and Self-Making in Nineteenth-Century America* (1997), Barrett's *Blackness and Value: Seeing Double* (1999), and Fred Moten's *In the Break* (2003) all acknowledge their debt to Spillers's work.

It is not surprising that many of these texts are informed by what is perhaps Spillers's most famous essay, "Mama's Baby, Papa's Maybe: An American Grammar Book" (1987). Of them, Holland's is most obviously indebted to Spillers's work, and it is a debt she acknowledges not only in the footnotes of her book but also in her opening, framing chapter as well as in her original and provocative reading of Morrison's *Beloved*. One of the most compelling things about Holland's use of Spillers to build her analytical framework is something that ought not be all that unusual but is: the sheer rarity of using the work of a black woman thinker, not only as a text to be analyzed but as a tool and lens through which to analyze culture and history. Spillers's essay "Interstices: A Small Drama of Words" (1992) contributes one of the building blocks for Holland's framework. In "Interstices" Spillers writes, "[the black woman] became instead the principal point of passage between the human and the nonhuman world. Her issue became the focus of a cunning difference—visually, psychologically, ontologically—as the route by which the dominant male decided the distinction between humanity and 'other'" (76). Holland elaborates upon this by noting that "What Spillers accomplishes in these two examples is astonishing. Black female bodies serve as passage between humanity and non-humanity as well as the articulation of that passage. I would suggest that this border, which is no border at all but a passageway, also encompasses the terrain between the living and the dead, between the ancestral and the living community. . . . Elaborating on Spillers's central point in 'Interstices,' that 'black is vestibular to culture,' I would like to add that this space is both material and linguistic—a chamber housing the flesh and its attending language" (2000, 43). From here, Holland is able to posit a reading of the dead in Morrison's *Beloved* and in Randall Kenan's *Visitations of the Spirit*. In bringing together Morrison and Spillers, Holland stages an encounter, a performance, and an engagement whose counterpart in the performing arts might be a stage shared by Jessye Norman and Aretha Franklin, different genres but powerful voices, born of a similar context, pushing each other, higher and higher. Holland's is a luminous work of criticism that establishes her not only as an important feminist voice but also as a critic who brings black feminist criticism to queer theory in her readings of Kenan.

If Holland is empowered by Spillers to insist on recovering mutilated bodies, so too is Alexander in her well-known and often reprinted essay on Rodney King, "Can You Be BLACK and Look at This? Reading the Rodney King Video(s)" (2004b), and throughout her recently published collection, *The Black Interior* (2004a). The very title of the collection and the charge around which it builds are inspired by Spillers, for so much of Spillers's project is concerned with the "interior": both with the "intramural" relations within black life, particularly as they are organized around lines of gender, and with the "interpersonal," with "interiority," and with "intersubjectivity" (Haslett 1998). Alexander writes:

> If black people are the subconscious of the Western mind, where is "the black subconscious," both individually and collectively articulated? My interest is not in psychotherapeutic culture and African American literature—though what a fascinating topic that is—but rather the marker such language offers for identifying complex unexplored interiority beyond the face of the social self. If black people in the mainstream imaginary exist as fixed properties deemed "real," what is possible in the space we might call surreal? . . . "The black interior" is not an inscru-

table zone, nor colonial fantasy . . . [but] inner space in which black
artists have found selves that go far, far beyond the limited expectations
and definitions of what black is, isn't or should be (2004a: 4–5).

Perhaps in an attempt to relocate, if not altogether recover, the flesh, Alexander looks for the spaces designated and created by black folk, spaces where the self is visible, in literal "black interiors" (2004a).

So, in many ways, *The Black Interior* itself is quietly involved with Spillers even though she is not most obviously there. But she is quite explicitly present in the collection's most famous essay, "Can You Be BLACK and Look at This?" (Alexander 2004b). Spillers's presence is felt not simply in the use of "Mama's Baby, Papa's Maybe" but also in Alexander's essay's bold insistence in its first line: "At the heart of this essay is a desire to find a language to talk about 'my people'" (2004b, 175). Alexander acknowledges that this phrase is romantic but insists on the necessity of using it in certain instances, such as in reference to the tape of the Rodney King beating. Yes, Alexander argues, race is a complex fiction but is "perfectly real in at least some significant aspects of our day-to-day lives" (175). In the version of the essay that appears in *The Black Interior*, she adds "'Post-Black'? Post-Script." Alexander asks, "What do black people say to each other to describe their relationship to their racial group, when that relationship is crucially forged by incidents of physical and psychic violence that boil down to the 'fact' of abject blackness?" (2004b, 176). It is Spillers, as well as a multitude of other African American thinkers, who helps build the case, who has done the difficult theoretical work from which Alexander explores these intramural moments. However convincing her case might be, in her postblack postscript Alexander is careful to acknowledge the critics who might accuse her of racial essentialism and those who have, particularly the loudest and perhaps most influential, Paul Gilroy. Gilroy sees Alexander's metaphorical notion of "collective memory" as veering toward "a dangerous kind of myopic nationalism" (Alexander 2004b, 175). Once again, Alexander politely reminds him that this is neither her aim nor her ideology: "I am thinking instead of how this particular metaphor can help explain the persistent and positively consolidating (non-nationalistic) aspects of collective identification" (176) between a group of people who share a historical, political, and spatial condition. So for Alexander, Spillers and others help provide a way out of the constriction. It is important to note that Alexander is not specifically concerned with questions of feminism in her text. However, I would argue that her focus on the interior grows out of a black feminist project. Writers and critics as diverse as Morrison, Spillers, and Washington have all noted that, while black male writers focus their attention on relationships and struggles between black and white men, black women most often turn their gaze to the relationships among black people. This is the focus that animates Alexander's project, and as such it demonstrates the way that a critical practice informed by and engaging with the work of black feminist critics can yield insightful, original, and exciting readings and analyses.

Spillers's influence is also evident in Hartman's discussion of the management of slave women's sexuality, especially in case law (Hartman 1997). For Hartman, understanding the mechanisms at work that allow sexual violence against black women to pass as seduction is central to understanding the quotidian violence necessary for the maintenance of slave society. Again, a reading informed by the insights of black feminism yields new insight into the conditions of the enslaved, both male and female.

Although I have focused on the works of feminist scholars here, it is important to note that male critics of this generation display the influence of Spillers as well. I am speaking in particular about the work of two scholars, Moten and Barrett, whose work I seek to champion every opportunity I get, not only because of their insights but also because they seriously engage and are in dialogue with the work of Spillers and a number of other black women intellectuals. In other words, they do not make patronizing nods or meaningless lists of names, but they are actually informed by and in conversation with the work of both their senior colleagues and their peers. I have focused here on Spillers because she is the theorist most consistently cited by these writers. However, it is clear, and I am certain that all of the younger writers cited above would acknowledge, that they stand on the shoulders of many of her contemporaries as well. What I hope these examples demonstrate is the way that black feminist literary theory and criticism laid the foundation for a new wave of important scholarship in the field of African American, African diaspora, and American literary and cultural studies.

Black feminist literary criticism and theory inform all these works, and all use these insights in order to read cultural and literary texts produced across boundaries of race, ethnicity, and gender. Similarly, scholars Jennifer DeVere Brody and Kim Hall are black feminist scholars of the Victorian and Renaissance eras, respectively. In *Impossible Purities: Blackness, Femininity, and Victorian Culture* (Brody 1998) and *Things of Darkness: Economies of Race and Gender in Early Modern England* (Hall 1995), Brody and Hall render black feminist analysis of texts and eras thought to be far removed from the project of black feminist literary criticism. In this way, all of these authors prove Valerie Smith's dictum that black feminism is a strategy of reading literary and social texts and contexts. As such, black feminist criticism has informed the emergence of newer fields of literary criticism, and it has animated analyses of film, theater, music, media, and politics as well.

From the beginning, brilliant black lesbian feminists have been central participants in the articulation of black feminism (see, e.g., Bethel and Smith 1979; Shockley 1979; Barbara Smith 1991). Black feminist criticism early offered insight into the relationship between sexuality, race, and gender. It is not insignificant that Barbara Smith in "Toward a Black Feminist Criticism" (1977) reads *Sula* as a lesbian text. Nor is it trivial that one of the most important voices in this body of work is Lorde, especially her collection of essays *Sister Outsider* (1984) and her bio-mythology *Zami* (1982). Even though these critics often engaged in arguments with other black feminists about their failure to adequately address issues of sexuality in the early 1980s, such a conversation was not yet taking place in the broader field of African American studies. Consequently, black feminist criticism provided a space that allowed for the emergence of black queer studies and black masculinity studies as well. Situated at the nexus of black studies and queer studies but subordinated by both, scholars interested in black gay, lesbian, and transgendered people provide a critique of both fields and a reading practice that lays claim to both. This field has given rise to exciting voices including but not limited to Phillip Brian Harper, Holland, Dwight McBride, and Robert Reid Pharr.

In addition to informing black queer studies and black masculinity studies, black feminist criticism has also been used to demonstrate ways that a black feminist strategy of reading has relevance outside of purely literary study. Critics such as Valerie Smith (1989), hooks (1995, 1996), Jacqueline Bobo (1995), Jacqueline Najuma Stewart (2005), Daphne Brooks (2006), Wahneemah Lubiano (1992), Davis (1998), Lisa Gail Collins (2002), and Patricia Williams (1991) have used black feminist reading strategies to analyze film, theater, the media, music, visual arts, and the law. In fact, hooks's oeuvre offers a testament to the growth and versatility of black feminist literary and cultural criticism. One of the earliest figures who sought to define black feminism, hooks has brought her sensibility to bear on literary texts, film, media, the visual arts, pedagogical practice, and studies of class and of black masculinity.[8]

## But Some of Us Are Brave

In the thirty years since the publication of Barbara Smith's "Toward a Black Feminist Criticism," the field has experienced a tremendous amount of growth and growing pains to accompany it. It helped institutionalize the study of works by black women of all nationalities, and along with the work of historians it led the way for the development of black women's studies as a distinct field within both African American studies and women's studies.[9] The project initially provided a discursive intervention that sought to address the invisibility and silence of black women in dominant critical discourses as well as those oppositional discourses that emerged from the black power and feminist movements. Since that time, black feminist critics have succeeded in calling attention to the works of contemporary black women writers, unearthed the writings of earlier artists, constructed and dismantled literary traditions, and provided a method of reading that centers an analysis based on the intersection of race, class, and gender. Along the way, the field has encountered critiques from within and without. It has withstood accusations of essentialism, political correctness, and crude nationalism. Although it continues to be a discourse in opposition to right-wing ideologies, it has often incorporated as well as challenged critiques of biological essentialism and U.S. national chauvinism. Finally, black feminist criticism has helped create the conditions for the emergence of other critical stances, such as black queer studies and black masculinities studies.

Work informed by the tenets of black feminist criticism continues to be important for a number of reasons: Readings that focus on the intersections of class, race, gender, sexuality, and nationality with an eye toward equality and justice are especially valuable today; a critique that emerges from those whose positionality has made them experience physical, psychic, and economic violence at the hands of the United States from within its borders provides a unique insight into the workings of this global, imperial power. Now, in the first decade of the twenty-first century, black feminist criticism finds itself at an important juncture. Given the misogyny of some of today's contemporary black popular culture as well as the impact of U.S. imperialism on the lives of women of color and poor women globally, the insights of black feminist criticism offer a mode of analysis worth heeding, for black feminist criticism provides a strategy of reading but also informs a politics that measures a society and its culture by the place that the poorest women and girls occupy within it.

## Notes

This article is dedicated to Nellie McKay, pioneering feminist critic, inspiring teacher, and devoted mentor.

1. For a comprehensive bibliography of black feminism see the extraordinary Web project compiled by Sherri L. Barnes, "Black American Feminisms: A Multidisciplinary Bibliography," http://www.library.ucsb.edu/subjects/blackfeminism/.

2. In fact, 1970 is an important year in the history of *Black World*. Prior to then, the journal had been known as *Negro Digest*. Though both were published by John H. Johnson, the later incarnation brought significant intellectual and editorial changes influ-

enced by the black power movement. For more on black women writers who published in *Black World*, see duCille (2005).

3. Washington also wrote the foreword to *I Love Myself When I Am Laughing* (Hurston 1979).

4. See Hudson-Weems 1993, 2004. Clenora Hudson-Weems contends that historically and culturally most black women are not feminists. She insists that dealing with gender issues does not automatically make one a feminist, thus the feminist has no monopoly on gender issues.

5. This archaeological endeavor also produced important biographical work such as Thadious Davis's *Nella Larsen, Novelist of the Harlem Renaissance: A Woman's Life Unveiled* (1994) and Alexis De Veaux's *Warrior Poet: A Biography of Audre Lorde* (2004).

6. See Bell, Parker, and Guy-Sheftall 1979; hooks 1981, 1984, 1989; Wade-Gayles 1984; Christian 1985, 1987, 1989; Spillers 1985, 1987; Carby 1986; Williams 1986; McKay 1987, 1990; Smith 1989; Wall 1989.

7. It should be noted that in *Psychoanalysis and Black Novels* (1998) Tate joins Spillers in the project of bringing psychoanalysis to bear upon the literature of Americans.

8. See hooks 1981, 1984, 1989, 1990, 1992, 1993, 1994, 1995, 1996.

9. Given this, it is somewhat ironic that the nation's only department of Africana Women's Studies, at Clark Atlanta University, seems to be primarily focused on the social sciences. The program defines itself as follows: "Founded in 1982, the Africana Women's Studies is the only degree-granting women's studies program located in an historically black college in the United States, the only women's studies program in the United States which offers the doctoral degree in Africana Women's Studies and the only Africana women's studies program in the world. AWS provides opportunities for the systematic analysis of the convergence of gender, class and racial bias. It also focuses on the comparative examination of the contributions, problems, strategies and concerns of Africana women. Analytical approaches that rigorously compare and contrast the lives of all women by class, age and color without regard to their geographic location are strongly encouraged. AWS is cross-cultural, national, international and interdisciplinary in its focus. Similar to many nontraditional, interdisciplinary programs and departments, AWS has a small, stable core faculty with faculty associates from traditional departments." See "Graduate Degrees Offered," then "Africana Women's Studies," at http://www.cau/edu/grad_stud/default.html.

# References

Alexander, Elizabeth. 2004a. *The Black Interior*. Saint Paul, MN: Graywolf.

———. 2004b. "Can You Be BLACK and Look at This? Reading the Rodney King Video(s)." In Alexander 2004a, 175–205.

Awkward, Michael. 1989. *Inspiriting Influences: Tradition, Revision, and Afro-American Women's Novels*. New York: Columbia University Press.

Baker, Houston A. 1984. *Blues, Ideology, and Afro-American Literature: A Vernacular Theory*. Chicago: University of Chicago Press.

———. 1991. *Workings of the Spirit: The Poetics of Afro-American Women's Writings*. Chicago: University of Chicago Press.

Barrett, Lindon. 1999. *Blackness and Value: Seeing Double*. Cambridge: Cambridge University Press.

———. 2005. "African American Literary Criticism since 1990." *Johns Hopkins Guide to Literary Criticism and Theory*. http://litguide.press.jhu.edu.

Bell, Roseann P., Bettye J. Parker, and Beverly Guy-Sheftall. 1979. *Sturdy Black Bridges: Visions of Black Women in Literature*. Garden City, NY: Anchor/Doubleday.

Bethel, Lorraine, and Barbara Smith, eds. 1979. "Conditions: Five, the Black Women's Issue." Special issue of *Conditions* 2, no. 2.

Bobo, Jacqueline. 1995. *Black Women as Cultural Readers*. New York: Columbia University Press.

Brody, Jennifer DeVere. 1998. *Impossible Purities: Blackness, Femininity, and Victorian Culture*. Durham, NC: Duke University Press.

Brooks, Daphne. 2006. *Bodies in Dissent: Spectacular Performances of Race and Freedom, 1850–1910*. Durham, NC: Duke University Press.

Cade, Toni. 1970. *The Black Woman: An Anthology*. New York: New American Library.

Carby, Hazel V. 1986. "It Jus Be's Dat Way Sometime: The Sexual Politics of Women's Blues." *Radical America* 20(4):8–22.

———. 1987a. *Reconstructing Womanhood: The Emergence of the Afro-American Woman Novelist*. New York: Oxford University Press.

———. 1987b. "Woman's Era: Rethinking Black Feminist Theory." In Carby 1987a, 3–19.

Chay, Deborah. 1993. "Rereading Barbara Smith: Black Feminist Criticism and the Category of Experience." *New Literary History: A Journal of Theory and Interpretation* 24(3):635–52.

Christian, Barbara. 1980. *Black Women Novelists: The Development of a Tradition, 1892–1976*. Westport, CT: Greenwood.

———. 1985. *Black Feminist Criticism: Perspectives on Black Women Writers*. New York: Pergamon.

———. 1987. "The Race for Theory." *Cultural Critique* 6(1):51–63.

———. 1989. "But What Do We Think We're Doing Anyway: The State of Black Feminist Criticism(s) or My Version of a Little Bit of History." In Wall 1989, 58–74.

Collins, Lisa Gail. 2002. *The Art of History: African American Women Artists Engage the Past*. New Brunswick, NJ: Rutgers University Press.

Combahee River Collective, The. 1977. "A Black Feminist Statement." In *Feminist Frameworks: Alternative Theoretical Accounts of the Relations between Women and Men*, ed. Alison K. Jaggar and Paula S. Rothenberg, 202–9. New York: McGraw-Hill, 1978.

Davies, Carole Boyce. 1994. *Black Women, Writing and Identity: Migration of the Subject*. London: Routledge.

———, ed. 1995. *Moving Beyond Boundaries: Black Women's Diasporas*. New York: New York University Press.

Davies, Carole Boyce, and Molara Ogundipe-Leslie, eds. 1995. *Moving Beyond Boundaries: International Dimensions of Black Women's Writings*. New York: New York University Press.

Davis, Angela Y. 1998. *Blues Legacies and Black Feminism: Gertrude "Ma" Rainey, Bessie Smith, and Billie Holiday*. New York: Pantheon.

Davis, Thadious. 1994. *Nella Larsen, Novelist of the Harlem Renaissance: A Woman's Life Unveiled*. Baton Rouge: Louisiana State University Press.

De Veaux, Alexis. 2004. *Warrior Poet: A Biography of Audre Lorde*. New York: Norton.

Dubey, Madhu. 1994. *Black Women Novelists and the National Aesthetic*. Bloomington: Indiana University Press.

duCille, Ann. 1994. "The Occult of True Black Womanhood: Critical Demeanor and Black Feminist Studies." *Signs: Journal of Women in Culture and Society* 19(3):591–629.

———. 2005. "The Mark of Zora: Reading between the Lines of Legend and Legacy." *S&F Online* 3(2). http://www.barnard.edu/sfonline/hurston/ducille_01.htm.

Evans, Mari, ed. 1984. *Black Women Writers (1950–1980): A Critical Evaluation*. Garden City, NY: Anchor.

Foster, Frances Smith. 1993. *Written by Herself: Literary Production by African American Women, 1746–1892*. Bloomington: Indiana University Press.

Fuss, Diana. 1989. *Essentially Speaking: Feminism, Nature, and Difference*. New York: Routledge.

Gates, Henry Louis. 1988. *The Signifying Monkey: A Theory of Afro-American Literary Criticism*. New York: Oxford University Press.

Hall, Kim F. 1995. *Things of Darkness: Economies of Race and Gender in Early Modern England*. Ithaca, NY: Cornell University Press.

Hartman, Saidiya V. 1997. *Scenes of Subjection: Terror, Slavery, and Self-Making in Nineteenth-Century America*. New York: Oxford University Press.

Haslett, Tim. 1998. "Hortense Spillers Interviewed by Tim Haslett for the Black Cultural Studies Web Site Collective in Ithaca, NY, Feb. 4, 1998." http://www.blackcultural-studies.org/spillers/spillers_intvw.html.

Hemenway, Robert E. 1977. *Zora Neale Hurston: A Literary Biography*. Urbana: University of Illinois Press.

Henderson, Mae Gwendolyn. 1989. "Speaking in Tongues: Dialogics, Dialectics, and the Black Woman Writer's Literary Tradition." In Wall 1989, 16–37.

Hine, Darlene Clark, with Kathleen Thompson. 1998. *A Shining Thread of Hope: The History of Black Women in America*. New York: Broadway Books.

Holland, Sharon Patricia. 2000. *Raising the Dead: Readings of Death and (Black)Subjectivity*. Durham, NC: Duke University Press.

Holloway, Karla FC. 1992. *Moorings and Metaphors: Figures of Culture and Gender in Black Women's Literature*. New Brunswick, NJ: Rutgers University Press.

hooks, bell. 1981. *Ain't I a Woman: Black Women and Feminism*. Boston: South End.

———. 1984. *Feminist Theory from Margin to Center*. Boston: South End.

———. 1989. *Talking Back: Thinking Feminist, Thinking Black*. Boston: South End.

———. 1990. *Yearning: Race, Gender, and Cultural Politics*. Boston: South End.

———. 1992. *Black Looks: Race and Representation*. Boston: South End.

———. 1993. *Sisters of the Yam: Black Women and Self-Recovery*. Boston: South End.

———. 1994. *Outlaw Culture: Resisting Representations*. New York: Routledge.

———. 1995. *Art on My Mind: Visual Politics*. New York: New Press.

———. 1996. *Reel to Real: Race, Sex, and Class at the Movies*. New York: Routledge.

Hudson-Weems, Clenora. 1993. *Africana Womanism: Reclaiming Ourselves*. Troy, MI: Bedford.

———. 2004. *Africana Womanist Literary Theory*. Trenton, NJ: Africa World Press.

Hurston, Zora Neale. 1979. *I Love Myself When I Am Laughing . . . and Then Again When I Am Looking Mean and Impressive*, ed. Alice Walker. Old Westbury, NY: Feminist Press.

Lorde, Audre. 1982. *Zami: A New Spelling of My Name*. Trumansburg, NY: Crossing.

———. 1984. *Sister Outsider: Essays and Speeches*. Trumansburg, NY: Crossing.

Lubiano, Whaneemah. 1992. "Black Ladies, Welfare Queens, and State Minstrels: Ideological War by Narrative Means." In *Race-ing Justice, En-gendering Power: Essays on Anita Hill, Clarence Thomas, and the Construction of Social Reality*, ed. Toni Morrison, 323–63. New York: Pantheon.

McDowell, Deborah. 1980. "New Directions for Black Feminist Criticism." *Black American Literature Forum* 14(4):153–59.

———. 1986. Introduction to *Quicksand and Passing* by Nella Larsen, ed. Deborah McDowell, ix–xxxvii. New Brunswick, NJ: Rutgers University Press.

————. 1995. *"The Changing Same": Black Women's Literature, Criticism, and Theory.* Bloomington: Indiana University Press.

McKay, Nellie Y. 1987. "Reflections on Black Women Writers: Revising the Literary Canon." In *The Impact of Feminist Research in the Academy*, ed. Christie Farnham, 174–89. Bloomington: Indiana University Press.

————. 1990. "Literature and Politics: Black Feminist Scholars Reshaping Literary Education in the White University, 1970–1986." In *Left Politics and the Literary Profession*, ed. Lennard J. Davis and M. Bella Mirabella, 84–102. New York: Columbia University Press.

Moten, Fred. 2003. *In the Break: The Aesthetics of the Black Radical Tradition.* Minneapolis: University of Minnesota Press.

Peterson, Carla L. 1995. *"Doers of the Word": African-American Women Speakers and Writers in the North (1830–1880).* New York: Oxford University Press.

Quashie, Kevin Everod. 2004. *Black Women, Identity, and Cultural Theory: (Un)becoming the Subject.* New Brunswick, NJ: Rutgers University Press.

Shockley, Ann Allen. 1979. "The Black Lesbian in American Literature: An Overview." In Bethel and Smith 1979, 133–42.

Smith, Barbara. 1977. "Toward a Black Feminist Criticism." *Conditions: Two* 1(2): 25–44.

————. 1991. "The Truth That Never Hurts: Black Lesbians in Fiction in the 1980s." In *Third World Women and the Politics of Feminism*, ed. Chandra T. Mohanty, Anna Russo, and Lourdes Torres, 101–29. Bloomington: Indiana University Press.

Smith, Valerie. 1989. "Black Feminist Theory and the Representation of the 'Other.'" In Wall 1989, 38–57. New Brunswick, NJ: Rutgers University Press.

————. 1998. *Not Just Race, Not Just Gender: Black Feminist Readings.* New York: Routledge.

Spillers, Hortense. 1985. "Afterword: Cross-Currents, Discontinuities: Black Women's Fiction." In *Conjuring: Black Women, Fiction, and Literary Tradition*, ed. Marjorie Pryse and Hortense Spillers, 249–61. Bloomington: Indiana University Press.

————. 1987. "Mama's Baby, Papa's Maybe: An American Grammar Book." *Diacritics* 17(2):65–81.

————. 1992. "Interstices: A Small Drama of Words." In *Pleasure and Danger: Exploring Female Sexuality*, ed. Carol S. Vance, 73–100. London: Pandora.

————. 1996. "'All the Things You Could Be by Now if Sigmund Freud's Wife Was Your Mother': Psychoanalysis and Race." *Critical Inquiry* 22(4):710–34.

Stewart, Jacqueline Najuma. 2005. *Migrating to the Movies: Cinema and Black Urban Modernity.* Berkeley: University of California Press.

Tate, Claudia, ed. 1983. *Black Women Writers at Work.* New York: Continuum.

————. 1992. *Domestic Allegories of Political Desire: The Black Heroine's Text at the Turn of the Century.* New York: Oxford University Press.

————. 1998. *Psychoanalysis and Black Novels: Desire and the Protocols of Race.* New York: Oxford University Press.

Wade-Gayles, Gloria Jean. 1984. *No Crystal Stair: Visions of Race and Sex in Black Women's Fiction.* New York: Pilgrim.

Walker, Alice. 1975. "In Search of Zora Neale Hurston." *Ms.* 3(9):74–90.

————. 1983a. *In Search of Our Mothers' Gardens: Womanist Prose.* New York: Harcourt Brace Jovanovich.

————. 1983b. "Zora Neale Hurston: A Cautionary Tale and a Partisan View." In Walker 1983a, 3–92.

Wall, Cheryl A. 1989. *Changing Our Own Words: Essays on Criticism, Theory, and Writing by Black Women*. New Brunswick, NJ: Rutgers University Press.

Wallace, Michele. 1978. *Black Macho and the Myth of the Superwoman*. New York: Dial.

Washington, Mary Helen. 1972. "The Black Woman's Search for Identity: Zora Neale Hurston's Work." *Black World* 21 (August): 519–27.

———, ed. 1975. *Black-Eyed Susans: Classic Stories by and about Black Women*. Garden City, NY: Anchor.

———, ed. 1980. *Midnight Birds: Stories by Contemporary Black Women Writers*. Garden City, NY: Anchor.

———, ed. 1987. *Invented Lives: Narratives of Black Women, 1860–1960*. Garden City, NY: Anchor.

———. 1994. "'The Darkened Eye Restored': Notes toward a Literary History of Black Women." In *Within the Circle: An Anthology of African American Literary Criticism from the Harlem Renaissance to the Present*, ed. Angelyn Mitchell, 442–53. Durham, NC: Duke University Press.

Williams, Patricia. 1991. *Alchemy of Race and Rights: Diary of a Law Professor*. Cambridge, MA: Harvard University Press.

Williams, Sherley Anne. 1986. "Some Implications of Womanist Theory."*Callaloo: A Journal of African American Arts and Letters* 9(2):303–8.

# FROM THIS MOMENT ON . . .

## Mission Statement

*Black Men for the Eradicaton of Sexism*

1994

We believe that although we are op-
pressed because of our color, we are privileged because of our sex and must
therefore take responsibility for ending that privilege. We live in a society that along with being racist, classist, homophobic, and capitalist, is also
fundamentally sexist. Just as all whites socialized in a white society will be
racists, so too will all men socialized in a sexist society be sexists. The fact
that we are black does not make us immune. We are dealing with a disease
that once within us remains for the rest of our lives. As long as the society
remains sexist all of our brothers to come will suffer the same fate. Because
we struggle to move forward as a people we accept our responsibility of
helping to dismantle this form of oppression that we help to perpetuate.

We believe that our relationships with women must be based on the
principle of equality. Our notions of sexuality are based on domination.
We are taught as boys to be sexual conquerors of women whose bodies
are objectified and declared to be the property of men to be bought, sold,
and traded. We reject relationships based on domination and the violence
against women and prostitution they create. We seek to establish relationships with our sisters based on equality. Men and women are complementary. We need each other in order to survive and to thrive. However two
people must be held in equal standing in order to be complementary.

We recognize that present Eurocentric notions of manhood and masculinity are damaging to the psyche of black men and must be replaced with a
holistic interpretation of manhood that acknowledges the oneness of men
and women. Patriarchal notions of manhood, which we have internalized
from our oppressors, demand that our existence as men be defined by our
sexual ability and our ability to produce economically and dominate others. Following this path in a society that denies economic equality and per-
verts sexuality is like committing suicide. Masculinity is a one-dimensional,
social creation that has nothing to do with biological reality. Notions of
"masculine" and "feminine" only serve to further sexism and to suppress

the abilities of both men and women. It is sexism, not biology, that confines men to being aggressive and women to being nurturers.

We believe that sexism is a global form of oppression of no less importance than any other form of oppression. All forms of oppression including sexism, racism, and classism are interconnected and support each other. For too long the struggle for the liberation of African people in the United States has been centered around the liberation of black men. This male-centered analysis inhibits us from fully confronting the oppression we constantly face and perpetuate within and without the black community. The struggle against sexism must become an issue of primary importance if we are to advance as a people.

We believe that sexist oppression against women pervades every aspect of our communities and must be eradicated. The oppression of women is a difficult issue for our community to deal with partly because it is such a personal one. It is passed on to us through media, schools, religious institutions, friends, and families. Although it has often been said that black women are held in high regard by the black community, the reality is that black women are either denigrated as whores and enemies or are placed on a confining pedestal as superwomen. The humanity of our sisters is lost in these classifications which only succeed in further dividing our people and preventing us from collectively dealing with other forms of oppression. Sexism is a radical problem that requires a radical solution. It will not be solved by simple reform. We support feminism/womanism and all efforts to eradicate sexist oppression. We ultimately demand a complete and fundamental change that eradicates oppression based on sex, race, class, and sexual orientation, both within and without.

We are not perfect. We do not claim to be. As we fight alongside our sisters we struggle to become whole; to deprogram ourselves. We have organized into one body because we know in our hearts and minds that as we hold our sisters back so will we hold ourselves back.

# Resting in the Gardens, Battling in the Deserts
## Black Women's Activism

*Joy James*

1999


Reminding you Sister
Its okay to rest your feet
from battles
But lay in gardens
warmed by sun
Not in spreading deserts
near convenient wells
            —Audre Lorde


## Introduction

The above epigram is taken from an inscription by Audre Lorde for *The Black Unicorn*.[1] Lorde is one of many black women writers, including Toni Cade Bambara, Sonia Sanchez, and Alice Walker, who have greatly influenced the growth and development, the genius, if you will, of womanist or black feminist theory and activism.

Tens of thousands of black women have furthered democratic politics and social justice through their activism and analyses. Black feminist politics display a radical singularity. In its revolutionary tendency (only one of many trajectories within black women's activism) one finds the framework for an alternative to liberal antiracist and feminist politics. Black women have tended incredible, secluded gardens within the expansive wasteland of this dysfunctional democracy.

What often distracts attention from the fruits of black women's labors are depoliticizing representations that obscure their contributions to democratic politics. Often commercial and stereotypical portrayals of black females center on fetishized and animalized sexual imagery; consequently, blacks, females, and politics become effaced or distorted. Racial and sexual caricatures corseting the black female body have a strong historical legacy. Progressive intellectuals and activists satirize denigrating stereotypes that recycle vilifying images of black females as "tragic mulattas," tricksters and *femmes fatales.* Nevertheless, commercial images of America's sexualized attraction as well as aversion to black females eclipse images of black female political agency in conventional culture. Deconstructing representations of black females as sexual deviants and of images that promote antiblack and antifemale contempt and violence has been a primary concern of black women writers and activists in the United States for centuries.

The political agency of black women still seems to be infrequently referenced, perhaps because black males remain the most influential petitioners and pugilists in contemporary American race politics. (Their ideological span stretches from the reactionary positions of California's antiaffirmative action czar Ward Connerly and Supreme Court Justice Clarence Thomas's anti–civil rights activism, through the liberalism and reconciliation politics of historian John Hope Franklin who headed Bill Clinton's President's Race Initiative, to the neoradicalism of elite black academics.) Although exceptions have occasionally been made for very extraordinary women, historically, the image of "freedom fighters" has been masculinized, a fact that furthers the erasure of black women activists.

## Historical Legacies

> [W]e find our origins in the historical reality of Afro-American women's continuous life-and death struggle for survival and liberation. Black women's extremely negative relationship to the American political system (a system of white male rule) has always been determined by our membership in two oppressed racial and sexual castes. . . . Black, women have always embodied, if only in their physical manifestation, an adversary stance to white male rule and have actively resisted its inroads upon them and their communities in both dramatic and subtle ways.
>
> —The Combahee River Collective Statement[2]

The search for antiracist and feminist community can be measured by the heroic efforts of ancestral and activist African American women. Most Americans are unfamiliar with the history of militant black female fighters, yet their stories are readily available. Memoirs such as *Crusade for Justice: The Autobiography of Ida B. Wells*; *Angela Davis: An Autobiography*; and *Assata: An Autobiography* touch a raw nerve among those who become politically stressed or polarized when facing radical and revolutionary social justice battles.[3] (Paradoxically, political autobiographies expand an intellectual base for progressive struggles while simultaneously providing a comfort zone that validates for the consumer society, images of revolution-

aries marketed as commodities through publications for consumers.) Reading such narratives reveals rebellions that democratized American politics.
Tens of thousands were and are inspired by Ida B. Wells's crusade against
lynching, Ella Baker's organizing for civil rights, Angela Davis's support
for prisoners (beginning with the Soledad Brothers in the late 1960s), and
Assata Shakur's revolutionary battles in the black liberation movement (a
movement eventually destroyed by the Federal Bureau of Investigation's illegal counter revolutionary program, COINTELPRO). The works of women
such as Wells, Baker, Davis, and Shakur, although not consistantly "radical"
or "revolutionary"—and containing contradictions—pushed beyond conventional politics. Seeking liberation, each offered models of black female
resistance to political, social, state or gender dominance.

Following the unique political maneuvers executed by Wells at the turn
of the previous century, African American women continuously organized
and shaped liberation leadership, leaving significant imprints on the movements of the 1960s and 1970s.

Black women who uniformly considered themselves "antiracists" but not
necessarily "feminists" nevertheless expanded antiracist women's politics,
community development, democratic power, and radical leadership. Given
the primacy of movements in the formation and articulation of black female
militancy, history plays a central role in contemporary analyses.

In the 1960s, black women participated in the Southern Christian Leadership Council, the Student Nonviolent Coordinating Committee, the Congress on Racial Equality, the Organization of Afro-American Unity, and
the Black Panther Party. Emerging from the black liberation and antiracist
movements that helped to redefine radical action, in the 1970s black wom-
en's organizations such as the Combahee River Collective issued cogent
manifestoes that articulated a revolutionary black feminism.[4]

Reviewing radical and revolutionary politics for contemporary struggles we see legacies alive and changing in the activism of prisoners rights
advocates and environmental organizers. At a time of mass, militant unrest,
through bold confrontations with state authority, black women activists
forged prototypes for late-twentieth-century, and early twenty-first-cen-
tury, black female radicalism.

Of the many branches of black feminism extending from battles for a
liberated African and female existence in America, the most imaginative
and transformative are rooted in black female radicalism. It is impossible
here to offer a comprehensive survey of the ideological diversity or plurality of black feminist activisms or the more subtle differences found even
within radical black feminism. Yet it is essential that we examine the limits

of liberalism or civil rights advocacy, as well as black women's challenges to state power and antiradicalism within conventional feminist and antiracist politics.

The most recognized political activism remains in conventional politics. Despite exclusionary practices set by racism, sexism, and class bias, African American women have made gains in the "public realm" of electoral politics and appointed office; these are the political victories most often seen and celebrated in antiracist feminist politics. The 1992 election of Carol Mosely Braun as the United States' first black woman senator (whose politics often fell short of progressive), and the reelections of Democratic leaders Maxine Waters (who helped to publicize the connections between the Central Intelligence Agency and cocaine trafficking in the Iran-Contra scheme), Cynthia McKinney (active in human rights advocacy in U.S. foreign policy), Corrine Brown, Carrie Meeks, and Eleanor Holmes Norton to the U.S. House of Representatives, stand as key examples of black female progress in electoral political power. Outside of congressional halls, black women also have mobilized the "private realm" of local and religious communities, neighborhood schools, and cultural centers. Directly or indirectly opposing institutional control, and social and state neglect or violence, they have informed American political culture by leaving indelible marks in antiviolence campaigns, resource redistribution for underresourced communities, youth and women's groups, and labor and civil rights activism. Both the highly visible congresswomen and the nearly invisible community activists shape models of political progressivism.

Black women activists and feminists are not uniformly progressive, although they all invariably face marginalization and opposition fueled by white supremacy, corporate capitalism, patriarchy, and homophobia. Radical or revolutionary black feminisms also face resistance from liberal and conservative feminisms and antiracism. Black feminist politics negotiates the "internal" opposition of antiradicalism among feminists and antiracists and the counterfeminism evident among some radicals.

Battling with state power, patriarchal culture, as well as antiradicalism and counterfeminism among progressives, subordinate women have forged a feminist politics through militant antiracist movements. Discomfort with black feminist speech and activism in its most radical expressions—those which confront exploitation tied to militarism, corporate dominance, and neoimperialism stems from and fosters restricted notions of "feminism" and "antiracism." Difficulties in accepting black feminisms on their own terms may stem from not only sexism and racism but a lack of familiarity with critiques of monopoly capitalism and neoliberalism.

Given our economic and ideological diversity, we cannot in good faith posit black women as a class. A homogenized view of women of African descent allows conventional politics to elide historical black militancy. There is no "master" narrative that frames the concerns of all black women and their organizations. The multiplicity of ideologies reveals varying degrees of political efficacy and risk for social change; this diversity is often obscured by the "framing" of feminism in ways that either erase the contributions of radical black women or depict a homogeneous black feminism as an (corrective or rebellious) appendage to either antiracist or feminist struggles.

Resistance has historically challenged and shaped black female praxis across a broad ideological spectrum. Black women's autonomy from the pervasive dominance of neoliberalism and corporate culture, however, opens new avenues for political activism.

## Continuing Crusades

Today, black women's struggles center on related but seemingly diverse issues, such as reproductive rights, environmental racism, childcare and health issues, sexual violence, police brutality, and incarceration. Key intersections along the American political curve of antiracist, feminist activism include community, ideology and identity, revolutionary iconography, state punishment, sexuality, black male patriarchy and profeminism, economic resources, and social and racial justice.

One area for concentrated focus has been the assault on affirmative action and the expansion of the prison industrial complex. Combined, these form a twinned hydra for racial, economic, and gender repression. A resurgent neoconservatism hostile to "racial preferences" in education and employment acquiesces to racial bias in imprisonment and state execution. The state of California, which leads the nation in incarceration, spends more on prisons than on schools. Of the nearly two million incarcerated in U.S. jails, prisons, and detention centers, over 70 percent are people of color. The Washington, D.C.–based Sentencing Project has noted that blacks convicted of committing similar offenses as whites are eight times more likely to be incarcerated.

Black women are increasingly becoming active around human rights abuses tied to policing and imprisonment given the destructive impact official and unofficial policies have on their families and themselves. A few striking examples illustrate the gross inequality and abuse rampant in the prison industry and state policing: the Thirteenth Amendment to the Constitution legalizes slavery for prisoners; anyone convicted of killing a white person is four times more likely to receive the death penalty, particularly if she or he is not white; over 65 percent of juvenile offenders sentenced to death since the reinstitution of the death penalty in 1976 have been either black or Latino.[5] One of the few democratic nations to execute minors and the mentally retarded, the United States has executed more youths than any other country.[6]

Although they are a minority of the prison population, women, particularly women of color, are increasingly facing the punitive powers of the state. In March 1999, the Amnesty International Rights for All campaign issued a report, *Not Part of My Sentence: Violations of the Human Rights of Women in Custody,* documenting the abuses of women in U.S. prisons and jails. By June 1997, there were 138,000 women incarcerated in the United States, triple the number since 1985 and ten times the number of women imprisoned in Spain, England, France, Scotland, Germany, and Italy combined.[7] Most of the women incarcerated in the United States are nonviolent offenders convicted of economic crimes or drug use. Eighty percent are mothers, eighty percent are poor; and the majority are women of color. The less common violent offenses are generally connected to domestic violence. Racial bias in sentencing means that women of color incarcerated for nonviolent and violent crimes will increasingly make up the growing population of incarcerated females. Serving time, this population of caged women finds itself subject to new forms of physical and sexual abuse; and, although the Convention Against Torture, which the United States ratified in 1994, defines rape of women in custody by a correctional officer as torture, the United States government has engaged in virtually no monitoring of the conditions and situations of imprisoned women in respect to human rights violations.[8]

In theory, human rights protections exist for both prisoners and nonprisoners in the United States under the International Covenant on Civil and Political Rights and the international conventions ban on racial discrimination, torture, and ill-treatment. The government, however, places itself above the law. In 1998, the United States continued to exempt itself from international human rights obligations that granted protections to U.S. residents and citizens—rights still not available under U.S. law. Even after ratification of key human rights treaties (generally the state weakens such treaties with reservations), the United States fails to acknowledge human rights law: It refused to ratify the International Children's Rights Convention; opposed human rights initiatives banning landmines, child soldiers; and undermined the International Criminal Court (ICC). At the Rome Diplomatic Conference in July 1999, 120 states voted for and seven, including the United States, against the ICC treaty.[9]

The above are only some of the battles which today's progressive activists face. Conscious of both U.S. domestic and foreign policies, many black women also continue to organize and theorize around other crises and conditions that erode freedom and democratic culture and destroy life. These include racial and homophobic lynchings; the international AIDS epidemic currently devastating parts of Africa and U.S. cities; refugees and regional wars; embargoes crippling Cuba and killing hundreds of thousands of Iraqi children; decolonization struggles in Puerto Rico and Ireland; Palestinian statehood; political prisoners in China and other countries as well as in the United States (which has over one hundred political prisoners, but only one on death row, Mumia Abu-Jamal); the war on drugs; addictions; the international resurgence of neo-Nazis; nuclear waste and toxic dumping; incest, rape, and domestic violence; underweight babies and infant mortality; dire poverty amid the increasing stratification of wealth; and, of course, hypertension and high blood pressure.

### Conclusion

In a culture that greets antiblack and antifemale violence, and the vilification and abuse of black females and their kin with considerable equanimity, many are compelled to act. Some African American women do so with distinct political intent to revolutionize rather than reform existing power structures, hoping to go to the root, to nurture and grow structural change that alleviates and diminishes oppressive conditions. Although for most Americans the recognized public fighters or advocates remain male, the Others, black female organizers, battle as outsiders, at times criminalized as cultural and political outlaws.

In these struggles, activists find that on one hand, the state has the power to extinguish a radical movement; on the other hand, it can modify and absorb that movement into the mainstream, so that it no longer functions as resistance to official policy. Sometimes the most convenient resting place seems to be in apolitical pursuits or politics that fit within conventional frameworks. Some retreat into isolationist politics of their singular, pressing cause, abstracted from other struggles which can provide important tributaries for growth and development. What we expect and demand of ourselves, society, and the state may fall short of our abilities to rethink and effectively counter corporate globalization, the stratification of wealth and poverty, the inhumane routinization of war (whether through bombing or embargo), and the increase of police powers (through the nefarious War on Drugs and President Clinton's 1996 Omnibus Crime Bill).

Despite the institutional force and prevasive presence of state and corporate policies, black feminist activism, like other insurgent action, reveals in its organizing and analyses its own peculiar power. Nowhere is this more evident than in the revolutionary potential of black feminism such as that found among women of Jericho 98, the Black Radical Congress, the prison and death penalty abolitionist movements, of activists who take rest and respite—just not by convenient wells.

> I may be able to speak the languages of men and even of angels,
> but if I have no love, my speech is no more than a noisy gong
>   or a clanging bell
>                                         —1 Corinthians 13:1

## Notes

1. This epigram is an excerpt from an inscription written by Audre Lorde to the author in September 1989 in Lorde's collection of poems *The Black Unicorn* (New York: W.W. Norton, 1978).

2. The Combahee River Collective, "The Combahee River Collective Statement," in Gloria Hull, Patricia Bell Scott, and Barbara Smith, eds. *All the Women Are White, All the Blacks Are Men, But Some of Us Are Brave: Black Women's Studies* (Old Westbury: NY: The Feminist Press, 1982).

3. See: Ida B. Wells, *Crusade for Justice: the Autobiography of Ida B. Wells,* ed. Alfreda M. Duster (Chicago: University of Chicago Press, 1970); Angela Y. Davis, *Angela Davis: An Autobiography* (New York: Random House, 1974); Assata Shakur, *Assata: An Autobiography* (Westport, CT: Lawrence Hill and Company, 1987).

4. For anthologies documenting the emergence of black feminist activism, see: Beverly Guy-Sheftall, ed. *Words of Fire: An Anthology of African-American Feminist Thought* (New York: The New Press, 1995); Toni Cade Bambara, ed. *The Black Woman* (New York: New American Library, 1970); and Barbara Smith, ed. *Homegirls: A Black Feminist Anthology* (New York: Kitchen Table: Women of Color Press, 1983).

5. Ibid., 6.

6. See Sklar, ed., *Torture in the United States,* 5.

7. Amnesty International, *Rights for All, Not Part of My Sentence: Violations of the Human Rights of Women in Custody,* New York: Amnesty International, March 1999, 15–16. Amnesty documents that these European countries combined have a combined population of 150 million women as compared to 120 million women in the United States.

8. The United States was to submit a report on its compliance with the Convention Against Torture in 1995 but no report to date has been released. In response, a coalition of over sixty non-governmental organizations (NGOs) issued a report in October 1998 titled Torture in the United States: The Status of Compliance by the U.S. Government with the International Convention Against Torture and Other Cruel, Inhuman or Degrading Treatment or Punishment. See Morton Sklar, editor, Torture in the United States, Washington, D.C., World Organization Against Torture, October 1998.

The report notes that the major areas of noncompliance in the United States center on: the death penalty, prison conditions and the treatment of refugee detainees; physical and sexual abuse of women in prisons; the return of refugees to situations of torture and persecution and their long-term detention under abusive conditions. Other violations noted in the report are: the United States' failure to extradite or prosecute torturers who worked with the Central Intelligence Agency or were trained at the School of the Americas; the United States' lack of adequate domestic implementation of the 1996 Illegal Immigration and Immigrant Responsibility Act; and arms sales and other assistance by the U.S. government that support torture in foreign countries (such as the sale of electronic stun gun equipment and some 10,000 shock batons to Turkey to be used against the Kurdish minority, the same equipment which Amnesty International has denounced in its use against U.S. prisoners).

9. See: the 1999 Human Rights Watch Report published on the Black-Radical Congress website: "subscribe brc-news" to <majordomo@tao.ca>; archive: http://www.egroups.com/group/brc-news; www.blackradicalcongress.org | BRG | blackradicalcongress@email.com

## Some of Us Did Not Die[1]

*June Jordan*
2002

          Once through the fires of September 11, it's not easy to remember or recognize any power we continue to possess.

Understandably we shrivel and retreat into stricken consequences of that catastrophe.

But we have choices, and capitulation is only one of them.

I am always hoping to do better than to collaborate with whatever or whomever it is that means me no good.

For me, it's a mind game with everything at stake.

For example, what has what kind of savagery blurred or blocked or buried alive?

This is an excerpt from my *Poem To Take Back The Night*:

> What about moonlight
> What about watching for the moon above
> the tops of trees and standing
> still enough to hear the raucous crickets
> chittering invisible beneath the soon lit stones
>
> What about moonlight
> What about moonlight
>
> What about watching for the moon
> through windows low enough to let the screams
> and curses of the street the gunshots
> and the drunken driver screeching tires
> and the boombox big beat and the tinkle
> bell ice cream truck
> inside
>
> What about moonlight
> What about moonlight. . . .

Luckily, there are limitless, new ways to engage our tender and possible responsibilities, obligations that our actual continuing coexistence here, in these United States and here, in our world, require.

For example, as the great Afghan poet, Rumi, has written:

> "Bird song brings relief
> to my longing. . . .
>
> Please, universal soul, practice
> Some song, or something, through me!"

Thank you so much, Barnard's Women Center, and thank you, Barnard College, for your notice and your faith! Thanks for asking me to speak, out loud, about the rough-hewn trajectories of my poet's life.

I am rather late as I try to tell you tonight about my gratitude.

Back in 1975, I wrote:

"To be honest, I expect apocalypse, or I look for and I work for defeat of international evil, indifference, and suffering, only when I am not otherwise stunned by the odds, temporarily paralyzed by the revulsion and grieving despair.

But life itself compels an optimism. It does not seem reasonable that the majority of the peoples of the world should, finally, lose joy, and rational justice, as a global experiment to be pursued and fiercely protected. It seems unreasonable that more than 400 million people, right now, struggle against hunger and starvation, even while there is arable earth aplenty to feed and nourish every one of us. It does not seem reasonable that the color of your skin should curse and condemn all of your days and the days of your children. It seems preposterous that gender, that being a woman, anywhere in the world, should elicit contempt, or fear, or ridicule, and serious deprivation of rights to be, to become, to embrace whatever you choose. . . .

At Barnard, there was one great teacher whom I was privileged to know, Barry Ulanov. And in freshman English I remember two assignments for which I will always feel gratitude. One was a paper that would pull together, I think he said somehow, Alfred North Whitehead's *Aims of Education* and Edith Hamilton's *Mythology*. Many of my classmates became more or less suicidal as they reflected on this task. But I thought, damn, if you can synthesize Whitehead with Greek mythology, then maybe you can bring the Parthenon to Bedford-Stuyvesant, and make it all real."[2]

Back then, I meant to say that Barnard College never gave me the connection between the apparently unrelated worlds of black and white. But that is not quite true: because there was no obvious given connection between Barnard and Bedford Stuyvesant, I had to discover and invent that connection for myself—which is worthy work for anyone, for sure.

And because this/Barnard was the Parthenon, I got to thinking about how some of us choose to remember, and why, and how: why we do not forget.

And I got to thinking about the moral meaning of memory, per se. And what it means to forget, what it means to fail to find and preserve the connection with the dead whose lives you, or I, want or need to honor with our own.

Before Barnard, I didn't even know there was a Parthenon, or a Pantheon—these are ideas at least as much as they are standing, if mostly ruined, remains of human pride and hope and a reaching for impossible, and imperative, accomplishments. So, however belatedly, thank you for that! And thank you for the man who became my husband and the father of my son.

"In between classes and in the middle of campus, I met him on a very cold day. He stood, without shivering, behind a small table on which an anti-McCarthy petition and pages of signatures lay, blowing about. He wore no overcoat, no gloves, no scarf, and I noticed that his cheeks seemed almost bitterly red with the wind. Although that happened some half century ago, I remember that he wore a bright yellow Oxford cloth button-down shirt, open at the neck, and no tie. He explained the petition to me. But I wanted to do something else. I wanted to excuse myself and find him a cup of coffee so he'd keep warm enough to continue standing out there, brave against Senator Joe McCarthy and the witch-hunts that terrorized America. He looked like a hero to me. It really was cold. He really didn't care. He stood there, by himself on purpose. I went away to bring him back a cup of coffee, and, as I recall, that same afternoon I told a couple of my friends that I had met the man I would marry.

That was 1954. He was a twenty-year-old senior at Columbia College. I was eighteen and a sophomore at Barnard College, across the street. It would be hard to say which one of us was younger or more ignorant of the world beyond our books, our NAACP meetings, school parties, ping-pong, running hikes through Van Cortlandt Park, or our exhaustively romantic letter-writing at the rate of two or three letters a day. But he was taller and stronger, and he was white. We were not the same."

And beginning then, inside that interracial, state criminalized relationship, I learned all the way to my knees, the sometimes terrible consequences of difference, the sometimes fatal response of religious, and of political and social systems set against differences among us, differences characterized by those most powerful as deviant, or pathological, or blasphemous, or beneath contempt.

That confrontation with heavyweight intolerance carried me through our Civil Rights Revolution and into our resistance to the War Against Vietnam and then into the realm of gender and sexual and sexuality politics. And those strivings, in aggregate, earned me from Brooklyn to Mississippi, to South Africa, to Nicaragua, to Israel, to Palestine, to Lebanon and to Northern Ireland, and every single one of those embattled baptisms clarified pivotal connections among otherwise apparently disparate victories, or among apparently disparate events of suffering, and loss.

Issues of community control in New York City's public schools plunged me into the complicated facets of self-determination. And, then again, my personal recovery from actual rape catapulted me into difficult questions about resistance as a reluctant attitude for anyone who believes he or she has been violated and debased.

In turn, several intricate problems of resistance have taken me into repeated attempts at overview constructions and analyses of the world-wide absurdity of endangered female existence: I mean, why is that our universal situation? And when will we revolt against our marginalized, pseudo-maverick status and assert our majority, our indispensable-to-the-species' power—and I do mean power: our verifiable ability to change things inside our own lives and in the lives of other folks, as well.

For example, I attended one of the best prep schools for girls in this country. And then I came here to Barnard.

And I did not know, I did not understand, the fantastic privilege such an education implied.

I think I more or less mostly tolerated school because, to me, it was just that, "school." And yet, here, in this new millennium, we are struggling with the consequences of the abysmal fact that education, that basic literacy, in fact, is not god-given, or a sovereign state entitlement. As a matter of fact, education is denied to most female human beings on the planet. And even if you disregard the significance of that for girls and women, you just might, nevertheless, begin to care about the documented correlations between illiterate female populations and the impoverishments, the barbaric hardship of every society maintaining and/or imposing such an unequal, such a literally suffocating status quo.

Before the Taliban took over most of Afghanistan, 90 percent of girls and women were illiterate. After the Taliban, it is virtually 100 percent. Now some of us knew about these deplorable conditions quite a while ago. In my 1993 essay, "I Am Seeking an Attitude," I wrote:

"It took longer than inexcusable indifference for folks inside the United States to even raise an outcry against the documented, systematic, genocidal rape of more than 20,000 mostly Muslim women, and girls, inside the former Yugoslavia.

It is still all quiet on the documented, horrifying fate of women, and girls, inside Afghanistan."

And yet it was years later, and not because our official government cared about the sisters of the Taliban, before USA policies stopped supporting the Taliban.

Indeed, it was American feminists including Jay Leno's wife, who agitated for censure of horrible Taliban practices. And, nevertheless, as recently as four months ago, George W. Bush gave the Taliban 43 million dollars. Why? To cajole Taliban cooperation with our War Against Drugs—Clearly a war way more important than a war against the maiming and annihilation of Afghan women.

I have evolved from an observer to a victim to an activist passionately formulating methods of resistance against tyranny of any kind.

And most important, I think, is this: I have faced my own culpability, my own absolute dirty hands, so to speak, in the continuation of injustice and powerful intolerance.

I am discovering my own shameful functions as part of the problem, at least. I no longer think "They" are this or that, but rather, "We" or "I" am not doing enough, for instance, or "I" have not done my homework, and so on.

Here is one poem from my Kosovo Suite:

### April 10, 1999

The enemies proliferate
by air
by land
they bomb the cities
they burn the earth
they force the families into miles and miles of violent exile

30 or 40 or 81,000 refugees
just before this
check-point
or who knows where
they disappear

the woman cannot find her brother
the man cannot recall the point of all
 the papers somebody took

away from him
the rains fail to purify the river
the darkness does not slow the trembling
 message of the tanks
Hundreds of houses on fire and still
 the enemies seek and find
 the enemies

only the ones without water
only the ones without bread
only the ones without guns

There is international TV
There is no news

The enemies proliferate
The homeless multiply
And I
I watch I wait.

I am already far
and away
too late

too late

And as I have wrestled with my own violence, my own instincts to strike back, to strike out and smash what hurts me, or my people, or my country, or my ideal aspirations for my beloved America I have written in part:

"the bombing
began and did not terminate for 42 days
and 42 nights relentless minute after minute
more than 110,000 times
we bombed Iraq we bombed Baghdad
we bombed Basra/we bombed military
installations we bombed the National Museum
we bombed schools we bombed air raid
shelters we bombed water we bombed
electricity we bombed hospitals we
bombed everything that moved/ we
bombed everything that did not move we
bombed Baghdad
a city of 5.5 million human beings"

And then, getting strictly personal, and strictly political, at the same time, I wrote *Soldier*, the story of my childhood:

"Maybe I should have been born a boy. I think I dumbfounded my father. Whatever his plans and his hopes for me, he must have noticed now and again that I, his only child, was in fact a little girl modeling pastel sunbonnets color-coordinated with puffy-sleeved dresses that had to accommodate just-in-case cotton handkerchiefs pinned to them.

I'm not sure.

Regardless of any particulars about me, he was convinced that a "Negro" parent had to produce a child who could become a virtual whiteman and therefore possess dignity and power.

Probably it seemed easier to change me than to change the meaning and complexion of power.

At any rate, he determined he'd transform me, his daughter, into something better, something more likely to succeed.

He taught me everything from the perspective of a recruiting warrior. There was a war on against colored people, against poor people. I had to become a soldier who would rise through the ranks and emerge a commander of men rather than an infantry pawn.

I would become that sturdy, brilliant soldier, or he would, well, beat me to death."

And sometimes, I suspect, whenever any of us feel defeated we may think maybe everybody should have been born a boy. Maybe everybody should have been capable of the awesome and inspiring heroism of our firefighters, and our police, who sought only to retrieve and rescue the living and the wounded from the infamy of September 11.

Maybe we should all of us be that strong that way.

Maybe that would be easier, all around.

But there is also the humble love of Ruth and Naomi I will place right next to the derring- do of David's love for Jonathan.

There is the bravery of the Women In Black who for more than a decade hold public, silent vigils to end the illegal Israeli occupation of Palestinian territory.

There are the ridiculed pink-beribboned people against violence in the bedroom, the kitchen, the streets, and in our domestic and foreign priorities. There is the bravery of women against the valorization of violence and force rather than the valorization of a negotiating wish and commitment to make merciful and just our coexistence with really different people trying, always, to fully and freely live on this one earth.

So, actually, I am ok with being a girl, and becoming a woman.

I am fighting breast cancer, and it's not a readily visible contest but you know, it's mine, and it's also the fight that a stupendous number of other women have no choice about.

### Ode #2 Written During Chemotherapy at UCSF
### or
### Ode to I'd Really Rather Be Sailing

Or failing to dive fast enough so fish
Marvel at the rapidity of my descent into the sea
So deep even sperm whales move on sound
So dark even what's electrical will not ignite into a luminous event

Oh, I'd rather be flying
Or lying beside somebody lift
My lips to lips
Averse to words
Lips articulate as colorings of an eye
About to blink me just beyond just lust
I'd rather be no answer
Or no cancer always stuck inside gray company
Of frail and bald and sagging melodrama
Intro-venous drips and problematic pokings in my veins
And daily pills that kill acuity of consciousness
And stats that say, "That's it! That's that!"

Oh, no lie!
I'd really rather be somebody's
Sweet potato pie!

In 1999, I published an essay, "Are You Hunting For Jews?"

"'You're looking for me.'
   With those four, casual words, Aryan Nation member Buford O. Furrow Jr. presented himself to the FBI in Las Vegas, August 11, 1999.
   One day earlier, Furrow was hunting for Jews. He wanted to kill Jews. He wanted America to wake up. He thought that killing Jews would help to interrupt a dangerous national sleep during which 'the spawn of the devil'—Jews, blacks, homosexuals—have gained something or other powerful and good at the expense of Christian white people. . . .

And then, a few weeks later, I heard an Auschwitz survivor, Elly Gross, in an interview with Laura Flanders on Pacifica Radio.
   Elly Gross is part of a class action suit seeking compensation for the slave labor forced upon her, and thousands of other Jews, in 1944.
   What struck me to my soul was her spontaneous, on-air declaration. She said: 'I guess it was my destiny to live.'
   She meant that her life hopes to honor the memory of her mother and her five-year-old brother who were waved to the left—to their death—by a

white-gloved Nazi officer, June 2, 1944, while she was waved to the right, first to Auschwitz, and then to the slave labor at Fallersleben.

She meant that to live is not just a given: To live means you owe something big to those whose lives are taken away from them."

And two things happened for me: I realized that regardless of the tragedy, regardless of the grief, regardless of the monstrous challenge, Some of Us Have Not Died.

Some of us did NOT die, for example, on September 11th. This is what Elly Gross meant by "I guess it was my destiny to live."

And I come among you, here, humbled by that attack against the World Trade Center, September 11, that atrocity against so many thousands of men and women, from more than 50 countries around the world and as I listen to and as I watch various New York City survivors express their rage and their terrified, seared consciousness, and their inconsolable longing for loved ones lost, and their sense of safety lost—may I just repeat this idea that, as Elly Gross said, I guess it was your destiny to live.

Indeed some of us did not die.

Some of you, some of us remain, despite that hatred that violence that murder that suicide that affront to our notions of civilized days and nights.

And what shall we do, we who did not die?

What shall we do now? How shall we grieve, and cry out loud, and face down despair? Is there an honorable nonviolent means towards mourning and remembering who and what we loved?

Is there an honorable means to pursue and capture the perpetrators of that atrocity without ourselves becoming terrorists?

I don't know the answer to that.

But I do believe that fundamentalist anything bodes ill for the irreducible diversity of our species.

I do believe that fundamentalist conflict burns at the core of our international fratricide.

I do believe we cannot even aspire towards safety without respectful reckoning with completely different, religious, world views, embraced by most of humanity.

This will take study, and time.

And even as I study and I respect and I beg others to continue to do likewise, it seems clear to me that only inside a *secular* political state can we harbor and cherish diverse religions, as well as other moral systems, and practices.

Religious belief must stay separated from political power because, otherwise, the secular human potential of democracy itself will be compromised, or snuffed out, entirely. The humane *secular* potential of democracy rests upon the conviction that just because you exist you—male/female/ Jew/Gentile/Muslim/poor/rich/smart/beautiful/lazy/scientific/artistic/gay/ straight/bisexual/ Republican—you are equal under the law and it is the law which reigns as the supreme organizing governance of our experiment, our United States. That is the humane secular basis for a democratic state.

And so I hope we can bestir ourselves not to "Rally Around Caesar," as the recent *Economist* recommends. I hope we will bestir ourselves to rally around an emergency/militant reconstruction of a secular democracy consecrated to the equality of each and every living one of us.

Some of Us Did Not Die
We're Still Here
I Guess It Was Our Destiny To Live
So Let's get on with it!

**Scenario Revision #1**

Or
suppose that gorgeous
wings spread
speckled
hawk
begins to glide
above my body lying
down
like dead meat
maybe start to rot
a little bit
not moving
see
just flat
just limp
but hot
not moving
see
him circle closer
closing closer
for the kill
until
he makes that dive

to savage
me
and inches
from the blood flood lusty
beak
I roll away
I speak
I laugh out loud

Not yet
big bird of prey
not yet

## Notes

1. Adapted from a keynote presentation at Barnard College, 11/9/01.
2. *Notes of A Barnard Dropout*, 1975. From *Civil Wars*.

# Racialized
## Gender/Gendered Racism
### Reflections on Black Feminist
### Human Rights Theorizing

*Stanlie M. James*

2002

       This paper represents the beginning of a process of thinking about and clarifying the ways in which U.S. Black Feminist perspectives might serve to enhance our understanding of the complexities inherent in the formulation of more comprehensive conceptualizations of international human rights. It is a product of my belief that Black Feminism specifically, but other feminists representing a diversity of standpoints and perspectives, can and do contribute new dimensions to the expansive processes of human rights development.

       Because I consider familiarity with international law as fundamental, not only to this specific project, but to our understanding of how human rights has and will continue to evolve into the twenty-first century, it is important to provide a brief overview of these two interrelated areas. International law evolved as a set of rules that were intended to regulate relations among states. Constructed within a "public" world that is distinct from domestic law, the focus of international law has been the relationship between sovereign states while the states' treatment of individuals residing within their own boundaries was considered to be a "private" matter beyond the jurisdiction of relationships between states.

       Horrified by the legal mistreatment of Jews, gypsies, and homosexuals in Nazi Germany, contemporary human rights rose as a collective international attempt to address the devastating realities of our inhumanity towards each other during World War II. It is the branch of international law that refers to a wide range of legal and/or moral values (the is and the ought of human activities) that would limit the power of the state while at the same time prescribing its responsibilities to individuals within its jurisdiction. Conceived as fundamental, as opposed to nonessential, human rights are quintessentially general or universal in character, so that in theory they should be extended to every person regardless of merit and without discrimination.

Early on, the position of civil and political rights was privileged in international human rights law. The underlying principle of these rights (which included the right to life, the right to vote and hold office, freedom of thought, conscience and religion, the right to peaceful assembly, and freedom of association) was the view that laws are principally a means of regulating state intervention in private life, with an emphasis on constraints of power rather than an affirmative duty to ensure rights. Thus, international law in general and, more specifically, human rights laws, were slow to address questions concerning liability of states in relation to the acts of private individuals or groups that cause damage to other individuals, groups, or the state.

Since 1948 human rights law has undergone, and continues to undergo, an evolutionary process of reevaluation and reformulation through the development of international conventions (or treaties). The claims of discrimination and oppression by individuals and groups are slowly attaining recognition as appropriate subjects for international law through this evolutionary process. Thus the individual is, in a sense, gaining standing in international law. Such recognition contributes to the task of redefining public/private distinctions at the international level.

Individuals and groups situated at the margins of society have challenged and continue to challenge international human rights theorists and advocates to recognize and respond to more and different kinds of discrimination and oppressions that may have been either fostered by, or ignored by, specific states or the dominant groups that control the states. In this regard, international feminists are to be applauded for their early endeavors to challenge human rights theorists, not only to recognize gender-based oppression that has marginalized women in their own societies, but to reconceptualize human rights in a manner that more fully acknowledges and incorporates the rights of women into new formulations of international human rights. This has been most apparent in their endeavors to reconceptualize international norms around the subject of family and, more recently, violence against women.

Traditionally, the state was called upon to protect the institution of the family with an emphasis on privacy rights. However, feminists argued that the notion of a sphere of private life which is protected from direct state intervention is extremely problematic because the family is the very site of many of the most egregious violations of women's physical and mental integrity. Thus, the blanket deference to the institution of the family and privacy rights within the family often has disastrous consequences for women. When private violations of women within the family were propagated the traditional distinctions between public and private life at both the domestic and international levels were challenged in a manner that eventually resulted in the creation of the omnibus Convention on the Elimination of all Forms of Discrimination Against Women (CEDAW).

Efforts by the international community to address the contentious problem of racial discrimination, most specifically through the Convention on the Elimination of all Forms of Racial Discrimination (CERD), has likewise been critical to those endeavors that seek to foster the development of just societies.

CEDAW and CERD (and the Convention on the Child as well), are part of a mutually reinforcing set of instruments designed to more fully develop the principles of human rights mentioned in the foundational international human rights documents the UN Charter and the Universal Declaration of Human Rights. Thus, explicit references to the principle of non-discrimination found in the Charter and the Declaration, are reiterated in both conventions. In Article 1, CEDAW defines discrimination against women as "any distinction, exclusion, or restriction made on the basis of sex which has the effect or the purpose of impairing or nullifying the recognition, enjoyment, or exercise by women, irrespective of their marital status, on a basis of equality of men and women of human rights and fundamental freedoms in the political, economic, social, cultural, civil or any other field."

Likewise Article 1 of CERD defines the term "racial discrimination" as "any distinction, exclusion, restriction or preference based on race, color, descent, or national or ethnic origin which has the purpose or effect of nullifying or impairing the recognition, enjoyment, or exercise, on an equal footing, of human rights and fundamental freedoms in the political, economic social, cultural or any other field of public life."

While antiracist advocates and feminists have had a positive impact on the development of international human rights law, as evidenced by these two Conventions, both instruments were conceptually compartmentalized in a manner that failed to articulate even the possibility of a relationship between the two. Rather both instruments seem to treat their respective areas as if they were discrete subjects. Thus CEDAW's intent to achieve comprehensiveness is compromised by an underlying assumption that all women experience gender discrimination in much the same fashion. Such an essentialist perspective fails to capture the complexity of women's identity that incorporates a variety of characteristics, including (but not limited to): ethnicity, religion, class, and sexuality. For purposes of this paper, I am particularly intrigued by CEDAW's failure to explore the impact that racist domination, discrimination, and exploitation has had on the lives of women within the context of their specific societies.

CERD, in the interest of equity, must also be critiqued for its failure to articulate a gendered understanding of race and racism. (I am using the term gendered here to refer to the processes, systems, and institutions etc. within a given society that reinforce the socially constructed roles ascribed to the different biological sexes.)

While CEDAW and CERD are to be commended for their pioneering efforts to clarify the definition of discrimination in a manner that incorporates nonintentional and international acts, as well as acts by state and non-state actors,[1] neither convention fully explores the multifaceted, interrelated nature of discrimination and oppression. Both conventions are limited by essentialized conceptualizations of gender and race that fail to examine the intersection of race and gender, nor does either convention question how the combined effects of these two aspects of identity might shape the nature and consequences of the particular experiences of women of color. Thus, both fail to fully exploit opportunities to enhance our understanding of the ramification of either racialized gender discrimination or gendered racial discrimination.

Clearly, racial discrimination does not always affect men and women in the same way. Indeed, as the International Human Rights Law Group notes, there are circumstances in which women suffer racial discrimination of a different kind or degree than men, or ways in which racial discrimination may only affect women. If women are essentialized in a manner that fails to account for the diversity of their experiences, then the particular consequences that may arise from women's differentiation by race may escape notice. The Law Group warns us that such discrimination often escapes detection because the monitoring of women's enjoyment of rights is not systematic and focused.[2]

Compelled to address the simultaneity of discrimination and oppression constructed around race and gender, Black Feminists and other racialized women in the U.S. and other parts of the world, unlike many of their White middle-class western feminists or male antiracists counterparts, are engaged in the critical processes of analyzing gender through the prism of race, while simultaneously viewing race and racism through the refraction of gender. Indeed they have also been compelled to grapple with the impact of other issues on their lives including class, sexuality, ethnicity, and religion.

Constructed within a particular social and economic context, U.S. Black Feminisms are indicative of a long tradition of oppositional agency to our encounters with a variety of oppressions at various points in our history, including enslavement and emancipation, historical and contemporary segregation, affirmative action, poverty and both inter- and intra-racial patriarchy. Thus, U.S. Black Feminisms are an assertion that despite their lowly status in society, Black women are indeed worthy of liberation. Such liberation would emerge from the critical characteristics of Black Feminisms including an emphasis on developing nuanced analyses of the multiplicity, simultaneity, and complexity of discrimination and oppression; acknowledgment of its similarities to and differences from feminist, antiracist, and other liberatory struggles; a commitment to forging communities of resistance dedicated to ensuring the equitable distribution of social, political, and economic resources; and a willingness to transgress boundaries to forge strategic alliances with other groups experiencing similar forms of discrimination and yearnings for liberation.

Although these brief remarks are of necessity limited to U.S. Black Feminist perspectives, it is important to acknowledge that such perspectives are not monolithic. Indeed there is a wide range of opinions among U.S. Black Feminists that have sparked lively, intense, and prolonged discussions among scholars and activists. Likewise, other U.S. women of color, including Chicana, Asian American, and Native American Indian feminists as well as women of color in other parts of the world are also engaged in critical efforts to reconceptualize and reformulate human rights in ways that are more reflective of their realities.

It seems highly likely that Black Feminist perspectives (as well as the perspectives of other women of color) have the potential to inform ongoing efforts to expand international human rights law in a manner that is sensitive to the nuances and complexities of multiple oppressions in at least three ways. First, they would challenge what Romany refers to as the "feminist essentialist impulse" through exposing the deficiencies of a "generic woman" as the subject of international legislation. Second, their gendered perspective would contribute to a less androcentric and thus a more profound understanding of the multifaceted nature of racism. Finally, they could inform efforts to reconceptualize distinctions between public and private, thus influencing the kinds of things that could constitute legitimate concerns within human rights formulations.

Vasuki Nesiah has observed that "the absence of women of color [in these discussions] conveys a loaded presence." She argues that women are often essentialized when differences are understood only through the lens of gender and not complicated by the mediation of other structures. Thus, asserting the primacy and sufficiency of gendered ideologies and institutional arrangements to explain oppression leads to the construction of woman as a generic transnational identity. Nesiah notes that such essentialism often results in defining women, especially those designated as "Third World" (or minority), as victims of oppression, a status that, I would argue, has often served to obscure any agency they might be deploying. Nesiah goes on to point out that feminists simply cannot invoke women without speaking to the specific politics and conditions of struggle through which women are socially constructed and against which women are socially situated. To complicate our understanding of the ways women negotiate gender, it is critical that we not only identify the similarities of the oppressions that we confront globally, but that we carefully examine the lives of women who are situated along such axes as race, class, and sexuality then analyze the simultaneity of the multiple oppressions they experience and struggle against.

Examples of how U.S. Black Feminist perspectives might broaden our understanding of human rights violations are in order here. Defined as "the identification of potential criminal suspects on the basis of skin color or accent,"[3] the contentious issue of "racial profiling" has recently captured the U.S. public attention. A report issued by the Leadership Conference on Civil Rights entitled *Justice on Trial: Racial Disparities in the American Criminal Justice System* states that:

> Practices like racial profiling . . . proceed in large part from the twin misperceptions that 1) Blacks and Hispanics commit most crimes and 2) most Blacks and Hispanics commit crimes—misperceptions that have justified everything from pretextual traffic stops to the entirely unjustified beatings and abuse of innocent individuals (i.e., Rodney King, Ahmadu Diallo and Patrick Desmond are the most visible examples of this kind of mistreatment). . . . [Profiling] and police misconduct contribute to the beliefs shared, to one degree or another, by Americans of all races and ethnicities that the police do not treat Black and Hispanic Americans in the same manner as they do White Americans, and the promise of fair treatment enshrined in the Constitution has limited application when police confront a Black or Brown face.[4]

While racial profiling of any sort has very serious ramifications, the assumption seems to be that men are most affected by racial profiling primarily because the emphasis has frequently focused on the "driving while Black" aspect of this particular phenomenon. However, another aspect of racial profiling that has received much less media attention is a belief among law enforcement officials that most international drug couriers are Black females. Thus, Black female citizens in the United States were "nine times more likely to be subjected to x-ray searches by U.S. Customs Officials than White female U.S. citizens [even] though Black women were less than half as likely to be found carrying contraband as *White* females."[5]

In addition to the driving while Black and the Black female as drug courier aspects of racial profiling, the report also documented the devastating impact of unequal sentencing patterns. The data not only reflect the deeply entrenched racism of United States society, but support the notion that the differentiation of women by race also has particular consequences both individually and for the community.

Despite the fact that overall drug usage among Blacks is less than White usage and declining, more Blacks are arrested than Whites for drug use. "Nationwide, Black males convicted of drug felonies in state courts are sentenced to prison 52 percent of the time, while White males are sentenced to prison only 34 percent of the time. Forty-one percent of Black female felony drug offenders are sentenced to prison as compared to 24 percent of White females."[6]

The massive incarceration of Black and Hispanic males in the United States has a destabilizing impact on their communities. While it contributes to a skewed male-female ratio, it often leaves women alone to raise their children. Because women are more vulnerable to poverty, children raised by their mothers alone are more likely to experience impoverished childhoods.

While the literature and the popular media refer to this phenomenon as "the feminization of poverty," Athena Mutua has taken issue with this construction. Mutua argues that the feminization of poverty phrase should be retired because "it fails to adequately capture the dynamics at work in the creation and maintenance of people, both women and men, in poverty." It along with the notion of "gendered poverty" fails to explicate the fact that even where women are not poorer than men they tend to be more vulnerable to poverty than men. Neither concept problematizes the intersections of race, citizenship and other status which may either be affected by or have a profound impact on, various economic processes.[7]

Mutua observes that the poverty of U.S. women of color can be attributed not only to gender inequalities and subordination but also arises as much or more from other subordinations based on class, national origin, race, etc. She concludes that while gender mediates (shapes and structures) poverty, the other existing interlocking subordinating practices and policies exacerbate or aid in maintaining women of color in poverty. Thus there is a substantial added disadvantage to being not only Black but also female in the U.S., a gendered "Black tax" as it were.

Just as gender and race have an impact upon poverty, race and gender are also crucial to an understanding of issues around women's imprisonment. The Justice on Trial report found that "Black women are incarcerated at a rate seven times greater than White women. Further the 417 percent increase in their incarceration rates between 1980–1995 is greater even than the increase for Black men. Three-fourths of the women in prison were mothers, and two-thirds had children under 18 years of age. More women in prison therefore means fewer mothers caring for their children, a trend that further exacerbates the deterioration of the minority communities and family structure." It would be appropriate to assume that the imprisonment of women may have an even more profound impact on the community than when men are imprisoned. Although it is beyond the scope of this paper at this time, such an assumption certainly warrants further investigation.

The international human rights community is currently grappling with the critical issue of violence against women that has focused on the ways in which women's experiences of war and as political prisoners often vary from men's as well as the ways in which women are subjected to violence in the home. This particular issue strikes at the very heart of the traditional dichotomy between public and private because it escorts what had been previously characterized as critical aspects of privacy and therefore beyond the scope of international law into the public domain.

While supportive of efforts to address this problem, Black Feminists are critical of analyses that fail to adequately incorporate recognition of the race of the victim and the perpetrator. The issue of the rape of Black women has a long history and is a complicated case in point. Very briefly, enslavement for Black women incorporated the added dimension of vulnerability to rape without access to legal protection. Indeed, there were no laws against assaulting one's own property. Even after emancipation and well into the twentieth century Black women were vulnerable to rape by both White and Black men, but because they were perceived as lacking in virtue and animalistic, they were unable to utilize the courts for relief from the violations of their rights to bodily integrity. Because of the deeply entrenched racism within the legal system, a system that assumed that Black women were unrapeable, they were often reluctant to subject themselves or their Black assailants to the degrading experience of court, especially since the results were not likely to be positive. Thus, in different ways throughout American history both White and Black men have appropriated the bodies of Black women without their permission and Black women were unable to find either protection from or punishment of, their assailants through legal avenues.

We are reminded by Neil Stammers that human rights are socially constructed so that the ideas and practices of human rights are created and recreated by human actors in particular social historical settings and conditions. Often these actors come together in social movements seeking "to make power visible" through challenging the relations and structures of power. Their task is to develop legitimate alternatives, values, norms, and lifestyles that would validate the perspective and identities of those who are oppressed by particular relations and structures of power. Celina Romany notes that both domestic law and international law reflect power differentials that would require us to extricate and examine those devices deployed for the inclusion and exclusion of various groups, while also exposing entrenched systems of domination and subordination.

As we commemorate the 35th anniversary of the Convention on Race it is appropriate to pause and recognize its importance as a pivotal political document in contemporary human rights history. It is equally as critical to acknowledge that it is a "living document." CERD, CEDAW, and the other human rights instruments were receptive to input from a plethora of sources including governments, NGOs, and human rights lawyers, and activists. While the original strategy of disaggregating race and gender discrimination may have been appropriate within their respective historical contexts, non-essentialist, feminist, and antiracist conceptualizations of women as a multidimensional category will advance more nuanced and complicated analyses of oppression at the multiple intersection of identities. This may, in turn, prove to be more effective in struggles to eradicate discrimination and exploitation. Thus, a Black Feminist perspective in concert with the perspectives of other women of color has the potential to provide another creative avenue for meeting the challenge found in the United Nations Charter to "promote and encourage universal respect for, and observance of, human rights and fundamental freedoms of all, without distinction as to race, sex, language, or religion." Certainly those perspectives could help foster more integrated and coherent strategies to expand human rights in the twenty-first century.

## Notes

1. International Human Rights Law Group. www.hrlawgroup.org/ site/~programs .html.

2. Ibid.

3. Leadership Conference on Civil Rights. Leadership Conference on Education Fund. *Justice on Trial: Racial disparities in the American Criminal Justice System*, 1.

4. Ibid.: 10–11.

5. Ibid.: 6–7.

6. Ibid.: 25.

7. Athena Mutua. "Why Retire the Feminization of Poverty Construct." *Denver University Law Review* 78: 2001.

## "Con-di-fi-cation"
Black Women, Leadership,
and Political Power[1]

*Carole Boyce Davies*

2007

Every colonized person who today accepts a governmental post must know clearly that he will sooner or later be called upon to sponsor a policy of repression, of massacres, of collective murders in one of the regions of . . . the [French] empire (Fanon 1958: 118).

The exigencies of projecting U.S. power, conditioned by the ever-present rhetoric of the threat of terrorism, but not determined by it, transcends party and racial affiliations and ensures that those black Americans—and for that matter other people of color and women—who rise to positions of strategic foreign policy construction will substantially represent state interests above all others (Lusane 2006: 197).

### Introduction

What happens when members of a subordinated group rise to power within an oppressive system? Who do these people end up representing? How does a black American woman manage the internal/domestic histories while understanding her location in diaspora and transnational spaces? What happens when a member of a subordinated group now ends up being the face of empire? How do class, status, and political affiliation affect the nature of one's participation in the political and intellectual process? How do we begin to subject the rise of black women to leadership positions to the kind of internal critique that is fair and necessary?

This article responds to these questions by examining the meaning of Condoleezza Rice, a black woman secretary of state of the U.S. (2005 to 2009), and therefore the international spokesperson for contemporary American imperialism.

The rise of black women to various positions in state power between 2005 and 2006 is one of the historical contexts in which Condoleezza Rice can also be placed. In many ways, it reflects decades of feminist activity that challenged the logic that leadership is always and only male. With Ellen Johnson-Sirleaf, the new president of Liberia; Portia Simpson Miller, Prime Minister of Jamaica; and Michaelle Jean, recently appointed Governor General of Canada, we have the beginnings for an analysis of their contributions and failings once they access political power. Earlier, Valerie Amos in London became Baroness Amos, appointed by the Blair government to a ceremonial position and title in the House of Lords. What is different, perhaps, is that Condoleezza Rice has risen to power in the belly of U.S. imperialism; and in order to be successful, she seems to have to work towards being the most efficient articulator of its machinations.

A brief comparison with other black women who have sought to make similar moves toward the centre of U.S. state power is worth considering. The variety of congresswomen of integrity and recognition such as Barbara Jordan of Texas (who distinguished herself during the Watergate hearings) and Barbara Lee of California (the only congresswoman to vote against the war) provide a different model. Rice has indicated in most interviews that she would never run for the office of president, preferring instead the kind of appointments she has had.

Perhaps more significant to this discussion is the former congresswoman from Brooklyn, Shirley Chisholm, who, in 1972, became the first African American and the first woman to run for the U.S. presidency. While she may be forgotten or unknown by a new generation, her example is worth recalling at least to provide some balance to the type of black woman like Rice who now serves as the media-driven black political role-model of choice. Congresswoman Chisholm, a member of the Brooklyn Caribbean diaspora community, campaigned with the slogan "unbought and unbossed," offering a political position of integrity, claiming to navigate power on her terms, actually being the person who ran for that same office Condoleezza now helps to keep alive—and without having to go down on her knees to powerful white men.

Based on a presence and politics that is the opposite of Chisholm, "bought and bossed" is one way of seeing Rice, given the range of benefits she has accrued on various boards of multinational corporations as she rose to this position. With a politics aligned with representing the interests of U.S. imperialism and multinational corporations, Rice has served the interests of big business, has been on the boards of directors of Chevron, TransAmerica Corporation, Hewlett Packard, J.P. Morgan, and Charles Schwab. Antonia Felix reports:

> Condi joined the Board of Directors of Chevron Corporation, a multinational with oil operations in 25 countries, immediately upon return-

ing to Stanford in 1991. Her expertise on the states that made up the former Soviet Union made her a valuable asset for Chevron's oil interests in Kazakhstan. She worked extensively on those deals, including their plan to help build the pipeline from the Tengiz oil field across southern Russia to a Russian port on the Black Sea. Like her Hoover Institution colleague, George Schultz, who served as a director of Chevron before she arrived at the company, Condi supplemented her Stanford income with fees from Chevron that included a $35,000-per-year retainer and $1,500 for each board and committee meeting attended. By her tenth year with the company, she held over 3,000 shares at Chevron, stock worth $241,000. Also like Schultz, she had a supertanker named after her—the 136,000-deadweight-ton SS *Condoleezza Rice*. (2005: 256–257).[2]

Often the only woman in the company of the world's most powerful men, with a Chevron tanker named after her, the SS *Condoleezza Rice*, her status as handmaiden to multinational corporations has been already metaphorically identified. By these means then, her name is no longer private property, and can also be moved from its personal to its corporate identification, as have the names of Oprah Winfrey and Martha Stewart.

But even more salient is the unabated loyalty she gives to one of the already-acknowledged worst presidents in U.S. history. While this is an analysis that has to be carefully nuanced, the fact is that all biographical coverage defines Condoleezza as perhaps the most loyal of supporters of the president. Because she is also now noted for her ability to offer a quick and professional articulation of the most inane Bush policy position, she is also now identified as the major ventriloquiser for U.S. imperialism.

### Ventriloquising Imperialism

Clarence Lusane offers a very detailed reading of the foreign policy operations of Rice and Powell in his *Colin Powell and Condoleezza Rice: Foreign Policy, Race and the New American Century*. He sees them as willing actors:

> That Powell and Rice committed themselves to an administration that let blind ideological rigidity override competence, fairness, tolerance, and restraint, says much. More than innocent bystanders or dupes, both are implicated in Bush's failed presidency as part of the insider team and council that created and implemented his vision and agenda. Neither, to this day, has disavowed the Bush domestic and international doctrine of hegemony and power politics at the expense of domestic progress and global cooperation and development (2006: 187).

It is this process of black ventriloquising of imperialism which deserves its own language by which we can chart this and future actions that follow this pattern. "Condification" defines the process of the conservative black and/or female subject in power and working publicly against the larger interests of the groups to which s/he belongs. It therefore refers to a particular agent of a form of neo-colonialism, one very specific to U.S. internal colonial dynamics and history. By these means, "condification" defines what happens when a black person, woman, or Latino enters these same power structures and never or rarely identifies with their originating group's interests, even when this is the status quo for white masculinity (i.e., representing its interests). "Condification" demands that one forgets one's group interests and instead works to ensure its continued dominance. "Condification" also offers a language to identify the process of intellectuals (in this instance, the black female intellectual) from oppressed groups, who enter the seats of power and then use their knowledge with calmness for the benefit of oppression—in this case, American imperialism. The term *condification* is beautifully already prepared by the subject's name that now lends itself to this definition. Thus, "cond-i-fi-cation" carries within it the "con" of conservatism; the "con" of being conned, along with the resonance of commodification, in the sense of being bought and/or sold for a particular interest. It also suggests the Fanonian self-alienating psychology of "conditioning" and "confusion" that is the ultimate product of racism, as it is colonialism,[3] that is, being conditioned to work in the interest of a repressive state and against one's own larger interest.

Being "condified", then, refers to the public positioning of oppressive black conservatism and the normalising of the same while supporting amazingly offensive policies and politics, and masquerading them when convenient under a black umbrella. Being "condified" means being treated to a public "sweetness" or politeness, which functions as a camouflage for more insidious policies. Being "condified" ultimately means being extremely colonised or subjected to "condification."

At the start of her appointment, the tendency was to see the former national security advisor (2001–2005) and current U.S. secretary of state, Condoleezza Rice, as someone to be admired for occupying such a central position—and therefore a role model for young black women, someone that they could emulate. There are in fact reports that among women in a variety of African countries, she is also seen as a type of ideal black woman, one who has made it to the top of U.S. state power by whatever means and that achievement itself was to be admired. This rise to power began in 2000 when, following a highly contested national election, President Bush was selected as president of the U.S. He created perhaps the most ethnically diverse cabinet in history when he appointed two African Americans and one Latino to key positions. Following the foreign policy debacle of, from all accounts, the pre-planned execution of the invasion of and War on Iraq (erroneously using the 9–11 terrorist actions on the U.S. as pretext), and with the Bush administration on the wane, these perceptions now seem rather different.[4] Indeed, in the wake of the treatment of New Orleans after Hurricane Katrina, the view is quite the opposite among black youth and adults: pride at her accomplishments,[5] dismay at the absence of any benefits to black Americans.

Sylvia Wynter's take on Condoleezza Rice is instructive. Seeing her up close at Stanford, she describes Rice as "a black Margaret Thatcher," not just for her manifestation of Thatcher's trademark rigidity but also for showing the tendency of some lower-middle class individuals (such as Thatcher was) to seek to escape their origins by all means.[6] Stuart Hall's definition of "Thatcherism" is appropriately invoked here, given that in much the same way, "condification" has become the public presentation in the body of a woman (in this case, a black woman) of a range of policies that dismantle long and hard-fought-for rights, while defending this process with an amazing level of aggression. Hall defines "Thatcherism" as follows:

> Thatcherism's project can be understood as operating on the ground of longer, deeper, more profound movements of change which appear to be going its way but which, in reality, it has been only occasionally and fleetingly, in command over the past decade. We can see Thatcherism as, in fact, an attempt to hegemonize these deeper tendencies within its project of "regressive modernization," to appropriate them to a reactionary political agenda and to harness to them the interests and fortunes of specific and limited social interests (1996: 224).

If Thatcherism is for Hall an attempt only partially successful in the task of "harness[ing] and bend[ing] to its political project circumstances which were not of its making" (1996: 224), then "condification" and "being condied" also involves being subjected to a certain maintenance of dominance under a cover of "sweetness", as in "con-dol-cee-za"—the original meaning of the name as given by her mother from the musical notation "with sweetness". Thus, cordiality and super-professionalism conveniently camouflage an appropriation of political movements as they simultaneously reject their larger historical implications.

"Condification" marks the limit, in my view, but can also be seen as the ultimate manifestation of a domestic black and/or feminist bourgeois discourse of women or black people's access to power—thus having equal opportunity to oppress. At the same time, it becomes an affront to black feminist positions as expressed in their earliest and therefore most radical formations.[7]

The intent here is not to make "condification" an ideology or an "ism" (a body of thought or ideology that percolates through the implementation of policies and the articulation of a particular set of ideological principles). Instead, I want to present "condification" as a tendency, a project perhaps, a behavioural process that marks the rise of a certain neocolonial elite in the U.S. imperial context, operating for the benefit of the dominant state and its rulers.

Aime Cesaire describes U.S. imperialism as the only imperialism from which one cannot recover intact (1972/2000: 76). Thus, within the framework of U.S. imperialist desires and practices, we are in the "American hour," in which "violence, excess, waste, mercantilism, bluff, conformism, stupidity, vulgarity, disorder" operates. So how does the intellectual navigate the contemporary globalised economies dominated by multinational corporations with a new "international division of labour," a global poor and urban "underclasses . . . left behind on every significant dimension of social opportunity"? (Hall 1996: 225).

Several other attempts have been made over the years to identify the nature of the co-optation of intellectual work in/for black communities. W.E.B. DuBois himself reversed his own formulation, finding in the end that he had not accounted sufficiently for the selfishness of the "talented tenth." Still, his double consciousness model lingers here as well, as does Zora Neale Hurston's formulation of the "pet negro system". Here she describes a certain mutual benefit to dominating white society as to the co-opted black intellectual or creative figure (1979: 156). Numerous examples of this abound regarding Rice's relationship with and service to the Bush family. Bob Woodward in *Bush at War* reports that after her parents died, George and Laura Bush became in effect Condi's family: she spent her vacations with them and was almost part of the household (2002: 34). Still, the "like one of the family" option for black subjects has an entirely other interpretation and history as it relates to the hierarchy of domestic service in white households, and generally to black service to white dominance.

Woodward's *Bush at War* (2002) and *State of Denial* (2006) reference several situations that are not very flattering of Rice, who as secretary of state seems to be bereft of the independence carried by her office, and too embedded in the Bush family pathologies. In *Bush at War* he gives examples in which the President states that Rice's job is to "bear the brunt of some of the fire . . . to take the edge off a little bit. And she's good at that" (2002: 158). He is further cited as providing a revision for his purposes of the secretary of state position:

I was growing a little impatient. I can be an impatient person. Plus I feel comfortable being—one of the things I can be totally unscripted or unrehearsed with Condi. That's the nature of her job, is to absorb my—is to help, you know, kind of say, well Mr. President I appreciate that point of view, and I think you probably ought to think this way a little bit (158) . . . She is a very thorough person, constantly mother-henning me (256).

Patricia Hill Collins had earlier suggested:

African American women intellectuals are nurtured in this larger black women's community [which has created] the outsider-within stance . . . leading to a generalized black woman culture of resistance. Out of the dialectic of oppression and activism come the experiences of African American women generally that stimulate the ideas of Black Women intellectuals (1991: 12).

However, any construction of a generalised and uniform black/women's community seems directly challenged in scenes such as captured by Woodward. As Rice entertains for the "Big House," plays the piano for the Bush family, spends weekends in Kennebunkport (where she coached the president-to-be), stays in the small house in the family compound in Crawford, Texas, during her vacations, and functions as the professor-as-homeschooler to an untrained and unprepared new president, the narrative is further complicated. For Condoleezza is also confident that she wants to demonstrate at each occasion that she is better at European culture than most white people, including the Bushes—and clearly she is.

    Condoleezza Rice functions fully inside this dominance and seems to live out the "equal opportunity to oppress" model that Lorde identified in her "Equal Opportunity Poem" (1986: 16–18). Thus her description of Bush to Oprah Winfrey as a smart and intelligent man, which flies in the face of all the evidence to the contrary. Perhaps this is all another grand performance in the masking tradition of Darlene Clark Hine's definition of dissimulation. One of the criticisms of Rice, both as national security advisor and secretary of state, is that she has functioned as the person who flatters the president most, operates with a fierce loyalty that Bush demands, and as a result has not been able to take a balanced and objective view of very dangerous world situations. In what has now been described as one of the world's most colossal foreign policy mistakes, the invasion of Iraq and the subsequent war seem to have been undertaken without any analysis or study of foreign policy or deep knowledge of the history and culture of that area of the world. Instead the cold war logic of Soviet scholar Dr. Rice has impacted policy. Woodward provides numerous examples where a more knowledgeable reading of Middle East politics would have avoided bungled policy. So, using the fall of Stalin as a model, Rice felt that Iraq would be chaotic for a while. . . . "But history predicted it would be temporary. In the end, she was confident, order would reassert itself, as had happened in the old USSR" (Woodward 2006: 158–9).

The more insidious reading of this process of "condification" is Rice's performing of a myriad of other service functions for an imperialist agenda, including participating intellectually in the construction of the Vulcan ideology. The Vulcans was the name given by Rice to an extreme right wing, foreign policy group, which included policy advisors from the Bush Senior administration and bridged to George W. Bush's regime. Vulcans include George Bush Sr, Richard Armitage, Robert Zoellick, Paul Wolfowitz (now head of the World Bank), Robert Blackwill and Richard Perle. As the coordinator and namer of the Vulcans, we are observing the operations of "condification" at its highest manifestation. Rice indicates that she chose the name "The Vulcans" from her hometown mascot: "the Roman god who created thunderbolts and hammered metal into tools for the gods ... I grew up right there in Birmingham with Vulcan. . . . I remember as a little girl that it was red if there was an accident or green if everything was clear" (Rice cited in Felix 2005: 30). In this case, the selected Birmingham, Alabama, image has to do with mythical European power. Given the multi-layered civil rights iconography of Birmingham, Alabama, this selection is telling. Felix's *Condi: The Condoleezza Rice Story* (2005) and indeed all the biographies written as children's success stories (see, for example, Ditchfield 2003; L. Wade 2003; M. Wade 2004; Cunningham 2005 ; Naden and Blue 2006) identify her as growing up in Birmingham, Alabama, in the 1950s and 1960s in a family that deliberately stayed outside of civil rights activity while attempting the impossible task of protecting their daughter from the very public and visible racism that surrounded them.

But Rice is also identified as not only serving, but formulating some of the repressive Vulcan policies. Elane Sciolino in "Bush's Foreign Policy Tutor: An Academic in the Public Eye" (2000) describes this advanced role Rice played in Bush's nuclear policy. Rice used her credentials as a political scientist at Stanford University and as a specialist on Russia as major credibility collateral at the National Security Council during the first two years of the Bush administration. Isikoff and Corn's *Hubris: The Inside Story of Spin, Scandal, and the Selling of the Iraq War* (2006) indicates a central role for Rice (along with Cheney, Rumsfeld, and Bush) in the selling and spinning of the war (using the most forceful rhetoric in persuading the nation that war was necessary) and the maintenance of the current US position. Following the very condemnatory Baker/Hamilton commission report, an interview with Rice on the PBS News Hour, 21 December, 2006, reasserted much of the Iraq War justification narrative as she defended the Bush strategy.

The conservative intellectual with power is well-represented here. The point is that major discussions about intellectual activism, such as Edward Said's, assume some sort of progressive ideological commitment. What happens when the ideological position is not in the interest of any progressive agenda, but is in fact its opposite, and that same energetic type of intellectual activism is used for the benefit of a dominating state? This is a paradigm in which Rice becomes a major player and exercises leadership. As we have already asserted, to be "condified" is to be subject to that sweet-and-sour home-grown approach to destruction by a member of one's formerly identifiable racial, ethnic, class, or gendered community. Therefore the actual practice of black and/or women scholars who occupy leadership roles has to be similarly interrogated, now that they have the potential of creating or affecting policy.

Related examples have already been provided by neocolonial elites in Africa and the Caribbean. Condoleezza Rice, a black woman as the face of U.S. foreign policy to the rest of the world, confirms that one cannot assume that one's contribution is automatically radical because it comes from a member of a subordinated group. As a black woman conservative with U.S. power, she articulates an identity that has not been seen to be publicly operating in this way before. Other conservative spokespeople from subordinated communities in myriad locations around the world resonate in minor ways but with similar effect, even with more localised impact. In Rice's case, the international implications demand the kind of scrutiny offered here.

### Exceptionalism as Strategy

The mythic media construction of Condoleezza as "the [exceptionally] smart black woman" also becomes a typical singling out of one member of a subordinated group as many others with similar talents are erased. In other words, there is a public sense that she is the only black woman who can answer questions in a professional style and presentation well recognised by those in the academy. Condoleezza, with normal academic credentials, herself admits in one interview that coming from Stanford, she is used to intellectuals producing many more books than she had in the same time frame. In her first eight years at Stanford, she is identified as publishing fifteen articles and subsequently her dissertation, *Uncertain Allegiance: The Soviet Army and the Czechoslovak Army* (Princeton University Press,

1984). This was followed by an edited collection, *The Gorbachev Era*, co-edited with Alexander Dallin (Stanford Alumni Press, 1986) and a jointly authored *Germany Unified and Europe Transformed: A Study in Statecraft* (Harvard University Press, 1995) with Philip Zelikow—average output for an academic at her level. What was significant, however, was her area of expertise, which few African Americans specialised in, and her grooming for international relations work at Denver and Stanford.

Condoleezza therefore describes herself as a Europeanist, in the sense that her research expertise focuses on Europe, discussing it within its own terms. Ironically, in today's world, lacking the kind of information or black world knowledge which African Studies develops represents a huge gap, indeed a lack of knowledge of most of the world. Being a Europeanist and being an Africanist are neither symmetrical in relation to the functioning of the academy nor assigned the same value, academic space, or size. Being a Europeanist in fact means specialising in the mainstream of the already European Studies–oriented academy in which Africana Studies is marginalised. According to Felix, when Rice was appointed national security adviser:

> She also had to discuss her own limitations and admitted that the candidate was not the only one with much to learn. Condi's career as a Soviet scholar gave her insight into that part of the world but little background in the political histories of other regions. She did not have a strong grasp of America's policies in Asia, Africa, Latin America, or other non-European nations, and had to undergo her own crash course in those areas (34). "I've been pressed to understand parts of the world that have not been part of my scope," she said. "I'm really a Europeanist" (2005: 34–35).

This means that she was uninformed (as she indicates in her own self-description) about the rest of the world, having earlier seen African Studies and other related "ethnic studies programmes" as not critical to her intellectual roundedness in terms of knowledge, the kind of information that attempts to account for lives outside the European world. Being a Europeanist thus also means a silencing and denial of colonialism, imperialism, and racial and sexual conquest.[8]

So in a world in which, as Wynter says, "everything Black has been negatively marked, and everything white has been positively marked" (2006), how does the black subject position her/himself? The best reading is offered by Fanon-defined black "self-alienation," which is significant as it suggests that "the black alienated subject carries a consciousness that does not function in his best interest . . . indeed it has to negate everything black in order to be that ideal representation of the human" (2006).

It makes sense therefore that it was under Rice's leadership that Black Studies at Stanford would be dismantled from a model that had developed, via St Clair Drake, with a diaspora orientation. In the eyes of black Stanford alumni who had struggled as students to make Black Studies a permanent feature of their university's experience, Provost Rice did nothing to advance this cause. Rice herself has conceded that some of the decisions she made at Stanford were perhaps too hard.

The issue of bourgeois American feminism in its general sense is perhaps the easiest lens with which to approach this issue.[9] In the case of the State Department, the rise of individuals such as Madeleine Albright was seen as evidence of women challenging the fraternity of men in leadership of the State Department. According to Antonia Felix, Madeleine Albright had throughout her career "been committed to the advancement of women in the field, and she considered her cabinet appointment a victory for all women" (2005: 309–310). If Madeleine Albright was seen as challenging the location of women in subordinate roles, one of the principles of U.S. bourgeois feminism, then Condoleezza turned out to be the most fitting representative of black and female success according to the model of the dominant society—highly accommodationist, conservative, clever—but not for the benefit of the wider black communities.[10]

The model of choice for Condoleezza, however, is not Albright, her female predecessor, but the late Jean Kirkpatrick, hard-line U.S. representative to the United Nations, who at her passing was identified by the secretary of state's office as follows: "This is somebody that the Secretary knew quite well. She looked up to her as a role model, somebody who as a more senior policymaker and a senior academic always had time for more junior people, people like Condoleezza Rice, who was then coming up through the ranks of academia."[11] But Kirkpatrick was also known for her extreme conservatism and also that same Thatcher-like rigidity.

There is no indication that I have seen so far that Rice sees herself as articulating any black and/or feminist positions, even as she benefits from their political work. Perhaps the closest one gets is in her speech to the American Baptist convention.[12] Here Condoleezza announces, to applause from a group of largely white men, that once she finishes her term it will be twelve years since a white man has held the position of secretary of state. The rhetorical question we can ask in response is: Has this made our world any better? From all accounts, the world seems a much worse place to those whose lives continue to be destroyed. Moreover, intellectuals in power operating for the benefit of an oppressive state, such as this one, bear some responsibility for participating in this process, even leading it at times.

The link between Fanon, *Les damnés de la terre* [The Wretched of the

Earth], and the logic of condemnation or election is fascinating in this context. Living out, if not publicly advancing, a bourgeois feminist position occupies the same pole as an effaced blackness. In other words, how do we account for the "damned" and the "wretched" who remain the sizable population of black communities wherever they are, even as selected black beneficiaries reap the rewards of struggle? The New Orleans Hurricane Katrina debacle makes this point clear, for the wretched were visibly abandoned without any support.[13]


## The Levees and the Limits

In "Towards African Diaspora Citizenship,"[14] I identified as constitutive the long history of forced migration, which displaced African peoples, moving them globally from a range of political formations in precolonial nations, empires and other smaller ethnic political structures. This logic of diaspora is what, in some contexts, drives some understanding of related formations and varied geographical conditions. One of the key features of this understanding is that the majority of these groups, exploited for centuries, remained consistently debased and disenfranchised in their new locations. African Americans are prominently located as one of these groups. In the U.S. in particular, conditions existed of labour abuse, the denial of rights, beatings, maimings and other forms of physical brutality which accompanied the processes of jim-crowing, sharecropping, and extreme racial segregation—all of which can be seen as the equivalent to an internal colonialism that succeeded plantation slavery.

The intent of Pan-Africanism was to make itself a practical and achievable political reality—one that went beyond the rhetorical articulations. And one can now see the results of the great deal of work that has gone into identifying the contours of the African diaspora. A dynamic library of and discourse on African diaspora studies (see, for instance, Harris 1993; Okpewho 1996; Boyce Davies 2002; Edwards 2003; Gomez 2003) is helping to shape the contemporary understanding of the diaspora. It is here that the relevance of St Clair Drake, who developed Stanford's Black Studies Program, becomes relevant to this discussion. Drake's "Diaspora Studies and Pan-Africanism" offers a thoughtful overview of the ways that diaspora and Pan-Africanism as concepts interact, function concurrently, and provide research agendas for the future. This was a project which at Stanford, perhaps with some imagination, could have provided an imaginative research agenda and even an African diaspora "think tank" along the lines of other versions at Stanford, if it had been well supported at the institutional level.

The maintenance of some clear connections—cultural, economic, demographic, and political—for the advancement of African-descended people has nevertheless remained a constant feature even as the critique of essentialised identities and imagined communities remain. Historically, black public intellectuals, including the conservative Booker T. Washington, have accommodated at least some minor version of this, even if strategies have differed.

And here the issue of the victims of Hurricane Katrina and the breaking of the levees reenters, as it revealed most starkly the frailty of citizenship rights for U.S. African Americans. Black people worldwide, by extension, descended again into Hurston's "infinity of conscious pain" as participants and as witnesses of another epic, slave-ship-like cycle of degradation. The absence of black political figures with the power that Rice has from this situation also has foreign policy implications, as it relates to the African diaspora policy aspect of international relations.

Recent activity on the diaspora at the political level offers perhaps the most important practical application of years of scholarship on African diaspora and the political activism of Pan-Africanism as identified by St Clair Drake. The African Union, after appropriate deliberations, has decided to account for the dispersed African populations in the traditional legacy of Pan-Africanism.

It has voted that the diaspora would be its sixth region, and various plans are in place to activate some practical features of diaspora exchange. The earlier identified inabilities of figures like Rice to be equipped intellectually to deal with these new developments resonates strongly as the U.S. remains unaccounted for in these developments. Brazil recently hosted the Congress of African Diaspora Intellectuals (CIAD II in July 2006) and Trinidad has already hosted a Caribbean meeting on the African diaspora sponsored by the African Union. Once again, African American interests were not represented at the official level (although many African American individual public intellectuals and NGOs were present), as they were also at the 2001 Conference Against Racism in Durban.

In many ways, the U.S. imperial project as developed in the Caribbean has been the building of its version of imperialism as European imperialism has waned. The more recent attempts in the Middle East, via Iraq, have been to create a series of what Greg Thomas calls "future super-colonies." The current disastrous result (which echoes the Cesaire formulation) is that at the end of 2006, with close to a million Iraqi people killed, worsening humanitarian conditions and a country totally destroyed, the Iraqis and their neighbours have refused to consign their country to the U.S. imperial project.

Yet in visits to Brazil and in the Caribbean, as in the U.S., Rice is not above using race and Jim Crow history to legitimate herself and thereby the policies of U.S. imperialism. Beyond that, and after those encounters, we see no visible recognition of the Afro-Brazilian experience, the Caribbean experience or the African experience in U.S. foreign policy under her leadership of the State Department—unless framed within U.S. interests. My search for policy material that specifies U.S. State Department policies on Africa and on the Caribbean, for example, continues to be unrewarding, except for sporadic stabs at genocide in Darfur. Repeated speeches instead describe the importance of building what Rice calls "transformational democracy." And under the Project for the New American Century ("Rebuilding America's Defenses: Strategy, Forces and Resources for a New Century"), the current administration's position supports an aggressive military as is being used in Iraq (as it was in Grenada, Panama, and Haiti). "Transformational democracy," then, can also be effected by preemptive military action if appropriate, shorthand for U.S. style–democracy and ultimately U.S. imperialism.

So on the issue of the diaspora, so far, African Americans remain officially outside of these frameworks. Some countries would say this is a good thing, being understandably wary of U.S. "transformational democracy" projects such as the Iraqi debacle. Still, this remains a weak spot for this secretary of state: the inattention to the political movement to operationalise the African diaspora on the one hand; the U.S. failed imperial projects in the "Middle East" on the other. Even a smaller project such as the inaugural Caribbean Heritage Month celebration, which took place in June 2006, seemed to happen without her public involvement. The particulars of U.S. attempts at global hegemony may mean that U.S. interests get acted on in this new form if the structure is malleable. In the meantime, the African-descended populations in South America have come up with their own human rights statements meant to identify their relationships to the rest of the African diaspora, their rights as linked to indigenous peoples, and the desire to be educated about the history and contours of their African and African-diaspora experience.

American imperialism, even as it wanes, has left U.S. African Americans in the unfortunate position of being within the belly of this beast notwithstanding, fighting its wars and representing its failed foreign policies.[15] Within the "diaspora" framework, the question of US hegemony itself has to be consistently readdressed. In a way, African American representation has a choice: either to walk out of Durban[16] officially (as Colin Powell did) rather than deal head-on with racism and imperialism, or participate in another diasporic geography that has nothing to do with having the benefit of U.S. power.

Thus, the internal colonialism model as applied to the U.S., raised by thinking African Americans in the U.S., is worth recalling, given the rise of people like Rice who are clearly functioning in a way recognisable to those who have seen neo-colonial elites operating in other parts of the world. The epigrammatically captive experience of the black people of New Orleans following Hurricane Katrina and the breaking of the levees, without access to any leadership that could represent them, is the other side of this neocolonial construct; and there are several others that fit the contours of internal US neo-colonialism.

Michael Dawson in *Black Visions: The Roots of Contemporary African American Political Ideologies* sees the ten-point programme of the Black Panther Party as one of the articulations of this internal colonialism. Black people in the U.S. have consistently argued for themselves as a separate nation confined within the borders of the United States, and therefore constituting an oppressed nation with the right to self-determination. The generations of early Pan-Africanists coming from the U.S., such as Anna Julia Cooper, and DuBois, seemed to articulate a similar point. And even before this, Martin Delaney and David Walker made similar connections. Walker's *Appeal* addressed the "colored people of the world" prior to the formation of a diaspora language. Malcolm X later characterised the plight of African Americans as that of an internal colony—oppressed and colonised people of the U.S. who needed to forge links with international communities. For Malcolm X, as for a variety of leaders, the links with other colonised peoples would be openly made during the civil rights era, with references to "brothers and sisters in Asia who were colonized by the Europeans, our brothers and sisters in Africa, who were colonized by the Europeans, and in Latin America, the peasants who were colonized by the Europeans" (Cobbs Hoffman and Gjerde 2002: 350–351).

Several complaints lodged before the UN by DuBois, Paul Robeson, Malcolm X, the Black Panther Party, and Claudia Jones have sought to have the dwindling human rights of African Americans redressed. As recently as the 2000 presidential elections in Florida, African Americans went to the UN to get their rights protected. And the devastating effects of Hurricane Katrina and the broken levees reveal that even if a foreign government offered help, unless the U.S. accepted it, then disenfranchised black communities in the South, dying from the effects of a devastating storm, could not be reached, bordered as they are in the U.S.

Within the internal colonialism model, then, one can see the rise of a neocolonial elite in much the same way as this has occurred in other geographical locations. A range of black political figures and moneyed folk, entertainers and the like, act from that position. In the case of the neocolonial elite, Condoleezza Rice, Colin Powell, Clarence Thomas, and a range of other political actors function publicly in the interest of the dominant state, and at the expense of the advancement of their communities, undoing previous and hard-won gains while repudiating these same communities' struggles. Thus, following Hurricane Katrina and the breaching of the levees, perhaps the worst disaster to befall a black people since enslavement, with all the signifiers and their referents attached, the black woman who has indicated that she can tell George Bush anything (according to an interview published in *O Magazine* in 2002); who has his ear and an amazing chemistry with him, behaved in a way that caused many to wonder how come the black woman who has the ear of the President did not make her people's life any better at a critical and historically definitive moment.

Given to using football metaphors and seeing herself as the administration's quarterback, when asked about the vision of African Americans stranded on rooftops in the aftermath of Hurricane Katrina, Rice, after denying that the range of failed responses by the Bush administration was because of the race of the majority of the victims, reserved her strongest anger for the people who dared to criticise the president's lacklustre response to the disaster: "But I will tell you what I deeply resented. I resented the notion that the president of the United States, *this* president of the United States, would somehow decide to let people suffer because they were black. I found that to be the most corrosive and outrageous claim that anybody could have made, and it was wholly and totally irresponsible." When pushed a bit more by the interviewer, she indicated that it was the storm of the century, "it was certainly not because anybody wanted to be negligent or cared less because these were Black Americans. That was a ridiculous lie" (White 2006: 187). In other words, in the range of things to be angry at in this situation, Rice is angrier at the attack on the president than on what happened to black Americans. And the misperception, in her eyes, that the Republicans have "blown off" African Americans and Africa (actually a response to singer Kanye West's claim "George Bush does not like black people") is also a lie in her view on the grounds that Bush has given huge increases in funding to historically black colleges and has tripled his development assistance to Africa. (However, according to those on the ground, a great deal of that monetary assistance has never been paid.)

Within the logic of PNAC (Project for the New American Century— actually an American imperialist project) and the official "transformational democracy" position of the Bush government, with Condoleezza, an African American as the primary face of U.S. foreign policy to the world, and given that "global hegemony" is one of the U.S. missions, Condoleezza and the process of "condification", represents for me the possibility of a global

U.S. hegemony articulated through the most deceptive and cynical of ways—the face of a black woman. From all reports, she thinks of U.S. foreign policy largely in terms of U.S. national and strategic interest, with the U.S. maintaining international leadership.

Although at the height of her professional career, still with many more miles to go, many U.S. African Americans still live in the seemingly false hope that someone with access to the ear of the president (especially given that in the understanding of politics in Washington, D.C., access means power) will at some point be able to *represent* them, thereby transforming that access power to something tangibly useful for the African diaspora.

## Practices of Power

A new subject of study for black feminist intellectuals must then be the practices of black women in power and political leadership. Condoleezza Rice, as we have established, is one of these seemingly powerful women, acknowledged as being the closest person to the president on his cabinet. The question is how someone who has acquired this level of power can best exercise leadership. Since Rice is also identified as intimate friend and confidante of the president, identified as having amazing chemistry with him, "home-schooling" him on international affairs, pronunciation of words, names of foreign leaders, and consistently creating much of the foreign policy that he articulates,[17] she must surely then be subjected to the same scrutiny as him. Bush himself has described her in the often-quoted phrase as able to "explain to me foreign policy matters in a way I can understand."

Rice's co-optation of the civil rights narrative and the women's movement is used for the purposes of war and imperialism, even as she maintains that her race and gender are irrelevant to her options. It is not unusual to hear Rice comparing the war on Iraq with the American Civil War and the liberation of the enslaved Africans. In a recent article in *Essence Magazine*, with its known black readership, she was asked by the interviewer about the $250 billion cost of the war, the deaths and wounding of tens of thousands of military and civilian people, and whether the war was a right thing since she had supported it from the start. Rice responded with perhaps one of the most incredible political cartwheels ever seen, claiming that slavery might have lasted longer in the U.S. if the North had decided to end the war early: "I'm sure there are people who thought that it was a mistake to fight the Civil War to its end and to resist that the emancipation of slaves would hold. I know there were people who said why don't we get out of this now, take a peace with the South, but leave the South with slaves?" (White 2006: 187). By these means, then, she appropriates the liberation of black people from enslavement to make the case for its opposite: the imperialist invasion and destruction of the once sovereign nation of Iraq, the resulting deaths of numerous U.S. soldiers and hundreds of thousands of Iraqi people, and the destruction of the physical infrastructure of Baghdad, once one of the world's most beautiful cities.

In the final analysis, this is the conundrum of accessing power in a context of domination that Lusane, following Fanon, articulates in the quotations that open this piece. One either acquiesces, as the Fanonian example suggests, or acts swiftly and with principle for the benefit of one's communities, knowing that this access to power may be short-lived. Appropriating those power positions and utilising political movements, even as they are denied or erased by one's institutional interests, is a less than admirable position in which to be placed.

While we are now seeing the actual presentation through "condification" of a certain version of black female leadership, Audre Lorde's "Equal Opportunity" poem had already imaginatively presented a black woman who has made it into the highest echelons of the U.S. military complex, and who in this role has to assist in the execution of the worst of U.S. policies—in this case, the invasion of Grenada. It closes tellingly with lines that present the diabolical result of this conjunction of US imperial power and black female identity:

> The American deputy assistant secretary of defense
> for equal opportunity and safety
> pauses in her speech licks her dry lips
> "as you can see the Department has
> a very good record
> of equal opportunity for our women"
> swims toward safety
> through a lake of her own blood.

## References

Boyce Davies, Carole et al. eds. 2002. *Decolonizing the Academy: African Diaspora Studies*. Trenton, New Jersey: Africa World Press.

Boyce Davies, Carole and M'bow, Babacar, "Towards African Diaspora Citizenship: Politicizing an Existing Global Geography," in Katherine McKittrick and Clyde Woods. eds. *Black Geographies and the Politics of Place*. Toronto: Between the Lines press/ Boston: South End Press, forthcoming, 2007.

Cesaire, Aime. 1972/2000. *Discourse on Colonialism*. New York: Monthly Review Press.

Childress, Alice. 1956. *Like One of the Family. Conversations from a Domestic's Life*. Boston: Beacon.

Cobbs Hoffman, Elizabeth and Gjerde, Jon. eds. 2002. *Major Problems in American History: Volume II Since 1865*. Boston: Houghton Mifflin Company

Collins, Patricia Hill. 1991. *Black Feminist Thought*. New York, London: Routledge.
Cunningham, Kevin. 2005. *Condoleezza Rice: US Secretary of State*. Chanhassen, Maryland: The Child's World.
Dawson, Michael C. 1991. *Black Visions: The Roots of Contemporary African-American Political Ideologies*. Chicago: University of Chicago Press.
Ditchfield, Christin. 2003. *Condoleezza Rice: National Security Advisor*. New York, Toronto, London: Franklin Watts.
Drake, St Clair. 1993 [1982]. "Diaspora Studies and Pan-Africanism" in Harris, Joseph. ed. *Global Dimensions of the African Diaspora*. Washington, DC: Howard University Press.
Edmondson, Jacqueline. 2006. *Condoleezza Rice: A Biography*, Greenwood Biographies Series. Portsmouth, NH: Greenwood Publishing Group.
Edwards, Brent Hayes. 2003. *The Practice of Diaspora: Literature, Translation, and the Rise of Black Internationalism*. Cambridge, Massachusetts: Harvard University Press.
Felix, Antonia. 2005. *Condi: The Condoleezza Rice Story*. New York: Newmarket Press.
Gomez, Michael. 2003. *Reversing Sail. A History of the African Diaspora*. Cambridge: Cambridge University Press 2003.
Hall, Stuart. 1983. *The Politics of Thatcherism*. London: Lawrence and Wishart.
Hall, Stuart. 1996. "The Meaning of New Times" in Morley, David and Chen, Kuan-Hsing. eds. *Stuart Hall, Critical Dialogues in Cultural Studies*. London: Routledge.
Harris, Joseph. ed. 1993.*Global Dimensions of the African Diaspora* (Washington, D.C.: Howard University Press.
Hurston, Zora Neale. 1979. "The 'Pet' Negro System" in Walker, Alice. ed. *I Love Myself When I am Laughing*: A Zora Neale Hurston Reader. New York: The Feminist Press.
Isikoff, Michael and Corn, David. 2006. *Hubris: The Inside Story of Spin, Scandal, and the Selling of the Iraq War*. New York: Crown.
Lorde, Audre. 1986. *Our Dead Behind Us*. New York: W. W. Norton & Co.
Lusane, Clarence. 2006. *Colin Powell and Condoleezza Rice: Foreign Policy, Race and the New American Century*. Westport, Connecticut and London: Praeger.
Malcolm X. 1965. *Malcolm X Speaks*. New York: Grove Press.
Naden, Corinne J. and Blue, Rose. 2006. *Condoleezza Rice*. Chicago: Raintree.
Okpewho et al. eds. 1996. *The African Diaspora: African Identities and New World Self-Fashionings*. Bloomington: Indiana University Press.
Said, Edward. 1996. "The Limits of the Artistic Imagination and the Secular Intellectual", *Macalester International: Special Issue on Literature, the Creative Imagination and Globalization* 3.
Sciolino, Elane. 2000. "Bush's Foreign Policy Tutor: An Academic in the Public Eye." Available on http://www.casi.org.uk/discuss/2000/msg00703.html.
Wade, Linda R. 2003. *Condoleezza Rice. A Real-Life Reader Biography*. Bear, Delaware: Mitchell Lane Publishers, Inc.
Wade, Mary Dodson. 2004. *Condoleezza Rice: Being the Best*. Brookfield, Connecticut: The Millbrook Press.
White, Timothy. 2006. "Being Condoleezza", *Essence Magazine*, October.
Woodward, Bob. 2002. *Bush at War*. New York: Simon and Schuster.
Woodward, Bob. 2006. *State of Denial*. New York: Simon and Schuster.
Wynter, Sylvia. 2006. "Proud Flesh Inter/Views Sylvia Wynter", *Proud Flesh: New Afrikan Journal of Culture, Politics and Consciousness*. Available at www.proudfleshjournal.com.

## Notes

1. This is a shortened version of a much longer paper presented at the Diaspora Hegemonies Conference, University of Toronto, October 2006. I thank the conference organisers for the opportunity to present preliminarily the first long version of this paper, which will be available in full on JendaJournal.com, the e-journal. The paucity of good material on this subject has prompted me to begin working towards a book on the subject. Thanks to readers Greg Thomas, Zillah Eisenstein, Monica Jardine, Babacar M'bow and anonymous reviewers of *Feminist Africa* for helpful comments at various stages of this paper's writing.

2. The S.S. Condoleezza Rice would be renamed in 2001, as it served as a visible reminder of the Bush administration's obvious ties to the oil industry, with the White House facing questions about the appropriateness of the tanker's name. A list of other related activities while Condoleezza Rice was on the board of Chevron were identified in a protest statement distributed at the 2002 Stanford graduation by a student group. The full document is available at http://www.stanford.edu/group/rats/condi.

3. This latter point about "conditioning" is owed to Ngugi wa Thiong'o in response to my telling him what I was working on, during his book tour visit to Miami, 13 October 2006.

4. In a 2002 survey, then National Security Advisor Rice was viewed favourably by 41% of African-American respondents. As her role increased, some African-American commentators began to express doubts concerning Rice's stances and statements on various issues. Other writers have also noted a distance between Rice and the black community. Some have described her invoking the civil rights movement to clarify her position on the war on Iraq as cynical and offensive. Bill Fletcher, Jr, the former leader of the TransAfrica Forum, a foreign policy lobbying organisation in Washington, DC, has described her as "only black by accident." In August 2005, American musician, actor, and social activist Harry Belafonte referred to African-Americans in the Bush administration as "black tyrants". While Condi has been supported by Dorothy Height of the National Council of Negro Women, there has not been much analysis by black feminist intellectuals. This is (as far as I know) one of the first attempts.

5. Conversations with students at a conference in honour of the 25th anniversary of the Women's Research and Resource Center at Spelman College in Atlanta, October 2006, indicated that while Rice might be the kind of woman that Spelman grooms in terms of poise and self-presentation, few could identify with her politically.

6. Available at http://www.proudfleshjournal.com.

7. See the positions of the National Black Feminist Organization and The Combahee River Collective, and even the earlier statements by Sojourner Truth, Harriet Tubman, Maria Stewart and Anna Julia Cooper. These articulated a radical critique of dominant US positions, rather than the "equal opportunity" model currently deployed in politics, the corporate world and some aspects of the academic world as well.

8. Zillah Eisenstein makes this point. Her own work on Hillary Clinton and Condoleezza Rice (*Sexual Decoys: Gender, Race And War In Imperial Democracy*, forthcoming from Zed Press) makes some important allied arguments about the failure of these practices for the meaning of feminism.

9. Elaine Brown, for instance, identifies both Colin Powell and Condoleezza within the context of neo-slavery as "New Age House Negroes" and "New Age House Negresses", and also suggests that within feminism, Condoleezza can be seen as a black feminist icon. See http://proudfleshjournal.com/vol1.2/interview-eb.html for more.

10. Conscious that one cannot assume any generic and uniform community, there is nevertheless a larger African-descended population that continues to be disenfranchised, and which many intellectuals and politicians have sought to represent. The question as to whether Condoleezza has any black "community" to which she owes anything came up as a question in the first presentation of this paper in Toronto, October, 2006.

11. Press briefing, 8 December 2006.

12. Available at http://www.state.gov/secretary/rm/2006/67896.htm.

13. Clarence Lusane sees the Katrina disaster as having even more impact than the Iraq war in unmasking horrendous domestic policies that have consistently disregarded the poor (2006: 181–197).

14. Forthcoming in the collection *Black Geographies*, edited by Katherine McKittrick and Clyde Woods.

15. An unpublished paper by Anton Allahar describes this "capitalist democracy" in his unpublished paper "The Other Side of Democracy: the US and the War on Terror," which he graciously shared with me in October 2006, following the presentation of a version of this paper at the University of Western Ontario.

16. Durban in South Africa hosted the International Conference Against Racism in 2001.

17. All of the biographies have identified this point. See, for example, Jacqueline Edmonson's biography of Rice, which indicates that she made lists of foreign leaders for him and would rehearse them with him while doing things like exercising together (64).

# The Relevance of
# Black Feminist Scholarship
## A Caribbean Perspective

*Violet Eudine Barriteau*

2008

Women's studies has offered one major challenge to the allegedly hege-monic ideas of elite white men. Ironically, feminist theory has also sup-pressed Black women's ideas. Even though Black women intellectuals have long expressed a unique feminist consciousness about the inter-section of race and class in structuring gender, historically we have not been full participants in white feminist organizations (Patricia Hill Col-lins 1990: 7).

## Introduction

In this article, I speak from a Caribbean feminist location to examine some of the core contributions black feminist scholarship has made to feminist epistemology, and to simultaneously call attention to its near-erasure. I doc-ument some of the main conceptual tools and analytical devices black femi-nist theorising brings to the process of creating knowledge, not only about black women's lives, but with relevance to all women's lives.[1] In the process of stocktaking, of synthesising some of these contributions, I reflect on the politics of knowledge production and what is perhaps the under-explored applicability of black feminist theoretical analyses to comprehending the lives of Caribbean and African women. This article is long overdue, and many of the questions I raise I cannot answer here, and in fact do not have answers for. Rather, I hope this piece will start a conversation about the rel-evance of black feminist theory to women across nationalities, ethnicities, and race. In the process, I hope to contribute to advancing feminist visions, irrespective of the geographic locations in which women experience the dynamic and constantly mutating power relations of gender.

Even as I hold mainstream and Western feminist theorists account-able for the refusal to fully acknowledge the contributions of black feminist theorists, I am compelled to consider whether or not Caribbean[2] feminist scholarship and practice have engaged with black feminist scholarship—

and if not, why not? What are some of the main issues Caribbean feminists attempt to address, and how do these intersect with the conceptual tools offered by black feminist theorists? Why haven't Caribbean feminists consciously utilised the theoretical tools of black feminist scholarship? How much do we know about these theoretical contributions?

Part of the motivation to write this article comes from a desire to disseminate widely what I see as the strengths of black feminist theory, and to begin to think through why Caribbean feminists have not made more use of it. I have suspicions (many of which I can substantiate) as to why black feminist scholarship is generally missing from the canonical anthologies of feminist theories, but why is it absent in the works of feminists who share an historical legacy of racist and colonial exploitation? Problematising race and exposing how racist practices complicate all other social relations of power is a central organising principle of black feminist theorising. As a black Caribbean woman and feminist, race and racism do not enter my life and the lives of most Caribbean women in the identical trajectories that they do for minority women in racist societies—the geographic and political locations for much of this theorising. This is not to suggest that racism and racist practices are not threaded through the social fabric of Caribbean life. They are, but they are experienced differently. As I stated 14 years ago:

> Black women's experiences of race in the Caribbean differ from that of black women in North America. With population composition ranging from 95,4 percent to 79,9 percent black in most Caribbean countries[3] [White, 1986: 65] there is the legacy of race rather than say the North American version of the day-to-day reality of racism. For example, in Barbados, indigenous whites dominate the corporate economy. They own or control economic activities within major industrial sectors. They maintain a web of corporate interlinkages based on ethnic or kinship ties [see Beckles 1989a]. *Yet for black Barbadians racial discrimination in the areas of health services, education, transportation, housing and public policy is an alien experience* [emphasis added] (1992: 25).

To what extent has the absence of state-sponsored racism in the post-independent Caribbean affected the engagement of Caribbean feminists with black feminist theorising that makes an interrogation of racism central to its analysis? If some feminists claim there is evidence of racism in state practices in certain Caribbean countries, why haven't the theoretical insights of black feminist theory been used to reveal these practices?

As it relates to black feminist theorising, the politics of creating knowledge about women's lives takes an internecine turn. Feminists have been theorising for centuries to correct the falsity, gendered hegemony and intellectual violence of patriarchal knowledge claims (see, for instance, Spender 1982; Rossi 1974; Schneir 1972; Martin 1972). Ironically, while most feminist theorists discern quite readily the exclusionary parameters of mainstream (i.e., androcentric) knowledge production, they replicate these exclusionary practices in the new generalisations they offer and the lived realities they investigate to distil these knowledge claims.

## A Caribbean Feminist Perspective

What do I mean by a Caribbean feminist perspective and by describing myself as a Caribbean feminist? It means that I define myself as a black woman, a feminist, and a political scientist—who reflects upon and negotiates, operates, theorises, and works within the trenches of gender relations in the Commonwealth Caribbean (Barriteau 2003b: 57). As a precondition to problematising the intersection where my multiple identities meet Caribbean realities, I believe I have a responsibility to generate new knowledges about Caribbean societies. I locate myself and my analysis at the juncture where regional experiences of rapid changes in the global political economy intersect with fundamental developments in the social relations of gender (Barriteau 2001). I attempt to work at the crossroads where a politicised, theoretical stance and the competing, complex realities and contradictions of everyday life in the Caribbean meet. I see this location as a ground-level vantage point that enables me to contribute to the ongoing dialogue on rethinking Caribbean society from a feminist perspective. This position enables me to argue that an understanding of the operations of the social relations of gender and gender systems is foundational to any assessment and critique of Caribbean society. It means that I am very interested in North-South relations, and the policies and politics of industrialised countries and their impact on children, women, and men in the Caribbean and other southern regions.

Even though Caribbean countries have achieved "flag independence," and our peoples and most of our leaders truly desire to be sovereign, the Caribbean has not escaped new versions of enduring colonial legacies, some of which have been wilfully maintained by newly minted independent governments (Barriteau 2004b: 136). We may look and wish to be beyond the political dimensions of colonialism, but many of our leaders and peoples have neither surrendered nor even interrogated the cultural and economic trappings of colonialism.

Even though the economic and political discussions now centre on globalization, in reality Caribbean countries are suspended somewhere between formal political independence and new forms of colonialism. An equal vote at the United Nations does not necessarily translate into equal treatment in the international arena. The post-Columbian[4] Caribbean is perhaps the original geopolitical configuration of globalisation. For more than five centuries, Caribbean realities have been violently punctured, punctuated and systemically redefined by international economics, politics, and cultures. Though decimated and plundered by and since the Columbian intrusion, the indigenous peoples of the Caribbean managed to survive alongside migrants from Europe, Africa, Asia, and the near, far, and Middle East.

In the 21st century, the Caribbean can still be comprehended as a misunderstood metaphor for the global. Misunderstood because as the ongoing processes of globalisation convulse, conquer, and reconfigure commerce, cultures, and citizenship, the Caribbean is increasingly neglected in internationalised, intellectual discourse and enterprise. Continuing to assess and reflect on the post-Columbian Caribbean would yield important lessons to the global community. One obvious but overlooked lesson is that in this confrontational world, the Caribbean exists as a zone of peace. This is part of the larger context in which particular issues affecting Caribbean feminism are played out.

## Issues in Caribbean Feminism

What concerns of Caribbean feminism can benefit from taking up the conceptual tools of black feminist theory? As reflected in the literature, much Caribbean feminist scholarship centres on Caribbean states, and state neglect of Caribbean women or complicity in issues negatively affecting women (see, for example, Reddock 1994; Barriteau 1995; 2004a; Bailey 2003; Harris 2003; Pargass and Clarke 2003; Vassell 2003; Maxine Henry-Wilson 2004; Robinson 2004; Rowley 2004). A special issue of *Feminist Review*, entitled "Rethinking Caribbean Difference," reveals additional concerns of Caribbean feminist theorising from interdisciplinary perspectives. Pat Mohammed locates the politics of identity as a central concern of feminism and feminist theory in the Caribbean (1998: 6). She also signals an unexplored demarcation of Caribbean and black feminist concerns when she cautions that she "cannot speak for or in the manner of a white middle-class academic in Britain, or a black North American feminist," even though she shares with both similarities that go beyond societal difference, and which are fuelled by shared commitment to gender equality (1998: 6). Hilary Beckles charges that Caribbean feminist theorists have failed to investigate why "institutional political projects such as independence took hegemonic precedence over women's liberation" (1998: 48). He specifically challenged me to "redefine and relocate Caribbean women's movements within the ideological space provided by postmodern feminism in order to create and promote social activism that reflects a coherent feminist opposition and vanguard" (1998: 51–52).

Rhoda Reddock explores and links the emergence of women's organisations and the development of feminist consciousness in the 20th-century Commonwealth Caribbean. She traces the evolution and changing character of women's organisations over the last two centuries, while highlighting the emergence of small radical or feminist-oriented groups (1998: 57, 61–62). Rawwida Baksh-Soodeen undertakes a critique of Caribbean feminism as largely Afrocentric and argues that the women's movement should reflect the experiences of women of other ethnic groups in the region: "The Caribbean post-independence and feminist discourses gave preeminence to the historical experiences and present-day situation of African-Caribbean people, leading to an Afrocentric rather than a multicultural paradigm" (1998: 83).

In a 2002 keynote address, I attempted to capture some of the challenges of Caribbean feminism as follows:

1. To unravel the knot that surrounds power, and to investigate how our difficulty with power influences what issues receive our attention; to grapple with feminists' ambivalence over power, how we come to power, claim it, respect it, and use it.

2. To begin to rethink the processes we can develop and use to ensure that democratic practices define how we create knowledge, and how we expose and avoid replicating hierarchies of power in the social relations we seek to disrupt.

3. To be aware that feminist scholarship and activism has to be distinguished by a commitment to interrogating, picking apart and honestly confronting how power works. In whatever avenues we work, we have to acknowledge that we are contesting and seeking to change relations of power.

4. The need to establish genealogical authority and continuity between feminist thought and gender studies. This is not a quest for theoretical primogeniture. It is about identifying conceptual frameworks that recognise and explore those relations of power that shape how women and men experience the same social and economic phenomena in fundamentally dissimilar and unequal ways.

5. To maintain and support meaningful dialogue with the study, issues, and questions of masculinities. We need to create a space within which to converse with masculinity beyond the necessary, but generally reactive responses that have been generated so far.

6. To tackle the knot of race/ethnicity/class, and deconstruct an us/them frame of analysis, which must transcend its origins in a post-colonial, nationalist treatise.
7. To engage with the challenge of class, another social relation of power and privilege that has not yet been satisfactorily interrogated in our work.
8. To address the fragility and vulnerability of the women's movement in the face of a frontal assault on Caribbean women that goes beyond a backlash (Barriteau 2003c).
9. The withdrawal of state attention from women and women's issues in a majority of Caribbean countries. Many states believe they have fulfilled their mandates towards women and must now focus increasingly on men.
10. The similar retreat from a focus on women by international development institutions.
11. The weaknesses in both scholarship and activism in linking the adversities in women's lives to larger structures of oppression and exploitation.
12. The gentrification and abuse of power by the leadership in both the academy and the political movement.

## The Theoretical Contributions of Black Feminism

Black feminist theorising has made critical contributions to feminist epistemology. Yet this is not reflected in anthologies of feminist thought, critiques of feminist scholarship, or even online encyclopaedic references. In a small attempt to redress the balance, I summarise some of these core contributions here.

### Rejection of an undifferentiated notion of sisterhood

The first major move by black feminist scholars was to discard the simplistic, undifferentiated notion of global "sisterhood". Black feminist theory comprises a body of work by black feminist intellectuals reacting to the failure of existing feminist explanatory frameworks to adequately comprehend the realities of black women. Sojourner Truth, Barbara Christian, Audre Lorde, Gloria Joseph, Toni Cade Bambara, Patricia Bell Scott, Barbara Smith, Gloria T. Hull, Beverley Guy-Sheftall, Paula Giddings, Michele Wallace, Stanlie James, Deborah King, Hazel Carby, Patricia Hill Collins, Angela Davis, bell hooks, Patricia King, Patricia Williams, as well as many others[5] from different disciplinary bases, interrogated existing feminist theories and found them lacking, as they myopically and wilfully ignored or denied black women's specific experiences.

For instance, Sojourner Truth's powerful statement at the Women's Convention in Akron, Ohio, in 1851 was a nineteenth-century deconstruction of the notion of a global, common womanhood and an insistence on inserting black womanhood in the concept of what it meant to be a woman.

Speaking of the United States in the 1970s, Audre Lorde stated, "By and large, within the women's movement today, white women focus upon their oppression as women and ignore differences of race, sexual preference, class, and age. There is a pretence to homogeneity of experiences covered by the word *sisterhood* that does not in fact exist" (1984: 116). And Zillah Eisenstein reminds us of Hazel Carby's theoretical stance: "there is no lost sisterhood to be found; . . . there are definite 'boundaries' to the possibilities of sisterhood" (Eisenstein 1994: 208; Carby 1987: 6, 19). Carby's statements contain echoes of the calls by Patricia Mohammed, Rawwida Baksh-Sooden and Neesha Haniff for a more differentiated reading of identities within Caribbean feminism (Mohammed 1998; Baksh-Sooden 1998; Haniff 1996). I hold that the more comprehensive and inclusive insights offered by black feminism strengthen all feminist knowledge.

### Prioritises and problematises race as a social relation, complicated by other social relations

A foundational contribution of black feminist scholarship is its exposure and problematising of race/racism as a social relation, which simultaneously complicates and is complicated by other social relations of domination. The intellectual and activist work of black feminists reveals hierarchies of power within categories of race, class, gender, patriarchal relations, sexuality, and sexual orientation. Black feminism demonstrates that white or other feminist theorising that refuses or fails to recognise race as a relation of domination within feminism and society, facilitates the continued oppression of black women within the feminist movement and within society. This is a very powerful argument, and many of the dynamics of power and privilege crystallise around this.

Barbara Ransby notes that one of the strongest ideological tenets around which black feminists have organised "is the notion that race, class, gender and sexuality are co-dependent variables that cannot readily be separated and ranked in scholarship, in political practice, or lived experience" (2000: 1218). The insertion and simultaneous theorisation of race and racism changes what constitutes feminist theory and what could be its subject matter. Radical, socialist, and liberal feminists had examined other oppressive social relations, but none had made race central to their analysis. Black feminist theory exposes racism and the politics of exclusion and denial embedded in feminist knowledge production in the same way that black feminist activism confronts racism in everyday life.

## Changes feminist methodologies and requires new methodological approaches

Feminist knowledge and feminist methodologies change when the specificity of the lives of black women/minority women/marginalized women inform feminist theory. Beside exposing racism and the politics of exclusion and domination, what we know and how we come to know it, what that ongoing body of knowledge looks like, and what purposes it serves, all look radically different when we recognise that other knowledge claims are less universal than they first appeared. Patricia Hill Collins insists that we understand and use black women's modes of resistance as a basis for examining the simultaneous oppressions women experience (1990). Zillah Eisenstein notes that black feminist theorist Barbara Christian is "troubled that the overtly political literature of African American women and of the women of South America and Africa is being preempted by a postmodern view that assumes that 'reality does not exist' and that 'everything is relative and partial' (Eisenstein 1994: 208; Christian 1988: 74, 73). She goes on to state that the critiques offered by Christian and others help to clarify an important difference between a postmodern focus on diversity and the political focus offered by black feminists. She recognises that black feminists focus on difference in order to understand problems of oppression: "They struggle to theorise a feminism that is diverse at its core, rather than to theorise difference as an end in itself" (208). This distinction that Eisenstein draws out of the work of black feminist theorists is critical, and yet it is goes unrecognised in the larger body of feminist work.

Audre Lorde's open letter to white radical feminist Mary Daly (1984) demonstrates how what we think we know changes when that knowledge is approached from another vantage point. In her critique and exposure of the racism in Daly's work on the nature and functioning of the Goddess, Lorde points out that Daly images white women as Goddesses, with African women entering her analysis "only as victims and preyers-upon each other" (1984: 67). Here Lorde exposes a key distortion that is very similar to the way that early development discourses constructed women in the Caribbean and Africa. Women in the South, whether Caribbean, Asian or African, were generally seen as helpless victims in need of international development intervention. To categorise black or any other grouping of women exclusively as victims is a persistent narrative seen all too often in discourses on women in development, minority women and abused women (Carby 1997: 47).

## A theoretical foundation shaped by women's lived experiences and subjectivity

Patricia Hill Collins states that black feminist theory needs a theoretical foundation that deals simultaneously with the experiences and effects of race, gender and class in examining and shaping the complex realities of black women's lives (1989). Black feminist theory holds that the constructed invisibility of black women's lives must be challenged. For example, much black/African American and West Indian history has focused on the activities of black men. Feminist historians in the Caribbean such as Rhoda Reddock (1985), Lucille Mair (1986), Hilary Beckles (1989b), Verene Shepherd (1993), Bridget Brereton (1994) and Patricia Mohammed (1995) have countered this by analysing the experiences of black and Indian women in order to address women's exclusion (or token inclusion) from West Indian history.

Black feminist scholarship underlines the importance of using lived experience as a criterion for generating knowledge. These experiences should be used to validate knowledge claims, and to create or refute generalisations. This insistence that theory should be built "from the ground up" rejects Western philosophy's fascination with and faith in rationality, objectivity and theory that move from the abstract to the concrete. The epistemological and methodological shift offered by black feminism also recognises and values black women's subjectivity.

## The concept of multiple jeopardies/multiple consciousness/multiple identities

Deborah King's concept of multiple jeopardies/multiple consciousness shifted the conception of women's oppressions as confined within ethnic and racial boundaries (1986). Like many other black feminists before her, King was concerned about the practical and theoretical invisibility of black women. She situates her analysis in the fluid and constantly mutating confluence of race, class, sexism (or relations of gender) and sexuality. Barbara Smith likewise informs us that "the concept of the simultaneity of oppression is still the crux of a black feminist understanding of political reality and, I believe, one of the most significant ideological contributions of Black feminist thought" (1983: xxxii).

I used Deborah King's analysis of the simultaneity of multiple oppressions to build a postmodern feminist theory for Caribbean social science research, noting that "theoretically and politically her contribution recognises that much of feminist theory represents white, Eurocentric feminist theorising and is therefore inadequate in not addressing the epistemological and practical concerns of other women, especially black women" (Barriteau 1992: 22–23).

Deborah King and Fiona Williams maintain that the simultaneous experiences of these relations of domination not only compound these oppressions, but reconstitute them in specific ways, an important theoretical breakthrough. Barbara Ransby states:

> Because any political agenda that addresses the realities of most African American women's lives must deal with the four major systems of oppression and exploitation—race , class, gender and sexuality—black feminist politics radically breaks down the notion of mutually exclusive, competing identities and interests and instead understands identities and political process as organic, fluid, interdependent, dynamic and historical (2000: 1219).

Yet such simultaneity of analysis is very difficult to achieve in practice. Even when there is a commitment to tracking simultaneous oppressions or relations of domination, there is tremendous political pressure to prioritise a particular oppression, to create hierarchies, to rank one as more debilitating, more devastating, more demanding of political activism than the others. All too often, the search for alternatives breaks down when confronted with the challenge of moving simultaneously on all oppressions, or recognising how the experiences of black women unite these oppressions. Even though black women exist at the intersection of all these oppressions, they are constantly asked to choose and identity with one only.

If we interrogate the powerful title of the book *All the Women Are White, All the Blacks Are Men, But Some of Us Are Brave* (Hull, Bell Scott and Smith 1982), this can clearly be discerned. "All the Women Are White" reveals that Gender = Race = Privileged Femininity. This kind of simplistic thinking, however, fails to mask the privileges available to women of the dominant race. In societies with institutionalised racism, race nuances adverse relations of gender for women of the dominant race. In other words, for members of the dominant race, relations of race mute or mediate adverse relations of gender. For example, in the United States, relations of race carry privileges to white women individually and collectively, whether or not they want to access them. These privileges await them, are bestowed on them and are available for their use.

Likewise, "All the Blacks Are Men" tracks how Race = Gender = Inferior Masculinity. The belief that all blacks are men equates race with masculinity, but with race (blackness) understood as inferior and pathological. So race in this equation brings relations of domination to masculinity in an obsessively patriarchal, capitalist society. Thus a wounded, inferior masculinity is created with expectations of the expression of that masculinity, irrespective of what individual black or minority men might contribute. And the black woman? She of course remains invisible, with no recognition of either her race or her gender. And yet society remains racist and sexist, is still driven by capitalist patriarchal racism, which means that merely to exist as a black woman requires bravery.

### Simultaneously problematises public and private spheres

A major contribution of black feminist theory is that it simultaneously problematises the public and private spheres from the perspective of race. Like radical feminist theory, black feminist theory is concerned with patriarchal relations in the private domain. However, unlike radical feminism, black feminism goes on to demonstrate how racist relations follow black women into the private realm and in the process reconfigure their household and intimate spaces very differently. Experiences of relations of oppression within households differ for black or minority women in a racist state, because the remedies of the state may be applied differently. For example, these oppressive relations may be read as "cultural" as a way of side-stepping engaging with or changing them. Alternatively, domestic or intimate practices that are not understood or accepted may be viewed as pathological in an attempt to avoid acknowledging their difference.

Hazel Carby informs us that black family structures in Britain have been seen "as pathological by the state and are in the process of being constructed as pathological in white feminist theory" (1997: 47). Patricia McFadden reminds us that in several African countries, archaic notions of culture are continuously invoked to curtail the advancement of women, to protect the sexual and socio-cultural privileges of men, and to deny women their property rights (2002: 18, 30–31, 34).

### Analysis is located in political economy

Like socialist feminist theorising, black feminist theory deliberately adopts a framework of analysis that is situated in the political economy of state systems. Material relations and class relations are intrinsic to this analysis, which identifies how working-class black women experience antagonistic capitalist relations more intensely, as a result of the ideological relations arising from race acting upon the oppressive relations arising from gender. Once more, a very different and far more nuanced rendering emerges when the political economy of a society is examined from a black feminist theoretical perspective.

In Western political thought and within Enlightenment philosophy, the public and private realms represent radically different spheres of existence for women, in which the private world is one of dependence, while the public world is one of freedom. One result is that the private sphere becomes dependent on the public sphere, which in turn is dominated by internal and external (i.e., international) capitalist relations, thus creating hierarchies of dependence. This is why liberal feminists have argued for women's inclusion in the public realm, so that they too might enter the world of freedom, the world of liberation.[6] However, black feminist theory reveals that both spheres represent hierarchies of dependence for black women. In a racist society, the state trivialises, misrepresents and infantilises women's citizenship and domestic concerns (Carby 1997: 47).

### Black feminist theory deconstructs patriarchal relations

Central to black feminist theorising is the knowledge that patriarchal relations structure women's lives very differently to their male peers. The "rule of the father" institutionalises men's power in the family and society. The notion that the source of this power is natural, supported by biology, and sanctioned by religion and state practices, complicates patriarchal relations for women in the family and the state. However, the crucible of racism exposes patriarchy as a construct that is neither natural, nor sanctioned by biology, nor ordained by religion, as it is clear that racism denies black men the patriarchal privileges held by white men, thus exposing the fallacy that maleness automatically confers power.

Yet this remains a powerful construct that grants domination, control and authority to men who wish to access the privileges of patriarchs. In the Commonwealth Caribbean, men of European, African and Asian/Indian descent have assumed the role of patriarchs. Black men who are minorities in racist societies often seek control and manifest their desire to be patriarchs in ways that are pathological. Meanwhile, through their everyday experiences, black women confront the falsity of the universalising tendencies of patriarchy in a racist state. This is vital, as women who do not understand the contradictory and antagonistic interactions of patriarchal and race relations can make arguments for the reinstatement or establishment of black or other ethnic patriarchies.

### Placing race at the centre alters basic concepts

By centralising women's experiences of relations of domination in race and racism, black feminist theorising radically alters the meanings and understandings of basic concepts critical to feminist analysis. Race-contesting-gender-contesting-class-contesting-race turns many concepts on their heads. In the process, black feminist theory destabilises the coherence and certainty with which certain concepts and constructs are regarded in the general body of feminist thought. I glance at several of these below.

**THE HOME.** Liberal, radical, and socialist feminist theories typically analyse the home as a site of oppression for women. Betty Friedan set the stage in her 1963 analysis in *The Feminine Mystique*: "It is very urgent to understand how the very conditions of being a housewife can create a sense of emptiness, non-existence, nothingness in women" (Friedan cited in Agonito 1977: 380–81). Likewise, think of radical feminism's emphasis on patriarchal relations beginning in the family and radiating outwards to civil society, the state and the economy. In the context of a hostile, racist society, black feminism theorises the home as a respite. Note this position does not romanticise the home or deny oppressive gender relations that may be present there. However, this position recognises that for black women, the home might well be a place of physical and psychic retreat from overtly racist practices and experiences.

Black feminist theory thus reveals that there are other dimensions to black women's experiences of home that are not captured by liberal, radical, and socialist feminist analysis—especially for those black women who for centuries have been obliged to work outside the home, whether in fields, factories or the homes of others. Many of these women, instead of longing to be liberated from the home, yearn for the opportunity to go home or stay at home. In the words of two scholars, "Black feminist Barbara Smith has argued that . . . families of people of color have been havens, even if the safety or buffer they have provided has been incomplete. The invasion of the state into black family life does not negate the protective functions of the family and community" (Eisenstein 1994: 204; Smith 1983: 64–72).

**THE FAMILY.** By extension, the family becomes in some instances a site of political and cultural resistance, or at least a place of respite from racism. Hazel Carby notes that ideologies of black female domesticity and motherhood have been constructed through black women's employment in chattel positions as domestic workers and surrogate mothers to white families, rather than in relation to their own families (1997: 47).

**SEXUALITY.** Black women's sexuality has been objectified, commodified and pathologised, with black women stereotyped as having wild and unbridled sexual urges. Alternatively, black women were presented either as unsexed or whorish—they are either Nanny or Jezebel (Stanton 1992). Evelyn Hammond has argued that black women's sexuality is constructed in opposition to that of white women (1993). However, it is perhaps more accurate to say that in the struggle for sexual liberation, many white women demanded reproductive technologies in order to say yes to sex, while many black women wanted autonomy and freedom from an intrusive and racist state in order to be able to say no.

Audre Lorde led the way in theorising sexuality as a source of power, exposing homophobia and heterosexism within black communities, especially towards black lesbians (1984). Patricia Hill Collins notes that for Lorde, "sexuality is a component of the larger construct of the erotic as a source of power in women. Lorde's notion is one of power as energy, as something people possess which must be annexed in order for larger systems of oppression to function" (1990: 166). How much of Audre Lorde's path-breaking work in theorising the range of women's sexuality has informed work on women's sexuality in the Caribbean?

Meanwhile, looking at the intersection of sexuality and slavery studies, Angela Davis has considered how the ending of slavery created new social and sexual realities for black women and men. She insists that it was not the economic status of former slaves that underwent radical transformation on emancipation—they were no less impoverished upon being emancipated than they had been during slavery. Rather, it was the status of their personal and sexual relationships that was transformed or revolutionised. She argues that for the first time in the history of the African presence in the Americas, masses of black women and men were able to make autonomous decisions about their sexuality and sexual partners. Whether this was respected or not, black women and men now had sovereignty over the decision about who they could or would sleep with, and it was this that marked an important divide between life during slavery and life after emancipation (1998: 7–8).

So we see that concepts of great interest to feminist scholars, including the construction of the family, the home and sexuality noted above, are transformed in the hands of black feminist scholars.

## The Politics of Creating Feminist Knowledge

Black feminist theorising presents scholars with some hard questions concerning the politics of generating knowledge, including feminist knowledge. Investigation reveals that many of the conceptual tools that "appear" (as if for the first time) in postmodern and feminist theorising of the past few decades in fact draw on the work done by black feminist scholars—but without acknowledgement of the genealogy or theoretical roots of these concepts. For example, the concept of multiple jeopardy/consciousness/identities, as well as Audre Lorde's conceptualisation of difference,[7] both predate their extensive and uncredited use by other scholars during the 1980s.

For instance, if we take the case of Rosemary Tong's *Anthology of Feminist Thought: A Comprehensive Introduction*, we find that she somehow manages to exclude any reference to black feminist thought in the eight schools of feminist thought she covers. She does, however, recognises the work, or perhaps more accurately, the personhood of Audre Lorde, whom she individualises. In making the point that "attention to difference is precisely what will help women achieve unity" (1992: 237), she states:

> Audre Lorde, whose very person is a celebration of difference—Black, lesbian, feminist, disfigured by breast cancer—and whose poetry is a voice against the duality of mind/body, wrote that as we come to know, accept, and explore our feelings, they "will become sanctuaries and fortresses and spawning grounds for the most radical and daring ideas— the house of difference so necessary to change the conceptualisation of meaningful action" (Lorde 1985: 126). Feelings lead to ideas and ideas lead to action, said Lorde (1992: 237).

Yet Tong neither analyses nor even notes Audre Lorde's substantive earlier theorisation of the concept of difference. In what claims to be a comprehensive anthology of feminist thought, we meet Audre Lorde as an individual whose life was a celebration of difference, rather than as a scholar credited for the analytical concepts that she created, and which have been repeatedly used in feminist theorising. Tong cannot claim to be unaware of the work of black feminists as her bibliography lists several of the important works of the 1970s and 1980s, including works by Angela Davis, bell hooks, Gloria Joseph, Alice Walker, and others. Her subject index makes no reference to black feminism or women of colour.

Exceptions to this kind of willful blindness do exist; for instance, Zillah Eisenstein is a self-defined white, middle-class feminist, whose work *The Color of Gender: Reimaging Democracy* (1994: 2) presents an uncommon appreciation of what black feminist theory offers feminist epistemology, in much the same way that Jane Flax's pedagogical and research strategies do (1998).[8] In *The Color of Gender*, Eisenstein engages fully with the collective works and contributions of black feminist theorists, offering new conceptual tools for building on this work. For example, she draws on the work of black feminist theorists to create the concept of "racialized patriarchy", stating that:

> Patriarchy differentiates women from men while privileging men. Racism simultaneously differentiates people of color from whites and privileges whiteness. . . . Like any other structuring of power, the racializing of gender is a process that always needs to be renegotiated. I use the

term "racialized patriarchy" to bring attention to the continual inter-play of race and gender in the structure of power (1994: 2-3).

Unfortunately, most contemporary feminist scholars continue to ignore the work of black feminists. Wikipedia, the popular online resource, lists six main schools of feminist thought, psychoanalytic, radical, liberal, socialist, Marx-ist, and postmodern. It goes on to categorise sixteen subtypes of feminism (including fat and religious feminism) without mentioning black feminism, even though the last subtype—womanism—is related (Wikipedia 2006).

## Toward a Conclusion

The issues that concern Caribbean feminists—the state and women, iden-tity politics, fractures and fissures within the women's movement (includ-ing exclusionary practices), the development of feminist consciousness, dialogues with masculinities—all resonate within black feminist theory.

In 1977, exactly 30 years ago, black feminists were addressing the ques-tion of identity politics, the claim that "the personal is political" and the need to dialogue with masculinities (all issues that Caribbean feminists are currently tackling). These issues coalesced in the statement issued by the Combahee River Collective, and explicitly called a Black Feminist State-ment. This constituted a powerful theorizing of the concerns confronting black women (Gloria T. Hull et al. 1982 [1977]). While expanding on the concept of identity politics ("we believe that the most profound and poten-tially the most radical politics come directly out of our own identity"), the Statement ruptured the continuity between biology, being, gender roles and politics: "although we are feminists and lesbians, we feel solidarity with progressive black men and do not advocate the fractionalization that white women who are separatists demand" (The Combahee River Collective, 1982 [1977]: 16).

The Collective also expanded the radical feminist principle or man-tra, "the personal is political", to include the notion of the personal as also cultural:

> A political contribution which we feel we have already made is the expansion of the feminist principle that the personal is political. In our consciousness-raising sessions for example, we have gone beyond white women's revelations because we are dealing with the implications of race and class as well as sex. Even our Black women's style of talk-ing, testifying in Black language about what we have experienced, has a resonance that is both cultural and political (The Combahee River Collective, 1982 [1977]: 17)

The Collective also anticipated the construction of gender roles and recognised that like women, how men express maleness and masculinity is due to how they have been socialised, rather than the result of some essential, inherent biological maleness that makes male behaviour inevitable, fatalistic and destructive. In the process, the Collective rejects biological determinism, paving the way for a fuller understanding of the ideological and material dimensions of relations of gender:

> We reject the stance of lesbian separatism because it is not a viable political analysis or strategy for us. We have a great deal of criticism and loathing for what men have been socialized to be in this society: what they support and how they oppress. But we do not have the misguided notion that it is their maleness per se, i.e., their biological maleness that makes them what they are. As Black women we find any type of biological determinism a particularly dangerous and reactionary basis upon which to build a politic (The Combahee River Collective, 1982 [1977]: 17).

The Collective highlighted some of the conceptual flaws of radical feminist theorising (specifically lesbian separatism as a political strategy) and advocated an inclusive politic strategy that would enable black women to struggle together with black men against racism while also challenging them on sexism (The Combahee River Collective, 1982 [1977]: 16). They were also beginning to explore the simultaneity of multiple oppressions. What is even more compelling is that as lesbians, these women could have easily privileged their sexual orientation in their feminist politics and gender identities. Instead, they chose to politicise race and use it as a base from which to build coalitions with black men whom they did not desire sexually, but whose survival in a racist, rabidly capitalist society mattered in their analysis of capitalism, racism and sexism. Nevertheless, the revolutionary theoretical insights of this comparatively early analysis and its potential value for future feminist strategies have not been appreciated. The theoretical insights from this Statement alone could be useful for feminist coalitions and agendas in Africa and the Caribbean.

We must ask how black feminist theorising could be relevant to African women and women of the African diaspora, such as those in the Caribbean? What is its significance to white women in Northern industrialised societies? Asian women? Muslim women in the Middle East? Black feminist theorising provides many important conceptual tools for rethinking our understanding of social institutions, especially if we wish to reveal and erase relations of dominations in everyday life. I believe that African and Caribbean feminists can benefit from assessing the conceptual tools offered by the vast body of work that comprises black feminist theory, and by examining the factors surrounding its relative absence in our intellectual and activist work. This article merely scratches the surface of black feminist theory. We need ongoing investigation of this body of scholarship, as well as interrogations of its applicability. Even while recognizing that the contributions of black feminist thought are confronted by the politics of knowledge production, the body of feminist knowledge is poorer for not acknowledging and disseminating the work of black feminist theorists.

## References

Andaiye. 2002. "'The angle you look from determines what you see': Towards a Critique of Feminist Politics in the Caribbean." The Lucille Mathurin Mair Lecture 2002, Centre for Gender and Development Studies, University of the West Indies.

Agonito, Rosemary. 1977. *History of Ideas on Woman: A Source Book*. New York: G. W. Putman and Sons.

Bailey, Barbara. 2003. "The Search for Gender Equity and Empowerment of Caribbean Women: The Role of Education" in Tang Nain, Gemma and Bailey, Barbara. eds. *Gender Equality in the Caribbean: Reality or Illusion?* Kingston: Ian Randle Publishers.

Baksh-Soodeen, Rawwida. 1998. "Issues of Difference in Contemporary Caribbean Feminism". *Feminist Review 59*.

Barriteau, Eudine. 1992. "The Construct of a Postmodernist Feminist Theory for Caribbean Social Science Research", *Social and Economic Studies* 41: 2.

Barriteau, Eudine. 1995. "Postmodernist Feminist Theorizing and Development Policy and Practice in the Anglophone Caribbean: The Barbados Case" in Marchand, Marianne H. and Parpart, Jane L. eds. *Feminism/postmodernism/development*. London: Routledge.

Barriteau, Eudine. 2002. "Issues and Challenges of Caribbean Feminisms." Keynote address delivered at the Inaugural Workshop on Recentering Feminisms, Centre for Gender and Development Studies and the Faculty of Law, University of the West Indies.

Barriteau, Eudine. 2003a. "Theorizing the Shift from 'Woman' to 'Gender' in Caribbean Feminist Discourse: The Power Relations of Creating Knowledge" in Barriteau, Eudine. eds. *Confronting Power, Theorizing Gender: Interdisciplinary Perspectives in the Caribbean*. Kingston: University of West Indies Press.

Barriteau, Eudine. 2003b."Confronting Power and Politics: A Feminist Theorizing of Gender in Commonwealth Caribbean Societies", *Meridians, Feminism, Race, Transnationalism* 3: 2.

Barriteau, Eudine. 2003c. "Conclusion: Beyond a Backlash—The Frontal Assault on Containing Caribbean Women in the Decade of the 1990s" in Tang Nain, Gemma and Bailey, Barbara. eds. *Gender Equality in the Caribbean: Reality or Illusion?* Kingston: Ian Randle Publishers.

Barriteau, Eudine. 2003d. "Issues and Challenges of Caribbean Feminisms", *Agenda Empowering Women for Gender Equity: African Feminisms* 58.

Barriteau, Eudine. 2004a. "Constructing Feminist Knowledge in the Commonwealth Caribbean in the Era of Globalization" in Bailey, Barbara and Elsa Leo-Rhynie. eds. *Gender in the 21st Century: Caribbean Perspectives, Visions and Possibilities*. Kingston: Ian Randle Publishers.

Barriteau, Eudine. 2004b. "Gendered Relations in a Post-Colonial/Modernizing Caribbean State" in Endeley, Joyce, Ardener, Shirley, Goodridge, Richard and Lyonga, Nalova. eds. *New Gender Studies from Cameroon and the Caribbean*. Department of Women and Gender Studies, University of Buea: Cameroon.

Barriteau, Eudine. 2006. "Engendering Development or Gender main-streaming? A Critical Assessment from the Commonwealth Caribbean" in Kuiper, Edith and Barker, Drucilla K. eds. *Feminist Economics and the World Bank: History, Theory and Policy*. London and New York: Routledge.

Beckles, Hilary. 1989a. *Corporate Power in Barbados—A Mutual Affair: Economic Injustice in a Political Democracy*. Bridgetown: Lighthouse Publications.

Beckles, Hilary. 1989b. *Natural Rebels: A social history of enslaved black women in Barbados*. London: Zed Books.

Beckles, Hilary. 1998. "Historicizing Slavery in West Indian Feminisms", *Feminist Review* 59.

Brereton, Bridget. 1994. "Gendered testimony: autobiographies, diaries and letters by women as sources for Caribbean history." Elsa Goveia Memorial Lecture, Department of History, University of the West Indies, Mona, Jamaica.

Brewer, Rose M. 1993. "Theorizing Race, Class and Gender: The New Scholarship of Black Feminist Intellectuals and Black Women's Labor" in James, Stanlie and Busia, Abena. eds. *Theorizing Black Feminisms: The Visionary Pragmatism of Black Women*. London and New York: Routledge.

Carby, Hazel V. 1987. *Reconstructing Womanhood: The emergence of the Afro-American woman novelist*. New York: Oxford University Press.

Carby, Hazel V. 1997 [1982]. "White Woman Listen: Black Feminism and the Boundaries of Sisterhood" in Mirza, Heidi Safia. eds. *Black British Feminism: A Reader*. London: Routledge. First published in *The Empire Strikes Back: Race and Racism in Seventies Britain*. London: Hutchinson.

Christian, Barbara. 1988. "The Race for Theory", *Feminist Studies* 14: 1.

Collins, Patricia Hill. 1990. *Black Feminist Thought: Knowledge, Consciousness, and The Politics of Empowerment*. Boston: Unwin Hyman.

The Combahee River Collective. 1982 [1977]. "A Black Feminist Statement" in Hull, Gloria, T., Scott, Patricia Bell and Smith, Barbara. eds. *All the Women Are White, All the Blacks Are Men, But Some of Us Are Brave: Black Women's Studies*. New York: The Feminist Press at the City University of New York.

Davis, Angela Y. 1998. *Blues Legacies and Black Feminism: Gertrude "Ma" Rainey, Bessie Smith, and Billie Holiday*. New York: Pantheon Books.

Eisenstein, Zillah R. 1994. *The Color of Gender: Reimaging Democracy*. Berkeley: University of California Press.

Flax, Jane. 1998. *The American Dream in Black and White: The Clarence Thomas Hearings*. Ithaca and New York: Cornell University Press.

Friedan, Betty. 1963. *The Feminine Mystique*. New York: W. W. Norton.

Hammond, Evelyn M. 1993. "Towards a Genealogy of Black Female Sexuality and the Problematic of Silence" in Alexander, Jacqui and Mohanty, Chandra. eds. *Feminist Genealogies, Colonial Legacies, Democratic Futures*. New York: Routledge.

Haniff, Nesha. 1996. *The Stereotyping of East Indian Women in the Caribbean*. Wand Occasional Paper 1, January/February.

Harris, Sonja. 2003. "Review of Institutional Mechanisms for the Advancement of Women and for Achieving Gender Equality 1995–2000" in Tang Nain, Gemma and

Bailey, Barbara. eds. *Gender Equality in the Caribbean: Reality or Illusion?* Kingston: Ian Randle Publishers.

Hull, Gloria T., Patricia Bell Scott and Barbara Smith. eds. 1982. *All the Women Are White, All the Blacks Are Men, But Some of Us Are Brave: Black Women's Studies.* New York: The Feminist Press at the City University of New York.

Lorde, Audre. 1984. *Sister Outsider: Essays and Speeches.* New York: The Crossing Press.

Lorde, Audre. 1985. "Poetry is not a Luxury" in Jardine, Alice and Eisenstein, Hester. eds. *The Future of Difference.* New Brunswick: Rutgers University Press.

King, Deborah. 1986. "Multiple Jeopardy, Multiple Consciousness" in Malson, Micheline R., et al. eds. *Feminist Theory in Practice and Process.* Chicago: University of Chicago Press.

McFadden, Patricia. 2002. *Impunity, Masculinity and Heterosexism in the Discourse on Male Endangerment: An African Feminist Perspective.* Working Paper 7, Centre for Gender and Development Studies, University of the West Indies.

Mathurin-Mair, Lucille. 1986. "Women Fieldworkers in Jamaica during Slavery." Elsa Goveia Memorial Lecture, Department of History, University of the West Indies, Mona, Jamaica.

Martin, Wendy. 1972. *The American Sisterhood: Writings of the Feminist Movement from Colonial Times to the Present.* New York: Harper and Row.

Mohammed, Patricia. 1998. "Towards Indigenous Feminist Theorizing in the Caribbean", *Feminist Review* 59. Mohammed, Patricia. 1995. "Writing Gender into History: The Negotiation of Gender Relations among Indian Men and Women in Post-Indenture Trinidad Society, 1917–47" in Shepherd, Verene, Brereton, Bridget and Bailey, Barbara. eds. *Engendering History: Caribbean Women in Historical Perspective.* Kingston: Ian Randle Publishers.

Painter, Nell Irvin. 2000. "Regrets", *Signs: Journal of Women in Culture and Society* 25: 4.

Pargass, Gaietry and Roberta Clarke. 2003. "Violence Against Women: A Human Rights Issue" in Tang Nain, Gemma and Bailey, Barbara. eds. *Gender Equality in the Caribbean: Reality or Illusion?* Kingston: Ian Randle Publishers.

Ransby, Barbara. 2000. "Black Feminism at Twenty-One: Reflections on the Evolution of a National Community", *Signs: Journal of Women in Culture and Society* 25: 4.

Reddock, Rhoda. 1985. "Women and Slavery in the Caribbean: A Feminist Perspective", *Latin American Perspectives* 12: 1.

Reddock, Rhoda. 1994. *Women, Labour & Politics in Trinidad & Tobago: A History.* London: Zed Books.

Reddock, Rhoda. 1998. "Women's Organizations and Movements in the Commonwealth Caribbean: The Response to the Global Economic Crisis in the 1980s", *Feminist Review* 59.

Reynolds, Tracey. 2001. "Caribbean Fathers in Family Life in Britain" in Golbourne, Harry and Chamberlain, M. eds. *Caribbean Families in Britain and the Trans Atlantic World.* London: Macmillan Education Ltd.

Robinson, Tracy. 2004. "Gender, Feminism and Constitutional Reform in the Caribbean" in Bailey, Barbara and Leo-Rhynie, Elsa. eds. *Gender in the 21st Century: Caribbean Perspectives, Visions and Possibilities.* Kingston: Ian Randle Publishers.

Rooks, Noliwe, M. 2000. "Like Canaries in the Mines: Black Women's Studies at the Millennium" *Signs: Journal of Women in Culture and Society* 25: 4.

Rossi, Alice S. ed. 1974. *The Feminist Papers: From Adams to de Beauvoir.* New York: Bantam Books.

Rowley, Michelle. 2004. "Bureacratising Feminism: Charting Caribbean Women's Centrality within Margins" in Bailey, Barbara and Leo-Rhynie, Elsa. eds. *Gender in the 21st Century: Caribbean Perspectives, Visions and Possibilities*. Kingston: Ian Randle Publishers.

Schneir, Miriam. ed.1972. *Feminism: The Essential Historical Writings*. New York: Vintage Books.

Shepherd, Verene. 1993. "Emancipation through Servitude: Aspects of the Condition of Indian Women in Jamaica, 1845–1945" in Beckles, Hilary and Shepherd, Verene. eds. *Caribbean Freedom: Society and Economy from Emancipation to the Present*. Kingston: Ian Randle Publishers.

Smith, Barbara. ed. 1983. *Home Girls: A Black Feminist Anthology*. Kitchen Table Women of Color Press: New York.

Spender, Dale. 1982. *Women of Ideas and What Men Have Done to Them*. London: Pandora Press.

Stanton, Donna C. 1992. "Introduction: The Subject of Sexuality" in Stanton, Donna C. ed. *Discourses of Sexuality: From Aristotle to Aids*. Ann Arbor: The University of Michigan Press.

Tong, Rosemary. 1992. *Feminist Thought: A Comprehensive Introduction*. London and New York: Routledge.

Truth, Sojourner. 1851. "Ain't I a Woman?" Available at http://eserver.org/race/aint-i-a-woman.txt.

Vassell, Linette. 2003. "Women, Power and Decision-Making in CARICOM Countries: Moving Forward from a Post-Beijing Assessment" in Tang Nain, Gemma and Bailey, Barbara. eds. *Gender Equality in the Caribbean: Reality or Illusion?* Kingston: Ian Randle Publishers.

White, Averille. 1986. "Profiles of Women in the Caribbean Project", *Social and Economic Studies* 35: 2. Wikipedia. 2006. "Feminist Theory." Available at http://en.wikipedia. org/wiki/feminist_theory.

## Notes

1. Black feminist scholarship is an exceedingly rich and heterogeneous body of work, spanning three centuries. This survey does not in any sense pretend to capture all the ideas, debates, theories, concepts and strategies that would comprise black feminist theorising.

2. I accept the Caribbean as the geographic grouping of island states and Latin American and South American countries bordering the Caribbean Sea – what has also been referred to as the Circum Caribbean. In terms of my theoretical work, I define the Caribbean as the independent Anglophone island states and British dependencies within the Caribbean Sea, including the Central American country of Belize and the South American country of Guyana. These are the former colonies of Britain, or, in a few cases, British Protectorates. They form the political grouping called the Commonwealth Caribbean (Barriteau, 2001: 3).

3. Trinidad and Tobago, and Guyana, are the exceptions in the Commonwealth Caribbean. In these countries, especially in the post-independence period, charges and experiences of racist practices centre on relations between Indo-Caribbean and Afro-Caribbean peoples, and the contours of state policies and governance when predominantly "black" or Indian-descended parties occupy state power.

4. This term refers to the period after Christopher Columbus, acting on behalf of the Spanish monarchs, made landfall in the Americas in the 1490s, while searching for a trade route to the East. This is generally accepted as the beginning of European colonisation of the Americas, including the Caribbean.

5. This list is merely meant to be representative, suggests no hierarchies of contributions, and makes no claims to being exhaustive.

6. Ironically, in order to facilitate women's participation in the public sphere, the approach of the Commonwealth Caribbean states has been to prioritise equality over freedom.

7. For an understanding of difference not as a polarised opposition, but a full, rich, complex location and basis from which to theorise, see Lorde's classic essay, "The Master's Tools will never Dismantle the Master's House" (1984).

8. In the late 1980s and early 1990s, Jane Flax, a white, Jewish, feminist philosopher, political scientist and psychotherapist, introduced me and many other postgraduate students at Howard University to the work of black feminist theorists. In courses on political theory, feminist theory and feminist philosophy, she routinely included the scholarship of black feminists, not as part of special topics on race, but as core components of the courses she taught. I am deeply indebted to her for exposing me to this rich body of scholarship.

## Epilogue
### On Dolls, Presidents, and
### Little Black Girls

*Cheryl A. Wall*

2009

The day after standing on the Mall in Washington to witness Barack Obama's inauguration, I met my first class of the spring semester. The first text for the course was Toni Morrison's *The Bluest Eye*, the heartbreaking story of a little black girl's destruction. The juxtaposition was stark. On Tuesday I felt as though I finally understood the meaning of "jubilee," a word that conjures up images of large crowds of enslaved people listening for the proclamation of their emancipation. For me, standing in that crowd in Washington, the word was reinvested with meaning. Jubilee signified not just freedom itself, but the sense of awe that accompanied its achievement. I understood that in the eerie quiet of the crowd, who responded to the sights on the jumbo screens with cheers, but who listened to the words—especially those of the president—in a stillness that I would not have thought possible for almost two million people to sustain. Many could not hold back their tears, which I realized no one could see until the speech ended, because we were all so focused on what was going on in front of us. As we turned to embrace, stranger to stranger, kin to kin, we met each other's tears. And then, the shouting began. That, too, captured the meaning of jubilee.

On Wednesday, I realized that I was not eager to turn to *The Bluest Eye*, one of my favorite novels, because it meant returning to the traumatic history that the nation seemed on the brink of overcoming. I wanted to live in the joy for just a little while longer. One of the most joyful moments of Tuesday had been the sight of Malia and Sasha Obama. The cheers that greeted them were second only to those for their parents. But it wasn't until I reread the story of Pecola Breedlove that I began to appreciate what a wonder it was that for the first time in history, if only for a day, the most adored children in the world were two little black girls.

It was surely unimaginable in 1970, the year that saw the emergence of "a community of black women writing," to use Hortense Spillers' phrase. Three of the signal texts of that year—Morrison's *The Bluest Eye*, Alice

Walker's *The Third Life of Grange Copeland*, and Maya Angelou's *I Know Why the Caged Bird Sings* marked the introduction of three of the most influential writers of the late twentieth century. It also marked the shift in the locus of African American literature from the preoccupation with the conflict between black and white men across the color line. Instead, Morrison and Walker's first novels and the initial volume of Angelou's autobiography looked behind the veil to explore broken families, domestic violence, and sexual abuse. They explored, in short, the profound and multifaceted impact of racism on intimate relationships. As different as they were in aesthetic terms, they shared the perspective that in a society ordered by hierarchies of power based on race, class, and gender, no one is more powerless—hence more vulnerable—than a poor black girl. Such girls were at the center of each narrative.

*The Bluest Eye* tells the story of Pecola, a girl so convinced of her own ugliness that she prays, "Please, make me disappear." She seeks to discover the secret of this ugliness that renders her invisible to white storekeepers and makes her the object of scorn to her black classmates. Most painfully, Pecola is despised at home. Her parents believe that they themselves are unworthy of love and their children bear the brunt of that self-hatred. The Breedloves are displaced southerners. Without the familiar signs of segregation, Pecola's mother, Pauline, feels out of place in the midwestern city to which they have come seeking opportunity. She even feels alienated from her black neighbors. She seeks refuge in the movies, but celluloid heroines only intensify her sense of inferiority. A domestic servant, Pauline believes ardently in the superiority of her white employers and of their children. And because she hates herself, she cannot love her daughter. Pecola's father, an abandoned child whose sexual development is stunted by the disfiguring gaze of racist white men, never achieves his own sense of self. When he attempts to express love toward his daughter, he rapes her. But Pecola's friends Frieda and Claudia help readers derive meaning from her story and convey a sense of hope through their own.

Not surprisingly for a novel of girlhood, *The Bluest Eye* features dolls of various kinds: Raggedy Ann dolls with round faces and mops of hair, and the blonde, blue-eyed baby dolls that the novel's adults think are every child's desire. Pecola is too impoverished to even own a doll. But she is so enthralled by the image of Mary Jane, the blue-eyed blonde girl on the peanut-butter candy wrappers, that she spends her precious pennies on candies to worship rather than to eat. And she is so mesmerized by the image of Shirley Temple, that she drinks three quarts of milk in order to hold the cup adorned with Temple's face.

Conventionally, dolls socialize girls to be women and mothers, a convention that becomes painfully ironic in a novel about a girl who gives birth to her father's still-born child. The novel's deployment of dolls and images, however, is also shaped in part by the 1954 *Brown v. Board of Education* Supreme Court decision. The doll test, developed and administered by psychologists Kenneth and Mamie Phipps Clark, was critical to the NAACP's case. Using four gender-neutral dolls, two pink and two brown, the Clarks demonstrated how children between the ages of three and seven understood the significance of race in America. By a wide majority, in the North and South, in cities and rural areas, black children preferred the white dolls over the brown. They had internalized society's racial hierarchy. The Court recognized these findings as evidence of the harmful effects of segregation.

Claudia, the character who sometime serves as narrator of *The Bluest Eye*, is also the voice of social critique. I think of her as a figure for the black feminist critic. Claudia refuses to love Shirley Temple. She finds the Raggedy Ann dolls revolting, and her impulse upon receiving one of the blonde, blue-eyed dolls is to dismember it to see what it is made of, "to find the beauty, the desirability that had escaped me, but apparently only me. Adults, older girls, shops, magazines, newspapers, window signs—all the world had agreed that a blue-eyed, yellow-haired, pink-skinned doll was what every girl child treasured." The passage identifies the ideology that constructs desire. In this regard it is aligned with the research of social scientists like the Clarks. But Claudia's deconstructive impulse enacts a more radical mode of critique. She wants to get at the root of the meaning of race. Her dismemberment of the doll reveals nothing substantive inside it. Race is a wholly ideological construction. This does not, of course, diminish its power.

Perhaps that is the reason that I was not immediately outraged by the reports that surfaced shortly after the inauguration that the Ty company planned to market Malia and Sasha dolls. I was certainly pleased with the fierce response of Michelle Obama, who immediately decried the exploitation of her children. I was thrilled to be alive in a world where a black mother was powerful enough to force a corporation to stand down. Yet the part of my imagination that had taken up residence in the world of *The Bluest Eye* pondered whether having dolls that looked like the Obama girls would have made a difference to Pecola. Let me reformulate that thought. As a trained reader, I know better than to confuse fact with fiction. So, consider this question: could dolls that look like those adorable presidential daughters mitigate the self-hatred of poor black children? Well, I think the answer is slightly yes, but mainly no.

Given children's capacity for imaginative play, there is no telling what empowering fantasies such dolls might engender. But, as ethnographer

Elizabeth Chin, reminds us in *Purchasing Power: Black Kids and American Consumer Culture* (2001), poor black girls in urban neighborhoods rarely acquire so-called "ethnically-correct" dolls. Moreover, even as they play with "white" dolls, they remain acutely aware of the social distance between the world the dolls represent and the world they themselves inhabit. How would we even begin to measure the distance between the White House and the inner city? Whether or not Malia or Sasha dolls would improve a child's self esteem, they would do nothing to change a child's social and material reality. Morrison's novel is conscious of this truth.

*The Bluest Eye* is not just about pernicious ideas of beauty and romantic love; it is mainly about the corrosive effects of racism, sexism, and economic exploitation. The "dying fire [that] lights the sky with a dull orange glow" in the novel's opening pages is pollution from a steel mill. It lingers over working-class neighborhoods but does not extend to the lakefront homes of the wealthy—where families like Pauline Breedlove's employers reside. The environmental pollution is analogous to the pollution of race, gender, and class oppression that the novel critiques. These oppressions persist today, and so do their deleterious effects on black families. In the 1990s Darlene Powell-Hopson and Derek Hopson, another husband-and-wife team of psychologists, repeated the doll test and recorded similar results. So did a New York City teenager, Kira Davis, who used the test as a framing motif for her 2005 film, *A Girl Like Me*. A much enhanced and pervasive media that commodifies young black women's bodies now runs twenty-four/seven with damnable consequences. According to Johnnetta Betsch Cole and Beverly Guy-Sheftall in *Gender Talk: The Struggle for Women's Equality in African American Communities* (2003), almost one in three black adolescent girls has experienced some form of sexual or physical abuse. Morrison's novel is as timely as it is timeless.

The emergence of black women's writing and the emergence of black women's studies are inextricably connected. Many of the founders of black women's studies—Barbara Christian, Beverly Guy-Sheftall, Akasha (Gloria) Hull, Nellie Y. McKay, Barbara Smith, and Mary Helen Washington—were English professors. They began their careers analyzing the new texts that were being published, beginning approximately forty years ago, and by rediscovering forgotten texts by authors including Gwendolyn Brooks, Zora Neale Hurston, and Nella Larsen. As these scholars formulated critical and theoretical methods of analysis, they developed theories of what we now call intersectionality that remain central to the methodology of women's and gender studies today. The first to articulate this theory was Barbara Smith, who in her 1977 essay, "Toward a Black Feminist Criticism," identified race, sex, and class as interlocking factors in black women's literature, as in black women's lives. By now black women's studies has reshaped critical inquiry across disciplines in ways that the academy has yet to fully recognize. If black women's studies has not transformed the academy, it has certainly influenced it.

Black women's writing and black women's studies were never about literary or academic transformation alone. They were always about social transformation. I am an optimist, so I believe that the election of Barack Obama makes social transformation more possible. Something fundamental has changed, of that I am sure. Yet I think back to that day of jubilee in 1863, and I know that almost 150 years of often traumatic history followed it. This year's inauguration does not represent the fulfillment of the goals of freedom, justice, and equality. It is not *yet* Jubilee.

As I reflect on the challenges ahead, I think again of Claudia, who never loses faith in the integrity of her own experiences and ideas. While she confesses that she did learn to love Shirley Temple—or, at least as I prefer to think, she learns to pretend to love her—it is Claudia's fearless, edgy determination as well as her wicked sense of humor that sets the standard to which we as feminist scholars should aspire.

# Acknowledgments
# and Permissions

## Acknowledgments

We are in the wonderful position of having entirely too many people to acknowledge and thank for their support and help as we embarked upon the *Brave* process. We realize that this is hardly sufficient, but we are hopeful that this generic but deeply heartfelt "thank you" will suffice. We would be remiss, however, if we did not specifically acknowledge a special group of people who learned first hand about the messy, exhilarating, frustrating process of constructing an anthology and who, as a part of their own learning processes, provided the editors with crucial support, including helping to identify essays, going to the library, making copies, reading and commenting on potential contributions, and listening to our deliberative thinking. They were the students of Nellie Y. McKay who were deeply impacted by the example of her scholarly life and her careful mentoring. Michelle Gordon, Rhea Lathan, Eric Darnell Pritchard, and David LaCroix served as graduate assistants for both Nellie and Stanlie M. James at various times throughout this process. Others who were less formally involved but no less important to the process included Lisa Woolfork, Kimberly Blockett, Gregory Routledge, David Ikard, Shanna Greene Benjamin, Keisha Watson Bowman, Gretchen Michlitsch, Lynn Jennings, Katherine Mellen Charron, Trudi Witonsky, and David Junker. This list also includes Mary Jatau, a graduate student at Arizona State University, who contributed to the completion of *Still Brave* by sharing in the proofreading process.

## Permissions

Alexander-Floyd, Nikol G. and Evelyn M. Simien. "Revisiting 'What's in a Name?': Exploring the Contours of Africana Womanist Thought." Copyright © 2006 Frontiers Editorial Collective. Reprinted by permission of the University of Nebraska Press from *Frontiers: a Journal of Women Studies*, vol 27, no 1 (2006).

Awkward, Michael. "A Black Man's Place in Black Feminist Criticism," from *Negotiating Difference: Race, Gender, and the Politics of Positionality* (Chicago: University of Chicago Press, 1995): 43–58. Reprinted with permission from the publisher.

Davis, Adrienne. "Don't Let Nobody Bother Yo' Principle: The Sexual Economy of Slavery." Copyright © 2002 by Adrienne Davis. Reprinted with permission of the author from *Sister Circle: Black Women and Work*, New Brunswick: Rutgers University Press, 2002.

Davis, Angela Y. and Cassandra Shaylor. "Race, Gender, and the Prison Industrial Complex: California and Beyond," Copyright © 2001. Reprinted with permission of Indiana University Press from *Meridians 2.1* (2001): 25.

duCille, Ann. "Phallus(ies) of Interpretation: Toward Engendering the Black Critical 'I'" from *Callaloo* 16.3 (1993): 559–73 © Charles H. Rowell. Reprinted with permission of The Johns Hopkins University Press.

Giddings, Paula. "The Last Taboo," copyright © 1992 Paula Giddings, from RACE-ING JUSTICE, EN-GENDERING POWER, edited by Toni Morrison. Used by permission of Pantheon Books, a division of Random House, Inc.

Grant, Jacqueline. "Womanist Theology: Black Women's Experience as a Source for Doing Theology, with Special Reference to Christology," from *The Journal of the Interdenominational Theological Center* (1986). Reprinted with permission from The Journal of the Interfaith Theological Center.

Griffin, Farah Jasmine. "That the Mothers May Soar and the Daughters May Know Their Names: A Retrospective of Black Feminist Literary Criticism," from *Signs: Journal of Women in Culture and Society* 32.2 (2007): 483–507, edited by Mary Hawkesworth. Copyright © 2007 by The University of Chicago. All rights reserved. Reprinted with permission from The University of Chicago Press.

Hammonds, Evelynn M. "AIDS the Secret, Silent, Suffering Shame," unpublished conference paper presented at the AIDS Conference as the Spelman College Women's Research and Resource Center, 2005. Copyright © 2005 Evelynn Hammonds. Reprinted with permission from the author.

hooks, bell. "Black Women: Shaping Feminist Theory," from *Feminist Theory: From Margin to Center*, © 1984. Reprinted with permission from South End Press.

James, Joy. "Resting in the Gardens, Battling in the Deserts: Black Women's Activism," from *The Black Scholar* 4 (Winter 1999): 2–7. Reprinted with permission from *The Black Scholar*.

James, Stanlie M. "Racialized Gender/Gendered Racism: Reflections on Black Feminist Human Rights Theorizing," from *Black Women, Globalization, and Economic Justice: Studies from Africa and the African Diaspora*. Copyright © 2002 Stanlie M. James. Reprinted with permission from the author.

Jordan, June. "Some of Us Did Not Die," Copyright © 2002 June Jordan. Reprinted with permission of the publisher from *Some of Us Did Not Die: New and Selected Essays of June Jordan*. New York: Basic/Civitas Books, 2002: 3–15.

Lorde, Audre. "The Uses of Anger: Women Responding to Racism," from *Sister Outsider: Essays and Speeches*. Reprinted with permission from Sister Outsider by Audre Lorde, copyright © 1984, 2007 by Audre Lorde, Crossing Press, Berkeley, CA. www.tenspeed.com.